THE ARMIES OF BRITAIN
1485 – 1980

Michael Barthorp

Field Marshal Sir Gerald Templer KG GCB GCMG KBE DSO Hon DCL (Oxon) Hon LLD (St. Andrews) 1898 – 1979
Chairman of the National Army Museum Building Appeal.
Member of the Council of the National Army Museum.
Chairman of the Executive Committee of the National Army Museum.

THE ARMIES OF BRITAIN 1485-1980

This book is dedicated to the memory of
Field Marshal Sir Gerald Templer KG
as a token of respect and gratitude for the many years of hard work he
gave to the preservation of the Army's history and heritage for the British Nation.

4

The National Army Museum wishes to acknowledge the generosity and interest of the following sponsoring organisations, without whose help the publication of this History would not have been possible:

A

AA - 274
Abbey National Bldg. Soc'y. - 13
AB Connectors - 173
Advance Linen - 28
Airfix - 80
Alcan - 193
Alvis - 207
Amalgamated Metal - 37
Amey Roadstone - 83
Arrow - 208
ATA Training Aids - 75
Atlas Hydraulic - 136
Australia & New Zealand Bank - 228
Avon - 185

B

Babcock International - 72
BACO - 165
Bank of Scotland - 191
Barr & Stroud - 51
Barclays Bank - 23
Beecham - 254
Bell & Howell - 92
Arthur Bell & Son - 284
Bentalls - 142
Bestobell - 204
BICC - 49
Black & Edgington - 162
Boots - 127
Bowater - 296
Bowring - 115
BP - 229
British Aerospace - 245
British Airways - 279
British Bata - 210
British Gas - 264
British Manu'g. & Research - 44
British Relay - 161
British Steel - 117
Brooke Bond Liebig - 249
Brown Shipley - 176
James Buchanan - 267
Burberry - 150
James Burrough - 145
Butlins - 60

C

Calor - 222
Canada Life - 235
Capper - Neill - 58
Champion - 241
Chelsea Bldg. Soc'y. - 282
Chiltern Hunt - 47
Chubb - 36
Chloride - 29
City of London Bldg. Soc'y. - 251
Coats Patons - 216
Cogswell & Harrison - 52
Coles - 181
Colonial Mutual - 178
Commercial Union - 16
J.Compton Sons & Webb - 144
Consolidated Goldfields - 201
Thos. Cook - 209
Corintra - 106
Costain - 139
Samuel Courtaulds - 82
CQC - 172
Crane Fruehauf - 184
Craven Tasker - 86
Crown Paints -212
C & S Antennas - 102
Cusson - 157
Czarnikow - 253

D

David Brown - 240
Delta Metal - 30
Dewhurst - 202
Michael Druitt - 119
Dunlop - 59

E

Earl's Court & Olympia - 272
Charles Early - 55
Edbro - 21
Eley - 22
EMI - 67
Ercol - 17
Esso - 261

F

Fairey Holdings - 242
Thomas Fattorini - 121
Ferranti - 174
Firmin - 31
FMC - 124
Fodens - 203
Fortnum & Mason - 149
House of Fraser - 188

G

Galt - 12
J.R. Gaunt - 148
GEC Marconi - 200
Geest - 260
Gieves & Hawkes - 151
Gillette - 63
Giltspur - 73
GKN - 154
Gloster Saro - 140
Grand Metropolitan - 10
Grindlay's Bank - 79
Guardian Royal - 84
Arthur Guinness - 76

H

Hamworthy - 74
Harrisons & Crosfields - 68
Harvey of Bristol - 103
Hawley - Goodall - 248
Hennell - 197
C.E. Heath - 236
Hi-Flex Inter'l. - 90
High Duty Alloys - 126
Jane Hodge Foundation - 24
Honeywell - 87
Hotspur - 65
Hunting - 180

I

IBM - 232
ICI - 64
ICL - 169
Ilford - 205
Inchcape - 113
Ind Coope - 111
International Wool Secre't. - 147
Inver House - 105
Invertron - 192

J

Johnson/Goddards - 196

K

Kismet - 141
Kiwi - 277
Kodak - 223
Kyle Stewart - 25

L

Lacre - 218
Laird - 107
Land Rover - 217
Leeds Perm't. Bldg. Soc'y. - 61
Letts - 175
Lipton Export - 66
London Life Assurance - 116
London Weekend TV - 268
Lovell - 34
Joseph Lucas - 130

M

3M - 20
Mabey & Johnson - 259
Marks & Spencer - 33
Matthew Gloag - 9
Mars - 263
McAlpine - 177
MEL - 41
MESL - 53
Metal Box - 54
Modern Materials Mang't. - 32
Moore Paragon - 46
Morse Equipment - 95
Muirhead - 120

N

Nationwide Bldg. Soc'y. - 182
National Provident Instn. for Assur. - 137
National Westminster Bank - 215
Nestle - 231
Northern Rock Bldg. Soc'y. - 243
Norwich Union - 123

O

Ocean Transport & Trading - 132
Overseas Container - 89

P

Parker Gallery - 104
Philips - 97
Pilkington - 43
Plessey - 85
Pontins - 108
William Press - 77
Purdey - 237

R

Radio Rentals - 114
Rank Organisation - 195
Rank Xerox - 225
Reckitt & Colman - 256
Redifon - 219
Rentokil - 93
Rolls-Royce - 152
Ross - 227
Royal Bank of Scotland - 189
Rubery Owen - 96

S

George Salter - 153
Scammell - 273
Scottish & Newcastle - 135
Scottorn - 71
Seagrams - 220
Seagull S.A. - 146
Securicor - 27
Sedgwick Forbes - 19
Serck - 262
Short Bros. & Harland - 110
Singer & Friedlander - 35
Smith, Kline & French - 199
W.H. Smith - 11
Solartron - 45
Sothebys - 62
Sperry Rand - 100
Stanley - 40
Starrett - 88
Sterling Armaments - 280
Sterling Metals - 42
Storno - 171
John Swire - 156
Systems Designers - 78

T

Tanqueray, Gordon - 198
Taylor Woodrow - 133
Tecalemit - 166
Tennant Industrial Exp. - 155
Telephone Rentals - 186
Texaco - 239
Thames TV - 224
Thorn - 48
Thomas Tilling - 91
Tirfor - 125
Tootal - 26
Touche, Remnant - 159
Tozer, Kemsley & Milbn. - 14
Trafalgar House - 69
Trusthouse Forte - 194

U

UBM - 38
Unigate - 206
United Biscuits - 158

V

Vauxhall/Bedford - 258
Vickers - 247

W

Wallis & Wallis - 101
Ward White - 252
Watney Mann Truman - 81
Westland - 270
Wheway Watson - 109
Whitbread - 168
Wickman - 50
Wilkinson Sword - 257
Williams & Glyn's Bank - 15
Wimpey - 163
Wilson & Garden - 70
Woolwich Eqble. Bldg. Soc'y. - 233
M.Wright - 183

THE ARMIES OF BRITAIN

FOREWORD

The armies of Britain and her empire have never been short of chroniclers. Major Michael Barthorp is especially well qualified to join their ranks. Throughout his career as a regular officer, and for some years before, he spent much of his spare time studying the history, uniform and traditions of the regiments of the British Army and of their overseas comrades-in-arms. He has since written several books and articles and is known as an authority on numerous aspects of the history of the profession of arms.

This, his latest work, is unique in two respects. It is the first history of the armies of the Empire to be financed largely by charitable, industrial and commercial sponsors. I am most grateful to them all for the contributions which, despite soaring publication costs, have enabled the museum to offer an important history at a very reasonable price. This is also the first major book to be illustrated almost entirely from the National Army Museum's remarkable collections. Although as Director of the museum since 1970 I have been deeply involved in every recent phase of its development, I still find it almost incredible that collections of so great a variety, richness and historical significance have been assembled in such a short time. That this has been achieved is due to the wisdom and generosity of thousands of friends and supporters who have seen the museum as the ideal resting place for family treasures that extend in variety from splendid portraits of great soldiers to the humblest of relics picked up on far-off battlefields; and in appeal from a posthumous medal for gallantry to the skeleton of Napoleon's little charger, Marengo.

Since 1960, when the museum was first installed within the Royal Military Academy Sandhurst, the first phase of the Chelsea building has been opened by Her Majesty the Queen and a 26,000 sq.ft. extension approaches completion as this book goes to press. Soon the story of Britain's armies, represented until now by displays cut off at 4th August 1914 will be extended to the present day, the exhibits marching in step with the chapters of Michael Barthorp's book from the origin of the army in 1485 to the retrenchment and rationalisation of recent years. The record of five hundred years of Britain's military heritage is no mere echo of distant trumpets, but forms a fascinating and integral part of the social history of the great empire that lives on in the Commonwealth.

Seagull S.A., suggested the form of the book, have handled all the financial details and have been largely responsible for the editorial process. I am sure that the company would wish to be associated with the gratitude the author and I feel towards my colleagues in the Department of Records.

The National Army Museum is proud of this concise account of the men who did so much to shape the world in the eighteenth and nineteenth centuries and who, in the twentieth, have done more than their share to defend freedom and to prevent new conflicts in many more places than the average layman can recall.

William Reid

ACKNOWLEDGEMENTS

The aim of this book is to recount the story of Britain's land forces in peace and war over the last five centuries. The term "land forces" embraces not only the Regular Army and the Militia, Yeomanry, Volunteers and Territorials of the Reserve Armies, but also the Indian Army and Colonial Forces, until the countries of the British Commonwealth and Empire from which they were drawn achieved their independence. Any account of land operations must inevitably touch upon the support lent to the Army by the Royal Navy and Royal Marines, particularly when they served ashore, and later by the Royal Air Force. Likewise no discussion of the great struggles of this century would be complete without mention of the magnificent contribution to British field forces of the Dominion Armies.

The audience for which this book is primarily intended has been defined by the Director of the National Army Museum as "the intelligent lay reader", although it is hoped that the military history specialist, as well as serving and retired soldiers, may also find it of interest. Its text is designed to complement and expand upon the displays contained in the National Army Museum.

Any attempt to compile a bibliography for such a vast subject must of necessity be either too lengthy or too inadequate, but some of the many works consulted can be found listed in the source references given for all quotations used. However, an author attempting such a task as this would be failing in gratitude if he did not single out for special mention the work of others who have tackled a similar undertaking: Sir John Fortescue's "History of the British Army" (1899-1920); H.M. Chichester's and G.Burges-Short's "Records and Badges of Every Regiment and Corps in the British Army" (1900); E.W.Sheppard's "A Short History of the British Army" (1940); Corelli Barnett's "Britain and Her Army" (1970); and the joint editors, Brigadier Peter Young and Lt.Col J.P. Lawford, and their collaborators in "A History of the British Army" (1970). Invaluable for the Indian Army have been Philip Mason's "A Matter of Honour" (1974) and T.A. Heathcote's "The Indian Army" (1974), and for the story of more recent times, Gregory Blaxland's "The Regiments Depart" (1971). No such list would be complete without acknowledgement of the work of the numerous Official Historians of British land operations and the authors of regimental histories. Of particular assistance have been several volumes of such military historians as the Marquess of Anglesey, W.Y. Carman, David Chandler, Michael Glover, C.C.P. Lawson, Sir Basil Liddell-Hart, John Mollo, C.W.C. Oman, H.C.B. Rogers, John Terraine, Jac Weller, and the many contributors to the Journal of the Society for Army Historical Research.

I am indebted to the Director of the National Army Museum, William Reid, for his faith in my ability to undertake the task, and to all his staff, particularly Boris Mollo and David Smurthwaite for their help, guidance and suggestions; Marion Harding for her work on the illustrations, and Ann Duhig for compiling the index. Heartfelt thanks are also due to Major-General J.B. Akehurst and various anonymous staff officers at the Ministry of Defence (Army) who spared time from their normal duties to supply answers to a host of questions about the Army of today. The library staff of the same Department who have been most helpful in providing books.

The book could not have been written in the time allowed for its completion without the selfless help of my wife, who both protected me against all extraneous interruptions and demands on my time, thus almost depriving herself of any social life, and, though no addict of military history, conscientiously performed the role of "the intelligent lay reader", perusing every chapter with great care and diligence, questioning the obscurities and suggesting improvements.

Lastly I must acknowledge a debt to my father of a less precise, but nevertheless important nature. A soldier himself, and the brother, son and grandson of soldiers, all of whom collected books, photographs, pictures and post-cards about the Army, he ensured the preservation of all this material, upon which I fell at an early age. Thus, from childhood, I became imbued with an abiding interest in the Army's history which my father always encouraged but never forced upon me. Such a grounding has greatly facilitated my task and has ensured that, whatever its defects, the work has been completed with affection for its subject.

M.J.B.
Jersey C. I.

CONTENTS

	Sponsors of The Armies of Britain	4
	Foreword	5
	Acknowledgement	6
	The National Army Museum	8
Chapter 1	The Beginnings 1485-1641	9
Chapter 2	The New Model 1642-1660	21
Chapter 3	Restoration and Revolution 1660-1701	31
Chapter 4	Marlborough's Glory 1702-1713	43
Chapter 5	The White Horse of Hanover 1714-1754	55
Chapter 6	Plucking the Lilies of France 1755-1763	67
Chapter 7	"Primus in Indis" 1600-1784	79
Chapter 8	The World Turned Upside Down 1775-1783	91
Chapter 9	Britain at Bay 1793-1808	103
Chapter 10	Under Wellington's Command 1808-1815	117
Chapter 11	Expanding the Raj 1804-1852	135
Chapter 12	Against the Russian Bear 1816-1856	153
Chapter 13	Sepoy Mutiny 1857-1859	165
Chapter 14	A Changed Army 1854-1899	175
Chapter 15	On the Frontier 1860-1904	183
Chapter 16	Soldiering Across the World 1816-1900	193
Chapter 17	From the Cape to Khartoum 1806-1898	201
Chapter 18	The Last of the Gentlemen's Wars 1899-1914	215
Chapter 19	Armageddon 1914-1918	225
Chapter 20	Proper Soldiering Again 1919-1939	241
Chapter 21	The Greatest Feats of Arms 1939-1945	249
Chapter 22	Retreat to Reform 1946-1980	267
	Appendix A	285
	Appendix B	289
	References	290
	Index	292

The museum was opened at Sandhurst in 1960 to display the history of the British Army from the reign of Henry VII. It also tells the story of the Indian Army up to partition in 1947 and of the armies of other Commonwealth nations up to their independence. The first phase of the present building in Chelsea, opened by H.M. the Queen in 1971, cost one million pounds raised entirely from donations.

There are four permanent galleries: weapons on the ground floor, a historical gallery depicting the army's battles, generals and development on the first floor; the art and uniform galleries above.

A 26,000 sq.ft. extension, also paid for by private subscription, will give additional exhibition area. Permanent displays will continue the story of the British Army and the land forces of the Empire from 1914 until today. A large gellery will house temporary exhibitions.

The National Army Museum still maintains a presence at the Royal Military Academy, Sandhurst, its first home. The Indian Army Memorial Room in the old chapel and the museum of those Irish Regiments disbanded in 1922 can be visited by arrangement.

CHAPTER 1
THE BEGINNINGS
1485 – 1641

From earliest times rulers and leaders have found it prudent to surround themselves with armed men to safeguard their persons and their position. Such bodyguards have ranged in size from a handful to a small army. Some have protected their overlords to the death, others have been the very instrument of their downfall. From the Praetorian Guards of the Roman Emperors, to the Scottish Archers and the 'Cent-Suisses' of the French kings, and continuing down the ages to formations of the twentieth century, like the 'Leibstandarte' of Adolf Hitler, these bodyguards have enjoyed fame or obloquy, sometimes both, but for the most part their names and deeds have faded into history with the dynasty or individual they were formed to protect. A few, like the Papal Swiss Guards, have survived, and to their number have been added new units which guard the heads of modern states. But none can claim the unbroken lineage of that corps which to this day still guards the sovereign whose forbears it has shielded for close on five hundred years – the Queen of England's Bodyguard of the Yeomen of the Guard.

When the last of England's Yorkist kings fell at Bosworth Field in 1485, the crown passed to Henry Tudor, Earl of Richmond, who ascended the throne as Henry VII. After the ruinous years of the Wars of the Roses, Henry set himself to restore peace and prosperity to England, which could best be done by removing power from the great nobles and centralising it in the monarchy. To pursue this task, one essential was the safety and prestige of the King's person and so:

"for the safeguarding and preservation of his own body he constituted and ordained a certain number, as well as of good archers as of divers other persons, being hardy, strong and of agility, to give daily attendance to his person whom he named Yeomen of his Guarde; which precedent men thought, that he learnt from the French Kings, for men remembered not any King of England before that time which used such a furniture of daily soldiers". (1)

This body of permanent troops, raised, as their name suggests, from the yeoman class, were picked men armed with bows and halberds† some of them being mounted. Originally about 60 in number, their strength rose to 200, a figure which remained more or less constant until 1660, except during Henry VIII's reign when they were increased to 600. They were dressed in the Tudor livery of green and white, which would be changed in the next reign to the red or scarlet still worn today and which subsequently became the colour of the British soldier's uniform for three hundred years.

While no Tudor Englishman could remember such a standing force of "daily soldiers", one had existed many centuries before. When the Danish king, Canute, conquered England and took the English throne, he formed a royal bodyguard chosen from his Danish troops and known as "house-carles", a force several thousand strong. The house-carles continued in existence as guards of the subsequent Saxon kings and fought their last battle on the hill at Hastings around the dead body of King Harold.

The house-carles were, however, only the nucleus of the English army of those times. The mass was provided by the "fyrd", a levy of freemen between the ages of 16 and 60, summoned to the king's service as occasion required, on the basis of land tenure. The fyrd had been reorganised by Alfred the Great, who divided the country into military districts, in which every five hides* of land were to provide an armed man complete with food and pay, while owners of more than five hides were required to do thane's service: to serve as a heavily-armed man at his own expense throughout the duration of a campaign. After the Norman Conquest the fyrd remained for a time as a reserve to the main military force of the Norman kings which was based on knight-service. Under this system England was distributed into knight's fees which obliged each military knight to rally to the king's service, with his retainers, when called upon to do so. Before long, however, the system degenerated into the practice of many knights offering money in lieu of service, with which the Norman kings hired

---

† A weapon combining a hook for pulling, a point for thrusting and a blade for cutting, mounted on a staff, about seven feet in overall length.

* A hide measured between 60–100 acres, according to locality.

mercenaries to fight their battles for them. With the coming of the mercenaries the fyrd fell into disuse but, because of the ever-increasing unpopularity in the country of the former and the inefficiency of, and scant numbers provided by, the feudal array of knights, it became clear to Henry II that the military resources of the country had to be reorganised. In 1181 therefore, he enacted the Assize of Arms, which re-established the fyrd as the national militia of England, and which required every knight and freeman to furnish himself with arms and armour according to a scale based on each individual's means. This enactment, though extended by succeeding monarchs, remained the basis for the provision of the defence force of England until Tudor times.

Edward I found the existing system of assembling a military field force so cumbersome that he instituted the Commissions of Array, under which one or two leading men in each county were commissioned to muster such forces as were required. By the Statute of Winchester in 1285 he confirmed and elaborated the Assize of Arms by dividing the freemen into classes of horse and foot armed with weapons according to their means. For the first time there was included a body of archers armed with the long bow, the weapon that was to make England's name as a military power, and which would restore to the foot soldier that supremacy on the battlefield, hitherto enjoyed by the armoured knight on his war horse. Whether the long bow was used defensively to repulse an enemy attack at long range, or in attack to weaken the enemy by missile-fire prior to a charge by armoured men-at-arms, it proved a battle-winning weapon which first endowed the English infantryman with a reputation on the continent of Europe that he would earn again and again, long after the bow had been superseded by more modern weapons.

From Crecy in 1346 to Agincourt in 1415 the English army, with its men-at-arms of knights and squires and its footmen of archers and Welsh spearmen, reached a pinnacle of fame and success. The men for these campaigns in France were raised chiefly by contracts, know as "indents", made between the king and men of position or military ability who undertook to serve with a mixed force of all arms for a fixed term at a stipulated rate of pay. Many of these bodies, once their services were no longer required, set themselves up as "free companies", hiring themselves out as mercenaries and spreading the fame of the English soldier as far as Spain and Italy. However, with France re-animated by the phenomenal Joan of Arc, English military power waned and degenerated until all the French conquests of Edward III and Henry V were lost except for Calais. The bands of men, who for years had known no trade but war, returned home and took service under the groups of nobles, then taking sides for the clash between the Houses of Lancaster and York known as the Wars of the Roses. When it ended with the accession of Henry VII, the nobility had been decimated, the professional fighting men exhausted or slaughtered, and the country as a whole was longing for peace and tranquility.

This Henry gave England. He imposed his authority on the great nobles by curbing their power and limiting the number of their retainers; he laid the foundations of a modern nation with a state revenue derived from taxation; and he pursued a careful and cautious foreign policy, eschewing all thought of military adventure on the continent. Although his formation of the Yeomen of the Guard was believed to have been in imitation of the French Kings' Scottish archer guard, he did not intend it as the nucleus of a larger standing force, such as was gradually being instituted in France. His foreign policy required none and for home defence there remained the obligations imposed by the Statute of Winchester on the people of the country to take up arms in times of civil emergency or under threat of foreign invasion.

With peace at home and no military involvement on the continent since the close of the Hundred Years War in 1453, English military ideas became stagnant and the weapons of the militia remained those of the great days of Agincourt — the long bow and the bill, the latter deriving from the two-handed battle-axe of the old Saxon infantry. Yet in Europe great changes in military organisation and technology were taking place. The mediaeval feudal hosts were being replaced by tough and ruthless professional soldiers, well-drilled, organised in tactical formations, and trained in the use of the new arms that began to appear during the struggles of the Italian Wars of the late fifteenth and early sixteenth centuries between France on the one hand and the Holy Roman Empire, with its Spanish allies, on the other. The supremacy once enjoyed by the English archers passed to the Swiss pikemen, employed mainly by the French, who fought in great solid blocks bristling with 18-foot pikes. They were rivalled in the Emperor's armies by the German 'landsknechte', disciplined mercenaries, armed with pikes, halberds and, increasingly, a proportion of firearms. The landsknechte were raised by their own captains in companies of some 400 which were then assembled into regiments of varying size under the colonel who had been commissioned to form a corps by the Emperor. In the early sixteenth century pride of place among the infantry of Europe began to be taken by the Spanish 'tercios', highly disciplined regiments, some 1500 strong, armed with pikes and swords, but principally with firearms. These were the arquebus, a heavy, cumbersome and inaccurate weapon fired from a forked rest but one which, in the hands of the Spaniards, ended the superiority of the Swiss pikemen.

Turning to the cavalry, the old feudal array of knights, doomed first by the English archers and then by the Swiss pikemen, had been replaced by better drilled and properly organised companies of mounted men-at-

Engraving by James Basire after a sketch by S.H.Grimm from a painting at Cowdray in Sussex, published by the Society of Antiquaries, 23rd April, 1788.

7010-16

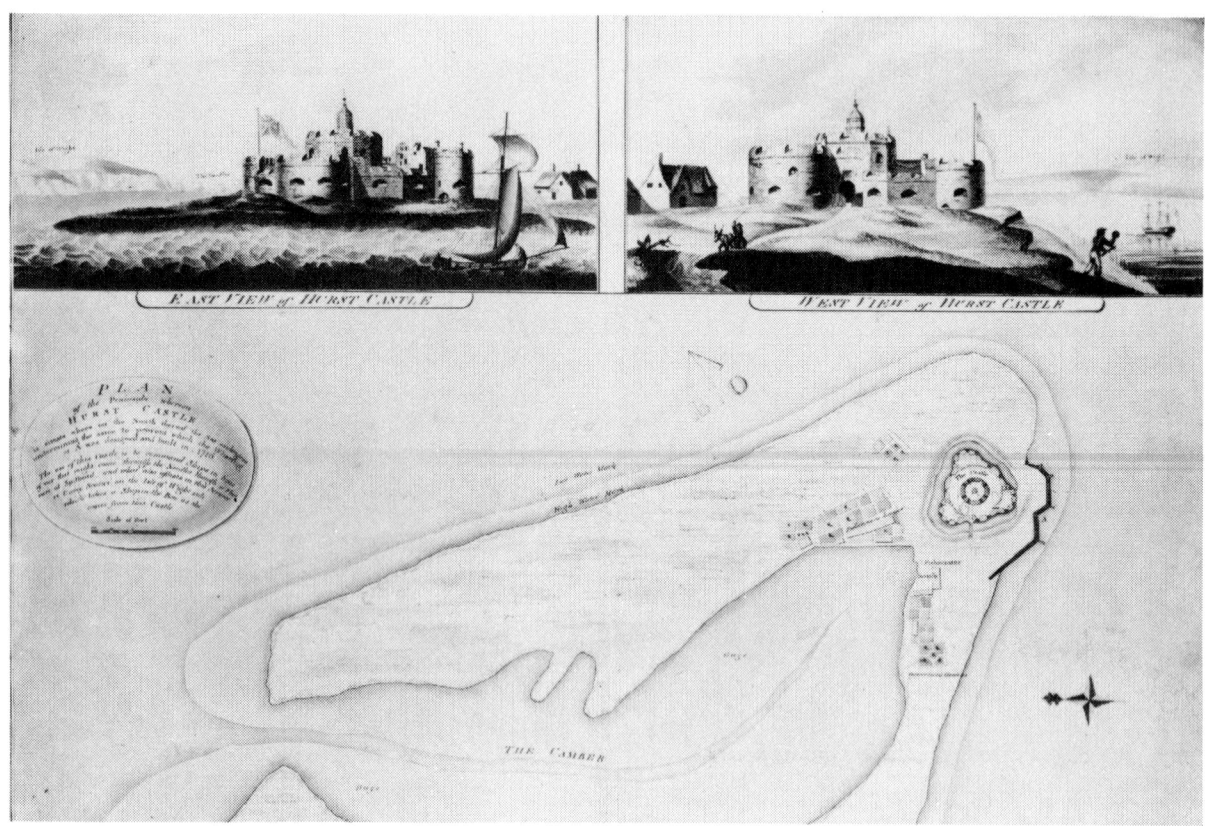

Hurst Castle, on the Solent, was built in 1541-44 to defend the approaches to Southampton Harbour.

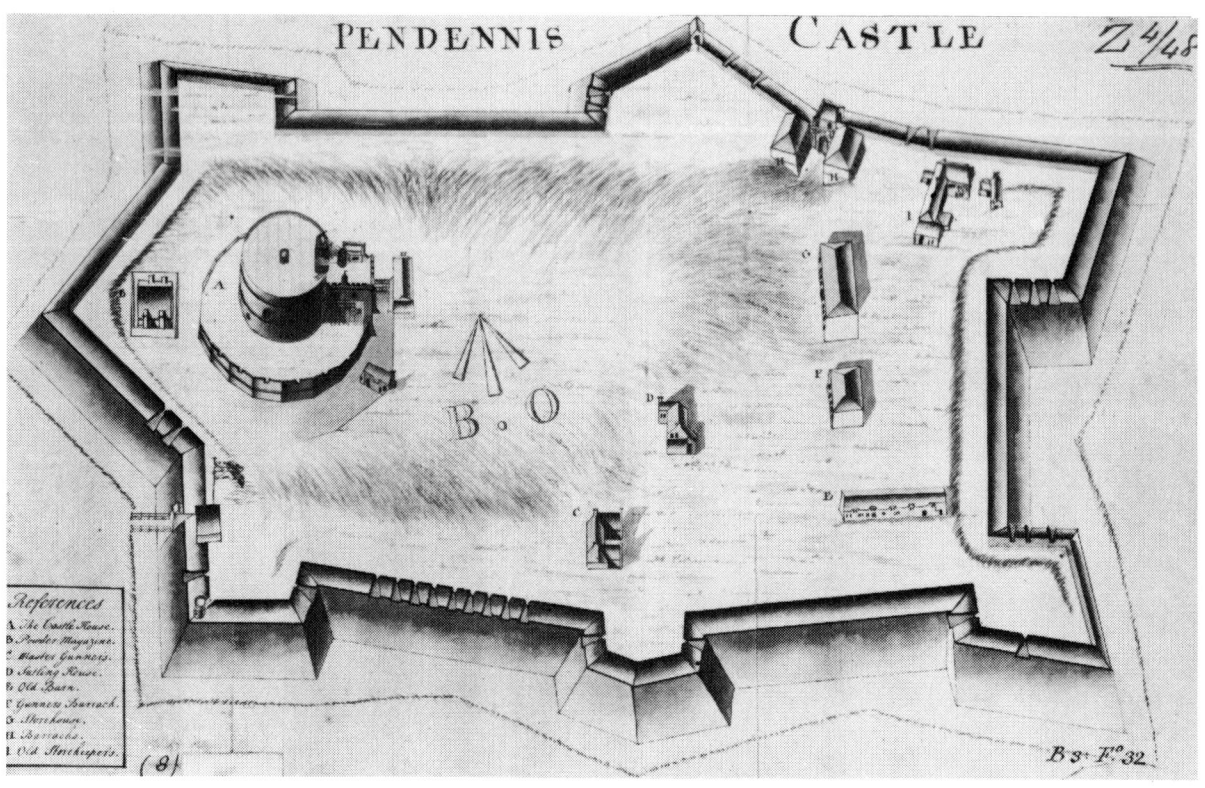

The construction of Pendennis Castle, at the entrance to Falmouth Harbour, was begun in 1540.

7104-40

arms, still armoured and with the lance as their main weapon. The developments in infantry weapons, however, saw the rise of a new type of cavalry who depended not on shock action, which had largely been countered by the long pikes and the arquebus, but on volleys of pistol fire delivered by successive ranks of horsemen arrayed in a square formation, a drill known as the 'caracole'. This originated with mercenary bands of cavalry raised in Germany called 'reiters', a fierce and brutal crew who rode with blackened faces but whose method set the tone of cavalry tactics for about a hundred years. Lastly, no army now moved without its train of artillery. Since guns had first appeared in the Hundred Years War, their development had proceeded apace, particularly in France, and the great train of over 300 cannons and bombards taken by Charles VIII into Italy in 1494 soon demonstrated the vulnerability of mediaeval fortifications.

Compared with such increased military professionalism England had only her amateur levies, the yeomen and peasants hurriedly summoned from their peacetime occupations to take the field, should occasion arise, under the equally amateur leadership of the nobles and gentry; bill and bow against pike and arquebus. The possibility of such an uneven match did not deter Henry VIII from embarking on a more robust and warlike foreign policy than that of his father. He allied himself with the Empire, Spain and the Pope against France, but before he could consider operations on the continent, he had to secure his rear against the Scots, the allies of France. This he did by issuing a Commission of Array to the Earl of Surrey for calling out the militia of the northern shires. To provide a field force for war in France he had to rely on such troops as could be induced to volunteer, mostly archers and billmen with some light horse from the Scottish border, supplemented by mercenary landsknechte and Burgundian mounted men-at-arms.

Surprisingly he enjoyed, in 1513, a quick and successful campaign, defeating a weak French force at the Battle of the Spurs and capturing Tournai. Meanwhile the Earl of Surrey's militiamen trounced the Scottish army at Flodden, the northern billmen cleaving windrows through the Scots, despite the latter being arrayed and armed like the Swiss pikemen and supported by artillery. James IV of Scotland was killed, the Scottish nobility suffered grievously, and the victory secured Henry's northern frontier for the rest of his reign.

Henry raised two more armies, both of similar content to that of 1513, part native volunteers, part mercenaries, for further expeditions to France in 1523 and 1542. Though he captured Boulogne in the last, the campaign had to be abandoned through lack of funds. These attempts to influence European affairs had made little impact on the continuing struggle in Italy, had emptied the Treasury, and had initiated no reforms to England's military system. Indeed his earlier successes confirmed Henry's faith in the old English weapons and the arrangements for mustering an army when one was required. Furthermore he went on to encourage the use of the long bow as the national weapon by compelling every man in the kingdom to practise archery regularly. Such conservatism and trust in old methods will be met again and again in the country's military affairs.

Despite Henry's attachment to the bow, firearms and pikes were gaining in popularity in England. In 1537 the Guild of St George was formed in the City of London *"to be overseers of the science of artillerie, that is to witt, long bowes, cross bowes and hand gonnes". (2)* That such a responsibility should be entrusted to a City livery company is some reflection on military affairs in Tudor England, although this particular guild subsequently became the Honourable Artillery Company then, as now, a regiment of the reserve forces of the Crown. In 1539 a great review was held by the King of the 15,000 London militiamen, or trained-bands as they were starting to be called. They were uniformly dressed in white and marched past in good order, led by their artillery who were followed by arquebusiers and pikemen with bowmen and billmen bringing up the rear. It was in the sphere of artillery that Henry made his greatest contribution to the defences of the country. Though indifferent to hand-guns, he showed great personal interest in cannon and established an officer of state, the Master of the Ordnance, with his own department to attend to the provision and storage of artillery and ammunition for the navy and land forces. At first the guns were purchased from abroad, but gun foundaries were being set up and by 1535 heavy guns were being cast in England by John Owen and experts hired from Europe. Connected with the introduction of an artillery train were the measures taken by Henry for the safety of the realm. As a second line to the navy, which he also organized as a state department, he constructed a line of forts along the south coast from the Medway to Cornwall. These were armed with his heavy cannon and manned by permanent garrisons. The latter, together with the Yeomen of the Guard and a second royal body-guard raised in 1509 from young noblemen, then known as Gentlemen Pensioners but now the Honourable Corps of Gentlemen-at-Arms, were the only permanent land forces of the Crown at the end of Henry VIII's reign. Since England was protected by the sea and its navy it did not require a large army such as continental powers were maintaining on an increasingly permanent basis. If invasion came the militia would be summoned as in the past.

The next two reigns, of the minor Edward VI and the Catholic Mary, saw the national unity achieved by the two Henrys rent by political and religious factions and a return to the internal disorder of the Wars of the

14

Sir Francis Vere.

Woodcut from "The Commentaries of Sir Francis Vere" published in 1657.

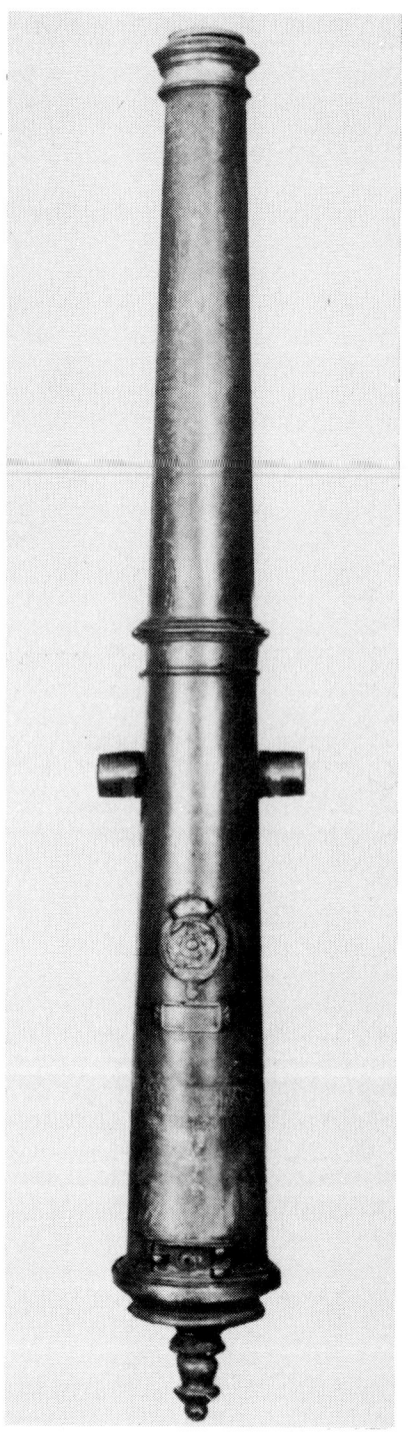

Bronze Cannon (Saker) dated 1538.

Cast with a crowned Tudor Rose within the Garter and incised with the names of Henry VIII and the brothers John and Robert Owyn of Houndsditch, the makers

Royal Artillery Museum, Woolwich.

7111-10

'A Yeoman of the Guard attending Queen Elizabeth on a progress'. c1570
Engraving after S.Hooper from Francis Grose, 'Military Antiquities', 1786.

Roses, if with less bloodshed. It was not therefore a period in which any improvement to England's land forces was likely, for only in times of danger from without have the English ever responded to the need for greater efficiency in their defences. In fact the period demonstrated how frail a first line the main defence of the realm, the shire militia, could be in times of civil insurrection. When the Protector, the Duke of Somerset, was faced in Edward's reign by Jack Ket's rebellion in Norfolk and a revolt of Cornishmen, he had to rely on Italian arquebusiers and German landsknechte to quell them. If the militia was called out in defence of causes which lacked popular support, the sovereign could look in vain for their obedience. When Sir Thomas Wyatt marched on London in protest against Mary's forthcoming marriage to Philip II of Spain, even the Yeomen of the Guard deserted the Queen.

The period saw another victory over the Scots at Pinkie in 1547, where the English army, still largely armed with bills and bows but stiffened by 600 arquebusiers, defeated a numerically superior force by the use of Henry VIII's carefully nurtured artillery and a preponderance of heavy cavalry consisting partly of the Gentlemen Pensioners of the Guard, some professionals from the permanent garrison at Boulogne, and foreign mercenaries. Pinkie was notable for the first use on British soil of the caracole tactics of the German reiters. This victory for English arms was however balanced eleven year later by the loss of Calais, the last possession in France, where the mediaeval defences were smashed by the French artillery.

Mary's only contribution to the reform of the military system was the supercession in 1553 of Edward I's Statute of Winchester, by which the militia had hitherto been regulated and which had authorised the Commissions of Array. The new Act, of 1558, in fact did little more than re-assert the obligations of all men between 16 and 60 to serve, provide for the supply of more up-to-date weapons, and re-define the responsibilities for the provision and upkeep of arms and armour according to a new rating system, in which men were divided into ten classes, from those worth £5½ a year to those worth £1,000 a year. The former had to keep a coat of plated armour, a bill or halberd, a long bow with arrows and an iron helmet; the latter had to provide 16 horses, 60 suits of light armour, 40 pikes, 20 bills or halberds, 20 arquebuses, 50 iron helmets and 30 long bows. Though the more modern weapons to be provided included pikes and arquebuses, a clause expressly permitted the bow as an acceptable and *"efficient substitute for the arquebus". (3)* In 1549 an Act of Edward VI had created the appointment of Lords Lieutenant of counties for the organising and controlling of forces in place of the Commissions of Array. In 1557 Mary defined their duties as being:

> *"To call musters of men, arms and horses; fine for absence forty shillings, prevention of false returns, making away with arms and armour, power to deal with offences of Captains and Petty Captains when assembled under Deputy Lieutenants, to appoint places of rendez-vous, attend to the razing of the beacons, look to places where the enemy may land, break bridges, cut trenches and throw down trees in the event of invasion." (4)*

The supervision and command of the county militia was therefore now vested in the Lords Lieutenant but as a precaution against any one of them abusing his powers, the appointment was only to be filled in time of emergency; a wise measure in uncertain and troubled times but not one conducive to the peacetime preparedness of the only military force available. Only one other military reform was made by Mary, small but of some consequence to the soldier: she raised his daily pay, when embodied, from sixpence to eightpence, a sum he would have to be content with for the next two hundred years.

Europe in the first half of the sixteenth century had been dominated by the long war between France and the Empire in Italy, a war in which England could play a peripheral part as and when she chose. In the second half it was dominated by the great conflict between Protestantism and Catholicism which, in national terms, witnessed a civil war in France, and the determination of Philip II of Spain, ruler of the richest and most powerful state in Europe, to re-impose his will and his religion on his rebellious Dutch Protestant subjects in the Spanish Netherlands and their only ally, Elizabethan England.

On ascending the throne in a dark and dismal period of English history, Elizabeth I intended to follow a cautious path in foreign policy but found herself drawn inexorably into war with Spain, a war for which, on land, she was totally unprepared. There was the fleet and the great generation of Elizabethan seafarers but on land, apart from the royal bodyguards and the fortress garrisons, there was only the militia. The reforms of Mary had not prevented the decline of this force into total inadequacy, almost non-existence, except on paper. The obligation for service had become increasingly unpopular, all attempted to avoid the annual musters, while the new drills required for proficient manoeuvring of formed bodies armed with pike and arquebus were time-consuming and lacked the jollity and friendship of the old archery contests. Yet if he was to face the steady and menacing ranks of the disciplined veterans in the Spanish tercios, the English militiaman would need more training than a few Sunday afternoons at the butts. It was realised that the efficient training of every fit man between the ages of 16 and 60 in the new weapons was impractical, therefore only a proportion were selected

for training. In 1575, out of 183,000 men mustered in 37 counties, only 12,000 received special training, while 63,000 were equipped but not trained. After a further 3,000 were drawn off as cavalry, the balance were classed as pioneers, neither trained nor armed. The trained men were formed into companies known as trained-bands, which were regarded as the nation's first line of defence.

When the Dutch revolted against their Spanish overlords in 1572, the latter moved with haste and ferocity to suppress the uprising. Fighting for survival the Dutch looked to their fellow Protestants in England for support but Elizabeth, still reluctant to embroil herself on the continent, would only send money and volunteers. From the trained-bands of London Captain Thomas Morgan raised a company of 300 picked men who arrived in the nick of time to help the Dutch prevent the recapture of Flushing. From then on further volunteers reached the Netherlands. Some met with ignominious defeat but others, led by professional soldiers like John Norris, acquitted themselves with honour against such foremost captains of the age as Don John of Austria and Alexander of Parma, proving that the dread tercios were not invincible. Their aid to the Dutch was, however, still unofficial and it was not until 1584, with Dutch resistance beginning to crumble following the assassination of William the Silent, that Elizabeth realised she must fight if England was not to face the might of Spain alone. Accordingly in 1585 an expeditionary force under the Earl of Leicester, hastily raised, untrained, and ill-equipped, was sent to Holland.

England's paucity of military resources was now manifest. With nothing but the neglected militia to call upon, forces had to be found, first, to defend the country against possible invasion, secondly, to mount foreign expeditions in Holland, against enemy bases in Spain and, as if this was not enough, to quell a serious rebellion in Ireland. As far as the first was concerned, the Lords Lieutenant set about the tasks of preparation. When news came that Philip's great Armada had put to sea and Englishmen began to realise the seriousness of the threat, patriotic feelings re-asserted themselves and men rallied to the musters. At the muster of the London trained-bands in 1588, there were found to be in arms: *"Capteynes and Colonells in all 47; Ensignes in all 45; Soldyers in all 7,100 whereof pykes 2,350, Calyvers† 4,750".(5)* Professional soldiers like Norris had been sent round on tours of inspection to supervise the training but generally were horrified by what they found among the raw levies. Thankfully the sea and the winds, with some help from the fleet, spared Englishmen from the lesson that enthusiasm and patriotism were no substitutes for military training and skill-at-arms.

Though the threat to England passed it was not the end of the war. Indeed it was almost only the beginning and the struggle against the formidable Spanish army among the dykes and fortified towns of the Netherlands went on into the next reign. To find the men for such a campaign and for the expeditions mounted against Lisbon, Cadiz and the Caribbean taxed the Tudor administration to the limit. Constitutionally only individual volunteers from the militia could be sent overseas but volunteers were not readily forthcoming. The Lords Lieutenant were ordered to provide so many from each county on a quota basis according to the population in each. Obviously the most likely volunteers were the better types found in the trained-bands but, in view of their importance for home defence, the authorities were unwilling to spare them for foreign service. Consequently the majority taken for such service were untrained. Some were gentlemen volunteers, the offspring of the nobility and gentry, eager for fame, adventure and the chance of becoming the captain of a company; since the latter enjoyed almost total responsibility for the management of his men, from their raising to their disbandment or death, he was afforded considerable opportunities, sanctified by custom, for enriching himself at the expense both of the government and his troops. A number of volunteers from the yeomen and craftsmen class answered the call of the recruiting drum but the bulk of the men had to be impressed. Some were honest men drawn from gainful employment who, though naturally reluctant to serve, eventually made good soldiers, but the press fell heaviest on the dregs of society, *"any idle fellow, some drunkard or seditious quarreller, a privy picker or such a one as hath some skill in stealing of a goose". (6)* When Lord Leicester's expedition was being formed in 1585, the Queen's Privy Council ordered the conscription of all able-bodied unemployed men in Surrey and Sussex; these were rounded up during carefully mounted raids on fairs and popular meeting places all on the same day. They were immediately escorted to Rye and embarked on ships for the Netherlands. These rogues and vagabonds were unpromising material with which to face the most feared infantry in Europe but it would not be the last time that the ranks would be filled from this level of society.

Much of the onus of raising cavalry for overseas expeditions fell upon the clergy who maintained numerous mounted servants among their establishments. Sometimes money was taken in lieu of men, as in 1585 when, the cost of putting a cavalryman in the field being assessed as £25, the clergy were ordered to raise £25,000 between them. Such levies inspired outcries about the Church's poverty and though the Bishop of Winchester's offer in 1587 to raise two companies of troops earned him the gratitude of his Queen, it also incurred the wrath of his fellow bishops. Though more than ready to offer up prayers for their country in its hour of need, the

† Arquebuses with a uniform bore, or calibre, hence caliver.

clergy shared the general reluctance of their countrymen to provide more tangible support – a reluctance that grew steadily as the campaign in the Netherlands and elsewhere dragged on.

Leicester's first action in the Netherlands in the spring of 1586 was at Zutphen, better remembered for the noble death of Sir Philip Sidney, than for the lost chance of a successful ambuscade of a Spanish convoy, due to a foolhardy charge of English horse led by the brave but undisciplined gentry. Leicester resigned his post in 1590 and was succeeded in overall command of the English and Dutch forces by Prince Maurice of Nassau. In 1594 the English troops were taken completely into Dutch service. Maurice realised that only with a trained, disciplined and organised army could he hope for victory. With the aid of one of the foremost English soldiers of the time, Francis Vere, who had been appointed "sergeant-major-general" of the English troops after Leicester's departure, Maurice set himself to reform and build an army to rival Spain's; with regiments of infantry in which pikemen and musketeers supported each other, and troops of horse armed with pistols or carbines on the reiter model. Vere's great work in this enterprise received its reward when English troops played a leading and decisive role in the crushing defeats inflicted on the Spaniards at Turnhout in 1597 and Nieuport in 1600. Despite an unpromising start, despite, (until taken into Dutch service) all manner of corruption displayed by the home authorities and captains of companies over pay, mustering of men, supply of food, clothing and munitions, the English army in Holland had been transformed from a rabble into regiments of brave, skilled veterans. Much was no doubt due to lessons learned in the hard school of experience, but it was Vere's skill as an organizer, administrator and tactician that enabled English soldiers to achieve a renown they had not known in Europe since Agincourt.

The first 40 years of the Stuart dynasty were notable in military terms for, on the one hand, the ultimate decay of the national military system dating back to the fyrd and the increasing struggle for control of that system between King and Parliament; on the other, for the experience gained by English and Scottish soldiers fighting as mercenaries in the continuation of the religious conflicts of the sixteenth century, known as the Thirty Years War.

Taking the latter first, we find that the English troops in the Netherlands remained in Dutch service until a truce was made with Spain in 1609. Of these a number under the command of Horace Vere, the brother of Francis, entered the service of the Elector Frederick, the Protestant prince whose defiance of the Habsburg Empire in assuming the throne of Bohemia had precipitated the Thirty Years War. When, as an extension of this war, fighting again broke out in the Spanish Netherlands in 1624, large numbers of English volunteers rallied to the Dutch cause, distinguishing themselves in such actions as Bois-le-Duc (1629) and the siege of Breda (1637). It was in these struggles with the Spaniards for the fortified towns of the Netherlands that many of those Englishmen, who would soon be arrayed against each other in the cause of King or Parliament, first learned the soldier's trade: Thomas Fairfax, Jacob Astley, Philip Skippon, George Goring and others who will be met later, including a young Devon captain, George Monck. At Breda, too, these men were joined in arms by the youthful sons of the Elector Frederick, the Princes Rupert and Maurice.

Meanwhile Scottish soldiers were gaining experience of new methods and tactics under one of the rising stars of the military firmament, Gustavus Adolphus, King of Sweden. A regiment raised by Sir Donald Mackay from Highland clans and Edinburgh gaols had been fighting with some distinction in the service of the King of Denmark against the Imperialists since 1626. Another, under Sir John Hepburn, had been raised to fight for "The Winter Queen", Elizabeth Stuart, daughter of James I and husband of the Elector Frederick, and after a short spell in Dutch pay, had offered its services to Gustavus Adolphus. Joined by Mackay's and two other Scottish regiments, Lumsden's and Stargate's, it formed, under Hepburn's command, the "Green Brigade" of the army Gustavus landed in Germany to fight in the Protestant cause. The name of this formation derived from the colour of its standards by which each brigade of the Swedish army was distinguised.

Gustavus made many innovations in organisation and tactics, based on his belief in the superiority of speed and mobility harnessed to increased firepower, and the mutual support of horse, foot and artillery, over the principles of weight and mass, seen in the unwieldy blocks of pikemen, musketeers and heavily armoured cavalry of the Spanish school, favoured by the great Imperialist captains, Tilly and Wallenstein. Gustavus' infantry was formed into eight-company regiments of about 1,000, each split into two 'battaglia' (hence, battalions), with a preponderance of musketeers over pikemen, formed in three or six ranks.† His cavalry were armed with two pistols and a sword and wore helmet and cuirass only; instead of the reiters' caracole delivered from a square formation, they were taught to charge in three ranks, pressing home with the sword after firing a volley with their pistols. The artillery was standardized and light mobile guns were attached to the infantry for close support. The order of battle was the customary seventeenth century one of infantry in the centre and cavalry on the wings, but the latter often had musketeers in support, and his regiments were deployed with plenty of space for manoeuvre.

† A company had 72 musketeers and 54 pikemen distributed in corporalships of 24 and 18 respectively.

18

London Trained Bands in the procession at the Obsequies of Sir Philip Sidney, 1587
Engraving by Th. Dirk de Bry after Thomas Land

Trained in these methods Hepburn's brigade fought in Germany until 1635, winning fame particularly at Breitenfeld in 1631 where it was said *"though there were brave brigadds of Sweds and Dutch in the field, yet it was the Scots brigadd's fortune to have gotten the praise for the foote service, and not without cause".(7)* Subsequently, when France entered the war against the Empire, Hepburn's brigade joined the French service as the 'Regiment d'Hebron'. They will be met again later under a different designation.

While British soldiers were earning their laurels under foreign paymasters, military events at home were a catalogue of shame and disgrace. James I ended the war with Spain and repealed the Militia Acts of Mary so that the force's obligations and duties rested once more on Edward I's Statute of Winchester. In the face of such kingly interest it is little wonder that national enthusiasm for the only defence force dwindled and died. Charles I, at the instigation of his favourite the Duke of Buckingham but with no military power at his back, decided to harass Spain by sending an expedition to Cadiz. The Spaniards had little difficulty in routing the disorganized, half-clad, press-ganged rabble that passed for an English army which had previously rendered itself senseless after discovering a warehouse full of wine soon after landing. Similar expeditions to relieve the French Huguenots in La Rochelle met with equally shameful ends, until the assassination of Buckingham by the embittered officer, Felton, put paid to these adventures.

In 1639 the Scots, angered by Charles' attempts to impose the Anglican prayer book upon them, raised an army to defend their religion under Alexander Leslie, a veteran of Gustavus. Already at odds with his Parliament over the Petition of Right, Charles could not accept this affront to his authority in the north and, in an astonishing throw-back to the feudal system, summoned the peers to join him with their retainers as a cavalry force, at the same time calling out the northern militia to provide his foot. The appalling inefficiency and unpreparedness of the force that reluctantly answered the summons was mercifully not further demonstrated on the field of battle, since Charles found he had no option but to make concessions to the Scots. He tried again the following year, this time summoning the militia from the southern counties. It was doubtless of little concern to a militiaman from Wiltshire or Kent which prayer book the Scots used, certainly not enough to induce him to leave his farm or trade and march north; as was seen in the days of Mary, when the militia, English society in arms, could or would not identify with the king's cause, it withheld its loyalty and obedience. Amid scenes of riot, insubordination and mutiny, a motley rabble eventually arrived in the north and met the Scots at Newburn, where Leslie quickly ensured that *"the whole army did run with so much precipitation".(8)*

In an effort to swell his numbers, Charles had issued Commissions of Array to the Lords Lieutenant. These had raised a storm of protest, with Parliament questioning their legality under the Petition of Right and refusing to provide the king with the wherewithal to meet the Scottish threat. Charles therefore dissolved Parliament. But now, defeated by the Scots, he was forced to agree to pay them huge indemnities, the money for which could only be voted by Parliament. This, the Long Parliament, was re-assembled and promptly passed an act to prevent its dissolution without its consent. As the rift grew, the final break came over who should control the militia, not that it was worth the struggle. Parliament asserted its right to do so and appointed county lieutenants with powers to quell rebellion, finally demanding that it should rule in the king's name. When Charles rejected this, Parliament levied an army of 10,000 men and declared all those loyal to the king to be in rebellion. So it came to war.

Thus a military system which, in essentials, had remained unchanged since Alfred the Great, which had survived the Norman Conquest, the feudal system, the long wars with France, the introduction of the modern state of the Tudors, the threat of Spain, the great conflicts in Europe between professional, almost permanent armies, in the end proved to be the catalyst that was to set Englishman against Englishman. It had long proved inadequate and inefficient, yet it was ironic that it would take a civil war, rather than peril from abroad, to change it.

20

Prince Rupert, c1641.

Portrait, oil on panel, attributed to G.Honthurst.
National Portrait Gallery.

King Charles I c1645.

Details from portrait, oil on canvas, artist unknown.
National Portrait Gallery.

'1653 Oliver Cromwell
Lord Protector of England, Scotland & Ireland.'

Line engraving by G.Vertue after a miniature by
Samuel Cooper from Rapin's 'History of England'
published in 1732.   0910-275

Lord George Goring, c1645

Portrait, oil on canvas, artist unknown.
National Portrait Gallery.

THE ARMIES OF BRITAIN

Acknowledgements

Illustrations:

Reproduced by Gracious Permission of Her Majesty The Queen 56, 63, 145; Crown Copyright, reproduced with permission of the Controller of Her Majesty's Stationery Office 12, 283; Army Museums Ogilby Trust 98; The Earl of Dartmouth 34 lower; P. Dineley Esq 52 left; Mr R. E. F. Green 28 lower right; Headquarters London District 151; Imperial War Museum 250 right, 255 upper, 256 upper, 259 centre; India Office Library and Records 80 upper; National Portrait Gallery 20 upper left, upper right, lower right, 34 upper right, 45 upper left, 138 lower right; Rifle Brigade Museum Trustees 115 upper; Royal Artillery Institution, Woolwich 14 right; Royal Irish Fusiliers Museum 121 right, 138 upper right; The Tate Gallery, London 45 lower; Victoria and Albert Museum 28 upper left; Mr. Jac Weller 112 lower; York and Lancaster Regiment Museum 238 upper right.

Maps:

A. J. Barker, *The Vainglorious War,* Weidenfeld & Nicolson 157; Correlli Barnett, *Britain and Her Army,* Allen Lane 42, 66, 74, 89, 192; Byron Farwell, *Queen Victoria's Little Wars,* Allen Lane 213; David Green, *Blenheim,* Collins 48; Jac Weller, *Wellington at Waterloo,* Longman 132, P. Young and J. P. Lawford, *History of the British Army,* Weidenfeld & Nicolson 132.

Errata

Page	Location	Correction
Page 20	upper left:	should read *Lord Newport, c1645 Detail from double portrait by Sir Anthony Van Dyke National Portrait Gallery*
	upper right:	*Details* read *Detail*
	lower right:	should read *Prince Rupert, c1645 Portrait, oil on panel, attributed to G. Honthurst National Portrait Gallery*
	lower left:	*0910-275* read *6910-275*
Page 22	line 2:	*Miliarie* read *Militarie*
Page 25	line 19:	*ship-chandlers* read *ship-chandler*
	line 43:	*infrantry* read *infantry*
Page 26	lower left and right:	transpose captions
	lower left:	should read *Regimental Colour*
Page 27	line 8:	after *artillery* insert *commanded*
	line 26:	*North-Hamptonshire* read *Northamptonshire*
Page 31	line 16:	*Fifty* read *Fifth*
Page 32		should read *A Captain, An Ensign, A Lieutenant and a Company of Pikemen*
Page 34	lower:	*Dirick* read *Dirck*
Page 37	line 34:	*five battalions* read *six battalions*
Page 40	line 29:	*Brandeburgers* read *Brandenburgers*
Page 41	lower centre:	should read *Detail of matchlock musket c1694*
	right:	insert *Cavalry* after *Ranks* and *c1670-80* after *pommel*
Page 42	line 8:	after *The* insert *Commons,*
Page 43	line 36:	*arny* read *army*
Page 51		transpose captions
Page 52	upper centre:	insert accession no *6308-48*
	lower centre:	insert accession no *7109-20*
Page 58	line 47:	*8,000* read *12,000*
Page 60	upper right:	insert after *coat (back view)*
	lower left:	should read *Royal Regiment of English Fuziliers*
	lower right:	delete *42nd* and substitute *Highland*
Page 63	upper:	After caption insert *Reproduced by Gracious Permission of Her Majesty The Queen*
Page 76	line 16:	*contiuedn* read *continued*
Page 89	upper right:	battle symbol should read *Plassey 1757*
Page 92	line 32:	*Germaine* read *Germain*
Page 96	line 30:	*replused* read *repulsed*
Page 97	upper left:	*I. S. Copley* read *J. S. Copley*
Page 101	upper right:	*Officer's cap,* read *soldier's cap*
Page 104	upper:	close inverted commas after *July 9th*
	lower:	should read *Stipple engraving by W. Bromley after P. J. de Loutherbourg*
Page 105	left:	delete *Light Infantry or.* For first *c1800* read *c1795*
Page 110	line 34:	*significnace* read *significance*
	lower:	*J. A. C.* read *Jac*
Page 112	lower:	*J. A. C.* read *Jac*
Page 116	line 18:	*made* read *mad*
Page 118	upper right, lower left and right:	*Leiut-General,* read *Lieut-General*
Page 120	line 45:	*demorilised* read *demoralised*
Page 121	lower left no 2:	should read *J. O. Vandeleur*
Page 126	line 5:	after *procure* read *a satisfactory artillery commander*
	line 11:	*intended* read *tended*
	line 17:	*developed* read *deployed* and *formal* read *normal*
	line 20:	*latert* read *latter*
	line 31:	*eneemy* read *enemy*
	line 55:	*quare* read *square*
Page 127	line 1:	*&* read *and*
	line 10:	*&* read *and*
	line 16:	*unparalled* read *unparalleled*
Page 130	line 14:	*mountred* read *mounted*
Page 134	lower:	insert *Watercolour by E. A. Judge*
Page 138	lower right:	*6007-317* read *6005-317*
Page 144	line 20:	*demeanuor* read *demeanour*
Page 148	upper:	*flank company* read *light company*
Page 151		should read *Her Majesty Queen Elizabeth II returning from the ceremony of Trooping the Colour*
Page 152		should read *The Royal Scots Dragoon Guards and the Queen's Own Highlanders at Catterick*
Page 160	lower left:	*c1854* read *c1845*
Page 167	lower:	*Detatchment* read *Detachment*
Page 169	line 48:	*order* read *ordered*
Page 176	line 15:	*Fleetword* read *Fleetwood*
Page 177	footnote line 4:	*to* read *by*

Page 179   lower right :   *watercolour* read *watercolours*

Page 182   lower right :   should read *General HRH The Duke of Cambridge. 1862* read *1860*

Page 187   upper left :   should read *45th Rattray's Sikhs*

Page 188   line 50 :   *northenmost* read *northernmost*

Page 191   line 40 :   after *then* insert *outbreaks*

Page 194   line 38 :   after *force* insert contents of footnote•

Page 197   *Richard Hennel* read *Robert Hennel III*

Page 199   upper :   *Wei-Hai-Wei* read *Wei Hai Wei*

Page 200   line 5 :   *Delegation* read *Legation*

Page 203   line 55 :   *it's* read *its*

Page 205   upper :   should read *10th Company Royal Engineers*

Page 209   line 39 :   *comapy* read *company*

Page 218   line 56 :   insert *began* at start of line

Page 220   line 56 :   *slough* read *slouch*

Page 230   lower :   should read *British Cavalry in Palestine, 1918. Photogravure after a painting by J. P. Beadle 6004-10*

Page 233   upper :   delete *Advance* and *contemporary photograph*

            centre right :   *21st October 1917. During* read *21st October 1917, during*

Page 234   line 43 :   *Deville* read *Delville*

Page 236   line 3 :   *surprises* read *surprise*

            line 31 :   *exchange* read *exchanges*

Page 240   line 7 :   . . . . read *had released men for*

            line 15 :   *naver* read *never*

Page 246   centre :   *Mohman* read *Mohmand*

Page 247   line 13 :   *men* read *man*

Page 249   line 8 :   *three - battalion brigades* read *three three-battalion brigades*

Page 251   lower :   *c1940* read *c1944*

Page 256   upper :   delete *contemporary photograph*

Page 259   centre :   should read *Bedford trucks of XII Corps*

Page 266   lower :   *plotters on* read *plotters for*

Page 269   upper :   delete *during the expedition of Pyongyang*

Page 274   before footnote insert +

Page 275   upper :   *Troudos* read *Troodos*

Page 277   line 13 .   *nusiance* read *nuisance*

Page 280   lower :   delete *ARM*

Page 284   line 13 :   *those other nations* read *those of other nations.*

Page 292   1st column line 21 :   *R. G. L. Alexander R. L. G.* read *'H. R. L. G. Alexander*

            2nd column line 7 :   delete *under Hore*

Page 294   1st column line 42 :   *Caridgan* read *Cardigan*

            1st column line 61 :   *citudad* read *ciudad*

            2nd column line 74 :   *Hafir* read *Haig*

Page 295   1st column line 36 :   delete *5th Eu*

            2nd column line 13 :   *Garwal* read *Garhwal*

Page 296   1st column line 48 :   After *(1899)* insert *216*

            1st column line 51 :   *trereat* read *retreat*

            1st column line 99 :   *Ragland* read *Raglan*

            2nd column line 6 :   *Romme* read *Rommel*

            2nd column line 38 :   *Jenkings* read *Jenkins*

            2nd column line 38 :   delete *war of*

            2nd column line 83 :   *Scotaldn* read *Scotland*

            2nd column line 84 :   *Namue* read *Namur*

            2nd column line 85 :   *Statue* read *Statute*

CHAPTER 2
THE NEW MODEL
1642-1660

When the King raised his standard at Nottingham on 22nd August 1642, thus signalizing his determination to fight, both sides were faced with the problems of finding the men, munitions, supplies and, above all, money, needed to form effective armies. The only military force of the country, the county militia with its arsenals, became the focus of local struggles for its control all over England. While men's allegiances were governed by the political issues, which had been increasingly dividing King and Parliament, and to a lesser extent by the religious differences between Puritanism on the one hand and the Anglicanism of Archbishop Laud on the other, their choice was also affected by ties of family and regional loyalties, local rivalries, obligations between landlord and tenant and between landlord and monarch. In addition both sides soon found that, while local forces may have been ready to declare for one or the other, they were reluctant to serve outside their own areas. For example, when the King marched from Nottingham only 500 of the local trained bands were willing to join him and the rest had to be disarmed.

The inefficiency of the militia and the difficulties of mobilizing it as a nucleus of a field army soon became apparent to both sides. Although some of the trained-bands were to provide useful service, such as those of London in defending the capital, or the Cornishmen in securing the west for the King, both Royalists and Parliament had recourse to raising new regiments in the areas which each gradually came to dominate. While some parts of the country tried to remain neutral and others contained isolated pockets of loyalty to one side or the other, generally speaking the south-west, Wales, the west midlands and parts of the north were for the King, while Parliament controlled the east and south, including the larger towns, the ports and, most important of all, London, thereby retaining the machinery of government, the Board of Ordnance, the fleet, and the resources of the City.

Strategically, therefore, the advantage lay with Parliament. In material and financial resources too it was superior, having the support of the mercantile classes and control of the ports and cities, while the King had to rely on contributions from his wealthy followers, even sending the Queen to the continent to pawn the crown jewels. In manpower the King had the support of most, but by no means all, of the great nobles, who could raise sizeable regiments from their tenantry, but the country gentry, more numerous than the nobility and also with considerable wealth, power and available manpower at their command, were fairly evenly divided in their loyalties. Puritanism was very strong in the urban populations but the allegiance of the lower classes generally was determined more by personal and local circumstances than by conviction; as Hobbes wrote, *"there were very few of the common people that cared much for either of the causes but would have taken either side for pay or plunder". (1)*

Neither side had a monopoly of the few professional soldiers in the country, the veterans of Holland and Germany, and in both armies regiments were raised and commanded by men who owed their rank to their social position rather than military ability. The standard of training of these hastily-raised regiments depended therefore on the degree of military skill which individual officers and men had, or had not, acquired in the militia, and such drill as the few men with proper experience of soldiering were able to impart before taking the field. Lacking the discipline of regular troops, their morale and obedience would depend on the frequency with which they were paid and the distances from their homes they would be expected to march. Since the former was anything but regular and the latter considerable, the ranks of both armies were soon depleted by men going off to loot and pillage or simply desert.

Although Parliament had one solid body of infantry in the London trained-bands, the Royalists were superior in cavalry. Drawn from the county squirearchy and their servants, the latter contained better horses and men with more latent ability as cavalrymen than anything Parliament could muster. Even so they were raw and undisciplined. Perceiving this, their commander, Prince Rupert, adopted a modified version of Gustavus' cavalry tactics, by instructing his troopers to charge home with the sword without pausing to discharge their pistols and to use the latter only when they had got to grips with the enemy. Though aged only 23, Rupert,

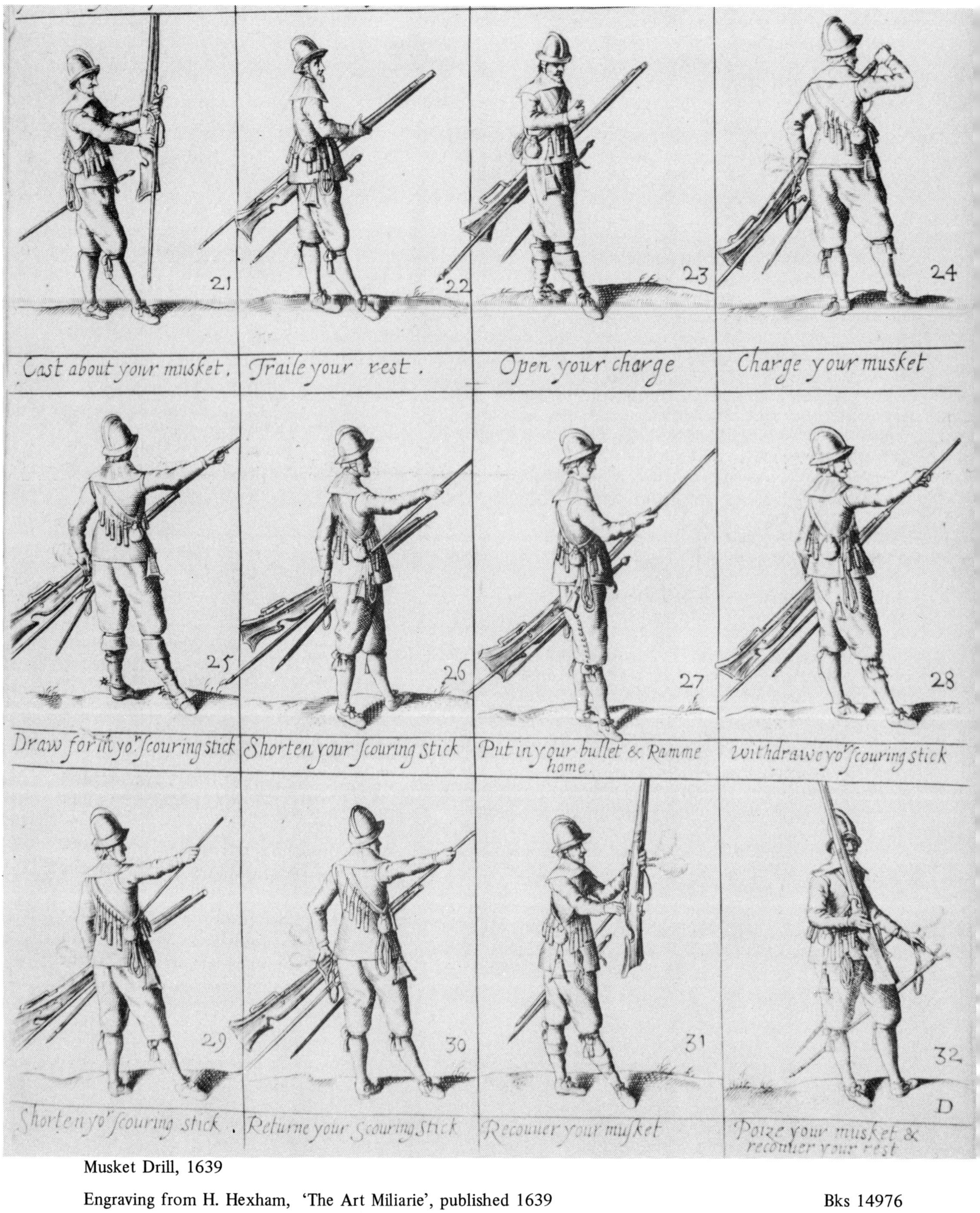

21	22	23	24
Cast about your musket.	*Traile your rest.*	*Open your charge*	*Charge your musket*
25	26	27	28
Draw forth yoᵘʳ ſcouring stick	*Shorten your ſcouring stick*	*Put in your bullet & Ramme home.*	*withdrawe yoᵘʳ ſcouring stick*
29	30	31	32 D
Shorten yoᵘʳ ſcouring stick.	*Returne your ſcouring stick*	*Recouer your muſket*	*Poize your musket & recouer your rest*

Musket Drill, 1639

Engraving from H. Hexham, 'The Art Miliarie', published 1639

Bks 14976

a tall, striking figure, *"very sparkish in his dress....clad in scarlet, very richly laid in silver lace and mounted on a very gallant black Barbary horse" (2)*, was already a veteran of the Thirty Years War. He was given command of the Royalist horse by his uncle, the King, but soon came to excercise his authority in the army as a whole, his forceful manner prevailing over the elderly noblemen appointed to the chief command. The King retained strategic control over his forces which, despite his often weak and vacillating leadership, at least made for more centralised command than existed in the Parliamentary forces, where their commander-in-chief the Earl of Essex, was subject to a host of often conflicting orders from both Houses of Parliament, resulting in no clearly defined strategy or purpose.

The King's aim in 1642 was to recapture London as quickly as possible. Advancing from Shrewsbury on 12th October, he unexpectedly encountered Essex at Edgehill, near Banbury, on 23rd. An indecisive battle followed with each side fighting stoutly but with little skill until exhaustion forced the combatants to draw apart. Two lessons stood out from the battle. The overwhelming superiority of the Royalist horse, trained in Rupert's shock tactics, carried all before them, but their lack of discipline showed in their failure to rally to the support of their hard-pressed infantry which was nearly overrun. The second was the importance of morale. Commanding the 67th troop of Parliamentary horse was the Huntingdonshire squire and Member of Parliament, Oliver Cromwell, then aged 43 and with no previous military experience. What he had seen at Edgehill confirmed his views made to John Hampden after the earlier skirmish at Powick Bridge, where Rupert's horse had routed Essex's advance guard: *"Your troopers are most of them old decayed serving men and tapsters and such kind of fellows, and their troopers are gentlemen's sons, younger sons and persons of quality. Do you think that the spirit of such base and mean fellows will ever be able to encounter gentlemen who have honour and courage and resolution in them? You must get men of a spirit that is likely to go on as far as gentlemen will go, or else I am sure you will be beaten still". (3)* His experience at Edgehill more than ever convinced him that a new type of recruit was needed, *"such men as had the fear of God before them, and made some conscience of what they did". (3)*

After Edgehill Charles pushed on to London but in such leisurely fashion that Essex was able to get there before him and organise its defences which, backed by the City trained-bands, baulked the Royalist advance. The King had missed his opportunity to end the war and withdrew to Oxford.

His plan for 1643 was a sound one, being based on a threefold advance on London. From the west Sir Ralph Hopton's Cornishmen were to strike through the southern counties and march on London from the south; the Marquis of Newcastle's Yorkshire army was to thrust southwards; while the King's own army, based on Oxford, was to deal with the main Parliamentary force under Essex. At first all went well: Hopton, after a string of victories, pressed on into Wiltshire; Rupert took Bristol, the second port in the Kingdom; and Newcastle defeated the Fairfaxes, father and son, in Yorkshire and moved down through Lincolnshire. Then the plan began to founder due to the increasing reluctance of local troops like Hopton's and Newcastle's to fight far from their homes, a reluctance that became ever more evident as Parliamentary garrisons held out in their rear. In the west Plymouth, Exeter, and above all Gloucester, astride the route to the King's recruiting ground in south Wales, remained steadfast for Parliament. Until these places were secured the plan could not proceed, but Gloucester resisted all attempts to take it and in early September was relieved by Essex. In the north the Fairfaxes held Hull, threatening Newcastle's rear, so that he felt compelled to return and besiege it. Reinforced by sea, the city was never in danger and Sir Thomas Fairfax was able to ferry his cavalry across the Humber, join up with Cromwell and recover Lincolnshire. Newcastle abandoned the siege and the threat from the north had failed.

Earlier in the year, to guard against such a threat, the county forces of Norfolk, Essex, Hertfordshire and Cambridgeshire had been grouped together in the Eastern Association. Cromwell had returned to this area after Edgehill, organising its preparations for defence and raising the new kind of soldiers he had earlier envisaged. His troop of 60 men had, by March 1643, become a regiment of five troops and by September of ten. His aim was to create a body *"inspired by a common zeal, welded together by a common discipline, sensitive like an instrument of music to the spirit of its commander". (4)*   The men he chose to fill the ranks were of some substance, yeomen farmers, freeholders and their sons from the eastern counties. The officers he appointed were chosen for their worth rather than their social standing: *"I would rather have a plain russet-coated captain that knows what he fights for, and loves what he knows than that which you call a gentleman and is nothing else". (4)* One captain, Henry Ireton, was the son of a Nottinghamshire gentleman; another, James Berry, had been a clerk in an ironworks. Cromwell chose good horses and insisted on scrupulous horsemastership; his men he armed with iron "pot" helmets and back-and-breast cuirasses, their arms being sword and pistols. He drilled them, disciplined them, fed and clothed them and did his best to see they were paid regularly. In August his new regiment formed part of the Earl of Manchester's Eastern Association army, organized to face Newcastle's southwards march before, as has been seen, the latter turned back to besiege Hull.

Charles' plan for 1643, initially so full of promise, had failed, but equally Parliament was no nearer victory.

Both armies lacked recruits and resorted to impressment. The Royal army had too many regiments of only company size, due to the custom of filling gaps by raising new regiments instead of reinforcing existing ones, and Parliament's,relying on the variable efforts of county committees, lacked uniformity of any sort. Both dwindled from the troops' aversion to moving far afield.

Parliament therefore looked for an ally and, by signing the Solemn League and Covenant†, obtained the support of the Scots who, in early 1644, despatched an army southwards under Alexander Leslie, Earl of Leven, the victor of Newburn in 1640 who had learned his trade in the Swedish service. To co-ordinate the military operations a Committee of Both Kingdoms was set up,an improvement on the Parliamentary direction of the war hitherto but in which the views of the civilians were soon at odds with the military members. Nevertheless the Scottish invasion disrupted the King's plans in the south and Rupert was sent north to relieve Newcastle, now besieged by Fairfax and Manchester in York. On 2nd July the armies of Rupert and Newcastle met the combined forces of Fairfax, Manchester and the Scots on Marston Moor. Though about equal in cavalry, the Parliamentary infantry outnumbered the Royalists' by two to one. In an area of about two square miles, 45,000 English and Scots fought out the largest and most decisive battle of the Civil War to date.

The usual deployment of infantry in the centre and cavalry on the wings brought some of the finest troops on both sides face to face, including the two foremost cavalry leaders of the war. On the Royalist right Rupert's horse opposed for the first time Cromwell's yeomen of the Eastern Association, who were supported by part of the Scottish horse. In the centre the predominantly Scottish infantry, their musketeers and pikemen trained in the Swedish discipline and arrayed in two lines, stood opposite two prime Royalist regiments of foot, Lord Byron's and Rupert's Bluecoats, backed by Newcastle's tough Yorkshiremen, the Whitecoats. On the Royalist left the horse was led by Lord George Goring, the archetypal cavalier and a veteran of the Dutch wars, who placed musketeers between his troops of horse in the Swedish manner. Against him was Sir Thomas Fairfax with some largely raw Yorkshire cavalry with three regiments of Scottish horse in reserve.

During the long summer's day interspersed with thunderstorms, the two armies watched each other across a ditch. As evening came with no sign of movement, Rupert decided no attack would come that day and ordered his troops to feed themselves. Then Cromwell struck. His horsemen smashed through the leading Royalist squadrons, were checked by the second line, but with the Scottish horse coming up in support, they pressed home their charge and put Rupert's men to flight. As Cromwell later said, *"God made them as stubble to our swords". (5)* In the centre the infantry came to push of pike and with their greater numbers the Parliamentary foot enjoyed an initial success but, on coming up against Newcastle's Whitecoats, the tide turned and their right centre began to give way. Meanwhile Goring had charged and routed Fairfax's recruits and although part of his force disappeared in headlong pursuit from the field, the remainder swung round to attack the right flank of the Parliamentary infantry. Pressed by the Whitecoats in front and Goring's troopers on the right, soon only three Scots regiments remained in fighting order. But now help came from Cromwell. Reforming his men after their success on the left, he led them across the field behind the Royal army to retrieve the shattered Parliamentary right. The drill and discipline so carefully inculcated in the months of training now told as he first swept Goring's disorganized troops from the field, and then turned on Newcastle's infantry. Though soon surrounded, the stubborn pikemen of the Whitecoats fell back step by step to a walled enclosure known as White Syke Close. Here, as darkness fell, they fought to the last until the rising moon revealed nothing but their dead.

The Royal army was shattered and the north was lost to the King. Cromwell's Ironsides — a name originally bestowed by Rupert on Cromwell himself — had proved what careful training, strict discipline and staunch morale could achieve, and Cromwell had made his mark as one of the foremost soldiers of the time. Leven, who had some experience of armies, said of Cromwell's men, *"Europe hath no better soldiers".(6)*

Despite this great success Parliament failed to follow it up. Their victorious northern army split up to pursue different tasks: The Fairfaxes to reduce Yorkshire, the Scots to besiege the city of Newcastle, while the Eastern Association under Manchester returned to its home ground. Worse was to follow, for two months later in the south Essex's army surrendered at Lostwithiel, and in October a supine Manchester let slip the chance of defeating the King's army at Newbury. By the end of the year the high promise of Marston Moor had sunk in a welter of dissension, weakness and hesitation. It was time for a radical change.

A month before Marston Moor, Sir William Waller, the Parliamentary commander in the west, ascribing his lack of success to the transitory and local character of the levies forming his army, wrote to the Committee of Both Kingdoms: *"I write to let you know that an army compounded of these men will never go through with your service, and till you have an army merely your own, that you may command, it is in a manner impossible to do anything of importance".(7)* In November Cromwell, bitterly disillusioned with the jealousies and rivalries of the Parliamentary leadership and the wasted opportunities of 1644, made a forceful speech in the House of Commons, echoing Waller's words and calling for a new and more positive handling of the war

---

† An agreement under which Parliament undertook to introduce Presbyterianism in England and Wales.

The Jane Hodge Foundation

effort: *"I do conceive if the Army be not put into another method, and the War more vigorously prosecuted, the people can bear the War no longer, and will force you to a dishonourable peace".(8)* Seized by the urgency of the situation, Parliament passed the Self-Denying Ordinance, which debarred all members of the Lords and Commons from military command, thereby excluding unsuccessful noblemen like Manchester and Essex and also Cromwell himself. On 23rd November the Commons instructed the Committee of Both Kingdoms *"to consider of a frame or model of the whole militia".(9)* This led, on 13th February 1645, to the passing of an Ordinance which authorised the formation of a national army for general service, with no local connections, which was to be of a standard organisation and regularly paid from national funds — a New Model Army.

The establishment was fixed at 14,400 infantry, 6,600 horse, 1,000 dragoons, and a train of artillery. To fill the ranks, the armies of Essex, Waller and Manchester were combined, with the shortfall made good by impressment, a method of recruitment which was to continue until the end of the Civil War. Supreme command was vested in the captain-general, a post given, with universal approval, to Sir Thomas Fairfax. Then aged 33, Fairfax had enjoyed mixed success in the war, but he was a brave, honourable and straightforward leader, who knew how to handle men and had always set an example of energy and determination. His second-in-command was Philip Skippon, a veteran of the Dutch wars, who was appointed sergeant-major-general and commander of the foot. The post of lieutenant-general in command of the horse was left vacant, the obvious contender being temporarily excluded by the Self-Denying Ordinance. The senior officers selected by Fairfax contained a high proportion of gentry of varying degree, but there were also men who had been *"tradesmen, brewers, tailors, goldsmiths, shoemakers and the like". (10)* Colonel Okey commanding the dragoons was a former ship-chandlers. Ability determined their selection and not, as previously, social position.

The cavalry was recruited from better educated and more highly motivated men than the urban and rural lower classes found in the infantry; Cromwell's own regiment of horse, now split into two, provided the model for the mounted arm. The sometimes mutinous material from disbanded regiments which Skippon had to weld into the new infantry required firm though tactful handling, but the promise of regular pay and the infliction of severe punishments on the more recalcitrant soon had the men from the old armies and the new conscripts pulling willingly together.

The horse was organized into eleven regiments, each of six troops of 100 men excluding officers. The regimental staff had a colonel and a major, who each had a troop of their own, while the other four troops were commanded by captains, the troop officers being a lieutenant, a cornet and a quartermaster, giving a total of 24 officers in the regiment. Included among the men were three corporals-of-horse† and a trumpeter. The horse were armoured with a lobster-tailed helmet, fitted with a three-barred face guard and a back-and-breast plate worn over a coat of thick buff leather; they carried a sword and two pistols. Their tactics resembled those introduced by Rupert in imitation of the Swedish horse, but the emphasis was on a steady, controlled advance at a smart trot, with the troopers locked in tightly together in three ranks, the aim being to shock the enemy with weight and mass, rather than speed. Their pistol fire was reserved until they were among their opponents and once these were discharged, it was a matter of hacking away with the sword, still keeping as tight a formation as possible, until the enemy broke. Where they differed from the Royalist horse was in discipline which, whether they prevailed or were beaten in the sword fight, enabled them to rally and reform to charge again or attack some other body.

The dragoons were mounted infantry who fought on foot with muskets, using horses as a means of greater mobility. They were used for scouting, outpost duties, advance, flank and rearguards, and the capture of important tactical features. They were organized in companies of 100 with the same proportion of officers as the horse, and to signify their primarily infantry function had drummers instead of trumpeters. Their normal formation was in ten ranks with ten men abreast, nine of which dismounted for action while the tenth held the horses.

The foot was divided into 12 regiments, each of ten companies. As in the horse, the field officers, the colonel, lieutenant-colonel and major, each had his own company, the strengths of which were 200, 160 and 140 respectively. The seven captains' companies were 100 strong, all companies having a lieutenant, an ensign, two sergeants, three corporals and one or two drummers. Within the company the proportion of musketeers to pikemen was two to one, although the latter enjoyed greater prestige, and since they had to handle the 18-foot pike and were armoured with pot, back-and-breast and thigh guards, they were chosen for their height and strength. The task of the pikemen was to protect the musketeers from cavalry, to which they were highly vulnerable, and in attack to follow up the musketry volleys with "push of pike", in which they were joined by the musketeers clubbing their muskets or wielding their swords. Although an improved firearm, the flintlock or firelock, had been developed, these were as yet too expensive for general issue, and the musketeers were armed with the heavy and cumbersome matchlock. The New Model infantry were usually arrayed in six ranks, but

---

† A rank still used by sergeants in the Household Cavalry to this day.

26

Soldiers of the Trained Bands c1640

Plaster casts of wooden figures in Cromwell House, Highgate, built in 1637-38 by Richard Sprignell, Captain of the London Trained Bands. The figures are assumed to represent his company.   7009-32

Royalist Army c1645

Regiment Colour, possibly of Fitton's Regiment.

6003-168

Parliamentary Army c1645
5th (or 2nd Captain's) Company Colour

Regiment unknown.   5912-76

could double up to form three, thereby widening the frontage and enabling all three ranks to fire a volley simultaneously, with the front rank kneeling, the second stooping and the rear standing. As a symbol of their new status as part of a national army, all the foot and dragoons were uniformly dressed in red coats, each regiment being distinguished by the colour of its facings. Although red had been worn by the only permanent force before the New Model, the Yeomen of the Guard, and had been seen occasionally in elements of the Tudor armies and some individual regiments during the Civil War, its use by the New Model was the first instance of its adoption as the uniform colour by an English army as a whole.

The army was completed by a train of artillery by a lieutenant-general of the Ordnance and also included an Engineer-general with an engineering staff. However, apart from the use of heavy guns in sieges, artillery did not play a decisive role in this period and this arm was the least effective element of the New Model. Since the draught-horses and their drivers were impressed or hired, the train was furnished with two regiments of infantry and two companies of firelocks (dressed in tawny coats), whose tasks were as much protection of the guns as prevention of the drivers' desertion.

At the head of the army was a proper headquarters staff, in which Skippon doubled his function as commander of the foot with that of chief of staff, and which included: three Commissary—Generals for musters, victuals and horse provisions; a Waggon-Master-General for the provision of transport; a Scoutmaster-General for intelligence gathering; a Judge-Advocate-General; eight civilian Treasurers-at-War for finance; and physicians, an apothecary and a chaplain. The foot and horse also had its own staff officers.

The New Model Army was thus organized on a thoroughly sound basis, drilled, disciplined and administered in a uniform fashion, in complete contrast to the 'ad hoc' arrangements of English armies in the past. Throughout March and April 1645 the work went on at Windsor, preparing the army for the field. At the beginning of May it was on the march to bring the King to battle.

Although Charles still held the west, his outlook in early 1645 was not promising. His only hope lay in the brilliant campaign then being waged in Scotland by the Marquis of Montrose, who had raised an army of High-landers and Irish for the royal cause. The King decided to move north to link up with him but on reaching North-Hamptonshire he became indecisive. Here Fairfax found him and on 14th June the two armies met at Naseby. On the day before, a great shout had rung round the Parliamentary camp, *"Ironsides is come" (11),* the result of Fairfax's succesful petition to Parliament for the release of Cromwell to take over the lieutenant-generalship of the horse.

Outnumbered two to one, the King's army was crushed at Naseby. The fatal indiscipline of Rupert's horse squandered their rout of the Parliament left and, while they busied themselves amongst Fairfax's baggage, Cromwell on the right bludgeoned his way through Langdale's untrained Yorkshire horse and turned his Ironsides on the Royalist infantry. Charles was persuaded to flee, his reserve went with him, and Rupert's Bluecoat infantry was left to fight and die. When Rupert himself returned the battle was lost and his men, with blown horses, would not face the victorious Parliamentarians.

Naseby was the end of the King's hopes for a military victory. During the next few months his forces in the west crumbled at Langport, Bridgewater and Bristol before the ever-increasing power of the New Model; Montrose was finally defeated at Philiphaugh; and eventually, having surrendered to the Scots, Charles was handed over by them to Parliament in January 1647. Having failed to preserve his cause by force of arms, he now tried to save it by negotiation, aided in his machinations by the growing differences which ensued between the New Model and its political masters.

The army had fulfilled the task for which it had been called into being by Parliament and, confident of its own power based on armed strength which it alone now possessed, was in no mood to put up with double-dealing from anyone. Throughout the army, and especially in the better educated horse, there was great religious fervour, even fanaticism. This manifested itself most strongly among the "Independents", who recognized no religious authority between man and his Maker, whether it be of the Catholic, Anglican or Presbyterian variety. Their dislike of authority in religion extended into politics where their views were radical, if not revolutionary, by the standards of the time. Their burning faith had made them a redoubtable fighting force but it also made them a political one.

Parliament, on the other hand, was predominantly Presbyterian and, in accordance with the promises made to the Scots under the Solemn League and Covenant, began to impose Presbyterianism on the country and to weed out the Independents from the army. Furthermore, with the fighting now over, it proposed to disband, or at least reduce, the army as an economy measure while, at the same time, giving no indication of any willingness to make good the arrears of pay which, despite the good intentions of 1645, many of the troops were owed.

These grievances brought the army near to mutiny. To avert widespread indiscipline Cromwell and Fairfax made common cause with their men and led the army into London. Having reminded Parliament where true power lay, Cromwell endeavoured to come to some agreement with the King, but this led to further unrest among

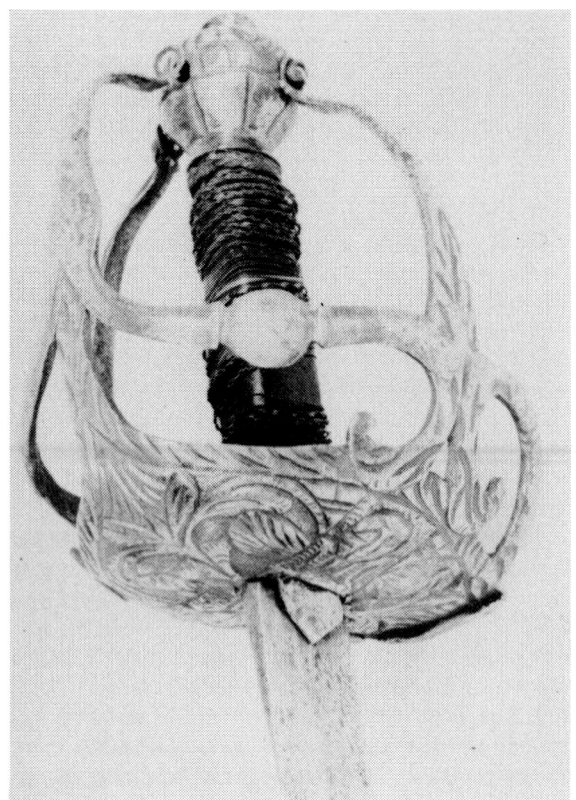

English mortuary sword, c1645   7512-126

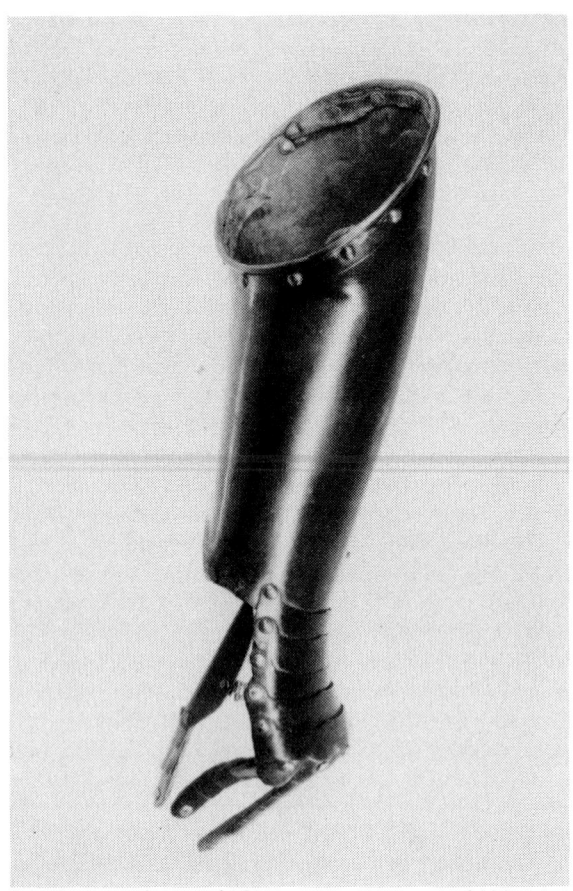

Bridle gauntlet, c1645   6408-34-1

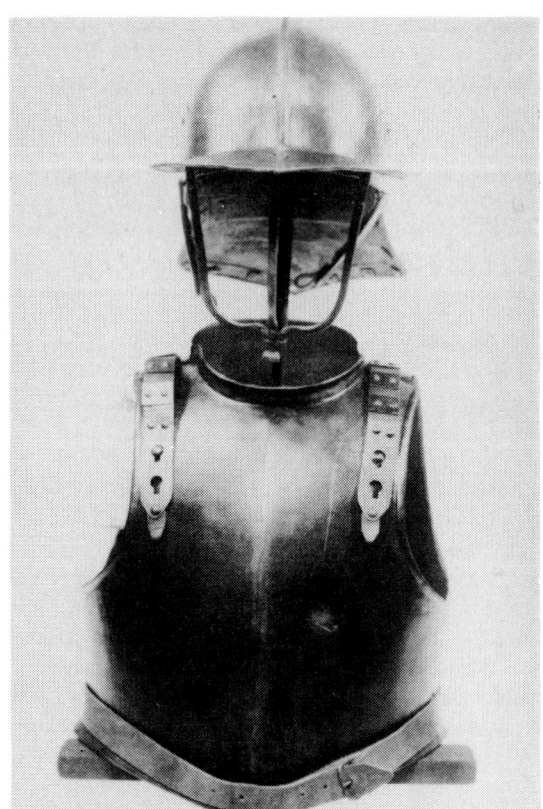

Trooper's pot helmet, breast and back plates
c1645   6408-34

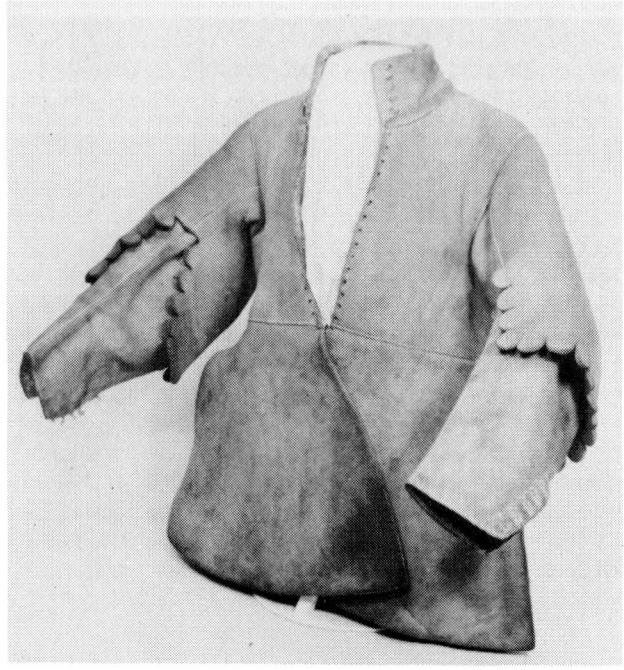

Buff coat worn by Major Thomas Sanders, Gell's Regiment
of Horse, c1645   7209-49-1

the lower ranks, where the ranting firebrands of an extreme sect known as the Levellers were fomenting discontent. Cromwell restored order, but his efforts to settle with the King were soon proved to have been futile. As a result of Charles' secret and devious negotiations, the Scots renounced their treaty with Parliament and sent an army across the border, while Royalist uprisings broke out in Wales and Kent. The army's quarrel with Parliament was temporarily set aside and, with Fairfax subduing the south, Cromwell moved hurriedly north and trounced the Scots at Preston.

This second Civil War finally convinced the army of the King's duplicity and it determined to be rid of him. Although Fairfax still held the chief command, the real authority lay with Cromwell and Ireton, while a new breed of colonels, men *"of a darker and wilder strain"(12)* like Pride and Harrison, had replaced the straight-forward, honest soldiers of the early days of the New Model. Once a believer in constitutional monarchy, Ireton was now a convinced republican, but the King was given a last chance. Ireton drew up proposals in which sovereignty was to be vested in the people's representatives, elected for biennial parliaments, and over whom the King would have no veto. Meanwhile Parliament, despite having been saved by the army from a royalist triumph in the second Civil War, entered into further negotiations with the king as a counter to the army's power. When it received Ireton's proposals it ignored them, and the King still hopeful of escape, rejected them. The army now lost patience with both King and Parliament. On 6th December 1648 Colonel Pride entered the House of Commons with musketeers at his back and ejected or arrested the Presbyterian majority, leaving only about 50 members of the Independent persuasion who would be obedient to the army's wishes; a collection which became known as the Rump. On 1st January this body ordered the King to be brought to trial and on the 30th he was put to death. With his execution the monarchy and the House of Lords were abolished and in May the Rump, at the behest of the army, set up the Commonwealth. Fairfax and some of the older officers, who had been growing more and more uneasy at the unconstitutional road the army had been following, disassociated themselves from the King's trial; the people of England, generally appalled at the execution, began to see the army as an even greater instrument of tyranny than that from which the army had originally been formed to save them.

Although government by the Commonwealth was supposed to be, according to the Act which established it, by *"the supreme authority of this nation, the representatives of the people in Parliament"(13)*, it was in fact an oligarchy, ruled by a Council of State whose power was nominally derived from the unrepresentative Rump but effectively from the army. Its authority was soon in danger, from within by the seditious activities of the Levellers, who had a strong following in the lower ranks, and from without by the hostility of most of Europe to the execution of the King, and the danger of Royalist invasions from Scotland and Ireland, where Charles II had been proclaimed. The Irish threat was the most pressing and Cromwell was appointed to command a force of 12,000 to deal with it. Before he could embark, however, mutiny inspired by the Levellers broke out in the army. While in sympathy with many of the Levellers' beliefs, he would brook no indiscipline among the troops and, by arresting 400 of the mutineers and shooting three of them, he rapidly restored order.

From August 1649 Cromwell subjected Ireland to fire and sword, throwing his well-trained troops against the Irish strongholds and teaching the people a lesson of severity and brutality that would never be forgotten. By May 1650 the back of the rebellion was broken and Cromwell returned to England, leaving Ireton to complete the pacification of the country.

A month later Charles II landed in Scotland and a Scottish invasion became imminent. A force of 10,500 foot and 5,500 horse was assembled and the command offered to Fairfax. However, out of sympathy with all that had occurred, he declined and Cromwell was appointed captain-general. Among the officers of this force, one in particular should be noted: the Devonshire captain last met in the Dutch wars, George Monck. A royalist at the beginning of the Civil War, Monck had changed sides in 1644. Impressed by his abilities, Cromwell offered him the colonelcy of a regiment of foot. The regiment concerned refused to accept Monck as colonel on account of his royalist past, so Cromwell, reluctant to lose the services of a good officer, formed a new regiment for him from two others, which had been part of the original New Model infantry.

At dawn on 3rd September Cromwell met Leslie's army at Dunbar. Though outnumbered and overlooked by the Scots on high ground, he placed a small force of infantry to check the enemy's left and centre, while he threw the bulk of his army against their right, turning their flank and hemming them in between a mountain and a deep burn. In an hour it was all over, with almost the entire Scottish army casualties or prisoners. Sir John Fortescue called it *"the greatest action fought by an English army since Agincourt."(14)*

Nevertheless Charles managed to raise a new Scottish army the following year and, though Cromwell moved against them, the Scots slipped past and invaded England. Cromwell pursued and on the anniversary of Dunbar he beat them at Worcester as soundly as he had done the year before. Charles fled to France and the danger to the Commonwealth was over. Three years later Monck completed the pacification of Scotland and the three kingdoms were united in one Commonwealth, a unity fought for and won by the New Model Army, an achievement claimed as its *"greatest and noblest work".(15)*

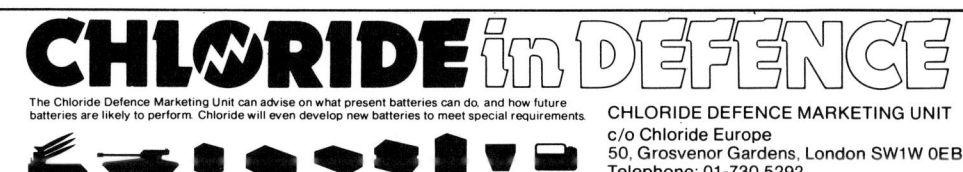

In the last six years of the Commonwealth the army enjoyed mixed fortunes. In the field of military endeavour, an expedition against Spanish possessions in the Caribbean suffered a fate that will become increasingly familiar as other British armies are sent to that theatre, wherein defects of organisation and preparation are exacerbated by the scourge of disease. Against this, the first appearance on the continent of England's red-coated professional soldiers was greeted with admiration and respect by their French allies with whom they were to operate against Spain in the Low Countries in 1657. Cromwell, by now Lord Protector of England, was keen to secure Dunkirk as a naval base against the dangers of a Royalist invasion from Spanish Flanders, where Charles II and his followers were under the protection of Spain, which was itself at war with France. Though disconcerted by the English soldiers' demands for beef and beer, the French were impressed by their discipline. At the sieges of St Venant and Ypres the redcoats, impatient with laborious trench-digging, showed the way into the Spanish redoubts. Again, at the Battle of the Dunkirk Dunes on 24th May 1658 the pikemen and musketeers of the English foot broke the Spanish right on their own by outstriding the more slowly moving French. In the French ranks that day was that old Scottish corps of the Thirty Years War, the 'Régiment d'Hebron' now the 'Régiment Douglas'. There were other men from the British Isles in the Spanish ranks at the Dunes; when, at the end of the battle, the only regiment still in formation on the Spanish side was summoned to surrender, it was found to be the King of England's Royal Regiment of Guards, which will be met again in the next chapter. Nearly 300 years later descendants of this regiment and those of their fellow-countrymen on the opposing side would again make a stand on the Dunkirk Dunes.

At home the Commonwealth army's reputation was less happy. After Worcester the army and the Rump parliament found themselves at odds, and since the latter would not dissolve itself, Cromwell closed it down by force of arms. In December 1653 he took over supreme authority as Lord Protector of England, Scotland and Ireland. His aim was to devise some permanent constitution with popular support at the same time as keeping the country stable, but the first Parliament he assembled was so clearly rent by the dissensions of different factions, that he dissolved it. The country was becoming increasingly restless with all manner of plots abounding. He therefore placed it firmly under military rule, dividing it into 12 districts, each under a major-general with a force of mounted constabulary to keep order. Peace was preserved, the administration was just and efficient, but it was bitterly resented by the gentry, unwelcome to the common people, and left in its wake a fear of military dictatorship and a distrust of professional soldiers and a standing army that has endured in the country to this day.

On 3rd September 1658 Cromwell died. His son, Richard, was proclaimed Protector but, without any of his father's strength and will, was incapable of controlling the army which, after a brief recall of the Rump, exercised the only authority in the realm over a people who, in all quarters and of most persuasions, now wanted nothing but the return of the monarchy.

Since pacifying Scotland in 1654, George Monck had remained there in garrison with his army of 10,000. A man of moderate views, he had seen in Cromwell the only alternative to chaos, into which, with Cromwell dead, the country now seemed in danger of falling. He caught, too, the rising demand for a return to kingship and the swelling hatred of military rule, and realised that, with England held down by the sword, only another sword could free it. He concentrated his army at Coldstream on the border, four regiments of horse and six of foot, including that granted to him by Cromwell. As 1659 drew to a close, news reached him that the army in England had begun to mutiny and disintegrate. On 1st January 1660 he crossed the Tweed and marched for London, greeted on all sides as a saviour. He quietly reinstated the Presbyterian Members of Parliament, thus outnumbering the Independents of the Rump, and, in its last act, the Long Parliament finally dissolved itself. A free election followed, the new Parliament invited the King to return, and on 29th May Charles II rode into London. England's first standing army had deposed one king, but restored another.

Gold Royalist badge of Charles I c1645   7105-8-2   Silver Parliamentarian badge of Earl of Essex   7505-3-1

CHAPTER 3
RESTORATION AND REVOLUTION
1660–1701

It is often believed that the creation of the country's standing army dates from the Restoration of 1660. This of course is not the case for, as has been seen, such an army was first established by Parliamentary ordinance of 1645. When Charles II returned to inherit his kingdom the same army, increased over the years to a strength of 40,000, was still under arms with George Monck, to whom the King owed his throne, at its head with the new title of King's Captain-General. However, having just emerged from under one regime sustained by armed might, the nation had no wish to grant the new monarch similar powers of coercion. With the country seemingly settled and at peace, there was no longer need for such an expensive and potentially dangerous force: this could now be disbanded and the safety of the realm once again entrusted to the old militia system. Despite the proved ineffectiveness of the latter in the past, the landed gentry, who would organise and officer it, believed it afforded a restoration of their power and influence and a counterweight to the authority of the king, whose prerogative of its command, endorsed by Act of Parliament in 1661, was somewhat diminished by financial limitations on his powers of embodiment over it, imposed by Parliament a year later.

In order that the army could be disbanded without turbulence, measures were taken to discharge arrears of pay and resettle the men in civilian life. Under the watchful eye of Monck, the Cromwellian military establishment was gradually reduced until by early 1661 all that remained was Monck's own troop of horse and his regiment of foot. These too might have passed into limbo had it not been for a sudden armed uprising of Fifty Monarchy men, a fanatically religious sect of extreme republicans. This was crushed by Monck's regiment but the danger it had presented for a time proved the need for a permanent force of troops to maintain order and ensure the safety of the King. Charles still had his bodyguards, the Yeomen and the Gentlemen-at-Arms, a small number of whom had accompanied him in exile, but the personal nature of their duties did not permit their use in a wider role.

Therefore, on 14th February 1661, Monck's regiment, which traced its lineage to Weldon's and Lloyd's regiments of the original New Model Army, laid down its arms in token of the formal abolition of that army, and promptly took them up again as the Lord-General's Regiment of Foot Guards, familiarly known as Coldstreamers, after the village from which they had marched on London in January 1660. After Monck's death in 1670 they became the Coldstream Regiment of Foot Guards and so have survived to this day, the only regiment of the Army that can trace an unbroken descent from the New Model. However, in 1661, their Cromwellian origin required them to yield precedence to the King's Royal Regiment of Guards, raised partly as a new corps by Colonel John Russell and partly from that other regiment of royal guards last seen on the Dunkirk Dunes in 1658. Though this regiment was subsequently designated the 1st Regiment of Foot Guards (and from 1815, Grenadier Guards), the Coldstream asserts its earlier origins by its motto, 'Nulli Secundus'.

Monck's troop of horse was retained in being but also had to yield precedence to two other troops, the King's and the Duke of York's all three of which are the forbears of the regiment now known as the Life Guards. These three were independent troops, composed chiefly of gentlemen, but in addition a new regiment of horse of eight troops was raised by the Earl of Oxford from disbanded cavalrymen of the New Model. Its distinctive uniform of blue gave it the colloquial title of Oxford Blues, of which the second word has formed part of the regiment's successive titles until the present day†.

To complete the Royal army at home, the King summoned from France a regiment that could boast even older origins. The Scots 'Régiment Douglas', the descendants of Gustavus Adolphus's Green Brigade, which had fought alongside the New Model at the Dunes, now became, after the two regiments of Foot Guards, the senior regiment of British infantry. Though it was returned to the French service until 1678, it was allowed to retain its precedence in the British Line which, as the Royal Scots, it still enjoys today.

Apart from a force to secure his throne, Charles II needed money. This he acquired by marrying a rich

---

† As the Royal Horse Guards (The Blues) it was amalgamated in 1969 with the 1st Royal Dragoons to form the Blues and Royals.

A Captain, a Lieutenant and a Pikeman c1680. Frontispiece and title-page from 'Military Discipline or the Art of War'. Published by Robert Marden, London, 1689.

Portuguese princess, Catherine of Braganza, who brought as her dowry half a million pounds and the overseas possessions of Bombay and Tangier. The latter was under constant threat from the Moors and to safeguard it a garrison had to be provided. Thus, in 1661, another troop of horse and the Tangier Regiment of Foot † were raised for service in this outpost, and so began the Army's long tradition of colonial campaigning against savage enemies. The Tangier garrison remained under almost constant threat until 1684 when, though reinforced by additional troops of horse and another regiment of foot (later 4th King's Own), its value as a possession was outweighed by the expense of its defence and it was abandoned.

Thus by the end of 1661 Charles II could command a standing force, or "guards" as they were categorized at the time, of four troops and a regiment of horse, and four regiments of foot, all of which, with the exception of the Tangier units, could claim links and origins with bodies raised before 1660. In addition there were a total of 48 independent companies providing the permanent garrisons for such places as the Tower of London, the coastal forts built by Henry VIII, the Channel and Scilly Islands, and various important inland castles. Such garrisons had existed since Tudor times. At this stage, therefore, it is clear that these guards and garrisons were neither a new standing force established at the Restoration nor, in view of their numbers, did they constitute an army such as the New Model had been. Nevertheless, they were the nucleus on which further increases of permanent troops would be grafted through the pressure of subsequent events, until such guards and garrisons could indeed be described as an army, despite frequent and bitter opposition to the establishment of such a force.

In 1665 the country blundered into a trade war with its old allies the Dutch, a war which revealed, with the Dutch fleet in the Medway, how weak England had become since Cromwell and how unprepared was the militia. But it also brought another regiment into the King's service. There were in the Netherlands three regiments of English foot, the successors to the volunteers who had won fame under Francis Vere in Elizabethan times. They were required to take an oath of fealty to their Dutch masters but since they refused to fight against their own country they were dismissed. They managed to make their way to England where they were formed into the Holland Regiment, better known from the colour of their facings as the Buffs, later the 3rd Foot.

The humiliations of the Dutch war brought Charles unpopularity and closer Parliamentary control over his finances. While England as a whole feared the expansionist policies of Louis XIV of France, Charles envied Louis' mastery over his country and longed to enjoy the same power himself but without money, which Parliament was unwilling to vote him, he was powerless. By a change of policy in 1668 he allied himself with Holland against France. Though this gave satisfaction to the country, Parliament still kept a tight grip over the purse-strings. Determining therefore that his best hopes of obtaining money and making himself independent of Parliament lay in alliance with Louis, he signed with him the secret Treaty of Dover, by which, in return for financial assistance, he undertook to aid France in war with Holland.

This treaty led to the despatch, in 1672, of a force of 6,000 British troops commanded by the Duke of Monmouth to serve under the great French captain, Turenne. Two years later Charles was forced to make peace with the Dutch and turned over certain regiments into their service. The rest of Monmouth's force continued to serve under Turenne against the Austrians until recalled in 1678. The regiments which formed the British contingent in these campaigns were all, with the exception of the Royal Scots, subsequently disbanded or merged into others, but one attracted considerable praise from Turenne owing to the marked abilities shown by its colonel, John Churchill, then in his mid-twenties, whose military career had begun in the 1st Guards and who had seen his first active service at Tangier.

The closing years of Charles' reign were marked by the threat of civil insurrection, as a result of the attempts by the Whigs in Parliament to exclude the King's brother, James Duke of York, from the succession, on the grounds of his Roman Catholicism. The unrest stirred up by the Whigs led Charles to dismiss Parliament, but not before he had received from Louis XIV the money Parliament would not grant him to carry on the business of state and to support the maintenance of the troops vital to the security of his position. Charles succeeded in discrediting the Whigs and the country swung back in his favour, but his reliance on Louis made it impossible for England to act as any sort of counter to the growing domination of Europe by France, against which only William of Orange offered implacable opposition.

Nor was opposition to Louis' designs likely from James II. Modelling himself on the French King, James was determined to consolidate the power of the throne and to make England a Catholic kingdom. For this he needed a strong army at his back, a course which would inevitably bring him into collision with a predominantly Protestant Parliament which, since the Restoration, had constantly striven to reduce the King's permanent troops. James was soon presented with a justification for an increase to his military establishment by the rebellion in 1685 of the Duke of Monmouth, the bastard of Charles II and a Protestant claimant to the throne. Monmouth's pathetic rustic levies from the West Country were soon despatched at Sedgemoor by the royal army commanded by John Churchill. But this early threat to his reign enabled the King to call for the raising of six

† Subsequently the 1st Royal Dragoons and the 2nd Foot, Queen's Royal Regiment.

King Charles II (1630-1685)
Portrait, oil on canvas, by J. Riley, c1665   6007-10

George Monck, Duke of Albermarle (1608-1670)
Portrait, oil on canvas, artist unknown c1665   6005-31

Review of the Army at Tangier, 1683. Painting, oil on canvas, by Dirick Stoop.   7012

new regiments of horse, two of dragoons, and nine of infantry, to which were added the regiments Charles II had made over to the Dutch in 1674†. The senior of the new foot regiments was designated the Royal Regiment of Fusiliers with a special function of providing a protective escort for the artillery train.

In November 1685 James reminded Parliament of the poor showing of the militia against Monmouth's rebellion and demanded, first, the voting of £1,400,000 to maintain a standing army instead of the militia, and secondly, that Roman Catholics should be included therein, both as officers and as soldiers. When Parliament demurred at this blatant attempt at enforcing the royal authority, James prorogued it and set up a military camp of nigh on 16,000 regular troops on Hounslow Heath, close to the capital. This camp remained in being for three years.

Apart from the army in England, there were, and had been since the Restoration, separate military establishments in Ireland and Scotland. From the latter one battalion now came south to provide the King with a third, or Scots Regiment of Guards. A regiment of Scots guards had been raised for Charles I in 1642 for service in Ireland but this was disbanded by Cromwell after the Battle of Worcester, where it fought for Charles II as the "Lyfe Guard of Foot", and was not reformed until 1660, remaining on the Scottish establishment until 1686*. By 1688 the combined strength of the three armies stood at 34,000 men, a force that could no longer be described as merely "guards and garrisons".

Had James simply confined his attentions to the army to increasing its efficiency, a task for which he was well qualified as he had a genuine talent for military administration and pride in his troops, his name might be remembered as one of the Army's great benefactors. The troops at Hounslow were certainly a fine spectacle and the London populace found it a place of interest and entertainment, rather than the muster-ground for an armed Catholic 'coup d'état' on their liberties. Sadly James went ahead with his scheme of infiltrating Catholics into the officers' ranks, while in Ireland his agent, the Earl of Tyrconnel, simply dismissed Protestant officers and men in droves, replacing them by Catholics, and even sending Irish peasants over to England to form nuclei of Catholics in the English regiments. In later periods the Irish would fill the ranks of the British Army and be welcomed as comrades by English soldiers, but to the redcoats of the Jacobean period, like their fathers in the New Model, these Irish appeared as alien savages, regarded in much the same light as both English and Irish soldiers of Victorian times would view Afghan tribesmen or Sudanese dervishes. In his blindness James failed to see the resentment and distrust his measures were building up in an overwhelmingly Protestant army, until he heard the cheers with which the troops greeted the news of the acquittal of seven bishops, who had been tried for refusing to read the declaration which suspended penal laws against Catholics. He then rapidly broke up the Hounslow camp and dispersed the regiments about the country.

The rising anger in the army was reflected in the country at large, and when James' queen was delivered of an heir, the prospect of a Catholic succession determined the leading Protestants to delay no longer. Advances were made to the Protestant champion, William of Orange, who was married to James' daughter Mary, to persuade him to assume the English throne. William was quick to realise that the accretion to his cause of the English army and navy would greatly strengthen his arm in his struggle with Louis XIV. Nevertheless he appreciated that the successful accomplishment of such an undertaking would depend largely on where lay the loyalties of the very sailors and soldiers he was anxious to acquire; particularly as, in the face of the ever-present French threat to Holland, he could only spare for the English enterprise a force about half that of James'.

On 5th November 1688 William landed at Torbay. James, who on first getting wind of William's plans some time before had further increased his forces+, now ordered his troops to concentrate at Salisbury to meet the invasion. Although a number of desertions occurred, a force of 24,000 under Lords Faversham and Churchill, who had been ennobled and promoted lieutenant-general in 1683, assembled at the rendez-vous on the 24th. The temper of many of the officers was uncertain and the King held a council of war. Faversham recommended a retreat to a position behind the Thames, but Churchill spoke strongly against such weakness in face of an inferior force, and urged the King to stand and fight. James hesitated, then decided on retreat. That night Churchill joined William. James had lost his best soldier, whose defection was followed by many noblemen and his own daughter, Anne, with her husband, Prince George of Denmark. The King ordered the disbandment of the army, an order which fell on deaf ears, and fled the country. On the night of 17th December a battalion of Dutch Guards took over from the Coldstream at the Palace of Whitehall, and the "Glorious Revolution" had become a fact.

---

† Subsequently the 1st to 6th Dragoon Guards, the 3rd and 4th Dragoons, and the 7th to 15th Foot. Two of these regiments from Holland became the 5th and 6th Foot.

* Two other regiments on the Scottish establishment were those which later became the 2nd Dragoons (Royal Scots Greys), formed 1678, and the Royal Scots Fusiliers, 21st Foot, formed 1678.

+ Two additional infantry regiments, later the 16th and 17th Foot, and extra companies for existing regiments.

When William III was declared king, he inherited an army that had changed greatly under Charles and James, in many instances for the worse. At the Restoration Charles had appointed Monck as commander-in-chief with very extensive powers over the whole administration of the army; thanks to Monck's character and abilities, the transition from a Cromwellian force to a royal one was carried out smoothly. After Monck's death Charles, and following him James, became their own commanders-in-chief, keeping all matters concerned with manpower in their own hands. Responsibility for material was vested in the Office of the Ordnance, presided over by its Master-General, a new title for the old post originated by Henry VIII, who also exercised complete control over the artillery and engineers. Financial matters were administered by the Paymaster-General but, since Parliament in its refusal to recognise the legality of the army consequently declined to vote any money for its upkeep, the money came, in Charles' case, from his privy purse and, in James', by diverting funds voted for the militia. Since Charles was always short of money and James' methods were illegal, it is not surprising, in an age where corruption became almost a way of life, that it was soon rife in the Paymaster-General's department, from which it spread right through the military structure, with consequent lack of efficiency and lowering of the army's reputation in the eyes of the country.

The practice of buying and selling appointments was quite common in public life in the seventeenth century and the army was no exception to the general custom. With regiments changing hands for money, and commissions being bought and sold, the various sub-divisions of the army became the personal property of its colonels and captains, who raised, clothed and, when money was available, paid them; a system in which private interest prevailed over public good, and which afforded countless opportunities for bribes, rake-offs and peculation. When officers found themselves out of pocket, either due to the machinations of contractors or the legal and illegal deductions by civilian clerks and officials (whose own inadequate pay drove them to extortion), they made good their losses by plundering, on one pretext or another, the soldiers' pay. This was divided into money actually paid to the soldier, his "subsistance"†, out of which he had to feed and accommodate himself, and "off-reckonings" made over to the colonel, from which a number of authorised payments for clothing and accoutrements, subscription to the Chelsea Hospital, and fees to various officials, were deducted, the balance being theoretically due to the soldier. Thus it was not difficult for a dishonest officer to invent further deductions, not only from the off-reckonings, but often from the subsistence money as well. An army riddled with fraud and officered by financial speculators was unlikely to attract soldiers of the calibre of Cromwell's Ironsides and, as it expanded, the ranks had to be filled up with all manner of rogues, vagabonds, cripples and wastrels, who could only be induced to join by dubious means and deterred from desertion by threat of hanging. So, to the ever-prevalent distrust by Parliament and people of a standing army was added a contempt for the very trade of soldier, and thus began the tradition of having to draw men for the ranks from the poorest and often criminal classes of society.

Only a stern and frequently brutal discipline could keep such poor material to its duty, or so it was thought at the time. However, to enforce such discipline, a code of military law was required. None such had ever been passed by Parliament which, since the Petition of Right in 1628, had feared its use being applied by the monarch to civilians as well as soldiers. Troops therefore were technically only subject to civil law, but because this was clearly inadequate to deal with many breaches of military discipline, military commanders had perforce to administer their own justice under Articles of War. As the size of the peacetime army increased, the need to have military justice put on a proper footing became more and more evident. To do so, however, called into question the whole constitutional position of the army, since although Parliament recognized the King's prerogative to maintain an army in time of war, it denied his right to do so in peacetime. Parliament had no intention of allowing William to follow James' example, and early in the reign passed a Declaration of Right which stated that the maintenance of armed forces by the crown in peacetime without the consent of Parliament was illegal. But, since William's accession to the English throne now involved his new kingdom in his war with Louis XIV, Parliament had no choice but to accept that, for the present, the army must remain in being. Furthermore, it was forced to attend to the problem of military discipline when the army's demoralisation, caused by the mismanagement of the Stuart kings and the uncertainties of the Revolution, culminated in a mutiny by the Royal Scots over the imposition of a Dutch colonel while on its way to Flanders.

In 1690 it passed the first Mutiny Act. This reiterated the prohibition of the Declaration of Right but recognized that the military crimes of mutiny, desertion and sedition could not be checked by civil law, and empowered the Crown to convene courts martial to deal with these offences, the maximum penalty for which was death. The Act went no further than this and was only a temporary measure, but its passing showed that Parliament at least acknowledged, though did not formally legalize, the existence of a standing army.

---

† For a trooper of horse, 2s. out of 2s.6d., for a dragoon, 1s.2d. out of 1s.6d., and for the infantryman, 6d. out of 8d., the same daily rate of pay granted by Mary Tudor.

As will shortly be seen, William was confronted by a multitude of dangers, which he had to face with an army weak in numbers and morale and no single government department to administer it. Strategy and operational matters were the responsibility of two Secretaries of State; finance that of the Lord High Treasurer; munitions, guns and war supplies the province of the Board of Ordnance. In addition there was the Secretary to the Forces, or Secretary-at-War. In Monck's time he had been little more than a clerical assistant to the commander-in-chief, but under Charles II the post had grown in importance and usefulness, roughly in proportion to the ability of the incumbent. William was fortunate that in 1683 the post had gone to William Blathwayt, an able and conscientious official, who developed the office to form a link between the king, the army and Parliament, until in the next reign Blathwayt's successors, St John and Walpole, both politicians, became virtually the equivalent of a modern Secretary of State for the Army.

Before turning to William's campaigns, two developments in the infantry of the period must be noted. As the efficiency of the soldier's musket improved, with flintlocks replacing matchlocks, so the numbers of pikemen decreased until, by giving the musketeer his own protection against cavalry in the form of a bayonet which he plugged into the barrel of his musket, the need for pikemen disappeared. Bayonets were first issued to the Tangier Regiment in 1663 and from 1672 began to be served out to all dragoons and infantry. The prestige enjoyed by the pikeman passed to a new type of infantryman, the grenadier, a company of which was added to each regiment by James II in 1678. Their task was to lead an assault by hurling small hand bombs, and since this would call for strength and courage, they were drawn from the tallest and most stalwart men of a regiment. As the civilian-type of broad-brimmed hat worn by all soldiers would not permit them easily to sling their fire-locks when throwing grenades, they were given special caps, at first no more than fur-trimmed stocking caps but which soon lost the fur and acquired an upright cloth front decorated with suitable insignia; these caps added to their height and made them more imposing in the enemy's eyes.

In 1689 William was faced, not only by the need to defend his Dutch realm from Louis XIV's efforts to take over the Spanish Netherlands, against which he formed the Grand Alliance†, but also by rebellions in Scotland and Ireland on behalf of James II, who had the support of France. The danger in the British Isles was the most pressing and only a small force of ten battalions could be spared for Holland. One of these, as mentioned above, was the Royal Scots. Its temper was not untypical of the whole force and William hurriedly despatched Churchill, now Earl of Marlborough, to restore it to order. Even with his abilities this was no easy task, the Dutch commander, Prince Waldeck, reporting that, *"M. de Marlbrouck had much trouble with them" (1)* Nevertheless, by August, in his first encounter with a Marshal of France, Marlborough had won a victory at Walcourt.

Meanwhile new regiments of horse, foot and dragoons, totalling 10,000 men, were being raised at home. In Scotland Graham of Claverhouse, "Bonnie Dundee", raised an army for James II from the Highland clans and routed a Williamite force of five battaltions at Killiecrankie; a savage melee in a highland glen, notable chiefly for a lesson it taught in weapon development. The charge of the Highlanders had been so swift that the royal troops, having discharged their muskets, had had no time to plug in their bayonets to meet the broad swords and were overrun. Their commander, Mackay, determined to obtain a new type of bayonet, then being developed on the Continent, which could be screwed over the barrel so that men could fire with the bayonet already fixed. The Highlanders pressed on to Dunkeld, held only by one regiment, newly raised three months before but of a singular character. Alone of the King's army it stood in the direct tradition of Cromwell's Ironsides, being raised entirely from a stern and fanatical sect of Covenanters, known as Cameronians*, whose discipline and fighting spirit were sustained more by their religious faith than their military structure. For four hours, with the town in flames around them, the Cameronians held Dunkeld until the Highlanders, dismayed by the tenacity of their resistance, fell back defeated and melted away. The revolt was over and Scotland secured for King William.

In Ireland he was challenged by a war which, for three years, would prevent him giving his full attention to the struggle in the Netherlands. Early in 1683 the Earl of Tyrconnel had called out the Irish Catholics on James' behalf and, with the regular regiments of the Irish establishment in which a few years earlier he had replaced Protestants with Catholics, succeeded in reducing the Protestant cause to the besieged towns of London-derry and Enniskillen. Although James himself arrived in Ireland in March with French troops and money, the two northern towns gallantly held out for William until July, when they were relieved by General Kirke with three regiments. In August reinforcements, mainly consisting of the new regiments raised in the spring but supplemented by some seasoned Dutch troops, were landed at Carrickfergus under the command of the veteran Dutch general, Marshal Schomberg, now aged 84. However the force was so ill-found, the men raw and undisciplined, the officers useless, the officials responsible for supplies and money corrupt and incompetent, that

---

† England, Holland, the Holy Roman Empire, Spain, Brandenburg (Prussia) and later Denmark and Sweden.
* Later the 26th Foot.

Schomberg, confident only of his Dutchmen, could do no more than maintain a bridgehead.

The following year more experienced troops, part English, the rest Dutch, Danes and French Huguenots, were brought over from England and Holland. Very popular in England at this time, and particularly with the army, was the anti-Catholic Irish song, *"Lilliburlero"*, which was played and sung so widely that it had helped to harden public opinion against James. On 1st July 1690, with William at its head, the army marched down to give battle to James' forces drawn up on the south bank of the River Boyne as,

> *"Drums they did beat and rattle,*
> *And Lilliburlero was the tune*
> *We played going down to battle". (2)*

With its mocking notes cheering one side and confounding the other, William's men stormed across the river and after a hard fight overthrew the Jacobite army. Seeing the day was lost, James fled, first to Dublin, then to France, never to return.

Notwithstanding their defeat the Irish fought on. To prevent further French reinforcements arriving, a force under Marlborough, who had returned from Holland, captured the southern ports of Cork and Kinsale. William took Dublin, but Athlone held out and Limerick was saved by the capture of William's siege train. The king left Ireland in August, leaving the Dutch general, Ginkel, to complete the campaign in 1691. After taking Athlone Ginkel pushed the Franco-Irish troops westwards to Aughrim, where the French commander, St Ruth, drew up his force for a last stand on a strong position defended by stone walls and a bog. A fierce fight ensued as Ginkel's infantry struggled forward through the bog to dislodge the Irish from their defences. They were forced back, but reformed and came on again. As evening closed in it looked as though the attack could not prevail, but then a narrow way was found through the bog along which cavalry could pass, though only two files abreast. Led by General Mackay and the Huguenot Marquis de Ruvigny, the Blues and two regiments of horse† poured through the gap under a heavy fire and, reforming on the other side, charged down on the Irish from the flank. The infantry made another effort in front, St Ruth was killed, and the Irish, having fought nobly all day, were broken. Limerick held out until October but, with no French reinforcements able to reach it, was forced to surrender. The Jacobite cause in Ireland was finished and William could now concentrate all his resources for the continental campaign against Louis.

The army in 1691 stood at four troops of Household cavalry, ten regiments of horse, five of dragoons, six battalions of Foot Guards, and 39 of foot*, some 50,000 men in all. After deducting the garrisons necessary for the safety of the British Isles, William was able to transport to the Netherlands for the campaign of 1692 a force of 23,000 British troops, to which would be added Dutch, Danes, Prussians (then called Brandenburgers) and numbers of mercenary regiments hired from sundry German princelings.

The war they were about to fight would be the first in a series of struggles against the ambitions and expansionism of a succession of French rulers which would last for over a hundred years. It would be fought in an area which, over an even longer period, would claim the lives of more British soldiers than any other part of the globe — the cockpit of Europe, northern France and Flanders. Its rich soil could provide sustenance for contending armies, its multiple waterways transported their stores and supplies, and its numerous towns, transformed into fortresses of enormous sophistication by the great engineers of the age like Vauban and Coehoorn, kept watch and ward over these vital elements. Owing to the difficulties of feeding and manoeuvring large armies in the winter months, warfare in this age was a seasonal business. Moreover, since commanders were unwilling to hazard unduly their expensive and often hardly-raised armies, it developed into a formalised affair with the opposing armies marching and counter-marching to draw each other from their fortresses or strategically important areas, punctuated, when such manoeuvres failed, by sieges and the occasional field action. When armies actually met in battle, the fighting could be fierce and costly but the campaigns were nevertheless conducted according to rules and conventions respected by both sides. The formality of this type of warfare is perhaps typified by an incident recorded in 1703 when the French commanders,

> *"Marshal Villeroy and the Duke of Berwick sent presents of Wine to the Duke of Marlborough, and he*
> *returned their civility in a large Present of English Beer and English Sack, in English Bottles Seal'd. Some*
> *of Our Officers being near the River and French Officers on t'other side, the latter called to Ours and told*
> *them they would come and talk with them if they would not fire on them, upon which they gave mutual*
> *assurances but al that passed was a few compliments and the French having Wine with them drank my*
> *Lord Marlborough's and other healths and so each party returned home." (3)*

† Later the 2nd and 3rd Dragoon Guards.

* The three regiments of Foot Guards and the Royal Scots each had two battalions, other foot regiments only one. The 1691 regiments included the Blues and those later numbered in the cavalry of the Line as the 1st Dragoon Guards to the 7th Dragoons (later Hussars) and in the infantry as the 1st to the 27th Foot. Other regiments were disbanded after the war.

39

7508-50

The Battle of the Boyne, 1690

Painting, oil on canvas, by Jan Wyck.

In 1691 the French had captured the fortress of Mons, thus breaking the Allied line between the rivers Sambre and Scheldt. Further success attended them in May 1692 when the French marshals Luxembourg and Boufflers took Namur, a vital fortress guarding the juction of the Sambre and the Meuse, before William could reach it from Brussels. Luxembourg then marched north-west, as though moving on Brussels, but in reality to draw William away from Namur. William followed and on 23rd July the two armies met at Steenkirk, some 20 miles south-west of Brussels.

William devised a sound plan based on a surprise attack on the weak French right by British and Danish infantry, whose advance would be masked by woods, but the delay of his commander, the Duke of Wurtemburg, in executing the attack allowed Luxembourg to reinforce his right. Thus, when Wurtemburg finally ordered the advance, William's infantry were met by superior numbers supported by artillery. Disregarding heavy losses, the 1st Guards, Royal Scots, Scots Fusiliers and the Danes pressed stubbornly on, tearing gaps in the first three French lines, while six other battalions came up in their support. Now was the time for William to throw in his reserves but, through an error of deployment, they were boxed up too far in the rear. So, when Luxembourg ordered the French and Swiss Guards to counter-attack, the isolated British infantry, their ranks decimated by the heavy fighting, were forced back. By resolutely contesting every yard, they gained time for reinforcements to get forward but by then it was too late and there was nothing for it but retreat. A battle which had begun so promisingly and in which the troops fought so stoutly had been lost by inept generalship. Steenkirk ended the 1692 campaign and the armies withdrew to winter quarters.

In 1693 Luxembourg, by first besieging Huy on the Meuse and then threatening Liege and Maastricht, drew William from an impregnable position on the River Senne. William reduced his strength to reinforce the endangered fortresses but, since he had earlier detached other troops to create a diversion on the Scheldt, found himself outnumbered by nearly two to one when Luxembourg confronted him at Landen. Furthermore, with a river at his back and a stream on his left, he had insufficient room to manoeuvre, while his frontage was too broad and his men too thinly spread to permit the reinforcement of one part of his line by another..

The battle that followed, said Alexander Shields, chaplain of the Cameronians, was *"great fury and fierceness in all manner of fighting, and was long from 4 of the clock in the morning until 5 at night".(4)* Luxembourg pushed the weight of his assault against the defended villages of Neerwinden and Laer, the key to William's position, which were held tenaciously by the 1st, Scots and Dutch Guards, the Scots regiments, and some Hanoverians and Brandeburgers. The fighting raged back and forth, with positions being lost and retaken by troops who never failed to rally. When the Scots were being overwhelmed for the second time in Laer, Shields said: *"Orders were given to face to the right about whereupon all withdrew out of the retrenchments and presently rallied on the plain behind. D'Offarrell's† men getting first out did first rally but ours first attacked the enemy within our deserted retrenchments and beat them quite out again, killing and taking many".(5)* Clearly inter-regimental rivalry was already a spur to action in the Williamite army. At one point in the centre the Coldstream and the Royal Fusiliers threw back five French brigades as well as beating off a flank attack by the French Household cavalry. In the end, however, the French numbers began to tell and with ammunition running low the line gave way; William himself brought forward six regiments of horse to cover the retreat. Once again the British infantry had made superhuman efforts to save the day and redeem William's errors, but Luxembourg had won a great victory. When the fortress of Charleroi surrendered shortly afterwards, the campaign closed with all the line of the Sambre in French hands.

In 1694 the advantage in the field lay with the French, but the war was draining away their resources, and the deaths of Louvois, Louis' brilliant War Minister, and of Luxembourg badly affected the efficiency of the French military machine. William, on the other hand, had increased his strength by two-thirds, and for the first time started the next campaign with the initiative, while the French sat behind their defence lines from Namur to the sea. Deceiving the new French commander, Villeroi, by a series of feints, William suddenly descended on the great fortress of Namur. After a brilliant action by the Guards on the outworks, the reduction of Vauban's massive defences continued step by step until at last the final breach was stormed by the Royal Regiment of Ireland (later the 18th Foot, Royal Irish), who ever after bore on their colours the motto, *"Virtutis Namurcensis Praemium"*.

The war dragged on for two more years but was eventually brought to a close by the Treaty of Ryswick in 1697. France gave up the territory it had conquered and Louis recognized William as King of England and Anne, William's sister-in-law, as his heir.

The army, by its endeavours and exertions, had emerged from the slough of disrepute into which it had fallen under the Stuarts, and the redcoat of the 1690s had done much to restore the prestige that his forbears of the New Model had enjoyed in the eyes of Europe. However the dangers they had endured and the blood they had spilled in their country's cause earned them neither gratitude nor consideration at home. With peace

---

† O'Farrell's, Royal Scots Fusiliers.

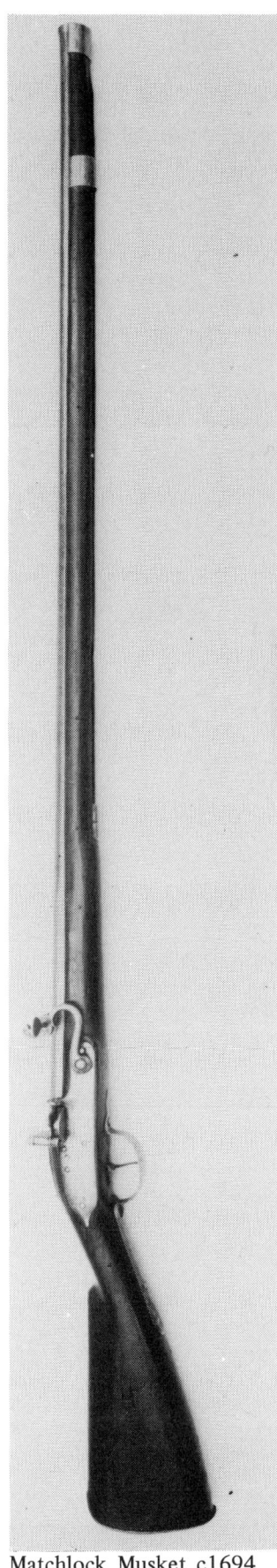

Matchlock Musket c1694
7009-26-1

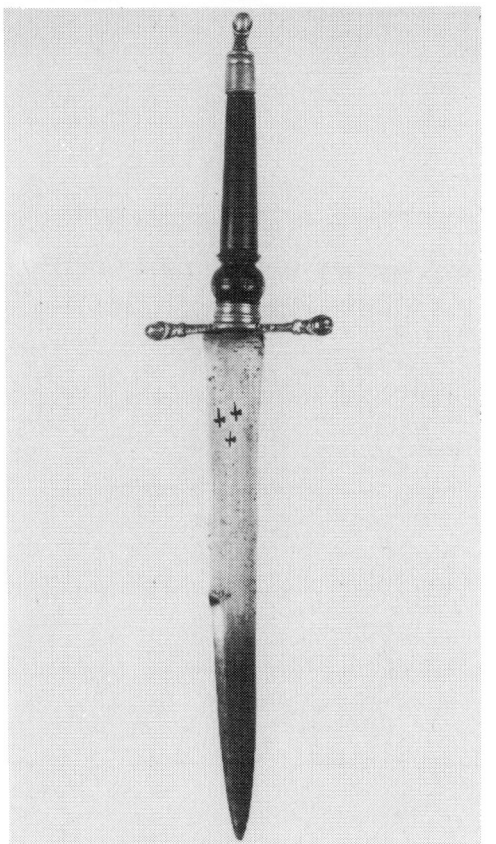

Plug Bayonet c1690   6310-145

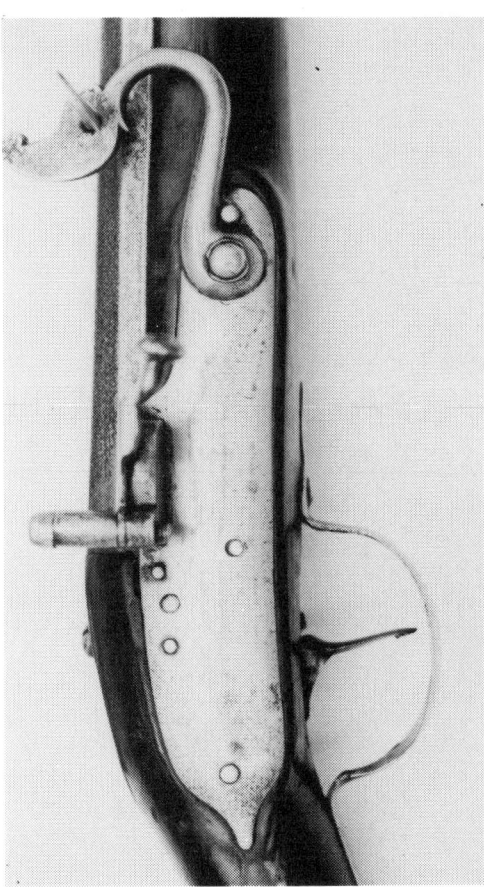

Cavalry, probably Royal Horse Guards.
c1670-80

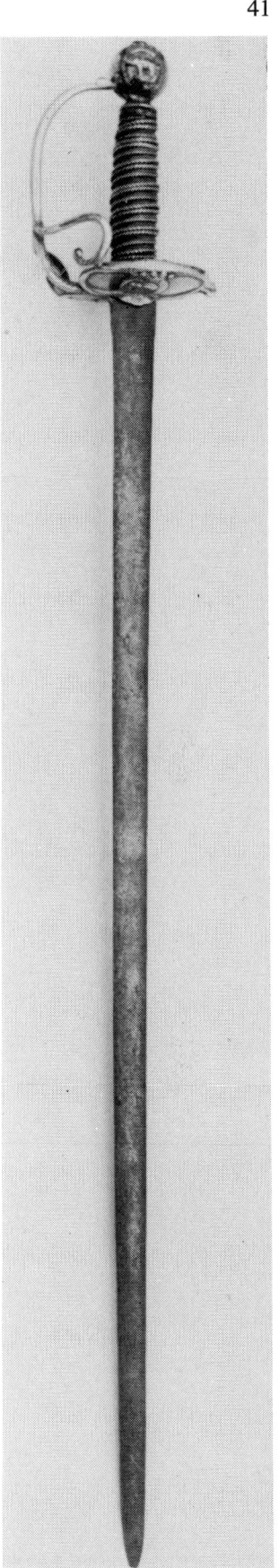

Other Ranks Sword with arms of Aubrey
de Vere 20th Earl of Oxford in pommel.
7208-31

42

temporarily restored and with no thought for the morrow or realisation that France was still the strongest power in Europe, *"the House of Commons saw its opportunity and turned savagely upon the Army. They actually passed a resolution to disband all regiments except the Guards and the Tangier regiments; and that without providing for payment of their arrears.....amounting to two millions sterling".(6)*

After the King had reminded Parliament that England must be kept safe from attack, the Commons grudgingly approved, in March 1699, an establishment for the army in England of a mere 7,000, with a further 12,000 for Ireland, and declared all other regiments not included in these establishments as disbanded. The scandal of the army's pay set men against their officers and all ranks against the officials responsible for pay. The never the soldiers' friend, were so inundated with angry petitions from officers and men that eventually and reluctantly a Commission was appointed to look into the debts due to the army. The threat of further turbulence was, however, averted by other influences, for by 1701 the French drums were again beginning to beat their call to arms.

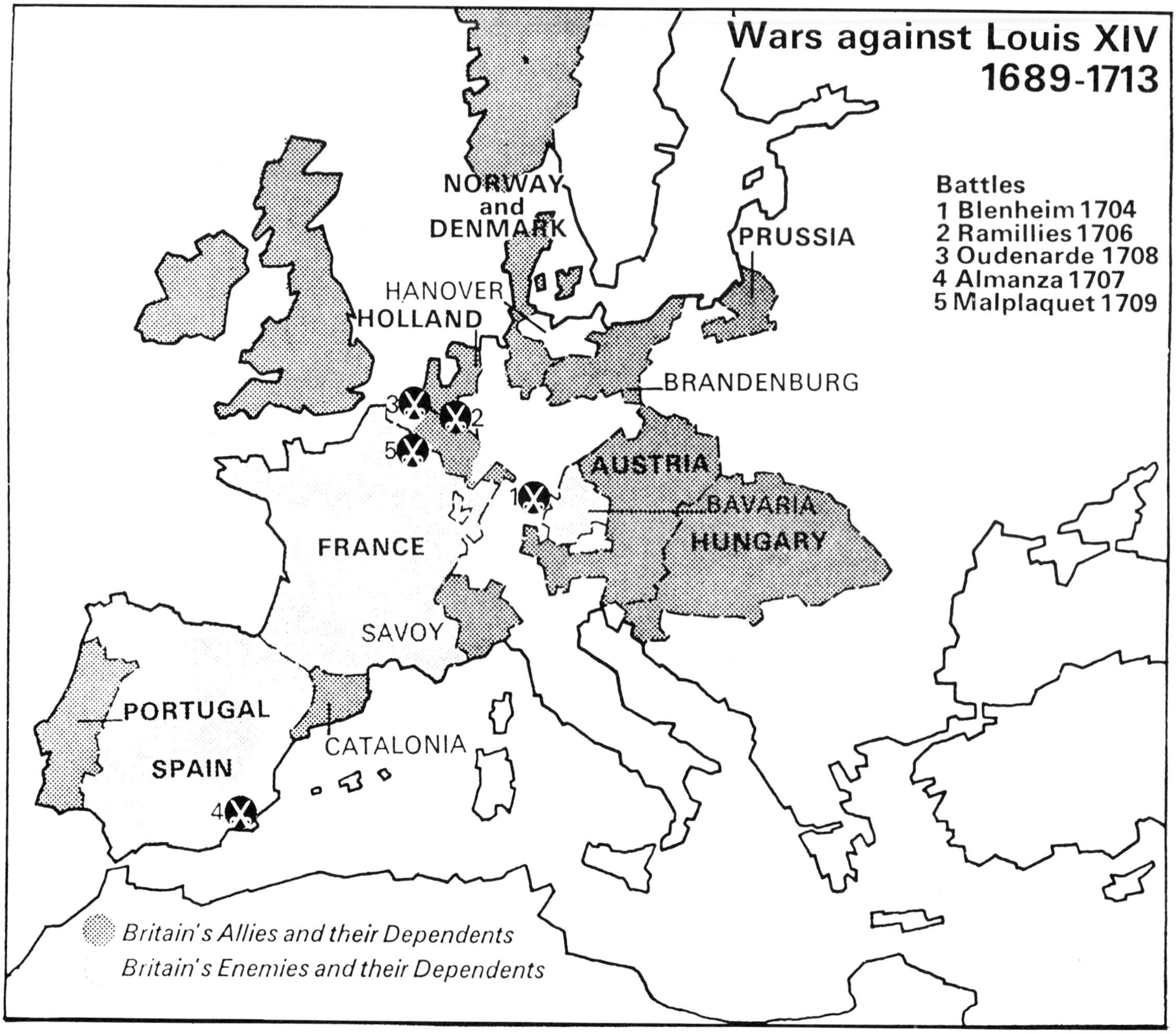

Wars against Louis XIV 1689-1713

NORWAY and DENMARK

PRUSSIA

HANOVER
HOLLAND

BRANDENBURG

AUSTRIA
BAVARIA
HUNGARY

FRANCE

SAVOY

PORTUGAL
SPAIN
CATALONIA

Battles
1 Blenheim 1704
2 Ramillies 1706
3 Oudenarde 1708
4 Almanza 1707
5 Malplaquet 1709

Britain's Allies and their Dependents
Britain's Enemies and their Dependents

CHAPTER 4
MARLBOROUGH'S GLORY
1702 – 1713

It was the death of a mad Spanish king, followed by the demise of James II, that decided the fate of many of King William's soldiers. The passing of these monarchs set off a chain of events, as a result of which these soldiers, instead of being dismissed to face poverty and neglect, would achieve a renown unparalleled in Europe under a great captain whose brilliance has never been surpassed and seldom equalled. When Charles II of Spain died in 1700 he bequeathed his throne, and the vast Spanish possessions in the Netherlands, Italy and the Americas, to Philip, grandson of Louis XIV. The other claimant to the Spanish throne was the Archduke Charles, younger son of the Habsburg Emperor Leopold. Louis had no wish to have the Habsburgs at his back or on his northern frontiers; at the same time he realised that to accept Charles II's will, thus, as far as he was concerned, uniting France and Spain, would inevitably bring him into conflict with the Emperor. The prize of Spain seemed worth the risk of war so he accepted the nomination of his grandson. By doing so he ensured the hostility, not only of the Empire, but also of Holland. Not content with that, he then earned the antagonism of England by acknowledging, on James II's death, his son as the rightful King of England in defiance of the Treaty of Ryswick. In 1701 William III re-organized the Grand Alliance while his Parliament, now convinced of the necessity to fight Louis, voted the necessary men and money. In March 1702 William died, to be succeeded by Anne, and on 4th May war was declared on France.

So the War of the Spanish Succession began. On one side France and Spain, joined by Bavaria, faced England, Holland, the Empire and Prussia, whose forces would be supplemented by contingents of Danes, Hanoverians and Hessians. The chief theatre of operations, as far as England was concerned, would again be the Spanish Netherlands into which Louis moved troops before the outbreak of war; but the strategic position of Bavaria, menacing Vienna as well as forming a barrier between the northern allies and the Imperialists, would carry the war into southern Germany. In addition, England's old alliance with Portugal and her need for bases in the Mediterranean would lead to operations in Spain, while a fourth theatre of war would be in northern Italy where the Imperialists confronted the Franco-Spanish forces around Milan.

With William, the architect of the Grand Alliance, dead and a new queen on the throne, England would need a man of great talents to direct her military effort in co-ordination with her allies. Fortunately he lay to hand in the person of John Churchill, Earl, soon to be Duke, of Marlborough, who emerged from the shadows into which he had temporarily fallen under William †, to be appointed Captain-General of the land forces, Master–General of the Ordnance and Ambassador to the United Provinces (Holland). His fall from William's favour had prevented him from taking any part in the previous campaign in the Low Countries, but William had re-instated him when the renewal of hostilities seemed imminent, and the successful negotiations to re-form the Grand Alliance had been chiefly in Marlborough's hands. The northern allies were therefore fully aware of his abilities; once operations began he was tacitly accepted, but never formally appointed, as the Allied commander-in-chief, though with limitations on his freedom of action where the Dutch troops were concerned.

To fulfil his great task he would need backing at home, allies on whom he could rely, and a well-found army. He and his Duchess, Sarah, enjoyed a long-standing friendship with the Queen, so her support was assured. While governmental control of the army was the responsibility of the two Secretaries of State, posts held by men of no great consequence, the successful prosecution of the war would depend on its financing, and therefore on the abilities of the Lord High Treasurer. Marlborough was fortunate in the appointment to this post of Sidney Godolphin, a brilliant and experienced public servant of complete honesty, admired by the Queen and a life-long friend of Marlborough himself. On the outbreak of hostilities the Secretary-at-War was still the admirable Blathwayt who was succeeded in 1703 by Henry St John, the first political holder of this post, under whom it

---

† Due to his resentment of William's Dutch favourites, his and his wife's loyalty to Princess Anne over a quarrel between her and her sister, Queen Mary, and his suspected Jacobite sympathies.

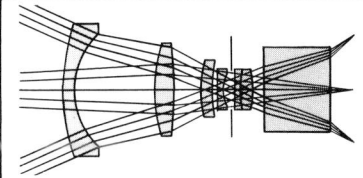

OPTICAL SYSTEMS

PILKINGTON P.E. LTD

gained in authority and influence; though able, his ambitions led him into intrigues against Marlborough and Godolphin, and, during a political crisis in 1708, he was replaced by Robert Walpole.

Among the allies the Dutch had a number of useful generals like Ginkel, the victor of Aughrim who had been created Earl of Athlone by William, and the great engineer, Coehoorn, but their caution and close adherence to purely national interests often impeded and hindered Marlborough's plans; only with Overkirk was he able to develop mutual trust. Among the Imperial forces, however, he found the perfect confederate in Prince Eugene of Savoy, a skilled and experienced soldier of great ability; their partnership must rank as one of the greatest military combinations in history. A significant aspect of their unity and success was a common belief, unusual in warfare of that age, that wars could only be won by crushing the enemy's army in battle, thus breaking his will to resist, and that the manoeuvres and sieges, so favoured by other commanders of the time, were only means to that end and not an end in themselves.

The prime instrument on which Marlborough would chiefly rely was the British Army†. Tested in William's war but greatly reduced thereafter, it was now expanded again by doubling the establishments of existing regiments and raising new ones. During the course of the war 50 new regiments of foot, including marines, would be added, of which those later numbered as 28th-39th Foot survived the peace; many of the new regiments were used to replace old ones when these were ordered from England or Ireland to Flanders or Spain. The increase in the cavalry was much lower, only seven new regiments being raised. The highest strength reached by the Army during the war was 70,000 men at home and abroad. The greatest number of units was six troops of Household Cavalry, 11 regiments of horse, 16 of dragoons, and 79 battalions of foot. Between 1702-12 the force with Marlborough in Flanders averaged just under 22,000, while that in Spain rose from 8,000 in 1704 to 26,000 in 1709.

Such a large expansion for an army technically maintained by voluntary enlistment required a massive effort by regimental recruiting parties, drumming up for men the length and breadth of the country. A ready source lay in the men disbanded in 1698 and there were always a number of genuine volunteers who would take the shilling, such as one Mathew Bishop who, after several years as a sailor, decided that the land forces offered greater chances of advancement. Lack of work, particularly in the winter months, drove many to enlist, while the bounty and blandishments offered by the recruiting parties attracted others, like those on whom, as Bishop described, *"we prevailed by reason of the beer and our talk".(1)* The majority had to be found by other methods. Capital offenders were offered the Army as an alternative to the gallows; Justices of the Peace were empowered to levy men who were without lawful employment or visible means of support; many prisoners were enlisted; and insolvent debtors were offered release if they joined or found a substitute. Though Parliament came close to passing a conscription Act, in the event only the impressment of the unemployed was tightened up. Finally recruitment was slightly improved by short-term enlistment for only three years.

Filling the ranks with such material foreshadowed the off-quoted remarks of the Duke of Wellington in the next century about *"scum of the earth"* and *"enlisting for drink"* but, in the same way that the Duke qualified these judgements with the words, *"it really is wonderful that we have made them the fine fellows they are"(2),* so it was with Marlborough's men. By his inspiring leadership, by giving them self-confidence through success in battle, and above all by his concern for their lives and welfare through careful planning and administration, he turned unpromising and generally unwilling material into the finest army in Europe.

He was supported by a hand-picked staff, among whom was the outstanding William Cadogan, the Quarter-master-General who also acted as his Chief of Staff, while his senior general officers included a number of able men like his brother, Charles Churchill, Lord Orkney and Lord Cutts, nicknamed "Salamander" on account of his courage in the hottest parts of a battlefield. The regimental officers varied in quality. There were still many who looked upon their commands as a source of income, while others made themselves conspicuous by absenting themselves as and when they chose to do so, sometimes when unpleasant or dangerous duty threatened. Against these must be set the likes of Robert Parker, captain in the Royal Regiment of Ireland, a true and dedicated soldier, and the dour Covenanter, John Blackadder of the Cameronians, whose sensibilities were pained by the *"swearing, profane talking, bantering or some impiety or other"(3)* of his fellows. Once on the field of battle, however, most officers, good or bad, could be relied upon to conduct themselves gallantly.

During Marlborough's campaigns four or five infantry battalions were grouped more or less permanently in brigades, which would be arrayed in one of two lines of battle, these lines being divided between the wings into which the army in the field was formed. Cavalry regiments were brigaded as required, again formed in two lines. General officers held no permanent command, such as in the later divisions and corps of the next century, but were assigned to the command of a wing, line, or specially detached force of a number of brigades as needed. At Blenheim, for example, Cutts was given a force of four brigades to assault the village of that name, while in the

---

† Strictly speaking it did not become British until after the Act of Union between England and Scotland in 1707, but for convenience it will be described as such from henceforth and dignified by the use of capital initials.

John Churchill, 1st Duke of Marlborough (1650-1722)
Portrait, oil on canvas, by John Clostermann
6005-312

George Hamilton, Earl of Orkney (1666-1737)
Portrait, oil on canvas by Martin Maingaud c1710
6108-27

War of Spanish Succession, c1710. A Camp Scene   Oil painting by Marcellus Laroon   7104-39

centre Charles Churchill commanded the first line, but with a general responsibility for the whole centre, and Orkney the second, between which were deployed two lines of cavalry.

Cavalry regiments, horse and dragoons, were generally organized into nine troops, each averaging three officers and about 40-50 troopers; three troops formed a squadron for action. The men were armed with sword and pistols in the horse, sword, carbine and bayonet in the dragoons. Marlborough's handling of cavalry continued the tradition of Rupert and Cromwell with his belief in the effect of shock action — two-squadron charges at a fast trot with men knee to knee in two ranks using only the sword. Pistols he would only allow for the protection of horses when grazing. Dragoons were gradually assimilating themselves more to the horse but were still used for dismounted action, as was seen at the storming of the Schellenberg in 1704 when Lord John Hay, commanding the Scots Greys, was ordered *"to dismount and charge the enemy on foot. This order was forthwith obeyed by that noble Lord, who dismounted and put himself at the head of his regiment and was marching up bravely to attack on foot just as the enemy began to give way. Hereupon he remounted and soon got over with our other squadrons which now put the enemy to flight and pursuing them killed a great many". (4)* Marlborough's use of massed cavalry proved the deciding factor at Blenheim and Ramillies, and under his command the British cavalry reached a standard of efficiency that would not always be achieved in its later history. Their fine appearance earned the praise of Prince Eugene who said he had never seen *"better horses, better clothes, finer belts and accoutrements"* and particularly commended *"that lively air I see in every one of these troopers' faces". (5)*

Apart from the Guards and the Royal Scots, the regiments of foot each had one battalion, divided into between 10 and 12 companies and a grenadier company. A company consisted of three officers, four to five sergeants and corporals, one, sometimes two drummers†, and between 50-60 privates, the larger figure being the official war establishment. Foot Guards had a slightly higher establishment. As the regiment was the property of the colonel, so it was known by his name; thus the Royal Welch Fusiliers, for example, (which did not become Fusiliers until 1714) fought at Blenheim as Ingoldsby's but at Malplaquet as Sabine's. Regiments took their seniority from their respective dates of formation. By 1703 pikes had virtually disappeared from the infantry, and every man in the ranks (corporals and privates) was armed and accoutred with flintlock musket, socket bayonet, and a pouch containing about two dozen paper cartridges holding the ball and powder; officers carried a short pike called a spontoon, except in the grenadier company where they had short muskets known as fusils, and sergeants a halberd; all ranks carried a sword in addition to their principle weapon. Though the company was the administrative sub-unit, for battle the battalion was drawn up in line, three ranks deep, with the grenadiers split between either flank, and divided into 18 platoons, told off into three "firings" of six platoons each. The platoons forming each firing were staggered along the line so that a continuous fire could be kept up from every part of the line, delivered, at the halt, when about 60 paces from the enemy. In each platoon the front rank would kneel, while the second and third ranks stood, the third firing between the intervals of the men in the second, all men firing together. This system was greatly superior to the French custom of rank-by-rank volleys, since it made for easier fire control, it produced relentless fire effect, and one third of the battalion was always reloaded to deal with any emergency*. The fire effect was also increased by the attachment to each battalion of two light guns firing canister from the flanks.

There was as yet no Royal Regiment of Artillery and a train of artillery had to be specially formed by the Board of Ordnance for a campaign. Since Marlborough was both Captain-General of the Army and Master-General of the Ordnance, the problems arising from the separateness of the Board from the Army were greatly mitigated. Field guns ranged from the 3-pounders attached to infantry battalions up to 24-pounders and had an average range of about 600 yards. There were heavier calibres used for sieges, supplemented by howitzers and mortars. All pieces, except for the light battalion guns, were heavy and cumbersome and required between eight and ten horses to draw them, animals and their drivers having to be hired from civilian contractors. Ammunition was either round shot, a solid ball of stone or cast iron, or canister, which discharged a spray of musket balls; hollow shot — globes filled with explosive — were fired from mortars and howitzers. Deficiencies in organisation, lack of mobility and supply problems all imposed limitations on the use of artillery but Marlborough fully perceived its importance both in attack and defence. He was well served by his chief artillery officer, Holcroft Blood, and himself closely supervised the apportioning of guns to batteries, their siting and movement, to ensure the co-ordination of artillery support with the tactical manoeuvres of horse and foot.

In view of the amount of siege warfare at this period, the engineering branch, also under the Board of Ordnance, was surprisingly little developed. The field army's staff included engineer officers to advise on sieges, fortifications, river crossings, maintenance of communications and so on. While some were excellent, like Colonel

---

† The Royal Scots were unique in the Army in having one piper in the colonel's company.

* For further details of organisation and tactics of all arms, see   David Chandler, "The Art of Warfare in the Age of Marlborough" (1976).

Armstrong, who alone of Marlborough's staff maintained that the siege of Bouchain in 1711 was practicable, there were others like those at the siege of Lille in 1708 of whom Marlborough complained; *"It would be a cruel thing if . . . we should fail of taking it by ignorance of our engineers". (6)* In the ordnance train, which included detachments of miners, pontooneers and pioneers, the officers to command these were drawn from foot regiments; for major engineering tasks, such as the construction of entrenchments, siege works, bridging, road improvement and the like, recourse had to be made to large bodies of locally-raised civilian labourers.

In the field of supply and transport all was in the hands of civilian contractors, working to the instructions of the staff through the agency of field commissaries appointed by Commissioners of Supply and Transport. The efficiency of these arrangements depended on the ready availability of money, the honesty of the contractors and the resources of the region of operations. For additional comforts each regiment had its own civilian sutlers, who provided such luxuries as meat and liquor and whatever they could add to their wares by plundering, an activity at which they were adept. In the relatively prosperous and fruitful lands of northern Europe the system, under the watchful eye of Marlborough, ever mindful of his soldiers' well-being, worked well enough and his troops were *"better fed than any of their predecessors except Cromwell's men".(7)* However, in the barren and poverty-stricken countries of the Iberian Peninsula, the English commanders, Peterborough and Galway, faced appalling administrative problems. Although the successful treatment of casualties was inevitably limited by the medical knowledge of the time, Marlborough did all he could to ensure the sick and wounded were properly cared for. Besides the 40-bed regimental hospitals presided over by the regimental surgeons and their mates, he arranged for marching and fixed hospitals manned by civilian surgeons engaged for the duration of the campaign. During the march to the Danube in 1704 men who fell sick were treated in a general hospital which followed the army by barge up the Rhine. First aid was given on the battlefield at casualty collecting posts from which the wounded were transported in requisitioned wagons and carriages to the main army hospital. Nevertheless, in spite of these careful arrangements, it has been calculated that *"a casualty had a one in three chance of surviving a serious wound".(8)*

When Marlborough arrived in the Low Countries in May 1702 France had occupied the Spanish Netherlands with all its important fortresses and was poised to invade Holland itself from the south-east near Cleves. In the first two years campaigning Marlborough, by skilful manoeuvring, removed this threat and captured the fortresses in eastern Flanders as far south as Huy and Liege. All his attempts to force a field action, however, were obstructed by the timidity of the Dutch field deputies attached to his headquarters for the purpose of safeguarding the interests of their national contingent. Meanwhile a combined French and Bavarian army had driven the Imperialists from the upper and middle Rhine and were ready to strike at Vienna.

It was clear to Marlborough in 1704 that this threat gravely endangered the Grand Alliance but that if he could link up with the Imperialists, not only would the danger be averted, but a great blow might be struck at the Franco-Bavarians. So, despite the formidable presence of other French armies in Flanders and eastern France, he began his epic and brilliant 250-mile march to the Danube, after hoodwinking the Dutch government as to his true intent so that he could take their troops with him. By secrecy and deception he also convinced the French that, first, he was planning to invade France by way of the Moselle, then, when he had passed Coblenz, that his objective was Alsace. It was only after he had turned east and met the Imperialists near Ulm, did the French divine his intention and send an army under Marshal Tallard to the aid of the Franco-Bavarian forces of Marsin.

For nearly six weeks between May and June, often in wet weather which turned the dusty roads to mud, the Anglo-Dutch troops tramped on through the forests and fields of southern Germany; cheered by the women- *"some of them much handsomer than we expected to find"* thought Captain Pope of the 8th Horse *(9)* — and always sustained by the careful administration of the Duke. Captain Parker wrote:

"As we marched through the countries of our allies, commissaries were appointed to furnish us with all manner of necessaries for man and horse. These were brought to the ground before we arrived and the soldiers had nothing to do but to pitch their tents, boil their kettles, and lie down to rest. Surely never was such a march carried on with more order and regularity and with less fatigue to man and horse".(10)

The perfection with which the march was conducted and the confidence it instilled in the troops was amply demonstrated by the gallantry and fortitude displayed on 2nd July, when, despite fearful casualties, Marlborough's men stormed the hill of Schellenberg and drove the Bavarians from their defences.

Just over a month later, on 11th August, the combined forces of Marlborough and Prince Eugene met those of Tallard and Marsin at Blenheim. This great battle drove Bavaria out of the war; freed the allied communications between Vienna and the Low Countries; and, by its total and crushing defeat of the French army, shattered its invincible reputation and raised that of Marlborough and his men to the heights. It witnessed the combination of Marlborough and Eugene in action for the first time: while the latter contained Marsin and the Bavarians, Marlborough attacked the fortified villages of Blenheim and Oberglau on the flanks of Tallard's position , thus neutralising them in preparation for his great and finally decisive blow in the centre. The furious

48

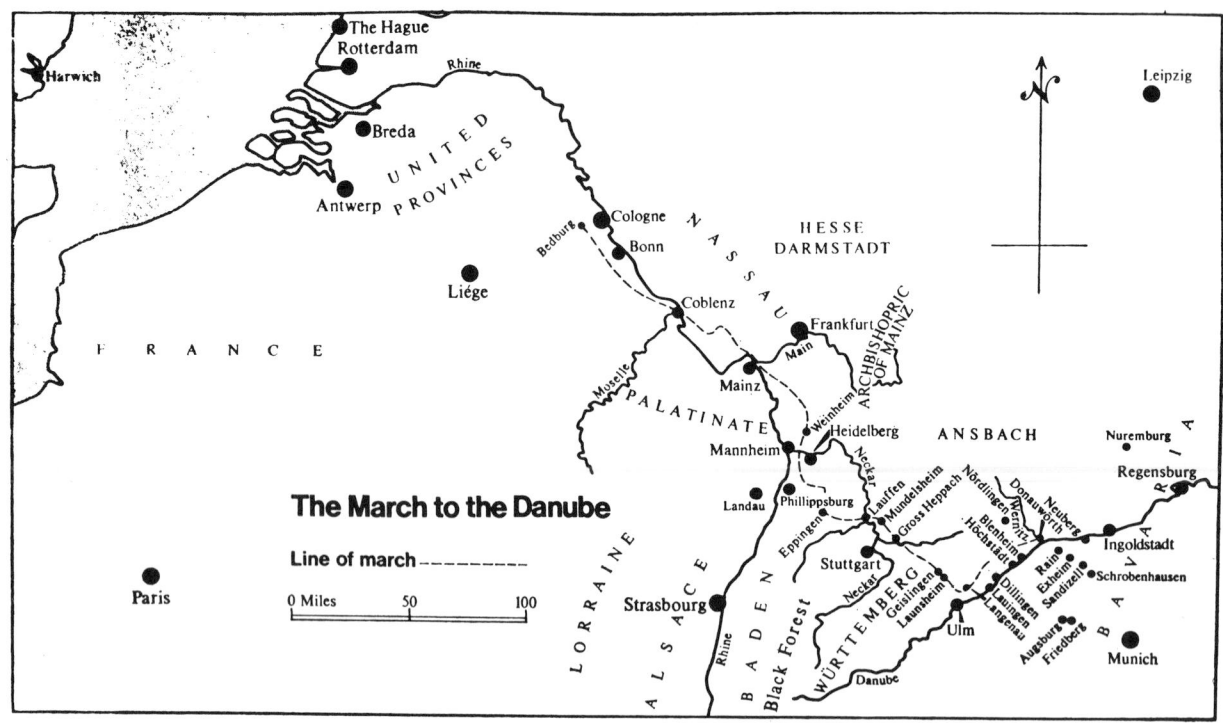

The March to the Danube

Line of march ----------

0 Miles   50   100

The Battle of Blenheim, 1704 Painting, oil on canvas by John Wootton   7511-82
Purchased with the aid of a grant from the National Art Collections Fund

and persistent attacks on Blenheim by Cutts and 16 British, Hessian and Hanoverian battalions, with the 1st Guards, Scots and Welch Fusiliers, North's and Churchill's† in the van, eventually tied down a total of 27 French battalions. When Marlborough advanced his centre, the British Cavalry* on its left were checked by fire from Blenheim and then pushed back by the French horse; but they recovered to come on again in the final break-out of the massed Allied cavalry, driving the routed enemy into the Danube which, after the battle, was, as Chaplain Noyes observed, *"ful of Jack Boots"* . Among the many prisoners was Marshal Tallard himself, brought to Marlborough by a Hessian dragoon officer . The Duke's triumph was complete. Noyes summarised the day's work by saying: *"Tho' Prince Eugene, if any man on earth, may eclipse the Duke of Marlborough's Glory, yet he ought not as to this Action. The Victory was gained by my Lord Duke and the whole Glory ought to be his". (11)*

In 1703 the war returned to Flanders but, as in 1703, Marlborough's plans for an advance into Lorraine and his subsequent out-manoeuvring of Marshal Villeroi came to naught through the hesitation of the Dutch. In Spain, following the capture of the great fortress of Gibraltar the year before, a force under Lord Peterborough+ landed on the east coast and, after capturing Barcelona, rallied Catalonia and Valencia to the cause of the Archduke Charles of Habsburg.

Marlborough had hoped, in 1706, to initiate a campaign in northern Italy in conjunction with Eugene but a French victory on the Rhine against the Imperialists again unnerved the Dutch who insisted on continuing operations against Villeroi in Flanders. The latter, thinking to catch Marlborough before he had concentrated his forces, left the safety of his lines behind the River Dyle and marched east with 60,000 men. The two armies met, somewhat to each other's surprise, near Ramillies. Villeroi, who had a slight superiority of numbers, drew up his troops in a concave arc facing east along the line of four villages. The most northerly, Autreglise, lay behind marshy ground and a river, the Little Geete, which ran southwards, passing to the east of Offuz, to its source at Ramillies. The last village, Taviers, on which Villeroi's right rested, stood on the River Mehaigne flowing east-west. In the decisive battle that followed, Marlborough again displayed his skill in outwitting an enemy, his acute perception of the terrain, his concentration of force at the decisive time and point, and not least his personal courage in rallying some beaten squadrons at enormous risk to his own life.

Appreciating that the battle could best be won in the open ground between Ramillies and Taviers, he first sent his Dutch to attack and fix Villeroi's right wing at the latter place. At the same time he launched the British foot under Lord Orkney, flanked by the British cavalry, against Autreglise and Offuz, to prevent the French withdrawing men from that sector to reinforce their centre and right. When Villeroi saw the lines of redcoats, against which he had been specifically warned by Louis XIV, advancing through the swamps of the Little Geete, far from withdrawing troops, he hurriedly reinforced his left. The Allied centre then went forward, the infantry directed on Ramillies with Overkirk's Dutch squadrons on their left. Fierce fighting ensued in the village but a counter-attack drove Overkirk back. Marlborough at once spotted the danger. In support of Orkney's advance on the right were 39 squadrons hitherto uncommitted which were now ordered to move to the centre under cover of a re-entrant. Orkney was ordered to disengage and retire behind the Little Geete. His English and Scots infantry had been making good progress against strong opposition and although, as he said, *"I think I never had more shot about my ears"(12),* it took ten ADCs and finally Cadogan himself to make him break off. *"I confess",* he said, *"it vexed me to retire. However we did it very well and in good order, and whenever the French pressed upon us, with the battalion of guards and my own ††I was always able to make them stand and retire".(12)* On reaching the ridge to the east of the Little Geete, one line faced about, continuing to poise a threat at the French left, while the other, its movements hidden by the ridge, followed the concealed way taken by the right wing squadrons and moved down to reinforce the Allied centre. Meanwhile General Schultz, with 12 Dutch battalions, the Buffs and Scots Fusiliers, had broken into Ramillies so that, with Taviers also in Dutch hands on the left, the flanks of the open central area were secure for Marlborough's cavalry, now reinforced from the right, to make their final assault. With the Danish horse riding wide on the left, the massed squadrons thundered at a heavy trot into the French centre, opening it up as though it were a door hinged on Ramillies; then, swinging north, they drove into Villeroi's left wing, which he tried hastily to re-deploy from where it had been watching Orkney's men across the Little Geete. The French retreat turned into a rout, with *"whole brigades running in disorder"(13),* and as they fled, so they were pursued far into the night by the English horse which, having been left to support Orkney, were the freshest of the Allied cavalry.

Over half of Villeroi's army were casualties or prisoners at a cost to the Allies of some 4,000. Following his defeat the great fortresses of the Spanish Netherlands, from the Meuse through Ath and Menin to Ostend,

---

† Later 10th and 24th Foot. Marlborough himself was Colonel of the latter. The other British infantry at Blenheim were: Royal Scots (2 bns.), 3rd Buffs, 8th, 15th, 16th, 20th, 26th Cameronians, 37th.

* The cavalry were the 1st, 3rd, 5th, 6th and 7th Dragoon Guards, Scots Greys, 5th Royal Irish Dragoons.

+ *"An eccentric genius",* Fortescue, *"History of the British Army",* Vol.I, p.489.

†† 1st Guards and Royal Scots.

began to fall one by one into Marlborough's hands. By the end of the campaigning year he stood on the French frontier.

The high hopes inspired by this wonderful campaign were not fulfilled in 1707. The capable veteran Marshal, Vendôme, took command in northern France and remained firmly on the defensive, refusing to be drawn into battle. Marlborough's own plans for an offensive in support of an attack by the Imperialists on southern France were first put back by the latter's delay in moving, and then hindered by an exceedingly wet summer. In Spain the Allied army was now under Galway, formerly the Huguenot de Ruvigny last met at Aughrim. After capturing but failing to hold Madrid in 1706, he advanced again from Valencia only to be defeated at Almanza. Although the British infantry on the left threw back the Spaniards opposing them, they were abandoned by their Portuguese allies and had to fight it out against a force three times their strength. On the extreme left Hill's, *"that poor single regiment"*, had to make a gallant lone stand against enemy horse and foot when its supporting battalion *"went off a little too fast"(14)*; they stood their ground until rescued by a charge made by Harvey's horse. It is said that, for their brave conduct, Steuart's†, which lost 24 officers and 300 killed and wounded out of 467, were awarded the badge of Britannia by Queen Anne*(15)*.

A wet spring delayed the opening of the 1708 campaign in Flanders and when it started, on 13th June, the French moved first, marching north from Mons and seizing Ghent and Bruges. The Duke immediately moved west from Brussels, making for the fortress of Oudenarde on the Scheldt which he guessed would be the next French objective. At the same time he summoned Eugene, who had been threatening France from the Moselle. The latter, leaving his army to follow, made haste to join Marlborough, whom he found unwell and plagued by reports of political difficulties in England. Nevertheless, cheered by Eugene's arrival and inspired by the chance of catching Vendome in the open, the Duke drove his troops forward towards Oudenarde.

By an outstanding forced march his advanced guard under Cadogan reached the fortress on 11 July just as the leading French troops appeared on the high ground to the north. When the battle began only Cadogan, with 15 squadrons and 12 battalions, was on the west bank of the Scheldt, while behind him the engineers were hurriedly constructing pontoon bridges to accelerate the crossing by the main body. Thus the army came into action piecemeal, hurried up by Marlborough to prolong Cadogan's line, which by now was being attacked by the entire French right wing. A fierce infantry fight developed among the close-set hedges and copses, the advantage now lying with one side then, as fresh troops came up, with the other. But while the volleys of his English and German battalions hammered out to repulse the French infantry, Marlborough's far-seeing eye had spied the road to victory: a high stretch of open ground above and to the left of the main battle. Overkirk's Dutch horse and foot were hurrying through the streets of Oudenarde and the Duke, leaving Eugene in command on the right, directed Overkirk to this high ground, forming two attacking lines: one, of horse and foot, to go for the French rear, the other, purely of foot, directed at Vendome's right flank. With about only an hour of daylight left, he launched this massive left hook. While the Dutchmen went in, Eugene advanced his right, pressing forward in the centre and curling round the French left. As dusk approached the luckless French began to crumble amid the encircling allies. Sergeant Millner of the Royal Irish wrote: *"We drove the enemy from ditch to ditch, from hedge to hedge, and from out of one scrub to another in great hurry, confusion and disorder". (16)* By nine o'clock the battle was over. Part of the French army under Louis' grandson, the Duke of Burgundy, had remained passive spectators of the whole fight and, when they saw the fate of their comrades, made off. Of the remainder, some 20,000 were killed, wounded or taken prisoner, against allied casualties of around 3,000. Marlborough had taken a calculated risk in giving battle with his army divided by the Scheldt, but had proved that his generalship was as skilfull in an encounter battle as in a set-piece like Blenheim or Ramillies.

With the French running for shelter behind the Ghent-Bruges canal, Marlborough now conceived the bold plan of a direct advance on Paris but his allies, even Eugene, were unwilling to take the risk. Instead it was agreed that Eugene should besiege Lille, the capital of French Flanders and Vauban's greatest fortress, while Marlborough covered him. The siege began in August with an exploit by a single British soldier, Sergeant Littler,* who swam a river to a French outwork and let down the drawbridge. In September a French attempt to intercept a large and important convoy to the siege works was defeated by General Webb at Wynaendael. Lille's formidable defences held out for the rest of the year but on 9th December Marshal Boufflers and his garrison marched out with the honours of war. Ghent and Bruges were retaken shortly afterwards and a successful year closed with news of the capture of Sardinia and Minorca in the Mediterranean.

So hardly had the French suffered in 1708 that Louis sued for peace, but so exorbitant were the terms

---

† Hill's, Steuart's and Harvey's later the 11th and 9th Foot and 2nd Dragoon Guards respectively. Other regiments at Almanza were: 3rd, 4th and 8th Dragoons, a mixed battalion of Guards, 2nd, 6th, 17th, 28th, 33rd, 35th and 36th Foot, plus two other regiments of Dragoons and five of Foot. The battalion that abandoned Hill's was Mark Kerr's, disbanded 1713.

* Of the 1st Guards according to some authorities, of the 16th Foot to others.

Battle of Malplaquet, 1709.
Painting, oil on canvas, by Louis Laguerre.

7308-10-3

View of the Battle of Ramillies.
Etching by J.V. Vianon after G.L. Mosburger, Contemporary.

7102-33-330

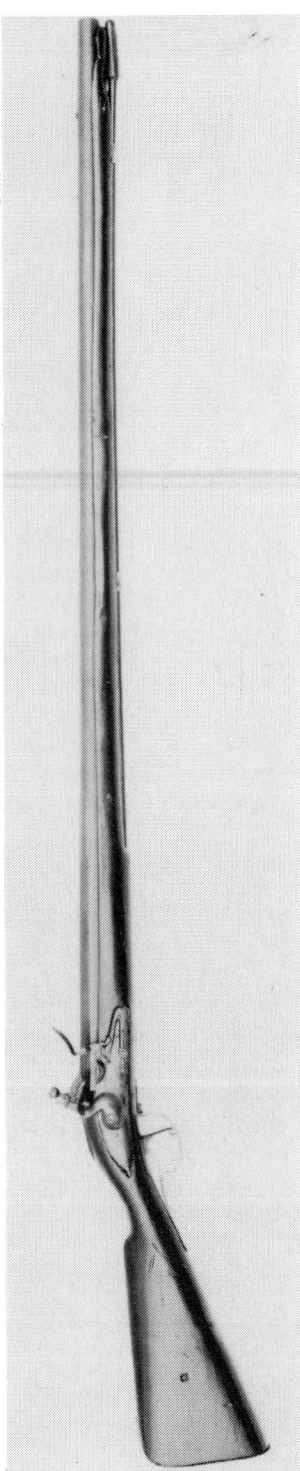

Flintlock musket c1695
7105-7-22

Holster cap used by the 1st Duke of Marlborough c1705

Brass hilted British
cavalry sword, first half
of the eighteenth century
7110-8

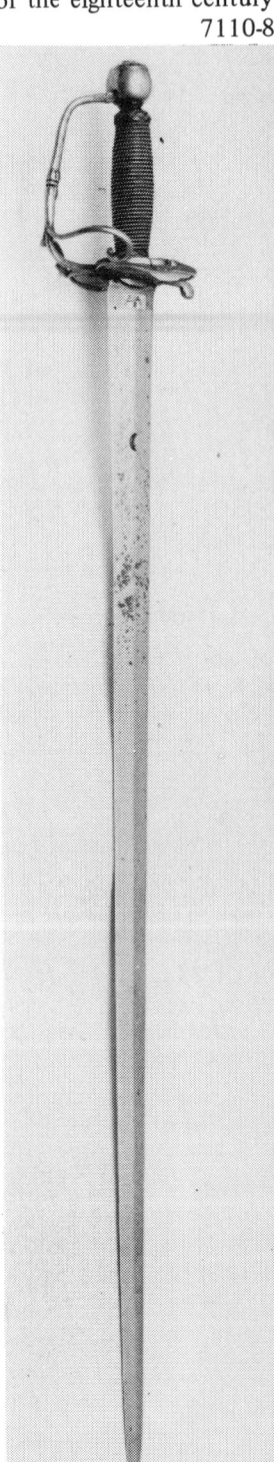

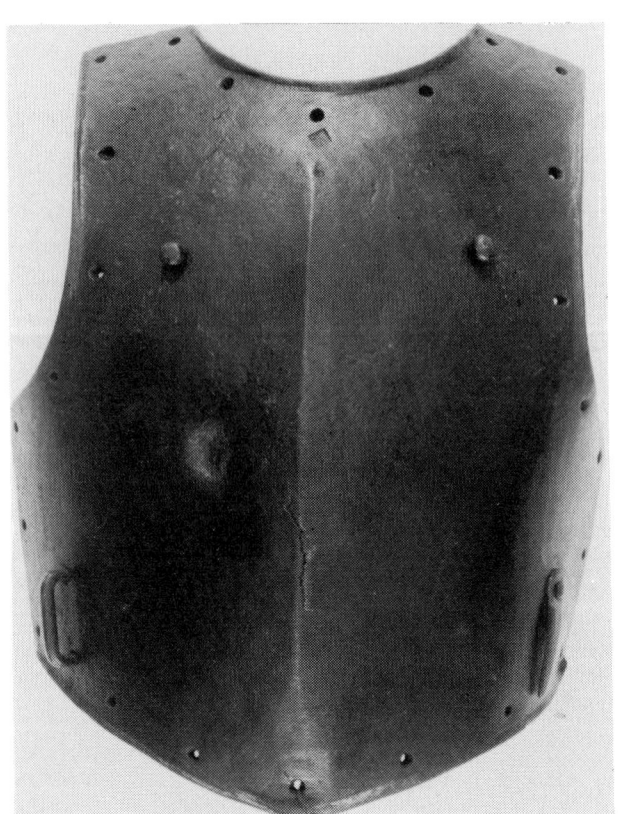

Cavalry breastplate c1700
Probably Danish, made for British service. This type of
breastplate was worn on cross-straps without a backplate.

offered by the Allies that they stiffened the French will to resist. By July 1709 another army under Marshal Villars had been mustered in strongly fortified lines between the Scarpe and the Lys. Marlborough, increasingly beset by the whiles of English politicians bent on undermining the Queen's confidence in him, was bitterly disappointed by the bungling of the peace terms. So too was the field army, whose great endeavours had nearly brought the war to an end, and its spirit lacked the brightness of earlier years. Now the work had to be done again. A two-month siege of Tournai in drenching rain did little to restore its enthusiasm though its loyalty and discipline still held. When Tournai fell, Marlborough marched rapidly to invest Mons but Villars, reluctant to lose another fortress, left his lines and moved in pursuit. On 11th September the armies met at Malplaquet. What followed was described by Richard Kane, commanding the Royal Irish, as *"the most desperate and bloody attack and battle that had been fought in the memory of men".(17)*

Villars had chosen a naturally strong position, based on two large woods with a mile-wide gap between them; this he made even stronger by constructing entrenchments, batteries and redoubts across the gap, which was enfiladed by further defences on the edge of the woods; within the woods additional obstacles were erected. The infantry and guns were deployed within the defences, with a preponderance on the flanks, and the horse were arrayed in rear. Marlborough's plan was to attack with Eugene's Austrians, the Prussians and the Dutch on the flanks to induce the enemy to weaken his centre, in preparation for the decisive thrust by Orkney's English foot, followed up by the cavalry; a not-unfamiliar tactic, *"perhaps all that a tired man with nagging personal worries could think of".(18)* A force under General Withers, of British and foreign battalions, which had not yet come up, was to deploy into action off the line of march to turn the extreme French left.

For eight dreadful hours the Allied infantry battled in the woods with appalling loss of life, advancing, recoiling, reforming and advancing again. On the right Orkney had to throw three of his battalions, Buffs, Godfrey's (16th) and Temple's, into the inferno to maintain the momentum, while on the left the Dutch were swept away in droves. Slowly and inexorably the carnage mounted, until Withers arrived to drive in behind the French left. At last the pressure in the wood forced the French to weaken their centre and, supported by fire from a 40-gun battery, Orkney led forward his redcoats to storm the redoubts. The cavalry went through, were twice counter-attacked but finally, with Eugene sending in the last reserves of Austrian horse, broke out. Seeing the day was lost, the French disengaged and retired in good order and unmolested, for the Allies were all too exhausted to pursue. It was an expensive victory as, compared with French losses of some 12,000, the Allies suffered nearly 20,000 casualties, amongst which the Dutch infantry lost half their strength. Marlborough was horrified and ill after the battle, writing to Godolphin: *"....in so great an action it is impossible to get the advantage, but by exposing men's lives; but the lamentable sights and thoughts of it have given me so much disquietude that I believe it is the chief cause of my illness; for it is melancholy to see so many brave men killed with whom I have lived these eight years, when we thought ourselves sure of a peace".(19)* Malplaquet achieved little, for in France the heroism of their troops served to strengthen their resolve to fight on; in England the Whig politicians, who had thrown away the chance of an honourable and advantageous settlement with France at the beginning of the year, now quarrelled among themselves, while the Tories intrigued for a compromise peace and the downfall of Marlborough.

In 1710 the pressures building up on the Duke, as a result of the uncertainties of his position at home and the burden of eight years' responsibilities in high command, might have broken the perseverance of a lesser man. Nevertheless he set to once more, reducing the French frontier garrisons one by one with a view to striking into France itself. Four had been taken when news came of the Whig government's defeat and the assumption of power by the Tories. At the beginning of 1711 Marlborough came home, to be humiliated, not only by the Tory ministers, but also by the Queen, whose reign he had done so much to enhance but whose ears now listened only to his enemies. His great friend and stand-by Godolphin, had already been dismissed, but since it suited the new regime, to retain him in command, for the moment, and since the Allies pleaded for his return, he sailed once more for Flanders.

Meanwhile the operations in Spain had yielded little success to the Allied cause. The Austrian general, Staremberg, who had replaced Galway, launched an offensive in the north-east. The British cavalry fought *"with great eagerness and fury"* at Almenara, pursuing the enemy to Lerida with shouts of *"Almanza, ye dogs! Remember Almanza!"(20)* This action and a further defeat of the Spaniards at Saragossa led to the second occupation of Madrid. However the approach of Vendôme with a French army forced Staremberg to retreat. Stanhope, with a small force of eight British battalions, was trapped by Vendôme's 20,000 in the little town of Brihuega. Hoping that Staremberg would come to their aid, Stanhope's men desperately contested every yard, the Scots Guards particularly distinguishing themselves. As they were forced back they set fire to the houses they had to abandon but in the end, with ammunition running low and no sign of Staremberg, Stanhope surrendered. The next day Staremberg was defeated at Villa Viciosa and by the end of the year was back in Barcelona, with Spain lost to the Allies.

During the winter of 1710-11 in Flanders Villars had constructed a 90-mile defence line, running from Namur through Valenciennes and Arras to the sea, protected by rivers and inundations and studded with fortresses. So strong did Villars believe these works to be that he called them the Lines of 'Non Plus Ultra'. Notwithstanding this formidable barrier, Marlborough, then concentrating his army around Douai, determined to break through it and capture the fortress of Bouchain, at the junction of the Scheldt and the Sensee, thus opening a path into France. The point at which he planned to cross the lines was some seven miles west of Bouchain, where some causeways crossed the river in front of the lines, the approaches to which were dominated by the small fortress of Arleux. This he disposed of with great subtlety. First seizing it by a surprise night attack, he left a garrison therein and moved away, hoping to induce Villars to retake it. This the latter did and, to ensure it could not be used again by Marlborough, demolished its defences — exactly as the Duke had hoped for. The Allied army was then concentrated westwards, near Vimy Ridge, opposite Arras where, through numerous strategems, Marlborough convinced not only Villars, but also his own army, much to their consternation, that it was there that he planned his break-through. On 4th August, after an ostentatious reconnaissance of the French defences, he ordered an assault for the following morning, all of which was reported in due course by spies to the French commander. That night, leaving his camp fires burning, he set the whole army in motion, hurrying eastwards through the moonlight towards Arleux. At 2 a.m. Villars discovered the deception and set off in pursuit, but he was too late. All through next morning Marlborough's men, having covered 40 miles in 18 hours, were pouring through the Lines of 'Non Plus Ultra' at Arleux and forming up to give battle. Villars however drew off southwards to take shelter in Cambrai and on 9th August Marlborough set siege to Bouchain.

To reduce the fortress with its garrison of 5,000 and, at the same time, to safeguard his rear against Villars' army of 100,000, Marlborough could only muster 90,000. Therefore, to protect his siege operations and his lines of communication, he dug his army in behind 30 miles of entrenchments, constructed by a work force of 6,000 labourers. Just over a month later, on 14th September, Cadogan was able to report to Whitehall, *"the happy conclusion of the siege of Bouchain, which has been attended by all the circumstances my Lord Duke's friends could wish for his Glory and Reputation"*. He went on:

> *"His Grace undertook it in sight of the enemy army, tho' superior to his by above 30 battalions, and commanded by a General that France looked on as its last hope and who, piqued even to rage by being duped in the Passage of the Lines, was resolved to leave nothing unattempted to repair his fault and relieve Bouchain. He indeed made a great many efforts towards it, but they all proved fruitless by the measures His Grace took to disappoint them, so that notwithstanding the French army's remaining within cannon shot of our approaches, yet our convoys of bread and artillery came regularly and safe, our communication was preserved with our great towns, and in 15 days after our batteries began to fire the place was surrendered".(21)*

So, despite increasing age and poor health, and feeling the politicians' knife already pricking between his shoulder blades, Marlborough brought to a triumphant conclusion his last and one of his most brilliant campaigns. Shortly after, his government, discarding their allies, opened negotiations for a separate peace with France. When Marlborough returned to England, Crown and ministers showed their appreciation of one who had wrought so long and so ably on their behalf, by first dismissing him from all his posts and then charging him with embezzling public funds. It was but one more example — and it would not be the last — of shameful ingratitude and disloyalty of British politicians towards her military men.

It might be asked, however, who now remembers Robert Harley, Earl of Oxford, or Henry St John, Viscount Bolingbroke, the men who plotted his downfall? On the other hand, the name of the great Duke of Marlborough, diplomat of supreme tact and skill, strategist of foresight and tactician of cunning and daring, is forever inscribed among the lists of great captains and great men. Much has been written of his fame in all these fields, but let his renown rest on the words of two men of the Army whose repute he raised to such heights. The Irish captain of foot, Robert Parker, wrote: *"He never led us on to any one action, that we did not succeed in".(22)* While of the man the soldiers called *"The Old Corporal"* or *"Corporal John"*, another corporal, Mathew Bishop, said: *"The Duke of Marlborough's attention and care was over all of us. The known world could not produce a man of more humanity".(23)*

CHAPTER 5
THE WHITE HORSE OF HANOVER
1714-1754

Under the terms of the Treaty of Utrecht, which finally ended the War of the Spanish Succession in 1713, Louis XIV's grandson, Philip, was confirmed as King of Spain on condition that the thrones of France and Spain should not be united. The Spanish possessions in Flanders and northern Italy were transferred to the sovereignty of the Emperor, the former thus becoming the Austrian Netherlands. Britain retained her conquests of Gibraltar and Minorca and received from France the New World territories of Newfoundland, Nova Scotia and Hudson's Bay. Lastly, Louis formally recognized the Protestant succession in England so that, when Anne died in 1714, the crown passed to the Elector of Hanover who ascended the throne as George I. Britain's foreign policy in future would therefore also be influenced by the interests of Hanover.

Even before the Treaty of Utrecht was signed, measures were in hand to reduce the size of the Army to an establishment of 22,000, of which two-thirds would be for garrisons overseas. The inadequacy of the force that remained for home defence was made clear in 1715, when a rebellion broke out in Scotland, with some support in the west and north of England, to restore the Stuarts, in the person of James, son of James II, to the throne. The disbandment of some regiments was cancelled and thirteen new regiments of dragoons† and eight of foot were hurriedly raised.

The rising began in the Highlands on 6th September. The few Royal troops in Scotland were hastily moved up to Stirling to block the exits from the Highlands. Some of the Highlanders nevertheless got through to join the Jacobites in the Lowlands and Northumberland and, having marched into England, reached Preston. Here they were forced to surrender on 11th November, coincidentally the very day on which their comrades in Scotland were defeated at Sherriffmuir. The latter's defeat was in fact more moral than tactical, since they overcame half the Royal force with ease but failed, despite their superiority in numbers, to finish off the remainder and simply retreated northwards. By February the rebellion was over. The poor showing of some of the Royal troops against what were little more than tribal levies showed how quickly the great army built up by Marlborough had deteriorated.

Another small flurry of Jacobite activity occurred in 1719 when two Spanish frigates landed a 300-strong detachment of Spanish troops with three Scottish peers on the west coast of Scotland at Kintail in Ross-shire; here they were joined by some 600 clansmen. General Whiteman marched down from Inverness with the Scots Greys and three regiments of foot and briskly dispersed them at Glenshiel on 10th June.

The early eighteenth century English or Lowland Scots soldier regarded the Highlands and their inhabitants in much the same light as in more recent times the British Army viewed the tribes of the North-West Frontier of India. The military problems in both areas were not dissimilar, requiring as they did the pacification of an unruly people living in mountainous terrain with poor communications. Forts and barracks had to be built to keep watch over the countryside and in 1725 General Wade began to open up the Highlands by building roads, the results of which are still visible to this day. On the principle that the best gamekeeper is an ex-poacher, independent companies of Highlanders were raised from clans loyal to the Hanoverian succession to police the disaffected areas. Similar companies had been raised in 1710 but these had been disbanded after the '15 Rebellion. Four companies were raised in 1725, a number which was soon increased to six. They wore the Army's red coat with Highland dress of a dark blue, black and green tartan which, in conjunction with the nature of their duties, earned them the colloquial name in the Highlands of "Am Freiceadan Dubh" — the Black Watch. On 7th November 1739 these companies were formed into a regiment, which in due course became the 42nd Royal Highlanders and later still (1881) adopted as their official title the original colloquialism.

Another important corps which dates its formation from the reign of George I is the Royal Regiment of Artillery. After the Treaty of Utrecht the train of artillery was disbanded and when the Board of Ordnance was required to reform one for the Jacobite rebellion it was unable to do so. Two companies of permanent artillery

---

† Of these, six later became light dragoon regiments and eventually the 9th and 12th Lancers, 10th, 11th, 13th and 14th Hussars.

An Encampment of the Royal Artillery in the Netherlands, 1748

Painting, oil on canvas, by David Morier. Loan HM The Queen

were therefore raised by Royal Warrant of 26th May 1716 and by 1727 this had increased to four. However it remained under the Ordnance Board and its officers were commissioned by the Board and not by the King. The first commandant to be appointed was a Dane, Albert Borgard, who had served with distinction in the British service at Steenkirk and throughout Marlborough's campaigns. By 1744 the regiment had a strength of eight companies, one of which was entirely composed of cadets training to become artillery officers. No other regiment, unfortunately, took such trouble over training its officers.

Apart from these innovations the reign of George I was not a happy one for the Army. The blame was not the King's for he did what he could to remedy the injustices, indiscipline and corruption which soon began to permeate the Army after the Treaty of Utrecht. He considered the system of officers buying and selling their commissions to be wrong and, although he was unable to abolish it, he instituted, in 1720, fixed tariffs for their prices and imposed certain limitations on their purchase based on rank and length of service. However, control of the Army was now firmly in the hands of Parliament. Its very existence depended on the annual passing of the Mutiny Act, which now specified the number of troops authorised for any one year. This procedure gave ample scope to voices clamouring for its disbandment, reduction or, when these failed, for measures which could only result in a breakdown of its administration and discipline. Calls for its replacement by the militia were heard anew. Those who were most vociferous in support of the militia and against a standing army when out of office were often the first to change their tune when confronted with the realities of power. Not only were there the threats of Jacobitism and foreign invasion, but in a highly politically-minded, singularly undisciplined and turbulent age with no police force, the Army was the only body available to maintain public order, whether this be the quelling of the riots and disorders that accompanied elections, the *"suppression of tumultuous weavers and other persons"(1)*, or the hunting down of highwaymen and smugglers.

Such duties made the Army unpopular with all classes of society: with the gentry, since it interfered with their often unscrupulous political activities; with the middle classes, since the absence of any barracks (except in Scotland and Ireland) saw the billeting of drunken and quarrelsome soldiers in their towns; and with the lower classes, since they regarded the soldier as an instrument of repression against their liberties and criminal activities. Held in such low esteem by the nation it was not surprising that many officers were inefficient, idle and corrupt, and that the ranks could only be filled with difficulty and then only by the dregs of society, who had to be kept in check by ferocious punishments. Not until a war with Spain in 1739 did recruits come forward in abundance. In the absence of a commander-in-chief, executive control of the Army lay in the hands of the Secretary-at-War, now a junior minister and therefore a political appointment, whose motivation was too often not the good of the Army but political advantage. This led to the Army being used as a pawn in the game of party politics. Moreover, since all matters affecting officers' careers were in the Secretary's hands, it inclined an officer to put political allegiance before his duty, particularly when that duty was questioned, derided or abused by contemporary opinion and events. Such interference by politicians with the internal workings of the service, which many senior officers were too powerless or lazy to resist, led to the remonstration by General Wade that *"the discipline of our army is in a very bad way".(2)*

In view of the tribulations that beset the Army in the long peace that followed the War of the Spanish Succession, it is surprising that in the wars of the mid-eighteenth century, as will shortly be seen, British soldiers would again display the gallantry and stubborn tenacity of Marlborough's day, if not always achieving the brilliant successes of those times. Sir John Fortescue was in no doubt that the Army was saved *"by the spirit, the pride and the self-respect of individual regiments"* in which *"there were always officers who worked hard and conscientiously for the credit of their own corps, and always men who were proud to take service with them and help them to maintain it"(3)*. It was also helped by the interest and beneficial influence of the House of Hanover and, once on the field of battle, the British soldier has ever been sustained by his sense of inbuilt superiority to foreigners, even when disaster has been staring him in the face.

The peacetime establishment of the Army in England and Scotland was eventually fixed in 1722, despite bitter opposition in Parliament, at 18,000 men. To this figure must be added the 8,000 on the Irish establishment which was always kept separate. Then there were the garrisons for the colonial possessions which had to be maintained. Since the beginning of the seventeenth century British colonies on the eastern seaboard of North America and in the West Indies were responsible for their own defence by implementing the same militia system that had pertained in England. Where there was an indigenous white population, as in the American colonies, this posed no problem; in the West Indies manpower was found from the victims of "transportation to the colonies". Since after the Restoration this source of supply ceased to be so plentiful, recourse was made to the raising of independent companies which, in the manner of the old "garrisons" of fortresses in England, were intended to be permanently stationed in the localities they were responsible for. The addition to the Crown after the Treaty of Utrecht of Minorca and Gibraltar necessitated the raising of further such companies, while the garrison for the newly-acquired provinces of Newfoundland and Nova Scotia was found by grouping four

companies from the West Indies and American plantations into a regiment which later became the 40th Foot. In the West Indies the garrisons were increased to regimental strength during the War of the Spanish Succession.

The principle of a garrison's permanence was adhered to whether it was an independent company or a regiment, with the result that the 40th remained in garrison for 46 years and the 38th Foot endured nearly 60 years in the Leeward Islands. Not only was no provision made for their relief but their needs suffered almost total neglect by the government at home. In 1711 the garrison at Gibraltar burned its huts for want of fuel and 19 years later they were still without proper accommodation. In 1739 the Bermuda garrison complained that no stores had been received in the colony since 1696! Under such conditions, to which must be added the high prevalence of fever and disease, particularly in the West Indies, service in these overseas companies and regiments was feared and detested. Despite offering high bounties to induce men to enlist for foreign service, it became increasingly difficult to obtain recruits for the overseas garrisons, and consequently men had to be drafted from regiments on the home establishment. In the next century foreign service would become the accepted lot of the soldier but this was not the case in the Georgian period. Men who enlisted realised that they might have to serve abroad in time for war but did not expect to have to do so in peacetime. Thus the system of drafting bred resentment and distrust, and, rather than accept the draft, men would mutiny or desert; crimes for which transportation to the foreign garrisons was often substituted for the death penalty. It seems never to have crossed the minds of English ministers that the economies they made by neglecting their troops overseas only resulted in weak garrisons of abandoned, fever-ridden and resentful men who can have had no military value whatever.

The parlous state to which the Army had been reduced by years of maladministration on the part of its civilian overlords and the constant sniping of power-hungry politicians was finally demonstrated in the only military expedition of the so-called War of Jenkins' Ear with Spain in 1739. The politicians who called loudest for war, as a means of revenge for Spanish threats to England's trade in the New World, were the same as those who protested at the increase to the Army's establishment such a war would need. The expedition fitted out to attack Spanish possessions in the Caribbean was a masterpiece of mismanagement. The generals quarrelled with the admirals; the attacks on Carthagena were a total failure; and the majority of the wretched soldiers who had survived the voyage and the incompetent operations finally succumbed to yellow fever. Perhaps what most typifies the whole sad story is that the only troops that could be scraped together for a subsidiary operation in Central America were 300 aged and infirm pensioners from the Chelsea Hospital.

Meanwhile the great powers were stirring in Europe once again. In Prussia King Frederick William I (1713-40) had built up a formidable army round which, unlike in England, the whole state revolved. With a highly professional officer corps drawn from the impoverished Prussian nobility, and a system of compulsory military service, Prince Leopold of Anhalt-Dessau, nicknamed the Old Dessauer, who had fought with Marlborough, drilled and drilled his troops until he had produced a magnificent fighting machine. In 1740 this army passed into the hands of a master of war, Frederick II, soon to be named the Great, who was determined to enlarge his kingdom. In October 1740 the Emperor Charles VI died, leaving the vast Habsburg possessions to his daughter, Maria Theresa. Quick to take advantage of a young and inexperienced Empress, Frederick marched into Silesia and defeated the Austrians at Mollwitz. Meanwhile France, seeing the opportunity of paying off old scores, allied herself with Bavaria, whose Elector had a claim to the Imperial throne, and prepared for war. Only in England and Holland was there support for Maria Theresa, compounded in England's case by George II's fears for his Hanoverian kingdom in the coming war.

In 1741-42 England prepared once more for a continental campaign. The Army's establishment was increased to 62,000, seven new regiments of foot were raised†, and the Earl of Stair was appointed to the command of a force of 16,000, destined to operate in Flanders in support of the Austrians. Though nearly 70, Stair was a commander of great experience who had first seen action at Steenkirk and had learned his trade at Marlborough's hand, both in command and on the staff. The fact that some three decades had elapsed since then was of small significance as warfare had changed but little. He appreciated that, since Maria Theresa had been forced to concede Silesia and make peace with Prussia, Austria was free to devote her attention to the Franco-Bavarians; the time was therefore ripe for an attack on the French army at Dunkirk by the English, Hanoverian and Imperial forces in the Austrian Netherlands, followed by an invasion of France.

Throughout 1742 this, and every other plan devised by Stair, all sensible, daring and capable of execution, were thwarted by the vacillilation and timidity either of the King, who was more concerned with the safety of Hanover, of the Allies, or of ministers at home. The Austrians wanted the Allied army to march into Germany for no very sound strategic reason, but since this would assist the security of Hanover, Stair was overruled. In February 1743 the army, 40,000 strong, marched east from Flanders. The British element consisted of the

† Six of these became the 43rd to 48th Foot.

60

Officer's coat worn by Lieut-General Richard
St George as Colonel of the 8th Dragoons, c1742
7107-30

Royal Artillery, c1750   6704-1
Kettle Drummer's Coat.

King's Own Regiment of Foot.   Royal Regiment of Dragoons of Ireland.   42nd Regiment of Foot

Engravings from 'A Representation of the Cloathing of His Majesty's Forces, 1742.'

Household Cavalry, nine regiments of horse and dragoons, and 12 of foot†.

Prevented from carrying out his schemes for invading France, Stair now planned a march on the Danube from which he could fall on the rear of the French army facing the Austrians, while the latter attacked in front. England and France were not yet officially at war with each other, both simply acting as auxiliaries for Maria Theresa and the Elector of Bavaria respectively. Lacking any of Stair's strategic vision and apprehensive of any manoevre that would take the army further from Hanover, George II forbade the plan, simply ordering Stair to occupy the heights of Mainz in order to command the confluence of the Rhine and the Main, a purely political objective concerned with the Electorship of Mainz and of no strategic value. Hearing that a French army under Marshal Noailles lay on the west bank of the Main, Stair planned to attack it, but was again prevented by the King, who on 19th June arrived in person and took command of the army. Meanwhile Noailles used his reprieve to cut the river above the Allies, thus preventing them from gaining any supplies from upstream; placed batteries of guns along the west bank of the river to command the road between the Allied camp and their base at Hanau; and prepared a force under Grammont to block the road downstream to cut off the King from Hanau. With the French ready to strike in front and behind him, the river with Noailles' cannon to the west, and an impassable range of wooded hills to the east, the King was now trapped. Since the army was also short of supplies he had no choice but to order a retreat on Hanau.

Once he saw the Allied army in motion, Grammont crossed the Main and took up position with 30,000 men near the village of Dettingen; Noailles prepared his remaining 30,000 to cross behind the Allies. As the Allied army advanced they could see Frenchmen across the river *"so near that in some places we saluted one another with our hatts as we passed, but. . soon . . . their artillery began to play upon us with great fury".(4)* This fire greatly impeded the deployment of the army into line of battle which the King had ordered as soon as he was aware of Grammont's presence. Many of the regiments, particularly the 3rd Dragoons and the British infantry on the left nearest the river, had to stick it out under the bombardment while the ponderous manoeuvres went on, until the Allied artillery came up to give counter-fire. At last all was ready: *"the King flourished his Sword and said 'Now Boys! - Now for the Honour of England, fire, and behave Brave, and the French will soon run".(5)* In the first line on the left were, from left to right, the 33rd, 21st, 23rd, 12th, 11th, 8th and 13th Foot, which now advanced with an Austrian brigade on their right, and beyond, the Blues, Household Cavalry, 6th and Royal Dragoons; filling the gap between the 33rd and the river were the 3rd Dragoons. The British brigade on the left *"was opposite the French Gensdarmerie* (Household Cavalry) *and when we came up within the distance of about 70 yards they rode up to us at a full trott, and tho' we gave them a very warm reception, yet a good many of them broke thro' us with more courage than conduct, for as they could not stop their horses, we faced upon them and brot. them down very fast, so that few or none of them went back".(6)* As the infantry poured their platoon fire into the 'Gens d'Armes', the 3rd Dragoons, though only mustering two weak squadrons, charged and charged again into the French flank.

After this first attack, *"the line of foot advanced to us, and the battle became general betwixt the two lines of infantry, which lasted about two hours when the French foot gave way and their horse advanced. We then made way for our horse to advance, which they did, but not with so much success; however their retreat seemed as if it had been done on purpose, for they brought the French line of horse after them upon our foot, where they suffered prodijiously from our fire" (7).* The British and Austrian horse now counter-attacked again; abandoned by their infantry, the French Household troops, who had fought valiantly all day, gave way, and the whole French army collapsed into rout.

Stair wished to pursue but the King decided to press on to Hanau and safety. Noailles, seeing the destruction of Grammont's army, curiously made no attempt to intervene. The King, making the last appearance of a British monarch on a battlefield, had been rescued from his folly by the stubborn fighting qualities of his troops; nevertheless he had displayed great personal courage and *"rode about like a Lion" (8).* until he was run away with, thereafter spending the rest of the day on foot. At the close of the battle he created a number of knights banneret: Lord Stair was the first, and the last, Trooper Thomas Brown of the 3rd Dragoons, who had charged single-handed into the ranks of the 'Gens d'Armes' to rescue a standard, receiving seven wounds to his face and body and three bullets through his hat.

The King went home to enjoy a great personal triumph, followed later by Stair who, not without just-ification, resigned his command, being replaced by General Wade. War was now officially declared on France.

---

† For ease of reference regiments will henceforth be referred to by their numbers. Although regiments continued to be called by their colonel's name until 1760 their numbers, indicating their precedence, appear in the Army List for 1742, which were confirmed by Royal Warrant of 14th September 1743. Royal Warrant of 1st July 1751 reaffirmed the numbers and in the Army List of 1754 the colonel's name was omitted for the first time. For subsequent and present titles of numbered regiments, see Appendix A.

and in 1744 the scene of operations returned to Flanders. Here the elderly Wade proved no match for the redoubtable Marshal Saxe, and by the end of the year, hamstrung by the obstructionism of his Austrian allies, he too resigned.

Early in 1745 the King's son William, Duke of Cumberland, was appointed commander-in-chief. Though only 25 he had been at Dettingen and had keenly studied the profession of arms. By the end of April he had mustered an army of 47,000, including 23,000 British, at Brussels and marched south-west to relieve Tournai, already invested by Saxe. On 10th May he found the French army, 59,000 strong, deployed on either side of the village of Fontenoy, dug in behind entrenchments and redoubts. Notwithstanding the strength of the position and his inferiority in numbers, Cumberland decided to attack next day. The Austrians were to attack the French right and the Dutch, whose army was now a shadow of its former self, were to take the village of Fontenoy itself, in order to cover the left flank of the British advance on the right against a line of entrenchments held by the cream of the French infantry; these defences were enfiladed from both sides by the village and a redoubt on the edge of a wood on the British right. This redoubt was to be stormed by a brigade under Colonel Ingoldsby.

The next morning the British cavalry rode forward to cover the deployment of the infantry into their lines of battle and immediately came under heavy fire from the French batteries. They sat motionless on their horses for an hour under this murderous cannonade until someone thought to withdraw them, an experience wryly described by one of the dragoons: *"I was forced to be very civil and make a great many bows to ye balls, for they were very near me, for both my right and left hand men were killed, and all round me there were men and horses tumbling about".(9)* With the cavalry out of the way, the infantry attack began.

On the right Ingoldsby, misunderstanding his orders, failed to move against the redoubt, while the Dutch recoiled from Fontenoy. The 42nd Highlanders, fighting their first battle in Europe, were thrown in to support the Dutch, charging in the Highland style with their broadswords after firing a single volley with their muskets. Despite a heroic attack, Fontenoy still held, but Cumberland impatiently ordered General Ligonier to advance the two lines of British infantry: ten battalions in the first, seven, with some Hanoverians, in the second.† Greeted by a hurricane of gunfire from the village and redoubt, the long red lines marched forward with measured tread, arms shouldered and drums beating. Though hundreds fell, the regiments still went on, closing up the gaps, until the French infantry came in view about a hundred yards distant. Opposite the Foot Guards on the right stood their counterparts, the 'Gardes Françaises' and the 'Gardes Suisses' in blue and red respectively. As the British line halted, Lord Charles Hay of the 1st Guards stepped forward, raised his hat and cried: *"I hope, gentlemen, that you are going to wait for us today and not swim the Scheldt as you swam the Main at Dettingen".* Turning to the ranks behind him, he said: *"Men of the King's Company, these are the French Guards, and I hope you are going to beat them today". (10)* The French replied with a volley and then the British musketry crashed out in answer, a ceaseless fusillade up and down the line. The French infantry were swept away and slowly the British lines advanced, halting and firing by platoons as they did so,* until they were within the French defences. There they stood, quite unsupported by their allies, as the French horse moved up. Three times the cavalry charged but each time the platoon volleys bowled them over as had happened at Dettingen. Then, still pounded on the flanks by the French guns, the red lines pulled back to reform and advance again, the volleys rolling out in succession at the French infantry who now came on once more. But without support on their flanks and with grievous losses, the French superiority in numbers gradually began to tell. When Saxe sent the French Household Cavalry against their left and his Irish brigade against their right, Cumberland saw it was time to retreat. The gallant infantry faced about and retired by succession of battalions as steadily as they had advanced, halting and firing every hundred yards. Two battalions, the 32nd and 34th, were aligned to cover the final part of the withdrawal. These two, supported by charges from the troops of Horse Guards+ and the Blues, held off the pursuing French to allow Ligonier's battered but undefeated infantry to get clear. Cumberland had displayed no feats of generalship and the failure of the Allies had cost the British dear but, as one historian has said, *"although a defeat, there is no battle in history that throws more lustre on the British infantry than that of Fontenoy".(11)*

Tournai fell to Saxe, and by the beginning of August Cumberland, outnumbered and with his allies in disarray, had had to surrender all of Austrian Flanders west of the Scheldt, including his base at Ostend. Crisis piled on crisis for urgent news then came from home that *"a very small spark at the beginning is now unhappily become a very great Flame".(12)* Prince Charles Edward Stuart, son of the Old Pretender, had landed in Scotland and raised the Highlands in rebellion to regain the throne for his House. Cumberland was ordered to return to England at once with most of his army.

---

† From right to left: 1st, Coldstream and Scots Guards, 1st, 21st, 31st, 8th, 25th, 33rd, 19th; second line: Buffs, 23rd, 32nd, 11th, 28th, 34th, 20th.

* See David Chandler, "Art of War in the Age of Marlborough" (1976), p. 126.

+ Later Life Guards.

Barrell's (later 4th King's Own) Regiment at the battle of Culloden, 20th April 1746
Painting, oil on canvas, by David Morier.

"H.R.H. William Duke of Cumberland with a view of the routed rebel army near Culloden."
Line engraving by B.Baron after J.Wootton.
Published 1747 by B.Baron.   7102-33-130

Silver tankard made for the Duke of Cumberland to commemorate the Battle of Culloden, 1746.

7011-12

Charles, encouraged by the news of Fontenoy, had arrived in the western Highlands with only seven followers. With the Highland clans rallying to his standard, he marched on Edinburgh, side-stepping General Cope who had advanced to meet him. The only resistance his army met was the spirited defence of Ruthven Barracks, near Kingussie, by a tiny detachment of the 6th Foot under Sergeant Mulloy, which successfully defied the might of Clan Cameron. Two raw regiments of dragoons drawn up to bar the road to Edinburgh panicked and fled and on the 17th September Charles entered the city. Meanwhile Cope had transferred his force of 2,300 by sea from Inverness to block the way south from Edinburgh. Here, at Prestonpans, the Jacobite army, now swelled to 2,500, fell on Cope's troops and utterly routed them. Charles returned to Edinburgh to recruit and, in early November, crossed the border with 6,000 men, captured Carlisle and advanced on Manchester: In England the militia, creaking from long disuse, was being called out, patriotic gentlemen were raising troops of volunteers at their own expense, and the battle-hardened regiments from Flanders were arriving home. Wade lay at Newcastle, Cumberland was advancing up the midlands, while the defence of London, where considerable panic reigned, was entrusted to militiamen, stiffened by some battalions of Foot Guards.

On 4th December Charles reached Derby. He had lost many men from desertion, only a minute number of Englishmen had rallied to his cause, and he knew he was in danger of being trapped between Wade and Cumberland. He therefore turned for Scotland and by the first week of January was laying siege to Stirling Castle in order to secure this gateway to the Highlands. Cumberland had returned south because of a rumoured French invasion, leaving Hawley, who had replaced Wade, to finish the business with 12 regiments of foot and three of dragoons. On 17th January the two armies met at Falkirk in a rainstorm. Hawley's dragoons fled, most of his foot were scattered, and had it not been for the two regiments on the right, the 4th and 48th, which alone stood firm and gave the rest time to rally, a total rout would have ensued. Cumberland came hastening north with reinforcements, berated the runaways of Falkirk, and hurriedly retrained the army to cope with a Highland charge. Then he set off after Charles who had retreated on Inverness.

On a cold, rainy morning on 16th April his force of 16 battalions, eight of them veterans of Fontenoy, faced the Highland army on Culloden Moor, east of Inverness. Near the right of the first line, in the ranks of the Royal Scots, stood Private Alexander Taylor, who later wrote: *"The Battle begun by Cannonading and continued for half an hour or more with great Guns. But our Gunners galling their Lines, they betook them to their small Arms, Sword and Pistol, and came running upon our Front-Line like Troops of hungry Wolves and fought with Intrepidity".(13)* Among the staff officers was a young major, James Wolfe, who had fought at Dettingen when no more than 16, and now watched the main Highland charge as it fell on the left of the British line, where stood his regiment, the 4th King's Own, or "Old Tangereers"† :

"They were attacked by the Camerons and 'twas for some time a dispute betweeen the swords and the bayonets; but the latter was found by far the most destructible weapon. The Regiment behaved with uncommon resolution, killing, some say, almost their own number. They were however, surrounded by superiority, and would have been all destroyed had not Col. Martin with his regiment (8th Foot) moved forward to their assistance, prevented mischief, and by a well timed fire destroyed a great number of them and obliged them to run off". (14)

This stalwart repulse by the 4th and 8th, well supported by the 25th and 37th, broke the Highlanders' spirit and the Jacobite cause was shattered into fragments.

There followed the remorseless harrying of Charles and his followers, which has ever since overshadowed Cumberland's many fine attributes as a soldier and the great work he later did for the Army as a reforming administrator. Though he undoubtedly quenched the remaining embers of rebellion with a hard and brutal hand, it must be remembered that he had been faced, in the middle of a great European War, with a most serious uprising in the home country. Its success could have led to a French invasion and the downfall of the House of Hanover, a dynasty that now enjoyed the support of most Englishmen and a high proportion of Scots, Lowland and Highland.

As it was, Saxe had been pursuing his conquests in the Low Countries, taking Brussels and Antwerp and laying siege to the fortresses along the Sambre and Meuse. With greatly superior strength, he attacked and defeated the Allied army at Roucoux in October. The British contingent, now only a handful of regiments but commanded by the able Ligonier, again displayed their battle spirit with a fighting withdrawal which contributed to the army's retreat in good order. By the following year, 1747, Cumberland had returned with the regiments from his Scottish campaign and in June he moved to intercept Saxe's thrust on Maastricht. At Lauffeld on 2nd July the failure of the allied troops again left the brunt to be borne by the British horse and foot who fought with all the valour of Fontenoy. Cumberland had to withdraw but he had saved Maastricht, though it fell to Saxe in 1748. By then both sides were ready for peace which was signed at Aix-La-Chapelle in October.

By their steadiness in battle, British troops had shown that, notwithstanding the misfortunes of the early

† Raised in 1680 for service in Tangier.

Georgian period, they were still as formidable in the field as soldiers, if not as an army, as their Marlburian fathers. Nevertheless Britain had little to show on land for their endeavours. The war in Europe had brought Britain and France into conflict on other continents. In French Canada a force of provincial militia from the British colonies of North America had captured the fortress of Louisburg, commanding the mouth of the St. Lawrence. The rising power and influence of the French in India, which will be considered in a later chapter, resulted in the loss of the British East India Company's trading post and fort at Madras. At sea, however, the supremacy of the Royal Navy, with its consequent threat to French trade and communications with her colonies, had compensated for the defeats in Flanders. By the Treaty of Aix-La-Chapelle Louisburg and Madras were returned to the former owners but, though peace returned to Europe, the colonial and commercial rivalries of Britain and France overseas contained the rapidly-germinating seeds of further conflict.

Although the war, and the Jacobite Rebellion in particular, had revealed the folly of not maintaining a large enough army, after the peace the usual reductions were made. Inevitably the old cries for even greater cuts were heard again but the poor showing of the militia in the '45 had led to a grudging appreciation of the need for the Army as a permanent institution. Despite its heroism in the field, the war had uncovered grave defects in its administration and discipline. When Cumberland took up the work of Commander-in-Chief in 1748 he set about re-asserting military, as opposed to civilian, control over the internal administration of the Army, establishing proper channels of communication and imposing discipline upon the officers. While he could not abolish the purchase system, which he disliked for the safeguards it provided for the elderly and inefficient, he did all he could to advance the able and deserving officer. His choices were not always fortunate since his strict interpretation of discipline tended to favour the martinet, but against these there were, here and there, a new type of officer coming forward, whose approach to the men was more humane, and who believed that an officer's duty was better   performed by encouragement and example than the imposition of punishment. Such a man was the young major, James Wolfe.

The successes of the Prussian Army led to the introduction of many of their drills and methods in the British service, although in musketry the British had proved they had nothing to learn from the Prussians, except for the use of the iron ramrod, instead of the wooden type, which greatly facilitated loading. For reasons of economy the regiments of horse were, in 1746, converted into dragoons but, in recognition of their long-standing seniority and superior status to the dragoon regiments, were granted the courtesy title of dragoon guards. In fact dragoons now were, to all intents and purposes, pure cavalry, the mounted infantry role having fallen into disuse. The increasing use of light troops by foreign armies for outpost and reconnaissance work led to the formation, in 1755, of a light troop in cavalry regiments, and in 1759 to the first regiment of Light Dragoons, the 15th. In the infantry further regiments of Highlanders were soon to be formed for this type of work. The ordinary infantry battalion now consisted of nine companies, and although the use of the grenade had gone out of fashion, the grenadiers remained the picked men of the battalion, and the custom of massing grenadier companies into elite battalions of storm troops for battle was gradually gaining favour. Finally, in an effort to regulate the Army's dress and to diminish the licence hitherto possessed by the colonels of regiments in this field, George II and Cumberland laid down, first in 1742 and again in 1751† precise instructions on the form and distinctions of the clothing of every regiment in the Army. By insisting on uniformity, at the same time as recognizing each regiment's particular insignia, discipline and 'esprit de corps' were encouraged. Though he had displayed no great skill as a commander in the field, Cumberland's work as an administrator from 1748 did much to prepare the Army for the great test it was soon to face.

---

† "A Representation of the Cloathing of His Majesty's Household and all the Forces upon the Establishments of Great Britain and Ireland", 1742, and the Royal Clothing Warrant of 1751.

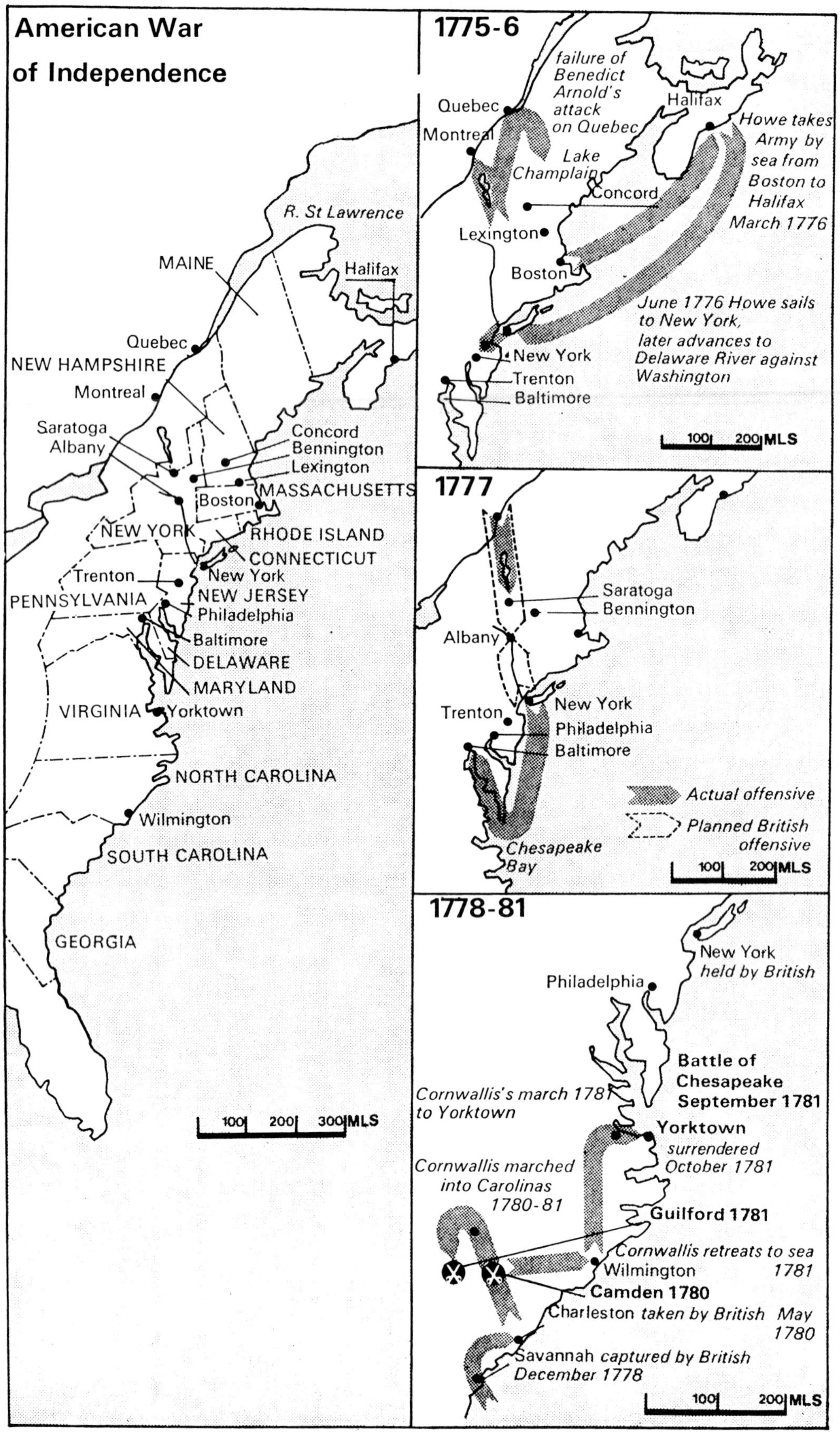

American War of Independence

1775-6

Quebec — failure of Benedict Arnold's attack on Quebec

Montreal

Halifax

Lake Champlain

Concord

Howe takes Army by sea from Boston to Halifax March 1776

Lexington

Boston

June 1776 Howe sails to New York, later advances to Delaware River against Washington

New York

Trenton

Baltimore

100 200 MLS

R. St Lawrence

MAINE

Halifax

Quebec

NEW HAMPSHIRE

Montreal

Saratoga
Albany

Concord
Bennington
Lexington

Boston

MASSACHUSETTS

NEW YORK

RHODE ISLAND

CONNECTICUT

Trenton

New York

NEW JERSEY

PENNSYLVANIA

Philadelphia

Baltimore

DELAWARE

MARYLAND

VIRGINIA — Yorktown

NORTH CAROLINA

Wilmington

SOUTH CAROLINA

GEORGIA

100 200 300 MLS

1777

Saratoga
Bennington

Albany

Trenton

New York

Philadelphia

Baltimore

Actual offensive

Planned British offensive

Chesapeake Bay

100 200 MLS

1778-81

Philadelphia

New York held by British

Battle of Chesapeake September 1781

Cornwallis's march 1781 to Yorktown

Yorktown surrendered October 1781

Cornwallis marched into Carolinas 1780-81

Guilford 1781

Cornwallis retreats to sea Wilmington 1781

Camden 1780

Charleston taken by British May 1780

Savannah captured by British December 1778

100 200 MLS

LIPTON TEA

We go a long way to bring you Quality

CHAPTER 6
PLUCKING THE LILIES OF FRANCE
1755 – 1763

With the signing of the Treaty of Aix-la-Chapelle in 1748 the armies ceased to march in Europe. Three months' sail away across the Atlantic, however, such treaties were of little account. Muskets began to flash along the Ohio river as British and French frontiersmen skirmished in the forests and the terrifying yell of the Indian war-whoop echoed round the isolated outposts; by 1755 such skirmishing had developed into war. Meanwhile, on the other side of the world, the rivalry between British and French interests in India continued unabated, and by 1751 had again erupted into open hostilities, as will be seen in the next chapter. Thus the overseas struggle, which had been a mere side-show to the continental war between Britain and France in 1742-1748, now flared up into a major contest over colonies and trade both in the New World and in India.

At the same time, in Europe, George II, in his anxiety for his Hanoverian possessions, contracted an alliance with Frederick the Great. His ally was soon to be beleaguered for Maria Theresa of Austria, determined to recover Silesia, now allied herself with France, Russia, Saxony and Sweden in an endeavour to humble the upstart Prussian monarch. Frederick, surrounded on all sides, struck first and invaded Saxony in 1756. Thus the Seven Years War began, a war which, with all the European powers sooner or later becoming involved and with fighting taking place all over the globe, has been described as *"the first world war".(1)*

Britain's prime aim was to expand her colonial empire, chiefly in the New World, at the expense of France and later Spain. Her strategy was based on the use of sea power to defeat France overseas while, at the same time, tying down French forces in Europe with operations conducted by allies paid with British gold and a limited military presence of her own. The overseer of such global strategy was a great patriotic leader, William Pitt, Earl of Chatham, who was appointed Secretary of State with full control over the war and foreign affairs. To implement his instructions where the Army was concerned, the post of Commander-in-Chief was given to Lord Ligonier, who had led the great infantry attack at Fontenoy. Born of Huguenot origins in 1680, he had seen action as a regimental officer in all Marlborough's battles, had conducted a fighting withdrawal by 12 battalions against 50 at Roucoux, and had been captured while leading a cavalry charge in an attempt to save the day at Lauffeld. To his bravery and ability as a fighting commander must be added his appreciation of the importance of sound administration.

After the peace of 1748 the Army had been reduced to a total strength of just under 40,000. By the end of the Seven Years War it would have risen to 150,000, a force of 32 regiments of cavalry and nigh on 150 battalions of infantry. To raise this number the old measures of the War of the Spanish Succession were re-introduced: the impressment of the unemployed, short-service enlistments of three, increased to five years, and clearing out the goals. The minimum height standard was reduced from five feet five inches to five feet two; Irish Catholics were permitted to enlist for service in America, where colonists were also taken into British regiments; and a new and fruitful recruiting ground was found in the Highlands of Scotland. The formation of the 15th Light Dragoons has already been mentioned in the last chapter and in 1759 six more light dragoon regiments were formed; of these, the 16th and 17th survived into a later age. The infantry was augmented by the raising of regiments numbered 50th - 115th, of which those up to the 70th would remain in the Army after the end of the war. Perhaps the most significant increase, both in numbers and competence, was in the Royal Artillery. From three marching companies in 1741, by 1761 it had 31 companies organized in three battalions, while in the previous year a quite distinct regiment of Royal Irish Artillery had been formed.

The 13 British colonies† in America lay along the eatern seaboard from south of the St. Lawrence estuary down to Florida, being bounded on the west by the Alleghanies. France held all Canada from the mouth of the St. Lawrence, down to the Great Lakes and, in the south, Louisiana along the Lower Mississipi. The French governor pursued an expansionist policy of pushing down the Ohio river from the Lakes to link up ultimately with Louisiana and cut off the British colonies from the lands west of the Alleghanies. In 1754 a force of Virginia

---

† From the north: New Hampshire, Massachusetts, Rhode Island, Connecticut, New York, New Jersey, Pennsylvania, Delaware, Maryland, Virginia, North Carolina, South Carolina, Georgia.

EMI Limited
20 MANCHESTER SQUARE, LONDON W1A 1ES
Telephone: 01-486 4488

militia under a Colonel George Washington was defeated on the Ohio while trying to check this expansion. To consolidate their position the French built a fort at the junction of the Ohio and the Monongahela, naming it Fort Duquesne. Alarmed at this threat to their rear the colonists sought help from home.

Early in 1755 General Braddock and two battalions, the 44th and 48th, arrived with orders to co-operate with the colonial forces against French incursions on the Ohio, the Hudson and elsewhere. Braddock decided to march first against Fort Duquesne but in doing so his small force was ambushed on 8th July by Indians under French leadership on the Monongahela. The British battalions, suddenly confronted by a new type of warfare for which they were totally untrained, fought back in the only way they knew against an enemy they could not see. They stood in their close ranks for two and a half hours, blazing away into the undergrowth, but with Braddock mortally wounded and most of the officers down, the tormented soldiers finally broke and fled. As he was borne dying from the field, Braddock said, *"Another time we shall know better how to deal with them".(2)* The lesson that the tactics of Fontenoy would not serve in forest fighting had been bitterly learned. By the end of the year Indian war parties in French pay were ravaging far and wide along the western borders of the British colonies.

At home 11 new regiments were formed, while in America a four-battalion regiment of Royal Americans† was raised from among the colonists. A new commander, Lord Loudon, was sent out with reinforcements in 1756 and an advance on the French fort at Ticonderoga on Lake Champlain was planned. However the French were also sending troops under the Marquis de Montcalm, who speedily took the offensive, reducing the British fort at Oswego on Lake Ontario to ashes and reinforcing Ticonderoga before Loudon had made a move. Worse was to follow for in 1757, while Loudon dallied over a plan to capture Louisburg, Montcalm captured Fort William Henry on Lake George and was unable to prevent his Indian allies from massacring part of the surrendered garrison.

By now Pitt had been appointed Secretary of State and threw himself into restoring the situation. Fifteen more battalions and two new regiments of Highlanders, Fraser's and Montgomery's were raised. A new scheme for the militia was drawn up: 32,000 men enrolled by ballot for a term of three years, divided into county regiments, each with a regular officer as adjutant, with the task of providing a force for home defence, so that regular troops could be released for service abroad. General Abercromby was sent out to replace Loudon and was accompanied by two younger officers of a new and more professional breed, Major-General Jeffrey Amherst and James Wolfe, now brigadier-general. Finally, a sizable force of some 26,000 regulars and 25,000 provincials was assembled in America for the 1758 operations, which envisaged a threefold advance on French Canada: 14,000 men under Amherst were to take Louisburg, with the view to opening the St. Lawrence for an attack on Quebec; Abercromby himself was to advance up the Hudson valley on Montreal; and a subsidiary attack was to be made on Fort Duquesne.

The lessons learned from Braddock's defeat had resulted in the formation of new units for forest warfare. First, there were the independent companies of Rangers, raised from trappers and frontiersmen and dressed in green hunting shirts for long-range reconnaissance and raiding; the most famous of which were those raised by a provincial officer, Robert Rogers. Secondly, a force of Light Infantry was trained for which *"regiments that have been any time in America are to furnish such as have been most accustomed to the woods and are good marksmen, and those from Europe are to furnish active marchers and men that are expert at firing ball, and all in general must be alert spirited soldiers able to endure fatigue". (3)* For their duties of scouting, patrolling and protection of the conventional infantry, they were given special training by the Rangers in forest craft, their clothing and accoutrements were adapted for work in close country, and they were armed with light muskets and tomahawks. Abercromby's second-in-command, Brigadier Lord Howe of the 55th, *"the best soldier in the British Army"(4)*, was one of the keenest enthusiasts for the new type of warfare and learned it by accompanying Ranger patrols in the forests. Scorning all the personal comforts deemed essential by most eighteenth century officers, he prepared his men for the field by ruthlessly cutting down on all officers' baggage and ordered all ranks *"to cut the Brims of their Hats off . . . and cut their Coats so as to scarcely reach their Waist". (5)*

Abercromby, who was not to prove one of Pitt's more inspired choices, moved his force by water to the head of Lake George, where he found Montcalm entrenched behind an enormously strong position at Ticonderoga. The death of the brilliant Howe in the opening manoeuvres was a disaster for the force as Abercromby, bereft of Howe's guidance, could devise no other tactic than to throw his battalions in a fruitless frontal attack against the concealed and protected French. An officer asked: *"What will our descendants say when they hear that 14,000 men with heroic courage but hopeless of success, for six consecutive hours sustained a triple fire from an enemy in entrenchments impregnable by small arms".(6)* The 42nd Highlanders alone lost 499 casualties. Abercromby, that *"aged gentleman, infirm in body and mind"*, as Wolfe scornfully described him *(7)*, had no choice but to retreat.

---

† Later the 60th Foot and subsequently King's Royal Rifle Corps.

A view of the landing of the New England Forces, in the Expedition against Cape Breton, 1745.

Coloured line engraving by Brooks after J.Stevens.
Published by John Bowles, 1745.

7102-33-227

Model of barge.
In barges like this Wolfe's army was carried up the St.Lawrence to attack Quebec, 1759.

6107-180

Meanwhile Amherst had transferred his force by sea and arrived on 3rd June off Cape Breton Island, from which the fortress of Louisburg looked out over the Atlantic. Bad weather prevented a landing, but on the 8th, covered by the guns of the fleet, Wolfe's brigade of 1,000 Rangers and Light Infantry and the massed grenadier companies stormed ashore under a heavy fire and seized a beachhead. The other two brigades were quickly landed, the fortress was invested, and after a siege lasting seven weeks, the garrison surrendered. The gateway to the St Lawrence was open, but the naval commander did not consider the river navigable. Receiving news of Ticonderoga, Amherst contented himself with destroying the French settlements round the coast and, leaving a garrison to hold Louisburg, returned to join Abercromby. In Amherst's force was Lord Howe's intrepid younger brother, the Honourable William, whose name will increasingly be encountered, then commanding the 58th, one of the new regiments raised in 1755, which, under *"his modest, diligent and valiant"* leadership, Wolfe considered to be *"the best trained battalion in all America".(8)*

The third thrust, on Fort Duquesne, had found it abandoned. A garrison was established on its site and at the same time a raid along the Mohawk valley captured Fort Frontenac on Lake Ontario. Pitt's overall plan had only achieved limited success in 1758 but footholds had been secured on the flanks of French Canada, whose communications with France were now threatened by the British fleet lying off the mouth of the St Lawrence. With Amherst replacing Abercromby in overall command, the plan for 1759 involved another attempt on Montreal by way of Lakes George and Champlain under the direction of Amherst himself; an expedition to the west against Oswego and Niagara; while Wolfe, now promoted local major-general, was to sail up the St Lawrence and take Quebec.

Wolfe's rise had been dramatic. Joining the Army in 1740 at the age of 13, he had attracted the attention of Cumberland during the War of the Austrian Succession and the '45, and when only 23 was promoted colonel in command of the 20th Foot, in which he displayed great skill as a trainer of troops. Tall and thin, with red hair, a receding chin and of uncertain health, he was not an imposing figure but he was possessed of an intense professionalism, very different from the dilettantism of so many officers of the period. He had never held an independent command and only at Louisburg had he commanded anything larger than a regiment. Now, at the age of only 32, junior in both years and, in his army rank of colonel, in seniority to many of his subordinates, he was selected by Pitt for the most important undertaking of 1759. With a force of only 8,500 he was to sail up the tortuous and uncharted waters of the St Lawrence, escorted by a fleet under Admiral Saunders, to capture a strongly fortified city garrisoned by Montcalm himself with an army of some 14,000, of which 3,500 were regular French infantry †.

Wolfe's army consisted of the 15th, 28th, 35th, 43rd, 47th, 48th, 58th, two battalions of the 60th, Fraser's Highlanders, the Louisburg Grenadiers (formed of the grenadier companies of the 22nd, 40th and 45th), 200 Light Infantry drawn from all these regiments under William Howe, six companies of Rangers, and three of Royal Artillery. He had three brigadiers, Monckton, Townsend and Murray, all able men but all, especially the arrogant, cynical Townsend, sceptical of their young commander's ability. The battalions varied in strength, from Fraser's 1,100 to the Grenadiers of only 300, but all, with the possible exception of the Ranger companies whom Wolfe found lacking in discipline, were solid and seasoned soldiers, well-experienced in American campaigning.

By 26th June, thanks to masterly navigation by the Navy, the army had been landed on the Ile d'Orleans, four miles downstream from Quebec. Apart from the city's own fortifications around the headland on which it stood on the north bank, the main French defences lay to the east between the city and the River Montmorency which, seven miles away, fell through a gorge into the St Lawrence. Opposite Quebec, where the St Lawrence flowed through a channel threequarters of a mile wide, the Point Levis formed a headland. Here Wolfe constructed a siege battery with a battalion to protect it and transferred most of the force to the north bank just east of the Montmorency.

Various maneouvres were made to tempt Montcalm from his defences but without success, so that on 31st July Wolfe tried to outflank the French positions along the Montmorency by a landing on the north bank of the St Lawrence in their rear. As Howe's Light Infantry demonstrated in the woods to the French front, the massed grenadier companies charged ashore while the 15th and the Highlanders waited in boats to follow up through the beachhead. The dash and enthusiasm of the grenadiers proved their undoing. Having swept over the beach defences, they started clambering, without any formation or waiting for orders, up the cliff face where *"the very first fire they received from the enemy was so well-directed, that it checked their impetuosity; and which being so well-maintained, that they were soon put into the utmost confusion, and were obliged to take shelter until all the troops were landed".(9)* With surprise lost and a sudden thunderstorm drenching the ammunition and rendering the cliff face impossibly slippery, Wolfe abandoned the enterprise and ordered a withdrawal.

† The remainder were colonial troops, originally recruited in France as the permanent garrison of French Canada, and Canadian Militia.

Lord Amherst c1758.

Painting, oil on canvas, artist unknown.

General James Wolfe, c1759.

Modern print after an oil painting by J.S.C. Schaak, 1766.

"The death of General Wolfe on the 13th September, 1759 at Quebec".

Mezzotint by Richard Housten after Edward Penney. Published by R.Sayer, January 1st, 1772.

7102-33-312

He next proceeded to lay waste the countryside about Quebec in the hope of inducing Montcalm's militia-men to desert the city and return to protect their homes. During August Murray's brigade was sent up river with Rear-Admiral Holmes' flotilla to raid and threaten French posts and supply depots along the north shore between 20-30 miles above Quebec. This danger to his communications with Montreal sufficiently worried Montcalm for him to detach troops from Quebec to reinforce Bougainville who was watching the line of the river in that area. The French commander was further perturbed by news from the south where Niagara had fallen to the British and Amherst had taken the fort at Crown Point which dominated the route to Montreal. Nevertheless he still held firm at Quebec.

In late August Wolfe fell ill and had to depute control of operations to his brigadiers, who suggested landing the army on the north shore above Quebec. Wolfe agreed in principle, so the camp opposite the Montmorency lines was evacuated and the troops embarked on the transports which sailed up to Cap Rouge ten miles above the city, leaving two battalions guarding the battery at Point Levis. Once recovered from his illness, Wolfe made a careful reconnaissance of the enemy shore to decide upon a suitable landing place. The area round Cap Rouge was carefully guarded by Bougainville but he spotted a narrow cliff track, protected at the top by only a small post, at a place called the Anse du Foulon, only some two miles above Quebec; between the top of the Foulon and the city stretched the open ground of the Plains of Abraham. He also learned that on the night of 12th September the French were planning to run a convoy of supply barges down river to Quebec. He therefore planned to transfer his troops from the shipping at Cap Rouge into boats under cover of darkness, row down-stream simulating the movement of the supply convoy and, while Saunders created a diversion with the fleet between the Montmorency and Quebec, land at the Foulon and give battle outside the city walls on the Plains of Abraham.

At about one-thirty in the early hours of the 13th the tide began to ebb and two lights appeared in the maintop-mast shrouds of HMS 'Sutherland'. On this signal the boats, now crammed with men, began to slip silently down river with muffled oars. Past the French sentries they stole, the challenges answered by a French-speaking Highlander, until the leading craft grounded on the beach at the Foulon. First ashore were the 24 men of the "forlorn hope"† under Captain Delaune who, closely followed by Howe and the Light Infantry, climbed stealthily up the narrow path and surprised the outpost at the top. The other regiments swarmed up behind them and, once formed, marched off to take up position on the Plains. Montcalm, who had always believed the British movements opposite Cap Rouge to be a feint, had been convinced that Saunders' demonstration presaged the real attack near the Montmorency and had deployed his troops accordingly during the early hours of the 13th. Now, as day broke, he looked west and saw the red lines forming on the Plains of Abraham. Wolfe had duped him.

Leaving the 3rd/60th to guard communications with the Foulon, Wolfe arrayed his battalions in a single line, from left to right: the 58th, Fraser's, 47th, 43rd, 28th, Louisburg Grenadiers and the 35th with its right resting on the river. The 15th and 2nd/60th were positioned to guard the left flank, while further to the left rear were the Light Infantry, to ward off marauding attacks by Canadian militia and Indians and to watch for any advance on the rear by Bougainville. The 48th, one of the strongest battalions, formed the single reserve.

At ten o'clock, having hastily redeployed his troops, Montcalm came on, his five regiments of white-coated French regulars in the centre and the colonials and militia on either flank. At 200 yards the French began firing as they advanced, the Canadians throwing themselves down to reload which somewhat disordered their formation. All the while the British line stood silent and motionless as the gap narrowed. At forty yards the muskets came up, one single massive volley slammed out and, as the smoke cleared, the French ranks were seen to be mangled. Another followed, then the line advanced with bayonet and broadsword, pursuing the broken French to the walls of Quebec. Wolfe himself, in his position between the 28th and the Grenadiers, had already received two wounds and as the line went forward another ball struck him in the chest. He was helped from the field by Lieutenant Henry Browne and Volunteer James Henderson of the 22nd's grenadiers but he was clearly dying and he knew it. An officer told him the French were giving way and he said: *"Go one of you to Colonel Burton – tell him to march Webb's Regiment (48th) with all speed to Charles's River, to cut off the retreat of the fugitives from the bridge".* Then he turned on his side, adding: *"Now, God be-praised, I will die in peace".(10)*

In Quebec Montcalm too was dying from wounds. A threat by Bougainville was easily repulsed and by 18th September the remains of the French garrison surrendered. Once again the disciplined musketry of the British infantry had proved its superiority on the battlefield. However, neither this nor Wolfe's daring and deter-mination could have prevailed had it not been for the efforts of Admiral Saunders and the officers and men of the Royal Navy, whose seamanship and skill had successfully transported and protected the army, and whose movements up and down the St Lawrence had threatened the supply lines and tested the nerves of the French

---

† A band of volunteers, always called for to lead hazardous enterprises.

49th Foot, Cholmondeley's Regiment 1747-48.
Grenadier's Mitre Cap.   6902-1

3rd Foot, Howard's Regiment c1740.
Officer's Mitre Cap.   6309-306

command. The fall of the capital of New France was truly a magnificent demonstration of inter-service co-operation.

Although this part of the plan for 1759 had been brought to a triumphant conclusion, Amherst had been unable to reach Montreal, so the French cause in Canada was not yet lost. Furthermore, Murray, who was left with a garrison of 7,500 at Quebec, had to hold it until the spring without the support of the fleet which had to sail away before the St Lawrence iced over. The victorious troops endured a bitter winter, beset by the cold, disease, shortage of food, endless labour and eternal vigilance to ensure the safety of the garrison. A French attack across the ice in January 1760 was beaten off, but in April they attacked again. Another battle was fought on the Plains of Abraham and Murray, who could only muster 3,000 men, many of them *"half-starved, scorbutic skeletons"(11)*, was driven back inside the walls and besieged by 9,000 French. However he held out until the thaw set in, and by 16th May British ships again lay off Quebec. By the following day the French had gone.

Throughout the winter Amherst had been making careful preparations for the final subjection of Canada by a concentric and simultaneous advance on Montreal. While Brigadier Haviland's 3,400-strong force of two British battalions, Provincials and Indians advanced up the Richelieu river from Lake Champlain, Amherst himself, with eight battalions, 500 Provincials and 700 Indians, would block any retreat westwards by a descent down river from Lake Ontario; Murray was to close in from the north. With nearly 400 miles between Amherst and Murray, and 200 between Haviland and the two former, the plan required the most careful organisation and timing. Nevertheless Amherst achieved it, and by 6th September all three forces, with a united strength of 17,000, were besieging Montreal. Deserted by his Indian allies, Vaudreuil, the French govenor, had only 2,500. Two days later he surrendered and the whole of Canada fell to the British. Though the most dramatic part of the campaign had fallen to Wolfe, its successful conclusion, with the loss to France of these vast possessions, was due to Amherst's patient and persevering powers of organisation and his ability to drive in harness with his often difficult Provincial allies, on whom so much depended in the way of men and resources.

While Canada was being won, operations were afoot in other parts of the New World to reduce French power. In 1759 a force of 6,000 started to attack the French sugar islands in the West Indies and, after five months fever-ridden fighting, captured the richest, Guadeloupe, and the following year, Dominica. The conclusion of the war in Canada freed forces for employment in the West Indies, so the veteran regiments of Ticonderoga and Quebec sailed south from the rivers and forests of Canada to the dense tropical vegetation and plantations of the Caribbean. In our present age these islands are highly regarded by rich tourists but to the eighteenth

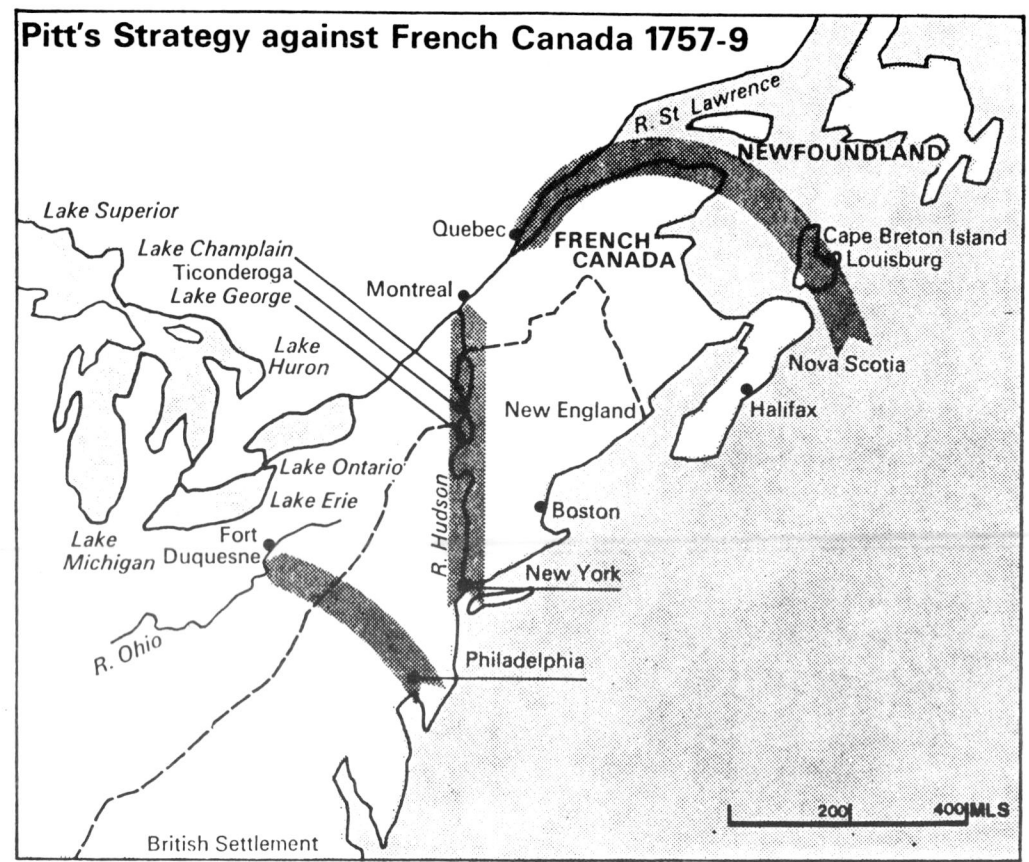

Pitt's Strategy against French Canada 1757-9

British Settlement

century redcoat they were a death trap. Hundreds of men who had survived Montcalm's muskets, ice-bound winters and the Indian scalping knives would fall victim to a deadlier foe in the West Indies, the dreaded yellow fever or "black vomit". At the capture of Fort Moro in Havannah in 1762 British casualties from enemy action were 1,000; over 5,000 died from disease. Still, the operations went forward. In January 1762 22 battalions under Monckton harried the French through the steep ravines and gulleys of Martinique. Its surrender paved the way for the rapid capture of St Lucia, Grenada and St Vincent. By March war had also been declared on Spain, as a result of the discovery of a secret treaty of alliance between the Spanish and French monarchs in contravention of the Peace of Utrecht. This led to the siege of Fort Moro which, after two months fighting in tropical heat under appalling conditions, ended in the whole of Cuba passing into British hands. When peace was signed the following year it was returned to Spain in exchange for Florida, while France ceded Grenada, Tobago, St Vincent and Dominica, to which of course must be added the great lands to the north in Canada. All over the New World the white, lily-strewn flags of France had been hauled down by British soldiers and sailors and now the Union Jack flew from the Caribbean to the St. Lawrence.

"America" said Pitt in 1761, *"has been conquered in Germany, where Prince Ferdinand's victories have shattered the whole military power of that great military monarchy, France".(12)* Ferdinand was a Prince of Brunswick, the brother-in-law of Frederick the Great and an experienced Prussian general of high repute. His services had been sought from the King of Prussia, following the defeat by France in 1757 of a mainly Hanoverian army under the Duke of Cumberland's command at Hastenbeck, after which the greater part of Hanover was overrun by French troops. This defeat was mitigated by Frederick's great victory over the combined French and Austrians at Rossbach, but the Prussians could not afford to have their right flank menaced by the victorious French in Hanover. Frederick therefore agreed to release Ferdinand to reform Cumberland's army of Hanoverians, Hessians and Brunswickers into an effective fighting force. This Ferdinand did to such good effect that during 1758 he forced the French to evacuate Hanover and Hesse and to fall back west of the Rhine. Throughout this year he repeatedly asked for British assistance and in August a force of six cavalry regiments and six battalions of foot arrived in Germany under Lord George Sackville†. Their theatre of operations would be Hanover, Westphalia and Hesse, much of which would become familiar 200 years later to the descendants of these regiments serving in the British Army of the Rhine.

---

† The command was originally given to Charles, Duke of Marlborough who died in October. The regiments were: Royal Horse Guards (Blue), 1st King's and 3rd Dragoon Guards, 2nd, 6th and 10th Dragoons; 12th, 20th, 23rd, 25th, 37th, and 51st Foot.

Early in 1759, while across the world Wolfe was preparing his move against Quebec, Ferdinand, with 45,000 men, found himself opposed by two armies, Contades' on the lower Rhine and de Broglie's on the lower Main, which together outnumbered him by almost two to one. Having struck first at de Broglie, who was nearest, he was repulsed and had to evacuate Hesse and Westphalia, falling back northwards to Osnabrück. On 11th July he heard that de Broglie had captured Minden on the Weser, and with Contades moving up from Herford to join de Broglie, Hanover lay open to the French. He therefore hurriedly marched east to find Contades in a strong position north of Minden with his right resting on the Weser, his front protected by marshland, and his left by the heights of the Wiehen Gebirge; de Broglie was across the Weser, watching the right flank. Ferdinand realised he would have to draw the French out. To effect this, he deployed his army in an arc to the north-west of Minden with his left, under Wangenheim, purposely unprotected on its left flank as a bait; at the same time he sent the Hereditary Prince of Brunswick, the Erbprinz, with a force of 9,700 round behind the Wiehen Gebirge to threaten the French rear.

When Contades heard of the Erbprinz's movements he responded exactly as Ferdinand hoped. He gave orders for his army to deploy forwards beyond the marsh during the night of 31st July, ready to attack Ferdinand at dawn the next day, following an assault on Wangenheim to expose Ferdinand's left flank by de Broglie, who was to cross the Weser the same night. By dawn Contades had his army drawn up with infantry and artillery on the flanks and 63 squadrons of cavalry in the centre. De Broglie's advance on Wangenheim's 15 battalions, all Germans with the exception of one British†, began rather hesitantly. Contades was about to order de Broglie to speed up his assault when he suddenly became aware that his own centre was under attack.

Ferdinand's advance had been somewhat delayed by the failure of his picquets to report the French movements, but by five o'clock his army was marching forward in eight parallel columns to take up their battle stations. In the third column from the right, commanded by Lieutenant-General Count von Spörcken, were the British infantry and two battalions of the Hanoverian Guards formed in two lines: the first, under Major-General Waldegrave, of the 12th, 23rd Royal Welch Fusiliers, 37th, the Hanoverians and a Royal Artillery brigade of nine 6-pounders; the second, under Colonel Kingsley, of the 20th, 25th and 51st. Through some misunderstanding this column, ignoring those on their left and right, pressed forward, the colours spread in the centre of each battalion and their drums thundering out a sharp step. Staff officers were sent galloping to stop them but, after a short halt, they advanced again, picking up as they did so another Hanoverian battalion from the column on their left. All the while they were inclining slightly towards their left, possibly because the French artillery was now beginning to pound their right flank, on a line of march which was taking them straight at the left front of the massed French cavalry, drawn up in two lines, with two regiments in reserve, in the centre of Contades' line. Such an attack by infantry on formed cavalry must have seemed incomprehensible to the French cavalry commander and he ordered 11 squadrons to the charge. At this the triple-ranked infantry halted, brought their muskets to the present, and at point-blank range delivered a volley. The blue- and grey-coated squadrons of the 'Royal-Cravattes' and the 'Mestre-du-Camp' were shattered by this fire and, as the few survivors reeled back in disorder, the lines of redcoats reloaded and waited the next onslaught. On they came, 22 squadrons this time, straight into the same deadly volley that had demolished the first charge. A few broke through, only to be brought down by the second line of infantry. Then the drums beat once more and the lines advanced over the tumbled heaps of men and horses. Now eight battalions of Contades' left moved against Spörcken's right flank. He quickly wheeled the 20th, 25th and 51st to meet them, while Ferdinand, seeing the danger, ordered Scheele's Hanoverian and Hessian infantry with 30 guns to advance in support of the British. At the same time, however, the French reserve horse, which included the 'Gens d'Armes' of the Household Cavalry, swung round to attack Spörcken's left and rear. The Welch Fusiliers and the Hanoverian Guards turned to meet the charge with levelled muskets. Hammered by these volleys in front and by those of another German column coming up on their right flank, half the resplendent French squadrons went down and the survivors made off. Meanwhile the French infantry on the right had been thrown into disorder by Scheele's guns. The undaunted redcoats reformed their ranks and marched forward again, right through the now completely broken French centre. The French infantry on the right were ordered to wheel inwards to make a flank attack but they were routed by a combined charge of Hessian infantry and Prussian and Hanoverian cavalry. At the other end of the field the Saxon infantry were sent forward against the now tired and depleted British, but the latter, with Hanoverian brigades on either flank, were able to throw them back. The French were lost, their broken regiments now being pulverized by the British artillery which moved forward at amazing speed to harrass their retreat. All that was needed was a final charge by the hitherto unused British cavalry under Sackville to complete the rout and pursue the beaten enemy. But despite repeated orders Sackville refused to move, and to the bitter shame of his magnificent squadrons, the remains of Contades' broken army were able to get away across the Weser, covered by de Broglie's rearguard.

† Formed of the grenadier companies of the six British regiments, under Colonel Maxwell of the 20th.

So ended the great battle of Minden, marked for ever by the valour and steadiness of six British regiments of foot and their Hanoverian comrades. Contades' himself expressed his astonishment at their achievement: *"I never thought to see a single line of infantry break through three lines of cavalry ranked in order of battle and tumble them to ruin".(13)* The British artillery too received high praise, but the cavalry for whom there had been opportunities enough to share the glory of their brothers-in-arms, were disgraced by the supine conduct of Sackville. He was relieved of his command, court-martialled, and forbidden to serve the King in any capacity, this sentence being read out to the Army as a warning to officers that *"neither high birth nor great employments can shelter offences of such a nature".(14)*

He was replaced by the Marquis of Granby. After Minden the French fell back southwards into Hesse and by the end of the campaigning year Ferdinand, having saved Brunswick and Hanover and cleared Westphalia, was back where he had started.

The splendid British feats of arms in 1759 of Minden and Quebec were further enhanced by Hawke's great naval victory over the French fleet at Quiberon Bay. Since this put paid to the ever-present danger of a French invasion of England, it released another 10,000 British troops for Germany, the so-called *"Glorious Reinforcement"*, which arrived in May 1760. However the French still mustered twice Ferdinand's strength and he was unable to repeat the success of the 1759 campaign. On the other hand, the Allied operations contiuedn to force France to keep large forces in Germany. For the British troops' part, the 1760 campaign gave the cavalry the chance to distinguish itself and redeem the fiasco it had been subjected to at Minden.

In July Ferdinand, outnumbered and with exposed flanks, ordered a diversion on the French base at Marburg, to be made by the Erbprinz with a detachment which predominated in light cavalry, including the newly-raised British 15th Light Dragoons. On the 16th the Erbprinz surprised a small force at Emsdorf. The 15th galloped hard to cut off the enemy's retreat and found themselves, with blown horses, facing four battalions. Nevertheless they charged straight in and despite heavy losses broke up the French, taking 1,600 prisoners. It was a spirited encounter for the first action of British light cavalry and rivalled the feat of their heavy comrades a week before at Korbach, where the 3rd Dragoon Guards and a squadron of the 1st had charged the French cavalry to save the allied guns and check the enemy's victorious advance.

Two weeks after Emsdorf the British cavalry again showed their mettle at Warburg on 31st July. Two infantry columns under the Erbprinz and Spörcken were launched against the left wing of de Muy's force, which was holding a ridge in front of the River Diemel, before the main army under Ferdinand had reached the field. The right column was led by a brigade consisting of two British grenadier battalions† and Keith's and Campbell's Highlanders. After some stiff close-quarter fighting these columns broke the French left, which decided de Muy to retire across the Diemel. Ferdinand's advance had taken him longer than he expected, so he sent the British cavalry under Granby on ahead to aid the Erbprinz's infantry. Having about five miles to cover Granby pushed on at best speed, trotting and cantering alternately, and forming his 22 squadrons into two lines as they rode: in the first line, the King's Dragoon Guards, the 3rd and 2nd Dragoon Guards, the Blues, 7th Dragoon Guards and the Carabiniers; in the second, the Greys, 10th, 6th, and 11th Dragoons. When they reached the battlefield the French horse were on the point of retiring and Granby, losing his hat and wig in the excitement, charged in amongst them at the head of the Blues, his bald head gleaming in the sunlight*. Following this beacon, the heavies thundered through the French ranks, demolished a counter-attack, and drove all before them into the Diemel.

Though Granby had his limitations as a commander and was thought by some officers to be too lenient a disciplinarian, he was much loved by the troops for his generosity and simple manners. Corporal Todd of the 12th Foot noted how, at an encampment, *"Lord Granby wrapt himself in his great coat and lay down upon the ground amongst us which greatly encouraged our men although we were in the greatest want of alsorts of Necessaries at this time and expecting to engage every moment".(15)* John Tory, soldier of the 3rd Guards, expressed the fervent hope that *"the PRAYERS OF THE SOLDIERY will attend him"(16)*, when Granby made a gift of 1,000 loaves to the brigade of Foot Guards, which arrived in Germany in late 1760 under the command of a major-general with the promising military name of Julius Caesar.

Ferdinand planned to surprise the French in 1761 with a winter campaign starting in February. Its success depended on the continuation of a hard frost to permit rapid movement and ease of supply on the indifferent winter roads. Initially all went well but then the weather broke and the roads became *"excessive deep; by which means the artillery had a great deal of difficulty to keep up, and the infantry marched up to their knees in dirt and mud". (17)* By 31st March the army was back behind the Diemel, whence it had set out in February. *"The whole expedition was upwards of 300 miles, in the midst of winter thro' inaccessible roads; both officers and*

---

† Maxwell's, which had been at Minden, and Daulhatt's, of the grenadiers of the 5th, 8th, 11th, 24th, 33rd, and 50th Foot.

* Hence the expression, going "bald-headed" at something.

GUINNESS

The Marquess of Granby relieving a sick soldier.   Painting, oil on canvas, by Edward Penny   6307-31

Seven Years War, Europe, Minden "The battle of Minden or Thornhausen where the allied army obtained a glorious victory over the French Army". August 1st 1759.
Tinted lithograph engraving. Published by Carrington Bowles c1759.   7102-33-255

soldiers exerting themselves in a manner worthy of the greatest applause"(18), but nothing had been achieved. The summer campaign compensated for this disappointing start, with Ferdinand outmanoeuvring and outwitting two French armies and defeating them at Vellinghausen, where the brunt of the action was borne by the British contingent.

By 1762 war-weariness was beginning to affect both sides and, for the first time in Germany, the French had to remain on the defensive. Ferdinand advanced down the Weser and surprised the enemy with an enveloping attack at Wilhelmstahl on 24th June. The French right withdrew in good order, but as their left prepared to meet an attack in front by British and Brunswick infantry, led by the 5th Foot, Granby surprised them from the woods in their rear with the Guards brigade, the two grenadier battalions and the two Highland regiments, supported by the 15th Light Dragoons. The French turned to counter-attack and sharp fighting ensued, until the 5th Foot charged in from the other side, taking double their own strength in prisoners.

Ferdinand pursued south, driving the French out of Hesse down to the Main, until a threat to his right by another French army from the Rhine forced him to fall back behind the Ohm. A brisk and rather pointless action was fought at the Brücke-Mühle, a vital bridge over the river. The bridge guard was subject to such heavy fire that the post had to be constantly relieved by fresh bodies of troops. When the Foot Guards' turn came, the commanding officer of the Coldstream launched his men with the words, *"Now show them what you are. Quick March!"(19)* Apart from the successful siege and capture of Kassel, this was the last action of the campaign and indeed of the war. Rumours of peace were already abroad when Brücke-Mühle was fought and eventually, on 14th November, there came news that the war was over at last.

The British troops in Germany under Ferdinand of Brunswick had always displayed great courage, daring and stubbornness, whether it be in attack or defence. These are fine battlefield qualities but battles, though they may decide the outcome of a campaign, are only a small, and often brief, part of it. In general military skills and discipline the British showed they had much to learn from their German allies. Their officers, though usually courageous, too often lacked or bothered to acquire the professionalism of the Germans in the responsibilities of administration, march discipline, encampments, reconnaissance and outpost duties. Furthermore they exhibited *"a quiet, natural arrogance which tempts them to despise the enemy as well as the danger. It is well known how much these people despise all foreigners; this of itself renders their co-operation with troops of other nations very difficult".(20)*

Their defects apart, the British Army of the Seven Years War could boast very considerable achievements. In the field of military development, perhaps the increasing use and understanding of the value of light troops was the most important. The lessons learned in America from the fighting methods of Rangers and Indians led to the formation, under the direction of Amherst, Wolfe and the brothers Howe, of light infantry as a protective screen for the more deliberate deployments and manoeuvres of the orthodox foot. In Germany the use by foreign armies of hussars and other light cavalry suggested the raising of light dragoon regiments. Although, on the face of it, the forests of North America offered more scope for light infantry than the open terrain of Germany, most European armies now had their units of 'jägers' or 'chasseurs' †, which inspired the formation of a British battalion of the same (oddly preferring the French title) drawn from volunteers of all the foot regiments in Germany. Its performance won the admiration of a Hessian 'jäger' officer who could not *"praise enough the bravery of these men and the skill with which Major Fraser led them".(21)* This battalion and the light infantry in America were disbanded at the end of the war but their skills would be resuscitated a decade later.

Before he sent troops to Germany, and to a lesser extent afterwards, Pitt had endeavoured to prevent France reinforcing her overseas possessions by raids on the French coast — on Rochfort in 1757, St Malo and Cherbourg in 1758, and Belleisle in 1761. Though some limited tactical successes were achieved, of strategic value there was nil. It was the long campaign in Germany, tying down large French armies, plus the supremacy of the Royal Navy, which enabled Britain to humble French power, not only in America and the West Indies, but in the great sub-continent of India, as must now be seen.

---

† 'Jäger' (German), 'chasseur' (French): literally a huntsman and by derivation a light infantryman.

CHAPTER 7
'PRIMUS IN INDIS'
1600–1784

Between 1526 and 1656 the Mogul Emperors, from their capital at Delhi, subdued the whole of northern India, then known as Hindostan, and most of the Deccan to the south. The main threat to their dominion came in the latter half of the seventeenth century from a race of Hindu mountaineers, the Mahrattas. Although the Emperor Aurangzeb eventually drove them back to their fastnesses in the Western Ghats and extended his rule far to the south into Mysore, the Mahrattas had revealed the weaknesses of the Mogul Empire. After Aurangzeb's death in 1707 Mogul power began to wane, and the governors, or nawabs, of the provinces into which the Empire was divided became virtually independent princes, particularly in the south.

The first Europeans to reach India were the Portuguese who established trading posts on the west, or Malabar, coast in the early sixteenth century. They were followed by English merchant adventurers who, in 1600, were granted a charter by Elizabeth I to trade under the name of the East India Company. In 1611 the Mogul Emperor allowed the Company to establish a trading post, or factory as it was called, at Surat on the west coast, north of Bombay. Further factories were set up on the east, or Coromandel, coast, including a headquarters at Madras where a fort, named St George, was built in 1639. When Charles II married Catherine of Braganza, her dowry, as mentioned earlier,added Bombay to the English Crown and in 1668 this was made over to the East India Company. Not long after, the Company extended its trading operations to the mouth of the Hooghly, with factories based around Fort William which was constructed at Calcutta. Thus the three centres of Company interest were established at Bombay, Madras and Bengal.

From the earliest days the Company had enlisted military guards for the protection of its factories. In 1662 a regiment, 400 strong, was sent from England to garrison Bombay. Many of the men died from disease but the numbers were kept up by enlisting other Europeans and some Deccanis. When the Company took over Bombay this body entered its service and,as the Bombay Europeans+,became the first regiment of the Company's armed forces, which grew in size until, nearly 200 years later, they became the Indian Army. In addition to this regiment and the European guards in the other centres, or presidencies as they subsequently were called, the East India Company began, in the early eighteenth century, to raise small units of half-castes and Indians but only in company strength. The latter were at first known as peons but gradually acquired the name of sepoys, or 'sipahis', from a Persian word 'sipah', an army.

These were not the only units of sepoys forming in the sub-continent. From 1668 the French, eager to get their share of Indian trade, began to establish, through 'Le Compagnie des Indes', their own factories down the east coast from Chandernagore on the Hooghly as far as Pondicherry, with their headquarters at the latter. Not only did they work much faster than the British, they also realised more quickly that their position would receive greater respect from the Indian princes if they had forces with which to back it, not simply a few factory guards. As early as 1674 they had perceived the possibilities of drilling and training Indians to perform like European soldiers, and continued to do so on a far wider scale than the East India Company. In 1739 they raised a force of nearly 5,000 Mohammedan soldiers organised on European lines. When, in the following year, a further rising of the Mahrattas menaced the territory of the Nawab of the Carnatic on the Coromandel coast, the French governor at Pondicherry, Dumas, sent these native troops to help the Nawab; this earned the French increased territory and greatly enhanced their prestige and power, including the title of Nawab for Dumas and his successors.

In 1741 Dumas was succeeded by Dupleix, a man of enormous energy and ability, who had ambitions of creating a great French empire in India, far beyond a few coastal trading posts. Arriving in India in 1720, he had turned Chandernagore into the most important European commercial centre in Bengal and now, inheriting

Subsequently, in 1849, the Honourable East India Company's 1st Bombay European Fusiliers; in 1860 the 103rd Foot (Royal Bombay Fusiliers); and in 1881, 2nd Battalion Royal Dublin Fusiliers (disbanded 1922).

80

Fort St. George, Madras, c1730   Oil painting by C. Lambert and S. Scott, c1730

India, c1753   Model of Trichinopoly Fort, made from balsa wood.   6402-2

the Nawab's mantle bestowed on Dumas, set about exploiting the divisions of the Indian rulers to further his own power, not only at their expense, but also at that of the East India Company.

In 1744, having learned of the outbreak of the War of the Austrian Succession, and that a British fleet was on its way to attack Pondicherry, he induced the Nawab of the Carnatic to forbid any hostilities in his territory. Having successfully forestalled any British land action against Pondicherry, he then obtained the Nawab's permission to make an attack in 1746 on Fort St George at Madras, by the simple expedient of promising it to the Indian ruler. Attacked by 1,500 Europeans and sepoys and bombarded from the sea by a French fleet, the English garrison of only 200 men were forced to surrender. Dupleix of course had no intention of handing over this prize and avoided doing so by turning his force on the Nawab. Though few in numbers, his soldiers quickly demonstrated that the horde armies of Indian princes, with their elephants and ancient cannon, were no match for European musketry and artillery in the hands of disciplined troops. This French victory, at St Thomé, taught the Indian rulers that Europeans could no longer be regarded as mere suppliants for favours; it made the English realise that where the French had showed the way they could follow.

In 1747-8 Dupleix attempted to take the British outposts of Fort St. David and Cuddalore, south of Madras, but he was thwarted in this enterprise by the arrival of a British fleet with reinforcements. In June 1748 he made another attempt on Cuddalore by a surprise night attack. However he now found himself opposed by an adversary worthy of his talents. In January Major Stringer Lawrence had arrived from England to take command of all the Company's forces in Madras. He outwitted Dupleix by ostentatiously withdrawing the garrison and guns from Cuddalore to St. David in daylight, but then secretly returned them under cover of darkness. When the French advanced at midnight expecting no resistance, Lawrence was ready for them, and so fierce a fight did his men put up, that the French panicked and retired in some haste. Lawrence now took the opportunity to reorganize the Company's forces in Madras on a sounder footing and formed the independent European companies into the Madras European Regiment.†

The danger to the Company's possessions in the Carnatic had now alarmed the Government at home into taking action. In November 1747 a force of eight men-o'-war and 1,400 troops under Admiral Boscawen had sailed to attack Pondicherry. His troops included a battalion of Marines and two battalions of "Independents". The ranks of the latter had been filled up with prisoners taken during the '45 Rebellion; men like James Miller, an Englishman, who had joined the Young Pretender's army at Preston and been captured at the seige of Carlisle when serving with the Manchester regiment, the only English body that had come out for the Stuarts and had been left to garrison Carlisle when the Jacobite army returned to Scotland. Many of these unfortunates had been sentenced to death, but, after some had been executed, the others were offered the alternative of service in the east, an option which most, including Miller, accepted. By August 1748 they found themselves on the Coromandel coast besieging Pondicherry.

Miller must often have wondered whether he had not chosen a fate worse than the gallows. On 10th September he wrote:

"We have had several killed and wounded in the trenches. We have had very bad weather of late, the Rains have been so great that our Trenches is fill'd with water and Mud, being almost unpassable, being so deep that it takes us to the wast and are oblig'd to stand in them twenty four hours. The Duty is very hard upon us, having scarce a night's rest in a week". (1)

These conditions, plus a prevalence of the "bloody flux" and the incompetence of Boscawen's engineers, rendered all their efforts fruitless. On 11th October, with the seige works completely inundated, Boscawen saw there was nothing for it but to abandon the operations.

The news of the peace of Aix-la-Chapelle, with its return of Madras to the British, brought a temporary halt to direct hostilities between France and Britain in the east. Towards the end of 1749 Boscawen's force sailed for home. Miller and his comrades in the Independent Battalions were offered a bounty of 40 rupees and a three-year engagement if they would sign on with the Company's forces. The numbers who initially volunteered were soon considerably increased for, *"when we came on Board our Men found the ship so throng and a great many other inconveniences that they went on shore in great numbers".(2)* Miller himself, however, had had enough of India.

With Dupleix's ambitions still unabated, and Indian politics offering a fruitful ground for intrigue, the peace did not last long. By setting up his own nominees as Nawabs in the Carnatic and Hyderabad, Dupleix planned to squeeze out the Company from its possessions on the Coromandel coast. Not to be outdone, the British decided to play Dupleix at his own game and lent their support to a rival contender for the Carnatic, Muhammed Ali, son of the earlier Nawab whom Dupleix had defeated at St. Thomé. Unfortunately Muhammed Ali, despite receiving British troop reinforcements, got himself besieged by the French and their Indian ally,

---

† Subsequently, in 1843, 1st Madras European Fusiliers; in 1860, the 102nd Foot (Royal Madras Fusiliers); and in 1881, 1st Battalion Royal Dublin Fusiliers (disbanded 1922).

the Nawab Chunda Sahib, in his rock fortress of Trichinopoly, 200 miles south of Madras. Though the armies of the Indian princes in these manoeuvres were numbered in thousands, the forces of the French and British, both European and sepoys, amounted only to hundreds. Even after three columns were sent to Trinchinopoly, the British therein mustered no more than 600 and this included the greater part of their European strength in Madras, as well as the majority of the officers. With the besieging force stiffened by 900 Frenchmen, Dupleix's scheme looked like coming to fruition.

The able Stringer Lawrence had gone home to England on leave and with such military talent as the Company possessed trapped in Trichinopoly, the civilian authorities at Fort St. George were at a loss to know how to save the situation. As so often happens, the hour of crisis produced the right man. Robert Clive, the son of an impoverished Shropshire squire, had been sent out to India in 1744 at the age of 18 as a clerk in the Company's service. Hating the work he had transferred to military duties and now, in 1751, had just been promoted captain. He suggested that the only way to relieve Trichinopoly was to mount a diversion against the city of Arcot, Chunda Sahib's capital, so as to induce the latter to draw off his forces from the siege. His plan was approved and, with a force of only 200 Europeans, 300 sepoys and three guns, he marched out of Madras in late August, heading for Arcot 65 miles away to the south-west.

Despite violent thunderstorms his small force covered the distance at such speed that the garrison abandoned the city at his approach. He marched in and set about restoring the dilapidated defences of Arcot fort. He had little time, for the fleeing garrison had encountered reinforcements sent by Chunda from Trichinopoly and by 23rd September an army of 10,000 with 100 French soldiers had returned to beseige him. Though he had a mile of walls to defend and only 120 British and 200 sepoys fit for duty, Clive was not content with a passive defence but made frequent sorties against the hostile camp by night. These raids, though risky, inspired his men with his own confidence and lowered the enemy's morale. By 10th November the besiegers had effected a breach in the walls with their siege train but Clive answered their calls to surrender with contempt. Meanwhile news of the epic defence of Arcot had reached the ears of the Mahrattas who, having been contemplating joining forces with Chunda, now decided to throw in their lot with Clive and sent 6,000 marching to his aid. Hearing this, the enemy commander, Chunda's son Raju Sahib, determined to assault before they could arrive. His hordes came on, led by elephants armed with great iron spikes on their heads to batter down the gates. Clive was down to only 80 Europeans and 120 sepoys, all exhausted by heat and lack of sleep, but he had prepared for the attack by training his few guns on the breach and arranging for muskets to be reloaded in relays, so that a continuous fire could be kept up. The fire thus produced was so hot and rapid that it maddened the elephants who trampled large numbers of the enemy underfoot. For an hour Clive's handful kept up their heroic defence until the baffled and frustrated enemy fell back. The following day Raju Sahib abandoned the siege and Clive was left triumphant in Arcot which he had held for 50 days.

Clive's defence of Arcot saved Trinchinoploy and gave him a reputation, in Indian eyes, to rival that of Dupleix; it also bred in the Company's soldiers, especially the sepoys, a tremendous pride and confidence in themselves. Many of Chunda's men deserted after Arcot and begged to be enrolled in the Company's service. From now on French power and influence gradually began to wane as British prestige grew.

Dupleix however was not beaten yet and in February 1752 he sent a force of 400 Frenchmen and 2,000 sepoys against Madras. Clive with a slightly smaller force went out to meet them but was ambushed in a moonlight battle at Covrepauk. By sheer cool-headed, determined leadership he extricated his troops from the trap and got them under cover from which they could return the enemy fire. For three hours they fought back until Clive spied a way by which he could withdraw part of his force unseen to attack the French in the rear. Surprise was complete and the French soldiers fled when their sepoys panicked.

Fighting went on for another two years around Trichinopoly. Lawrence, who had now returned from England, finally defeated the French forces which had remained in the area in June 1752. But in January 1753 his Indian allies, stirred up by Dupleix's constant intrigues, changed sides and he found himself besieged within Trichinopoly by overwhelming forces, backed by French reinforcements. By leaving only a small garrison inside the fortress and conducting a series of brilliant raids on the besiegers he held his own until August 1754. Then Dupleix was suddenly recalled to France and much of the impetus went out of the French effort in Madras. In January 1755 the French and British Companies agreed to a suspension of hostilities. To some extent the British position in India had gained a breathing space through Dupleix's recall, but had it not been for the endeavours and abilities of junior officers like Lawrence, Clive and their subordinates, none of a higher rank than major, the Company might well have been driven from India altogether.

In late 1754 evidence that the British Government was beginning to take some interest in Indian affairs was shown by the arrival of the 39th Foot and a detachment of Royal Artillery, the first regular elements of the King's Army to reach India. Their coming was timely for trouble next broke out in the Company's possessions in Calcutta. In August 1756 information reached Madras that the Nawab of Bengal, Suraj-ud-daula, perturbed by the spread of foreign influence within his domains, had attacked, captured and demolished Fort William at Calcutta, incarcerating many Europeans in the prison known to history as "the Black Hole", where numbers died from suffocation.

The news put the Company in a dilemma. The French were still strong in the Deccan and there were rumours from Europe, first, that war with France was again imminent, and second, that an expedition was being prepared in France for India. A few decades earlier the embryo Company had treated native rulers circumspectly, but after the events of recent years, an outrage, like the Nawab of Bengal's, was not to be tolerated. Clive was appointed to command a force of three companies of the 39th, detachments of the Madras and Bombay Europeans, and 1,200 sepoys. He reached the mouth of the Hooghly in December and briskly recaptured the town of that name and Calcutta before the year turned. A short pause ensued in which he took the opportunity to raise, for the first time, a sepoy battalion under a British officer, a new departure from the independent companies into which sepoys had hitherto been organized. This was the first, red-coated Indian regiment of the Company's Army, which took rank as the 1st Bengal Native Infantry; its men were not Bengalis but adventurers and mercenaries from the north. At the same time he also formed,from a number of independent European companies, a regiment of Bengal Europeans †.

Having achieved his initial objective Clive sent envoys to the Nawab to discuss peace. The latter temporized, at the same time assembling a huge force of over 30,000 men which began a ponderous advance towards Calcutta. Irked by the Nawab's evasions and by now contemptuous of Indian armies however large, Clive decided upon a surprise dawn attack on the enemy camp. His plan was thwarted by a sudden thick fog but his threat caused Suraj-ud-daula to seek terms in earnest. On 9th February 1757 peace was signed, the Company's position in Bengal restored, and a treaty of alliance agreed with the Nawab.

Clive, though keen to return to Madras, was unwilling to leave Bengal while the French still held Chandernagore, close to Calcutta, particularly in view of the likely re-opening of hostilities with France as a result of the outbreak of the Seven Years War. To move against the French, however, he required the sanction of Suraj-ud-daula in whose territory Chandernagore lay. The Nawab vacillated, then gave his permission, only to withdraw it 24 hours later. He was too late. Clive had already moved and, after a stiff fight supported by the fleet in the Hooghly, captured the French post. There were still other French possessions to be reduced but the Nawab was now thoroughly alarmed at the British success and again collected an army to halt it. Clive was unmoved by this danger as he had already made a secret agreement with one of the Nawab's discontented generals, Mir Jafar, for him to join the British with his contingent. Clive therefore advanced but was somewhat disconcerted not to find Mir Jafar waiting at the appointed rendez-vous. Instead he found himself confronted at Plassey by the Nawab with an enormous horde of 50,000, against which he could only muster 750 British troops, 2,500 sepoys, eight 6-pounders and two howitzers. Uncertain about Mir Jafar's intentions and knowing that a French force was only three days' march away and the monsoon was imminent, Clive held a council of war. The majority of his officers voted for a withdrawal, to which Clive himself assented. Then, during the night of 21st-22nd June, he changed his mind and decided to fight.

The following morning the Nawab's host swarmed out of their encampments with their horse, foot and elephants, encircling Clive's slender line in a great arc. The battle began with a cannonade but after several hours a torrential rainstorm caused the enemy guns to fall silent. The British gunners, who had managed to keep their powder dry,continued to fire and Clive brought up his infantry from where they had been sheltering from the enemy bombardment. Then the Nawab sent forward a mass of infantry against the British line but the disciplined musketry and steady fire of the guns sent them reeling back in panic. Clive immediately ordered the advance. Suraj-ud-daula had already fled and his mighty army simply dissolved, while Mir Jafar, who had watched the action from the flanks, doubtless waiting to see who would emerge victorious, came forward to greet Clive and to be appointed the new Nawab of Bengal. With his own nominee on the throne, Clive was undisputed master of Bengal, a victory won by his iron nerve and stern resolution. Plassey was his last battle for the Company in India but he remained in Bengal for two years where there was much to be done to consolidate his position.

The French had to be rounded up and Major Eyre Coote of the 39th made an epic march of some 300 miles to the borders of Oudh in pursuit of them. He had a tiny force of sepoys and two companies of Europeans, some of which were French deserters or prisoners, others Swiss and Germans, and the rest British. Apart from the climate, the terrain and dangers from the local population, he had to contend with two minor mutinies among his troops, first the Europeans, then the sepoys, all protesting at the length and hardships of the march. Overcoming all difficulties, he brought his expedition to a successful conclusion and proved himself as an officer of great promise.

---

† Later, in 1846, the 1st Bengal European Fusiliers; in 1860, the 101st Foot (Royal Bengal Fusiliers); and in 1881, 1st Battalion Royal Munster Fusiliers (disbanded 1922).

84

Robert Lord Clive (1725-1774)
In general officers state coat, 1757.

Portrait, oil on canvas, artist unknown.   6305-12-1

General Sir Eyre Coote, c1760

Portrait, oil on canvas, by G.Morland   7112-49

Major-General Stringer Lawrence

General Sir Joseph Smith, c1780.
Miniature.   6012-218

Meanwhile the French had been trying to restore their power in the Deccan. In April 1758 a French fleet carrying reinforcements from France under the Comte de Lally arrived off Fort St David at Cuddalore and captured it. His next objective was Madras but, short of money to pay his troops, he resolved first to raid the treasury of the Rajah of Tanjore. The expedition was a failure, his men grew disheartened and undisciplined, and he had to fall back on Pondicherry. After the fall of Fort St David the authorities at Madras sent urgent messages to Clive in Bengal for help, but the latter, faced with many difficulties and determined to hold Bengal with all its riches, refused. However, he then saw the opportunity of relieving French pressure in Madras by raiding their possessions in the Northern Circars, between the Carnatic and Bengal. Accordingly he despatched an expedition under Colonel Forde of the 39th with 500 Europeans† and three battalions of sepoys to attack the Marquis de Conflans, an officer new to India but with a larger force than Forde's. The latter conducted a brilliant campaign, first defeating Conflans at Condore on 3rd December. Despite shortages of supplies, cash and ammunition, a minor mutiny, and the ever-present threat of being overwhelmed by superior force, he made a daring and completely successful night attack on the French fort at Masulipatam, *"by far the strongest situation in India".(3)* Forde's accomplishments completely undermined French power in this area, eased the situation in Madras, and resulted in the powerful Nizam of Hyderabad, in whose domains the Circars lay and who hitherto had been entirely under French influence, concluding a treaty with the British.

Meanwhile Lally, having earlier summoned help from Bussy, the French commander in Hyderabad, had laid siege to Madras in December 1758 with 2,300 French troops and 5,000 sepoys. Opposing him was Stringer Lawrence with just over half that number of troops. Despite advancing years Lawrence conducted the defence with such vigour and resolution that Lally, beset by the indiscipline and desertion in his ranks and short of ammunition and supplies, could not prevail. On 16th February 1759 a British squadron arrived off Madras and Lally was forced to retire on Pondicherry.

With Madras now safe and Forde victorious in the Northern Circars, the French position in the south began to disintegrate, their posts falling one by one into British hands and more and more local rulers in the Carnatic changing their allegiance. In November Eyre Coote, now a colonel with his own regiment, the 84th,* lately raised in England, arrived to take the field in Madras and captured Wandewash. Lally advanced to meet him and on 22nd January 1760 the two armies met in battle. Coote had two King's battalions, his own and Draper's*, two of Madras Europeans and about three of sepoys, against Lally's four French battalions and 1,300 sepoys. Coote first manoeuvred Lally out of his chosen position; then, once battle was joined, outfought him in a struggle in which only the European troops of both sides were really engaged, until a lucky shot from a British gun exploded a French ammunition wagon, which caused panic and confusion in the enemy lines. Utterly defeated Lally again fell back on Pondicherry. Coote advanced slowly, systematically reducing all the French outposts. In August, having insufficient force to besiege Pondicherry, he threw a blockade around it. Eventually he was able to begin siege operations and on 15th January 1761, with the garrison almost on the brink of starvation, the fortress surrendered. Thus French power and influence in the Carnatic was terminated and, with Bengal now firmly under British control, the East India Company was supreme from Calcutta to the Coromandel coast. Although the French were allowed re-possession of some unfortified factories after the end of the Seven Years War in 1763, their military power in India was crushed.

It had taken 15 years to reverse the dominance so quickly and so widely achieved by Dupleix. It had been done by the determination, drive and courage of a handful of comparatively junior officers, operating with minute forces over vast distances, in burning heat, torrential monsoons, dressed in unsuitable eighteenth century clothing, with musket and bayonet and a few light field guns. With never more than, at best, five European battalions of foot, the British commanders had perforce to rely on the uncertain fighting qualities and willingness of locally-enlisted native troops to accept European discipline and training. But with success came confidence, both to the sepoys themselves and to their European leaders in their reliability, and gradually the independent native companies began to take shape as the Company's military arm.

Much of this was due to Stringer Lawrence, often called the father of the Indian Army. Not only did he have the character and presence to inspire Indian soldiers, but he also possessed the organizing ability to construct a proper and lasting framework on which a native army could be built. Following the example of Clive in forming a battalion of Bengal sepoys, Lawrence started the same process in Madras. In 1758 he formed a number of independent companies into the 1st and 2nd Battalions of Coast Sepoys. More were raised in 1759 and by the end of the Seven Years War ten such battalions had been formed, all of which were subsequently designated regiments of Madras Native Infantry. Over the same period 17 battalions of Bengal Native Infantry were formed. These were the nucleus of what later became the armies of the Bengal and Madras Presidencies of the East India

† Detachments of the Bengal and Madras Europeans.
* Disbanded after the Seven Years War.

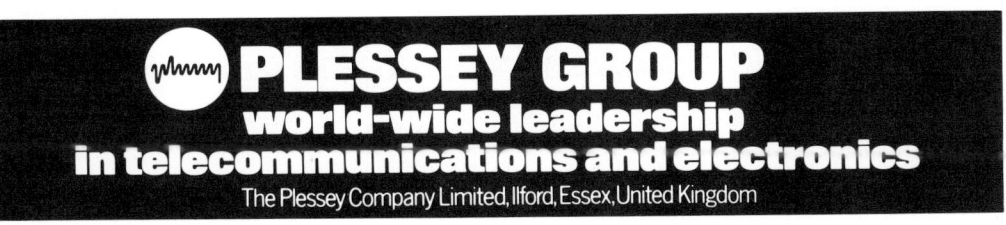

Company. The same process began in Bombay in 1768†. A battalion consisted of a grenadier company and eight line companies, each of 120 men, later (1766) being increased to ten but of the same overall strength. The companies had Indian officers, subadars and jemadars, and each battalion had a "Black Commandant", but with two European subalterns to advise and supervise and three white sergeant-majors to drill and train the sepoys; the last five being drawn from the Company's European regiments. In 1766 a European captain was placed in command of each battalion. Finally, to build up their prestige in the eyes of other natives and to assimilate them as much as possible to British troops, they were put into uniforms of mixed European and Indian styles in which a red coat predominated; a step which, as over the years the uniform became more and more European in cut, was to prove of mixed blessings. Perhaps the best testimonial to Lawrence's work with his sepoys is a remark made as early as 1759 by the Comte de Lally. *"You would be surprised"*, he wrote, *"at the difference between the black troops of the English and ours; it is greater than that between a Nawab and a cooly. Theirs will even venture to attack white troops, while ours will not even look at their black ones".(4)*

Having overcome French power in India, the Company now had to face threats to its position from Indian potentates. In Bengal, nominally under Clive's puppet, Mir Jafar, the activities of the Company attracted the attention of the Mogul Emperor, Shah Alam, who, enlisting the aid of the Nawab of Oudh, began to take steps to recover this province of his fragmented Empire. Between 1760 and 1764 there were numerous encounters between his forces and the Company's, culminating in the Battle of Buxar on 23rd October 1764. The British commander, Major Hector Munro, a King's (as opposed to a Company) officer, with ten companies of Bengal and Bombay Europeans and eight battalions of sepoys, about 7,000 in all, faced a force of between 40,000 and 60,000. After a fierce battle, in which the British found their opponents far more resolute than other native armies, Munro drove the enemy's left wing in upon its centre, and forced the whole tangled mass, elephants, camels, horses and men, into a mud-filled gulley from which there was no escape. 2,000 of the enemy were killed on the battlefield and thousands more perished in the gulley, while 167 guns and plunder to the value of £12,000 fell into British hands. They pushed on into Oudh as far as Allahabad and there dictated peace terms, under which the Emperor recognized the sovereignty of the Company over the whole of Bengal, Behar and Orissa.

Two years after this enormous increase to the Company's lands, trouble broke out in the south. In 1767 the ruler of the powerful state of Mysore, to the west of British possessions in the Carnatic, was an able and ambitious soldier of fortune, Hyder Ali, whose activities and those of his successors would threaten the Company's position in the Carnatic until the end of the century. What came to be known as the First Mysore War (there would eventually be four) occurred through the authorities at Madras being duped by the Nizam of Hyderabad into undertaking a campaign against Hyder Ali, only to find that the latter and the Nizam were in league with each other. The chief interest of the operations, which lasted from 1767-69, lies in the character of the British commander, but for whose sterling qualities the outcome might have been even more unfortunate for the Company than it actually turned out.

Joseph Smith was another of those young British officers cast in a heroic mould who are so often encountered in the story of British India. Smith had first attracted notice for his courage and presence of mind when serving as an ensign under Clive in 1752. In 1767, when aged 34, he was a colonel commanding the Madras Army. He was sent out to join the Nizam against Hyder Ali with one battalion of Madras Europeans and five of sepoys. When he learned that the Nizam had changed sides, he found himself in enemy territory, with mountains between him and the Carnatic, and opposed by a combined enemy army of over 70,000 with 109 guns. Nevertheless he managed to extricate his troops from this dangerous situation and fell back through the mountains towards a place called Changamah, where he had been promised supplies and reinforcements would meet him. These the Madras authorities failed to send but, undiscouraged, Smith attacked and threw back Hyder Ali's vastly superior forces. After a vigorous action lasting over three hours, he then continued his withdrawal marching *"for twenty seven hours without the least refreshment for man or beast who were never unloaded".(5)* Three weeks later he again overthrew an army twelve times his own strength in an action for which he gave all credit to his sepoys who attacked *"with a firmness that will ever do them honour, for notwithstanding all efforts from cannon, musketry, rockets, and horse, they (the enemy) could not discompose our lines".(6)* It was this praise and concern for his sepoys that made Smith an outstanding leader and earned him their total loyalty, no matter what the dangers and hardships. He was a modest, even diffident man yet his demeanour and reputation inspired devotion in his followers and fear in the enemy. At a crucial moment in a battle at Mulwagal, where Smith was not present, a tiny group of mainly wounded sepoys were rallied on a hill by Captain Brooke, who urged them to shout, *"Huzza! Huzza! Smith! Smith!" (7),* as though their leader was arriving to turn the

---

† For dates of formation, subsequent titles, uniform and battle honours of Indian regiments, see the Marquess of Cambridge, "Notes on the Armies of India", Journal of the Society for Army Historical Research, Vol.XLVII, page 23 et seq.

Surrender of Pondicherry to Col. Eyre Coote, January, 1761.   6609-115

Painting, oil on canvas, by Francis Hayman.

British infantry, native infantry and native cavalry drilling outside a fortified town.

Watercolour by F.L. Rothmeyer, 1786.   7412-128

tide. The most common English surname is an unlikely rallying call on a stricken field but in this case it served to stem the enemy's victorious advance. All Smith's efforts were hampered by the Company's failure to provide adequate supplies and resources. In November 1768 the Madras authorities committed the unbelievable folly of recalling him from the operations. His successor in the field had none of his ability and in March 1769 Hyder Ali appeared at the very gates of Madras. A peace was patched up between the Company and Mysore but the driving ambition of Hyder Ali gave little hope that it would be a lasting one.

In an effort to relieve the pressure on Madras before the peace was signed, a small force from the Bombay Army, which in 1768 comprised the three-battalion regiment of Europeans and two battalions of sepoys†, had attacked Mysorean possessions on the Malabar coast. However the chief threat the Bombay troops would have to face was the great Mahratta Confederacy of western and central India, made up of several powerful states, whose armed strength was based on hordes of fierce light cavalry, an arm of which the Company's forces were totally deficient*. In 1778 the involvement of the Bombay authorities in the politics of rival Mahratta states led to the despatch of a force to Poona, where the ruler had been intriguing with the French, with whom, as will be seen in the next chapter, Britain was again at war as a result of the American Revolution. The force, under the incompetent Colonel Charles Egerton, *"a bedridden invalid"(8)*, became surrounded at Wadgaon by a great host of Mahrattas. Despite a heroic rearguard action by six sepoy grenadier companies+ and the Bombay Europeans, the troops were hopelessly outnumbered and were only allowed to return to Bombay in safety after agreeing to the most humiliating terms. This did not end the fighting and the Bombay troops were reinforced by six battalions of Bengal sepoys, which, on the orders of Warren Hastings, appointed the first Governor-General of the East India Company in 1774, had made a celebrated march right across India from coast to coast. On 10th February 1780 the Mahratta stronghold at Ahmedabad was taken by storm. In October the British laid siege to Bassein, during which a covering force of six battalions under Colonel Hartley, who had commanded the grenadiers at Wadgaon, held off the Mahrattas for six weeks, finally inflicting a resounding defeat on them at Devghar. In his despatch Hartley said of his sepoys, *"their performance only confirms me in the high opinion I shall ever hold of them".(9)* The campaign closed with a treaty in 1782 but the Mahrattas would continue to pose a threat to British supremacy for nearly another 40 years.

Meanwhile Britain's renewed hostilities with France had induced Hyder Ali to test his strength once more against the Carnatic. In 1780 he poured into the British possessions with a formidable army of 100,000, laying waste everything in his path and massacring a detached British force at Pollilore. The British fell back to Madras, except for a small garrison of 100 sepoys under a single white officer, Lieutenant Flint, who held out at Wandewash, defying every attempt against them for nearly six months until relieved. The situation in the Carnatic became very grave. It was saved by Sir Eyre Coote who, now aged 54 and in indifferent health, came down from Bengal for his last Indian campaign. Throughout 1781-82, with one King's regiment, the 71st Highlanders, two under-strength battalions of Bengal and Madras Europeans, and ten sepoy battalions, Coote defeated Hyder on every occasion he fought him in the field — at Porto Novo, at Pollilore, Sholinghur and Arnee. But without cavalry and a crippling lack of transport and supplies, he was unable to match Hyder's mobility and bring the operations to a decisive conclusion. Nevertheless, by his skill, his dauntless spirit, and above all by the trust, loyalty and devotion he inspired in his men, particularly the sepoys, he saved Madras from being overrun. This achievement, together with his noble work in the Seven Years War, makes him one of the outstanding soldiers of British India. A year later, in 1783, he died, worn out by the long years of service to the Company whose cause he had done so much to advance. His death was preceded by that of Hyder himself who was succeeded by his ferocious son Tippoo, an inheritor of all his father's hatred of the British. In 1784 Tippoo made peace but it would only be a truce until he again saw his opportunity to fulfill his father's long-held ambitions for conquest.

Thus in 184 years the East India Company had laid the foundations of a great empire in India and established itself as the supreme European power in the sub-continent. Although the French had participated on a small scale against the Company's struggles with Mysore and the Mahrattas, they were finished as a power in India. Henceforth it would be only the Indian states and rulers that stood in the way of further British expansion. From its early days as a small trading organization, the Company had grown to be a mighty force in the land, its position and prestige sustained by its rapidly increasing sepoy armies, drilled and trained to a European discipline by a small number of British officers and supported, when occasions required, by King's regiments from home. This great achievement was perhaps due above all to those officers, aided, it must not be forgotten, by a

---

† Later becoming the 8th and 3rd Bombay Native Infantry (1824) and subsequently (1922) the 3rd/4th Bombay Grenadiers and 1st/5th Mahratta Light Infantry respectively.

* The first regiments of native cavalry were not raised until 1776 in Bengal, in 1784 in Madras and 1804 in Bombay.

+ The Bombay Army now had eight sepoy battalions.

few British non-commissioned-officers, who together, *"trained early to responsibility, to self-reliance, and to a study of their profession by isolation with a handful of sepoys among treacherous and quarrelsome native chiefs, ...learned to meet every emergency with skill, coolness and resource".(10)* Well might such men claim to share the proud boast enshrined in the motto of the 39th Foot, the victors of Plassey, that they too, and the sepoys they commanded, were *"Primus in Indis"*.

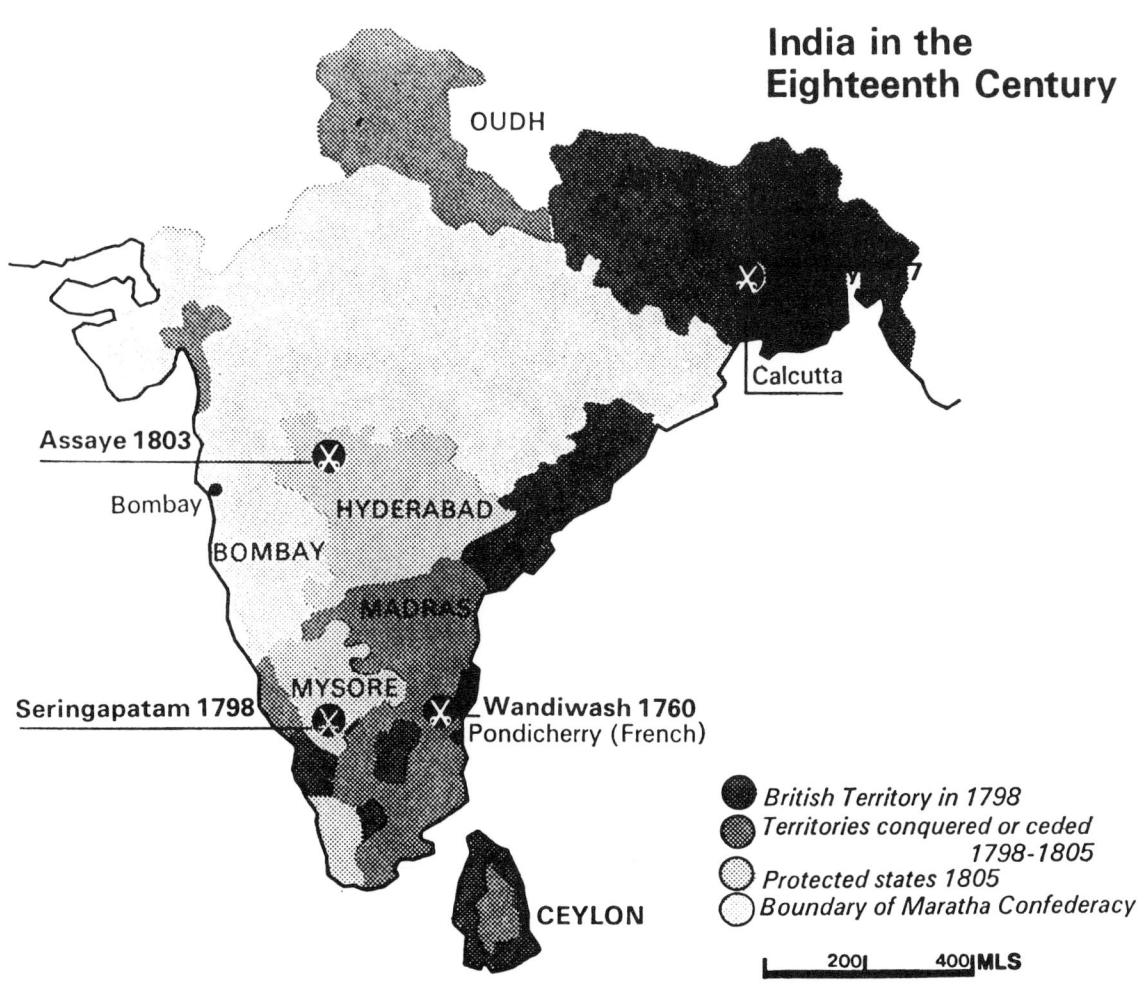

India in the Eighteenth Century

OUDH

Calcutta

Assaye 1803

Bombay

HYDERABAD

BOMBAY

MADRAS

MYSORE

Seringapatam 1798

Wandiwash 1760
Pondicherry (French)

● British Territory in 1798
◐ Territories conquered or ceded
1798-1805
◯ Protected states 1805
◯ Boundary of Maratha Confederacy

200 400 MLS

CEYLON

Minorca 1771   Lord George Lennox with men of the 25th Regiment

Lt-Col. Watson with soldiers of the 25th, 11th and 3rd Regiments.
Paintings, oil on canvas, attributed to Guiseppe Chiesa

7402-12

CHAPTER 8
THE WORLD TURNED UPSIDE DOWN
1775 – 1783

At the end of the Seven Years War in 1763 the British flag flew triumphant from Hudson's Bay to Florida in America, in the Caribbean, the Mediterranean and around the coasts of India. Twenty years later all of America except Canada was lost, France had re-asserted her presence in the West Indies, and British possessions in India were under attack by native princes abetted by the French. Above all British prestige had been gravely humbled. This remarkable reverse of British fortunes was the result of the rebellion of the American colonies against the Crown, compounded, when things began to go ill for Britain, by France and Spain seizing the opportunity to avenge old scores, thus turning a colonial revolt into another world war. Apart from the operations in India which have been touched upon in the last chapter, the British Army, seriously reduced after 1763, had to face a widespread confrontation with its country's enemies from Quebec to the Caribbean, in the Mediterranean, and even to the very shores of the British Isles. As always, the outcome of British land operations depended on supremacy at sea but the Royal Navy too had suffered economies and neglect during the years of peace. Once the European powers entered the struggle it found itself outnumbered and unable always to provide the support the Army so urgently needed in its endeavours.

Since the war witnessed the surrender of two British field armies to forces not highly rated for their military abilities at that time; since important possessions were lost; and since no battle honours were awarded to British regiments for their efforts in America, the war is sometimes regarded as a discreditable episode in the history of the Army. In some quarters a legend has evolved of its regiments floundering in tight European formations under incompetent leaders, helpless against American sharpshooters and forest fighters. Yet its officers and men had little to reproach themselves for. Its generals, Howe and Burgoyne, Clinton and Cornwallis, were able if not brilliant; some excellent junior officers made their mark; the regiments adapted quickly to North American terrain and warfare; and in battle after battle the troops so emulated the example of their forbears as to emerge victorious. This chapter will attempt to show how, in a lost war, the Army lived up to its traditions but were deprived of victory by faulty direction of the war and forces over which it had no control.

After the Seven Years War all regiments of infantry junior to the 70th Foot and all cavalry above the 18th Light Dragoons were disbanded. When the disturbances in America began, with the attacks at Lexington and Concord on 18th April 1775 against British troops sent to seize the arms stores of the Massachusetts militia, the British Army numbered about 48,000, of which only 8,000 were stationed in America. Recruiting was particularly difficult, due largely to the soldier's appalling rate of pay, still the eightpence per day† of Mary Tudor, and the general rise in living standards in all walks of life other than the soldier's. The prospect of fighting in what amounted to a civil war, against men with a common ancestry and with whom dangers had been shared in the conquest of Canada, did nothing to induce men to enlist, and between 1775 and 1778 only one new regiment was raised. Once begun, the rebellion quickly gained momentum and the shortfall in troops had to be made good by the hiring of German mercenaries, chiefly Hessians and Brunswickers, and the raising, in America, of Loyalist Provincial regiments. As a general rule, but one to which there were a number of notable exceptions, the former proved the most reliable. Not until the entry of France into the war in 1778, and Spain the year after, did recruiting improve sufficiently for the Army to be expanded. Partly through patriotic response and partly through the well-tried recruiting devices of earlier wars, enough men volunteered or were impressed to form 31 new regiments of foot and four of light dragoons between 1778 and 1781, bringing the Army's overall strength to 110,000. By the time this improvement started, however, the first major disaster had occurred in America; when it was completed, America had virtually been lost.

With this shortage of troops on the one hand and the vast expanses of the 13 Colonies, with a population of four million in which rebels outnumbered loyalists, on the other, the Army's strategic tasks of defeating the rebel armies and re-asserting control over re-conquered territory were conflicting and well-nigh insuperable.

---

† Before deduction of stoppages for food, clothing and necessaries.

As early as 1775 the Army's senior staff officer, General Harvey, the Adjutant-General, wrote: *"Taking America as it at present stands, it is impossible to conquer it with our British Army. To attempt to conquer it internally by our land force is as wild an idea as ever controverted common sense".(1)* To these difficulties must be added the fact that 3,000 miles of sea formed a time barrier of up to three months between the Army in America and the source from which came its directives, reinforcements and supplies. Once hostilities began in earnest, the fighting qualities of the rebels soon disproved the notion held by some in authority that they were merely opposed by "a rabble in arms". Tactically, as well as strategically, the Army's task would be akin to a householder trying to mop up a flooded basement with a pocket handkerchief.

The problems of subduing the rebels soon became apparent to commanders on the spot, for some of whom the task was made even less palatable by their own misgivings about the justice of their cause. Brigadier-General Lord Percy, whose energy and presence of mind had saved the troops retreating from Lexington from complete disaster and who later fought with distinction in a higher rank, returned home in 1776 in disgust at the war. When the chief command in America was offered to Amherst, he refused it since he was unwilling to fight against men who had served under him in Canada. In October 1775 the post went to Sir William Howe, last met scaling the Heights of Abraham with the light infantry in 1759. He too had much sympathy for the grievances which had driven the colonists to rebel and only accepted the command out of loyalty to the King. The lack of energy in prosecuting the war, of which he was subsequently accused, was due more to his wish to bring hostilities to an early and honourable close for both sides, than the laziness and love of comfort to which his failure was attributed, although his reputation as a 'bon viveur' was not unmerited. His successor, Sir Henry Clinton, was also not without doubts about the rights and wrongs of the whole affair. Despite their personal feelings and the difficulties confronting them, each commander in the field did his best to fulfill the task entrusted to him. But their views on how to prosecute the war, and their efforts to do so, were always subject to their political masters in London.

Although King George III was castigated by the American rebels as the chief perpetrator of all their injustices, it was not the King but Parliament which had levied the taxes upon them and denied them what they conceived as their rights. It was Parliament which, in ignoring their aspirations, had driven them to rebellion. Likewise it was Parliament which had reduced the Navy and Army and failed to heed the warnings of senior officers. Once the rebellion had broken out, it was ministers sitting in London who, misappreciating the support likely to be forthcoming from loyalists in America, and hampered at every turn by the Opposition, made tardy and inadequate preparations to support the troops already in America. The hour demanded a leader of Chatham's calibre, but with the Prime Minister, Lord North, happily admitting to his ignorance on military matters, conduct of the war fell to the Secretary of State for the Colonies, Lord George Germaine. Certainly Germaine had military experience, of a sort, for he was none other than Lord George Sackville, who had been court-martialled and dismissed for his dubious conduct at Minden. He had never forgotten his court-martial and his behaviour in office, it has been said, demonstrated *"a malignity towards all the principal commanders in America which bears very strong marks of personal vindictiveness".(2)* Whatever the merits of such a charge, there can be no doubt that it was Germaine's folly which led to the first major disaster of the war from which all else stemmed.

After the fight at Lexington the rebellion quickly spread and from April 1775 the Americans, with some 16-20,000 militiamen, besieged 11 under-strength British battalions in Boston. In May reinforcements of seven battalions and the 17th Light Dragoons reached Boston. A month later, on 17th June, the British attacked the rebel position on the heights overlooking the town, in the battle known as Bunker's Hill. After two frontal attacks in close order up a bullet-swept hillside, in which the American marksmen decimated the British ranks, Howe's infantry, with invincible courage, rallied and made a third such attack, trusting in the bayonet only. With the Americans' ammunition running low, the redcoats finally carried the position but with appalling losses of nearly half their strength. The battle had been marked by the determined gallantry of the regimental officers and men, a lack of imaginative tactics on the part of the British commanders, and the unflinching resistance of the Americans. It is perhaps this battle and Lexington that have given rise to the legends of British military incompetence mentioned earlier. Bunker's Hill certainly made clear that bulldozing tactics would not suffice in the future. Stunned by the losses, Howe withdrew into Boston to spend the rest of the winter there until, in the following March, he was forced, by increasing American pressure, to evacuate the town and sail for Halifax. During this winter's pause at Boston, to which he was condemned, first, by the lack of resources with which to resume offensive operations, and second, by lack of shipping once evacuation had been decided, a separate American attack on Quebec was narrowly averted by Sir Guy Carleton. In May 1776 Carleton was relieved by a force of 10,000 under Sir John Burgoyne, on whose arrival the Americans in Canada withdrew to Ticonderoga.

Once arrived at Halifax, Howe set about reorganizing his army and preparing for the next campaign. His unimaginative tactics at Bunker's Hill had been out of character for he had made his name in command of light troops in the Seven Years War. It was largely due to his influence that light infantry had been restored in the

Army in 1770, with the addition of a light company to every battalion of infantry. In 1774 he had established a camp of exercise for these companies, which he had trained in a combination of European discipline and the open-order methods of fighting he had observed practised by Indians and ranger companies in Canada. He was thus by no means reactionary where tactics were concerned, as indeed in future battles his troops would prove. Strategically he appreciated the importance of New York as the centre of the most widespread loyalist sympathies, the southern gateway of the route up the Hudson to Canada, and a more centrally placed base for the Royal Navy than Halifax, far in the north. He also realised that to take and hold it would require the concentration of all available forces, and that diversions, such as that ordered by the Government in early 1776 to rally the loyalists in the Carolinas, merely dissipated the main effort. In the event this diversion failed and the troops involved rejoined in time for Howe's offensive against New York.

On 3rd July, the day before the American Congress declared the independence of the 13 Colonies, Howe landed with 9,000 men on Staten Island. Here he had to await reinforcements from England, which soon began to arrive escorted by a fleet under his brother, Lord Howe. By August he mustered a force of 30 British battalions, from which he extracted the grenadier and light companies to form four battalions of the former and three of the latter, and a division of Hessians. The whole totalled some 25,000, including three batteries of Royal Artillery and the 16th and 17th Light Dragoons. In and around New York the Americans disposed of some 19,000 under George Washington, who had fought alongside Braddock on the Monongahela in 1755. Part of his force was provincial militia but the rest were drawn from the new "Continental" or regular army, that he had created in June 1775.

On 22nd August Howe attacked. Between 8 a.m. and noon 15,000 men, 40 guns and the horses of the light dragoons were put ashore on Long Island. The battalions of light infantry and grenadiers, the 33rd and 42nd were pushed forward to form an outpost line, while the rest of the army landed and reconnaissances were made of the enemy positions. By the 26th Howe's plan was ready. Advancing his army under cover of darkness towards the forward American defences along the heights in front of Brooklyn, he directed General Grant's brigade and the Hessians against the enemy right and centre to distract attention from the movement of his main body round the enemy left flank through an unguarded pass. At 9 a.m. two guns gave the signal for an advance on all fronts. Part of the 7,000-strong American force managed to withdraw to their last lines of defence but they suffered some 2,000 casualties against the British loss of under 400. Two nights later under cover of darkness, and thanks to winds which prevented the British ships from cutting off his retreat, Washington contrived to extricate the rest of his force on Long Island back to Manhattan.

After this promising start Howe landed on the west bank of the East River on 15th September and, by a series of outflanking movements round Washington's left, forced the Americans to retreat northwards to White Plains, some 25 miles from New York, leaving behind them 5,400 men to garrison their two forts on either side of the Hudson. Having defeated Washington at White Plains on 28th October, thus cutting off the forts from their main army, Howe turned south and captured them before Washington could return down the west bank of the Hudson to their relief. So Howe secured New York and opened the Hudson to the British Fleet. Washington fell back south-westwards to re-group his forces on the far side of the Delaware. Howe cleared New Jersey and left a garrison of Hessians at Trenton to watch the Delaware. Satisfied with the success of his operations he retired into comfortable winter quarters at New York to prepare for the next year's campaign. His peace of mind received a rude shock when he learned that Washington had re-crossed the Delaware in the depths of winter, surprised the Hessians at Trenton on Christmas Day, and driven in the British outposts to re-establish himself in New Jersey some 30 miles west of New York. Notwithstanding this setback Howe planned to continue his operations the following year by an attack on Philadelphia, the seat of Congress and the centre of American resistance. However, Lord George Germaine was now to take a hand in affairs.

At the turn of the year Howe informed Germaine of his plans to attack Philadelphia. At about the time his letter reached England in late February 1777, Burgoyne, who had been serving under Carleton in Canada but had gone home to England for the winter, submitted a plan of his own to Germaine. He envisaged cutting off the American forces in New England by leading an advance from Canada down the Hudson to be met at Albany by Howe's army striking north up the Hudson from New York. On 3rd March Germaine wrote to Howe approving his attack on Philadelphia. On the 26th Burgoyne sailed for America, bearing an instruction from Germaine to Carleton, ordering the latter to provide Burgoyne with 7,000 men for his advance on Albany. Germaine sent a copy of this instruction to Howe, but with no orders for the latter to amend his Philadelphia plan. Some weeks later, in about mid-May, Germaine received a copy of a letter, written by Howe on 5th April to Carleton, saying that since he, Howe, would not be receiving the reinforcements he had asked for, he would be unable to assist any operations by Carleton from Canada. Burgoyne had by now reached Quebec and was preparing for his expedition in accordance with Germaine's directive of 26th March. Germaine must have realised from Howe's latest letter that Burgoyne's project was now endangered, but contented himself with writing

General Howe, c1778   6705-20-11
Oval stipple engraving by J.Chapman, published April 1st, 1801

General John Burgoyne, in the uniform of Light Dragoons
(possibly as Colonel of the 16th), 1789. Etching by James
Sayer, published by C.Bretherton, 1789.   7403-14

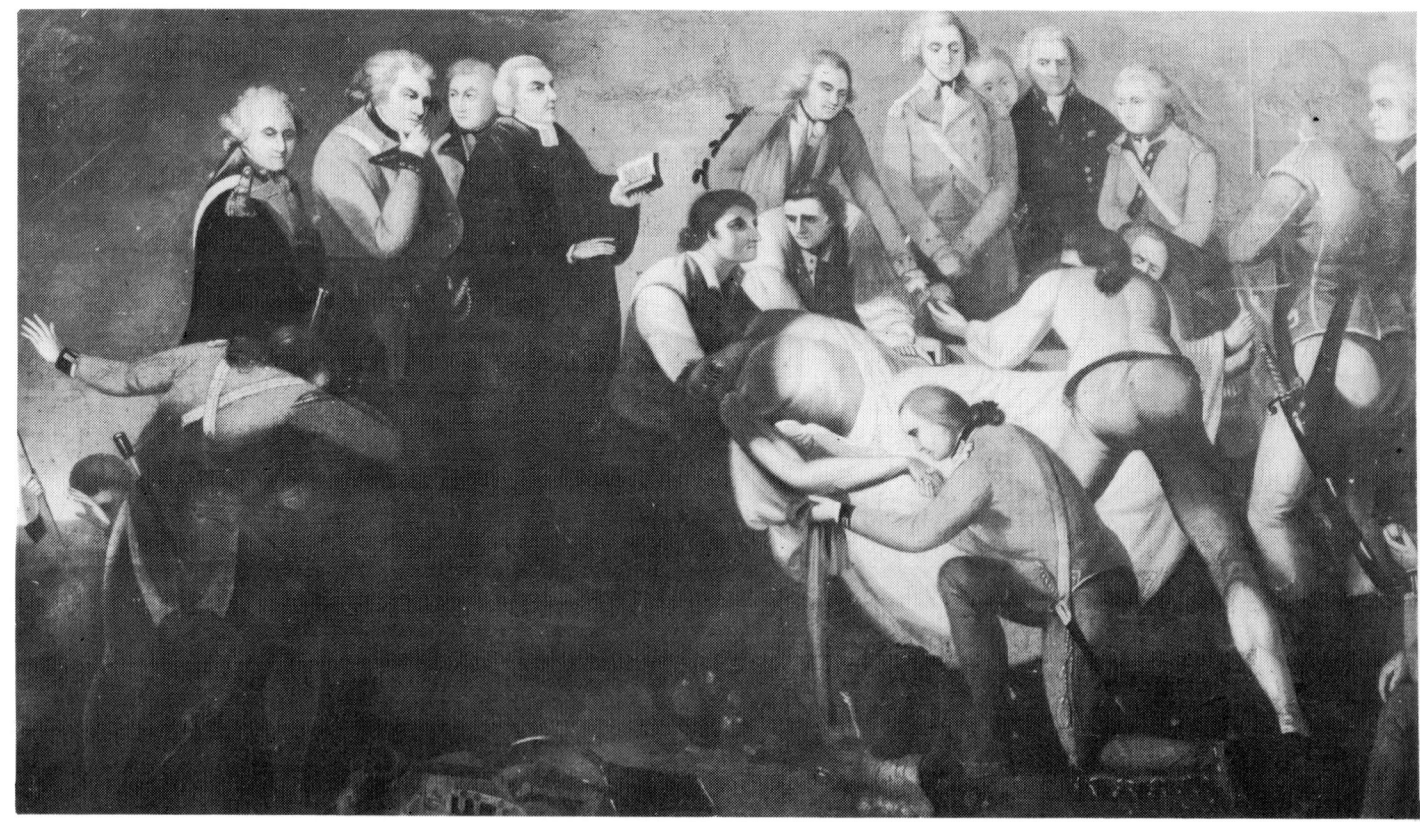

The Funeral of Brigadier-General Simon Fraser after the Battle of Saratoga, 9th October 1777   6012-200
Painting, oil on canvas, by J. Graham.

to Howe on 18th May repeating his agreement to the Philadelphia plan but adding a vague hope that Howe's operations might be completed in time for him to co-operate with Burgoyne's advance. A few days later he had afterthoughts and drafted a further directive to Howe, giving him firm orders to march up the Hudson to meet Burgoyne. The day he did so he was due to leave for the country but since the despatch was not ready for his signature by the time he wished to depart, he left without signing it. It was therefore never sent. At the beginning of May Howe had received Germaine's approval of his Philadelphia plan (sent on 3rd March), followed on 5th June by the copy of the 26th March orders to Carleton for Burgoyne's advance. Since this contained no order for Howe to change his plans, he began his campaign. He was not to receive Germaine's last letter (of 18th May) until 25th August, by which time he was in action against Washington on the road to Philadelphia. Burgoyne, meanwhile, had begun his southward march on 29th June, under the impression that he was to meet Howe at Albany. Thus Germaine, by first intriguing with an officer subordinate to both Howe and Carleton, then by issuing imprecise orders and making no allowance for the time correspondence took to cross the Atlantic, and finally by putting his country pursuits before his duty, ensured a divided effort by British forces in 1777 with, as will shortly be seen, disastrous results.

Howe had originally intended to advance overland on Philadelphia but Washington's presence in New Jersey decided him to move his force by sea, first to land in Delaware Bay then, when this was objected to by the Navy, in Chesapeake Bay farther south. Leaving Clinton to hold New York with 9,000 men, he sailed with 14,000 but owing to contrary winds landing was delayed until 22nd August.

On 11th September he fought a skilful battle at Brandywine Creek, defeating the Americans by turning their right flank and completely routing part of their force, while the remainder under Washington retreated northwards uncovering Philadelphia. On the 26th Howe marched in to find that the Congress had hurriedly decamped. Just over a week later Washington counter-attacked Howe at Germantown but was again repulsed. His defeat was largely due to a masterly delaying action by the 2nd Battalion of Light Infantry and the 40th Foot. The Light Infantry fell back slowly on the main body while six companies of the 40th took up position in Chew's House, a strong, brick-built, two-storey mansion, from which they put up such a stout defence as to upset Washington's plan of attack. Howe then withdrew to Philadelphia to ensure the safe passage of the Delaware, on which he would be dependent for supplies, during the coming winter. He had achieved what he had set out to do but, seeing no chance of bringing the war to a successful conclusion in 1778 without the reinforcements he had consistently requested, he wrote to Germaine asking to resign his command. Then, ignorant of what had befallen Burgoyne, he prepared to spend the winter at Philadelphia in comfort, while Washington, his army reduced by sickness and desertion to only 3,000 men, was without comfort of any sort in a miserable camp at Valley Forge, 20 miles to the west.

John Burgoyne, "Gentleman Johnny", was an accomplished soldier, popular with his men, an M. P., a man of fashion, a spendthrift and a gambler. The last, added to his personal ambition, was to lead to his downfall, with of course some help from Germaine. His force of 7,500 British, Brunswickers, Provincials and Indians pushed south down Lake Champlain, taking Ticonderoga and the forts covering the approches to the Upper Hudson by 7th July, while a diversionary detachment under Colonel St. Leger followed a roughly parallel course down the Mohawk river with the view to joining Burgoyne at Fort Edward, 45 miles north of Albany. Instead of continuing by water down Lake George to the next objective at Fort Edward, Burgoyne chose to take an overland route through very thick country which greatly tired his troops and imposed severe supply problems, already aggravated by the length of his lines of communication. On reaching Fort Edward he sent a force of Germans to capture an American stores depot at Bennington to the south-east, but this was defeated with heavy loss. Worse was to follow for St. Leger was beaten in the Mohawk valley and had to fall back on Canada. Nevertheless, in pursuance of his orders, Burgoyne pressed on down the west bank of the Hudson until he was halted by the Americans in a strong position at Stillwater. An inconclusive battle was fought on 19th September in which the 20th, 21st and 62nd Foot fought off attacks for four hours. On 7th October the Americans counter-attacked and Burgoyne's tired, hungry but valiant soldiers could not prevail against the ever-increasing numbers opposing them. His situation was now acute. He faced overwhelming odds, his supplies were almost at an end and his rearward communications were being cut by partisans. He had heard on 21st September that Clinton was attempting to come to his aid up the Hudson but he knew this force could not be near enough to effectively relieve the pressure against him. He fell back to Saratoga, where he learned that another American detachment was now positioned across his rear at Fort Edward. With his effectives reduced to 3,500 starving men†, surrounded on all sides by nearly 20,000 Americans, Burgoyne saw he had no choice but surrender. On 17th October his men marched out of Saratoga with the honours of war on the understanding given by Gates, the American commander, that they would be sent to Boston for immediate repatriation to England. Gates' word was broken by the politicians of the Congress who condemned the surrendered army to a long spell of imprison-

† There were in addition over 1,000 sick and wounded.

ment under atrocious conditions. Burgoyne himself eventually went home where he was disowned by Germaine, the architect of his fate. Carleton, who himself had been slighted by Germaine, wrote of Saratoga: *"This unfortunate event, it is to be hoped, will in future prevent ministers from pretending to direct operations of war in a country at three thousand miles' distance, of which they have so little knowledge as not to be able to distinguish between good, bad or indifferent advices, or to give positive orders upon matters which from their nature are ever on the change".(3)*

Although the force surrendered at Saratoga was not large, the blow to British prestige had world-wide repercussions. In February 1778 France signed an alliance with the Congress, followed a year later by Spain and Holland declaring war on Britain. The vultures were beginning to gather over the expiring corpse but it would prove it had life in it yet. The centre of British attention now had perforce to focus on the sugar and spice islands of the West Indies, where Britain and her enemies all had possessions, which to the eighteenth century economies were of enormous strategic importance. Operations against the Americans had to be deferred. As the expansion of the Army, grudgingly forced on British politicians by the new world crisis, would take time to effect, Clinton, now commander-in-chief following Howe's resignation, was ordered to make troops available for the West Indies and in Florida, and to withdraw from Philadelphia to New York. Washington, who had made good use of the winter to reform his army with the aid of Prussian drill-masters, moved against him, but Clinton carried out his retirement with some skill and by 5th July was back in New York.

Successful operations in the West Indies depended entirely upon naval supremacy. Throughout 1778 this was enjoyed by the Royal Navy, resulting in the well-devised capture of St. Lucia, where five companies of light infantry, all veterans from America, caused the French 1,600 casualties for the loss of only 13 killed. However, with the arrival of a French fleet at the end of 1778 and the Spanish entry into the war, the Royal Navy's resources became overstretched, and with fleets in the Atlantic, the Channel and the Bay of Bengal, it was unable to maintain supremacy in the Caribbean. Hence it bcame a matter of small British garrisons having to hold on where they could with no hope of a counter-offensive. Between 1779 and 1782 a number of islands were lost and the whole of Florida fell into Spanish hands. Yellow fever proved as fatal as in the Seven Years War.

While these operations were going on and a stalemate ensued around New York, Germaine had conceived the idea in 1778 of exploiting the then current naval supremacy to open a new front against the Americans in the southern states, which were supposedly highly loyalist. In November 1778 Colonel Campbell, with a force of Highlanders,† Hessians, and Provincials, captured Savannah; by the end of 1779, Georgia had been cleared of rebels and a Franco-American attack on Savannah replused. Clinton then followed from New York with a force of 8,000 and by May had captured Charleston in South Carolina, taking 6,000 prisoners. He returned to New York, leaving Cornwallis to subdue the Carolinas, an area of some 75,000 square miles with only 4,000 men. Cornwallis' paucity of numbers was supposed to be counter-balanced by the raising of loyalist militia, but in the event this support was to prove sadly lacking and far outweighed by the multiplicity of rebel guerilla bands, which were greatly to harass all Cornwallis' operations.

His force included British and German infantry and two of the best loyalist units brought from New York, both of mixed light horse and light infantry: Simcoe's Queen's Rangers and the British Legion under Barnastre Tarleton, a British officer of great ability in the command of light troops. His Legion included a troop of the 17th Light Dragoons. He demonstrated his skill at the opening of Cornwallis' campaign by his pursuit and destruction of a small American force after a march of 105 miles in 54 hours.

Cornwallis' main offensive opened in August 1780 with his resounding defeat of General Gates at Camden, where the light infantry, the 23rd and 33rd Foot showed they had nothing to learn from the Americans in the arts of woodland fighting. He pressed on into North Carolina but the defeat of his flanking column under Major Ferguson,* plus a shortage of supplies and harassment by guerillas in his rear, forced him to retire to Winnsborough. Reinforced in December by two composite battalions of Foot Guards, the 82nd+ and some Hessians, he advanced again in January 1781. He was now opposed by the able Nathaniel Greene who retreated steadily, leading the British ever deeper into North Carolina, as guerillas menaced their flanks and rear. The pursuit of over 200 miles left Cornwallis' troops exhausted and short of supplies, and the British commander had no choice but to retreat. The roles of the two armies were now reversed as Greene, reinforced to double the British strength, took up the pursuit. On 15th March they met at Guildford Courthouse. Despite their fatigue the British fought with courage and skill in the thick woods and eventually drove the Americans from the field after a desperate battle lasting four hours. However the fight had cost Cornwallis a quarter of his strength and he had to fall back to Wilmington on the coast, leaving South Carolina open to Greene, who proceeded to mop up the isolated British garrisons there and in Georgia. By the end of the year the Americans had recovered the whole area except for a coastal strip between Charleston and Savannah.

† Two battalions of the 71st (disbanded 1783)

* The designer of an early breech-loading rifle which he issued to his detachment during the war.

+ Disbanded 1783.

7307-93

Charles, Marquis Cornwallis, in Lieut-General's plain coat. Stipple engraving by B.Smith after I.S. Copley RA Published by J & J Boyden, September 1st 1798.

6612-4-1

George Eliott Lord Heathfield (1717-1790), background of Gibraltar   Portrait, oil on canvas, by A. Poggi c1783

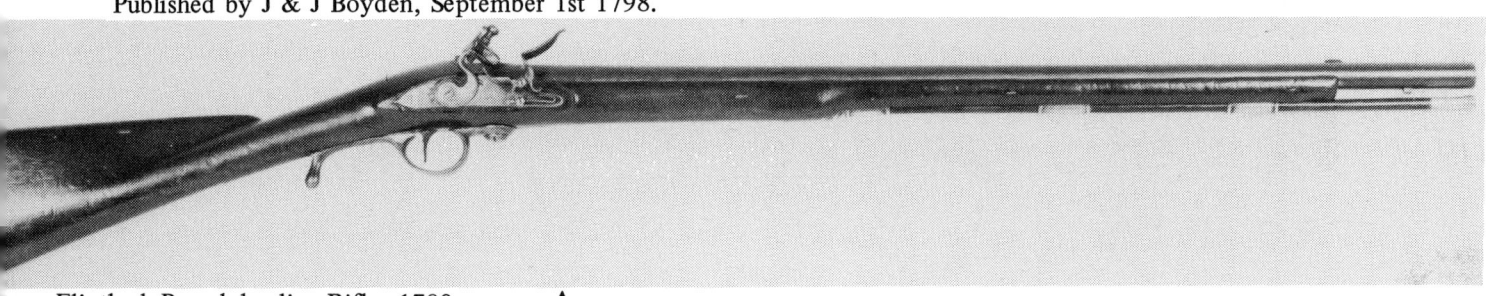

...son Flintlock Breech-loading Rifle c1780
...by Joseph Hunt   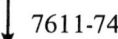 7611-74

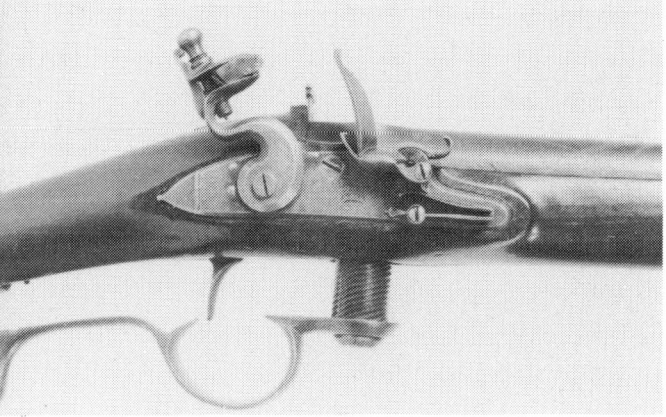

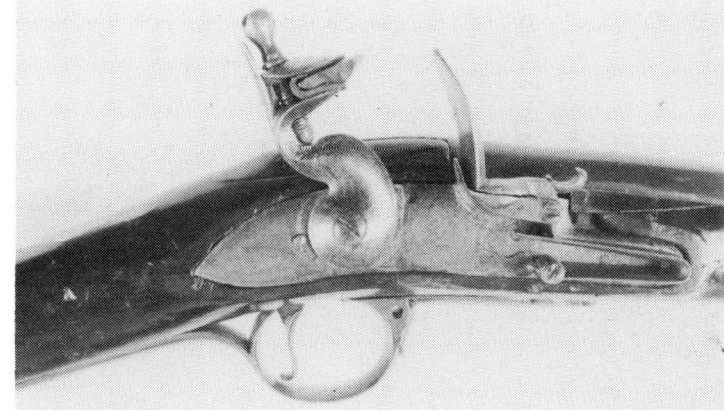

Musket, Flintlock, Long Land Pattern
Lock dated 1742   7403-130

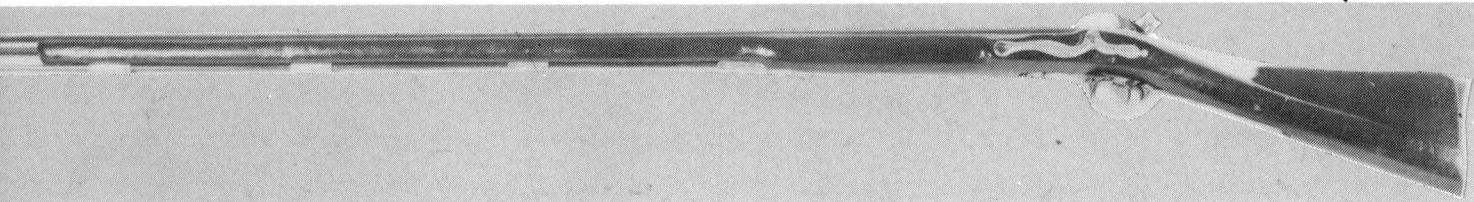

General Eliott at the Siege of Gibraltar, September 14th 1782

Painting, oil on canvas, by G. Carter

No aid was forthcoming from the Carolinas for Cornwallis. After a complex, three-cornered exchange of correspondence between himself, Clinton in New York and Germaine in London, which left everyone at cross purposes, he advanced north into Virginia to link up with a small British force operating near the mouth of the Chesapeake. Following some inconclusive operations against the Frenchman, Lafayette, and the arrival of American reinforcements, Cornwallis retreated to the coast so as to be near the protection of the Royal Navy and fortified himself at Yorktown in early August 1781. Meanwhile Washington, then facing Clinton at New York, had sent requests for aid to the French fleet in the West Indies under Admiral de Grasse. Then, leaving a force to hold Clinton's attention, he concentrated his own army of 9,500 with the 7,000 French troops of Rochambeau and marched south to join Lafayette, now watching Cornwallis in Yorktown. In early September de Grasse defeated a weak British naval force and Cornwallis, instead of having the Royal Navy at his back, found himself blockaded in Yorktown by the French fleet. A fortnight later Washington and Rochambeau arrived to close the trap on the landward side. With about 7,000 men, which included a large number of sick in hospital, Cornwallis held out against 20,000 Franco-Americans for three weeks, sustained by reports that Clinton was sailing to his aid. But with no sign of Clinton, nearly a third of his force incapacitated by sickness or wounds, and most of his guns out of action, he surrendered. On 19th October 1781, with their bands playing "The World Turned Upside Down", his British and German troops marched out of Yorktown into captivity between ranks of the victorious French and Americans. Five days later Clinton arrived but, finding Yorktown in enemy hands, sailed back to New York. There he held out for another two years but all military operations in America were virtually at an end and the American colonies lost. The campaign in the West Indies dragged on with increasing lack of success for Britain and only across the Atlantic did any gleam of victory shine on British arms.

In 1778 the activities of American privateers, and especially the raids on the Scottish and Cumberland coasts by the daring John Paul Jones, led to the raising in Scotland of regiments of Fencible Infantry, that is to say regular troops enlisted for home service only and for the duration of hostilities. In Ireland voluntary associations of Protestants were formed for local defence. When Spain joined France in 1779, an invasion of Britain seemed imminent and further regiments of Fencibles and Volunteers were raised, many of them at private expense. Fortunately the Franco-Spanish fleet was blown out of the Channel by an easterly gale. In the same year France contemplated a descent on the Channel Islands but it was not until two years later that such a project was undertaken. After a surprise night attack on Jersey in January 1781, a French force captured the British governor who agreed to surrender the island. But a young major, Francis Pierson, aged only 24, rallied the garrison and led his own regiment, the 95th, together with the 78th Highlanders† and the Jersey Militia, to attack the French, completely routing them but losing his life at the very moment of victory.+

In the Mediterranean Spain set its hand to the conquest of the British garrisons at Minorca and Gibraltar. At Minorca General Murray, Wolfe's brigadier at Quebec, disposed of only two British battalions, the 51st and 61st, and two of Hanoverians, men already weakened by fever. Attacked in August 1781 by 16,000 French and Spanish troops, Murray held out for six months. In December his men were stricken by scurvy which spread like fire through the confined spaces of the fortresses. Still they fought on, crawling and even being carried to their posts by the fitter members of the garrison, until at last, on 5th February 1782, with only *"six hundred wasted, decrepit, figures" (4)* left, Murray surrendered. The fall of Minorca enabled the Spanish commander, the Duc de Crillon, to transfer his forces against Gibraltar, then already under siege.

In command at the Rock was Sir George Eliott, who since his appointment in 1777 had urged on the improvement of its fortifications. Apart from the Royal Artillery manning the guns of the fortress, Eliott had as garrison the 12th, 39th, 56th and 58th Foot, later reinforced by the 72nd, 73rd* and three Hanoverian regiments; one of the latter, Hardenberg's, had shared the glory of Minden with the 12th Foot. In June 1779 Spain began a blockade which soon caused shortages within the garrison. The British retaliated by opening fire on the blockaders. On 12th September: *"An officer's lady was encouraged to discharge the first gun, and having taken a lighted match pronounced in a true heroic style, 'Britons strike home', and immediately every battery bellowed with rage, and vomited forth the most tremendous flames".(5)* The Spaniards made no attempt to begin siege operations until November 1780 but Eliott's supply problem grew steadily more acute, bringing hunger and disease, until in April 1781 a convoy of stores got through the blockade. On the very day of its arrival the Spanish batteries opened a bombardment which they were to keep up without intermission for 15 months.

---

† 95th, raised 1780, disbanded 1783. The 78th was re-numbered 72nd in 1783, later becoming the 1st Seaforth Highlanders.

* The subject of a painting by Copley in the Tate Gallery.

+ 72nd Manchester Volunteers, raised by public subscription in Manchester in 1777, disbanded 1784. 73rd Highlanders, disbanded in 1783.

97th Foot 1794-96
Drummer's fur cap.   6609-64-1

Light Company Officer's cap, 5th Regiment c1775
Military Heritage Museum, Lewes.

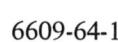

The Death of Major Pierson, Jersey, 8th Jan. 1781   6705-4-3
Line engraving by J. Heath after J.S. Copley Published by J.O.J. Boydell April 1796

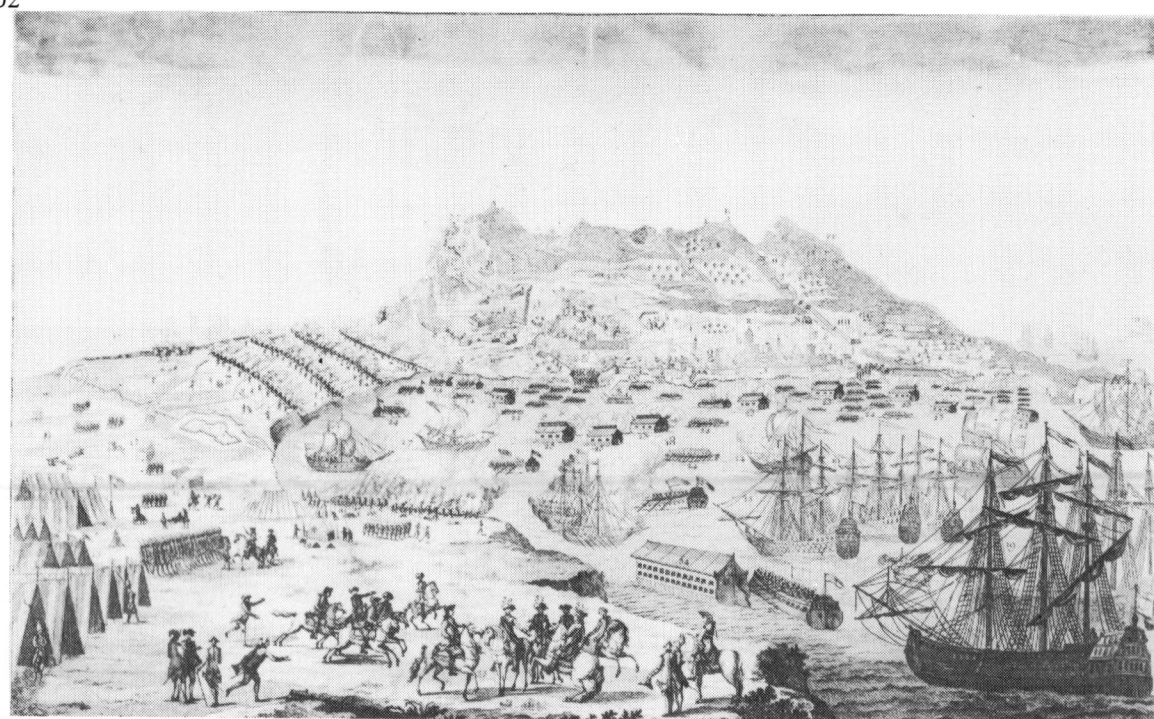

A view of the Rock and Town of Gibraltar 1782   Contemporary line engraving   7102-33-180

Sergeant Ancell of the 58th wrote: *"Between the land and sea fires we scarce dare close our eyes. The hurry of the times, the noise of the mortars, howitzers and cannon render the mind so confused; shot and shells are my near companions; smoke and wounded brother-soldiers are constantly in view; we have heavy duty, hard watchings, and little rest".*

Some of the infantry were trained as additional gunners while a company of snipers was formed from the best marksmen. The Royal Artillery were constantly in action with counter-bombardment but for most of the infantry the siege was an endless round of guards, picquets, working and carrying parties to improve and repair the defences. On 26th November 1781 Eliott launched a night sortie against the Spanish batteries. In two hours the light and grenadier companies, the 12th and the Hanoverians attacked and destroyed the works and magazines it had taken the Spaniards months to construct. This gave the garrison some respite but the works were repaired and the siege went on. The conditions under which the men endured led to occasional breakdowns in discipline and Eliott, a genial and humane man, had to hang and flog offenders to maintain order and vigilance; but for every man he punished, he always had words of cheer for the remainder. In September 1782 the French and Spaniards assembled a fleet of 44 warships and ten immense floating batteries to hammer the garrison into submission. Supported by the land guns this armada opened fire on the 13th. All day and far into the night the bombardment rained down upon the Rock but undismayed the British fought their guns, sinking the supposedly indestructible floating batteries with red-hot shot, and blazing away across the isthmus to deter any land assault. At last the enemy fire died away and Sergeant Ancell could write, *"the battle is our own".*

No land attack was ever attempted against Gibraltar and, though the artillery exchange continued for several months, the Spaniards' will was waning. In October Lord Howe's fleet escorted reinforcements and supplies into the harbour, and the garrison easily rode out the remaining months of the siege until news came of a general peace being signed on 2nd February 1783. By his unswerving example and determination Eliott had sustained his garrison in a defence lasting three years, seven months and twelve days, and shed some lustre on British arms amid a series of unfortunate and bitter reverses. Though no battle honours grace the colours of British regiments to commemorate the victories so ably and valiantly won in America in the face of overall defeat, the resistance of those at Gibraltar was rewarded with the right to bear upon their badges, colours and appointments, the name of the fortress they had defended and its arms of the Castle and Key — the first honour to be so awarded to a number of regiments.†

† The honour "Emsdorff" had been officially approved for a single regiment, the 15th Light Dragoons, in 1768. The word "Gibraltar" was granted to the regiments concerned on 14th April 1784, the Castle and Key on 2nd May 1836. Other honours for battles fought prior to the Great Siege were all awarded after 1784. Minden 1759, for example, was not granted until 1801; the Marlburian victories not until 1881.

CHAPTER 9
BRITAIN AT BAY
1793-1808

When France decided to support republicanism in America in 1778, little did the King and the ruling class realise they were helping to advance a political philosophy which a decade later would turn their own world upside down. Within three and a half years of the outbreak of the French Revolution the King and the moderate revolutionaries, who had hoped to establish a constitutional monarchy, had all been swept away in a welter of blood, as the extreme Jacobin faction sought by terror to impose their rule within France and to deter their enemies without. By 1792 the ancient monarchies of Europe were on the march against the dangerously subversive monster that had erupted in their midst, but their stiff and formal arrays proved no match against the new phenomenon of a nation in arms. The explosive citizen armies of the Revolution made up for their lack of equipment and training by their ideological fervour and were in any case stiffened by the old royal army which had undergone considerable modernization since the American war. The two coalesced into a type of army hitherto unknown in Europe, with leaders and led drawn from a complete cross-section of the French nation, and characterized by enthusiastic morale and a much higher individual intelligence than that found in the ranks of the old professional, monarchical armies. It fought a new, rapid and ruthless kind of war, its units grouped into wide-ranging formations living off the land, and bewildering its opponents, so long accustomed to the stately measures of eighteenth century campaigning with their formalities of winter quarters and ponderous sieges. It fought at first in defence of the Revolution and France's frontiers, but gradually its successes inspired in the new republic a thirst for conquest, far more overwhelming in its power and inspiration than anything dreamed of by Louis XIV. To this mood was harnessed the entire resources of the French nation, first by its ferocious new rulers and ultimately by Napoleon Bonaparte. In her determination to impose her new order far beyond her frontiers, France plunged Europe into war for nearly a quarter of a century. Only Britain would remain constant against a tyranny that threatened to engulf the world.

When Britain entered the war in 1793 an expeditionary force under the Duke of York was sent to the Low Countries to assist the Austrians and Prussians against the French who had invaded the Austrian Netherlands. Corporal George Robertson of the Royal Artillery hopefully reassured his family that *"there is none equal to the British Army"*, but added with caution, *"God knows how it will be this war".(1)* His caution was not misplaced for the Army was in no condition to undertake a campaign. Though the contemporary water-colours of Edward Dayes show British regiments at one of their most elegant periods, underneath the finery they were suffering from ten years' financial stringency and neglect. For the Army, the previous decade had been not unlike the reign of George I after Marlborough's wars, with establishments reduced, political interference, inefficient officers dependent on money and influence for their advancement, an undermining of discipline, bad recruiting both in quality and quantity, and indifference to the men and their requirements. That there was gold among the dross would be proved in the years that followed. In addition to the many rich young fops who purchased lieutenant-colonelcies and whose incompetence was demonstrated in the Low Countries, there were also the likes of the 20-year-old Edward Paget, who commanded *"an uncommon fine Battalion"(2)* of the 28th, or Lieutenant-Colonel Arthur Wellesley of the 33rd, then embarking on his first campaign. Nevertheless the general state to which the Army had been reduced by neglect and poor administration is best summed up in the words of the Duke of York's Adjutant-General who wrote: *"We are the most undisciplined, the most ignorant, the worst provided army that ever took the field".(3)*

When hostilities first broke out British ministers failed to appreciate the nature of revolutionary warfare and William Pitt, the Prime Minister, fell back on the traditional methods of subsidizing allied armies, sending limited British land forces to the continent, and using sea power to launch the main military effort against French colonies, primarily in the ill-fated West Indies. The major fighting in that theatre took place between 1793-98, with British troops having to contend with negro uprisings as well as French resistance, but operations continued as long as 1810 and to a lesser extent up to 1815. French power in the islands was virtually eliminated, but at appalling cost and with no effect on the French ability to wage war in Europe. Between 1793 and 1815 Britain

"Light Infantry of the Foot Guards. Four of these rais'd Companys embarked to join the Duke of York in the Siege of Valenciennes July 9th Coloured etching by T.W. published by S.W. Fores, 1793 7311-83

"The Grand attack on Valenciennes by the combined armies under the command of HRH the Duke of York, on the twenty-fifth of July,1793". Stipple engraving by P.J. de Loutherbourg after W. Bromley, 1801
7102-33-407

An officer, Light Infantry or Light Company of Line Infantry c1800. Watercolour, artist unidentified c1800.

'His Royal Highness Frederick Duke of York in the uniform of Colonel of the Coldstream Guards'. Watercolour by Robert Dighton Senior c1793.

lost 70,000 Europeans dead in the West Indies, of which less than ten per cent were due to enemy action. After 1798 the burden on British troops was mitigated by the formation of the West India Regiments, but even these indigenous soldiers suffered 5,000 fatal casualties. The total number of sick, wounded, missing and dead from the West Indian campaigns, excluding those incurred during the dreadful sea voyages to and from the theatre, has been calculated at the horrifying figure of 424,000†. Recruiting for the Army was difficult enough without such losses,not to mention their effect on the minds of men warned for West Indian service and potential recruits. Regiments, notably some raised in the Highlands, mutinied rather than face the yellow fever.

The Duke of York's army in the Low Countries eventually consisted of 22 battalions and 15 under-strength cavalry regiments. Many of the men were untrained, ill-equipped, hastily-raised recruits, with young, newly-joined officers who knew and cared nothing for their duty, and owed their place, sometimes even command of the green battalions, to political interest or the depth of the parental purse. The arrangements made by the Government for transport and commissariat were a disgrace and medical support almost non-existant.Fortunately there were a few sound regiments, like the Guards, the 27th and 28th, and the cavalry, though weak, performed well. York's army was further increased by numbers of solid Hessian mercenaries and various foreign regiments in British pay raised by French 'emigrés', German princelings and sundry adventurers. Between 1793 and 1802 about 80 of the latter were formed, of all arms. Some, like the Loyal Emigrants, were excellent and others, like Löwenstein's Jägers and the York Chasseurs, did good work as light troops. Against these there were units which were little more than armed gangs of criminals and deserters.

The campaign began in the time-honoured way of reducing fortresses. At first all went well, but after the Duke of York had failed to take Dunkirk,due to insufficient men and a lack of siege guns,a rapid French advance, with huge columns covered by swarms of skirmishers, compelled him to retreat to avoid being cut off from his base at Ostend. The following year a furious French offensive split the allies, forcing the Austrians to retreat eastwards, while the British and Prussians withdrew into Holland. The Revolutionary armies were no respecters of winter quarters and in the bitter weather of 1794-95 the retreat went on into north Germany. The army suffered dreadful privations: *"The cold was so intense that our breath was freezing as soon as emitted, and lodged in heaps of ice on our faces and on the men's blankets that were wrapped about their heads".(4)* At last the sorely-tried troops, now little more than a starving rabble, reached their transports at Bremen and embarked for home.

The campaign had been a disaster and an indictment of the politicians who had failed to maintain an army fit for war and provide it with the essentials necessary for its survival, let alone success. Only the never-failing fighting spirit of individual regiments lighten this dismal episode: the colonel of the 14th Foot ordering his drummers to strike up the Jacobin air, *"Ça Ira"*, to cheer his men into the attack at Famars*; the big guardsmen of the 1st Guards cuffing and booting the dirty, little Republican soldiers out of their positions at Lincelles as though they were dispersing a London mob; the amazing charge against six battalions in square by the 15th Light Dragoons at Villers-en-Cauchies; and the total overthrow of the French infantry at Beaumont by the Blues, the 1st, 3rd and 5th Dragoon Guards, Royal Dragoons and 16th Light Dragoons.

The chief weakness of the Army was the division of responsibility between the Secretary-at-War, the political executive chief with his legion of civilian clerks at the War Office; the Treasury; the Commander-in-Chief at the Horse Guards, provided with a proper headquarters staff for the first time in 1795; and the Master-General of the Ordnance, responsible for all matters concerned with artillery and engineers. In addition Pitt appointed, in 1794, a senior minister with full responsibility for military affairs: the first Secretary of State for War. This was Henry Dundas who unfortunately had to combine his new duties with those of three other departments unconnected with the Army. His endeavours during the latter part of the Flanders campaign had inspired little confidence, and it was not until the appointment to this post in 1805 of Lord Castlereagh, that Britain acquired a really able War Minister.

In 1795 the Duke of York replaced the now aged and infirm Amherst as Commander-in-Chief and soon proved that, though an unlucky commander in the field, he was an admirable administrator. The later successes of the Army in the Napoleonic Wars owed much to the improvements York made to the military system as he found it. The abysmal ignorance and inefficiency of many officers during the late campaign had stemmed from the purchase system, in which commissions could be bought even for children, and the custom of rewarding recruitment with commissioned rank. There was little York could do at the time to abolish these methods of commissioning which, despite their obvious defects, also had advantages†. However he set a minimum age limit

† See Dr R. N. Buckley, *"The Destruction of the British Army in the West Indies 1793-1815"*, J.S.A.H.R., Vol.LVI,p.79. The term "sick" only refers to major hospital cases, not men sick in quarters or barracks.

* This tune passed into the British military music of the Napoleonic Wars as *"The Downfall of Paris"*.

+ For these and other problems facing the Duke of York, and his reforms, see Richard Glover, *"Peninsular Preparation"* (1963).

of 16 for officers and demanded a recommendation from a field officer for any candidate for a commission. In future no subaltern could purchase a captaincy before completing two years' service, while six years were mandatory for a majority. He instituted a system of confidential reports on officers and did what he could to advance the able but needy. The whole matter of officers' promotions and appointments passed from the hands of the political Secretary-at-War into those of the Military Secretary, a staff officer working under the Commander-in-Chief. In 1802 the Royal Military College was founded at High Wycombe, with a Senior Department for training officers in staff duties (later the Staff College), and a Junior Department for training potential officers (later the R.M.C.Sandhurst)*. Lastly York established a tighter control over all officers by insisting upon the observance of the proper channels of communication and command, but he also made himself approachable to any officer with a genuine grievance by holding weekly military levées. All his measures concerned with officers were designed to bring them under discipline and improve their military competence.

Discipline among the rank and file was maintained by widespread use of the lash. Brutal though this may seem today, it was less so in the context of the times and was considered by men of all ranks, including the better stamp of soldier, as the only effective sanction on the very rough material from which the ranks were recruited. Later in the Napoleonic Wars large numbers of good men were inducted into the Regular Army from the Militia, which was conscripted by ballot, but, in the 1790s and before, most recruits came from the dregs of the working class, many of whom were rogues and criminals. In reply to the opponents of flogging, James Anton, an N.C.O. of the 42nd, wrote: *"The good soldier thanks you not for such philanthropy; the incorrigible laughs at your humanity, despises your clemency, and meditates only how he may gratify his naturally vicious propensities".(5)* The Duke of York nevertheless endeavoured to introduce more humanity into the maintenance of discipline, by limiting the maximum award of regimental courts martial to 300 lashes, and by exhorting regimental officers to pay greater attention to the prevention of crime. He wrote: *"The timely interference of the officer, his personal intercourse and acquaintance with his men (which are sure to be repaid by the soldiers' confidence and attachment) and, above all, his personal example, are the only efficacious means of preventing military offences".(6)*

The disasters of the Low Countries campaign had highlighted the regiments' faulty training. Until 1792 there had been no standard tactical drill in the Army, which made the handling of several battalions in a brigade difficult and uncertain. Furthermore the looser formations adopted in the forest fighting of the American War were thought by some unsuitable against continental armies in the open terrain of Europe. In 1792 a drill book devised by General Sir David Dundas and based on the exact movements of the Prussian Army was adopted as the official manual for the infantry.+ Many thought it too mechanical but York insisted on compliance to ensure standard tactical manoeuvres throughout all regiments. In 1795 a similar manual was introduced for the cavalry.

One of the chief defects of Dundas' regulations was his omission of light infantry. York's experience in Flanders of the French skirmishers, masking the movements of their columns, had impressed upon him how light infantry techniques had been neglected in the British service notwithstanding the high standards achieved in America. He set out to restore the light infantry companies of regiments to their true function as a protective and delaying screen, behind which the battalion could move or deploy from column into the maximum fire-productive formation of the line. He established experimental camps of exercise for light troops and introduced into the Army the rifle, a weapon of greater range and accuracy than the musket†, which had been used successfully in skirmishing tactics by German 'jäger' troops and the Americans. In 1797 the 5th Battalion of the 60th, largely composed of Germans, was equipped with rifles and put into a green uniform as a rudimentary form of camouflage. In 1800 York formed an *"Experimental Corps of Riflemen"* under Colonel Coote Manningham to train selected detachments from regiments of the Line with the view of providing each regiment with a platoon of green-jacketed riflemen as scouts and snipers. While still under training this corps was sent on an expedition to Ferrol and having thus served as a regiment in the field, so it remained. In 1801 it was numbered as the 95th Foot or Rifle Corps. Within ten years it had become a 'corps d'elite' of three battalions and after 1815, as a reward for its outstanding services, was taken out of the Line and styled the Rifle Brigade. A major contribution to the development of light troops was a pamphlet written by a German officer in the British service, the Baron de Rottenburg. These *"Regulations for the Exercise of Riflemen and Light Infantry"* formed the basis for the training of all such companies and, later, whole regiments of light infantry. In 1803 York appointed Major-General John Moore to train a brigade at Shorncliffe, consisting of the 43rd, 52nd and 95th, in light

---

* The Royal Military Academy at Woolwich had been founded in 1741 for the training of artillery and engineer officers. After 1945 the R.M.A and R.M.C. were combined to form the Royal Military Academy, Sandhurst, where all officers are now trained.

+ *"Rules and Regulations for the Movement of His Majesty's Army".*

† The rifling, or grooves, in the barrel made it slower to load than the smooth-bore musket.

Landing of British troops under Sir Ralph Abercromby and Vice-Admiral Mitchell on the Texel, Holland 27th August 1799. 63C
Painting, oil on canvas, by R.Dodd.

The Battle of Alexandria, 21st March 1801
Painting, oil on canvas, after P.J. de Loutherbourg.

690

tactics. Moore, whose ideal was *"the thinking, fighting man"* rather than the Prussian-type automaton, believed that, providing officers were trained and knew their duty, men could and should be encouraged to give of their best out of self-respect and not simply deterred from evil by harsh punishments. By applying all his undoubted brilliance as a trainer of men, he turned his Shorncliffe regiments into that magnificent fighting formation, the Light Brigade, later Division, of the Peninsular War. Three years later de Rottenburg himself converted three other battalions, the 68th, 71st and 85th, into light infantry regiments.

The cavalry in 1795 included 21 regiments of light dragoons, of which three would be converted into hussars in 1806†, in imitation of a type long popular in continental armies. However the distinction between the light cavalry of the British service and their comrades of the dragoon guards and dragoons was largely one of title and appearance, since Dundas' cavalry manual prescribed the same drill for all. The training of cavalry in England at this date was impaired by the lack of sufficiently open ground on which to train more than a couple of squadrons, hence few officers of the rank of lieutenant-colonel and above had experience of handling sizeable bodies of cavalry.

The Ordnance arms were fortunate in having the abilities of the Duke of Richmond as Master-General. He formed the Royal Horse Artillery to provide close support for cavalry, and relieved the foot artillery from their reliance on civilian drivers by raising the Royal Corps of Artillery Drivers, ill-disciplined though they proved to be. In 1788 he formed the engineering branch of the Ordnance into an all-officer Corps of Royal Engineers, which provided officers as required for a body of military workmen, known as the Royal Military Artificers. In 1812 the latter would become the Royal Corps of Sappers and Miners. Richmond also founded the Ordnance Survey to provide a map-making organization and much was done during his administration to improve the design and production of ammunition and explosives.

The effectiveness of all these reforms took time to mature and meanwhile the war with France still had to be fought. By 1797 Britain stood alone, Austria and Prussia having made peace. France had occupied all the Low Countries, the Rhineland and northern Italy. Only the sea and the Royal Navy stood between Britain and invasion, the fear of which evoked considerable patriotic response. As in the American war, Fencible regiments were formed; patriotic associations raised units of Volunteers and Yeomanry cavalry; and the regiments of county Militia were embodied by ballot for compulsory service in home defence. A small French force actually landed in south Wales but was easily rounded up by the Castlemartin Yeomanry. A greater danger occurred the following year when the initial success of a large-scale rebellion in Ireland encouraged the French to despatch a force to the rebels' aid. The latter were beaten at Vinegar Hill by General Lake so that, when the French arrived, they found no Irish support and were forced to surrender at Castlebar. The Irish Militia, however, had not shown up well and the large numbers of Irish filling the ranks of regular regiments as the Army expanded made it unwise to send such regiments against their fellow countrymen. Much of the work had to be done by English and Scots Fencibles and foreign corps.

In 1798 Bonaparte, now France's leading general, led an expedition to conquer Egypt and Syria. He had no sooner advanced on Cairo when a squadron under Nelson attacked and destroyed his fleet in Aboukir Bay, leaving him stranded in Egypt. This great victory of the Nile restored British sea power in the Mediterranean, led to the capture of Minorca, and so roused Europe as to enable Pitt to form the Second Coalition of Britain, Russia, Turkey, Austria and Naples. Allied hopes rose again as the Austrians and Russians drove the French out of Italy and Switzerland.

In June 1799 Pitt and Henry Dundas conceived a plan for the recapture of Holland in conjunction with a force of 18,000 Russians, paid for with British gold. The lifting of the invasion threat by the French adventure to Egypt and the destruction of their fleet now made the services of the home defence units less essential. Therefore when large numbers of militiamen volunteered for European service, partly out of patriotic spirit and partly to earn the ten pounds bounty offered for such service, they were hastily drafted into regiments of the Line. These men were good material, far better than the normal infantry recruit, but many lacked training. Instead of allowing them a further period of training, in which they could be thoroughly assimilated into their new regiments, they were packed off by Pitt and Dundas as soon as they were assembled to Holland. When they arrived in late August, a force of 12,000 men under the able and popular Sir Ralph Abercromby had already effected a landing against stiff opposition on the Helder Peninsula and captured the Dutch fleet. Hampered by a lack of transport and supplies with which, as usual, Abercromby had been but ill provided by the Government, the British commander was unable to follow up this early success. On 10th September the French commander, Brune, counter-attacked but his headlong offensive was thrown back, chiefly by the steadiness of the Foot Guards and the gallantry of the newly-arrived militiamen of the 20th and 40th. Abercromby then received more reinforcements of largely untrained militia but had to hand over to the Duke of York who had been sent out to command the combined Anglo-Russian forces, the first divisions of the latter arriving at the same time. Unfortunately Dundas failed to send administrative backing for such a force and desperate shortages of transport,

---

† 7th, 10th and 15th.

clothing, supplies and medical support soon became apparent, aggravated by the worsening weather. Two whole brigades did not even have greatcoats. Once again ministers had embarked upon a campaign under the delusion that all that was required for an army in the field was numbers. Furthermore the Dutch were nothing like as friendly as had been anticipated and the Russians were ill-trained and badly disciplined. Although the Duke pressed on and again defeated the French at Egmont-op-zee, he found any further advance increasingly hazardous. The approach of winter, the worsening supply situation over extended and inadequate rearward routes, the lack of shelter in a desolate, water-seamed landscape under everlasting cold winds and rain, all persuaded him he must retreat to his base at the Helder. Luckily the French proposed an armistice and York was able to evacuate his army from Holland.

The campaign had achieved little other than the capture of the Dutch fleet but it had demonstrated some hopeful signs for the Army's future. An up-and-coming cavalry leader, Lord Paget †, had displayed dash and skill at the head of his own regiment, the 7th Light Dragoons. John Moore's command of an always steady brigade * had marked him as one of the most promising men in the army. The indomitable spirit and reliability of the Foot Guards is epitomised by an incident during a withdrawal when the important village of Krabbendam had been abandoned by other troops. The 1st Guards were ordered to return and hold it but their commander, Maitland, demurred on the grounds that his men were exhausted, had suffered heavy casualties and were short of ammunition. *"At this moment a grenadier, lifting his chin from the muzzle of the musket on which he was leaning, said in a loud and steady voice, 'Give us some more cartridges and we will see what can be done'. Maitland cried, 'Shoulder Arms!' and they marched for Krabbendam".(7)* The raw militiamen, with inexperienced officers, had shown up well despite the miserable conditions; they and their like would prove a valuable source of manpower for the Army. The campaign witnessed the baptism of fire of the Royal Horse Artillery and also the first appearance of another new corps — the Royal Waggon Train +. Having only been formed when the campaign began, their ability to rectify Abercromby's shortage of transport had been limited but their existence would, in future, help to overcome the drawbacks of hired civilian drivers.

As the eighteenth century drew to a close, Bonaparte, having abandoned his army in Egypt and sailed to France, seized power as First Consul. With his return France went on to the offensive, throwing the Russians out of Switzerland, defeating one Austrian army in Germany and attacking another in northern Italy. The Second Coalition was collapsing. The only response of British ministers was a series of futile, pin-pricking raids based on naval supremacy. In May 1800 Henry Dundas appointed Abercromby to command the land forces in the Mediterranean, based on Gibraltar and Minorca, saddling him with a multitude of tasks quite beyond the resources at his disposal, with objectives as far apart as Teneriffe and Malta, not to mention assistance to the Austrians in northern Italy and French royalists on the Riviera. In May and June Bonaparte defeated the Austrians at Marengo and Ulm and forced an armistice upon them. It was not until October, after more fruitless operations of which only the capture of Malta was of any significnace, that Dundas devised a worthwhile task for Abercromby's army and even that held considerable risks. With 17,000 men Abercromby was to reduce the 27,000-strong French army in Egypt, in co-operation with the Turks and supported by a small force from India and the Cape of Good Hope †† under General Baird.

The plan was for Abercromby to land near Alexandria and advance on Cairo, while Baird was to approach across the desert from the Red Sea. John Moore was sent to assess the Turkish forces and soon reported them to be worthless. Between December and January 1801 Abercromby prepared his troops with careful rehearsals at Marmorice Bay near Rhodes for an assault landing. Despite the hazardous nature of the undertaking the men were in high spirits. Edward Paget of the 28th wrote: *"There is a certain devil in this army that will carry it through thick and thin. It is the first fair trial between Englishmen and Frenchmen during the whole of this war and at no former period of our history did John Bull ever hold his enemy cheaper".(8)* The army contained some fine troops: a brigade of Guards, some excellent foreign regiments, chiefly Swiss** three battalions of Highlanders, the 42nd, 79th and 92nd, a well-trained battalion of light infantry, the 90th, and 15 more regiments of foot in good order, of which the cream formed the body known as the Reserve ++ under Moore. The cavalry were drawn from the 11th, 12th and 26th Light Dragoons, though rather short of horses.

On 8th March Moore's Reserve stormed ashore at Aboukir Bay and drove the French from their positions among the sand-dunes. The march on Alexandria began and a sharp action was fought on the 13th at Mandora

---

†   Later Earl of Uxbridge and Marquess of Anglesey. Elder brother of Edward Paget of the 28th (see above).
*   1st, 25th, 49th Foot, 79th and 92nd Highlanders.
+   The forerunner of the Royal Army Service Corps, now Royal Corps of Transport.
†† Captured from the Dutch in 1795.
** Dillon's, de Roll's and the Minorca Regiment. Also the Corsican Rangers and Hompesch's Mounted Rifles.
++ 23rd, 28th, 40th (flank companies only), 42nd, 58th and Corsican Rangers.

where the 90th and 92nd, covering the advance, resisted determined attacks by French cavalry to give the rest of the force time to deploy. Abercromby then took up a defensive position four miles from Alexandria, with his right on the Mediterranean shore and his left on the edge of the dried-up Lake Mareotis. Moore held the right, with the 58th in some ruins on the shore, the 28th to their left front in a redoubt, and his other battalions ready to support this vital flank. The position was prolonged to the left by the Guards and two other brigades, while the remaining three and the cavalry formed a second line.

On the 21st, just before dawn, the French made a feint against the British left, but then hurled their main weight at the 28th and 58th to turn Moore's right flank. Heavy fighting ensued in the semi-darkness with Moore's supporting battalions joining the struggle. The Reserve held firm, even when the French cavalry was thrown in against them, and, with Stuart's foreign brigade coming forward, defeated all attempts to drive them from their positions †. Meanwhile other French attacks had been repulsed by the Guards. Everywhere the British musketry, delivered from a line only two ranks deep instead of the old three-deep arrangement, had proved decisive over the French columns. The impetus went out of the French attacks and they withdrew to Alexandria, leaving over a thousand dead on the field. The British lost 243 killed, mostly from the Reserve, but amongst them was Sir Ralph Abercromby.

Sir John Hely-Hutchinson took over command and, leaving 6,000 to contain the French in Alexandria, advanced on Cairo where the balance of the French army surrendered in mid-June. Having escorted his prisoners to the coast, he laid siege to Alexandria which finally capitulated on 26th August. Meanwhile Baird's force of five British and three sepoy battalions had made a staggering march of 400 miles across the desert in searing heat but its efforts had not been necessary. On 1st October Britain and France ended the Revolutionary War with the Peace of Amiens. The reformed British Army had enjoyed its first real success of the war and the French military writer, Jomini, considered that the Egyptian campaign marked *"l'époque de sa régénération"*. (9)

One of the dangers of the French presence in Egypt in 1798 had been its potential threat to India. Between 1790-92 the East India Company's old quarrel with the state of Mysore, under its ruler Tippoo Sultan, which had been dormant since 1784, burst into renewed hostilities. Lord Cornwallis, the defeated commander at Yorktown, was now Governor-General. He captured Bangalore and besieged Tippoo in his capital at Seringapatam. Tippoo sued for peace and lost half of Mysore to the Company and its Indian allies. Burning for revenge and encouraged by news of the outbreak of the Revolutionary War, he began to intrigue with the French who sent agents, money and military advisers. When Bonaparte began his conquest of the Near East in 1798 there was always present in his mind the possibility of an advance on India, an enterprise which would be greatly assisted by a rising against the British by ill-disposed rulers like Tippoo. However, the distant threat to India, posed by a French army astride the Near East, had not escaped the British authorities and, further alarmed by reports of Tippoo's flirtation with the French, they struck first in February 1799. From Bombay in the west and Madras in the east two British armies slowly converged on Seringapatam. Their combined forces totalled two King's and four Madras native cavalry regiments, eight King's infantry battalions, the Bombay Europeans, and 23 sepoy battalions. Among the European battalions was one Swiss regiment, de Meuron's, and the 33rd Foot, still under the command of Colonel Arthur Wellesley, whose elder brother, the Marquis, had recently been appointed Governor-General. After a laborious approach march greatly hampered by the enormous baggage trains and hordes of followers that always accompanied armies in India, the two forces met in mid-April and by the 19th Tippoo's great fortress was besieged. By 2nd May a breach had been made and two days later two columns, chiefly of British infantry, went into the assault. After some savage carnage in oppressive heat, the fortress fell. The atrocities that had been committed in the past on European prisoners by Tippoo ensured that no quarter was given and some 10,000 of his followers perished. Beneath the heaps of slain his own corpse was eventually found. With the fall of Mysore and the Nizam of Hyderabad completely under British domination, the whole of southern India was now controlled by the Company.

Northwards lay the warring princes of the Mahratta Confederacy, whose domains stretched from the Himalayas to Hyderabad and from the Bay of Bengal westwards to Gujerat. The Marquis Wellesley was determined to establish British supremacy over those vast areas; this could best be done by exploiting the internal rivalries of the various chieftains. Though the struggle with the Mahrattas forms no part of Britain's campaigns against Napoleonic France, it must be noted here since it was on the plains of central India that the Army's greatest commander of those campaigns fought his first battle as a general officer and one which, in later life, he always regarded as his best.

After the fall of Seringapatam Arthur Wellesley had remained in Mysore to restore order. On 29th April 1802 he was promoted major-general, though only in India. Later that year the defeat of one Mahratta chief, the Peshwa of Poona, by another gave the Governor-General the opportunity to intervene by supporting the

---

† For their gallantry in fighting off the French with their two ranks back to back, the 28th, later Gloucestershire Regiment, earned the right to wear a badge at the back as well as the front of their caps.

The Death of Col. Moorehouse, Madras Artillery, at the Siege of Bangalore 1791, showing men of 36th Regiment. Painting, oil on canvas, by Robert Home.

7

Seringapatam, the fortifications.
Photographs taken by J.A.C. Weller in 1968.

6911-

Peshwa. This alliance eventually united the other principal Mahratta chiefs, Holkar, Sindia and the Bhonsla of Berar against the British. While Lord Lake, the commander-in-chief in India, took command in the north, General Wellesley was ordered by his brother *"to restore the tranquillity of the Deccan".(10)*

In August 1803 he took Sindia's mighty hill fortress of Ahmednuggar so expeditiously that a Mahratta chief complained that the British *"came here in the morning, surveyed the wall, walked over it, killed the garrison and returned to breakfast".(11)* He headed off Sindia from an attack on Hyderabad and, in the course of advancing to catch the enemy infantry before they retired, came unexpectedly on the whole of Sindia's army camped along the north bank of the River Kaitna to the west of the village of Assaye. From his position on the south bank Wellesley could see that he was faced by a mass of some 30,000 Mahratta light horse on the enemy right with, on their left and extending as far as Assaye, 10,000 of Sindia's regular infantry with over 100 guns, trained, as he knew, by European instructors. With the addition of some irregular infantry this mighty host was about 40-50,000 strong. Against it he could only muster just over 7,000: the 19th Light Dragoons, the 74th and 78th Highlanders, three regiments of Madras native cavalry and five battalions of Madras infantry, with 14 guns of the Company's European artillery. To attack such a horde across a river barrier with men who had already marched 24 miles that day was a dreadful gamble, but to retreat was to risk being cut up on the march by swarms of Mahratta horse. His quick eye for ground spotted a possible ford a mile and a half east of the Mahratta left, leading to a triangle of ground about a mile wide, formed by the Kaitna and its tributary, the Juah, which ran back north-westwards round Assaye. He believed this triangle could provide a forming up area wide enough for him to deploy his small force, prior to rolling up the Mahratta line from the east. The plan depended on the proverbial slowness of Indian armies to react but, as he formed his two battle lines of infantry with cavalry in the rear, he saw the Mahratta infantry and guns rapidly changing front to meet the attack so that their right now rested on the Kaitna and their left on the Juah at Assaye. He sent orders to the commander of his right, Colonel Orrock, to avoid Assaye which was strongly held, and directed his attack on the enemy right and centre, calculating that once this was driven back the Mahratta round the village would retreat. In the teeth of a furious bombardment the 78th and the sepoys pushed forward with great determination, overrunning the enemy guns and driving the infantry before them, away from the Kaitna, back towards the Juah. But then disaster struck on the right. By some miscalculation Colonel Orrock led his troops, followed by the 74th, straight into the guns of Assaye. His sepoys broke back on the 74th, who were left exposed to a heavy fire from the village, followed by the Mahratta horse charging in on their flank. The Highlanders, hampered by the fleeing sepoys and a thick belt of cactus, fell in scores but the remainder rallied round their colours until salvation came from a charge by the 19th Light Dragoons and the 4th Madras Cavalry. Meanwhile Wellesley had wheeled his left wing round and, supported by the cavalry on his open flank, drove the enemy in front of him across the Juah after fierce and bloody fighting. The rest of the Mahratta army to the west, seeing their best infantry and their guns lost, made off to the north. It had been a very risky business but Wellesley throughout had remained calm and cool, always in control, despite being in the thick of the action and having two horses shot under him. The losses had been severe, especially in the 74th who in their gallant stand had suffered 384 casualties out of a strength of 500 and every officer, save one, killed or wounded.

After Assaye Wellesley continued his advance through Berar, again defeating the Mahrattas at Argaum and finally besieging the Bhonsla's hill fortress of Gawilghur. Its fall drove the Bhonsla to sue for peace and Wellesley's task in the Deccan had been successfully completed.

Meanwhile Lord Lake in the north had advanced on Delhi from Cawnpore against Sindia's main host. His force came from the Company's Bengal Army and included the 8th, 27th and 29th Light Dragoons but only one King's infantry battalion though a good one. *"Bring me my boots and the 76th Regiment of Foot,"* Lake said, *"and I am ready to go anywhere".(12)* In spite of facing odds of four to one, Lake attacked and routed the enemy outside Delhi. He then turned southwards after them, drove them out of Agra and pursued them to the west. At dawn on 1st November Lake's cavalry caught up with the Mahrattas at Laswari and attacked to hold them until the infantry could arrive. After charging repeatedly with great gallantry against the Mahratta guns, they were at last succoured by the infantry who had covered 25 miles under a blazing sun in eight hours. Lake gave his exhausted men an hour's rest, then threw them against the enemy right. A fearful struggle followed, with the 76th always showing an outstanding example to the Bengal battalions, until the superior discipline of the British told and the Mahrattas' resistance collapsed. Lake, a veteran of the American war, the Low Countries and the Irish rebellion, wrote: *"The enemy fought like devils, or rather like heroes. I never was in so severe a business in my life".(13)*

At this defeat Sindia sought peace and by the end of December 1803 much of his and the Bhonsla's territories had passed into the Company's hands. The other Mahratta chief, Holkar, showed no intention of coming to terms but the outcome of his intransigence must be left for a later chapter, since war had now broken out again in Europe.

The Peace of Amiens had turned out to be no more than an armistice. By May 1803 Britain and France were again at war and Bonaparte was massing an army of invasion, 160,000 strong, across the Channel at Boulogne. The Army's prime task in 1803 was the defence of the home base. The brigade then being trained at Shorncliffe under Moore, mentioned earlier, was one of the front-line formations for this task. However the Army's numbers were nothing like sufficient; out of some 100,000 regulars, only 40,000 were available for home defence, the rest being employed in the West Indies, the Mediterranean, India and elsewhere. They were backed by 50,000 balloted men again embodied for home service only in the Militia, for which an additional 20,000 were balloted soon after the outbreak of war; these provided a second line in various states of training. The regular, home service, Fencible regiments had been discontinued in 1801 because they were seen to be of limited value as well as a drain on men who might otherwise have enlisted in the Line; in fact, when they were disbanded, many had volunteered for the latter. Patriotic response to the country's danger again brought out a multiplicity of part-time Yeomanry and Volunteer units: the London and Westminster Light Horse, the Honourable Artillery Company of Tudor times, the Bank of England Volunteers, the Cinque Ports Volunteers, Cumberland Rangers, Loyal North Britons Association and hundreds more the length and breadth of the Kingdom. In London alone the Volunteers numbered 46,000 by October 1803. Nevertheless they were only enthusiastic amateurs whose likely effectiveness against Bonaparte's veterans was mocked by the satirical cartoons of Gillray. Furthermore many men joined the Volunteers simply to escape induction into the Militia by ballot.

Though these home service units of Militia, Yeomanry and Volunteers swelled the numbers, if not the efficiency, of the land forces confronting the invasion threat, they were also competing with the regular Army in the manpower market. The latter's recruiting potential was further diminished by the practice whereby men selected by ballot for the Militia could purchase substitutes. Though supreme at sea, the Royal Navy could not alone win a war against a predominantly land power like France. Sooner or later offensive land operations would have to be undertaken, which only a strong regular Army could perform.

The means of regular recruiting were the traditional regimental recruiting parties, *"drumming and fifing in the streets",(14)* their uniforms bedecked with ribbons, and the less savoury methods of the crimp, an agent who delivered up men for money. Some men looked to the Army as a release: from the gallows or prison; from *"having increased the population of their parish without permission of the clergy"(15)*; from unemployment, poverty and destitution, particularly amongst the Irish. Others, like simple ploughboys, were tricked into it by tales of *"glory, honour, drums, trumpets, deathless fame and all that".(16)* Finally there were the few genuine adventurers or patriotic spirits. All were attracted by the bounty, many by hopes of plunder and travel, and some by the uniform. Army life had been improved by the Duke of York's reforms which earned him the title of *"the Soldier's Friend".(17)* Proper barracks were being built; the standard of officer had been improved; the private's pay had at last been raised, in 1797, to a shilling a day; the abolition, in 1795, of the time-consuming and unhygienic practice of dressing the hair with powder would be followed in 1808 by doing away with the queue, or pigtail; even the uniform had been modernized, the hats, full-skirted coats and breeches, worn by all branches of the Army with various differences and modifications since the seventeenth century, now giving way to a variety of shakos, helmets, caps and busbies worn with short-tailed jackets, trousers and overalls. These dress changes not only gave the soldier a more practical and comfortable costume but also offered a dazzling variety of uniforms to entice simple country lads, compared to the relative sameness in all branches of eighteenth century dress. The dashing dark green of the Rifles proved particularly successful in attracting recruits. But despite all these and other improvements the bad old reputation of the Army deterred men from coming forward in sufficient numbers to fill the ranks for an offensive against France.

Numerous schemes of varying merit were introduced by successive Secretaries of State for War, first, to raise a sufficiently effective force for home defence, thus releasing regulars for service overseas, and second, to improve the strength of the regulars. As in the eighteenth century wars, short service enlistments were introduced but with limited success. Experience had shown that once men had become used to a soldier's life in the Militia, they were often willing to volunteer into the regulars and, being trained, were excellent material. But not until the extremely competent and hard-working Lord Castlereagh took over as Secretary of State for War, first in 1805 and again in 1807, was the manpower problem put on a proper footing. He abolished substitutes for the Militia, enforced the ballot, and by offering bounties to militiamen, induced really worthwhile numbers of them to volunteer for the regulars. Although the threat of invasion had abated when Bonaparte, or rather the Emperor Napoleon as he was from 1804, had marched away to defeat the Austrians at Austerlitz in 1805, a home defence force was still required in the absence of the Regular Army overseas. The Volunteers had decreased in numbers and efficiency since 1803 so, to back up the regular Militia, Castlereagh established a part-time Local Militia, into which many Volunteer units transferred bodily, and which was made up by voluntary enlistment or balloting. Such men could also volunteer for the regular Line.

The Army still contained a number of foreign regiments — the Chasseurs Britanniques, de Roll's, de Watte-

Rifle Regiments, 1804   6003-165
Coloured etching by and after J. Jones, from the book 'Rifle Manual and Firing' published by J. Thomas Smith, London, 1804

Presentation of Colours to the Temple Bar and St. Paul's Association (Volunteers), St. Paul's Cathederal, 7th December 1798   6510-1
Watercolour by Henry Matthews

ville's and Dillon's being some of the more prominent — and a valuable source of recruits accrued as a direct result of French conquest. In 1803 France overran Hanover and disbanded its army. Considerable numbers of these men made their way to England where they were formed into the King's German Legion, an excellent force of all arms which at its greatest strength in 1812 totalled some 15,000 men.

Although by 1808 the manning of the land forces was on a satisfactory basis, a sensible scheme of using them to prosecute the war had so far escaped ministers, who had continued to fritter them away in "penny-packet" operations. In 1805, while Napoleon was marching to defeat the Austrians and Russians at Austerlitz, an attempt was made to recapture Hanover but when the anticipated co-operation of Prussia was not forthcoming, the expedition was withdrawn. Between 1805-06 a force of 8,000 was used in southern Italy but, despite winning a notable victory against the French at Maida, achieved little. A thoroughly ill-conceived project to damage Spain, France's ally, by attacking Buenos Aires in South America came to a humiliating end. Meanwhile Napoleon had crushed Prussia at Jena and, after defeating the Russians at Friedland, concluded an alliance with the Tsar at Tilsit. This led Britain to mount the most useful expedition so far: the capture of Copenhagen and the Danish fleet in 1807 to deny its use by the French. The operations witnessed some fine work by Moore's light infantry and riflemen from Shorncliffe who, with the 92nd Highlanders, formed the picked Reserve brigade commanded by the recently returned victor of Assaye, now Major-General Sir Arthur Wellesley K.B. The following year, the invasion by Napoleon's new ally, the Tsar, of Sweden's possessions in Finland led to a small force under Moore being sent to bolster up the Swedes, but the erratic behaviour of their made king led to a withdrawal without even landing. In none of these operations was the British Army being used with any effect against the chief threat, the French Army, supreme in Europe. Eventually Napoleon himself provided it with its opportunity. In his determination to close all European ports to British commerce, he took steps to force Portugal, Britain's ancient ally, into his system. To ensure Spanish compliance with his plans he expelled the Spanish royal family, installed his brother Joseph on the Spanish throne, and poured troops into the Iberian Peninsula. In Spain and Portugal the people rose in revolt against the invasion and appealed for help from Britain. On 1st August 1808 Sir Arthur Wellesley, with a force of 14,000 men, landed in Mondego Bay, 100 miles north of Lisbon. The Army's chance had come.

'The Grand Triumphal Entry of the Chief Consul into London'

Coloured etching, probably by and after Isaac Cruikshank published by S.W. Fores, No.50 Piccadilly, October 1st 1803   7804-35

CHAPTER 10
UNDER WELLINGTON'S COMMAND
1808 – 1815

In 1808 Wellesley was aged 39 and the most junior lieutenant-general in the Army. The task given him by Castlereagh was the *"final and absolute evacuation of the (Iberian) Peninsula by the troops of France".(1)* It would take him six years to complete, at the end of which he would be a field-marshal and the Duke of Wellington, the name he will henceforth be called by here.† Within a month of landing in Portugal he had given the French a foretaste of the capabilities of a British army under his command by defeating them at Roleia and Vimiero. But then a hiatus occurred, for the British Government, in sending out reinforcements, also despatched two more senior generals to command the enlarged force. Wellington found himself superseded by two ageing nonentities who concluded the disgraceful Convention of Cintra with the French commander, Junot, by which the enemy forces in Portugal were permitted to return to France in British ships. The perpetrators of this feebleness were recalled to face an enquiry in England and as some of the odium caused by their actions quite unjustifiably attached itself to Wellington, he had to go as well. The command of the British troops in Portugal now passed to Sir John Moore, who arrived with the force that had been assembled for the Swedish expedition.

The isolated success of the Spaniards in defeating a French force at Baylen inspired in British ministers a completely erroneous impression of the effectiveness of the Spanish army. This led to Moore being ordered to co-operate with the Spaniards in driving the French out of Spain. Moore advanced to Salamanca with his 35,000 men but soon discovered that the Spanish army was no more than a fragmented collection of separate armies, ill-equipped and in poor condition, without any supreme commander with whom he could formulate plans. Meanwhile Napoleon, alarmed at the course of events in Spain, had entered the country at the head of 200,000 men, smashed the Spaniards in his path and was marching on Madrid. Moore well knew that any further advance on his part would hazard the only disposable field force Britain possessed but that to retreat could mean the loss of Spain and probably Portugal as well. Outnumbered by six to one, any direct advance on Napoleon was out of the question but Moore thought it might just be possible, by striking at the Emperor's lines of communications with France at Burgos, to take pressure off Madrid and draw the French away from southern Spain and Portugal.

This daring plan was set in motion in mid-December. Then, two days before Christmas, Moore learned that Napoleon had swung north-west from Madrid and was advancing rapidly to cut him off. There was nothing for it but to fall back to Corunna on the north-west coast where he could embark his army before he was crushed by overwhelming French forces. The retreat was initially covered with great skill and gallantry by Lord Paget's cavalry brigade, the light battalions of the King's German Legion and Moore's own Shorncliffe regiments, now under command of the stern and highly competent Robert Craufurd. The two light brigades were then detached to cover the southern flank of the main army, along the track to Vigo, while the task of rearguard fell to Edward Paget and his five battalions of the Reserve. As the retreat went on through the bitter, snow-covered Galician mountains, the morale of the men, so high before Christmas, now disintegrated under the hardships of a march, the need for which they could not comprehend. Only the brigade of Guards and Paget's Reserve kept their discipline. Not until Corunna was reached did the demoralised regiments pull themselves together, for then a battle had to be fought to ensure a safe evacuation. The disgraceful scenes of the retreat were redeemed by such stubborn fighting on the battlefield that the French were left too exhausted to hinder the embarkation.

The dreadful appearance of the troops when they reached England caused furious controversy about the campaign but Moore was spared it all, having fallen in action in the closing stages of the Battle of Corunna. He was a man of noble character, of great courage and humanity, whose faith in the innate qualities of the ordinary soldier made him a man before his time and one of the greatest trainers of soldiers the Army has ever had. As a field commander he was unlucky: his Swedish expedition failed through no fault of his own and in Spain he had been confronted by circumstances which he had not the means to overcome. Nevertheless his bold march into

---

† He was created Viscount Wellington in September 1809, Earl and Marquess in February and August 1812 and Duke in May 1814.

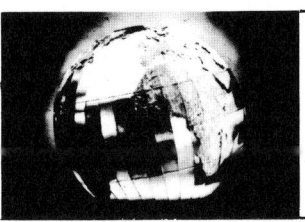 

William Carr Viscount Beresford (1768-1854)   7703-28
Commander in Chief, Portuguese Army, c1812

Portrait, oil on canvas, artist unknown

Leiut-General Sir John Moore (1761-1809)   6607-22
in Lieut-General's coatee

Portrait, oil on canvas, by Sir Thomas Lawrence, c1805

Lieut-General Lord Hill GCB (1772-1842)   6210-108
in Leiut-General's plain coatee

Portrait, oil on canvas, by George Dawe, c1819

'Leiut General Sir Thomas Picton GCB'   5602-500

Mezzotint by C. Turner after M.A. Shee ARA,
published by Welch & Gwynne, 24 St. James's Street,
London, 1843

Arthur Duke of Wellington against a mountainous background, possibly the Pyrenees c1813
Watercolour by Thomas Heaphy

6008-57

northern Spain, when prudence had dictated a rapid retreat to Lisbon, had so disrupted Napoleon's plans, that the Emperor left the Peninsula in disgust, the south and Portugal had been saved from French domination, at least for a time, and the British toehold around Lisbon had been preserved, thus keeping alive the inhabitants' will to resist.

Wellington, who had emerged unscathed from the Cintra scandal and had retained Castlereagh's confidence, was now sent back to Portugal but with more limited objectives than in 1808. His immediate task was the defence of Portugal. He quickly realised that a successful campaign in the barren lands of the Peninsula necessitated a sound system of supply and transport. His supply lines from England were secured by the Royal Navy's supremacy at sea, while the French armies opposing him were dependent on long land routes back to France over bad roads through a hostile countryside, in which Spanish guerillas would not only attack French convoys and reinforcements, but also tie down sizeable bodies of French troops who would otherwise be deployed in their main armies. Wellington's first task therefore was to establish a reliable commissariat to supply his army in the field from the base at Lisbon. At the same time the reform of the Portuguese army was taken in hand by General Beresford and a team of British instructors. To ensure he was fully aware of the enemy's movements and intentions and the nature of the terrain over which he would have to operate, Wellington put in hand the makings of an intelligence service, using guerillas, agents and special "observing officers", the most famous of whom was Colquhoun Grant of the 42nd, who rode far and wide behind enemy lines, always dressed in uniform.

Wellington's campaign in the Peninsula fell into three main phases: the defence of Portugal from 1809-10; the preparation for and execution of his first offensive in Spain, 1811-12; and the final victorious advance into France in 1813-14. In April 1809 Portugal was threatened by two French armies: Soult in the north and Victor on the Tagus in Estramadura. Wellington determined to strike first against Soult who was nearest. With 25,000 British and 16,000 Portuguese he turned Soult out of his position at Oporto by a daring crossing of the Douro and forced him to retreat in some disorder into the Galician mountains. He then turned south-east to link up with a Spanish army under Cuesta, in order to bring a combined force of 60,000 to attack Victor's 20,000. However Cuesta moved so slowly that he was driven back by Victor, now reinforced to double his former strength, to Talavera where Wellington took up a defensive position to block the French advance. In the battle that followed, on 27th and 28th July, Victor threw all his weight against Wellington's 20,000 British troops but each attack was repulsed with heavy loss. It was an expensive victory for Wellington who lost a quarter of his strength; furthermore he was unable to follow up Victor's withdrawal as news was received that Soult was advancing with 50,000 from Salamanca against his left rear. His experience in the Talavera campaign had convinced him that no reliance could be placed on the Spanish armies, so he therefore withdrew to Portugal. No French attack materialised and he was able to spend the winter of 1809-10 and the following spring constructing a defensive system of fortifications and entrenchments, known as the Lines of Torres Vedras, some 25 miles north of Lisbon, between the Tagus and the sea.

In 1809 Napoleon, having defeated Austria at Wagram, had forced her to make peace, thus releasing troops for employment in Spain where, by early 1810, the French armies totalled some 300,000 men. The Army of Portugual, under Massena, began preparing for an advance while Wellington maintained a watch on the possible approaches. At last it became clear that Massena was moving down the Mondego valley and Wellington concentrated his force along the ridge at Busaco to stop him. On 27th September, in a typically Wellingtonian battle, the British infantry stopped all Massena's frontal assaults. When the French marshal tried to turn the British left, Wellington fell back slowly to Torres Vedras, stripping the countryside of all possible resources as he went. Throughout the winter of 1810-11 the British lay secure behind the Lines, receiving supplies and reinforcements through Lisbon, while Massena's army, 25 miles away around Santarem, suffered increasing hardships, short of food and shelter and harrased by guerilla activity. For six months Massena maintained his positions before the impregnable Lines until March 1811 when he withdrew his by then demorilised army north-eastwards back into Spain.

Meanwhile other French armies had been attempting to subdue Spanish forces in eastern and southern Spain. A British force under Sir Thomas Graham moved to raise the siege of Cadiz but, after defeating Victor at Barrosa, the failure of the Spaniards to exploit the victory restored the situation to the French advantage. In Portugal Wellington followed up Massena's retreat and began operations to reduce the frontier fortresses of Almeida, Ciudad Rodrigo and Badajoz, which controlled the routes between Spain and Portugal. Massena hastily reformed his army and marched to Almeida's relief, only to be defeated by Wellington at Fuentes d'Onoro and compelled to fall back; nevertheless his attempt had allowed the Almeida garrison to break out through their besiegers. Beresford had been investing Badajoz when he was forced to suspend operations to counter Soult who was marching to relieve it. Beresford had worked wonders with his reorganization of the Portuguese army but lacked the flair and decisiveness for an independent command in the field. In a battle of appalling ferocity and cost at Albuera he managed to halt Soult, thanks to the heroic and stubborn gallantry of the British infantry,

5905-157

_1

310-47-2

_2

1. Army Gold Medal for Salamanca awarded to Lt-Col
   Thomas Lloyd, 94th Foot The Medal with Clasps for
   Vittoria and Nivelle was later mounted with the
   Gold Sarcophagus

2. Peninsular Gold Cross, 1812-14 Awarded to Maj-Gen.
   J.O. Vandaleur

3. Replica of the baton of Marshal Jourdan captured by
   the 87th Fusiliers at Vittoria, 1813

3_

6003-132

The landing of the British Army at Mondego Bay, Portugal 1808

Watercolour by Henri L'Eveque   7812-1-1

Battle of Fuentes D'Onoro taken from the right of the position occupied by the 1st, 3rd and 7th Divisions on the 5th May 1811
Aquatint by C. Turner after Major T. St. Clair from the series 'Campaigns in Spain and Portugal', published by Colnaghi, 1812-15

7102-33-507-6

who lost half their strength, and a brilliant counter-stroke launched at the critical moment by Lowry Cole. The French armies re-grouped and Wellington, now outnumbered, withdrew into Portugal for the winter, leaving Ciudad Rodrigo and Badajoz still in French hands.

Wellington began his 1812 operations with assaults on these two fortresses. Rodrigo fell in January and Badajoz, after a most determined defence, in April. With Portugal now secure, Wellington was ready for his offensive into Spain; his aim was the destruction of Massena's Army of Portugal, now under Marmont's command, which lay around Salamanca. To occupy the French Army of the North, he arranged for constant guerilla activity in Galicia, aided by a British fleet off the north coast. In the south a detached force under Rowland Hill was to sever communications between Marmont and Soult's Army of Andalusia by destroying the important bridge over the Tagus at Almaraz and then to keep Soult occupied. Lastly a British force from Sicily was to land in eastern Spain to distract Suchet's Army of Catalonia.

In June the advance began and after considerable manoeuvring the two armies met at Salamanca on 22nd July. Hitherto all Wellington's victories had been defensive battles in which successive French attacks expended themselves against an unyielding British line, deployed in carefully chosen positions of great tactical strength. At Salamanca he proved he was equally a master of the offensive battle, laying his army along Marmont's flank, watching for his opportunity, then swinging in a carefully poised striking force of all arms to roll up the over-extended French divisions in detail from a flank, while the rest of his army assailed them along their length. The French were routed and while the remnants sought safety north-eastwards behind the Douro, Wellington entered Madrid in triumph on 12th August. Salamanca stirred all the French in Spain into activity. In the south Soult abandoned his siege of Cadiz and evacuated Andalusia, marching to pick up reinforcements from Suchet in the east, prior to advancing again towards Madrid. Wellington meanwhile had marched north to besiege Burgos, leaving Hill with 30,000 men to cover the capital. However Burgos held out and the Army of Portugal, now under Clausel and reinforced by the Army of the North, moved to its relief. Wellington therefore raised the siege and retreated towards Salamanca, at the same time sending word to Hill to fall back and abandon Madrid. Clausel and Soult united their armies with King Joseph's, which together numbered 90,000 men, against which Wellington, even after he had linked up with Hill, could only muster some 70,000. Obviously nothing more could be done that year, so Wellington withdrew to Portugal. Though the campaign as a whole had been indecisive, Wellington had shown he was as formidable in attack as in defence. The French had abandoned the south and their whole position in Spain was growing less secure, with more and more troops tied down to protect their rear areas and lines of communication against ever-increasing hostile activity by the Spaniards. Furthermore they could look for no help from France, for far to the east the pitiful fragments of Napoleon's immense 'Grande Armée' were staggering out of Russia. Indeed, the French commanders in Spain would soon be forced to return troops to France to meet the anticipated counter-offensive of the united monarchs of Europe.

Wellington's plan for 1813 was to mount an apparent offensive from Ciudad Rodrigo towards Salamanca, but in reality to launch a great left hook out of northern Portugal, north of the Douro, aimed at the enemy's communications with France beyond Burgos; faced by this threat to their rear the French would have no choice but to fall back. Since he would be lengthening his lines of communication, while the enemy shortened theirs, Wellington planned to cut adrift from his depots in Portugal and subsist from new bases opened for him by the Navy on the north coast of Spain. All went as he had planned. Beginning his advance on 22nd May, a month later he trapped the rapidly retreating French at Vittoria, north-east of Burgos. He mounted an enveloping attack against King Joseph's army, taking an immense amount of booty and all the French artillery. His left wing under Graham cut the enemy's main road of retreat but did not move far or fast enough to block other side roads to the east, down which the beaten remnants, including the King himself, narrowly made their escape. The other French armies in Spain hastily beat their way back to the Pyrenees by devious routes, leaving only Suchet holding out in Catalonia against the ineffective movements of the British force that had come from Sicily the year before. Though Vittoria was not as decisive as Wellington anticipated, the whole of northern and central Spain was clear of the French, and when the news reached Vienna it induced the Austrian Emperor to throw in his lot with the Russians and Prussians, then advancing through Germany.

Wellington now closed up to the barrier of the Pyrenees where French resistance stiffened under the leadership of Soult, despatched personally by the Emperor to rally the beaten armies. Soult acted with great drive and resource and within a fortnight of his arrival had launched a counter-offensive to relieve the besieged fortresses of St. Sebastian and Pamplona. Much hard fighting ensued in the Pyrenean valleys, the broken nature of the country and the broad frontages forcing Wellington to delegate far more to his subordinate commanders than he would otherwise have wished to do. But no matter how determined the French attacks were, the British held on, and wherever a crisis occurred Wellington was there with his calm and steadying presence. By the end of October all Soult's efforts had been foiled. The Bidassoa had been crossed, St. Sebastian and Pamplona had fallen, and Wellington's men looked down into France. A fortnight earlier Napoleon's army had been shattered at Leipzig

by an allied army of 300,000 Russians, Prussians, Austrians and Swedes in one of the greatest battles mankind had yet known;even the British were represented by a rocket brigade of the Royal Artillery.When the news reached Soult, he was being driven from his positions along the Nivelle and falling back into south-west France. The year closed with his desperate but fruitless attempts to prevent the British forcing his next line astride the Nive, in front of Bayonne. 20 years after the outbreak of the French Revolutionary War the British Army was fighting on the very soil of France.

Any investment of Bayonne and its garrison was hindered by the River Adour which ran through it.Furthermore Soult's main army lay in its immediate vicinity. Wellington therefore began to manoeuvre to the east so as to induce Soult to follow to avoid being outflanked and encircled. Towards the end of February Soult had abandoned Bayonne to its own resources and Sir John Hope, with 18,000 men was left to complete its investment. On the same day Wellington attacked and defeated the French at Orthez, nearly 50 miles to the east. Soult was able to withdraw and again moved eastwards in the hope of dissuading Wellington from advancing further into France and for the chance of linking up with Suchet,whom he thought might reach him from Catalonia.Since Wellington knew the allied armies were now fighting in France to the north, Soult remained his main objective. Detaching a force to advance north to Bordeaux, which was known to be royalist in sympathy, he continued after the French marshal who stood to fight on the Garonne at Toulouse. On 10th April Wellington attacked to try and pin the French within the city but Soult once again managed to break out before he was encircled. These final labours of both sides had been in vain for two days later came news that Paris had fallen and Napoleon had abdicated on 6th April. The long struggle was over.

For six years in the Peninsula Wellington had tied down and finally ejected French armies of some 300,000 men, many of whom were veteran and experienced troops. He accomplished this with an army that never exceeded 60,000, supported by some 27,000 Portuguese troops. He was aided, sometimes hindered by Spanish armies of varying quantity and quality which at least drove the French to disperse their forces all over Spain. Above all he was operating among a population the bulk of which was bitterly hostile to the French, and which not only formed the guerilla bands that so constantly harassed the enemy, but also provided much of the manpower for Wellington's logistic arrangements on which his success so greatly depended.

Wellington's achievement in the Peninsula was the result of foresight, careful preparation, and never undertaking any enterprise that was beyond the capacity of his own resources. It was founded on the thoroughly reliable military system he built up and his superior tactics on the battlefield. He set his stamp of calm, methodical, painstaking work upon his own headquarters, of which the most important member was his Quartermaster-General, George Murray, always quick, accurate and reliable in the execution of his master's orders. Murray built up and trained a team of carefully selected staff officers and aides-de-camp, the young officers who provided the chief means of communication with the component parts of the army. Murray was also responsible for the working of the comprehensive intelligence department, whose work was so vital in the formulation of Wellington's plans. Wellington's appreciation of the importance of logistic backing, the neglect of which had so often caused British armies to founder, has already been touched on. It included the establishment of secure bases and supply depots, the training of an efficient and conscientious body of commissaries and the provision of adequate transport, much of it based on the Spanish muleteer and his hardy beast of burden. Wellington was well aware of the need to preserve his men and was insistent on regimental officers showing constant attention to their troops' health and well-being. He knew that sickness could be a greater killer than the enemy and that much of it could be avoided by the imposition of strict discipline and the supply of regular food and shelter. He looked for serviceability rather than smartness in dress and always endeavoured to see that the men were supplied with tents, blankets, cooking utensils and footgear. Of course shortages occurred and his men often had a ragged and patched appearance, but they seldom starved as other armies did, and sickness was kept within reasonable bounds, especially after 1812 when Dr James McGrigor was appointed surgeon-general. The latter exercised an energetic supervision over the medical services and introduced the use of portable, wooden field hospitals so that the sick and wounded could receive early treatment.

An essential part of Wellington's system was the grouping of his army, in 1809, into self-sufficient divisions. Prior to that date there had been no tactical formation larger than the brigade of between three to six battalions. A division had as a rule three infantry brigades, its own headquarters including logistic staff, and its supporting artillery. This grouping greatly assisted problems of command and permitted much increased scope for manoeuvre, including the detachment from the main force of one or more divisions for specific tasks, as for example Hill's covering operations in 1812. Except for the 1st Division, whose brigades were usually Guards and King's German Legion, each division contained two British and one Portuguese brigade . Each of the former had three battalions and a company of riflemen drawn from the 5th Battalion of the 60th; the latter had five battalions, one of which was of Portuguese riflemen or 'caçadores'. The riflemen of a brigade provided an outlying screen of skirmishers and supplemented the services of the light companies of the battalions. In the same way that the

main body of a division was covered by these light troops, so the army as a whole was covered by the famous Light Division, formed initially from Craufurd's Light Brigade of the 43rd and 52nd Light Infantry and the 95th Rifles, to which was added a Portuguese brigade of 'caçadores' and Ross's troop of Royal Horse Artillery. By the end of the war Wellington thought the Light Division was *"the flower of the Army, the finest infantry in the world".(2)* Equally distinguished on the battlefield as at the outposts, its finest achievement in the latter role was its guardianship of a 40-mile stretch of the River Agueda in north-east Portugal during the first five months of 1810. Opposed by a force six times its strength, its line was never pierced, its posts were never surprised and the enemy was denied any intelligence of what was going on in its rear.

Eight infantry divisions were formed in all and, as the war progressed, acquired characteristics and nicknames of their own, as regiments had always done. The 1st Division were "The Gentlemen's Sons" because of its guardsmen; the 2nd, "The Observing Division", since it was frequently detached under its own commander, Hill, to contain other forces not engaged by the main army; the 3rd, ever foremost in siege and battle, "The Fighting Division"; after the bloodbath of Albuera the 4th became "The Enthusiastics"; the Light Division was simply *"The* Division", though probably only to its members.

The Light was the only division to have cavalry attached to it, in the form of the 1st King's German Legion Hussars, one of the finest regiments in the army. The K.G.L. cavalry as a whole were more professional than their British counterparts who, though full of dash and fire, too often allowed such qualities to overcome prudence and the need to maintain formation. After Vittoria for example the failure of the British cavalry to sustain a controlled pursuit greatly assisted the escape of the beaten French. For most of the war the cavalry were grouped in a single division, of a varying number of brigades, but this was largely for administrative purposes as there were few occasions when it was possible to manoeuvre more than one brigade as a tactical formation. The cavalry were the weakest element of the Peninsular army but were not without their successes, notably Le Marchant's heavy brigade's decisive charge at Salamanca†, and the action at Garcia Hernandez a day later where four squadrons of the 1st and 2nd Heavy Dragoons of the King's German Legion routed four French battalions, three of which were in square.

As the army grew larger and the frontage of operations broadened, Wellington found it difficult to exercise over his divisions the close control he preferred, and began to group numbers of them into corps, though their composition was flexible and he resorted to this device only when he had to. This was partly because he had few senior officers whom he was prepared to trust with a formation larger than a division. Only Rowland Hill was considered reliable enough for such a permanent task; in his case the containing force in Estramadura of the 2nd Division, a Portuguese division* and two cavalry brigades.

Wellington had little say over the appointment of his general officers who were sent out by the Military Secretary in London. Besides the ever-dependable Hill, whose care and affection for his men earned him the nickname of "Daddy Hill", there were, among officers of sufficient seniority for a corps command, the admirable Sir John Hope, but who unfortunately came late to the Peninsular army, and Sir Thomas Graham, a noble character but of failing health and eyesight+. Edward Paget was a highly capable officer but was deprived of realising his full potential through wounds and being captured in 1812. Compared with such men there were the likes of the "puzzle-headed" Brent Spencer, who always called the Tagus the Thames.

Among the divisional commanders was the brilliant but sometimes unpredictable Robert Craufurd, one of the best qualified officers in the Army, whose death at Ciudad Rodrigo lost the Light Division their most gifted leader; he was succeeded by the reliable Hanoverian, Charles von Alten. In command of the 3rd Division was the valiant and irascible Thomas Picton, a stern disciplinarian and a determined, far-sighted leader, whose mighty frame, clothed usually in untidy civilian dress, and bellowing voice, *"with the power of twenty trumpets", (3)* made him well-known throughout the army. Lowry Cole was the popular and competent commander of the 4th Division, always good-natured and kind-hearted, whose finest hour was at Albuera. Edward Pakenham, though not *"the highest genius", (4)* led Wellington's counter-stroke at Salamanca with the greatest skill and did fine work with the 6th Division in the stiff fighting in the Pyrenees. These men, however, were the cream of his generals. He also had to contend with the likes of Sir William Erskine, *"upon whose sanity much reliance cannot be placed",(5)* the incompetent and self-satisfied Skerrett, and that *"paltry, plundering old wretch"* Hay.*(6)* Of his good commanders Wellington said: *"They are really heroes when I am on the spot to direct them, but when I am obliged to quit them they are children".(7)* Of the bad: *"Really when I reflect upon the character and attainments of some of the General officers of this army, I tremble".(7)*

† 5th Dragoon Guards, 3rd and 4th Dragoons.

* This was the only Portuguese division. All other Portuguese units were incorporated into British divisions.

+ Later the Earl of Hopetoun and Baron Lynedoch respectively. Graham did not take up a military career until the age of 46 when he was inspired to do so by the excesses of the French Revolution, in particular the violation by French customs officials of his wife's coffin.

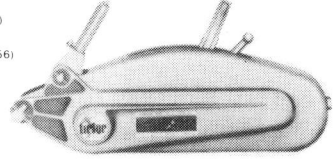

The most able cavalry leader of the time, Lord Paget, had lost his chance of service in the Peninsular army due to an escapade with Wellington's sister-in-law. His place was taken by Stapleton Cotton †, a man of magnificent appearance and a good horsemaster, but of limited though generally adequate capabilities as a cavalry commander. Despite the greater professionalism of the Royal Artillery compared with the cavalry, and even the infantry, Wellington was unable to procure artillery a satisfactory commander until 1813, when he promoted the comparatively junior Alexander Dickson over the heads of several of his seniors. At the same time the horse artillery passed into the capable hands of Augustus Frazer. Wellington was well served throughout the war by his Chief Engineer, Colonel Richard Fletcher, under whose direction the Lines of Torres Vedras had been constructed, but the lack of trained engineering troops was sorely felt at the great sieges of Ciudad Rodrigo and Badajoz, a deficiency which led to the formation of the Royal Sappers and Miners in 1812.

Though Wellington proved at Salamanca and Vittoria his mastery of offensive tactics, he intended to prefer the defensive battle. This afforded the most effective means of capitalising on his greatest asset, controlled musketry delivered from the broadest possible frontage, i.e. with infantry in a two-deep line, countering the French reliance on the weight and momentum of solid blocks of infantry formed in column, or their more flexible 'l'ordre mixte', a combination of line and column. In its simplest form this meant that a British battalion of 600 men in line could bring all its muskets to bear against a French battalion of equal strength, of which, when developed in its formal battle order of column of double companies, only the two ranks front, 132 men, could shoot; that is, until those two ranks were mown down, by which time the ranks behind were being fired at by the overlapping wings of the British battalion. The chief drawback of the line formation was its lack of depth and vunerability to cavalry; the latert being horribly demonstrated at Albuera when Colborne's brigade* was caught in line by a surprise attack of French lancers and hussars and destroyed. Wellington therefore insisted on certain refinements to its use.

The line was, as far as possible, always deployed under cover from the enemy's artillery and out of sight of their infantry until the moment came to engage. The concealment of the main battle line in this way at Busaco so deceived the French columns that by the time they had struggled up to the crest behind which the British infantry had been hidden, they found they were attacking, not Wellington's left but his centre, and consequently found themselves outflanked. At Salamanca Marmont was manoueuvring to outflank what he thought was a retreating army, only to find himself attacked in front and flank by Wellington's divisions emerging from behind a low range of hills.

The line was further protected and given depth by the use of skirmishers deployed in advance, whose task was to prevent the eneemy's light troops harassing the line in preparation for the advance of their columns, and also to cause as much confusion and casualties in the densely packed columns as possible. A French advance against an Anglo-Portuguese division of six British and five Portuguese battalions would first come under fire from two British and six Portuguese rifle companies. After engaging as long as possible, the riflemen would fall back to a flank or behind the skirmishers of the six British and four Portuguese light companies from the battalions. Gradually all the skirmishers would fall back, galling the French ranks with their fire, until it was time to run in upon their battalions. By then the main battle line had advanced from cover and the French, somewhat blown by their uphill climb and their ranks disordered by the skirmishers' fire, saw what awaited them:

> "The English, silent and impassive, loomed like a long red wall. More than one amongst us began to reflect that the enemy's fire would be very unpleasant when it did break forth. Our ardour began to cool. At this moment of painful expectation the English line would make a quarter-turn — the muskets were going up to the 'ready'. An indefinable sensation nailed to the spot many of our men, who halted and opened a wavering fire. The enemy's return, a volley of simultaneous precision and deadly effect, crashed in upon us like a thunderbolt. Decimated by it we reeled together, staggering under the blow and trying to recover our equilibrium. Then three formidable 'Hurrahs' termined the long silence of our adversaries. With the third they were down upon us, pressing us into a disorderly retreat". (8)

The line would not pursue far but the light troops would now come forth again to speed the fleeing enemy with fire and resume their former protective positions.

The third requirement for the security of the line was that its flanks must be protected, either by the ground or by other forces. At Talavera one end was covered by a precipitous hill, the other by thick olive groves. The advance of the 3rd Division, the striking force at Salamanca, had its flanks covered by two cavalry brigades. The result of not doing so was demonstrated at Albuera in the instance already quoted, but at the same battle Cole ensured the safe and victorious counter-attack of his 4th Division in line by a battalion in column on one flank, and one in quare, supported by a cavalry brigade, on the other. Over and over again

---

† Later Baron Combermere.
* 1st Battalion 3rd Foot, 2nd Battalions of the 31st, 48th and 66th.

this use of the line formation, accompanied by the necessary safeguards, prevailed both in attack & defence over the French armies which had hitherto overcome all the forces of Europe.

Ultimately the system and the tactics, the victories, sieges, advances and retreats depended above all on the quality of the regiments of the Line, in their battered shakos, faded red jackets and ragged trousers, weighed down by knapsack, pouch and musket, marching, fighting and enduring across blazing sierras, snow-covered mountains and in flea-ridden villages. The years of campaigning welded together a collection of regiments into a powerful and cohesive force, with a spirited, aggressive and self-confident character all of its own. An arduous, open-air life and shared dangers narrowed the divisions between the ranks; on the one hand the officers, sons of the gentry and professional classes, boys just out of school, ageing captains too poor to buy their promotion, off-spring of rich tradesmen, quarrelsome squireens, and proud Highland gentlemen; on the other the rank & file, ploughboys, gaolbirds, riotous Irish, well set-up militiamen, out-of-work weavers, pale-faced youths from the new slums, most of them illiterate but a surprising number with some education, and almost all with a bottom-less capacity for drink; between the two, the real professionals, the sergeants, hard, tough and experienced, guiding the young officers and ever watchful of the men.

Undoubtedly there were occasions, notably in the plundering that followed sieges like Badajoz, when men's worst characteristics came to the surface, with unparalled scenes of drunkenness, rape and violence amid a total breakdown of discipline. But equally the rigours of war brought out surprising qualities. George Napier of the 52nd, when wounded, was visited by one of his Irish privates, who walked seven miles to see him despite just having had his arm amputated. Another officer recorded that: *"A 43rd man, shot through the thigh, lost his shoes in the marshy ground. Refusing to quit the battlefield, he limped on under fire with naked feet and blood streaming from his wound, and thus marched for several miles over a country covered with flinty stones".(9)* Whatever the failings of Wellington's men, lack of courage and loyalty to each other was not among them.

What cemented officers and men together in the face of danger and hardship was regimental pride, a determination to uphold the honour of what for many of them was the only home they knew. It was this pride that sustained the half-battalion of the 92nd Highlanders which stood at bay against a whole division in the Pyrenees *"until half their blue bonnets lay beside those brave northern warriors"(10)* and which inspired the exhausted survivors to join in the counter-attack. As Hoghton's brigade at Albuera was swept by grapeshot, his men of the 29th, 48th and 57th closed in upon their tattered colours, maintaining a constant musketry and even advancing their shattered line. Such fortitude must have been inspired in the 57th by their colonel's exhortation to *"Die hard!"* and in the 48th by knowledge that they had saved the day at Talavera. The 28th, a regiment which had served in almost every campaign since its formation, was not present at the siege of St Sebastian but its yellow facings were seen among the storming parties, worn by Sergeant Ball and six men, who, arriving at the British camp as a fatigue party, had volunteered to take part in the assault for no other reason than *"the credit of their regiment".(11)* The sacrifices demanded and freely given by infantrymen for their colours were equalled by artillerymen's devotion to their guns, and it was this urge to save their 6-pounders that inspired Norman Ramsay's troop of Royal Horse Artillery, when isolated and surrounded by French cavalry at Fuentes d'Onoro, to first limber up and then charge at a gallop through the ranks of the enemy horsemen. There are countless examples of such regimental spirit to be read in the many memoirs and reminis-cences of men of all ranks of the Peninsular army. But perhaps the most remarkable is the regiment that pro-duced more such accounts than any other — the 95th Rifles. Formed only in 1800, it had none of the traditions and past glories of other, older regiments to live up to, yet in 14 years it became probably the most renowned in the Army, due to its unique character, uniform and above all its proud boast of being *"the first in the field and last out of it, the bloody, fighting Ninety-Fifth".(12)*

When the Peninsular War ended many of the regiments, far from returning home to the heroes' welcome they deserved, were shipped across the Atlantic for the closing stages of a futile war with the United States, which had broken out in 1812 over commercial disputes and supposed infringements of American neutrality. Not only did many Peninsular veterans needlessly lose their lives, but when Napoleon suddenly returned from Elba to threaten the peace of Europe again, and a new army had to be assembled to fight him in the Low Countries, several of the most experienced regiments were on the wrong side of the Atlantic. Nevertheless, although the British element of the army placed under Wellington's command in Belgium in 1815 had to be brought up to strength with new recruits and men drafted from the Militia, it was not so green as Wellington's reference to it as *"infamous"* and some accounts would indicate.†

By mid-June Wellington was preparing to combine with the Prussians under Field-Marshal Blücher. He had about 72,500 men and 156 guns, of which just over 32,000 were British and King's German Legion,* the

† See C.T.Atkinson, "An 'Infamous Army' ", J.S.A.H.R., Vol.XXXII, p.48. In any case Wellington's remark was made before the majority of British regiments arrived in Belgium.

* 32,210 in all. Infantry, 20,776; cavalry, 7915; artillery, 3519 and 96 guns.

Attack on the British squares by French Cavalry, Waterloo, 1815.

Watercolour by Denis Dighton.

7505-7-2

remainder were Hanoverians, Brunswickers, Dutch-Belgians and Nassauers, many of whom were raw and of uncertain quality. Some of his old commanders from the Peninsula were missing but Hill and Picton were there and the Earl of Uxbridge, formerly Lord Paget, commanded the cavalry.

Napoleon's plan was to deal first with the Prussians, whom he attacked and defeated at Ligny on 16th June, sending Grouchy with a third of his army to pursue and contain them. Meanwhile Wellington, having held the French left under Ney at Quatre Bras, fell back on the 17th to his previously selected position at Waterloo in front of Brussels. Here he would hold Napoleon until the help promised by Blücher arrived.

The great battle of 18th June has probably been more written about than any other, though its fascination lies more in the titanic struggle and decisive outcome than any tactical brilliance or innovation. An ailing Emperor expended his troops' valour and loyalty in headlong assaults, without any attempt to manoeuvre, against a typical Wellingtonian defensive position. For hour after hour the French columns trudged up the greasy slopes of Mont St Jean against the levelled muskets of the British line; each attack crumbled under the volleys. When the infantry failed the cavalry were thrown in, charge after charge, only to find the lines transformed into squares tipped with bayonets, round which the finest mounted troops in Europe milled helplessly. Then it was the infantry's turn again but still the line held. As Wellington said later: *"Never did I see such a pounding match. He (Napoleon) just moved forward in the old style and was driven off in the old style".(13)* The pounding went on until darkness fell, as Napoleon waited for Grouchy and Wellington waited for Blücher, but the old Prussian proved the most stalwart and the Napoleonic Empire crumbled into ruin.

Three examples from this mighty contest will suffice to show the quality of the British Army at the close of the Napoleonic Wars. When D'Erlon's corps, supported by a brigade of cuirassiers, began to force back the British infantry near La Haye Sainte, Lord Uxbridge threw his two brigades of heavy cavalry into the counter-attack. On the right, the Household Brigade, the 1st and 2nd Life Guards, the Blues and the King's Dragoon Guards, smashed into the cuirassiers. On the left the Union Brigade, Royal Dragoons, Greys and Inniskillings, drove through the tightly packed columns, hacking and slashing with their long swords at the French infantry, scattering all before them. In the ranks of the Greys rode Sergeant Ewart, 6 ft 4 inches tall and a splendid swordsman, who captured the eagle of the French 45th Regiment, while Captain Clarke and Corporal Stiles of the Royals took that of the 105th. The two brigades swept the slopes clear of D'Erlon's men but then, drunk with the excitement of the charge and deaf to Uxbridge's trumpeter sounding the recall thundered across the valley and up the other side right into the French position, cutting down the gun crews and everything in their path, before fresh reserves of French cavalry charged into their disordered ranks. With blown horses they were speedily overwhelmed and the survivors, only one in every three men, had a hard fight to regain the safety of their lines. Though the crisis at La Haye Sainte had been averted by their timely charge, their uncontrolled pursuit, in the true tradition of Prince Rupert, had resulted in the loss of a quarter of Wellington's mounted arm. It had displayed all the best and worst of the British cavalry: tremendous dash and gallantry but a fatal inability to rally and reform.

In contrast was the coolness and steadiness of the British gunners. When the infantry formed squares to meet the French cavalry charges, the artillery, whose guns were deployed in advance of the squares, were ordered to maintain their fire until the last possible moment and then run for shelter inside the nearest square. The closest square to Captain Mercer's troop of Royal Horse Artillery was composed of Brunswickers, mere boys who had never been in action before. As the cavalry came on Mercer *"glanced at the Brunswickers, and that glance told me it would not do; both squares appeared too unsteady, and I resolved to say nothing about the Duke's order, and take our chance".* His troop therefore stood to their guns, pouring grape-shot into the French ranks until *"it did seem they would ride over us"*, but, *"at the instant I thought it was all over with us, they turned to either flank and filed away rapidly to the rear".* When the next attack came Mercer saw that his men's example had served its purpose, for the Brunswickers *"stood firmly, and eyes fixed on us, ready to commence their fire".* Again Mercer's men remained at their posts, *"the discharge of every gun followed by a fall of men and horses like that of grass before the mower's scythe".(14)* Though some of the French dragoons rode through between the guns, hacking at the gunners as they passed, most bore off before they reached the muzzles. When the charges died away Mercer's six guns still stood in line, their crews about them, and the heartened Brunswickers still in square behind.

As the long day drew to its close and the Prussians were seen advancing from the east, Napoleon made his last throw by launching his final reserve, the Imperial Guard, at the right of Wellington's attenuated but undaunted line. Here stood Maitland's brigade of the 1st and 3rd Battalions of the 1st Foot Guards with, on their right, Adam's brigade of solid Peninsular regiments, the 52nd and 71st Light Infantry and two battalions of the 95th. The steady advance of the Guard was headed towards an apparently open sector of the British line, but where the 1st Guards lay concealed in four ranks behind a bank, sheltering from the French artillery

Coatee worn by L/Cpl. Gill, 1st Life Guards c1815
5812-72

Officer's coatee worn by Lt H. Anderson, 69th Foot, at Waterloo c1815
5012-48

Sabretache of a General Officer of Hussars
Worn at Waterloo by Lt-Gen. the Earl of Uxbridge
who commanded the British cavalry   6002-123

Round hat and silver spurs worn by Lt-Gen. Thomas Picton
who was killed at Waterloo, 1815   6112-92
6309-285

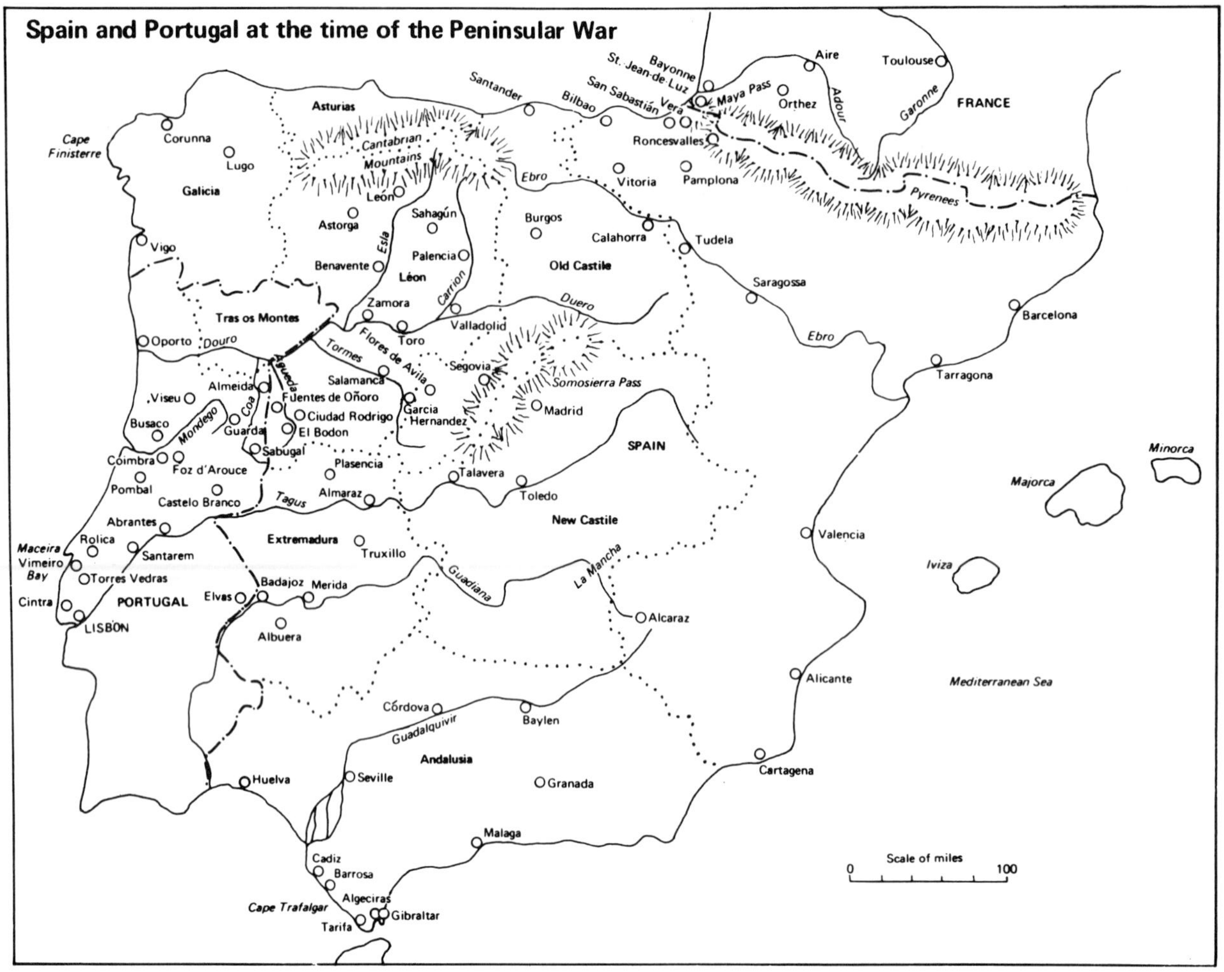

Spain and Portugal at the time of the Peninsular War
FRANCE
SPAIN
PORTUGAL
Mediterranean Sea
Pyrenees
Cantabrian Mountains
Cape Finisterre
Corunna
Lugo
Galicia
Asturias
Santander
Bilbao
San Sebastián
St. Jean-de Luz
Bayonne
Aire
Toulouse
Maya Pass
Orthez
Adour
Garonne
Vera
Roncesvalles
Vitoria
Pamplona
Ebro
León
Astorga
Sahagún
Burgos
Calahorra
Tudela
Vigo
Benavente
Palencia
Léon
Old Castile
Esla
Carrion
Zamora
Valladolid
Duero
Saragossa
Barcelona
Tras os Montes
Oporto
Douro
Toro
Tormes
Flores de Avila
Segovia
Somosierra Pass
Tarragona
Agueda
Almeida
Salamanca
Fuentes de Oñoro
Viseu
Ciudad Rodrigo
Garcia Hernandez
Madrid
Busaco
Mondego
Coa
Guarda
El Bodon
Sabugal
Coimbra
Foz d'Arouce
Plasencia
Pombal
Castelo Branco
Talavera
Toledo
Minorca
Majorca
Tagus
Almaraz
Abrantes
New Castile
Extremadura
Valencia
Rolica
Truxillo
Maceira Bay
Vimeiro
Santarem
Torres Vedras
Iviza
Guadiana
La Mancha
Badajoz
Merida
Elvas
Cintra
LISBON
Alcaraz
Albuera
Alicante
Córdova
Baylen
Guadalquivir
Andalusia
Huelva
Seville
Granada
Cartagena
Malaga
Cadiz
Barrosa
Algeciras
Gibraltar
Cape Trafalgar
Tarifa
Scale of miles
0
100

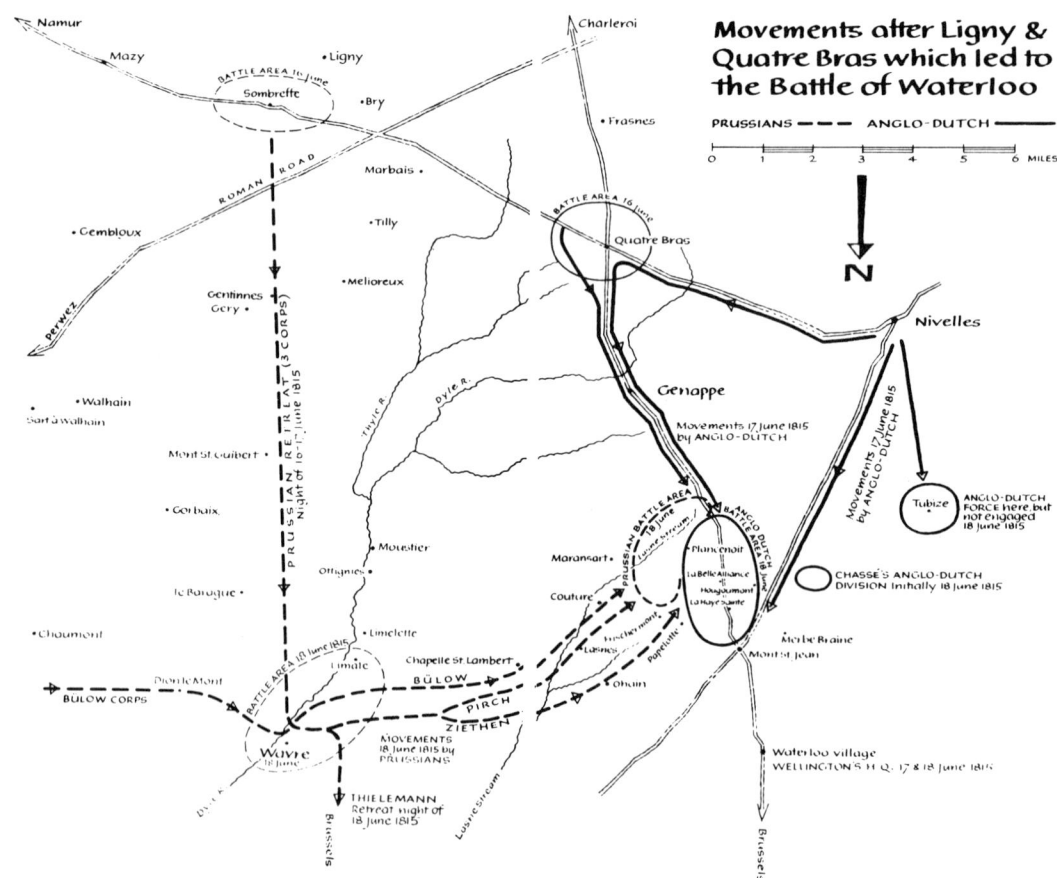

Movements after Ligny & Quatre Bras which led to the Battle of Waterloo
PRUSSIANS — — — ANGLO-DUTCH ———
0 1 2 3 4 5 6 MILES
N
Namur
Mazy
Ligny
Bry
BATTLE AREA 16 June
Sombreffe
Charleroi
Frasnes
ROMAN ROAD
Marbais
Tilly
Gembloux
Melioreux
BATTLE AREA 16 June
Quatre Bras
Perwez
Gentinnes
Gery
PRUSSIAN RETREAT (3 CORPS) Night of 16-17 June 1815
Nivelles
Walhain
Sart à Walhain
Genappe
Dyle R.
Thyle R.
Movements 17 June 1815 by ANGLO-DUTCH
Movements 17 June 1815 by ANGLO-DUTCH
Mont St. Guibert
Corbaix
Tubize
ANGLO-DUTCH FORCE here, but not engaged 18 June 1815
PRUSSIAN BATTLE AREA 18 June
ANGLO-DUTCH BATTLE AREA 18 June
Mousty
Ottignies
Maransart
Plancenoit
La Belle Alliance
Hougoumont
La Haye Sainte
CHASSÉ'S ANGLO-DUTCH DIVISION initially 18 June 1815
le Baraque
Couture
Chaumont
Limelette
Merbe Braine
Mont St. Jean
Chapelle St. Lambert
BATTLE AREA 18 June 1815
Limale
Lasnes
Dion le Mont
BÜLOW
BÜLOW CORPS
Ohain
PIRCH
ZIETHEN
Wavre 18 June
MOVEMENTS 18 June 1815 by PRUSSIANS
Waterloo village
WELLINGTON'S H.Q. 17 & 18 June 1815
THIELEMANN Retreat night of 18 June 1815
Brussels
Lasne Stream
Brussels

fire. *"Suddenly"*, wrote Captain Powell, *"the firing ceased, and as the smoke cleared away a most superb sight opened on us. A close column of Grenadiers† were seen ascending the rise 'au pas de charge' shouting 'Vive l'Empereur!' "(15)* When the leading ranks were about 50 yards away, Wellington, who had galloped over to the right, called out, *"Stand up Guards!"(16)* The guardsmen sprang from their cover and poured their volleys into the dense ranks. It was the classic manifestation of the concealed line against the column, but with the rate of fire doubled by the two rear ranks reloading as the front two fired. *" 'La Garde', who had never before failed in an attack, suddenly stopped. In less than a minute about 300 were down. They now wavered, and several of the rear divisions (companies) began to draw out as if to deploy".(15)* Then the bayonets came down as the 1st Guards drove forward in the charge. The French column recoiled before them but at that moment another battalion, of the 4th 'Chasseurs à Pied', came up towards the guardsmen's right flank. Seeing it, Maitland gave the order to retire, but his command was lost in the battle din; some heard it correctly, others thought they were to form square.Momentarily confused,the guardsmen's line was in some disarray until their officers told them to fall back as they were to their original position.There, their ingrained discipline instantly responded to a firm and audible command, whereupon the ranks were reformed with immediate steadiness. Meanwhile the situation had been restored by one who was the acme of Sir John Moore's *"thinking, fighting man"*. Commanding the 52nd was John Colborne, Moore's most accomplished disciple, who now, without orders from anyone, advanced his battalion in line, wheeled it left and deployed it along the flank of the 4th Chasseurs. The 52nd, one of the finest regiments in the Army and all veterans of the Light Division, fired a volley into the Chasseurs and sprang forward with the bayonet. The French column broke and, with the 71st and 95th coming forward on the flanks of the 52nd, Wellington waved them on to begin the long-awaited advance of the whole British line. As the broken ranks of Napoleon's élite Guard fell back, there was heard for the first time the fearful cry of *'La Garde recule'*, and panic spread through the French army. Thus the cream of the Napoleonic war machine was defeated by two elements that epitomised all that was best in the British infantry: the lethal volleys and disciplined response to danger demonstrated by the Foot Guards and the verve, speed and initiative of the light infantry and riflemen.

When reflecting after Waterloo how close the battle had been and paying,for him, an unusual compliment to *"that best of all instruments, British infantry"*, Wellington felt constrained to add, *"By God! I don't think it would have done if I had not been there".(17)* Such a remark might indicate conceit, of which he was not entirely devoid, but it was no more than the truth, applicable as much to his other battles as Waterloo. As the 7th Royal Fusiliers advanced into Beresford's shambles at Albuera, one fusilier said to another: *"Whore's ar Arthur?"* The second replied, *"I don't know, I don't see him".* *"Aw wish he wor here"*, said the first.*(18)* This was the nub of it. He was never loved by his men like Marlborough and indeed his cold, blunt, aristocratic manner discouraged any vestige of affection from his troops. Nor had he any fondness for them, regarding them simply as an instrument which, when the Napoleonic Wars were over, he discarded without a backward glance or thought for their subsequent well-being. His care for their administrative needs stemmed purely from his realisation that such measures were essential for their efficiency as a fighting force. He was a hard taskmaster and a stern disciplinarian with less compassion for the vices and weaknesses of the common soldier than the failings of senior officers. For the brave, cheerful, loyal rank and file who fought his battles he frequently made no attempt to conceal his contempt though appreciating their worth as a fighting machine. Yet his strict sense of duty, his prudence, foresight and skill were so apparent and penetrating that his men could not but respond with their loyalty, respect and trust. The qualities he applied to the pursuit of victory and the welding together of one of the finest field armies Britain has ever had were crystallized by the rifleman, John Kincaid, in words that bear comparison with Robert Parker's view of Marlborough: *"In all his battles Lord Wellington appeared to us never to leave anything to chance. However desperate the undertaking, we ever felt confident that a redeeming power was at hand, nor were we ever deceived".(19)*

---

† The French were in fact two battalions of the 3rd 'Chasseurs à Pied'.

Types of the 40th Madras Native Infantry c1835
Contemporary watercolour by a native artist

6003-90

The Sirmoor Rifles (later 2nd Gurkha Rifles) at Dehli, c1858.

5602-518

CHAPTER 11
EXPANDING THE RAJ
1804 — 1852

The Battle of Waterloo not only marked the final overthrow of Napoleon but also the end of the long series of wars with France and major British involvement on the Continent. For the next hundred years the Army would be employed in the expansion, consolidation and security of the British Empire. Some of its operations — though often hazardous and rigorous — would be of quite small scale involving only a handful of regiments, but all, whatever their scope, would turn the British Army into an Imperial force of a closed and exclusive character, far removed from the life of the country as a whole and very different from the mainly conscript armies of Europe. Only once, in the Crimea, would it be used against a major European power. As the British nation grew ever more prosperous and powerful, its long-service soldiers would be enduring, fighting and often dying while imposing and maintaining order in those distant parts of the globe from which most of its prosperity came: as far afield as Canada, Africa, the Antipodes, China and, above all, India.

Although the victories of Lake and Wellington in 1803 had forced two of the Mahratta chieftains, Sindia and the Bhonsla of Berar, to make peace, in the following year the third, Holkar, challenged the Company's authority. Once again Lake took the field but through the incompetence of his subordinates part of his force was routed by Holkar. Lake however was tireless in his efforts and, though British prestige suffered another blow from his failure to take the huge fortress of Bhurtpore, eventually succeeded in driving Holkar north into the Punjab. The pressures of the war in Europe compelled the Company to make peace, but on terms so advantageous to the Mahrattas that much of Lake's work was undone. Furthermore the whole of Central India was soon being subjected to the depredations of the Pindaris, a great host of lawless robber bands, who rode far and wide pillaging and terrorising the countryside. By 1812 these gangs were raiding into British territory and the Governor-General, Lord Hastings, determined on crushing them once and for all. Before he could do so, danger threatened from another quarter.

In the latter part of the previous century the Gurkhas, a hill race of Mongolian stock, had conquered the whole of Nepal and, having extended their presence over the Himalayan foothills, began raiding into the plains beyond. An expedition was mounted in 1814 to subdue these formidable warriors who, often armed with little more than bows and arrows, put up a heroic resistance and checked the advance of three of the Company's four columns. The British tried again in 1815 but it was not until a year later that General Ochterlony, by a rapid advance to Khatmandu, managed to convince the Gurkhas that it was time to seek terms. The respect for each other's fighting qualities engendered during the campaign led to a treaty of friendship and the recruitment of Gurkhas into the Company's Bengal Army. Indeed three battalions had been formed during the war, the Nasiri, Sirmoor and Kumaon; these were followed by others as the century progressed, eventually becoming the ten regiments of Gurkha Rifles of the Indian Army, four of which still form part of the British Army at the present day,† while the others joined the Army of the Republic of India in 1947. Thus, from a few skirmishes fought in the mountains of the Himalayas while Napoleon was being defeated in Europe, there developed a lasting bond from which has sprung a body of some of the bravest and most devoted soldiers of the British Crown.

In 1817 Lord Hastings began the delayed subjugation of the Pindaris, whom he planned to crush between a concentric advance of forces which together totalled over 100,000 men, the largest army the Company had yet put in the field. As the net closed round the Pindari bands, the Mahratta chieftains saw their chance to regain lost power and struck at the British rear. Fortunately they were disunited and the army, despite a major outbreak of cholera in its ranks, was able to defeat them in turn. Sindia was manoeuvred into surrendering without a struggle. The Company's old ally, the Peshwa of Poona, treacherously attacked his British Resident, but his host of 26,000 horse and foot was soon routed by a single brigade* of the Bombay Army at Kirkee. An even smaller force of two weak Madras battalions and the 6th Bengal Cavalry overthrew the Bhonsla of

---

† 2nd (formerly Sirmoor), 6th (formerly Kumaon), 7th and 10th. The Nasiri battalion became the 1st Gurkhas.

* Bombay Europeans, 1st, 6th and 7th Native Infantry.

Berar at Sitabaldi in November. A month later the most troublesome chief, Holkar, was brought to battle and defeated at Mahidpur by a Madras army, including detachments of the 22nd Light Dragoons and the 1st Foot, which, though larger than those employed at Kirkee and Sitabaldi, was still outnumbered by four to one. With these defeats there only remained the hunting down of the Peshwa and the Bhonsla who had avoided capture, and the final extermination of the Pindaris. These tasks were entrusted to a number of light columns of mounted troops which, with a little help from a tiger which accounted for the boldest and most elusive of the Pindari leaders, managed finally to subdue the entire area. By 1819 all the territories of the Mahratta Confederacy had passed into the Company's control.

Five years after the defeat of the Mahrattas the Company was compelled to undertake a campaign in Burma, which will be considered later, but, this apart, there followed two decades of peace in India, broken only by a month's operations in 1825-26 to subdue the fortress of Bhurtpore. This siege witnessed the first use of the lance† by British regular cavalry, in this case by the 16th Light Dragoons who, with the 9th, 12th and 23rd, had been converted into lancers in 1816 as a result of the numerous successes by Polish, and later French, lancer regiments in the Napoleonic army.

The British garrison in India now consisted of two elements. First there were the King's, soon to be Queen's, regiments of cavalry and infantry which came out for tours of duty, often as long as 20 years, and then returned home when relieved by others. As their ranks thinned through expiry of a man's service or death, so they were reinforced by drafts sent out from England. Many soldiers therefore might spend their whole service in India and indeed, when a regiment returned home, men had the option of transferring to an incoming regiment; some took their discharges in India and entered the Company's service. By 1835 the King's regiments in India numbered 20 of infantry and four of cavalry. The latter were usually light dragoons, lancers or hussars since the big men of the heavy cavalry required big horses which were not readily available in India, though later these too will be found serving there. Only the Household troops were exempt from Indian service.

The second element was the Company's armies of the Bengal, Madras and Bombay Presidencies. Each had a proportion of Europeans, now almost entirely of British, frequently Irish, origin, who were enlisted by the Company for a lifetime of service in India, either in the white battalions of infantry maintained by each Presidency, or in the artillery, horse and foot. They were a strange, hard breed these Company Europeans, who relieved the tedium of their peacetime life in sweltering cantonments with copious draughts of rum, and who welcomed the chance of active service *"with an instinctive fierceness and alacrity, (making) almost fiendlike superhuman efforts".(1)* The tenacity in battle of the Bengal Horse Artillery, a corps d'élite known as *"The Red Men"* from the colour of the horse-hair manes on their Roman-style helmets, has been immortalized in Rudyard Kipling's poem *"Snarleyow"*, while the very nickname of the Bombay Europeans was the *"Old Toughs".*

The bulk of the Company's armies were formed by the native regiments of cavalry and infantry. In 1824 the latter were reorganized into single-battalion regiments, of which Bengal had 69, Madras 51 and Bombay 26. In addition Bengal had 15 "local battalions" which included the Gurkhas. By the 1850s the Bengal Army had increased to 74 battalions. The mounted branch was of two types: the regular regiments of light cavalry, of which Bengal and Madras had, in 1824, eight each and Bombay three, all being dressed, trained and equipped like British light dragoons; and the irregular, or 'silladar' horse* of which the prototypes were the regiments raised by the half-caste, James Skinner, and William Gardner, who had fought as a mercenary for Holkar and married a 13-year-old Indian princess. In the 'silladar' regiments, the troopers or 'sowars' provided their own horses and accoutrements, consequently attracting a better class of man, and their whole character was much more "Indian" than the light cavalry, with at most only three British officers, whereas in the latter all the squadron and troop leaders were British. In the infantry battalions the number of British officers had risen from the three of Stringer Lawrence's day to as many as 23,with consequent downgrading of the Indian officers' responsibility and prestige.

The Bengal Army fancied itself a cut above the other two, partly because it was the largest and partly because both its British officers and Indian sepoys considered themselves socially superior. In Bengal the ranks were filled with high-caste Hindu Brahmans and Rajputs from Oudh and Behar, who were more imposing than the smaller, darker-skinned men of the other armies, and to whom the whole complex question of caste+ was all-important and hence was given every consideration in the Bengal Army, even to the prejudice of discipline. Though less impressive in appearance, the Bombay and Madras sepoys were hardier, and since men served together in the ranks regardless of caste — *"we put our religion in our knapsacks when our colours are unfurled" (2)* — their pride was in their battalions rather than, as in Bengal regiments, in their caste.

---

† An ash staff, tipped with a steel point and butt, at first 7ft long, increased to 9ft in 1829. Ash was superseded by bamboo in 1877.

* Only in Bengal and Bombay.

+ See Philip Mason, "A Matter of Honour"(1974) pp.123-126.

Whatever their variations the Company's native armies could, by the 1830s, look back with some satisfaction on nearly a hundred years of almost unqualified military triumph, and the sepoys displayed the loyalty and self-respect that comes from membership of any successful organization. Their fidelity and reliability was, however, beginning to be taken for granted by their British officers who were increasingly less committed to their sepoys as individuals than their forbears had been. A perceptive civilian observed that the sepoys' attachment to their officers rested upon the character of the latter, and on the lack of *"some powerful cause of discontent and excitement".(3)* Although there had been isolated instances of discontent, little had so far occurred to crack the seemingly invincible structure of an army which was, after all, recruited from a subject people and commanded by an alien race.

In 1838 British fears for India as a result of Russian expansion in Asia led to the replacement, by force of arms, of the Amir of Afghanistan, Dost Mohammed, with a British nominee, Shah Shujah. Between British India and Afghanistan lay the great Sikh Empire of Ranjit Singh which straddled the Punjab, Kashmir and most of north-west India. Ranjit Singh would not permit the passage of a British army through his territory, so the advance into Afghanistan had to take the long route to Kabul through the Bolan Pass and Kandahar. After eight weeks' operations, beset by disease, shortage of water and supplies, Shah Shujah was installed in Kabul in August 1839. It soon became clear that his rule could only be sustained by a British army of occupation. This was established in cantonments outside the city and by 1841 was reduced to a large brigade, composed of the 44th Foot, the 5th Bengal Light Cavalry, three regiments of Bengal Infantry†, and some irregular horse. The force was commanded by the elderly, infirm and hopelessly indecisive General Elphinstone. Meanwhile the rest of the army marched back to India, meeting such rapidly increasing opposition from the Afghan tribes along its routes that, although the Bombay force got through, Brigadier Sale with his own regiment, the 13th Foot, and some Bengal troops was forced to take shelter in an old fort at Jellalabad, where he was besieged for five months.

In the closing months of 1841 the situation of the garrison at Kabul daily grew more critical through the irresolution of the command, the onset of the bitter Afghan winter, shortage of supplies, and the all-pervasive menace of the tribes. While the officers quarrelled and complained, the morale of the Bengal sepoys crumbled in the intense cold and the 44th was not much better. When an out-lying post manned by a picquet of the British regiment and some sepoys was attacked by Afghans, Lady Sale, who had been left by her husband at Kabul, contemptuously noted: *"They all ran away as fast as they could – all cowards alike".(4)* This stout-hearted woman, the archetype of the British 'memsahib', seems to have had more spirit than the rest of the garrison put together.

On Christmas Eve the British envoy in Kabul, Macnaghten, was murdered within 600 yards of the British camp by Afghans led by Akbar Khan, the son of the deposed Dost Mohammed. Elphinstone did nothing, but a few days later contracted with Akbar Khan to withdraw the garrison to India under the latter's protection. On 6th January 1842, amid scenes of appalling muddle in sub-zero temperatures, the long unwieldy column, with a huge quantity of baggage, set out. The conditions were atrocious: *"Men frozen to death...women and children left on the roadside to perish...the men bivouacked all night in the snow, without a particle of food or bedding or wood to light a fire. Discipline was clearly at an end".(5)* All the while the treacherous Afghans hung like vultures on the flanks and rear of the wretched column, massacring the stragglers. On the 9th Akbar undertook to save the women and children, including Lady Sale, who was to endure eight months' captivity. In three days Elphinstone's brigade had been reduced from some 5,000 men to about 700 effectives, of which only some troopers of the 5th Cavalry and the 44th, whom adversity had somehow restored to discipline, could be counted upon. Indeed had it not been for the 44th, who again and again threw back the marauding Afghans, the miserable remnants would have succumbed even earlier. The end finally came on the 12th at Gandamak, in the Jagdalak Pass, where the last tiny handful of the 44th stood at bay and fought off successive attacks until they were overwhelmed. A few wounded men were taken by the Afghans, including Captain Souter who had tied the Regimental colour round his waist to save it, but only one man of the entire force, Dr Brydon, managed to escape to the safety of Sale's garrison at Jellalabad.

Such an affront to British prestige could not go unpunished and in March an avenging army under General Pollock set out from Peshawar to march on Kabul. The advance was hotly contested and Lieutenant Cumming of the 9th Foot wrote to his father: *"We have all to do over again,...at an immense cost of life.* The warfare is of a more trying and harassing kind than any before experienced in this country. Every eminence, every crag shelters an enemy. Such a warfare is calculated to try, to its utmost stretch, the fortitude of man".(6)* Though greatly hampered by shortage of transport, Pollock relieved Sale at Jellalabad and pushed on to Kabul, using his British regiments, 3rd Light Dragoons, 9th, 13th and 31st Foot, for the hardest fighting, finally reaching the Afghan capital on 15th September, where he was joined two days later by General Nott's force from Kandahar.

---

† 5th, 37th and 54th BNI.
* Including his own. He was killed in the Khyber Pass on 5th April, 1842.

138

Lord Lake and his son Colonel Lake
at the battle of Laswari, 1803
Stipple engraving by R.Cooper after Place,
published by Edward Orme, 1807   7102-33-222

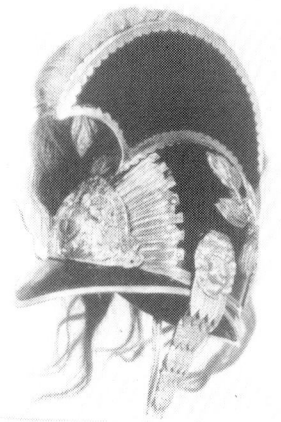

Lieut-General Hugh, Viscount Gough c1850
Portrait, oil on canvas, artist unknown   6003-130

2nd Regt   7002-14
Madras Light Cavalry
Officer's helmet c1830

1st Madras Native Infantry c1838
Shoulder belt plate   5705-5

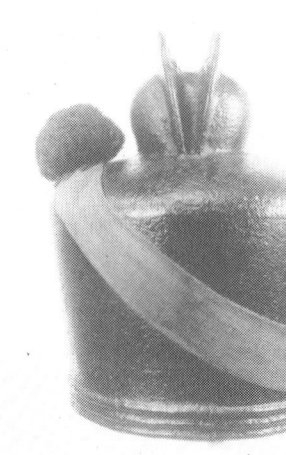

25th Regiment Bombay Native Infantry
c1846 Shako plate   7012-107-1

Madras Native Infantry c1850
Sepoy's shako   7109-21

General Sir Charles Napier c1850
Portrait, oil on canvas by S.P.Smart   6007-3

Skinner's Horse at Exercise, c1840
Painting, oil on canvas, by J.R. Gwatkin, c1840

6812-32

1st Afghan War 1842
Advance on the fort of Mamoo Khaul
Watercolour by G.A. Croley

6610-13

The British prisoners were released, part of Kabul was burnt, and the whole force returned to India, harassed all the way until it emerged from the Khyber Pass. That nothing had been achieved by the whole futile undertaking was proved by the immediate return of Dost Mohammed to his throne. That a great deal had been lost was obvious from the thousands of corpses of British soldiers and Indian sepoys scattered over Afghanistan. Even more significant were the facts that British power had been humbled in the eyes of the peoples of the East, that the legend of the invincibility of the Company's armies had been broken, and, above all, that confidence had been undermined, of the sepoys in their masters and indeed themselves, and of the British in the sepoys. The facade had sustained its first cracks, which before long were bound to endanger the whole edifice.

During the First Afghan War the British had made use of the territories of the Baluchi Amirs of Sind, a turbulent and ill-governed land which lay astride the River Indus. In order to retain their bases there and keep control of the Indus after the war, they again repeated their Afghan policy of replacing one ruler, Mir Rustam of Sind, with their own nominee. As in Afghanistan, the Baluchis sprang to arms and attacked the British Residency in Hyderabad. Fortunately the British commander in Sind was of a very different metal to those of the Afghan War. Sir Charles Napier, one of three famous military brothers who had all fought with distinction in the Peninsular War†, was a vigorous, fearless leader, albeit of eccentric appearance, with a great sympathy for the ordinary soldier. In a campaign as swift in execution as it was dubious in legality, Napier, with a small force of 2,500 including only one Queen's regiment, the 22nd Foot, defeated the Baluchis at Meanee and Hyderabad and completed the conquest and annexation of Sind in the first six months of 1843, notifying the Governor-General of his success with his famous punning telegram, " 'Peccavi' – I have sinned." The campaign witnessed Napier's remarkable dash, with 350 men of the 22nd mounted on camels in pairs and 200 of the Sind Horse*, across the desert to destroy the fortress of Imamgarh, so as to convince the Amirs that neither its supposed impregnability nor the desert wastes could deter British troops. The 22nd was a regiment of young soldiers who had never been in action before but who, in their first battle at Meanee, displayed a notable instinct for tactics. Forming the right wing of Napier's line, they had been ordered to charge with the bayonet but, on being suddenly confronted by a mass of Baluchis concealed in a dried-up river bed, they quickly realised, despite repeated orders to charge, that the musket would be far more effective. *The continued and destructive roll of musketry, delivered from the edge nearly of the river bank, levelled every being before it".(7)* Their action paved the way to victory and Napier, who was Colonel of the Regiment, seeing their thinned ranks after the battle, said with tears in his eyes: *"I can't make you a speech, my lads, but by God you are all gentlemen".(8)*

The questionable ethics of the annexation of Sind caused misgivings among all the semi-autonomous princes of India who began to fear for their own lands. It also alarmed the sepoys of the Bengal Army who were called upon to garrison it. For foreign service, as in Afghanistan, they received a special allowance, or 'batta', which, since Sind was across the Indus and therefore outside the Bengal Presidency, they expected to get there. However, as Sind was now annexed to the Company's domains, this claim was deemed by the authorities to be inadmissable. Serious unrest ensued in the regiments concerned and was only overcome by court-martialling the ringleaders, disbanding one regiment, and turning Sind over to the Bombay Presidency. However the incident, with its challenge to discipline and betrayal, as they saw it, of the sepoys' trust, further damaged the cohesion of the Bengal Army. The next campaign was not to make them any happier.

By 1845 it was becoming increasingly obvious that sooner or later the Company would clash with the Sikhs of the Punjab. Under Ranjit Singh the Sikhs had developed into a great nation with a powerful army, the Khalsa, particularly strong in infantry and artillery, which was trained and equipped on European lines by European adventurers, many of them ex-soldiers of Napoleon's armies. The Sikhs were big, hairy men who rejoiced in martial prowess and beside whom the Bengal sepoys, famed for their appearance, were almost insignificant. The high-caste Brahmans from Oudh loathed and feared the Sikhs as uncouth barbarians; the Sikhs merely held them in contempt. Towards the British, Ranjit Singh had pursued a policy to ensure mutual respect without confrontation. After his death in 1839, with the state rent by feuding factions, the Khalsa gradually began to usurp control and, conscious of British weakness displayed in the Afghanistan fiasco, determined to test its strength against the Company as a diversion from the internal squabbling. In December 1845 the Khalsa crossed the Sutlej and invaded British territory with 50,000 men and 100 guns, advancing to Ferozeshah while part of the army threatened an outlying British garrison under General Littler at Ferozepore.

The struggle with the Sikhs consisted of two campaigns: in the first, fought during the cold weather of 1845-46, four pitched battles were fought after which the defeated Sikhs were allowed to retain sovereignty of the Punjab under British protection once various concessions had been exacted; two years later the Sikhs rebelled, only to be defeated and have the whole of the Punjab annexed by the Company. The war was, however, to see some of the most fiercely contested battles ever fought in India. The British commander-in-chief

† His younger brother, William, was the author of the classic, *"History of the War in the Peninsula".*
* A 'silladar' regiment, raised by a brilliant leader of such troops, John Jacob.

was Sir Hugh Gough, a genial, fire-eating Irishman for whom the ultimate in tactical expertise was the bayonet charge, or what an officer described as *"the Tipperary rush (which) though effective, is rather expensive in good material".(9)* His best material was his Queen's regiments of cavalry and infantry, but the bulk of his force came from the Bengal Army. The cavalry were grouped in two-regiment brigades, while the infantry were formed in divisions of a varying number of brigades, most of which contained one Queen's and two Company battalions. Despite 30 years having elapsed since Waterloo, tactics had hardly changed since that era, reliance still being placed on the two-deep line for attack or defence with its front covered by skirmishers. All companies of a battalion, not simply the light company, were now trained to perform the latter role and a more reliable musket, based on the percussion principle, was gradually replacing the old flintlock. The volley was still used for fire effect but, in the words of the 1833 infantry manual, *"the most essential and usual mode of firing upon active service"* was file-firing, in which the two men of a file† worked together, one covering the other, each file firing independently. Even the soldier's dress had undergone but few modifications since 1815, most designed to increase smartness at the expense of comfort, and the only concession to the Indian climate was a white cover for their shakos or forage caps; many regiments in India tended to favour undress uniform for campaigning, rather than full dress. For artillery Gough largely relied on the cream of the Bengal Army, the splendid Europeans of the Horse Artillery, but their guns were inferior in calibre and range to those of the Sikhs.

On 18th December 1845 Gough encountered the Sikhs at Mudki, after an approach march of 100 miles covered in five days. Despite the fatigue of his men and with only an hour of daylight remaining, he launched his infantry at the Sikh lines, while the 3rd Light Dragoons made a spirited attack on the enemy guns from a flank. The Queen's regiments* doggedly fought their way into the Sikh positions through the all-enveloping dust and smoke, both sides blazing away at each other as night fell, until the darkness allowed the Sikhs to withdraw.

Two days later the armies met again at Ferozeshah in a 48-hour battle of even greater ferocity and carnage. Gough was forced to delay his attack until the arrival of Littler's division+ which had evaded the Sikh containing force at Ferozepore. When he reached Gough, Littler attacked prematurely and his division was decimated by the Sikh guns; the 62nd Foot, against which most of the fire was directed, lost 17 out of their 23 officers and 250 men. Their supporting sepoy battalions hung back, leaving the remains of the British regiment, exhausted after their long approach march, to stand their ground until ordered to retire. Having wasted valuable time, Gough then threw his force against the Sikh entrenchments but the enemy guns were so well served, and since most of the work again devolved on the five Queen's regiments†† and the 1st Bengal Europeans (now Light Infantry), only part of the position had been captured by nightfall. Gough therefore withdrew his tired, scattered infantry to resume battle next morning. Despite a sleepless night under constant fire from the Sikh artillery, his men responded with great determination and finally drove the Sikhs from their batteries at the point of the bayonet. Then, as the weary troops rested from their heroic endeavours, a fresh Sikh force, the army from Ferozepore, appeared in front of the captured position and opened fire with 40 guns. The British, worn out with fighting, short of food, water and sleep, their ranks wasted by casualties and their ammunition exhausted, could do nothing but endure the bombardment while maintaining as formidable an appearance as possible, until astonishingly the Sikhs suddenly ceased fire and pulled away. A half-crazed British staff officer had ordered all the cavalry and artillery to withdraw, a movement the Sikh commander fortunately interpreted as a threat to his rear. Gough's men had sustained nearly 2,500 casualties of which over half were British troops, despite their forming less than 30 per cent of the entire force.

A lull in the campaign followed, while Gough received reinforcements and awaited a column of heavy guns from Delhi. In the middle of January 1846, hearing that a Sikh force of 20,000 was moving to intercept the Delhi column, Gough detached 10,000 under Sir Harry Smith, a veteran Rifleman of the Peninsular War, to head them off. Smith caught up with the Sikhs and defeated them in a brilliant engagment at Aliwal. The 16th Lancers made a series of magnificent charges, first against the enemy horse, and then smashing four squares of the finest infantry the Khalsa could muster, trained by a famous Italian adventurer and soldier, Avitabile. The 16th suffered severely, however, and at one point one troop was commanded only by a sergeant.

After Aliwal the Sikhs withdrew to a strong, semi-circular entrenchment, with 16 ft-thick earthworks, backing on the Sutlej at Sobraon, defended by 70 guns in three rows and manned by 20,000 men. On 10th February, having duly received his heavy guns and reinforced to 15,000 men, Gough attacked. After a two-hour bombardment, which had little effect on the massive earthworks, the guns ran out of ammunition.

---

† One in the front rank, one in the rear.
* 9th, 31st, 50th and 80th Foot.
+ 62nd Foot, five battalions Bengal Infantry, two regiments Bengal Light Cavalry.
†† The 29th Foot had joined the army after Mudki.

"Thank God!" said Gough, *"Now I can be at them with the bayonet!"(10)* On the left, among Sir Robert Dick's division stood a recently arrived regiment, the 10th Foot, fiercely disciplined by their colonel, a martinet named Franks, who, as they were about to advance, announced to his men: *"I understand you mean to shoot me today, but don't kill me until the battle is over".(11)* Immediately opposite their advance was a Sikh gunner who afterwards described their onset:

> *"Nearer and nearer they came, as steadily as if on parade, in perfect silence. At last the order came, 'Fire', and our whole battery as if from one gun fired into the advancing mass...what was my astonishment, when the smoke cleared, to see them still advancing in perfect silence, but their numbers reduced to one half... On they came in that awful silence till they were within a short distance of our guns... Then, with a shout, they made a rush... In ten minutes it was all over... who could withstand such fierce demons, with those awful bayonets".(12)*

Dick's division broke into the entrenchments but then met such a determined counter-attack that they were forced back to the outer line. In the centre and on the right Gilbert's and Smith's divisions made similar attacks to relieve the pressure on Dick but everywhere met savage resistance. No sooner were they repulsed, however, than they reformed and came on again. Three times the 29th, in the centre, attacked but each time were driven off with heavy loss. On the right, Smith's men, 31st, 50th and two Gurkha battalions, clambered on each other's shoulders to scale the earthworks. As they got up, both officers carrying the colours of the 31st were killed, but Sergeant McCabe seized the Regimental colour and planted it high on the ramparts; the men surged in, driving the Sikhs before them. *"The old 31st and 50th laid on like devils"*, wrote Harry Smith later, *"This was a brutal bulldog fight".(13)* A gap was made in the earthworks and the 3rd Light Dragoons poured through in single file, galloping and slashing through the Sikh camp. Unable to hold back the flood of men now engulfing the position on all sides, the Sikhs, still fighting ferociously, were gradually pushed back and across the single bridge over the river. Suddenly the bridge collapsed under the weight, and with the British guns firing grape-shot at the survivors, the gallant Sikhs were finished. Their army was shattered by huge casualties of some 10,000 and the First Sikh War was over.

In the uneasy peace of the British protectorate that followed, Henry Lawrence, the British Resident at Lahore, set about restoring sound administration to the Punjab, assisted by a team of outstanding young officers from the Company's armies, who were all to make names for themselves in India: John Nicholson, Herbert Edwardes, Reynell Taylor and several others. One of them, Harry Lumsden, was entrusted with the formation of a body of troops, part cavalry, part infantry, to gain intelligence and to maintain security. Lumsden filled its ranks with hillmen from across the Indus, Pathans and Afridis, a very different breed from the normal run of Company sepoys; he gave them a uniform of loose-fitting clothing dyed the colour of the ground, the forerunner of khaki, from a Persian word, 'khak', meaning dust. This body of men was to become one of the most famous and distinguished regiments of the Indian Army — the Corps of Guides.

In 1848 rebellion broke out at Multan. Herbert Edwardes, with a hastily raised force of hillmen, drove the ringleader, Mulraj, and his followers into Multan where, in response to his appeals for help, General Whish presently arrived with a force of 7,000, including the 10th and 32nd Foot, to besiege the city. He was later reinforced by units of the Bombay Army and the 60th Rifles. By late November the revolt had spread to the northern Punjab and Gough again took the field against the re-formed Khalsa with a force of about 16,000, including six Queen's regiments† and the 2nd Bengal Europeans.

After an unfortunate cavalry skirmish at Ramnuggar on 22nd November, Gough encountered the main Sikh army at Chillianwallah on 13th January 1849. In another of his "Tipperary rush" battles he threw his line in a frontal attack against a strong Sikh position and suffered fearful casualties, though gaining a technical victory. Misinterpreting the "advance" for the "charge", the 24th Foot, a very fine, strong, but inexperienced battalion of mainly young soldiers, made a gallant attack with the bayonet, far outstripping the sepoy battalions of their brigade, and were cut to pieces* when they reached the Sikh lines. In contrast, the 61st, on the left, made a masterly attack, file-firing as they advanced, and began to roll up the Sikh right, capturing a battery of 13 guns. However, they too were unsupported and had it not been for charges by the 3rd Light Dragoons which protected their flank and rear, they could have suffered the same fate as the 24th. The infantry on the right, though losing heavily, got into the Sikh positions but disaster struck the cavalry on that flank. Due to the incompetence of their elderly, short-sighted brigadier and a misheard order, a controlled advance suddenly turned into a panic-stricken rout+, in which even the 9th Lancers and the 14th Light Dragoons were caught up. All in all, with over 2,300 casualties, it was an unhappy day for Gough, and when the news reached England, Sir Charles Napier was sent out to replace him.

---

† Cavalry: 3rd and 14th Light Dragoons, 9th Lancers. Infantry: 24th, 29th and 61st Foot.

* They lost 13 officers and 203 men killed, nine and 266 wounded.

+ See the Marquess of Anglesey, "A History of the British Cavalry", Vol. I, pp. 279 — 282.

Charge of the 16th (Queen's Royal) Lancers at the battle of Aliwal, 1st Sikh War, 1846
Coloured aquatint by J.Harris after H. Martens published by R. Ackermann, 1847

6206-30-5

The Battle of Chillianwala, 13th January 1849
Painting, oil on canvas, by C.B. Young

6702-46

Chobham Camp 1853, troops effecting a passage across Virginia Water on pontoons
Coloured lithograph published by Read & Co 1853

7502-119

However, long before Napier could arrive, Gough redeemed himself by decisively defeating the Sikhs at Gujerat, having been reinforced by Whish who, after several setbacks, had finally taken Multan in January. The remnants of the Sikh army were pursued with vigour and on 30th March 1849 the Punjab was formally annexed as a British possession.

The war had shown how much reliance had to be placed on the Queen's regiments and the Company Europeans for, with a few exceptions, the Bengal Army, cavalry and infantry, had not been impressive. At Ferozeshah, *"the native cavalry did not behave well"* and at Chillianwallah the 5th Light Cavalry *"ran away to a man".(14)* An infantry brigadier referred to his *"blackguard Sepoys . . . . who fell from the ranks from exhaustion or funk"(15)*, Lieutenant Bace of the 61st said of the sepoy battalions in his brigade at Chillianwallah that, although the 46th N. I. *"kept up pretty well"*, the 36th *"behaved shamefully . . . an armed rabble . . . the Sepoys firing in terror and at random, some discharging their muskets straight up towards the sky". (16)* British officers could not but compare the performance of the Bengal troops with the indomitable fighting spirit of the Sikh infantry and gunners. Indeed Sikhs and Punjabis were soon being enlisted into the Company's army, some into the Bengal regiments, where they made a strange contrast with the Brahmans of Oudh, but more importantly into special regiments of a Frontier Brigade, for service against the turbulent tribes of the north-west across the Indus. This was the beginnings of one of the finest components of the Army in India, the Punjab Irregular, later Frontier Force — the "Piffers".

For their part the Sikhs, while respecting and admiring the qualities of the British troops, grew ever more contemptuous of the Bengal sepoys and longed to revenge themselves on these representatives of an army that had defeated them, with results that will be seen later. Their fierce and aggressive demeanuor, even in defeat, and the obvious admiration the British had for them, further undermined the sepoys' morale, confidence and trust, already weakened by the Afghan and Sikh wars, and by yet still more injustices over their pay. Moreover, as mentioned earlier, many of the British officers of the native regiments, especially the younger and more recently joined, were showing an ever more evident unconcern for their duties and indifference towards their men. The cracks were developing into clefts but there were few who had the time or inclination to spot the danger to the edifice.

By the end of 1852 British India encompassed the whole of the sub-continent, from Peshawar in the north-west to Ceylon in the south and including the Burmese coastline down to Rangoon. In 1824 depredations by the Burmese against British territory in east Bengal had led to the First Burma War, a campaign of river and jungle operations largely carried out by the Madras Army, supported by Queen's regiments. After two years' fighting the Burmese Court of Ava signed a treaty which ceded to the Company the provinces of Assam, Cachar, Manipur and part of the Arakan coast. In 1852 violations of the treaty and oppression of merchants trading in Rangoon led to the despatch of a 20,000 strong expedition under General Godwin, part from Bengal and part from Madras, which included three Queen's regiments and, notably some Sikhs†. The fighting that followed centred on the Irrawaddy Delta around Rangoon, the chief feat of arms being a spirited attack in tropical heat by the 18th and 80th Foot, who stormed the strongly held, 350 ft-high Shwe Dagon pagoda, set on a terraced hill all ringed about with walls and stockades. Further skirmishes took place among the towns, rivers and swamps of the Delta but by the end of the year most resistance had ceased and the whole of the Burmese coast, from Chittagong down to Rangoon and Pegu, passed into British possession.

It was now nearly a hundred years since Clive defeated the first major Indian threat to the East India Company. In that time the Company had grown from a primarily trading organization into a mighty agency through which Britain, 10,000 miles away by sea, governed a vast territory nearly twenty times its own size. Its authority had been achieved by, and now rested upon a handful of British regiments, Queen's and Company's, and a much larger native army, which together had not only successively overcome all the warrior races of India, but offered many of them the chance of service in its cause. This service had been freely and loyally given, so unquestioningly that over the years the Company's officers had come to assume it as their right. The consequences of such carelessness were soon to be felt, after a momentous interlude elsewhere, on the very centenary of Plassey.

---

† The 4th Sikh Infantry and the Ludhiana Regiment. The Queen's regiments were the 18th, 51st and 80th.

'The Field of the Cloth of Gold' 1513. Detail of painting showing Henry VIII and the Yeomen of the Guard.

H.M. The Queen

145

Col. Francis Hawley, 1st Foot Guards c1685
Oil painting, artist unknown

Lady Louisa Lennox with her husband's regiment, the 25th, at Minorca, with Fort S. Philip in the background
Painting, oil on canvas, attributed to Guiseppe Chiesa 1771   7402-123

Lieut John Clayton Cowell 1st Foot, 1796

Portrait, oil on canvas, attributed to Sir William
Beechey   Purchased with the aid of the National
Art Collections Fund   6311-133

A Sergeant, 2nd Foot, c1805

Painting, oil on canvas, artist unknown

6208-77

147

Defence of the Chateau de Hougoumont by the flank company. Coldstream Guards, Waterloo. c1815
Watercolour by Denis Dighton

7505-7-1

Skinner's Horse at Exercise, c1840. Painting, oil on canvas, by J.R. Gwatkin, c1840.

6812-31

'The Welcome Arrival' A scene in the Crimea c1855
Painting, oil on canvas, by J. D. D'A Luard

5808-18

'Home Sweet Home' A Corporal of the 11th Hussars home on leave
Painting, oil on canvas, by C. M. Hodges, c1890

7508-25

149

British Officers of Indian Cavalry Regiment c1910.
5th Cavalry, 23rd Cavalry, 17th Cavalry, 26th Cavalry, 11th Lancers (Probyns Horse), 4th Cavalry, 16th Cavalry.
Watercolour by A.C. Lovett

5302-7

Guardsman - Service Dress   Officer - Service Dress   Subaltern - Service Dress   Sergeant - Service Dress
Fighting Order   Drill Order   Marching Order   Drill Order

The First or Grenadier Regiment of Foot Guards, 1925.

Her Majesty Queen Elizabeth II Trooping The Colour.

The Royal Scots Dragoon Guards at Catterick March 1978 Infantry - Tank co-operation.

Rolls-Royce B-Range engines.

Rolls-Royce Motors is one of the world's leading specialists in the design, development and manufacture of military engines—the B-Range engine is currently in service with the defence forces of 28 nations.

ROLLS-ROYCE MOTORS
Specialist and Light Aircraft Engine Division

CHAPTER 12
AGAINST THE RUSSIAN BEAR
1816-1856

On day after day in early 1854 the streets and docksides of the ports of Britain echoed to the sound of military bands as they crashed out a rousing popular tune of the day, *"Cheer, boys, cheer!"* Though not much given to acclamation of the despised redcoat, the solid, worthy, mid-Victorian citizens did surely cheer as, for the first time in nearly 40 years, they watched their soldiers going off to war. They cheered in anticipation of seeing the British lion savage, not the French eagle as in their youth, but a new adversary, the Russian bear. Indeed this time lion and eagle were to be brothers-in-arms, so strange a reversal of past practice that the troops' elderly commander would never be able quite to grasp it.

The sudden bellicosity of the British populace was perhaps more a flexing of the national muscle than any passionate belief in the cause their government had embraced on their behalf and at their behest. To be sure the underlying motives for the coming struggle were not that easy to apprehend since they involved support for a Moslem power, the Ottoman Empire, by two Christian nations, Britain and France, against a third, Russia. The quarrel arose from a dispute at Jerusalem, then in Turkish territory, between the Greek Orthodox Church, under the protection of Russia, and the Catholic Church, under the protection of France, over the custody of the Holy Sepulchre. Concessions made to France by the Turks in this regard incensed the Tsar, who demanded safeguards for the whole Greek Church in the Ottoman Empire and sent troops into the provinces of Moldavia and Wallachia along the Danube to enforce his demands. Alarmed at the possibility of a Russian partition of Turkish territories, with its consequent Russian command of the Bosphorous and the Dardenelles, which would threaten the Mediterranean and the route to India, Britain and France moved fleets up to the Dardenelles. On 23rd October 1853 Turkey declared war on Russia, who retaliated by destroying the Turkish fleet at Sinope on 7th November. This outraged public opinion in Britain, forcing the Government, already under pressure from the French Emperor, Napoleon III, into a more belligerent attitude towards Russia. In early 1854 both countries sent troops to Malta as an indication of their serious intent, followed in March by an ultimatum to the Tsar, requiring him to withdraw from the Danubian provinces. On 28th March, the Tsar having declined to comply, war was declared on Russia. In Britain Government and people now looked for a speedy victory from their Army, which they had reduced, ignored and neglected since Waterloo.

After the end of the occupation of France in 1818, the Army was cut to an establishment of 104,000 cavalry and infantry, of which 52,000 were garrisoned in the United Kingdom, 18,000 in India, and 34,000 in the colonies: Canada, the West Indies, the Mediterranean and Ionian Islands, West Africa, the Cape and Australia. The Ordnance arms totalled some 6,000. Four years later the overall establishment was further reduced to 100,000. All cavalry regiments above the 17th Lancers had been disbanded and the junior regiment of infantry was now the 93rd, the 95th Rifles having been taken out of the Line after Waterloo and designated the Rifle Brigade. The Royal Waggon Train, which had proved so useful in the Napoleonic Wars, was reduced to a strength of 120 all ranks and by 1833 had been abolished altogether, thus losing to the Army all the accumulated expertise in the field of transport and supply. All the divisional and brigade organization and all the staff system were swept away and the Army again reverted to being simply a collection of regiments scattered, often in small detachments, all over the British Isles and the overseas possessions.

In the two decades after Waterloo the need for national economy and the old distrust of a standing army ensured a concerted attack by Parliament on all military expenditure and consistent hostility towards the Army as an institution, both from politicians and people alike. Had it not been for the turbulent nature of the times, with rumours of rebellion, riots, conspiracies and radical agitation springing up everywhere in the wake of economic hardship, the Army would have been reduced even more. Until the Metropolitan Police was placed on a proper footing in 1829 and the formation of borough police forces ten years later and county police in 1855, the Army, though it had no love for the task, was the main bulwark against public disturbances, supported by the part-time Yeomanry cavalry which rendered invaluable service in maintaining order, though incurring the odium of the radicals for its part in the so-called "Peterloo Massacre". Although some of the Militia had to be called out during serious riots in Bristol in 1831, the force as a whole existed only on paper, with Parliament refusing to vote money for its upkeep and finally abolishing the ballot and reducing its permanent staff in 1835.

The soldier of the 1820s and 1830s was once again enlisted for unlimited service, usually from the lowest levels of society and increasingly from Ireland, as famine and destitution stalked that unhappy country. He was wretchedly housed in overcrowded and unhygienic barracks in which he was allowed 300 cubic feet of air as opposed to the convict's entitlement in prison of 1,000 cubic feet. His rations were one pound of bread and three-quarters of a pound of meat per day for which the only means of cooking was boiling in the two coppers allowed for each barrack room. His pay was a shilling a day, of which, after deductions for his rations, maintenance of his equipment and laundry, he received twopence halfpenny. Most of this went on drink, the dubious delights of the wet canteen being the only facilities provided, by often unscrupulous contractors, for his recreation. The widespread drunkenness that ensued, coupled with crowded conditions in the barrack rooms, resulted in outbreaks of indiscipline which could only be kept in check by flogging. While officers necessarily were insistent on maintaining good discipline in their regiments, at the same time it was only through their efforts that the soldiers' existence was made more endurable, though what they could do was limited by the extent of their own, often slender resources which had additional calls upon them.

The easy-fitting uniforms of the Napoleonic Wars had been smartened and tightened up with evermore imposing and impractical headgear to top them off. For the men such finery required constant cleaning with inadequate facilities, but for the officers, who had to pay for their own uniforms, the frequent dress changes and quantities of gold embroidery and decoration that so delighted the eye of George IV put them to never-ending expense. During the great increase of the Army during the Napoleonic Wars all manner of folk had received commissions, but after Waterloo officers generally came from the younger sons of the country gentry who, though usually possessing some private income, were not, except for some in the Guards and cavalry, rich men. Nor were they well paid. Once the interest on the money each had invested in purchasing his rank†, plus regimental expenses and income tax, had been deducted, the net annual pay for an ensign resulted in just over £75, rising to £114 for a lieutenant-colonel. An officer could realise the value of his commission by selling it at any time but, if he did so, he forfeited the interest on it, and, if he died while still serving, its value passed, not to his dependents, but to the next senior officer who was promoted without purchase into the vacancy caused by death. Such financial windfalls also accrued to officers who were fortunate and senior enough to fill rank vacancies caused by an increase to a regiment's establishment. However, in a relatively peaceful age, with more reductions than increases, the purchase system could condemn an able but penniless officer to spending long years in the same rank, while richer, younger men could buy their advancement over his head. The system was "illogical, iniquitous and indefensible"(1) but it appealed to a nation parsimonious where its Army was concerned since it avoided the need to provide pensions for officers.

The general neglect and stagnation of the Army under indifferent politicians and highly conservative commanders largely continued up to the outbreak of war in 1854 but from 1837 a few improvements were made. Following the report of a commission inquiring into military punishments, it was agreed by many officers from the Duke of Wellington downwards that, in view of the type of man enlisted and the conditions of service existing in the Army, discipline could not be maintained without use of the lash. However the maximum number of strokes had been reduced the previous year* and since the total number of floggings in the Army at home had fallen from 246 in 1835 to 163 in 1836, the commission hoped that in time flogging could be abolished as a punishment; by 1846 the maximum sentence from any court had been reduced to 50 lashes. The commission also recommended the awards of badges and extra pay for good conduct. By 1847 enlistment had been restricted to a term of ten years in the infantry with the option of re-engaging for a further eleven; in the cavalry and artillery the terms were 14 and 12 years. The need to improve barracks had been recognized, each man now had his own bed instead of, as previously, having to share a four-berth crib, schemes for regimental libraries and savings banks had been instituted, and the regulations regarding the sale of ruinous spirits in regimental canteens had been tightened up. Money had even been voted for the education of soldiers' children living in barracks. The uniform, though still impractical and increasingly old-fashioned compared to those of some European armies, had been shorn of its more fanciful and expensive embellishments. The percussion musket and carbine were

† The regulation prices for Infantry were: lieutenant-colonel £4,500; major £3,200; captain £1,800; lieutenant £700; and ensign £450. In the Foot Guards and cavalry the prices were much higher. These sums were frequently, though illegally, exceeded. The regulation price for a cavalry lieutenant-colonelcy was £6,175 but Lord Cardigan was alleged to have spent £40,000 in buying command of the 11th Hussars.
* To 200 from a general court-martial; 150 from a district court-martial; 100 from a regimental court-martial.

replacing the old flintlocks and would soon, from 1852, be superseded by a rifle, the Minié, still a muzzle-loader but with greatly improved range and penetration. Although the Duke of Wellington, still Commander-in-Chief of the Army and nearing the end of his life, approved it, he forbade its being called a rifle, otherwise he thought the soldiers *"will become conceited, and be wanting next to be dressed in green, or some other jack-a-dandy uniform".(2)*

A number of colonial campaigns, particularly the Sikh Wars, had forced an always reluctant Parliament to vote increases to the Army's establishment which, having risen to 144,000 in 1848, dropped to 130,000 in 1851, only to rise again to 135,000, including 30,000 for India, when a new danger threatened in 1852. In France another Bonaparte, Louis Napoleon, nephew of the great Emperor, had seized power and would shortly proclaim himself Napoleon III. Not only was the regular Army increased but a new Militia Bill was passed, providing for the embodiment of 80,000 men, who were to be raised voluntarily, or if insufficient were forthcoming, by ballot, and were to receive 28 days training annually. Later the same year an inspection of the Royal Artillery disclosed that there were only 40 guns of all calibres, most with unserviceable carriages, in the whole of Great Britain. For once urgent steps were taken to rectify the deficiency and a further 1,000 men were authorised for that arm. In 1853 a novel experiment was tried out: the establishment at Chobham in Surrey of a camp of exercise for formed brigades of cavalry and infantry with supporting artillery, engineers and a pontoon-train. It revealed many failings in the troops' training, particularly in the artillery, and highlighted the lack of attention that had been paid to the handling of bodies above battalion or regimental level— an almost inescapable defect due to the lack of manoeuvre areas in Britain. This led to the purchase of a large tract of land around Aldershot, initially as a training area but which after the Crimean War became the largest concentration of troops in the country. All these belated attempts to put right the neglect of the previous decades had gone some way to rendering the Army fitter for the struggle it was about to face, but the rigours of active service would soon reveal just how destructive of efficiency the hostility and indifference of its political masters and the conservatism of its military chiefs had been.

The expeditionary force, or "Army of the East" as it was called, that was sent to Turkey in 1854 included five regiments of heavy cavalry and five of light; three battalions of Foot Guards, 27 of the Line and two of the Rifle Brigade; two horse artillery troops, eight field batteries and a siege train; and 300 Sappers and Miners. By the end of the year a further eight battalions had joined the army and, as the war progressed, four more regiments of cavalry and 12 battalions of infantry were sent out. Of the original force, only the 50th Foot and the 1st Battalion Rifle Brigade had seen active service in the preceding ten years, the former in the Sikh War and the latter at the Cape. The men were nearly all *"veterans of from five to fifteen years' service; strong, hardy, well-intentioned fellows, whom no nation on earth could match".(3)* The merit of this claim can be judged to this day by the fine faces and strong physique of these long-service soldiers, caught by the cameras of Robertson, Fenton and other practitioners of the new art of photography. Splendid though the individual regiments undoubtedly were, no attempt was made, before sending them to the east, to form them into a field force, with the necessary staffs, organization and supporting services. Not until the army began to concentrate in Turkey were they grouped into five divisions of infantry and one of cavalry, each of two brigades with artillery attached, and their commanders appointed.

With the exception of the 35 year old Duke of Cambridge, the Queen's cousin, commanding the 1st Division of the Guards and Highland Brigades, all the other infantry divisional commanders were in their sixties. The Chief Engineer, Sir John Burgoyne, was 72. Sir George Brown, commanding the Light Division—Light in name only since it had but one battalion of that nature, the 2nd Rifle Brigade — and Sir G. de Lacy Evans, commanding the 2nd Division, were both veterans of the Peninsular War, while the 4th Division's Sir George Cathcart had had recent experience of a field command in 1852 during the Eighth Kaffir War at the Cape. In command of the Cavalry Division was the Earl of Lucan, then aged 54, on whom the forthcoming campaign was to impose its greatest burden in the personality of his detested and already notorious brother-in-law, the Earl of Cardigan, appointed to command the Light Cavalry Brigade. Had the Duke of Wellington not died two years before at the age of 83, it is not inconceivable, in the climate of the time, that he would have been offered the chief command. As it was, the mantle fell on one who had been his right hand since the Peninsular War, Lord Raglan, aged 66, formerly Lord Fitzroy Somerset, an able and conscientious staff officer, but a man who had never commanded so much as a company in the field, and whose military horizons had been bounded for the last few decades by the walls of Whitehall offices, working in the shadow of his great master. He was brave, courteous, self-effacing — almost to the point of invisibility where his troops were concerned — the epitome of the English gentleman, but in the conditions to be faced by an army suffering from 40 years of neglect, it might have been better, as one modern historian has suggested, if he had been *"a bloody-minded careerist bastard".(4)*

The deficiencies of the senior commanders might have been somewhat mitigated had their staffs been made up of officers trained and experienced in staff duties, but they were not. Out of 291 officers serving on the staff in May 1854 only 15 had been trained at the senior department of the Royal Military College. Most obtained their appointments, not through technical training or experience in India or other colonial campaigns, but through interest and influential connections, and *"with some bright exceptions, were neither more nor less than regimental officers, be-plumed and on horseback".(5)* The Commissariat Department was in the hands of a few Treasury clerks with no knowledge of or training in wartime duties. Since the Royal Waggon Train had long since been abolished and since only a handful of mules and carts were sent out by the Government, transport had to be improvised from local resources. The medical department was under-manned and under-supplied, the manufacture of ambulances was not even begun until after most of the force had left England and their drivers were found by calling up elderly service pensioners from retirement. Most casualty evacuation would have to be by stretchers carried by regimental bandsmen and drummers, many of whom were no more than boys. As the regiments and battalions were paraded at Constantinople for inspection by their French and Turkish allies, the steady ranks of well set-up, sunburned men, in their red, blue or green uniforms, their helmets, busbies, bearskins, shakos and feather bonnets, made a fine show but behind the magnificent facade lay serious defects of command, organization and administration.

In June 1854 the combined British and French armies were moved to Bulgaria with a view to supporting the Turks then facing the Russians along the Danube. However the Turks proved quite capable of dealing with the Russians on their own and forced them back across the Danube. Then Austria took a hand, undertaking with the Turks to ensure the Russian evacuation of Moldavia and Wallachia and to garrison those provinces with her own troops. By late August this had been accomplished and the British and French presence in Bulgaria was largely superfluous. But Napoleon III's belligerence and British popular opinion were not to be so easily assuaged. In mid-July the French commander, Marshal St Arnaud, had been ordered by the Emperor to prepare an attack on the Crimean peninsula with the aim of reducing the Russian naval base at Sevastopol. In England a public outcry, spearheaded by "The Times", demanded the same operation, thus not only forcing the Government's hand into ordering an enterprise to which no-one had given any consideration of the difficulties and dangers, but also giving the enemy due and clear warning of where the next Allied blow was likely to fall. While the deliberations went on and the telegrams flew back and forth between the commanders in the field and their Governments, dysentry, typhus and cholera struck the British and French camps in Bulgaria, reducing the two armies by death and sickness before either had fired a shot.

Despite the ill-health of the troops and the administrative weaknesses it disclosed, despite the misgivings of both army and naval commanders about the practicability of the operation, the invasion of the Crimea was determined upon and towards the end of August the embarkation of both armies began. On 13th September the fleet of ships arrived off the Crimean coast and on the following day the landing began on the shores of the unfortunately-named Kalamita Bay. This disembarkation luckily was unopposed but it took five days to get the troops ashore. By the 18th there stood on Russian soil about 26,000 British with 66 guns, 30,000 French with 70 guns and about 4,500 Turks. Of cavalry, only the British Light Brigade had as yet been disembarked. Sevastopol lay 30 miles southwards along the coast with five rivers intervening, but of information about the enemy's strength and dispositions there was none. The armies had no base other than the fleet. To make good the complete dearth of transport and ambulances in the British force, parties had to be sent to requisition all the native carts and their drivers that could be found in the vicinity; some 300 of various sizes were mustered by this means. The spell at sea had effected some improvement in the men's health but many were still weak from sickness and cholera still lurked in their ranks. They had no tents, only one blanket and greatcoat per man, and for cooking purposes there was one pot for every ten men and whatever fuel the men could gather and carry on their persons. All ranks were in full dress, the Guards, for instance, being uniformed exactly as for mounting the Queen's Guard in London, while Captain Maxwell of the 88th recalled that he wore *"the identical coat in which I had appeared at a ball at the Tuileries, which was not very comfortable in a ball room and quite unsuited for a wet night in a ploughed field".(6)*

The armies began their advance on the 19th, the French on the right or seaward flank, British on the left, and, after an inconclusive cavalry skirmish at the River Bulganak, closed up to within four miles of the River Alma, on the heights beyond which lay the first Russian defence line before Sevastopol. The Battle of the Alma on 20th September, the first of the Crimean War and of the British Army against a European enemy since Waterloo, was supposed to be a joint Franco-British attack, in which the French would turn the Russian left while the British performed the same service against the enemy right. Such was St Arnaud's understanding of the plan but Raglan merely promised him his general co-operation. In the event one French division established itself at the seaward extremity of the Russian line but was so feebly supported by the rest of the French army that Raglan had to commit his troops in a frontal attack against the bulk of the Russians. Having once

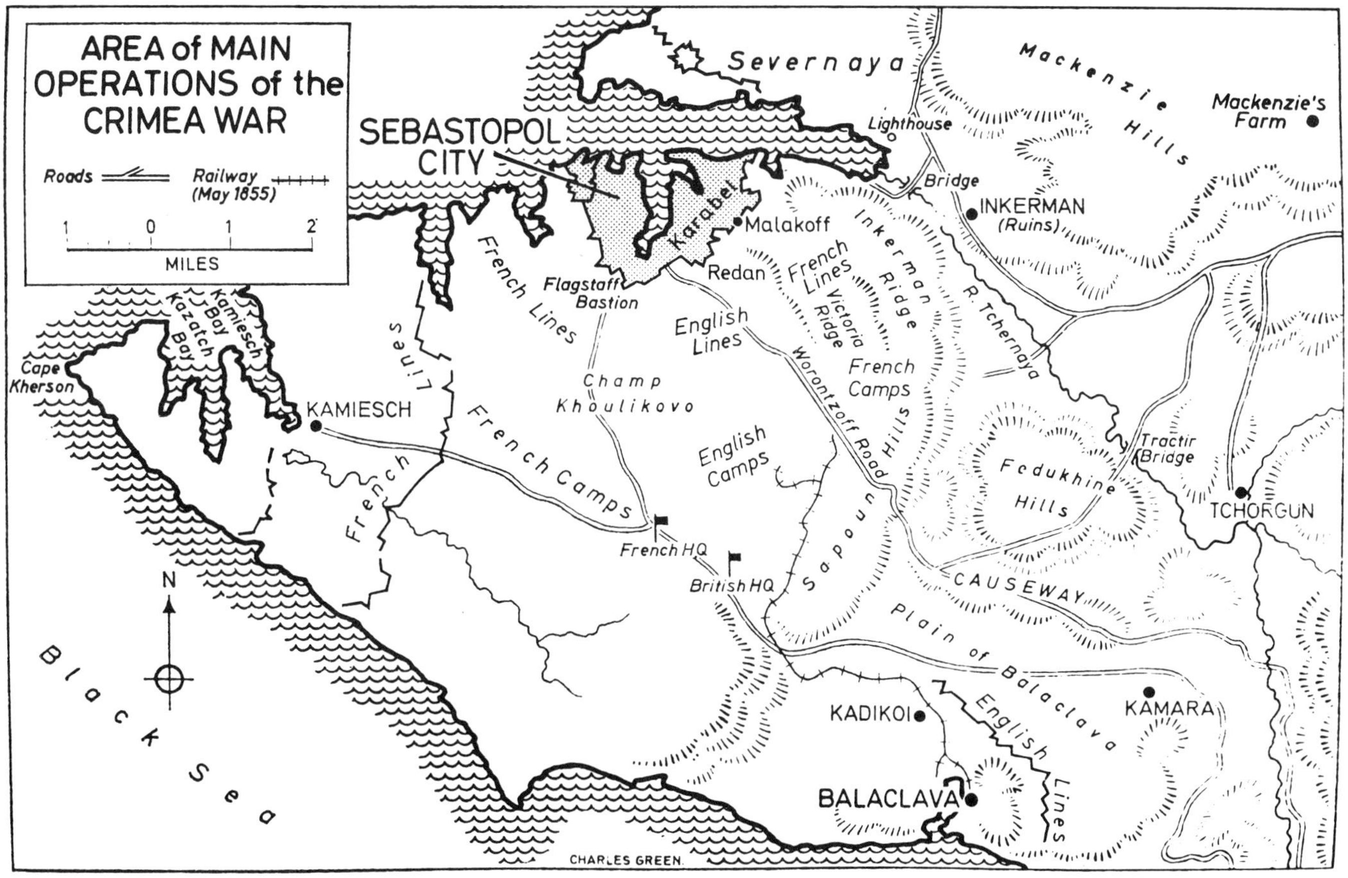

AREA of MAIN OPERATIONS of the CRIMEA WAR

Roads · Railway (May 1855)

MILES

CHARLES GREEN

given the order to advance, he rode with a small staff to a knoll midway between the Russian centre and left, well behind their advanced posts from which position, other than summoning up and directing the fire of two guns, he took no further part in the battle.

That the Russians were driven from a strong position was due entirely to the sense and drive of a few brigade and battalion commanders and the gallantry, determination and discipline of the British regimental officers and men. To attack the Russians they had first to negotiate the steep-banked river on which stood the village of Bourliouk, set on fire by the enemy and surrounded by numerous vineyards and enclosures in which skirmishers were posted. Beyond the river, on the British front, the ground sloped upwards to the Kourgane Hill where the Russians had deployed 16 battalions with supporting field batteries around two earth-works, the Great Redoubt holding 12 heavy guns and the Lesser Redoubt containing another field battery; on their extreme right and rear were 27 squadrons of cavalry. The advance was led by the Light Division on the left and the 2nd on the right, the front being covered by skirmishers of the 2nd Battalion Rifle Brigade, who led the attack in fine style, briskly clearing the river bank of the enemy outposts. Both divisions attacked with each of their two brigades in line covering a frontage of two miles, but since the 2nd Division had been left insufficient room to deploy, and since the burning village broke up its formation, its battalions advanced more or less independently, the 95th Foot† on its left wing actually joining the Light Division's attack. The latter's formation was also disrupted by the river and enclosures and, with two of its left wing battalions, the 77th and 88th, being halted by their brigadier to watch the left flank against a possible counter-stroke by Russian cavalry, its remaining four battalions, 7th, 19th, 23rd and 33rd, with the 95th, surged up the slopes

† Formed in 1824, taking the number vacated by the Rifle Brigade, formerly 95th Rifles.

158

in some disorder but nevertheless drove the Russians from the Great Redoubt. Unfortunately the victorious battalions were so intermingled that, when the inevitable Russian counter-attack came in, aided inadvertantly by a mysterious order to retire, the Light Division men began falling back except for the 7th Royal Fusiliers which, under their hated but respected colonel, Lacy Yea, continued an epic fire fight against four Russian battalions for upwards of half an hour.

The Duke of Cambridge had previously been ordered to support the Light Division's attack but, totally inexperienced in high command, had failed to advance his division soon enough until prodded into action by the wise old commander of the Highland Brigade, Sir Colin Campbell. After crossing the river the two flanking battalions of the Guards Brigade, 3rd Grenadiers and 1st Coldstream, halted to reform their lines, but the 1st Scots Fusilier Guards† in the centre were hurried forward up the hill. Here, the left wing of the battalion got thoroughly entangled with the retreating Light Division and was carried back with them, while the right wing, led by the colour party, pressed on until attacked and forced back by two Russian battalions. Meanwhile the Grenadiers and Coldstream, notwithstanding the gap between them, advanced in perfect order with unfaltering steadiness, opening a most effective fire on the Russian columns coming down to oppose their attack and re-capturing the Great Redoubt, as the Scots Fusilier Guards, having hastily reformed, advanced again to their aid. To the left of the Guards the Highland Brigade, 42nd, 79th and 93rd, attacked in echelon of battalions which enabled them successively to defeat by fire further Russian Battalions moving down across their front towards the Great Redoubt. With the Guards and Highlanders crowning the heights and the 2nd Division, with the 3rd in support, coming up on the right, the Russians abandoned the position and the battle was won. The French refused to pursue and as Raglan was unwilling to hazard his cavalry alone in such an enterprise, the Russians were able to retreat unmolested.

The Allies now had to decide how to proceed against Sevastopol. At the same time that they came to the conclusion that an immediate assault on the city from the north would be too costly, and that it would be better to open siege works on the southern side, using the harbour of Balaclava as a base, Menshikov, the Russian commander, decided to withdraw his army to the interior of the Crimea, leaving a garrison in the fortress of some 36,000, half of them sailors from the fleet. The British and French armies therefore circled round Sevastopol to the east making for the plateau known as the Chersonese Upland, narrowly missing Menshikov's troops as they withdrew. Sevastopol had in fact been but poorly defended, but the time taken to disembark the Allied siege train at Balaclava and bring it up to the plateau was put to excellent use by the Russian commander in Sevastopol, Todleben, who so strengthened his defences that by the time the first bombardment was opened on 17th October, the damage caused was insufficient to risk an assault.

Meanwhile Menshikov, who was now free both to reinforce Todleben and operate from outside the fortress, was preparing a counter-offensive, the first blow of which fell on 25th October against the base at Balaclava. That day witnessed three of the most famous incidents in the annals of the British Army, of which the second and most successful has received less acclaim than the other two. In the first, "The Times" correspondent's *"thin red streak tipped with a line of steel"*, the 93rd Highlanders, frightened off four Russian squadrons by opening fire with their Miniés at extreme range; a creditable example of infantry steadiness in the face of a small cavalry force but hardly the epic depicted in art and legend. The second witnessed a magnificent charge by Scarlett's Heavy Cavalry Brigade, no more than 800 sabres, against a solid column of Russian horse 3,000 strong. Scarlett himself, aged 55, and accompanied only by his A.D.C, Lieutenant Alexander Elliot,his giant orderly,Private Shegog, and Trumpet-Major Monks,charged 50 yards ahead of the first line of two squadrons of the Greys and one of the Inniskillings, which were followed up by the 5th Dragoon Guards, the Royal Dragoons and the second squadron of the Inniskillings. As they battled their way through the engulfing Russian squadrons, the 4th Dragoon Guards came in at a right angle against the Russian flank and, as one dragoon said afterwards, *"it was all push, wheel, frenzy, strike and down they went".(7)* Within eight minutes the Russians were in flight, offering a perfect opportunity for the Light Brigade, sitting on their horses ready and eager for action 500 yards away. But Cardigan remained oblivious to all appeals for a charge and the chance to complete the work so bravely done by Scarlett's heavies was lost.

The circumstances under which Cardigan's Light Brigade — 4th and 13th Light Dragoons, 8th and 11th Hussars, and 17th Lancers — eventually did charge on 25th October have probably been written about more than any other episode in British military history, except possibly Waterloo, yet it lasted no more than 20 minutes from the moment it was launched until the pathetic return of the shattered survivors.* Just under half of the 673-strong brigade were sent to their deaths, wounds or into captivity+ through a combination of Raglan's imprecise orders, hurriedly transcribed by his Quartermaster-General, Airey, and transmitted by a highly

† Title bestowed on the 3rd Guards in 1831. The 1st Guards had been named Grenadier Guards after Waterloo.
* For a good modern account, see John Harris "The Gallant Six Hundred" (1973).
+ Killed 113, wounded 134, prisoners 56. 463 horses were lost.

The Duke of Cambridge and the Grenadier Guards at the Battle of the Alma, 1854
Painting, oil on canvas, artist unknown

6th Inniskilling Dragoons at Balaclava, 25th October 1854   6608-1
Coloured lithograph by E. Walker after A. de Prades Published by W. H. Mason, 1st Jan. 1858

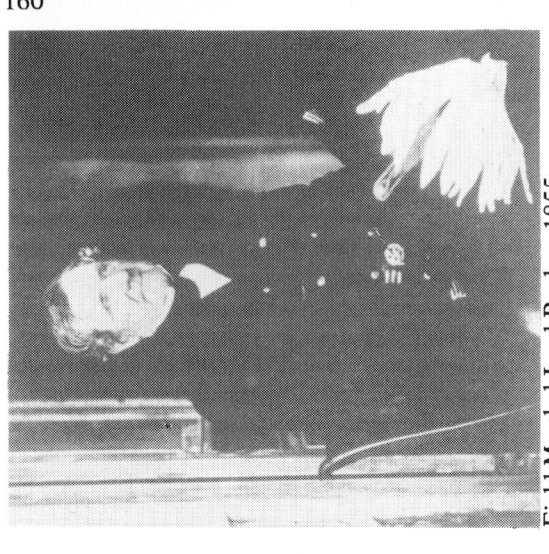

Field Marshal Lord Raglan, 1855
Photograph by Roger Fenton

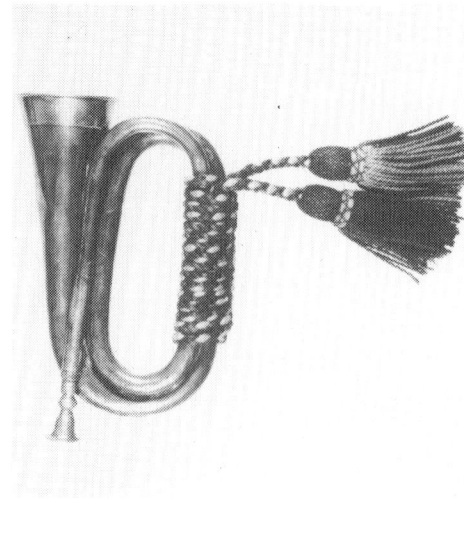

Bugle used by Trumpet Major Henry Joy, 17th Lancers, who was Lord Lucan's trumpeter at the battle of Balaclava   6310-190

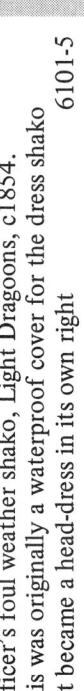

Percussion pistol carried by Sgt. Joseph Wickstead, 5th Dragoon Guards at Balaclava
5911-224

Lord Lucan, Commander of the Cavalry Division, Balaclava   7201-7
Mezzotint

Lt-General Sir George Brown, c1855
Mezzotint by Thomas L. Atkinson after the Hon. Henry Graves, 1st Jan 1859   7209-69

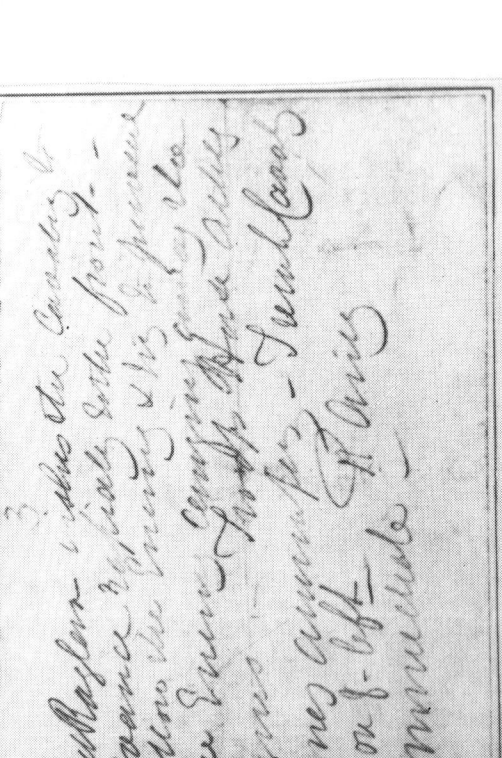

COPY. LORD RAGLAN WISHES THE CAVALRY TO ADVANCE RAPIDLY TO THE FRONT, FOLLOW THE ENEMY AND TRY TO PREVENT THE ENEMY CARRYING AWAY THE GUNS. TROOP OF HORSE ARTILLERY MAY ACCOMPANY. FRENCH CAVALRY IS ON YOUR LEFT. IMMEDIATE.
R. AIREY.
62114

Crimean War, Balaclava 1854   The order, carried by Capt. Nolan to Lord Lucan,

Maj-Gen. The Earl of Cardigan in the uniform of Colonel of the 11th Hussars   6702-19
Portrait, oil on canvas, by A.F. de Prades, c1854

Officer's foul weather shako, Light Dragoons, c1854. This was originally a waterproof cover for the dress shako but became a head-dress in its own right   6101-5

qualified, but impatient and contemptuous staff officer, Nolan, to the mutually antipathetic Lords Lucan and Cardigan, neither of whom shared the view of the battlefield enjoyed by their commander. Cardigan may have been stupid and arrogant, but his courage in leading his brigade down a valley flanked by artillery and riflemen against a 12-gun battery supported by cavalry cannot be disputed; once there, however, he abdicated all further responsibility for his hard-pressed men. It was the matchless gallantry and superb discipline of the regimental officers and men, counterpointing the follies and blunders of commanders and staff, that have endowed the Light Brigade's charge with such lasting fame; a comparison typical of so much else in the Crimean War. The events of the day undoubtedly saved the base at Balaclava, but by capturing some of the redoubts protecting it, the Russians gained control of the Woronzoff Road, the only metalled highway between Balaclava and the British camp on the Chersonese Upland—a loss that would cost the Army dear in the months to come.

On the day after Balaclava the Russians made a reconnaissance in force against the British right wing on the plateau but were everywhere repulsed by the picquets of the 2nd Division. On 5th November they launched a major attack under cover of darkness and fog in the same area. In this the Battle of Inkerman, the infantry of the 2nd Division, reinforced by the Light and 4th Divisions and the Guards Brigade, battled for eight hours in the swirling mists against four times their numbers. Rightly has Inkerman been called *"the soldiers' battle"* for of overall direction there was none, save for the spirited and courageous leadership of one brigadier, John Pennefather†, temporarily in command of the 2nd Division. It was fought, not by divisions and brigades, but by companies, detachments and small groups of men who, as they reached the battle, piled in with rifle and bayonet wherever danger threatened. *"Where the enemy was thickest there each soldier forced his way without regard to regiment and there he fought or fell, drove the enemy before him or was repulsed as fate and fortune ordained". (8)* No tactical brilliance marked this grim struggle, only the dogged and unyielding tenacity of the old long-service infantryman, highlighted by the individual initiative of junior ranks and outstanding acts of courage. By the end of the day, with the French coming belatedly to their aid, over a quarter of the British infantry engaged were casualties* and the survivors were exhausted, but only the Russian dead remained upon Mount Inkerman. As the gallant Pennefather triumphantly remarked: *"I tell you, we gave 'em a hell of a towelling". (9)*

Winter was now approaching and with its onset came deprivation and appalling suffering to the troops on the Chersonese Upland. No provision of any kind had been made for a winter campaign. Frozen to the bone or soaked to the skin, in frayed, threadbare uniforms, the stout-hearted infantry manned the snow or slush — filled trenches in front of Sevastopol with only sodden, leaking tents, pitched on a sea of mud, to return to when relieved. With no communication to Balaclava other than a rutted, slippery track and without transport, no supplies of any kind could reach the army save on the backs of sickly, exhausted and under-nourished men or on the few remaining, skeletal cavalry horses. The medical services were unable to cope with the rapidly increasing sickness and the nearest hospital was 300 miles away across the Black Sea at Scutari, where even there the conditions were intolerable until the arrival of Florence Nightingale with her nurses began to improve matters, despite the hostility of the Army Medical Department. When an N.C.O., who missed the worst of the winter through wounds received at Inkerman, rejoined his battalion, he was horrified at the appearance of *"the old Fusiliers, once one of the finest corps in our service, now poor, half-starved, miserable looking wrecks of humanity"* but he also noticed how *"the older hands had still that unconquerable look about them".(10)* In the dreadful winter of 1854-55 administrative incompetence and neglect condemned to death the heroic, long-suffering and uncomplaining old soldiers of the once splendid Army of the East.

The wretched plight of the army in the Crimea as reported to "The Times" by its war correspondent, W. H. Russell, and by letters from officers raised a public outcry at home. The Prime Minister and Secretary of State for War, Lord Aberdeen and the Duke of Newcastle, resigned and under Palmerston's administration urgent measures were taken in hand for a more effective prosecution of the war. Reinforcements, warm clothing, huts, and all manner of war material were sent out. A Land Transport Corps was raised and a railway constructed from Balaclava to the plateau.At Scutari the tireless endeavours of Florence Nightingale had done much to save life and improve conditions for the victims of that terrible winter. At home the disclosure of the state of the army resulted in the setting up of various commissions of enquiry, whose reports instituted far-reaching changes in Army administration. These will be considered in a later chapter but it should be noted that they only materialised after the Government of the day had been impelled to action by public wrath.

In the spring of 1855 operations were resumed for the reduction of Sevastopol. A joint Franco-British force was sent to destroy supplies and shipping at the Russian base of Kertch on the east of the Crimean peninsula. Batteries totalling 500 guns, many of them manned by the Royal Navy, maintained a constant bombardment against the Russian defences at Sevastopol and a general assault was ordered for the 18th June. The

† He had commanded the 22nd Foot at Meanee in 1843 (see Chapter 11).
* Killed 459, wounded 1933, missing 198.

A Private of the 28th Regiment in the Crimea, 1855
Photograph by Roger Fenton. 6412-151-6-15

Crimean War, 1855
Officer, 42nd Highlanders (Black Watch)
Photograph by Roger Fenton 6810-73-20

Officers and men of the 89th Regiment, in the Crimea, 1855
Photograph by Roger Fenton.

6412-151-6-29

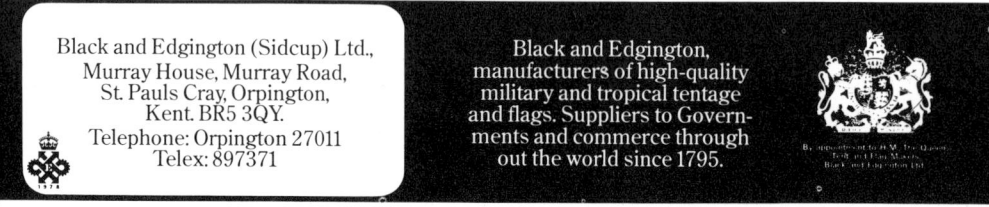

French assault was badly synchronized, the Russians were ready for them and their attack faltered. To maintain the momentum, Raglan ordered the British to advance. They had to cover 400 yards of open ground, swept by grape-shot and musketry, a daunting enough task for any troops, but a hopeless one for the green, inexperienced recruits, many of them mere boys, who now filled the ranks instead of the old stalwarts of the year before. A few brave men reached the Russian ramparts but, with over 1,500 casualties, the assault collapsed. For Raglan, already ailing in mind and body, bowed by his responsibilities and harassed by communications from the Government looking for scapegoats, this disappointment hastened his end and on 28th June he died. A guardsman wrote: *"Poor old man! It was his very kind heartedness that prevented him being a great general".(11)* He was succeeded by General Simpson, a colourless man of mediocre talents with little confidence in his own ability. On 8th September a further attempt was made against Sevastopol but though a spirited French attack captured a strongpoint known as the Malakoff, their other attacks failed and the British assault against the Redan met with ignominious failure. However the Russians inside the fortress saw the loss of the Malakoff as the beginning of the end and that night began to withdraw from the town, setting it alight and destroying everything of value.

The abandonment of Sevastopol meant to all intents and purposes the end of the fighting although peace was not finally signed until March 1856. A successful expedition to capture the important base and harbour of Kinburn, near Odessa, together with the loss of Sevastopol, convinced the Tsar of the futility of continued operations. The army, now properly clothed, housed and supplied, spent another winter in the Crimea without any of the tribulations of the previous year. Sir William Codrington, who had commanded a brigade† at the Alma, took over from Simpson in November 1855 and by the spring he had under his command a very fine force of 60,000 men. A much better stamp of man than the pathetic boys of the 1854-55 reinforcements had been reaching regiments, many of them volunteers from the Militia, which had been embodied during the war to relieve regular regiments for foreign service. To swell the overall size of the Army, Parliament had, in 1855 approved the raising of foreign legions of Swiss, Germans and Italians, of whom some 13,000 were enlisted, but in the event there was no need for their services.

To most people the Crimean War means the charge of the Light Brigade and Florence Nightingale but significant though these may have been, particularly the latter, there was a good deal more to it. In spite of the years of almost criminal negligence displayed by politicians towards the Army, in spite of inert direction from the Horse Guards, for which the Duke of Wellington must bear part of the blame, and in spite of the bungling prosecution of the war by Government and senior officers, a British army had nevertheless been transported on to enemy soil far from its home or, indeed, any other base; it had, in conjunction with a not always co-operative ally, defeated an army superior in numbers and operating on its own soil in at least two major battles; and it had endured dreadful suffering to finally emerge victorious in the cause it had originally been sent out to uphold — the halting of Russian expansionism in the Near East. Its sacrifices and heroism at the Alma, at Balaclava, at Inkerman and in the first bitter winter of the war had not only hastened the long-needed overhaul of an outdated military system, but awakened the realisation in the minds of the British public, at least for a time, that the despised, often hated redcoat was a human being of surprising, often noble qualities, whose valiant steadfastness deserved better of his countrymen. Sadly the best of them had to perish before this was grasped.

In one quarter at least there was no doubt about the need to reward deserving soldiers. In 1856 Queen Victoria instituted the Victoria Cross as an award *"to those officers and men (of both services) who have served us in the presence of the enemy, and shall have then performed some signal act of valour or devotion to their country".(12)* The first awards for the Crimean War were gazetted on 24th February 1857. Heading the list for the Army were Sergeant-Major Grieve of the Scots Greys and Private Parkes of the 4th Light Dragoons for gallantry at Balaclava, but the first acts in time to be rewarded were those of Sergeant O'Connor and Captain Bell, both of the 23rd Royal Welch Fusiliers, during the capture of the Great Redoubt by the Light Division at the Alma. 83 Crosses were awarded to officers and men of the Army in the Crimea. While it might be said that they were distributed more liberally than in later wars, it should also be remembered that all the recipient's acts were performed before the Victoria Cross was instituted, and thus there was no special incentive for their gallantry, other than their sense of duty and regimental pride.* As has ever been the case since its institution, there were doubtless other deserving men who never received it through lack of witnesses to their gallantry. Many older officers were sceptical of the need for such an award and in some cases its bestowal was treated with cynicism by the men. There were also men who thought they had earned it but failed to receive it. But for them and for others eager to distinguish themselves there would soon be opportunities in plenty, as a year after returning from the Crimea many would be sailing east again, this time to India, where a new and fearful menace threatened.

---

† 7th and 23rd Fusiliers, 33rd Foot.

* In 1879 a recipient of the V.C. announced on the morning before he won it, "I'm going for the V.C. today".

Major John Nicholson, 1851   Photograph   6511-115

Lt-Gen. Sir James Outram, 1857   Portrait, oil on canvas,
artist unknown   6308-42

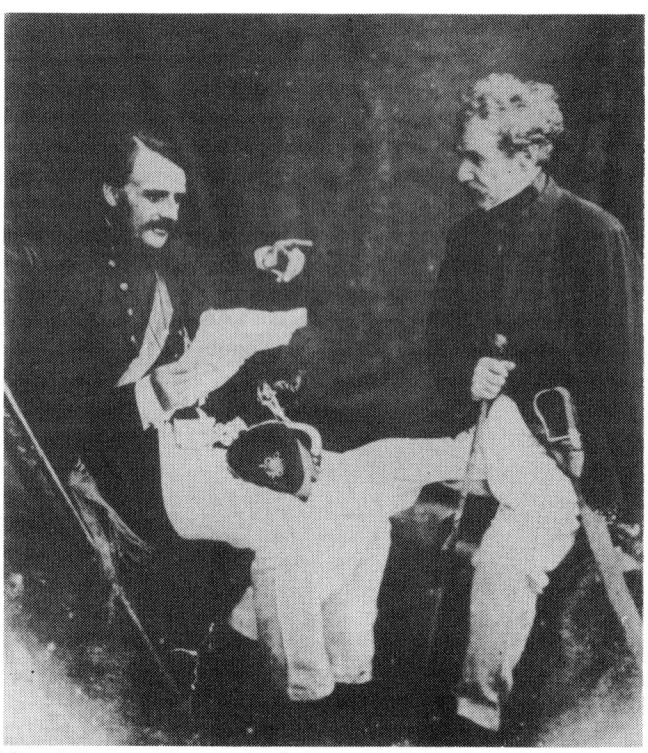

'Good News in Despatches'; Gen. Sir Colin Campbell and
Maj-Gen. William Mansfield, India, 1857
Contemporary photograph   6211-63-1

General Sir Henry Havelock KCB   Mezzotint by and after
A. H. Ritchie Published by The 'Albion', New York 1859
                                                    7402-41

CHAPTER 13
SEPOY MUTINY
1857–1859

On Sunday 10th May 1857 at Meerut, 50 miles north-east of Delhi, the 60th Rifles fell in for church parade at five in the evening, the mornings at that time of year being too hot even for religious observance. On this Sunday, however, no church service would ever take place; as the battalion was about to march off the sound of firing was suddenly heard and smoke was seen rising from the sepoy lines to the south-west. Within minutes frantic, white-faced men came galloping with news that the native troops were in a turmoil and that a mob, pouring up from the bazaar, was falling upon the British cantonments, massacring women and children and burning everything in their path. The mysterious rumours and reports of the last few days, discounted on all sides, had been proved correct. The unthinkable had happened as all over Meerut the loyal, faithful sepoys and sowars of the splendid Bengal Army turned on their British masters, embarking on an orgy of murder and pillage from which there could be no turning back.

The signs that trouble was in the wind had been there for a long time but most in authority were too blind or complacent to heed them. The rifts in the Bengal Army that had begun to develop between British officers and their sepoys after the Afghan and Sikh Wars† had widened. The regiments were weakened by the draining off of their best officers to the political and civil services which were expanding to administer the newly annexed territories. Too many of the younger officers joining regiments had no notion how to treat the sepoy. *"He is sworn at. He is treated roughly. He is spoken of as a 'nigger'. The younger (British) men seem to regard it as an evidence of spirit and as a praiseworthy sense of superiority over the sepoy to treat him as an inferior animal".(1)* The more senior officers, many of them too old, their energy sapped by years of Indian summers, were lazy, self-indulgent and unperceptive. As the white officers lost interest in and contact with their sepoys, so did the latter lose their respect. To this were added fears for their religion. In 1856 all recruits had to accept an undertaking for overseas service; since sea travel would render high-caste Hindus outcastes, many sepoys regarded this as an attempt to convert them to Christianity by violating their beliefs. A rumour began at Calcutta in January 1857 that soon all sepoys would be forcibly baptised at Queen Victoria's order while another held that Crimean War widows were to be married off to Indian princes, so that the children of such unions, brought up as Christians, would inherit their lands.

Unrest and uncertainty spread beyond the confines of the Bengal Army. In their urge to bring reform, justice and order to the chaotic, corrupt and feudal territories they had conquered or annexed, the Company's administrators had trodden on many toes. Princes and landowners had been dispossessed of their privileges, lands and pensions, old hallowed customs like *'suttee'*, the ceremonial burning of widows, had been forbidden, and new taxes proved burdensome on the ordinary people. All the measures taken to impose good government on the land were initiated through the highest motives, but everywhere they rode roughshod over native social, cultural and religious customs. All over northern India, during the forties and fifties, tension was building up. It became most highly charged in the vassal-state of Oudh, whence most of the Bengal sepoys were recruited, which in 1856 was formally annexed by the Company and its King deposed on the grounds of his misrule. By this act, the Bengal sepoys and their families lost many privileges they had hitherto enjoyed in their native state, landowners and dependents of the King were dispossessed, and even the peasants, whose lot the annexure was most likely to benefit, felt more threatened by the Company's rule than by the King's corrupt and overbearing officials. By 1856 the British in northern India were sitting on a powder keg of fear, frustration and resentment. All that was wanting was a spark to set it off.

During the later stages of the Crimean War an improved rifle, the Enfield, had been introduced in the British Army. Its cartridge was a cardboard cylinder containing powder and a bullet, closed at the top with a twist of paper. The loading drill required the paper to be bitten off prior to pouring the powder down the barrel, after which the bullet, still in its cylinder, was rammed down. To ease its passage the cylinder was coated in grease. In 1856 this weapon began to reach the Bengal Army but almost immediately a rumour

† See Chapter 11.

Enfield musket pattern 1853 and cartridge. The bullet lubricant of tallow and beeswax was one of the causes of the outbreak of the Mutiny.

6310-205

spread among the sepoys that its introduction was yet another subtle attack on their religion. The grease, it was said, was made from cow or pig fat. To the Hindu, the cow was sacred and for the Moslem the pig was unclean; either way the loading drill was a contamination, threatening the soldier with eternal damnation. The rumour spread like fire throughout the Bengal Army, while everywhere the agents of the discontented elements among the native population played upon the sepoys' fears, inciting them to overthrow their masters. Various attempts were made to calm the sepoys — they could make up their own grease, they could tear the paper with their fingers — but the fear of pollution took deep and rapid hold.

In January 1857 an outcaste taunted a Brahman sepoy with his defilement. In February the 19th Bengal Native Infantry refused the cartridges and had to be disbanded under guard of a Queen's regiment specially brought back from Burma; a fact the agitators quickly perceived as evidence of how few British troops there were in northern India. Indeed, the demands of the Crimean War and the annexation of the Punjab had resulted in the British regiments being so thinly spread that there were no more than four white battalions and a few batteries over the 800 miles between Agra and Calcutta. Officers' bungalows mysteriously caught fire, strange signs appeared on walls and buildings, reports came of 'chupatties', flat cakes made of flour, being passed by runners from village to village, signifying no one knew what. All these curious incidents and the sepoys' unhappiness over the cartridges were reported by the more conscientious and alert officers and officials, most of which eventually reached the Governor-General, Lord Canning, and the elderly Commander-in-Chief, General Anson, but any urgency in the original reports was lost by the time they had percolated upwards through the bureaucracy. On 29th March a young sepoy of the 34th Native Infantry, Mangal Pande, ran amok, fired at his British adjutant and sergeant-major, and called upon his comrades to join him. He was fearlessly confronted by General Hearsey, the garrison commander, and, having failed to commit suicide, was duly hanged. But his name was soon to resound as a rallying cry throughout northern India.

Meerut was one of the few military stations where, besides the Company's 3rd Bengal Light Cavalry and the 11th and 20th Native Infantry, there was a sizeable British garrison in the shape of the 6th Dragoon Guards, 60th Rifles and a troop of Bengal Horse Artillery. It was therefore an unlikely place for wholesale mutiny to break out and once it had it should have been easily quelled. Yet the reverse happened. On 23rd April 85 sowars of the 3rd Cavalry refused the cartridges and were ordered to be court-martialled by the regiment's unintelligent and unpopular commanding officer, George Carmichael Smyth. They were all found guilty and on 9th May were disgraced and shackled before their comrades under the guns and bayonets of the British troops, before being marched to the guardroom, after which they were due to begin long terms of hard labour. That night an Indian officer warned Lieutenant Hugh Gough of the regiment that a mutiny was being planned for the next day, Sunday. Gough reported to Carmichael Smyth who derided him for his fears. Gough therefore went to the garrison commander, Brigadier Archdale Wilson, only to meet a similar response. Other warnings were passed by loyal servants but all were ignored and disbelieved. The next evening, goaded by taunts in the bazaar and rumours that the 60th were coming to attack them, the sowars of the 3rd Cavalry rushed to free their imprisoned comrades. The mob came out of the bazaar, the fury contaminated the two native infantry regiments, sepoys of the 11th murdered the colonel of the 20th, and Meerut was ablaze in a night of horror. In face of it and despite the ready availability of British troops, Archdale Wilson and the divisional commander, General Hewitt, a man so obese that he could not mount a horse, both proved incapable of either dealing with the outbreak or of even mounting a pursuit against the sepoys who, leaving the mob to do its worst, all marched away towards Delhi.

The walled city of Delhi was of great strategic and political importance. It stood on the main route up the Ganges valley from Calcutta to the new territories of the Punjab and the North-West Frontier, so that its possession by the mutineers would cut off the British to the east of it from the Punjab where most of the European troops were disposed. It contained a huge magazine of guns and munitions and had a garrison of the 38th, 54th and 74th Bengal Native Infantry but no British regiment. It was also the old capital of the Mogul Emperors, whose last descendent, the 82-year old Bahadur Shah still lived there, without power and on a pension from the Company in his once-splendid but now squalid palace, surrounded by a seedy retinue which occupied its time with debauchery and intrigue but amongst which were men who longed for revenge against

Mutineers surprised by HM 9th Lancers.   Lithograph after G.F. Atkinson, published by Day & Son 1857-58.   7102-33-495-6

View from the Doomree Bungalow. A Detatchment of British infantry moving off, Indian Mutiny, 1857.
Lithograph after Capt. D. Sarsfield Greene. Published by Thos McLean, 1859.   7210-46

the Company. When the triumphant mutineers from Meerut arrived at Delhi they hailed Bahadur Shah as Emperor of Hindustan and were welcomed as liberators by the intriguers of the court who now saw their chance of power. Far too aged and effete for this role of leader of his people, and as terrified of the sepoys as of the British, Bahadur Shah was a prisoner of his fate. Within hours of the mutineers' arrival the British civilians in Delhi had been butchered by the mob and all three native regiments, with the exception of a single sepoy of the 74th, had joined the mutineers. Only the gallantry of three officers and six N.C.Os., all British, of the Commissariat Ordnance Department, in blowing up the magazine saved it from falling into the mutineers' hands. Three of them perished in the explosion, Lieutenant Willoughby escaped but was caught and murdered, while the others, Lieutenants Forrest and Raynor, Conductors Buckley, Shaw and a Sergeant, also named Shaw, miraculously all survived to be awarded the Victoria Cross.

News of the events at Meerut and Delhi spread rapidly throughout northern India, sparking off further mutinies and unrest among the Bengal troops, followed by attacks on Europeans. In nearly all the military stations throughout Oudh, Rohilkand, Behar and Central India units of the Bengal Army mutinied sooner or later. In some areas they were joined by native chiefs and villagers, in others the civilian population preferred to wait and see what happened; elsewhere there were Indians who gave refuge to Europeans, often at great risk to themselves. Where there were British troops in the neighbourhood under a vigorous commander, some sepoy battalions were disarmed before they could mutiny, but the decision to do so was often a difficult one since it was hard to predict their loyalty, and to disarm one battalion as a precautionary measure could prove just the spur to disaffect another which might otherwise have proved loyal. Moreover, few of the Company officers could believe their men were disloyal — a pathetic trust which often proved fatal for them. By the end of May most of the area between Delhi and Benares was hostile territory; Sir Henry Lawrence, the Chief Commissioner for Oudh, was isolated in Lucknow with a small garrison consisting of the greater part of the 32nd Foot and a handful of loyal sepoys and European volunteers, and Cawnpore was in imminent danger of attack.

As soon as news of Delhi reached General Anson, the Commander-in-Chief at Simla, he, appreciating that its recapture must be the first priority, assembled a force† at Ambala which moved off southwards after some delay caused by the need to improvise transport, supplies and medical support, none of which were readily available. Anson died of cholera on 27th May after handing over to Sir Henry Barnard, a Crimean officer, who joined forces with Archdale Wilson's troops advancing from Meerut. On 8th June the combined force, further increased by the Sirmoor Gurkha battalion *, drove some 30,000 mutineers from a strong position at Badli-ke-serai, six miles from Delhi, and established itself to the north of the city along a line of high ground known as the Ridge. Although this success greatly cheered the British troops, the task before them was daunting. They numbered no more than 3,000, had no heavy guns and were short of all types of ammunition and supplies. From their position, only two miles long, they could look down on the great walled city, seven miles in circumference, into which daily there poured more battalions of mutineers to join those of the Delhi and Meerut garrisons. The hot weather was now as its height, there was little shelter on the Ridge and before long sickness would be prevalent. The younger officers had pressed for an immediate assault as soon as the force arrived before Delhi and continued to do so throughout the siege, while their seniors insisted on waiting for reinforcements and a siege train. In the meantime they became as much besieged as besiegers, for almost every day the sepoys, their numbers constantly growing, sallied forth from Delhi to try and drive them from the Ridge.

The only quarter from which reinforcements could come was the Punjab, then administered by John Lawrence, the brother of Sir Henry. Although the bulk of the British regiments were stationed there, it was but recently conquered, its inhabitants were warlike and possibly eager to avenge their defeat in the Sikh Wars, while beyond it lay the fierce tribes of Afghanistan. If the peoples of the Punjab and the north-west were to join the mutineers, the fate of the British in northern India would be sealed. But Lawrence and his subordinates were made of sterner stuff than their colleagues further south. He appreciated that the hostility and contempt felt by the Sikhs and the Punjabi Moslems for the Hindu sepoys† would outweigh any sympathy for the latter's cause, but that any weakness by the British would most likely be exploited by them. As soon as he heard of the outbreak at Delhi therefore, he took immediate measures to disarm all sepoy regiments and by means of a movable column quelled without hesitation the slightest signs of disaffection. To increase his strength he planned to raise new levies from the frontier tribes and the Punjab, whose inhabitants he rightly guessed would be strongly motivated by the chance of loot and the paying off of old scores against the hated Brahmans. In so doing he knew he was taking a risk by arming these martial people but it proved to be justified. Sikhs, Punjabis and hillmen all gave loyal and valuable service throughout the Mutiny and Lawrence felt confident enough in the security of his own territory to send down to Delhi further British

---

† 9th Lancers, two troops Bengal Horse Artillery, 75th Foot, 1st and 2nd European Bengal Fusiliers.
* Later 2nd Gurkha Rifles.
† See Chapter 11.

units and battalions of the Frontier Brigade, by then re-designated the Punjab Irregular Force. The Corps of Guides had already reached Delhi on 9th June having covered 600 miles in 22 days and gone straight into action immediately on arrival.

Throughout June and July attacks by the mutineers on the Delhi Ridge continued but none, not even a major effort on 23rd June, the centenary of Plassey when it had been foretold that British power would fall, could prevail against the stubborn defence of the British and Gurkha infantry and the Guides. Apart from the need for constant vigilance the troops were afflicted by the stifling heat, followed by the monsoon which brought cholera in its wake. Reinforcements continued to trickle in but it was not until 14th August that a really substantial increase of some 2,000 arrived under Brigadier John Nicholson. Nicholson, a tall, dark, serious man of 34, was *"one of the Titans of the Punjab,.... of more than human energy and an intense devotion to duty which permitted no relaxation".(2)* The whole force drew inspiration from his arrival and nine days later he routed 6,000 mutineers who had left Delhi to intercept the advance of the siege train which Lawrence had been assembling in the Punjab. Nicholson's troops in this action,† though outnumbered by three to one, inflicted 800 casualties on the enemy, taking 13 guns and all their baggage and transport, for a loss of only 100, and that after a punishing approach march of 20 miles in monsoon conditions.

With the safe arrival of the siege train and its 32 heavy guns on 4th September, the force before Delhi was now nearly 9,000 strong, about a third of which were Queen's or Company Europeans*, the rest Sikhs, Punjabis, Gurkhas, Guides and a Baluch battalion. Barnard had died of cholera and the senior command had devolved on Archdale Wilson. In poor health, apprehensive of the strength of the city's defences and the possibility of his comparatively small force, daily weakened by sickness, being swallowed up in its maze of streets and buildings, he was reluctant to order an assault. However his hand was forced by Nicholson and the younger men. Working day and night, often under heavy fire, the necessary battery positions were constructed for the siege guns which, by the evening of the 13th, had blasted practicable breaches in the northerly walls of the city. An assault was ordered for the following morning: three columns to attack the north wall, one the Kabul Gate at the north end of the west wall, and one in reserve; the columns averaged about a thousand men in each, with the European battalions spread more or less evenly between them.

The storming parties advanced covered by 200 skirmishers of the 60th Rifles. Two made for the breaches but the third had to wait for the Kashmir Gate to be blown in by a party of Bengal Engineers led by Lieutenants Home and Salkeld and accompanied by Bugler Hawthorne of the 52nd Light Infantry, who was to sound the advance once the gate was blown. The task was carried out with great gallantry under heavy fire+ and the 52nd, 1st Punjab Infantry, and the Kumaon Gurkhas†† poured into the city. The fourth column, at the Kabul Gate, was repulsed but the other three, despite the fiercest resistance everywhere, had by nightfall secured a toe-hold within the walls for the loss of a thousand casualties including the mortally-wounded Nicholson. Little else was achieved that night or during the next two days for the British troops were utterly *"demoralised by hard work and hard drink"(3)* — due to liquor that had been purposely left in the streets by the mutineers. Fortunately the latter did not follow up this advantage and once all such supplies had either been consumed or destroyed, the methodical clearance of the city continued, though not without savage street fighting, until, by the 20th, the whole city was in British hands. The old Emperor was taken, his sons executed without trial, the city ransacked and a bloody vengeance exacted for the Europeans who had been murdered therein.

While the operations at Delhi had been going on, a critical situation had arisen in Oudh. Lying across the British road and river communications between Calcutta, Delhi and the Punjab, this highly volatile area was of great strategic significance yet in the whole province there was only one Queen's regiment, the 32nd Foot at Lucknow where Sir Henry Lawrence had his headquarters as Chief Commissioner. The military commander in Oudh, Major-General Sir Hugh Wheeler, was based at Cawnpore where there was a sizeable European population and a brigade of native infantry but only a few European artillerymen. When news of the outbreak at Delhi was received in mid-May, Lawrence began preparing his Residency for defence and stockpiling provisions; he also spared a company of the 32nd for Cawnpore where Wheeler order the construction of an entrenchment around two barrack buildings as a possible refuge for the European population.

At Calcutta the Governor-General, Canning, realised that reinforcements would be urgently needed in Oudh but he had few European troops to spare. Part of the 84th Foot, recently arrived from Burma, was sent forward up the Ganges Valley, followed by the 1st European Madras Fusiliers under Colonel Neill, hastily

† 61st Foot, 1st Bengal Fusiliers, two battalions Punjab Infantry, 400 cavalry (Guides, Punjabis and Multanis).
* 6th Dragoon Guards, 9th Lancers, 8th, 52nd, 61st, 75th Foot, 60th Rifles, 1st and 2nd Bengal Fusiliers.
+ V.Cs. were awarded to both officers, Hawthorne and L/Corporal Smith. Two other Sergeants and one corporal were killed.
†† Later 3rd Gurkha Rifles.

Cawnpore, the scene of the massacre, 1857   Chromolithograph by E. Walker after Lieut. Sankey published by Day & Son, 1858

'Interior of the Residency Billiard Room' c1858   Tinted lithograph after Lt. C.H. Mecham, published by Day & Son, Oct. 1st 18∷
6307-30-2-

summoned up from Fort St George. At the same time orders were sent to Brigadier Henry Havelock, then returning to Bombay by sea with the 64th Foot and 78th Highlanders after a campaign in Persia†, to sail on to Calcutta. By 18th June Neill, an energetic and ruthless officer, had reached and restored order in Allahabad where mutiny had broken out among the sepoys on the 6th. However, with only 300 men at his disposal, many of whom were suffering from sunstroke and cholera, he could not press on to Cawnpore through what was by now enemy territory until reinforcements reached him from Calcutta. He therefore set about accumulating the necessary supplies and transport for an advance.

Meanwhile, 80 miles to the west at Cawnpore, the three sepoy battalions and the 2nd Light Cavalry had mutinied on 4th June and offered their services to the Nana Sahib, a local Indian potentate with whom Wheeler had understood he was on friendly terms and who had led Wheeler to believe that the mutineers would make off to Delhi. On the 7th the British general saw he had been deceived for the mutineers, now equipped with artillery, returned to attack him. Within his entrenchment, a feeble rampart of dried mud only four feet high, Wheeler had nearly 400 women and children, and only about 240 soldiers and civilians to man the defences: the 32nd company, a handful of men from different corps, some hundred civilians, and the white officers of the mutinied regiments together with a few sepoys who had remained loyal. The enemy numbered some 3,000 with 15 guns and a plentiful supply of ammunition. For 18 days, in searing heat and under almost constant artillery fire, part of which was permanently directed at the garrison's only well and the route to it, with little protection either from the sun or the bombardment, Wheeler's tiny force maintained an heroic defence, beating off enemy attacks and even mounting sorties against the sepoy guns. The only shelter for the women, children and wounded was in the barrack blocks, one of which was burned down on the fourth day. Food supplies began to run out, every attempt to draw water sustained casualties, and by the 25th the ammunition was almost expended. That day the Nana Sahib offered, under a flag of truce, safe-conduct for the garrison to proceed by boat to Allahabad. To save the women and children Wheeler agreed to evacuate, though not without grave misgivings and against the wishes of the younger officers, who were all for fighting to the last. On the morning of the 27th the remnants of the garrison left their battered entrenchment and escorted the women and children, who had survived their horrific experience with such fortitude, down to the boats provided by the Nana at the riverside. No sooner had the boats pushed off, overloaded with toil-worn, exhausted men and women, when the mutineers opened a heavy fire from the bank. Out of forty boats, only one, with three officers and two soldiers, got away to safety. All the other men were killed at the river and the 200 surviving women and children were herded ashore to be incarcerated in a small house known as the Bibighur. There, two weeks later on 15th July, when news of an approaching British force reached the Nana Sahib, they were all butchered and their bodies thrown into a well.

On the day this atrocity took place, a British column under Havelock had defeated a body of mutineers 22 miles from Cawnpore. Havelock had linked up with Neill at Allahabad on 24th June and by 7th July his column, mainly consisting of the Madras Fusiliers, elements of the 64th, 78th and 84th and the Ferozepore Sikh battalion, was marching at best speed on Cawnpore. His rate of advance was slowed by the need to conserve his troops' strength, already affected by cholera and the oppressive heat; the 64th and 78th had only their winter serge uniforms in which they had come from Persia. Despite the hardships of the march all ranks were seized with the need to press on and after twice brushing aside mutineers sent to delay their advance, they finally entered Cawnpore on 17th July. Here the appalling evidence of the bloody massacre at the Bibighur so sickened the men that henceforth no mercy would be shown to the mutineers, and many innocent Indians would suffer with the guilty from the avenging fury of the troops, for whom the words, *"Remember Cawnpore!"*, became a rallying cry all over India. Fury already existed as a result of the murders at Meerut and Delhi, but Cawnpore fired it to a white heat which could only be assuaged by hangings, blowing men from guns, and omitting no opportunity to inflict maximum degradation on the religious sensibilities of any Indian suspected of being in rebellion. It was the compelling need to exact retribution for the murder of women and children, more than the saving of India from mutiny and chaos, that drove British troops to superhuman efforts on the march and in battle, and to inflict terrible punishment on those who had once been loyal and faithful servants.

Though his force had been whittled away to 1,500 effectives by enemy action, cholera and sunstroke, Havelock knew he must try and reach Lucknow, 40 miles away and now closely invested by the enemy. Leaving Neill and 300 men to hold Cawnpore, he crossed the Ganges and began his advance. Between 29th July and 16th August he fought five successful actions against sepoy forces sent against him from Lucknow,

† From December 1856-March 1857 to punish the Shah for his seizure of Herat from Afghanistan. Besides the two Queen's battalions and the 14th Light Dragoons, the troops were entirely from the Bombay Army. See Barbara English, "John Company's Last War" (1971).

inflicting heavy losses, but with his British and Sikh infantry reduced to less than 900 overworked and exhausted men and gravely hampered by his sick and wounded, he had to fall back on Cawnpore. Havelock and his valiant men had done their best, battling against always superior numbers, the punishing climate and the ever-present cholera, but without reinforcements it was clear he could not get through and, to make matters worse, his failure to do so now brought out in support of the mutineers all those local chiefs who had been waiting to see how events turned out.

When Havelock regained Cawnpore on 16th August, Lucknow had been besieged since 30th June. The bulk of the four sepoy regiments there had mutinied on 30th May but had evacuated the city to join other mutinous units in the vicinity. Hearing of their approach to Chinhat, eight miles from Lucknow, Sir Henry Lawrence moved out to attack them on 29th June but, outnumbered and outmanoeuvred by the Indian commander, he had to fall back on the Residency, having had 115 killed in his single Queen's battalion, the 32nd, a loss he could ill afford. The victorious mutineers pushed on into Lucknow and by the following day Lawrence's defences around the Residency were invested by the enemy, whose numbers rose throughout the ensuing siege from 6,000 to 10,000. To defend his mile-long perimeter Lawrence had the 32nd Foot, less those lost at Cawnpore and Chinhat, a company of the 84th, most of the officers from the mutinied regiments, some 150 civilian volunteers, a few Sikh troopers, and just over 700 loyal sepoys from the 13th, 48th and 71st Bengal Native Infantry†, about 1,600 in all. In addition there were 500 women and children and 50 European schoolboys of the Martinière College. The defences were based on a series of permanently garrisoned strong-points, linked by a low earth wall, and backed by a central reserve. On 4th July Sir Henry Lawrence died from a wound received during the mutineers' first bombardment of the Residency and command of the defence was assumed by Colonel Inglis of the 32nd, a brave, practical and resolute man of 42.

The mutineers kept up a constant artillery and musketry fire on the defenders. Some of the opposing gun positions were only separated by the width of a street and everywhere sepoy snipers lay in wait for the unwary. Often the only means of silencing a particularly destructive enemy battery was by a sortie to blow up the gun positions; though the determination of the defenders usually prevailed, such ventures always suffered casualties which, together with sickness due to the heat, the monsoon and the cramped conditions, inflicted a steady drain on the already slender manpower resources of the garrison. A constant threat to the defences were the mines exploded by means of tunnels dug from the enemy posts to underneath the strong-points. These could only be prevented by counter-mining and frequent underground encounters took place between the enemy tunnellers and a team, mostly of Cornish miners from the 32nd, led by an engineer officer, Captain Fulton. On 20th July the mutineers launched their first all-out assault on the Residency. *"On they came like so many demons in human forms – all round the position with their bands playing all our National airs, their bugles sounding, flags flying, etc. Scores of times they advanced to the charge and of course on each occasion were beat back".(4)* It began in the morning and lasted until four in the afternoon but at every post the defenders, whether they were British soldiers, loyal sepoys or civilians, all fought like tigers to hold their ground and repulse the attacks which were pressed with vigour and courage. In the following weeks three other such assaults were made but each in turn was defeated. In the meantime there was the constant bombardment, the ceaseless watching and listening by day and night, the mounting toll of dead, sick and wounded and steadily deteriorating living conditions, but through it all the unflinching resolution of the garrison never faltered, their spirits buoyed up by hope of Havelock reaching them.

On 16th August, the day Havelock abandoned his attempt to get through, Inglis wrote to him, urging him to lose no time in advancing to their relief:

"I have upwards of 120 sick and wounded, and at least 220 women and about 230 children...Our provisions will last us till about 10th September...We are daily being attacked by the enemy, who are within a few yards of our defences. Their mines have already weakened our post, and I have every reason to believe they are carrying on others. Their 18-pounders are within 150 yards of some of our batteries... and consequently the damage done hourly is very great. My strength now in Europeans is 350, and about 300 natives, and the men are dreadfully harassed".(5)

Communications between Inglis and Havelock were maintained by an Indian pensioner, Angad, who passed through the enemy lines at considerable risk of his life. On receipt of Inglis' letter, Havelock replied that he expected reinforcements within 25 days and would then march for Lucknow. In mid-September he was joined by Major-General Outram with the 5th Fusiliers and the 90th Light Infantry. Though Outram was the senior he allowed Havelock to continue in command of the enlarged force so that the honour of relieving Lucknow might be his. On the 19th Havelock began his advance and after routing an enemy force at the Alambagh, four miles from Lucknow, entered the outskirts of the city on the 25th. To reach the Residency

† After the Mutiny these became the 16th B.N.I. and subsequently (1922) the 10th Bn. (The Lucknow Regiment) 7th Rajput Regiment.

his men had to fight their way through narrow streets lined with loop-holed houses from which the sepoys poured a continuous musketry. As dusk began to fall at about five o'clock, Mrs Harris, one of the besieged, heard

> *"a very sharp fire of musketry close by, and then a tremendous cheering; an instant after, the sound of bagpipes, then of soldiers running up the road. Our compound filled with our deliverers, and all of us shaking hands frantically and exchanging fervent 'God bless yous' with the gallant men and officers of the 78th Highlanders. The big, rough, bearded soldiers were seizing the little children out of our arms, kissing them with tears running down their cheeks, and thanking God they had come in time to save them from the fate of those at Cawnpore".(6)*

The cost of getting through had been high, over 500 being killed or wounded in the fight through the streets, the 78th alone losing a third of its strength. Moreover large numbers of mutineers still remained under arms in the city and with no transport to evacuate the sick, wounded, women and children, Outram, who now assumed overall command, found he had no choice but to remain where he was, though extending the perimeter and leaving an outlying detachment at the Alambagh. However, with an additional 3,000 men to contend with, the mutineer forces were much less aggressive than before and, as cooler weather approached and a hitherto undiscovered food store was found, conditions within Lucknow became more bearable. On 7th November came news that a strong relief force, led by Sir Colin Campbell, was on its way from Cawnpore.

Campbell, one of the few commanders to have emerged with credit from the Crimean War, had been appointed Commander-in-Chief, India, after the death of Anson and had arrived at Calcutta on 13th August. His first task was to assemble a force for the relief of Lucknow but he also had to take account of a possible threat to Cawnpore by a large body of revolted troops from Gwalior under the command of Tantia Topi, a henchman of the Nana Sahib. Campbell left 1,700 men under General Windham to hold Cawnpore and moved on to the Alambagh where by 9th November some 4,500 troops were concentrated with 42 guns, of which eight were manned by a Naval Brigade under Captain Peel R.N. This use of sailors ashore in support of troops was becoming a feature of nineteenth century colonial campaigning. Campbell's force consisted of a brigade released by the fall of Delhi on 20th September†, detachments of the battalions in Lucknow, half the 53rd Foot from Calcutta, and the 23rd Royal Welch Fusiliers and 93rd Highlanders, both of which had been diverted to India while en route for China.

On 16th-17th November, with the 53rd, 93rd and the Sikhs of the 4th Punjab Infantry leading the assault, Campbell's men fought their way with a determined fury into Lucknow against fierce resistance. At the taking of the Sikander Bagh, a high-walled enclosure, the Sikhs and Highlanders encountered 2,000 sepoys of whom only three or four escaped alive. The mutineers in the city outnumbered the relief column by eight to one and were defending a succession of fortified buildings but by the evening of the second day's fighting the incoming troops had linked up with Outram's men and the garrison had been relieved. The Residency, which had been held for 160 days, was abandoned, all the women and children were evacuated and Campbell withdrew from the city, leaving Outram with 4,000 men in garrison at the Alambagh. A week after the relief Havelock, who had done so much to save Lucknow, died from an attack of dysentry which his exhausted body was not strong enough to withstand.

Not until March 1858 was Campbell able to return to Lucknow and complete the final overthrow of the rebels still in the city. Before that could happen he had to await the arrival of reinforcements sent out from England. In the meanwhile more pressing matters engaged his attention for on 28th November a rebel army under Tantia Topi had defeated Windham's force outside Cawnpore. Having despatched all the civilians from Lucknow down-river to Allahabad, Campbell attacked and routed Tantia Topi and the Nana Sahib at Cawnpore on 6th December. He then began clearing the Doab, the country between the Ganges and the Jumna, so as to open up communications with the Punjab.

By the end of February he had some 20,000 troops under command, which were joined by a substantial contingent of Gurkhas sent by the King of Nepal. Facing him in and around Lucknow were over 100,000 mutineers. Using the Alambagh as a firm base he began operations against Lucknow on 2nd March. By the 21st the whole of the city was once again in British hands but Campbell's slow and methodical tactics, governed by his wish to reduce casualties in the costly business of street fighting, enabled large numbers of mutineers to escape. Over the next nine months Campbell pursued the remaining but still sizeable rebel forces, first clearing Rohilkand and then, from June onwards, harrying the enemy in Oudh with mobile columns, gradually driving them north towards the foothills of the Himalayas. By the end of the year all resistance, except for the activities of a few guerilla bands, had ceased and British authority over northern India had been restored. The Nana Sahib took refuge in the Himalayas and was never seen again but his general, Tantia Topi, had escaped Campbell's clutches after his defeat at Cawnpore and had transferred his attentions to a different quarter.

---

† Including the 9th Lancers, 8th and 75th Foot, 2nd and 4th Punjab Infantry.

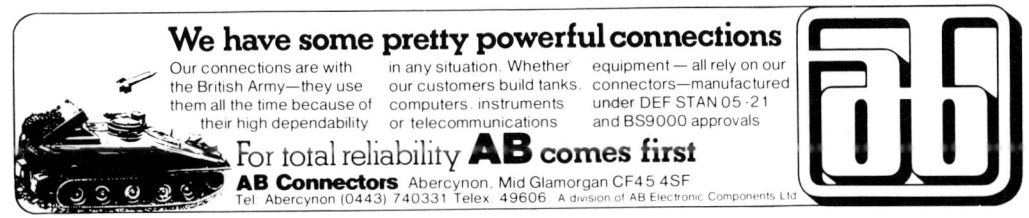

In June 1857 the sepoy regiments at Jhansi in Central India had mutinied and massacred the Europeans in the station. Their action had been encouraged by the Rani of Jhansi, who nurtured a fierce hatred of the British for annexing her territory in 1854 and now saw in the sepoy uprising her opportunity for revenge. By July all the land between the rivers Jumna and Tapti had passed entirely from British control. Not until the end of the year, when Sir Hugh Rose was appointed commander of the Central India Field Force, could anything be done to restore the situation. Rose's force, initially only about 6,000 strong, was largely made up of Bombay native troops with the 14th Light Dragoons, the 86th Foot, and the 3rd Bombay Europeans; in May he was joined by the 71st Highland Light Infantry and a Camel Corps, drawn from the Rifle Brigade, the 88th and some Sikhs. Rose, an intelligent, strong-willed man of boundless energy, pushed northwards from Mhow in January 1858 to besiege the Rani in Jhansi. Here Tantia Topi with 22,000 men came to join her but, before they could link up, Rose defeated him in the field, following up his victory by storming Jhansi itself in early April. The Rani fled while Rose pursued Tantia north-east to Kalpi where he again defeated him. This seemed to have finished the campaign but Tantia escaped and, having joined the Rani, together they made off to Gwalior where they incited the local ruler's troops to rebellion and occupied the city. Rose heard the news on 4th June and directed all the forces he could muster — only 5,000 in all — to converge with all speed upon Gwalior. In a series of actions over four days, in one of which the Rani was killed during a charge by the 8th Hussars, Rose defeated the enemy forces and drove them from the city. Only Gwalior fort, built upon a huge rock rising over 300 feet above the plain, remained in enemy hands but this was surprised and captured in a bold and daring stroke by Lieutenants Rose and Waller of the 25th Bombay Native Infantry on 20th June. For six months the Central India Field Force had kept up a relentless and sustained effort against the rebels, marching and fighting over a distance of nearly a thousand miles in the height of the hot weather with temperatures sometimes reaching 130 degrees Fahrenheit, but always drawing strength and the will to go on from the determination and example of their indomitable commander, Sir Hugh Rose. These operations broke the back of the rebellion in Central India but Tantia Topi still remained at large with a body of loyal followers. Small mobile columns were sent after him but for nine months he kept just ahead of his pursuers, twisting and turning all over Central India. The pursuit was as indefatigable as he was elusive — a troop of the 8th Hussars and one of the 17th Lancers were reputed to have covered 2,000 miles — but not until April 1859, when he was betrayed by one of his own followers, was he finally captured and executed.

With his end the long struggle of the Mutiny, with all its horrors and atrocities, its heroic endeavours and stubborn endurance, was finally brought to a close. The sepoys had fought with undoubted courage, a tribute perhaps to their training, but though enjoying vastly superior numbers had been unable to prevail. Their defeat was due in part to the incapacity and inexperience of their Indian officers in handling bodies of over company strength and to the lack of any effective overall direction. But it was also due to the inflexible determination of the British troops of all ranks to stamp out and punish all the perpetrators of mutiny and massacre. It was this resolve that kept them going, often in the worst heat of the Indian climate, defying death and disease, on arduous marches and amid ferocious fighting. Without lessening their achievement, the debt they owed to other Indians must not be forgotten. The Mutiny was almost entirely confined to the Bengal Army. Although about a third of the Bombay Army were Brahmans and Rajputs of the type that filled, and mutinied in, the Bengal regiments, only parts of two battalions were disaffected. In Madras not a single regiment mutinied. If the Bombay and Madras soldiers had not stood loyal, India could hardly have been held. Then there was the great contribution made by the Sikhs, Punjabi Moslems, and Gurkhas, as well as by Afghans and Afridis from across the North-West Frontier. Perhaps they were motivated more by dislike of the Brahman sepoys than love for the British redcoat; nevertheless they gave their loyalty and their courage freely and in so doing instituted a bond that would serve the Army in India well in the future. Lastly there were the thousands of non-combatant Indians, who as servants, labourers, messengers, transport drivers, cooks, and water carriers, supported the British columns; to their numbers must be added all the humble peasants who at the risk of their lives sheltered British fugitives from the mutineers.

The greatest single effect of the Sepoy Mutiny was the dissolution of the East India Company. It had long ceased to have any trading function and from 1st November 1858 the direct sovereignty of India became vested in the Queen. The Governor-General became the first Viceroy, ruling India in her name and responsibile to, in London, the Secretary of State for India, with his own department, the India Office. In India itself the three Presidencies remained in being, with the Viceroy doubling his duties with those of the Governor of Bengal, while the Governors of the two smaller Presidencies, though remaining responsible for their own territories, were subordinate to the Viceroy on matters affecting India as a whole. All this of course had considerable implications for the future of the Army in India, British and Indian troops alike, but the changes that ensued must be left for a later chapter.

CHAPTER 14
A CHANGED ARMY
1854–1899

The need for radical changes in the Army's administration, the chief essentials of which had remained unaltered since the early eighteenth century, was forced upon the Government by the disclosure to an angry public of its soldiers' sufferings in the first Crimean winter. Indeed the first of these changes had occurred before the invasion of the Crimea when, in June 1854, the Secretary of State for War was relieved of his additional responsibility for the Colonies. From December of that year, as ministers came to realise the consequences of their inertia and that of their predecessors, other changes followed in rapid succession, though of course it would be some time before they became effective.

The Commissariat was transferred from the Treasury to the War Office in belated recognition that it should be a military and not a civil department. In February 1855 the ancient office of Secretary at War was merged in that of the Secretary for War. A month later administration of the Militia and Yeomanry was transferred from the Home Office to the War Office, though command of such forces and power to issue commissions in them remained vested in the Lords Lieutenant of counties, as had been the practice, in the case of the Militia, since Tudor times. Next to feel the blast of reform was the old and separate army of the Master-General of the Ordnance. The responsibilities of the Board of Ordnance for fortifications, munitions and equipment passed to the Secretary of State for War; henceforth all military stores would bear the legend "WD" instead of the old "BO". The two Ordnance Corps, the Royal Artillery and Royal Engineers, both soon to be augmented after the abolition of the East India Company's Armies, passed from the Master-General's control to join the cavalry and infantry under the Commander-in-Chief. The character of the Royal Engineers, hitherto an all-officer corps, was changed by the incorporation of the Royal Sappers and Miners so that in future engineers of all ranks were concentrated in one corps.

Two other changes of 1855 concerned the provision of the soldier's small arms and clothing. Since the eighteenth century the manufacture of the Army's muskets had largely been in the hands of private factories although Government factories had been tried out during the Napoleonic Wars. Lack of money had caused the latter to lapse after Waterloo but in 1854 the excessive profits being made by private manufacturers led to the expansion and modernisation of the Government Small Arms Factory at Enfield, and in 1855 the first Superintendant was appointed. It was here that the Enfield rifles, whose cartridges sparked off the Indian Mutiny, were manufactured on American machinery. The clothing of cavalry and infantry soldiers had, from the beginnings of a standing army, been provided by the colonels of their regiments out of "off-reckonings", money made over from the soldiers' pay; in the Ordnance corps men had been clothed by contract. From 1855 it was decided to abolish the colonel's responsibility for clothing (and the profits he made thereby) and to dress all arms by contract, superintended by a new Army Clothing Department. Various changes in the basic design of the uniform, which as mentioned in Chapter 12 was becoming increasingly old-fashioned in 1854, had been under consideration before the Crimean War broke out, but it was not until 1855 that the appearance of the Army was completely altered.† The old coats and jackets of the heavy and light cavalry and the swallow-tailed coatees of the infantry gave way to the tunic, a more easy-fitting garment with skirts all round, which had been introduced in some European armies, notably the Prussian and French, in the 1840s; this, with various minor modifications, remained as the soldier's full dress garment up to 1914 and to the present day in the case of the Household troops.*

With the final end to the divided administration of the Army, a system which had grown up as a means of checking the Army's, and through it the Sovereign's, power, Parliamentary and civil control was now fully established over it. Theoretically the entire responsibility for the Army was now vested in the Secretary of State for War under whom the War Department was charged with all supply and finance matters, including provision of weapons, clothing and equipment, transport and medical services. The internal administration

† With the exception of the Royal Horse Artillery.
* The first patterns were double-breasted but changed to single-breasted in 1856.

and training of the Army was in the hands of the office of the Horse Guards, under the Commander-in-Chief, which remained outside the War Department but constitutionally subordinate to the Secretary for War. In practice, however, the Commander-in-Chief's department, which from 1856 was to be presided over for nearly 40 years by the Queen's cousin, the Duke of Cambridge, remained independent, a division of responsibility that was to diminish the effectiveness of the 1855 centralisation of administration as the Duke grew older.

Whatever the shortcomings of the 1855 changes, the period of the fifties and sixties saw reforming zeal at its height. The ignorance of staff duties displayed in the Crimea led to the expansion of the Senior Department of the Royal Military College which was transformed into the separate establishment of the Staff College, Camberley, wherein potential staff officers would be educated and examined in such duties before being eligible for appointments on the Staff. The training of regimental officers and men, too, received attention. The camp of instruction at Aldershot, which in the post-Crimean period developed into a permanent cantonment, has already been mentioned and by 1862 similar camps for all arms had been set up at Shorncliffe, Colchester and at the Curragh in Ireland. The replacement of smooth-bore muskets by the more sophisticated rifles, first the Minié, then the Enfield, disclosed the need for skilled instructors in their use and Schools of Musketry were opened at Fleetword and Hythe.

Though the Enfield was greatly superior to the old musket, the pace of weapon development was now such that it was soon rendered obsolete by new types of breech-loading rifles introduced in America and on the Continent. A design by Jacob Snider for converting Enfields into breech-loaders was accepted and by 1869 the new Snider rifle was in the hands not only of the Regular Army but also the Militia. No sooner was this in general issue when another rifle, the Martini-Henry, the first without an external hammer and with greatly improved range and accuracy, was undergoing troop trials prior to issue in the early 1870s.

The changes affecting small arms were paralleled in the Royal Artillery. The development of rifled and breech-loading guns, of which the Armstrong type was most favoured, greatly increased the scope of the whole science of artillery. This led to the opening of a School of Gunnery at Shoeburyness in 1859. Two years later over 1,000 rifled Armstrong guns of all calibres were ordered. The old brass cannon were set aside and in future all pieces were to be made of iron, later steel, while production would increasingly be concentrated at the Royal Arsenal, Woolwich instead of at private factories.

The lack of any proper transport system in the Crimea had called into being the Land Transport Corps. At the end of the war it was reduced to a total strength of 1,200 and renamed the Military Train, formed in six battalions. The men were drawn from cavalry and artillery volunteers and indeed when the 2nd Battalion arrived in India during the Mutiny, such was the shortage of cavalry, that it was employed entirely in that role under Outram's command around Lucknow. Although in the Mutiny *the Military Train bore a part which would have reflected credit upon the oldest and most experienced Cavalry soldiers",(1)* it proved less satisfactory elsewhere as a transport corps and was disbanded in 1870. This was largely because the supplies it was designed to carry were the responsibility of the entirely separate Commissariat Corps which, though administered by the War Department, was manned by civilians. This corps, within its limitations, did good work in the supply of food to the troops but, as its officials and the officers of the Military Train pointed out, *"it was unsound in principle to make one authority responsible for the waggon and another for its load".(2)* Various attempts were subsequently made to combine the two but the problem was not satisfactorily resolved until the formation by Sir Redvers Buller in 1888 of the Army Service Corps, granted the Royal title in 1918.

The Crimean War had particularly highlighted the deficiencies of the medical services which, apart from general hospitals under the supervision of Inspector-Generals and Staff-Surgeons, were entirely a regimental responsibility, each having its own surgeons and providing for its own hospitals. A Medical Staff Corps came into being in 1855 to man hospitals, becoming the Army Hospital Corps after the war with responsibility for all hospital and ambulance duties. In 1859 a medical school was established at Chatham where probationers received training in military surgery, medicine and hygiene. This was followed by the construction of two model hospitals, one at Netley, the other at Woolwich, to the first of which the Chatham medical school was transferred in 1863. Ten years later the long-standing practice of appointing medical officers permanently to regiments was abolished, and an all-officer Army Medical Staff was formed. In 1898 this was united with the Army Hospital Corps, which had been retitled Medical Staff Corps in 1884, into a medical corps of all ranks — the Royal Army Medical Corps.

The body today designated the Royal Army Ordnance Corps underwent several changes of titles and responsibilities, and the gradual conversion from civilian to military staff, after the transfer of the Board of Ordnance to the War Office. In broad terms the tasks concerned with all types of stores were dealt with by a department which undertook the office work and an independent staff of soldier-workmen which actually handled the stores. By 1896 these two branches had evolved into the Army Ordnance Department and the Army Ordnance Corps, which were not finally unified until 1922.

Even the spiritual needs of the soldier were not omitted from the changes of the post-Crimean period. In 1854 there were but seven chaplains for the whole Army. Following a substantial increase two years later, the Army Chaplains Department was formed in 1858 of which 57 were Church of England, 19 Roman Catholics, and five Presbyterians; all, regardless of denomination, were divided into four classes, those of the first ranking as colonels and the fourth as captains. Closely connected with the establishment of this Department was the restoration or new construction of special churches for garrisons' use, of which All Saints' at Aldershot, built in 1863, is a typical example.

In the same way that medical officers were transferred from regiments into a separate department in 1873, so too were regimental paymasters and veterinary surgeons, in 1878 and 1881 respectively. In 1893 the function of the military clerks who assisted the officers of the Army Pay Department was regularized by their incorporation, with the officers, into the Army Pay Corps.

So, over the course of the latter half of the nineteenth century, the various logistic agencies and departments were gradually removed from civilian or regimental control and reorganized into separate, functional corps, each with its own rank structure approximating to those of the combatant arms and each providing its own specialised service without which the fighting troops could not efficiently exist, whether in the field or in peacetime garrisons. It was a long, slow process, with many problems and inter-departmental rivalries to be overcome but, by the end of the century, that part of the Army now known as its Services, as opposed to the Arms — Cavalry, Artillery, Engineers and Infantry,— had become fully integrated within the Army, with their importance at last recognized by military and civilian overlords alike.

If the hard-learned lessons of the Crimean War had given rise to a reorganisation of the Army's higher administration, its training, weapon development, and logistic arrangements, the world situation in the years that followed drew attention to the Army's capacity to fulfill its functions. First there was the Empire to police and defend, a task intensified by the events of the Indian Mutiny, the need for an enlarged garrison in Canada following the outbreak of the American Civil War in 1861, and the possibility of larger commitments in Africa, both in the north due to the opening of a fast route to India through the Suez Canal in 1869, and in the south due to growing restlessness of blacks and whites; even in distant China and New Zealand the 1860s were to require a sizeable deployment of troops.†

The Army's second task was the security of Britain and the possible requirement to intervene in Europe where the ambitions of Napoleon III and the rising power of Prussia gave cause for increasing concern. In 1859 the establishment of the Army was fixed at 237,000 which, apart from the Household Cavalry and the Foot Guards, allowed for 25 regiments of cavalry and 132 battalions of infantry ; the latter to be deployed with 50 in India, 37 in the colonies and 45 at home. In some quarters there were doubts whether these would be enough, particularly at home.

By 1859 the alliance with France during the Crimean War had turned sour and the bellicosity emanating from that country inspired alarm in Britain as to the intentions of Napoleon III towards his late ally. This gave rise to a spontaneous, patriotic response in the shape of the "Volunteer Movement", a revival of the part-time, civilian army that had sprung up during the Napoleonic Wars. In May 1859 the Government sanctioned the raising of volunteer corps, provided there was no cost to the public. Within a year over 150,000 volunteers had been enrolled, mainly of the middle and skilled working class, rising sections of the community which hitherto had had little connection with or enthusiasm for soldiering of any sort. All over the country units were formed: mainly companies of Rifle Volunteers but also of Light Horse, Mounted Rifles, even of Artillery and Engineers. Apart from a quantity of Enfield rifles provided by the Government, everything else — uniforms, equipment, stores and drill halls — was supplied at private expense. In keeping with their style as Riflemen, most units adopted a uniform in which green or grey predominated but some were fanciful in the extreme: a North Cornwall corps paraded in scarlet Garibaldi shirts and broad-brimmed hats with feathers, while the Lancashire Light Horse Volunteers belied their description by affecting a costume similar to the heaviest of cavalry, the Life Guards.

Government approval for the Volunteers had not been achieved without considerable military and political opposition. The Duke of Cambridge pronounced such corps to be *"an armed and dangerous rabble"* who, in countering an invasion, might well prove to be *"quite as much in the way"(3)* of the regular forces. Political hostility ranged between mockery of the whole concept, objections as to its likely cost and radical fears about the growth of militarism. However, popular feeling forced recognition upon the Government which, though fully conscious of the financial considerations, was not averse to getting *"the middle classes imbued with an interest in our means of defence".(4)*

---

† Events in all these areas will be covered in later chapters.
* The 1st — 25th Foot by now each had two battalions; the 26th — 100th one each; the 60th Rifles and Rifle Brigade four each. In the following year a further three cavalry regiments and nine infantry battalions would be added to the dissolution of the East India Company's Armies (see next chapter).

To begin with, the absence of Government control, the multiplicity of units, and the lack of any unified system of recruitment, equipment and terms of service naturally diminished the value of the Volunteers as a military force. Many units were short-lived, soldierly enthusiasm often proved to be no more than a liking for the uniform and military rank, but elsewhere the characteristic efficiency, enthusiasm and improving zeal of the Victorian middle class proved that the Movement was more than a flash in the pan. Gradually its potential as a permanent supplement to the Regular Army and the Militia came to be recognized; from 1860 regular instructors and adjutants were seconded, though at the Volunteers' expense, and the individual companies and small detachments were grouped into administrative battalions.

While the Volunteer Movement made some contribution to the needs of home defence, the week-end drills of a few lawyers, tradesmen, clerks and mechanics were clearly not going to provide a trained reserve to swell the ranks of the Regular Army in the event of a European emergency. While the system of long-service existed, voluntary recruitment had served well enough, prior to the 1860s, for the provision of Indian and colonial garrisons, but it meant that there were no reserves of trained men who could be recalled to the colours should it suddenly be necessary to expand the Army. In any case voluntary recruiting for long service was becoming more difficult in an age of growing prosperity and increasing emigration; even Ireland, with its greatly diminished population, was no longer as fruitful as in the past. British inability to influence events in Europe had been displayed in 1864 when Prussia and Austria seized Schleswig-Holstein from Denmark and again in 1866 when Prussia shattered the Austrians in a six weeks' campaign. It was all too evident that in no way could Britain match the ability of Prussia to mobilise an army of 400,000 with astonishing speed, due to its system of universal conscription for three years with the colours and four in the reserve, added to its army's localized and identical organisation for peace and war. The superiority of the Prussian system, not to mention its technological advances in weapons and its mastery of mass movement and supply, was again to be demonstrated in 1870 by its overthrow of France, hitherto the pre-eminent military power in Europe. Before this crushing defeat occurred, however, a War Office committee had already formed the opinion that the Prussian system of recruitment had much to offer but its implementation in Britain was out of the question due to certain basic differences between the two countries: first, conscription was politically unthinkable in Britain, and secondly, while Prussia was purely a European power, Britain was both a European and an Imperial power with world-wide commitments.

The measures taken to fashion an army capable of fulfilling its dual function and, at the same time, to improve conditions of service, and thereby recruitment, were the product of the fertile and brilliant brain of Mr Edward (later Lord) Cardwell, who was appointed Secretary of State for War in Gladstone's Liberal Government of 1868. In 1870 Cardwell abolished long service in favour of enlistment for 12 years: six with the colours and six with the reserve, although men in regiments at home could pass into the reserve after three years. By this means a reserve of trained men would be built up, foreign garrisons could be manned without the constant turnover a shorter term of colour service would involve, and a better type of man would, it was hoped, be attracted into the ranks. At the same time pay, food and living conditions were improved and flogging was at last abolished, except upon active service.

Next, Cardwell planned to modernize the regimental system which hitherto had embraced a number of quite independent regiments, some with two battalions but the majority with only one, each with its own depot companies for recruitment, training and drafting to the parent battalion. Although the Line regiments had been allotted county titles to supplement their numbers as long ago as 1782†, these affiliations had been of no practical significance either as recruiting areas or as the location of their depots. A regiment's pride was in its number, not in the name of a county it happened to bear upon its appointments; the *"Die-Hards"* of Albuera fame were universally known to be the 57th and few cared that they happened also to be West Middlesex. A regiment's depot moved with it if it was at home and was situated wherever convenient if abroad. On the other hand, Militia battalions* and those of the Volunteers were all localized. Cardwell saw in the Militia a valuable source of recruitment for the Line and, aware of the Prussian success with localization, planned to link Line and Militia within territorial areas so that the close association between Militia battalions and their own districts might spread to the Line, thus stimulating recruitment through local pride.

In 1872 66 districts were formed, each including two Line battalions, two of Militia, the Volunteer battalions and a depot. For example, the 48th Regimental District was formed with its headquarters at Northampton to embrace the 48th (Northamptonshire) Foot, the 58th (Rutlandshire) Foot, two battalions of the Northampton and Rutland Militia, and the Northamptonshire Rifle Volunteers, while similarly the 28th (North Gloucestershire) were linked with the 61st (South Gloucestershire) and the Militia and Volunteer battalions of Gloucestershire. Cardwell intended to equalize the number of Line battalions serving at home and

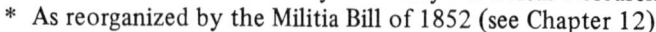

† See Journal of the Society for Army Historical Research, Vols. XIV, pp. 223-225 and XXXVI, pp. 34-38.
* As reorganized by the Militia Bill of 1852 (see Chapter 12).

Types of the Army Medical Services 1865   6803-38
Watercolour by James Ferguson

Uniforms of the Army 1865-66

Top Right: Foot Guards
Left :   Scottish Regiments
Bottom: Line Infantry Regiments

Lithograph after and watercolour by James Ferguson

21st Middlesex (Civil Service), RVC, c1860 Danger flag down
Photograph from 'Souvenir of the Camp at Wimbledon', by Vernon Heath

9th West Middlesex Rifle Volunteers, c1862   Battalion Twenty   5912-166
Photograph by Lucas Bros.

NCOs & gunners of the Royal Artillery examining the Whitworth Gun, c1864

5708-2-247

abroad so that the home battalion of a linked pair in a district trained drafts for its counterpart abroad; in due course the two would alternate. For Line regiments which already had two battalions, as in the 1st-25th Foot, this system posed no undue difficulty, but for the remainder, each with its own long traditions of autonomy, such close association with another proved hard to stomach. Having gone so far Cardwell had not gone far enough and it was left to his successor, Hugh Childers, to rationalise his system in the teeth of opposition beside which objections to Cardwell's scheme were of little account.

In 1881 the old, treasured numbers, separate identities, individual insignia, even the long-hallowed facings, were swept aside and henceforth all battalions of a district, Line, Militia and Volunteers were to become parts of a single, territorial regiment with two Regular battalions, one or two of Militia and one or more of Volunteers. All battalions of each regiment would wear the same badge and the facing colours were reduced to four: blue for Royal regiments, white for English and Welsh, yellow for Scots and green for Irish. Throughout the infantry the sense and practical advantages of the scheme were obscured by feelings of horror, disbelief and rage at the loss of ancient traditions and precious dress distinctions; it seemed nothing more than a blatant attack on regimental pride. For some the new designations were at least comprehensible if not palatable; even the most reactionary could not escape the logic of the 37th (North Hampshire) and the 67th (South Hampshire) becoming the 1st and 2nd Battalions of the Hampshire Regiment. But how to grasp the transformation of, say, the 31st (Huntingdonshire) into the 1st East Surrey or the 69th (South Lincolnshire) into the 2nd Welsh Regiment? Overnight the 75th Foot, for years uniformed as an English regiment despite a comparatively recent link with Stirlingshire, became the 1st Gordon Highlanders, having all the appurtenances of its junior partner, the 92nd, thrust upon it. Although the seniority which granted them two battalions spared the old Scottish regiments — the 1st Royals, 21st Scots Fusiliers and 25th Borderers — the loss of individuality, they had never, as befitted their Lowland origins, felt the need to emphasise their nationality by adopting anything resembling the garb of the vastly junior Highland regiments; yet now they were to be compelled to wear the Highland doublet and tartan trews, though topped incongruously with the headdress of the English Line.† That old regiment of Covenanters the Cameronians, 26th Foot, now found itself joined to the 90th Light Infantry; though both had always worn red, without any vestige of tartan, they were now to be uniformed in green with tartan trews as Scotland's first Rifle regiment, the Cameronians (Scottish Rifles). Such was their distaste that for years afterwards the 1st Battalion referred to themselves as the Cameronians and the 2nd as the Scottish Rifles. Some battalions simply ignored the new designations altogether: up until recent times the 1st and 2nd Battalions of the Oxfordshire and Buckinghamshire Light Infantry never described themselves as anything but 43rd and 52nd and their union was, on the face of it, one of the more acceptable in view of their long association in the Peninsular War. For some the loss of their old facings was more painful than that of the numbers; even the 3rd Foot, known officially since 1747 as the Buffs, had to adopt the new white facings of the English Line although the name remained, coupled with East Kent Regiment.* It would take many years for regimental sentiment to be appeased and for the theory behind localization to be accepted but in the course of time pride in the territorial titles became as strong as that for the old numbers and a new affection, between regiments and the counties and districts of the British Isles they represented, developed. Though it was to prove more effective on paper than in practice, Cardwell's plan, as completed by Childers, did result in an improved system, both for maintaining the overseas garrisons at sufficient strength, and providing a force in the British Isles for home defence or despatch overseas if required, within the limitations imposed by voluntary enlistment and the conflict between European and Imperial commitments.

One element of the home defence forces which escaped absorption into the new system was the Militia of the Channel Islands whose regiments included infantry and artillery. Each island's Militia remained a separate entity and furthermore retained the age-old method of filling its ranks by imposing a compulsory obligation to serve on all men between the ages of 16 and 60, unlike the United Kingdom Militia regiments which relied primarily on voluntary enlistment. The Channel Islands Militia were thus the only forces of the Crown in which a form of universal conscription prevailed.

For the implementation of Cardwell's reforms two other institutions of very long standing had to be removed. Unity of Line, Militia and Volunteers clearly could not be achieved while the two latter remained under command of the Lords Lieutenant of counties. Nor could the system work as long as the officers of the Militia and Volunteers were granted commissions by those same authorities while the Line continued to

† The blue cloth, spiked helmet for the Royal Scots and King's Own Scottish Borderers (adopted for all infantry, less Fusiliers and Highlanders, in 1878) and the sealskin cap for the Royal Scots Fusiliers (adopted by Fusiliers in 1866). In 1903 the two former received Kilmarnock caps, which were simply a stiffened and smartened-up version of the forage cap worn by all infantry from c.1830-c.1870, embellished with blackcock feathers.

* Their buff facings were restored in 1890, and between 1899 and 1913 19 other regiments regained their old facings (see Journal of the Society for Army Historical Research, Vol.X.p.210).

purchase theirs. In any case, now that all Arms were under control of the War Department, it was anomalous to have one set of regular officers, the cavalry and infantry, obtaining commissioned rank by purchase, while those of the artillery and engineers, who had never suffered the purchase system, did not. With the Regulation of the Forces Act of 1871, despite fierce opposition, Cardwell succeeded in abolishing purchase and bringing the Militia and the Volunteers under the same authority as the Line. In future first commissions were only to be obtainable through competitive examinations followed by training as a gentleman cadet at Sandhurst for cavalry and infantry and Woolwich for artillery and engineers, except for those who transferred from the Militia into the Line. Promotion was henceforth to be by seniority, theoretically tempered by selection, and controlled by compulsory retirement at certain ages and limitations on the tenure of battalion or regimental command.

Cardwell also attempted to complete the 1855 reforms of the higher administration of the Army by constituting the War Office and the Horse Guards as a single department, thus officially subordinating the Commander-in-Chief to the authority of the Secretary for War. It would however require more than an Act of Parliament to achieve this in practice for at the head of the Horse Guards there still sat the Royal personage of the Duke of Cambridge. The older he grew the more resistant to any sort of change he became, most of all to any diminution of his powers. Behind Cambridge was the Queen, the court and not a few of the older officers who deplored the rapid changes to the Army they had grown up in, viewing the modernization of the infantry as hopelessly destructive of regimental pride, the abolition of purchase as an encouragement to time-servers and the short-service soldier as a feeble substitute for the old long-service man.

In contrast to Cambridge and his ilk was the band of forward-looking officers led by Sir Garnet Wolseley, a highly ambitious man and zealous for reform and modernization. When at the War Office in 1871 Wolseley had been a fervent supporter of Cardwell's reforms and subsequently made a brilliant reputation for himself as *"Britain's only general"* in the course of a number of colonial campaigns, beginning with the Red River Expedition in Canada in 1870, as will be seen later; a reputation which, in view of the small scale of these operations, was perhaps overrated. A master self-publicist and propagandist for change, he was at constant loggerheads with Cambridge and the forces of reaction and from 1885, when appointed Adjutant-General at the War Office, he continued his struggle at close quarters against the dead hand of the ageing Commander-in-Chief, though by then his own prestige and influence was on the decline. On balance Cambridge emerged the winner, and when at last he lay down the office of Commander-in-Chief in 1895 and was succeeded by Wolseley, the latter, by then a shadow of his former self in intellect and energy, found that the post to which he had so long aspired had finally succumbed to reform and was reduced to the same level in the hierarchy as the Adjutant-General, the post he had held in 1885.

The long reign of Cambridge at the Horse Guards, though motivated by a sincere love for the Army, had done much to ensure that the modernized force envisaged by the well-intentioned reforms of the 1855–1881 period had not in fact kept pace with the rapidly changing political, military and technological facts of life in late nineteenth century Europe and the World. Not only that but some of Cardwell's reforms had developed weaknesses. An imbalance between the number of battalions at home and abroad had grown up. A drop in recruiting had given ammunition to the opponents of short-service. A threat of war with Russia in Afghanistan in 1885 coinciding with a campaign in the Sudan revealed how Cardwell's measures had failed to provide for the contingency of simultaneous emergencies. Even the increase in professionalism, expected to ensue from the establishment of the Staff College, schools of instruction and the abolition of purchase, had failed to materialise. Writing of his battalion in 1881, a regimental officer observed: *"No officer from the Regiment had ever entered for the Staff College. That was one of their numerous, die-hard boasts. Schools of instruction..had been invented by...the Horse Guards to enable slackers to sneak away from good, honest, regimental parades....Professionally speaking the Colonel, Adjutant and Sergeant-Major held the bullet to be a fool and the bayonet to be still the last argument of Kings".(5)* Such sentiments, which would continue to be prevalent throughout the eighties and nineties, were hardly appropriate in an age that witnessed the frightening efficiency of the Prussian General Staff, and the development of the machine-gun, the rapid-fire magazine rifle, smokeless powder and quick-firing, long range field guns. It was perhaps significant that the very same battalion, within a year of earning a high reputation in Afghanistan, was put to flight by a handful of Boer farmers equipped with modern rifles and using fire power to cover movement, coupled with superb fieldcraft.

In the decades following the late fifties and early sixties, when the possibility of British involvement in Europe had highlighted the Army's unreadiness for such a contingency, European powers had been preparing for conflicts on the pattern of the Franco-Prussian War of 1870 — conflicts which would depend on the rapid mobilization of the entire trained manpower of a nation and the application of modern technology to warfare. The British Army, on the other hand, had plentiful experience of fighting but in mountains, jungle, desert or veldt, against savage enemies who, though often ferocious and numerous, were not organized in highly-trained,

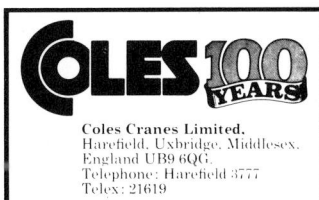

well-equipped army corps or armed with machine-guns and quick-firing artillery. It was the age of the heroic skirmish on far-flung frontiers, often against great odds and sometimes ending in bloody disaster. Through the words and sketches of war correspondents and artists like Archibald Forbes, Bennet Burleigh and Melton Prior, and stirred by the verses and stories of Rudyard Kipling, the late Victorian public thrilled or agonized over their breakfast tables at the adventures in distant lands of the *"Soldiers of the Queen"*. The once-despised redcoat now became Tommy Atkins, rivalling Jack Tar in the affections of the nation. Furthermore, though occasional reverses stunned the public, Tommy, with his public-schoolboy officer, always won through in the end, giving the taxpayer a comforting sense of pride and confidence in the superiority of his Army. It was public outrage over governmental neglect of its soldiers that had galvanized politicians into long overdue reform in 1855, but when the same public was content to bask in a blaze of Imperial glory kindled by the bayonets of its regiments, few politicians would stir themselves to enquire whether all was as well as it seemed to be. In 1899 politicians, public and Army were about to receive a rude shock, one for which romantic exploits in India, Africa and elsewhere, now to be considered, had left them all ill-prepared.

Rt. Hon. Edward Cardwell c1880
Photograph by Hill & Saunders

6408-218

Field Marshal The Duke of Cambridge
Painting, oil on canvas, by John Lucas, 1862

6011-15

CHAPTER 15
ON THE FRONTIER
1860-1904

After the Indian Mutiny military operations in India changed in character, in the terrain on which they were fought and to a large extent in the type of men who undertook them. From the eighteenth century up to 1857, with the sole exception of the First Afghan War, the enemy had been first the French with their native auxiliaries and allies, followed by the armies of Indian princes and potentates, against all of which the tactics employed had been largely those of European warfare. The scene of operations had gradually moved north from Mysore to the Punjab but the chosen fields of battle had been usually in open country favourable to the deployment of line and column. They had been fought predominantly by the Company's sepoy armies, drilled and trained to resemble as closely as possible the Queen's regiments with which they were stiffened. After 1859, when British authority, now vested in the Crown, was re-asserted all over India, no threat remained within the sub-continent, other than the possibility of civil disturbance. Great care would of course have to be taken to avoid any repetition of the events of 1857, but the focus of political and military attention now shifted to the north-west, across the Indus and beyond to Central Asia where, as the century progressed, Russian encroachments seemed increasingly threatening. Between British India's North-West Frontier and the Russians lay the independent state of Afghanistan and between Afghanistan and the Frontier lay the tribal territories, a wild and inhospitable terrain of jagged mountains, steep and rocky valleys, subject to extremes of heat and cold, where every man went armed and where the only law was that of the bullet and the knife. It was here for the next 50 years that the Army in India, re-organized after the Mutiny, would be chiefly employed.

One of the lessons of the Mutiny had been that there must be maintained in India an adequate proportion of British troops to Indian. In 1856 this had only been about one to nine but in future it was to be kept at about one to two; in 1863, when the reorganization was complete, there were 62,000 British and 125,000 Indian. When the East India Company was broken up it was decided to transfer to the Queen's Army all the Company's European regiments, which by then included five of cavalry, belatedly raised during the Mutiny, nine of infantry and the white elements of all three Presidencies' artillery and engineers. This caused some unrest, the men claiming that if they were required to transfer their allegiance from Company to Crown, they should be allowed either to claim a free discharge or the normal bounty then paid on enlistment into the Queen's Army. After some alarming scenes of indiscipline and near-mutiny, in the course of which one soldier was executed and the 4th and 5th European Light Cavalry were disbanded, discharges were allowed for those who wanted them. The remaining regiments were then transferred to the cavalry and infantry of the Line and the artillery and engineers incorporated into the Royal Artillery and the Royal Engineers. From these transfers there emerged the 19th, 20th and 21st Hussars, the latter converting to Lancers in 1897, and the 101st-109th Foot. In 1881 the 101st and 104th (previously the 1st and 2nd Bengal Fusiliers) became the regular battalions of the Royal Munster Fusiliers, while the 102nd and 103rd (Madras and Bombay Fusiliers respectively) became Royal Dublin Fusiliers. The 105th-109th were converted into the 2nd Battalions of the Yorkshire Light Infantry, Durham Light Infantry, Royal Sussex Regiment, Royal Inniskilling Fusiliers and the Leinster Regiment. The strong Irish character of the Company's Europeans was thus continued in the majority of the new designations.

The lengthy deliberations after the Mutiny on the future of the native forces came down in favour of retaining the three separate armies of Bengal, Madras and Bombay, the steadfastness of the two latter having, it was thought, proved the value of such segregation. Each continued to have its own Commander-in-Chief but the head of the Bengal Army was also Commander-in-Chief India with a general control over the two smaller armies. Outside his command was the Punjab Irregular Force, renamed Frontier Force in 1865, whose five cavalry regiments, 11 battalions, the Corps of Guides and four mountain batteries came under the orders of the Lieutenant-Governor of the Punjab.† This system remained until 1895 when the Presidency organization was

---

† Until 1886 when it was placed under the Commander-in-Chief Bengal. Besides the Guides cavalry and infantry it included, in 1865, the 1st-5th Punjab Cavalry, the 1st-4th Sikh Infantry, 1st-6th Punjab Infantry and the 5th Gurkhas.

abolished in favour of four Commands: the Punjab, Bengal, Madras (including Burma) and Bombay (including Sind and Baluchistan).

The Madras and Bombay Armies, having suffered little, if at all, from mutiny, stayed as they were, although a number of regiments were disbanded for reasons of economy. In Bengal, however, a major reconstruction was required. During the Mutiny all the regular cavalry regiments and 64 of the 74 infantry battalions had either mutinied or been disarmed. A few of the latter were re-admitted but the rest were all swept away. The new Bengal Cavalry was formed from eight irregular regiments, headed by Skinner's Horse, all of which had remained loyal, and eleven regiments raised during the Mutiny. The infantry was completely re-numbered into 45 single-battalion regiments, headed by the senior of the old, loyal regiments, the 21st, which now became the 1st Bengal Native Infantry. A majority of the new regiments were Sikhs and Punjabi Moslems, commonly called Mussulmans, which had been raised for service against the mutineers. In addition there were the Gurkha regiments, now numbered separately, and various irregular corps. Over the course of the rest of the century, due to periodic economies or emergencies, the number of regiments in the Indian Army as a whole fluctuated, but by the time of the next major reform, in 1903, there were 38 cavalry regiments, 138 infantry battalions and three corps of Sappers and Miners. The only artillery manned by Indians were the mountain batteries of the Punjab Frontier Force.

The heyday of the old high-caste Hindu sepoy from Oudh and Behar was now over and although a few such regiments remained, recruiting was henceforth to be confined more and more exclusively to what were known as "the martial races" of the north-west, Sikhs, Punjabi Mussulmans, Pathans, Afridis, Dogras, Jats, Baluchis and of course Gurkhas. The Bombay regiments continued to enlist large numbers of Mahrattas, but the Madras sepoy, the backbone of the armies of Clive and Stringer Lawrence, no longer found favour as a fighting man, though acceptable as a sapper, and the Madras regiments were increasingly recruited in the Punjab. In the latter half of the nineteenth century, it was the firmly-held view of most British officers in India that only the martial races were hardy and tough enough, not simply for tribal warfare on the Frontier, but also, as the Russian threat loomed larger in their imaginations, to face and hold a European enemy.

In 1861 the Company's officer-producing college at Addiscombe was closed and henceforth all British officers for Indian regiments were to be trained at Sandhurst. On commissioning they were posted, not to individual regiments as in the past, but to a pool of officers in whichever Presidency they were destined for, known as the Bengal, Madras or Bombay Staff Corps, from which all appointments — civil, staff or regimental — were filled. In order to develop the Indian officers' powers of command, the number of British officers in regiments was reduced, their duties being more of a supervisory nature, except at battalion level. Experience later in the field showed that a higher proportion was required to allow for casualties, and in 1890 the old eight-company battalion organization was changed to one of four double-companies, each commanded by a British officer with another as his second-in-command.

The rigours of campaigning in the hot weather during the Mutiny had demonstrated the unserviceability of the regulation uniform and many regiments, British and Indian, had followed the example of the Guides by adopting looser-fitting clothing dyed a khaki colour. After the Mutiny the dress of the Indian regiments was redesigned to give it a more comfortable and indigenous style, with turbans replacing the old shakos, and although the Indian version of the red tunic was widely worn in full dress, many of the regiments, particularly those of the Frontier Force and the Punjab, wore khaki, or drab as it was officially called, even in full dress. By the early eighties British regiments in India were dyeing their white summer clothing khaki for active service, a practice which led to the development of a permanently dyed khaki uniform for wear by British and Indian troops on all field service. †

Operations against the hill tribes on the North-West Frontier had first begun in 1847 after the First Sikh War and from 1860 were to continue for the rest of the century and into the next at an average of one expedition a year. Some were quite small, involving no more than a brigade, but the largest of all, in 1897, saw a force of over 30,000 men deployed. To the west of a line running roughly from Abbotabad in the north, through Peshawar, Kohat, Bannu and Tank, the limit of British administration in the sixties to eighties, lay the tribal territories — Buners, Mohmands, Afridis, Mahsuds, Khels of various descriptions, and Wazirs. All were bred to fighting and robbery from birth and were renowned as much for their bravery as for their cruelty, their hospitality as much as their treachery. Though constantly beset by tribal and individual feuds, which they would prosecute to the death no matter how long it took, they would also defer such feuds and unite together in the face of a common enemy. Many enlisted in Indian regiments, in which they would fight as valorously against their own kith and kin as they had against the same regiments before enlistment, and would do so again after their discharge. As formidable at long range with the rifle as at close quarters with knife and sword, they made their rock and scrub covered landscape a death trap for the unwary.

---

† For the British Army outside India, khaki was not officially adopted for foreign service until 1896. Troops on manoeuvres at home still wore red up until the turn of the century.

In the three decades after 1860 the policy adopted towards these tribes was to leave them to their own devices, until these led them, as they frequently did, to raid and plunder in the plains to the east. Then retribution had to be exacted, first by the imposition of fines, by blockade if these were not paid, and finally by punitive expeditions. What began as a simple operation to demolish a few villages and raze their crops could develop into a bitter and costly small war. In 1863 a force of 5,000 British and Indian troops under Brigadier Neville Chamberlain, sent to punish a tribe in the Chamla Valley, was surrounded by other tribes in the Umbeyla Pass. A further 4,000 reinforcements had to be sent up to their relief and an operation, originally anticipated to take no more than three weeks, lasted three months at a cost of nearly 1,000 casualties.

Underlying British policy towards the tribal areas was the conflicting argument over how best to counter the possible Russian threat. One school favoured a forward policy of extending British rule into and beyond the mountains that lay between the Indus and Afghanistan, to impose a physical barrier between India and an Afghanistan-based invasion. To be effective such a policy would require the subjugation of the tribes, with all the considerable military effort and expenditure that would entail. The opposition favoured the more economical policy of holding the line of the Indus, thus forcing an invader to channel his advance and extend his lines of communication through the mountain passes, where he would find the tribes as unfriendly as had the British. If, however, the Russians could, by diplomatic pressure, win over the Amir of Afghanistan and through him influence the tribes to their favour by promises of gain for them in the plains, then the mountains would prove no barrier and the Army would have to fight on the Indus, without any physical obstacle on which to fall back and with a huge, subject population in its rear. Therefore the Russians must be kept out of Afghanistan at all costs.

In 1877 Russia had gone to war with Turkey and the renewed threat to the Dardenelles, as in 1854, sent a British fleet to Constantinople. The danger of war spreading in Europe was averted by the Congress of Berlin but Russian troops had been moved to the Afghan border and a Russian mission sent to Kabul. To counter this the Viceroy, Lord Lytton, received governmental permission to send a British envoy to the Afghan capital but the Amir, Sher Ali, refused to accept him, threatening to prevent his entry into Afghanistan by force. Although by this time the Russians were preparing to leave Kabul, Lytton construed Sher Ali's refusal as being instigated by them and sent an ultimatum threatening invasion unless the British envoy was accepted. On 22 November 1878, no reply having been received, three British columns invaded Afghanistan with 35,700 men and 138 guns.

The Second Afghan War was fought between, on the one hand, comparatively small British and Indian forces of all arms and, on the other, the regular Afghan army, which was equipped with artillery often superior in calibre and quantity to the British guns, and whose operations were aided, either directly or indirectly, by hosts of tribesmen. The British infantry were armed with Martini-Henrys but the Indian regiments only had Sniders, and the column's manoeuvres were always hampered by the need to protect their lines of communication and the unwieldy baggage trains which had always been and still were such a feature of armies in India. It was the first major campaign since the convulsions of the Mutiny of the reformed native army and although there were some manifestations of unreliability, even treachery, the majority showed up well, with the Guides, Sikhs and Gurkhas always foremost in dependability and fighting prowess. It was also the last major campaign of the British long-service soldier for a number of the battalions and regiments engaged had been in India since before the introduction of short-service. It was generally thought that such battalions performed better than more recent arrivals with predominantly young soldiers in their ranks.

While the northerly column under Sir Sam Browne† fought its way up the Khyber Pass to Jellalabad and the southerly under Sir Donald Stewart advanced to Kandahar, the operations of the centre column saw the emergence as a field commander of a man who was to become one of the great Victorian military figures. Commissioned from Addiscombe in 1851 into the Bengal Artillery, Frederick Sleigh Roberts won the Victoria Cross in the Indian Mutiny for capturing a colour and saving the life of a sowar single-handed. Subsequently he had seen service as a staff officer and as a colonel had organized a minor frontier expedition but, as he wrote just before the war broke out, *"It was a proud, albeit a most anxious, moment for me when I assumed command of the Kurram Field Force; though a local major-general, I was only a major in my regiment, and save for a short experience on one occasion in Lushai, I had never had an opportunity of commanding troops in the field".(1)* His command was not large, only 6,600 men and 18 guns, which included battalions of Punjab infantry, the 5th Gurkhas and two British battalions, the 8th Foot and 72nd Highlanders; the latter were mainly experienced old soldiers but the 8th's men were of its young 2nd Battalion, only recently arrived in India and not fully acclimatized. His task was to force the Peiwar Kotal, a pass over a 2,000-ft, pine-covered ridge barring the exit out of the Kurram Valley and held by an Afghan force which outnumbered his by three to one.

† Having lost an arm while winning the V.C. during the Indian Mutiny, he devised the famous belt to carry his sword and revolver which was later adopted officially by the British and Indian Armies and subsequently by armies all over the world.

Roberts' plan was masterly. Having taken elaborate deceptive measures to suggest preparations for a frontal assault, he led part of his force on a night approach march up another pass to the north, ready to turn the enemy's left flank at first light, when the troops he had left in the valley under Brigadier Cobbe would advance frontally. The flank march in the dark was a hard climb. *"Onwards and upwards we slowly toiled"*, wrote Roberts later, *"stumbling over great boulders of rock, dropping into old water channels, splashing through icy streams, and halting frequently to allow the troops in the rear to close up".(2)* Secrecy was nearly lost through the treachery of some Pathans in the 29th Punjab Infantry discharging their rifles but, as the first streaks of dawn appeared, the Highlanders and Gurkhas went into the sttack at the summit of the pass, driving the Afghan regulars from their positions. The advance then began on the main position on the Kotal, as Cobbe launched the 8th Foot and 2nd Punjab Infantry from the valley floor, supported by the 12th Bengal Cavalry and Royal Horse Artillery. Hard fighting followed on both fronts as the troops pushed forward across deep ravines and through the pine forests, but when the Afghans realised that Roberts' men were getting round behind them, they began to give way. By the time the 12th Cavalry charged up the track at the head of the Kotal, the Afghan retreat had turned into a rout, leaving the whole of the immensely strong position and all their guns in Roberts' hands.

By January 1879 the three columns were firmly established in central Afghanistan. The Amir fled and in May his successor, Yakub Khan, signed a treaty with the British at Gandamak. The Afghans ceded control of the Khyber Pass and the Kurram Valley and accepted a British Resident at Kabul with supervisory powers over Afghan foreign policy. In return the British undertook to guarantee the country against foreign aggression. All that Lord Lytton had hoped for seemed to have been achieved and the possibility of Russian domination over Afghanistan thwarted. Then, on 3rd September, a horde of indisciplined Afghan regiments suddenly attacked the British Residency which was protected by a small detachment of the Guides, only 70 strong, under Lieutenant Hamilton V.C. The envoy, Sir Louis Cavagnari, was killed early on but the Guides fought heroically against enormous odds from morning till sunset. Finally only a handful under a Sikh officer, Jemadar Jewand Singh, were left alive. Though offered quarter and a safe conduct by their attackers, they preferred to sell their lives dearly rather than yield the post with which they had been entrusted. *"The annals of no army and no regiment can show a brighter record of devoted bravery than has been achieved by this small band of Guides".(3)*

When news of the tragedy reached India, Roberts was at once despatched with a column from the Kurram Valley to restore order in Kabul whence Yakub Khan had fled in panic. Having routed a large Afghan force at Charasiah, he entered the capital in mid-October. However he was now on his own and by early December the Afghans began massing in large numbers around Kabul. By a series of well-conducted offensive operations Roberts kept the enemy at arms' length for a few days but, with their strength daily increasing to around 100,000, he decided to bring in his outlying detachments and concentrate his whole force in the Sherpur cantonment which was prepared for defence a mile outside the city. He had about 7,000 cavalry and infantry, including the 9th Lancers, the 67th Foot, the 72nd and 92nd Highlanders, the 2nd Gurkhas, battalions of Sikhs and Punjabis, and the recently-arrived Guides Infantry which made had a forced march through hostile and snow-bound country from Jagdalak. By 16th December Sherpur was closely invested and Roberts completely isolated from the world outside, all the approaches to Kabul being blocked by the bitter Afghan winter. An hour before dawn on the 23rd wave after wave of screaming Afghans hurled themselves against the walls of the cantonment but each attack was beaten back by the Martinis and Sniders of the defenders, aided by star shells fired by the artillery. The sun came up and still the tribes came on in their thousands but at length, after about six hours' fighting, they began to lose heart and started streaming away in disorder. Roberts at once loosed his cavalry who galloped out to cut off the fugitives from the surrounding hills and the city. The victory was complete: for a loss of only five killed and 33 wounded, Roberts' men had inflicted 3,000 casualties and the area round Kabul was suddenly at peace.

As soon as the winter snows melted from the passes, Sir Donald Stewart advanced from Kandahar with 7,000 men to join Roberts and after a fierce battle at Ahmed Khel with 15,000 Afghans marched into Kabul on 2nd May 1880. The vacant throne of Afghanistan was now offered to Abdur Rahman, a nephew of Sher Ali, who, having agreed to abide by the Treaty of Gandamak, was proclaimed Amir in July. The British were about to evacuate Kabul and return to India when there came news that a British force had been almost annihilated to the west of Kandahar and that the garrison therein was now under siege.

In the west of Afghanistan, which had not hitherto been penetrated by British troops, Ayub Khan, Yakub's brother and a rival contender for the throne, had raised his standard at Herat and, having collected some 9,000 Afghan regulars with 30 guns, had begun to march on Kandahar, his numbers daily growing as thousands of the western tribes flocked to join him. Some local levies from Kandahar had gone out to oppose his advance, followed by a British brigade under Brigadier Burrows consisting of the 66th Foot, the 1st and 30th

5504-40-1

The fortified camp at Sherpur outside Kabul, 1879

5504-74

Maj-Gen. F. S. Roberts 1880

General Sir Sam Browne VC 7004-53-1

5504-39-58

2nd Afghan War, 1878-79
Halt of Prisoners from Bassaule with escort, 45th rattray's Sikhs on the
Khurd, Khyber

5504-22

92nd Highlanders at Kandahar, 1880
Sepia photograph after Vereker Hamilton 1910

Bombay Infantry, a weak cavalry force of the 3rd Sind Horse and 3rd Bombay Cavalry, and E Battery, B Brigade, Royal Horse Artillery. The levies had bolted and joined Ayub so that Burrows, with only 2,600 men, had found himself confronted on 27th July by an enemy host of some 25,000 regulars and tribesmen near the village of Maiwand. In the hopelessly uneven battle that followed, fought on completely open ground without any natural feature on which to base a defence, the 30th Infantry, a young regiment under-strength in British officers, broke and fled, their panic infecting the 1st, or Bombay Grenadiers, while the two cavalry regiments refused to charge. The men of E Battery fought their guns to the last possible moment before limbering up to avoid being overrun, and the 66th, abandoned by the native regiments except for a few of the Grenadiers, doggedly battled their way back to the cover of a small village. Here they fought to the end around their Colours until only nine men were left with two officers, Lieutenants Chute of the 66th and Hinde of the Bombay Grenadiers. When almost out of ammunition, this tiny band made one last gallant charge and were cut down to a man. The totally demoralised and exhausted survivors of the brigade, including Burrows himself, managed to make their escape by rallying round the guns of E Battery, which alone kept its order and discipline. After a harrowing march through the night, they straggled into Kandahar where, with the troops that had been left to garrison it, they were soon besieged by Ayub Khan's victorious army.

When this terrible news reached Kabul, all plans for evacuation were halted and Roberts was ordered to march with 10,000 men to the relief of Kandahar, 320 miles away. He had a brigade of cavalry, including the 9th Lancers, three British battalions, three of Gurkhas, three of Sikhs and three of Punjabis.† For artillery he had only mountain guns borne on mules and all baggage and supplies were cut to a minimum. On 8th August the relief column marched out of Kabul heading south-west through the mountains. With daytime temperatures at between 84 and 92 degrees Fahrenheit, each day's march began at four in the morning, camp being made at about two in the afternoon, although the baggage train, which had to be closely escorted, was not usually up until five. Not a baggage load was lost and hardly a man fell out. On 31st August Roberts reached Kandahar, having averaged about 14 miles a day with only one day's rest, which, over rough, stony mountain tracks in the height of summer, through possibly hostile country requiring constant protective measures for the column, and with all his force and baggage intact, was no mean achievement. The following day he completed his great march by attacking Ayub's army which was entrenched along a ridge outside Kandahar. In a two-brigade attack, led by the Highland battalions, the 2nd Gurkhas and 2nd Sikhs, Roberts' men drove the tribesmen in fierce hand-to-hand fighting from the walled enclosures protecting Ayub's right flank, prior to attacking his regulars on the far end of the ridge. Despite heavy enemy artillery fire the attack, supported by the mountain guns, was pressed home vigorously and, as the Highlanders and Gurkhas stormed into the last Afghan entrenchments, Ayub's army scattered in all directions. Kandahar was relieved and the last battle of the war had been fought.

Roberts' epic march set the seal on his growing reputation. Already a hero to his men, British and Indian alike, he found, when he returned to England on leave after the Afghan War, that he had become a legend. Though his greatest fame was yet to come, he always remembered with pride the Kabul-Kandahar Field Force. Years later he wrote: *"I hear the martial beat of drums and the plaintive music of the pipes; I see Riflemen and Gurkhas, Highlanders and Sikhs, guns and horses, camels and mules, with the endless following of an Indian army, winding through the narrow gorges. I shall never forget . . the men who had done so much for me". (4)*

By 1881 no British troops remained in Afghanistan. Abdur Rahman was securely on the throne and harmonious relations prevailed between the Indian and Afghan governments. However the continued Russian advances towards the Afghan frontier still posed a threat, both to Afghanistan and India, and war with Russia was only narrowly averted in 1885 following a dispute over a border incident in western Afghanistan. Furthermore there still remained the problem of the turbulent tribal territories many of which, after the formal demarcation of the Indian—Afghan border in 1893, came directly under British administration. Though this regularized affairs where two governments were concerned, the new border, or Durand Line as it was called, meant nothing to the tribes who continued their raiding and plundering as before.

In 1895 there occurred an incident which had all the ingredients of the archetypal frontier operation: a beleaguered garrison with relief columns hurrying to its aid, their advance delayed by ambush and hazards of terrain. In March of that year Dr. Robertson, the British Resident at Chitral at the northenmost end of the Frontier, became besieged by large numbers of tribesmen in a small stone fort garrisoned only by a company of the 14th Sikhs and some Kashmiri levies of doubtful value. For six weeks the little force resolutely held out while a column of 15,000 British and Indian troops under General Low battled its way northwards up the Swat Valley from Nowshera, 150 miles away. Meanwhile news of Chitral's plight had reached Gilgit, 200 miles to the east in the north of Kashmir. From here, Lieutenant-Colonel Kelly set out on 28th March with 500 men of the

† 60th Rifles, 72nd and 92nd Highlanders; 2nd, 4th and 5th Gurkhas; 2nd, 3rd and 15th Sikhs; 23rd (Pioneers), 24th and 25th Punjabis.

32nd Punjab Pioneers and two mountain guns. Both columns found their advance opposed; though Low met the stiffest resistance, with heavy fighting at the Malakand Pass and at the crossing of the Swat and Panjkora rivers, Kelly had further to go, over wild and precipitous country traversed only by narrow tracks all deeply covered in snow, which afflicted his men with frostbite and snow-blindness. The relief became a race between the two columns, but in the end the honour went to Kelly's men who marched into Chitral fort on 20th April to find Robertson and his Sikhs still holding their own.

Two years later, in 1897, a great tribal rising erupted. From the Swat and Buner territory in the north, down through the Mohmand country, the Khyber, the Afridi lands west of Kohat, and as far as the Tochi valley, the whole frontier was ablaze as outlying forts and outposts were attacked. In the north Sir Bindon Blood's Malakand Field Force relieved the besieged posts in the Malakand Pass and the fort at Chakdara, where 200 men of the 45th (Rattray's) Sikhs had resisted continual attacks by thousands of tribesmen for six days. Blood then began restoring order in the valleys before linking up with the Mohmand Field Force under Brigadier Elles to complete the pacification of the tribes north of the Kabul river. In the south the Tochi Field Force was formed to punish a tribe which had treacherously attacked a political officer and his small escort of the 1st Sikh and 1st Punjab Infantry. In this attack all the British officers were killed or wounded, but a steady and disciplined retreat was conducted by the Indian officers, thus disproving a commonly held view that no matter how brave Indian ranks were personally, they always relied on British officers in times of grave danger and difficulty. During this action Subadar Sundar Singh and 12 men of the 1st Punjabis sacrificed their lives to enable the remainder to evacuate the wounded. By late September most of the insurrections had been quelled and there only remained a large force of Afridis and Orakzais to be dealt with in the Tirah: a mountainous area, some 50 miles by 30, to the west of Kohat, bounded on the north and south by the Safed Koh and Samana ranges respectively, where no British force had ever been before. Tribesmen had already attacked British posts on the Samana range in September but two companies of the 36th Sikhs had held out in Fort Gulistan, although an outlying signal post at Sarighari had been overrun after a heroic defence for six hours by 19 men of the same regiment.

A large column of two divisions, each of two four-battalion brigades† with divisional troops, and 60,000 baggage animals was assembled at Kohat under Lieutenant-General Sir William Lockhart for the invasion of the Tirah from the south across the Samana range; further smaller columns of brigade strength were formed as reserves and for the protection of the lines of communication. In crossing the Samana range the force found its route blocked by 12,000 tribesmen holding a steep ridge at Dargai; this could only be approached on a one-battalion front up a narrow track, between the end of which and the heights above was a completely open stretch of ground. Covered by fire from the British and Indian mountain batteries, the 2nd Gurkhas attacked first with great dash but were pinned down by heavy fire at the foot of the final ascent, after suffering many casualties in crossing the open ground. They were followed by the 1st Dorsets and 2nd Derbyshires* but neither could get through the murderous hail of bullets that rained down from above. Next it was the turn of the 1st Gordons, commanded by Colonel Mathias who, forming his battalion for the attack, called out: *"Highlanders! The General says the position must be taken at all costs. The Gordons will take it!" (5).* With their pipers playing "Cock o' the North", the Highlanders charged across the open ground, followed by the 3rd Sikhs. Though about 50 men went down, they kept on, storming up to the crest line and driving the Afridis from the summit, thus clearing the way for the rest of the force. Of the five Victoria Crosses awarded for gallantry at Dargai, the action that most caught the public imagination was that of Piper Findlater of the Gordons, who, though shot through both ankes and lying under heavy fire, continued to play his pipes to cheer his comrades into the attack.

With Dargai won, Lockhart's column fought its way forward through the Sampagha Pass and into the Tirah proper. A fortified camp was established at Maidan in the heart of the territory from which, over the next six weeks, columns went out to exact retribution in all the surrounding valleys. When troops moved in sufficient strength and obeyed the rules of frontier warfare they were usually left alone but any small detachment or rear-guard was always vulnerable to sudden and violent attack. The perilous nature of such warfare was demonstrated on 9th November when a reconnaissance in force of the Waran valley was made from the high pass of Saran Sar with the 1st Dorsets. 1st Northamptons and the 36th Sikhs. As the withdrawal began large numbers of tribesmen opened fire on the rearguards. This caused several casualties, particularly amongst the Northamptons in the centre, whose rate of movement became slowed by the need to evacuate their wounded who could never be left behind in frontier warfare. In the gathering dusk their three rear companies became separated from the main body of the battalion, as well as from the flanking Dorsets and Sikhs, and on entering a defile which led down to the camp four miles away they came under heavy close-range fire from tribesmen concealed among the rocks on either side. The Northamptons fought desperately to cover the evacuation of the wounded from this death-trap. Eventually a company of the 36th Sikhs came back to assist their withdrawal but their rearguard of Lieutenant MacIntyre and a dozen men, who delayed too long in covering the retreat, were all killed and

† Each brigade had two British and two Indian battalions.
* From 1902 the Sherwood Foresters (Notts and Derby).

'The Defenders of Chitral', 1895 British officers involved in the siege   6307-56-13

The 13th Bengal Lancers charging tribesmen at Shabkadar, NW Frontier, 1897   5412-5
Watercolour by E. Hobday, 1899

mutilated. In this little action alone the three companies suffered nearly 50 casualties. The Northamptons were inexperienced in frontier fighting, having only just come up from Central India before the campaign began, and made mistakes which more seasoned battalions would have avoided but, as a contemporary account observed, *"the way in which they stuck to their wounded and brought them through that terrible nullah was a display of heroism and devotion worthy of a regiment that fought at Albuera". † (6)*

By the beginning of December most of the valleys and peoples of the Tirah had felt the effect of Lockhart's vigorous operations and, with the approach of the winter snows in which the force would not be able to exist, it was time to evacuate. The two divisions withdrew from Maidan towards Peshawar, one moving down the Waran valley which ran through the middle of the Tirah, while the other followed a parallel route down the Bara valley to the north. The former's march was unopposed but the two northerly brigades were constantly harassed and attacked. The brigades alternated between advance and rearguards with the mass of baggage animals in the middle, while the heights along the flanks were picquetted by the 3rd Gurkhas, whom no troops could match for speed and endurance up and down hill. The weather conditions grew steadily worse with rain, sleet and snow and the tracks churned into mud by the mass of men and animals. Throughout 13th December heavy and unremitting attacks were kept up but all were held off by the battalions of the rearguard, 2nd King's Own Scottish Borderers, 36th Sikhs and the 3rd Gurkhas, each behaving with utmost coolness, supporting one another and never hurrying their withdrawals. Two days later the force emerged from the mountains to link up with a supporting brigade that had been sent out from Peshawar.

From late December into January 1898 operations were resumed to quell the Zakha Khels in the Bazar valley, west of Peshawar, and to re-occupy the forts in the Khyber Pass which had been lost the previous summer. The 2nd Yorkshire Light Infantry, a battalion new to the Frontier, had a hard fight at the Skin Kamar Pass on 29th January, losing 59 casualties in their first action, but *"they were kept together and well handled by their officers and fought like men". (7)* Shortly after, those tribes which had not tendered their submission came in to do so and the Tirah campaign was at an end. It had been the largest and most widespread of all the frontier expeditions but it brought peace to the area, except for minor skirmishes, for ten years.

Although the Army in India was, from 1860, chiefly employed on the North-West Frontier, there had also been flurries of activity on the Himalayan border with Tibet and another war in Burma. Two expeditions, in 1861 and 1888, had to be sent into Sikkim, to the east of Nepal, and one, in 1865, to Bhutan, further to the east. The inhabitants of these areas were in no way as formidable as the tribes of the north-west, having only the most primitive firearms supplemented by bows and arrows and relying on stockades for protection, but the nature of the terrain and lack of communications imposed considerable strain on the administrative arrangements of any expedition entering their mountains.

In 1885 the hostility towards British interests and negotiations with the French in Indo-China of King Theebaw of Burma led to the despatch of 12,000 British and Indian troops, the latter chiefly from the Madras Army, to dethrone the King and take over Upper Burma*. Encountering little opposition the force sailed up the Irrawaddy to Mandalay, captured Theebaw and on 1st January 1886 the whole of Burma became a province of India. However this was only the beginning for the troops as it soon became clear that the whole of Upper Burma, a largely impenetrable country of swamp, jungle and mountains, was infested by bands of lawless brigands, or dacoits, who terrorised the ordinary people everywhere. The pacification of this territory was to take three years and even then outbreaks of trouble still occurred. All over the country fortified posts were established from which small flying columns of cavalry and mounted infantry went out to hunt down the dacoits wherever they appeared. The strength of the British and Indian troops employed rose to 25,000, backed up by several thousand military police recruited in India. As areas were brought under control, roads and tracks were built to open up the land, but it was a long and wearisome business, greatly beset by the high prevalence of disease among the troops. In charge of operations was Brigadier George White, who had won the Victoria Cross as a major in the 92nd Highlanders during the Afghan War and was to achieve greater fame later. When he handed over his command in April 1889, the greater part of Upper Burma had at last been fully pacified.

Some of the dacoits moved north and incited the Chins of Manipur state to insurrection and in 1891-2 expeditions had to be sent against them and their neighbours, the Lushais, while further north still the Kachins began to prove unruly, requiring the periodic despatch of columns into their mountain fastnesses to bring them to submission. After the turn of the century the focus of attention swung back to the Himalayas. In 1903-4 a peaceful mission under Colonel Younghusband to the Dalai Lama of Tibet turned into a military expedition of 3,000 men, after various attacks had been made by the Tibetans. In August 1904 the troops entered Lhasa where a treaty was concluded with the Dalai Lama, after which all returned to India.

---

† As 48th Foot they had formed part of Hoghton's brigade at Albuera in 1811 (see Chapter 10).

* For earlier British involvement in Burma, see Chapter 11.

In addition to keeping watch and ward on the frontiers and maintaining internal security within the sub-continent, the Army of India also had to provide troops for areas that lay in the spheres of influence of the Indian Government and even beyond. As long ago as 1838 Company troops had been sent to occupy Aden, followed two years later by an expedition to China to attack Canton and the island of Amoy, while the war with Persia in 1856 has already been noted in Chapter 13. After the Mutiny, expeditions mounted from India increased in scope and number. Some of these will be considered later but they included further operations in China in 1859-60 and again in 1900; in Abyssinia in 1868; Malaya in 1875; Egypt in 1882 and the Sudan in 1885. When war with Russia seemed a real possibility in the late seventies Indian troops had to be sent as far afield as the Mediterranean to strengthen British garrisons in Malta and Cyprus. All this was a far cry from the days of the Brahman sepoys for whom a sea voyage was an affront to their caste. Fortunately for the mainten-ance of the 'Pax Britannica', the ranks of the new Indian Army were filled with men whose prime motivation was loyalty to their officers and their regiments and wherever those were sent, the sepoy of "the martial races" willingly followed.

While the small frontier wars never approached in scale or magnitude the great conflicts in Europe before or since, they gave to generations of British and Indian soldiers a valuable training experience in which they were made aware of the need for marksmanship, fieldcraft, alertness, self-reliance and mutual support. Young officers and N.C.Os. acquired the arts of leadership and survival in the field, while defending a sanger on some mountain top or meeting the Khyber knives with bayonets in a dark defile taught young soldiers more in a few hours than they learned in months on the barrack square or peacetime manoeuvres. After one British regiment's first action on the Frontier, an officer wrote: *"The battalion is a better battalion now than it was a week ago".(8)*

Around such operations, particularly those against the fierce and warlike tribes of the north-west, there grew up a legend and a tradition which came to colour the picture the Army had of itself and the public had of the Army. In many respects the whole character and image of the late Victorian British and Indian Armies was enshrined in those dusty coloumns tramping through the passes: British infantry in their tropical helmets, big, bearded Sikhs, Bengal Lancers, the stocky, cheerful Gurkhas, Punjabis, the splendid Guides, jingling mountain batteries with their mules and screw-guns, all in crumpled khaki blending into the harsh terrain, while far above Afghans and Afridis, Mohmands and Mahsuds lurked among the crags watching for their opportunity. It was a hard life, breeding stamina and endurance, comradeship and mutual respect between the British and Indian soldier. Sudden death from knife or bullet was never far away and for the wounded it could be grim indeed, as the laureate of the soldier in India, Rudyard Kipling, made plain:

"When you're wounded and left on Afghanistan's plains,
And the women come out to cut up what remains,
Jest roll to your rifle and blow out your brains
An' go to your Gawd like a soldier." (9)

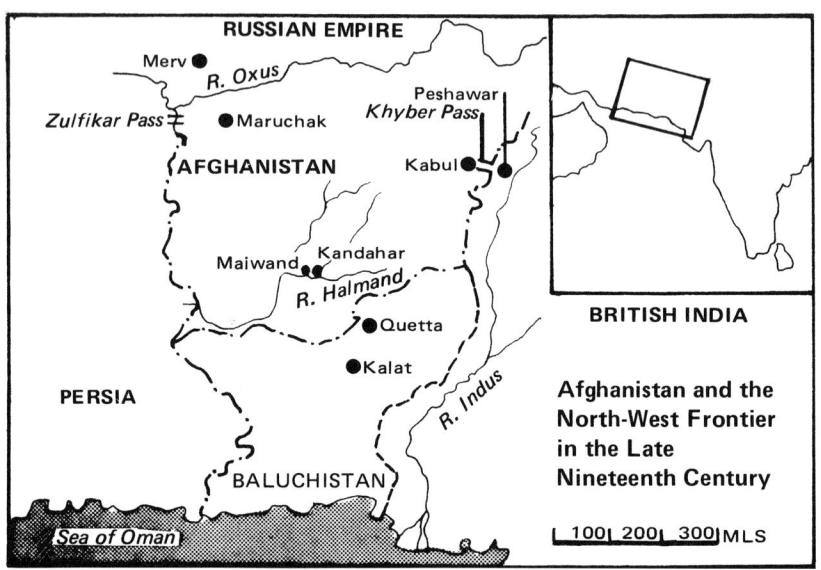

Afghanistan and the North-West Frontier in the Late Nineteenth Century

CHAPTER 16
SOLDIERING ACROSS THE WORLD
1816 – 1900

Although the Army after the Napoleonic Wars was employed chiefly in India and, as will be shown in the next chapter, in Africa, there were also other parts of the world under the Crown for which garrisons had to be found to protect British interests from either external or internal threats. The provision of such forces imposed considerable burdens on a small army dependent on voluntary enlistment and successive governments endeavoured to reduce their world-wide commitments wherever possible by replacing British soldiers with locally-enlisted forces.

In the British Isles, apart from the Army in England, a sizeable garrison of regular troops was always maintained in Ireland which could be supported, when necessary, by the Irish Militia; after the 1881 reorganization seven of the Irish regiments had three Militia battalions and the Royal Irish Rifles four, making 25 in all, but there were no Volunteer battalions in Ireland. One or two regular battalions were also permanently stationed in the Channel Islands to supplement the local Militia there. The two Mediterranean stations of Gibraltar and Malta were both important naval bases, strongly fortified and with a combined infantry strength of some ten battalions. In 1863 one Mediterranean garrison disappeared when the Ionian Islands, a British protectorate since 1815, were ceded to Greece. This reduction was balanced in 1878 by the acquisition from Turkey of Cyprus, as a convenient base in the eastern Mediterranean at which an expeditionary force could be assembled, if necessary, for employment in Asia Minor or on the Suez Canal. Four years later its value would be nullified by the British occupation of Egypt

Across the Atlantic the threat posed by the United States to Canada, already manifested in invasions during the War of Independence and that of 1812-14, necessitated the building of forts along the border and a permanent garrison of 11 British battalions to strengthen the Canadian Militia. In 1837-8 Canada's internal security was threatened by political discontent in the predominantly French province of Lower Canada breaking out into open rebellion, followed by an uprising in Upper Canada which was fuelled by American sympathisers. These outbreaks were quickly quelled by the prompt and decisive action of the Commander-in-Chief in Canada, Sir John Colborne, the brilliant pupil of Moore and Wellington, but they caused sufficient alarm at home for two cavalry regiments and four battalions† to be sent with all speed across the Atlantic. Subsequently the permanent garrison was increased to 19 regiments.

The proximity of the United States also offered a tempting refuge for would-be deserters from regiments stationed on the border, and in 1840 a regular Royal Canadian Rifle Regiment was formed for duty on the frontier *"to prevent desertion by occupying those advanced posts from which soldiers could with facility escape into the U.S.A". (1)* Its men were carefully selected out of volunteers from the British garrison who had to be of good character and with more than 15 years' service, reduced to 10 years in 1849. In the mid-sixties this regiment manned a total of 15 posts along the frontier over a distance of 1,500 miles, the most westerly being at Fort Garry on the Red River in Manitoba. It was disbanded in 1870 when the British Army ceased to serve in Canada. The sixties were a time of increasing tension on the border following the outbreak of the American Civil War and the British garrison was reinforced to a strength of 18,000 men. Fortunately no clash with the United States occurred, but an American-based organization of Irishmen, the Fenian Brotherhood, began raiding across the border in 1866 and were to do so again in 1870. Containment of the Fenian activity proved to be within the capacity of the Canadian Militia, which had been reorganized on a more efficient basis in 1855.

In 1867 Canada became a dominion and three years later its defence was placed entirely in Canadian hands, following the departure of all British troops except for a small garrison at the Royal Navy's base at Halifax. Before the withdrawal was completed, however, the transfer to the Crown of the Hudson Bay Company's lands in the north-west provoked a rebellion in the Red River area led by a half-breed, Louis Riel, who with 500

---

† King's Dragoon Guards, 7th Hussars, 2nd Battalions of the Grenadier and Coldstream Guards, 71st and 73rd Foot.

followers established himself in Fort Garry. Two special Militia battalions were formed† which, with 350 men of the 60th Rifles and detachments of Royal Artillery and Royal Engineers, made up the 1,200 strong expedition sent to restore order. After sailing up the Great Lakes from Toronto, the force then had to negotiate a further 600 miles of wild country — lakes, rapids and forests — before they reached the Red River, yet they dispersed the rebels without firing a shot or losing a man. The undertaking was a masterpiece of organisation which made the name of an officer whose later career has already been mentioned, Garnet Wolsey. It was perhaps appropriate that the last British regiment to be actively engaged in Canada should have been the 60th which had originally been raised in North America for service against French Canada in the Seven Years War.

Of British possessions in the western Atlantic, the naval base of Bermuda claimed a battalion for its garrison but, as mentioned in Chapter 9, the dreadful mortality of British troops in the Caribbean during the seventeenth and eigtheenth centuries led to much greater reliance being placed on locally-enlisted men. In the Napoleonic Wars 12 West India Regiments were raised but by 1819 these had been reduced by two, although the 3rd, 4th and 5th Regiments were re-raised for short periods during the rest of the century. All the officers were British, as were the N.C.Os. in the early days, but gradually all ranks up to and including sergeant were filled by coloured men, who in the 1st Regiment were generally Jamaicans and in the 2nd, Barbadians. In addition to quelling revolts in the Caribbean Islands and British Honduras, of which the most serious was an insurrection in Jamaica in 1865, they were also used to garrison British possessions in West Africa, taking part in some 22 expeditions in that region up to 1900, during which two Victoria Crosses were won, by Pioneer Hodge, 4th W.I.R., and Lance-Corporal Gordon, 1st W.I.R., in 1866 and 1892 respectively. It is curious, incidentally, that although coloured men of the West India Regiment were eligible for this decoration, it was not open to Indian soldiers until 1912. Up until 1858 the West India Regiment's dress followed that of the British infantry but in that year, at Queen Victoria's express wish, a highly-distinctive Zouave-type of uniform was adopted for all coloured ranks.

The loss of the American colonies in 1783 deprived the British legal system of a much-used sentence for convicted felons — transportation to the plantations of those colonies. The problem was solved by establishing a penal settlement in 1788 at Botany Bay on the east coast of Australia. To maintain order there, a regiment known as the New South Wales Corps was raised under Major Grose in 1789 and arrived at Sydney the following year. As the number of convicts in Australia grew, so the regiment was increased, being taken into the Line in 1808 as the 102nd Foot. It was relieved in 1810 by the 73rd and returned to England where it was disbanded in 1818. Thereafter until 1853, when transportation of convicts virtually ceased, the maintenance of order among them, both during the voyage out and in the settlements in Australia, Tasmania and Norfolk Island, became yet another of the normal commitments of the Army; by the 1840's the permanent garrison required four battalions.

After 1818 the arrival of respectable colonists and the establishment of farms and townships in New South Wales and South Australia presented tempting pickings for gangs of bushrangers: escaped convicts who took to the bush and terrorized the countryside with every type of violent crime. The hunting down of these criminals became another task for the military garrison from whose ranks picked men were formed, in 1825, into a body of mounted military police so as to provide a more mobile force* in the state of Victoria in 1851 led to the only "battle" fought on Australian soil, when, on 3rd December 1854, men of the 12th and 40th Foot, with mounted and foot police, had to attack the Eureka Stockade near Ballarat where 200 armed and insurgent gold-diggers had entrenched themselves in defiance of the colonial authorities. The diggers were surprised by a dawn attack and the troops' effective action prevented the spread of disaffection to other gold fields. A British garrison remained in Australia until 1870 when it was withdrawn, and thereafter each state became responsible for its own defence forces, based on very small permanent staffs, with part-time Militia and Volunteers, some units of which had first been raised in patriotic response to the outbreak of the Crimean War.

In 1840 the British garrison in Australia was called upon to send a company of the 80th Foot to New Zealand, which that year was formally, though reluctantly, annexed as a colony by the British Government as a result of the sometimes unscrupulous land purchases made by the London-based New Zealand Company which had been formed in 1839 to settle English immigrants in the country. All the land belonged to the Maori tribes whose rights, laws and customs received scant regard from the hustling agents of the Company. To safeguard the Maoris from exploitation, the first Lieutenant-Governor, Captain Hobson R.N., drew up a treaty with the chiefs whereby the Crown would protect their way of life and act as the sole agent for any land they wished to sell, in return for which they were to cede their sovereignty to the Crown. Many chiefs signed this Treaty of Waitangi but others remained suspicious of the white man's good faith, suspicions which were aggravated by the arrival of more and more immigrants and the tactless actions of the Company's agents. In 1843 the latter provoked some Maoris in the south of North Island into killing 19 Europeans, while in the north, around the

† 1st Ontario Rifles and 2nd Quebec Rifles.
* For the tracking down of the highly elusive bushranger. The discovery of gold

Bay of Islands, a somewhat unstable chief named Hone Heke, his mind inflamed by dire warnings from French and American traders, began to conceive the idea that British rule meant slavery for his people. After thrice cutting down the British flag that flew above the settlement of Kororareka at the Bay of Islands, his frustration broke out into open revolt by attacking the settlement and burning it to the ground in March 1845. Thus began the First Maori War.

The British garrison at that time consisted only of a detachment of the 96th Foot. This was hurriedly reinforced by the 58th, recently arrived in New South Wales, followed a few months later by elements of the 99th. This small force, aided by number of friendly Maoris and parties of sailors and marines landed from warships in New Zealand waters, was hurried into the field against Heke and his confederates with but the scantiest of administrative support and no artillery other than a few ships' guns. Initially the force was commanded by Lieutenant-Colonel Hulme of the 96th but he was superseded by the more senior Colonel Despard of the 99th, an elderly, opinionated man of little ability, whose contempt for the Maoris and belief in the bayonet as the solution to all tactical problems was to cause his men endless hardship and severe casualties. The Maoris were a brave and tough people with a natural aptitude for war which they waged with skill, ferocity and cruelty, oddly intermingled with a kind of sporting chivalry towards their opponents. They were no strangers to firearms, the most modern types of which they had acquired from American traders, and preferred to fight from their 'pas', strongholds constructed from huge timbers bound with flax, inside which were dug rifle-pits, underground shelters and communication trenches.

To reach these fortresses the British troops had to hack their way through forest and bush, over hills and swamp, often in torrential rain and manhandling the naval guns on their shipboard carriages. The dearth of transport limited the amount of ammunition that could accompany the guns which alone could hope to effect entry into the massive defences of the pas . Even the 32-pounders could not be relied upon to open a practicable breach. At the siege of Ohaeawai Pa in December 1845, Despard, in a fury of frustration at the failure of the bombardment, launched his storming parties at the unbroken stockade where, as a corporal of the 58th described, *"we were met with such a fusillade, I can only describe it as the opening of the doors of a monster furnace".(2)* The luckless infantry cut at the binding flax with their bayonets and tried to fire through the timbers at the Maoris in their trenches but, with men falling in dozens, Despard had to call off the assault. Even when things went better for the British, it availed them little, for rather than face defeat and capture the Maoris would slip away into the forest and construct another pa elsewhere. With so few troops, there was little that could be done but follow the Maoris from pa to pa . Eventually Heke was surprised at Ruapekapeka when a detachment of 58th and friendly Maoris got into his pa on a Sunday while his followers, many of whom were Christians, were at prayers. Although he himself escaped he felt he had done enough for honour and in late January 1846 he and his chief ally made peace with the Governor. No sooner was the north restored to order than trouble broke out in the south of North Island which was not finally subdued until the end of 1847.

After the First Maori War New Zealand became another of the Army's permanent garrisons, with one battalion based on Auckland and a second on Wellington. In addition the colonists began to form themselves into Militia units, some of which had been raised during the war. By 1860, when the white population of both islands had swelled to 80,000, and internal self-government had been granted in 1852, the garrison had been reduced to one battalion, the 65th Foot, with detachments of artillery and engineers. The Maori population was about 56,000, almost all in the North Island, and although they had been peaceful since 1847, many were far from happy at the rapidly growing number of Europeans and the increasing encroachments on their lands.

In March 1860, following a dispute over a land sale in Taranaki on the west coast, British troops opened fire on a pa whose inhabitants had interfered with a survey party. The Maoris retaliated by attacking some outlying farms and soon the Taranaki area was in revolt. Reinforcements of the 12th and 40th Foot arrived from Australia but the failure of a badly-coordinated attack encouraged more tribes to take the field. Major-General Pratt assumed command and with his force further increased by the 14th Foot, he pursued the insurgents into the interior, driving them from their pas and gradually gaining the upper hand until the enemy sued for peace in March 1861. In this little campaign Pratt eschewed Despard's methods of using his men's bodies as a battering ram; instead he adopted the old siege tactics of sapping up to the defences and constructing protective redoubts as he went forward. This tempted the Maoris into the open where it was easier to kill them with musketry from the redoubts and by counter-attack.

The campaign also revealed growing antipathy between the settlers and the military. Although the Taranaki Militia had served in the field and some, usually ex-soldiers who had taken their discharges in New Zealand, had given good service, the indiscipline and defiance of orders of others, added to the general reluctance of the colonists to assist in their own defence, earned the contempt of the British troops. The settlers, for their part, resented being ordered about by officers of an army whose disciplined structure represented everything they were trying to escape from by emigrating. Furthermore the soldiers, on whom the brunt of the fighting fell,

came to respect and admire the Maori as a gallant and chivalrous foe and to feel that the hardships and dangers they were expected to endure stemmed more from the colonists' greed for land than Maori aggression; a view the Governor felt compelled to share when he recognized that the land deal which had sparked off the trouble had been unjust to the Maoris. The colonists and their elected representatives,on the other hand, simply regarded the Maoris as a threat to their lives and settlements which they wanted eliminated and expected the troops to do the work for them. The antipathy spread upwards through the civil and military hierarchies, a state of affairs which not only adversely affected control of events in New Zealand, but also led to the Colonial Office in London becoming increasingly irritated by the New Zealand Government's inability to put its own house in order, while at the same time expecting Imperial financial and military support. Only when London threatened to withdraw troops was the New Zealand Government spurred into measures to improve the local Militia, which was raised to nearly 10,000 men, though only by the dubious expedient of encouraging volunteers by the offer of confiscated Maori land.

In 1863, however, the immediate need was for reinforcement, not withdrawal of the garrison, since a further uprising broke out in the heart of North Island where the Waikato tribe, still smarting over the 1860-1 campaign, set up a king of their own and attacked outlying settlements. Lieutenant-General Cameron had come out from England to take over the chief command which, in addition to the four battalions employed in the previous campaign, had been augmented by the 57th and 70th from India, while four more were on the way†. In July, having detached troops to guard his communications and isolated communities, Cameron was ready to lead a punitive expedition up the Waikato river to strike at the heart of the rebel territory. His troops were all dressed in blue as jackets of that colour were thought more suitable for bush warfare than the normal red tunic, and these Maori campaigns of the sixties were the only time when British infantry fought neither in red nor khaki. After a successful skirmish at Koheroa Cameron's further advance was delayed by attacks on his rear, and it was not until October that he was able to take the offensive against the Maoris' main defences at Rangariri. Hard fighting by the 12th, 14th and 65th attacking frontally, while the 40th came in at the rear, carried the flanking defences but a strongly fortified redoubt in the centre held out. Its palisades could not be scaled as the ladders were too short and the guns of Captain Mercer's Royal Artillery battery only managed to open a very narrow breach. Seeing the attack foundering, Mercer ordered his men to abandon their guns and make a dash for the breach. This gallant charge by gunners armed only with revolvers and short swords was repulsed with heavy loss, Mercer himself being mortally wounded. Seeing him lying in the open under fire, a Waikato chief, Te Oriori, leaped from the palisades and, though hit himself, carried the dying officer out of the line of fire. At dawn next day the Maoris surrendered and as they emerged from the redoubt the British soldiers ran forward to shake them by the hand. Although Cameron was now able to advance and occupy the Maori King's capital, the campaign dragged on and not until April 1865, with an attack on Orakau Pa , was the Waikato rebellion finally pacified.

The time it had taken encouraged other tribes in the east and west to take up arms and it was during the operations in the former area that the Maoris once again displayed what formidable warriors they were. On 29th April Cameron, with 1,700 men and three heavy guns, confronted 200 Maoris at the Gate Pa . Passing the 68th Light Infantry round to the rear to cut off the enemy's retreat, he opened a bombardment against the stockade. When a practicable breach had been made, the storming columns, 300 of the 43rd Light Infantry and an equal number of sailors, were ordered to attack. They charged into the pa with little loss but once inside were met by a fusillade of rifle-fire as the Maoris rose from their underground shelters. Nearly every officer was shot down and within minutes 112 men had fallen. Trapped in a confined space and with the Maoris rushing forward, the survivors panicked and fled from the pa . During the night the Maoris abandoned the pa and it was not until two months later, when a force of them were caught digging in along a ridge at Te Ranga, that the 43rd were able to redeem themselves with a magnificent charge alongside the 68th which completely cleared the position. After this, operations in the east petered out but trouble still remained in the west which was not finally subdued until January 1866.

With the European population having grown rapidly since 1860 to some 200,000, and the arguments between the local administration and the military commanders showing no signs of diminishing, London felt enough had been done and that it was time New Zealand undertook its own security. In the course of 1866-7 all the regiments were withdrawn except the 18th Royal Irish, whose planned departure in 1869 was further delayed after frantic pleas by the Governor, following a fresh series of raids by bands of outlaw Maoris. It took 18 months to restore order, but the work was done almost entirely by New Zealand forces and in 1870 the Royal Irish departed, the last of 14 British battalions to serve in the country.

While British soldiers had been fighting the Maoris in 1860, others had been in action 7,000 miles to the north in China. In 1840, following a commercial dispute between Britain and China over the opium trade, an expedition of British and Madras troops under Sir Hugh Gough, later to command in the Sikh Wars, had stormed

† The 18th from England, 43rd, 50th and 68th from India and Burma.

6004-26

One of the fine pieces of silver to be seen at the National Army Museum.
Silver model pagoda 1861 commemorating the Peace of Nankin, August 1842.
Made by Richard Hennell, London, 1860-61

Canton, occupied Shanghai and laid siege to Nanking. In 1843 the Chinese surrendered, re-opened their ports to European trade and ceded Hong Kong, which became a British colony and acquired a garrison. Fifteen years later the proverbial Chinese hostility to foreigners again erupted with the murder of a French missionary and the seizure of an English ship. In co-operation with the French, a British force of sailors, marines and the 59th Foot† from Hong Kong took Canton in December 1857 and then, sailing north, captured the Taku Forts guarding the approaches to Tientsin and Pekin at the mouth of the Peiho river. A new treaty was signed with the Chinese Emperor but when the British and French envoys arrived at Pekin to ratify the treaty, they were refused entry. A naval attempt to force the Taku Forts, now greatly strengthened, was repulsed with heavy loss. After this setback a strong military force of 10,000 British and Indian troops under Sir Hope Grant was assembled at Hong Kong in 1860 to co-operate with 7,000 French troops in an attack on Pekin to force the Chinese to abide by the treaty. The expedition comprised a cavalry brigade of the King's Dragoon Guards and two Indian regiments, Fane's and Probyn's Horse, two infantry divisions, each of two three-battalion brigades*, three field batteries Royal Artillery and a company of Royal Engineers.

By 12th August 1860 all the Allied troops had been landed at Pei-tang, about ten miles north of the Taku Forts. A march south-westwards brought them to the north bank of the Peiho where they turned east and, after two skirmishes with the Chinese, took up a position in the rear of the two forts on the north bank of the river. Supplies and artillery were brought up, batteries were constructed, and on 21st August the assault on the western fort went in, covered by the field guns and naval gun-boats which had entered the mouth of the river. The French on the right attacked the west gate while the British, led by the 44th and 67th Foot, made for the north gate, swimming the ditches that surrounded the fort under a heavy fire. A small breach had been made in the wall but it was too high up to clamber through until the foremost officers, Lieutenants Rogers of the 44th, Burslem and Lenon of the 67th, thrust their swords into the brickwork to make a step ladder so that they could help each other through the opening. Close behind them was Ensign Chaplin carrying the Queen's Colour of the 67th followed by Private Lane of the same regiment. Though both were wounded they raced through the battling Chinese towards the highest point of the fort to win the honour of being first to plant their Colour on the ramparts before the French could do the same. For their dash and leadership all four officers and Lane were subsequently awarded the Victoria Cross. As the storming parties poured in, fierce hand-to-hand fighting followed in which almost the entire Chinese garrison was annihilated. With this fort captured, the others put up little resistance and by the end of the day the way to Pekin was open.

The advance now began up the Peiho river. Tientsin fell without a fight and though the Chinese played for time by first seeking terms and then taking the British envoys as hostages, the Allied armies pressed on towards the capital. The Chinese commander, San-ko-lin-sin+, made a stand at Palikao, but after a fine charge by the King's Dragoon Guards and Fane's Horse which routed his Tartar cavalry, the infantry mopped up the remainder of the opposition and on 9th October the Allies entered Pekin. The Chinese agreed to abide by the 1858 Treaty of Tientsin and in due course the expedition withdrew. Although there had been some difficulties with the French, the operations reflected great credit on Sir Hope Grant who, in the view of Sidney Herbert, the Secretary for War, had displayed *"firmness, temper, skill, success"* and had organized *"a capital staff, an excellent commissariat, and a good medical department"*,(3) three essentials which had been so sadly lacking in the Crimea six years before.

After this, the Third China War, British relations with China remained peaceful for 40 years. Garrisons were maintained temporarily at Tientsin and permanently at Shanghai to protect British interests and the large trading communities. A European Volunteer Corps of several nationalities but under British command had been formed at Shanghai in 1853 for the defence of the foreign settlement and a similar, all-British corps was formed at Tientsin in 1898. Following the Third China War a number of British officers were loaned to the Chinese Emperor for service against the Taiping rebels from the south of the country. The most notable of these was a captain of the Royal Engineers, Charles Gordon, who with a handful of European and American officers, mostly soldiers of fortune, trained a force of 5,000 Chinese on British lines and led them to a series of victories over the Taipings in 1863-4 which earned them the name of the "Ever-Victorious Army". The main British base in the Far East continued to be at Hong Kong whose boundaries were increased in 1898 by the acquisition on a 99-year lease from China of the New Territories, north of Kowloon across the bay from Hong Kong island. The regular garrison was supplemented by a Volunteer Corps of Europeans formed in 1862, and in 1894 the Hong Kong Regiment was formed, but with Indian, not Chinese, other ranks and British and Indian Officers.

† Additional troops sent out from England for this expedition were diverted to India where the Mutiny was now at its height.

* Each brigade contained two British battalions and one Indian.

+ Known to the soldiers as "Sam Collinson" and alleged by some to be an Irish renegade from the Royal Marines.

Wei-Hai-Wei Regiment, China, 1900   6510-214-89

Indian troops in China, c1900   5911-345-5
The Native General Hospital at Wei Hai Wei

In the early summer of 1900 a fanatical, nationalist Chinese sect know as the Boxers began attacking and murdering all Christians among their countrymen and all foreigners in a serious of outrages which the Chinese authorities, at the behest of the Dowager Empress, did nothing to suppress and soon connived at. By mid-June the Boxers had gained control of Pekin and laid siege to the European community in the city, who collected together in the area of the British Delegation under the protection of some 400 troops of different nationalities who had formed the legation guards, including a detachment of Royal Marine Light Infantry. A relief column of sailors and marines from various European, American and Japanese warships lying off the mouth of the Peiho tried to get through to Pekin, but had to turn back to Tientsin which itself was soon threatened by the Boxers. In late June relief columns, including the Royal Welch Fusiliers from Hong Kong, arrived at Tientsin to reinforce the garrison and after a month's fighting had driven the Boxers from the neighbourhood. A contingent of Indian troops under General Gaselee, which earlier had been ordered to China, arrived at Tientsin in late July and these, together with other foreign reinforcements, made up a force of 20,000 which included Japanese, Russians, Americans, French, Germans and Italians. Leaving Tientsin on 4th August, the Allies reached Pekin on the 13th, storming the city next day against fanatical Boxer resistance, each national contingent vying with one another to be the first to reach the besieged legations. As the 7th Rajputs and 1st Sikhs fought their way through the Chinese city, a message was signalled by the defenders for them to enter the European perimeter through the sewer. Breaking through the grille at the base of the wall, the two Indian battalions, followed by the Welch Fusiliers, clambered through to be the first to greet the beleaguered garrison which had held out for 55 days. The Boxers still fought on in the city and it was not until the evening of the next day that resistance finally ceased. Under the overall command of the German Field-Marshal von Waldersee, the allied troops now began the pacification of the county round Pekin. Although a few more skirmishes took place, the relief of the legations had broken the back of the Boxer rising. The Chinese accepted the Allied terms in early 1901 and later that year the international army dispersed.

Two other British garrisons remain to be noticed in this world-wide survey. The growth of Singapore into a great trading centre and important naval base, following its acquisition by Sir Stamford Raffles in 1819, led in due course to British influence spreading into the Malay states which became a Crown Colony in 1867. As in Hong Kong, Volunteer Corps of Europeans were raised in Singapore, Penang and Malacca, and in 1896 several locally-enlisted units were amalgamated into a regular regiment, the Malay Corps of Guides, to back up the regular British garrison. The next link westwards in the Imperial chain of bases was Ceylon, with its valuable harbour at Colombo. After capturing the coastal areas from the Dutch in 1795, the whole of the island fell into British hands after a war with the King of Kandy in 1815. Four native regiments were formed, from Malays, Sinhalese, East African negroes and men from the East Indies. In 1827 these were amalgamated into the Ceylon Rifle Regiment which did not form part of the East India Company's forces but enjoyed a similar status in the British Army as the Royal Canadian Rifle Regiment mentioned earlier. However, recruiting for it was always difficult as the Sinhalese had little aptitude for soldiering and in 1874 the regiment was disbanded. Thereafter, apart from the regular garrison, the only local troops were a European Volunteer Corps.

Having thus travelled from Canada to Ceylon, with a brief insight into the enormous variety of places and peoples the nineteenth century British soldier was likely to encounter either on active service or maintaining the peace in static garrisons — a far wider field than his eighteenth century counterpart experienced — it is now time to turn to the Army's other chief area of employment, apart from India, in the period — the continent of Africa.

The West India Regiment, c1896.

New South Wales Regiments, c1900.

Chromolithographs after Richard Simkin, published by the Army and Navy Gazette.

CHAPTER 17
FROM THE CAPE TO KHARTOUM
1806 − 1898

Perhaps the most important consideration influencing British colonial policy in the nineteenth century was the need to preserve communications with India. Initially these followed two courses: the seaward route round the Cape of Good Hope and the overland route from the eastern Mediterranean to the Red Sea. Both had been threatened during the Napoleonic Wars, the former by France's defeat in 1794 of the Dutch, whose harbours at the Cape were then opened to French ships, and the latter by the French expedition to Egypt in 1798. In retaliation British troops had occupied the Cape in 1795 and, after returning it to the Dutch following the Peace of Amiens, again in 1806, while Abercromby's campaign had ejected the French from Egypt in 1801. Thereafter most British traffic to the east used the Cape route until the opening of the Suez Canal in 1869. Until that date, therefore, Britain was chiefly pre-occupied with the security of southern Africa, though not without keeping a wary eye on Russian designs in the Near East, as witnessed by the Crimean War. However, with the opening of a much faster route to the east through the Canal, strategic interest naturally shifted from south to north. The safety of these vital links in the Imperial chain necessitated the presence of naval and military forces, but the external security they provided led, for one reason or another, to internal disorder and rebellion from the inhabitants. In quelling these outbreaks the forces were drawn ever deeper into the hinterland of the peripheral bases, until they found themselves engaged on warlike operations, whose causes and outcome had little direct bearing on their original reason for being there − the security of the Imperial life-line. This was particularly the case in southern Africa after 1869, although by then other commercial and political factors had arisen which rendered their continued presence necessary. In addition to these two main theatres of interest, trade and other considerations led to British involvement in West and East Africa, and it may be as well to focus on these to begin with, before considering the Army's more significant role first in the south, and then in the north of the continent.

British interest in West Africa originated in the slave-trading activities of the Africa Company which established forts along the coast in Gambia, Sierra Leone and the Gold Coast. After the slave trade was abolished in 1807, the Company's forts were taken over in 1821 by the British Government which maintained order and protected the coastal tribes with a garrison of the West India Regiment and a body known as the Royal African Corps, partly recruited from negroes and partly from British deserters and other military criminals. Among the tribes of the interior, who had done well out of the slave trade and resented the new order of things, were the ferocious and aggressive Ashantis of the Gold Coast whose king claimed jurisdiction over the coastal tribes. In 1823 the Governor, Sir Charles Macarthy, led an expedition against them which ended in total disaster and his own death. Thereafter the Ashantis continued to threaten the coast until they were defeated by a force of the Royal African Corps and native levies in 1826, though peace was not finally made until 1831. The use of the African Corps as a penal regiment for white soldiers was discontinued after 1826 and its black element was eventually incorporated into the 3rd West India Regiment in 1840.

In 1873 the Ashantis attacked the Fanti tribe, then under British protection, and menaced the fort at Elmina on the coast. The danger was contained by the 2nd West India Regiment and some local levies, but it was decided to send an expedition from England to punish the Ashantis by destroying their capital of Kumasi, 160 miles inland. Three battalions, the 23rd Royal Welch Fusiliers, 42nd Highlanders and the 2nd Rifle Brigade, were earmarked and the command given to Wolseley, fresh from his successful Red River Expedition in Canada, who made all his preparations with great care, including the issue of a special grey uniform. For artillery he had a battery of mountain guns and a naval detachment with rocket tubes. Although the Ashantis greatly outnumbered the small British force, they were only armed with antiquated muskets, and the expedition was more a test of Wolseley's logistic arrangements and the ability of British soldiers to survive in dense country and the debilitating climate. Advancing from the coast in early January 1874, Wolseley encountered the main Ashanti army at Amoaful. The enemy fought with great courage, taking every advantage of the thick jungle and bush that surrounded the axis of the British advance, but superior armament and discipline finally overcame their

resistance, though not before considerable casualties had been sustained, the 42nd losing 104 killed and wounded out of 450 effectives. The Ashantis fell back, contesting Wolseley's advance with ambushes and surprise attacks, but on 3rd February the 42nd made a dash for Kumasi and found it abandoned. The king's palace and the town, with all its grisly remains of mass human sacrifice, were razed to the ground, a humiliating treaty imposed, and the force withdrew to the coast, the troops embarking for home only two months after the campaign had begun. The 1st West India Regiment remained to garrison West Africa and Wolseley returned in triumph to England to be awarded the G.C.M.G., the K.C.B., votes of thanks from Parliament and the City, a grant of £25,000 and a sword of honour—a not ungenerous reward for a fairly small scale, albeit highly successful campaign.

Failure by the Ashantis to observe the treaty and their continued barbarities led in 1896 to another expedition composed of locally-raised troops, the 2nd West Yorkshire Regiment and a Special Service Force, formed from detachments of regiments in England. No fighting took place, the king was exiled and the Ashanti country became a British protectorate with a Resident and garrison at Kumasi. Four years later the Residency was besieged following a considerable uprising of the Ashantis. In the ensuing operations, all of which were conducted by African troops under British officers, the Residency was relieved and, after five months' fighting, the Ashantis were finally subdued. Their territory was annexed as part of the colony of the Gold Coast and the Gold Coast Regiment was formed to police it. The Sierra Leone Frontier Force had been formed in 1891 to keep order in that area and in 1899 the Nigeria Regiment was raised from the Royal Niger Constabulary. The latter had been organized by the Royal Niger Company, which since 1885 had administered the Niger coast as a British protectorate, and had had to undertake various expeditions to pacify the tribes of the interior and bring under British rule the Kingdom of Benin, where a British envoy and his escort were massacred in 1897. In the north of the country clashes occurred with the Moslem emirs and with the French colonial authorities. Agreement was reached with the French but northern Nigeria was not subjected to British administration until 1903. Shortly after the Nigeria Regiment's formation it was incorporated into the West African Frontier Force which had been formed in 1898 to embrace all locally-raised troops in the Gold Coast, Sierra Leone and the Gambia. By the turn of the century the garrisoning of all British possessions in West Africa was the responsibility of the West India Regiment, the West African Frontier Force, which had its own supporting artillery, engineers and ancillary services, and a third and independent corps, the West African Regiment, raised in 1898. The only British troops in these territories were the officers of these units and a proportion of N.C.Os.

On the other side of the continent the first British involvement in East Africa was somewhat unusual for it was impelled, not by strategic necessity, commercial interest, or even simple colonial expansion, but one of humanitarian considerations, coupled with the need to demonstrate the strength and reach of Britain's Imperial arm. Between 1864 and 1867 Theodore, the half-demented and tyrannical King of Abyssinia, imprisoned two British diplomatic representatives and 58 other Europeans of various nationalities, mostly missionaries, artisans and their families. Endless negotiations having failed to free the hostages, it was decided to send an expedition from India to try and effect their release from Theodore's capital at Magdala, 400 miles inland across barren, mountainous and largely unknown country. The task was given to Lieutenant-General Sir Robert Napier, Commander-in-Chief of the Bombay Army, who had distinguished himself in the Indian Mutiny and the Third China War. With no base on the African coast from which to mount such an operation, and with little intelligence as to the likely strength of the opposition or what natural resources, if any, might be available, Napier appreciated that he must have sufficient strength, both to make the thrust to Magdala and secure his bases and line of march in potentially hostile country, and that his force must be entirely self-supporting. He therefore formed a striking force of two and a half Indian cavalry regiments with a squadron of the 3rd Dragoon Guards, three batteries and a naval rocket detachment, one British and three Indian companies of engineers, and five and a half battalions, including the 4th and 33rd Foot,† all organized in a division of two brigades under Major-General Stavely. A slightly larger division, also of all arms, under Major-General Malcolm was to guard the lines of communication. To maintain this force in the field, Napier assembled 16,500 native drivers, labourers and followers, 36,000 horses, mules, camels and bullocks and 44 elephants. Although the majority of the Indian troops were from the Bombay Army, there were also Bengal cavalry, Punjab infantry and Madras sappers. A novelty in a field force was the inclusion of a photographic detachment in the 10th Company, Royal Engineers. The force presented a varied aspect as although some of the British and Punjab infantry wore greyish khaki—its first use outside India—the remainder had their normal red or blue, while the colourful 27th Baluchis appeared in green tunics and red trousers.

The expedition began landing on the Red Sea coast at Annesley Bay near Massowa in late October 1867 but in view of the time it took to construct a harbour and establish a base and forward depots, including a 12-mile stretch of railway, plus getting all the troops ashore and making reconnaissances, it was not until 25th January 1868 that the advance to Magdala began. On 14th February the leading elements reached Antalo,

† Joined later by the 45th Foot.

200 miles from the coast, where they halted while the wherewithal to establish an advanced base for the final stage was brought forward and set up. The march was resumed a month later and on 9th April the foot of the great plateau on which Magdala stood was reached. Hitherto no resistance had been encountered but here, at Arogee, Napier's 1st Brigade found its way blocked by Theodore with a horde of some 10,000 warriors and some artillery manned, under duress, by German artisans. The Abyssinians came on at speed, their right wing curling round to get among the baggage train which could well have been overrun but for a determined bayonet charge by the 23rd Punjabis, while their centre and left hurled themselves at the double line of the 4th Foot, the Baluchis and 10th Company R.E. However, under the sustained fire of the Sniders supported by the mountain guns and the sailors' rockets, the vastly superior numbers and undoubted courage of the Abyssinians could not prevail; with their right wing in flight, the rest of the host pulled away, leaving 700 dead and 1,200 wounded, against which Napier's men only suffered 20 casualties.

Three days later Magdala was stormed. The fortress stood high above a cliff face, approachable only by a single path the head of which was barred by a stout gateway. After a preliminary bombardment, the 33rd and 10th Company R.E. advanced up the track, but on reaching the top, where they came under fire from the defenders, it was found that no explosives had been brought up to blow in the gate. The sappers attacked it with axes and crowbars but could make little progress as it had been reinforced from behind with boulders. Some of the 33rd moved off to try and find a way over the 12-foot wall to the right of the gate. A tall private named Bergin, having heaved Drummer Magner up on top of the wall, was then hauled up by the drummer, who continued to pull up other men while Bergin opened fire on the enemy who were directing a heavy musketry upon them.† Ensign Wynter with the Regimental Colour was lifted up by his excited men on to the wall where he waved the Colour to signal the successful entry. *"I shall never forget"*, he wrote in his diary, *"the exhilaration of that moment, the men firing and shouting like madmen".(1)* As more and more men got in, some rushed to open the gateway for the main body, while others charged the second line of defences. After bravely resisting for a time, the Abyssinians lost heart when word spread that Theodore had shot himself, and soon Magdala was in British hands. The hostages were found to be still alive and having thus accomplished what they had come so far to achieve, the troops withdrew from Magdala and Abyssinia. The happy outcome of Napier's expedition caught the imagination of the Victorian public, whose confidence in the Army had been badly shaken by the Crimean War, and when the British regiments returned home they were greeted as heroes, while Napier's painstaking arrangements were rewarded with promotion and a peerage.

The last two decades of the century witnessed the scramble for African possessions among the European powers, in the course of which Britain established protectorates in Somaliland, Zanzibar, East Africa (now Kenya) and Uganda, as a counter to possible domination of the Nile Valley by the French and Germans in central and eastern Africa respectively; it was thought that if the Upper Nile fell into foreign hands, the lately-acquired British control of Egypt, and with it the Suez Canal, might be threatened. Possession of these territories was obtained more by diplomacy than conquest – Uganda, for instance, being transferred by Germany in exchange for the island of Heligoland in the North Sea – but their pacification, policing and protection of a railway line that was to run from Mombasa to Lake Victoria required the mounting of a number of small military expeditions between 1897-1901. These were largely undertaken by Indian troops but, as had happened on the West Coast, three locally-enlisted regiments under British officers were raised: the East Africa, Uganda and Central Africa Rifles, which in 1902 were amalgamated to form the King's African Rifles.

Reverting now to the original sphere of British influence in Africa, the Cape, its second occupation in 1806, like that of 1795, had been undertaken purely to retain in British hands this important outpost on the route to India. The British Government had no interest in extending the limits of the colony, which already, due to the spread of Dutch settlers, reached 450 miles eastwards to the Great Fish River, nor, at the height of the Napoleonic Wars, the resources to do so, but the authorities at the Cape found the peace threatened by incursions of the Kaffir tribes across the Fish River. Two campaigns against these tribes, the vanguard of a great black wave which had been pressing down from the north for 200 years, had been fought by the Dutch in 1779 and 1789, and during the first British occupation of the Cape they had attacked British troops who had been sent to quell an armed uprising of Dutch farmers; skirmishing went on against them until the British evacuation of 1802. Two further outbreaks occurred in 1812 and 1819, after which forts began to be constructed along the border and, in an attempt to swell the European population who could assist in its defence, immigrants from the British Isles were persuaded to settle in the eastern region of Cape Colony.

For the next dozen or so years all remained quiet and the settlements slowly prospered. However, much farther to the north, the Zulus were being turned into a great military machine by their chief, Chaka, who by 1825 had expanded his empire into the north of Natal. This surge southwards, with it's consequent dispersal or annihilation of all rivals, inevitably built up pressure on the Kaffir tribes, whose own progression had been halted

† Both men were subsequently awarded the Victoria Cross.

at the Fish River. In December 1834 some 17,000 Kaffirs burst over the border, raiding the outlying farms, stealing cattle and generally terrorizing the border settlers. Colonel Harry Smith, a Peninsular and Waterloo veteran of the 95th Rifles, hurried up from Cape Town to Grahamstown, the chief township of the frontier district, calmed the settlers' fears, and with a mixed force of two regular battalions,† part of which he converted into mounted infantry, armed burghers, Hottentots and a locally-enlisted regiment, the Cape Mounted Rifles,* drove the invaders back across the Fish River in a few weeks' skillful operations. A punitive expedition was then sent into Kaffraria as far north as the Kei River, driving the tribes and confiscating their cattle until they sued for peace after which the frontier was advanced to the Keiskamma River.

From 1836 thousands of Dutch in Cape Colony, or Boers as they were now known, began trekking north to escape from the constrictions of British rule and to find wider lands where they could pursue unhindered their own way of life. Some made for the country north of the Orange and Vaal Rivers while others moved over the Drakensburg Mountains into the fertile coastal belt of Natal. Here they came into contact with the Zulus, now under Dingaan, who first tolerated, but then attacked them. The Boers took their revenge, defeating the Zulus at Blood River in 1838 and establishing their settlements around Port Natal, later Durban, and Pietermaritzburg. However, the British Government, piqued at the insult offered to their colonial rule by the Great Trek, and conscious of the importance of Durban, as another harbour on the route to the east, annexed Natal up as far as the Buffalo and Tugela Rivers in 1843. Many of the Boers in Natal moved westwards, an exodus which Sir Harry Smith, now returned to the Cape as Governor after his successes in the Sikh War, endeavoured to halt in 1848 but, having failed to do so, annexed the territory between the Orange and the Vaal into which the Boers were moving. The latter resisted but were defeated by a British force of three battalions+ and Cape Mounted Rifles at Boomplaats. Four years later the Boer community north of the Vaal was recognized as the independent republic of the Transvaal, followed, in 1854, by the renunciation of British jurisdiction over the lands south of the Transvaal and the establishment of a second Boer Republic, the Orange Free State.

The British change of heart had come about largely through the Government's reluctance to add to the financial burden already imposed by the maintenance of security on the eastern frontier of Cape Colony. After quelling a further Kaffir uprising in 1846, which had required a larger force than the 1834 outbreak, Smith again had to start operations in December 1850 against the tribes raiding the settlements from their fastnesses in the Amatola Mountains between the Kei and Fish Rivers. The situation was aggravated by disaffection among his native levies, including the Cape Mounted Rifles, and with only four British battalions there was little he could do other than stand on the defensive until reinforcements were sent out from England. The first having arrived in June 1851, by October the number of battalions had been doubled††and his only Regular mounted force, the European element of the C.M.R., reinforced by the 12th Lancers. Nevertheless it took until December 1852 to subdue the tribes in the Amatolas. It was a war of sudden ambush and arduous patrols, of long harassing marches to scour the thick bush and forest for concentrations of the elusive and swiftly-moving enemy. The nature of the fighting was described by a sergeant of the 74th Highlanders:

"The enemy. . . never dared to appear without the boundary of the forest; so that the skirmishers, on their advance to the dense bush, were repeatedly saluted with volleys of musketry from the hidden foe, and all they could do was to return the fire and double as swiftly as they possibly could to the bush, which having been gained, not an enemy was to be found. They had retreated deeper into the jungle as the troops advanced but when the troops began to retire from the bush, the enemy, emerging from their lair, sent volley after volley at the retiring skirmishers".(2)

The troops soon learned to abandon the close formations and rigid drill movements of European warfare and to move quickly and silently, taking cover and thinking for themselves. Regulation uniforms were replaced by broad-brimmed hats, stocking caps, canvas smocks and corduroy trousers while their accoutrements were replaced by lighter articles of local manufacture. Even so the conditions of bush warfare left *"their clothes hanging in rags; their shoes worn off their feet, some of the men actually marching barefoot"(3).*

† 72nd Highlanders and 75th Foot.

* Raised from Hottentots in 1817 as the Cape Corps with British officers and N.C.Os. Over the years the number of British increased until by 1851 the ranks were being filled by volunteers from the Line cavalry and infantry. Its uniform largely followed that of the Rifle Brigade with light dragoon touches. The men were armed with swords and double-barralled carbines. Disbanded as an Imperial force in 1870.

+ 45th, 91st and 1st Rifle Brigade.

††2nd, 6th, 12th, 45th, 60th, 73rd, 74th, 91st.The 43rd and 1st Rifle Brigade arrived later, the latter having returned home in 1850.

Entrance to Magdala c1868
Photograph taken by 40th Company Royal Engineers

Zulu War c1879
Rorke's Drift Camp.

5104-22-17

By keeping up a continual pressure and never giving the tribes any respite, the troops gradually drove the enemy from their mountain hiding-places. Sir Harry Smith was recalled by an impatient Government in 1852 but by the time he left the Cape the bulk of the work had been done and its successful outcome owed much to his drive, perseverance and popularity with the troops.

The frontier now remained quiet for a quarter of a century, order being maintained by an all-European para-military force raised in 1855, the Frontier Armed and Mounted Police. Many of its recruits came from the German Legion raised, but never employed, in the Crimean War †, who after that war were offered the opportunity of emigrating as military settlers to South Africa. In 1877 an inter-tribal dispute led to the ninth and last of the Kaffir Wars but the scale of the insurrection never reached that of the previous campaign and proved well within the capacity of the F.A.M.P., supported by two regular battalions* and various colonial volunteers, amongst whom some of the most useful were the German settlers.

Although the Zulus had continued to feud with the Transvaal Boers, which had led to British annexation of the republic in 1877, they had not hitherto displayed any evil intent towards Natal. Nevertheless, Sir Bartle Frere, the British High Commissioner, conceived the proximity of such a formidable, martial nation as a permanent threat to the colony which must be restrained. Using a few minor border incidents as his justification, he sent an ultimatum to the Zulu King, Cetshwayo, setting out conditions which he well knew would be unacceptable. No reply having been received, an army of 16,000 men under Lord Chelmsford invaded Zululand on 11th January 1879, to advance on Cetshwayo's capital at Ulundi in three columns: the right under Colonel Pearson of the 3rd Buffs from the mouth of the Tugela; the centre, which Chelmsford accompanied, from the Buffalo at Rorke's Drift; and the left under Colonel Evelyn Wood of the 90th from the Transvaal border.

The main strength of the centre column rested on two battalions of the 24th Foot, the 1st Battalion being long-service men who had been in South Africa since 1874, while the 2nd were predominantly young soldiers; the rest of the force was made up of 350 European volunteers and police, 2,600 native horse and infantry, with one field and one rocket battery, Royal Artillery. Having established a camp at the foot of the hill of Isandhlwana, Chelmsford moved out on 22nd January with 2,500 men, including most of the 2/24th, to search for the enemy who had been reported to the south-east, leaving 1,800 to guard the camp under Colonel Pulleine of the 1/24th. At around midday the main Zulu army of some 23,000 appeared on Pulleine's left front and hurled themselves in a huge arc at the fighting line he formed in front of the camp, their right wing sweeping round the rear of Isandhlwana to cut off the line of retreat. By four o'clock that afternoon Pulleine's force had been obliterated; only 85 fugitives managed to escape across the Buffalo. Of the survivors, no more than two men were from the 24th's six companies+. Abandoned by the native levies and overwhelmed by the speed and weight of the Zulu charge, the 24th's steady line was broken up into small groups which fought on desperately until the last men were mercilessly hacked down, nearly 600 perishing under the assegais.

Part of the Zulu army pressed on to attack the mission station at Rorke's Drift, where B Company of the 2/24th under Lieutenant Bromhead, aged 33 and nearly deaf, had been left to protect the Buffalo crossing and a few sick men in the hospital. Command of the post was assumed by the senior officer present, Lieutenant Chard of the Royal Engineers, who on hearing of the attack at Isandhlwana had hastily organized a defensive perimeter of mealie bags and biscuit boxes. From four thirty in the afternoon until four the following morning, the hundred-odd men at Rorke's Drift held 4,000 Zulu warriors at bay, throwing back attack after attack in fierce hand-to-hand fighting, the whole savage scene being lit by the flames from the burning hospital, until in the early hours the Zulus melted away into the darkness. After it was over, a soldier wrote: *"I shall never forget the place about as long as I live".(4)* When day broke, the leading elements of Chelmsford's column reached the Drift, having returned from the wrecked camp at Isandhlwana which it had reached after nightfall, following its fruitless reconnaissance the day before.

Although the defence of Rorke's Drift, which was rewarded by the unprecedented number, for a single action, of 11 Victoria Crosses,††had saved Natal from invasion, Chelmsford's plans were in total disarray for, apart from the disaster to the centre column, Pearson was cut off and besieged in Eshowe. Wood in the north was ordered to hold fast in a fortified position at Kambula Hill until reinforcements arrived from England, the first of which began to reach South Africa in mid-March. While Wood demonstrated against the main part of the Zulu army, inflicting heavy casualties on them at Kambula on 29th March, Chelmsford set out to relieve Pearson, defeating the Zulus at Gingindhlovu on 2nd April and bringing the Eshowe force safely back behind the Tugela.

† See Chapter 12.

* 1/24th and 88th Foot.

+ Including G Company, 2/24th.

†† Lieutenants Chard, R.E. and Bromhead, 24th; Surgeon-Major Reynolds, Army Medical Department; Assistant -Commissary Dalton; Corporal Allen, Private Hitch, Hook, W.Jones, R.Jones, J.Williams, 24th; Corporal Schiess, Natal Native Contingent (a Swiss).

With his original force now increased by two cavalry regiments and five battalions, Chelmsford planned a new offensive in which one division would link up with Wood prior to striking at Ulundi, while another division under Major-General Crealock would advance up the coast. Meanwhile it had been decided at home to replace Chelmsford with Wolseley, who sailed for the Cape a week before the second invasion of Zululand began on 31st May.

Chelmsford's initial movements were marred by the death in an ambush of the Prince Imperial, the son of Napoleon III, who much against Chelmsford's wishes had been allowed to join the field army. Apart from this the advance went smoothly, if slowly, without resistance from the Zulus, and by 2nd July was within four miles of Ulundi. Here Chelmsford received a telegram from Wolseley, who had reached Durban on 28th June, ordering him to undertake no serious operations. However, Chelmsford was not to be denied at this stage and two days later, forming a large square, he advanced against Cetshwayo's army. The Zulus came on in their usual horn formation, their wings encircling the square, but, in the face of concentrated artillery and rifle fire, their courage and speed could not prevail. A corporal wrote: *"Our firing was in volleys, and the Bullets went flying as thick as rain. They were falling down in heaps as though they had been tipped out of carts. On they still came till they were up to the Square all but about sixty yards . . . We made up our minds to fight in close quarter with our Bayonets but the enemy Began to shake in front of our fire, they halted dead for a few Seconds, then turned and flew for their lives".(5)* Chelmsford launched the 17th Lancers in pursuit and in less than an hour it was all over, for the loss of only 12 killed and 88 wounded. Four days later Chelmsford resigned his command, having left the ambitious Wolseley nothing to do but organize the final mopping-up operations, including the hunting down and capture of Cetshwayo, and the dismemberment of the Zulu State.

Although the crushing of the Zulus had relieved the Transvaal Boers of their oldest enemy, they had been growing increasingly restive under the British yoke imposed on them in 1877. In December 1880 the 94th Foot was ambushed by Boers at Bronkhorst Spruit on a peaceful march from Lydenburg to Pretoria and shortly afterwards the small British garrisons in the Transvaal were all under siege. Commanding in Natal was Sir George Colley, thought to be Wolseley's most brilliant protegé, who, though disposing of only a small body of troops — the garrison having been greatly reduced after the Zulu War —, immediately formed a relief coloumn: two half-battalions of the 58th Foot and the 3/60th Rifles, a squadron of King's Dragoon Guards and mounted infantry, four guns and some naval rockets, just over a thousand men in all. On reaching the border between Natal and the Transvaal, he found his way blocked by 2,000 Boers holding strong positions on a semi-circle of high ground astride the road at Laing's Nek. On 28th January 1881, unperturbed by either the steep and open approach or the enemy's numerical superiority, and utterly contemptuous of the Boers' fighting abilities, Colley ordered the five companies of the 58th to take the position with the bayonet, while the mounted squadron was to charge the Boer left where it curved forward along the right flank of the infantry's line of advance. With their red coats and white helmets bright against the green slopes and the Colours flying bravely in the centre, the 58th began the ascent. Though mostly young, short-service soldiers, they were not novices having fought at Ulundi but they were soon to find the concealed Boer rifles a different proposition to the Zulu assegais. The mounted attack failed completely and the Boer left started to fire into the 58th's exposed right flank. Hurried on by mounted staff officers, the sweating infantry pressed on until they neared the crest where they came under heavy point-blank fire. Every attempt to charge was shot away, most of the officers went down, including the two ensigns with the Colours which were saved by a colour-sergeant, and eventually the order was given to retire. Still under fire from the front and on the flank, the luckless regiment fell back steadily and in good order to the foot of the slopes where they reformed under the single unwounded officer, a lieutenant. Rather than commit the 60th, who had been held in reserve, to a similar fate, Colley withdrew. The Boers had demonstrated that old-fashioned tactics based on the bayonet were no match against well-concealed marksmen armed with modern rifles. At least one lesson was learned for, when news of Laing's Nek reached the Horse Guards, orders were issued forbidding Colours ever again to be carried into action †

Just over a week later the Boers again displayed their mobility and fighting skill with an attack on the 60th, who had been sent to clear Colley's line of communications for the reinforcements he was expecting from Natal. Among these were the 92nd Highlanders, a battalion of old soldiers fresh from their triumphs in the Second Afghan War, full of confidence in their superiority both to the Boers and the young soldiers of the 58th and 60th. With this valuable addition to his force, Colley determined on turning the Boer right by a night occupation of Majuba Hill, which towered 2,000 feet above the positions astride Laing's Nek. Instead of using the strong, seasoned Highland battalion for this task, he formed a mixed force of three companies of Highlanders, two of the 58th and one of the Naval Brigade, detailing other companies of the 92nd and 60th to provide linking posts between Majuba and his camp.

† The Colours carried by the 58th at Laing's Nek, the last to be carried by any regiment in battle, are today displayed in the National Army Museum.

The force, led by Colley himself, safely occupied the summit during the night of 26th-27th February, but during the morning the Boers, unconcerned at this threat to their flank and rear, began to scale the hill, covering their movements with well-directed rifle fire. Colley, seemingly still oblivious of the mettle of the men he was up against, had made no attempt to entrench his position so that, at noon, when the Boers suddenly appeared over the rim and opened a deadly musketry at short range, his men were caught without protection and began to lose heavily. They fought back for a while but, with the three detachments soon inextricably mixed up, control became difficult, cohesion was lost and, when Colley was killed, panic infected the survivors, with Highlanders, 58th and sailors flying for their lives down the slopes up which they had so laboriously climbed. Of the 600-odd men on Majuba, 480 were killed, wounded or taken prisoner at a cost to the Boers of only one man killed and 11 wounded — the latter statistic highlighting the masterly fieldcraft of the Boers as much as the poor standard of musketry then pertaining in the British infantry, whether long — or short-service men.

Although the British garrisons in the Transvaal† had meanwhile repulsed all attacks made upon them, the fiasco at Majuba closed the campaign and peace was signed on 23rd March, giving the Transvaal self-government, followed, three years later, by complete independence; an outcome which contained within it seeds of further trouble yet to come. However this must be left to a later chapter as the centre of military interest now shifts to the north of the continent.

British concern for the security of Egypt, after the opening of the Suez Canal, led to increasing involvement in the chaotic affairs of that country, although its government remained nominally in the hands of its ruler, the Khedive. In 1882 foreign interference provoked an uprising of the Egyptian Army under the Minister of War, Arabi Pasha, who took over the country. In reprisal for riots in Alexandria in which Europeans were massacred, a British fleet bombarded the harbour on 11th July and landed sailors and marines to restore order. Despite this, Arabi and the Egyptian Army, which had been trained and equipped on European lines, were still defiant and at large, so an expeditionary force was formed of a cavalry brigade and two infantry divisions from England and the Mediterranean, and a further cavalry brigade and one of infantry from India; the whole totalled some 35,000 men and the command was given to Wolseley, then the Adjutant-General at the War Office.

His plan was to simulate an attack against the Egyptian positions south of Alexandria, while actually seizing the Canal from both ends, thus obtaining control of the freshwater canal and railway running west from Ismailia, up which axis he intended to advance on Cairo which, he anticipated, would most likely be defended by Arabi at Tel-el-Kebir, half-way between Ismailia and the capital. Such a course of action not only offered a shorter route and better going than an advance up the Nile from Alexandria, but by using the Canal and railway, he would be able to offset his shortage of land transport. All went as planned. While a brigade from Cyprus feigned offensive operations from Alexandria, the main force sailed down the Canal to Ismailia as the Indian contingent from Bombay seized the southern end at Suez, all being safely in British hands by 22nd August. During the disembarkation of the main body, advance guards were pushed forward up the railway to protect repair work on it and the freshwater canal. A number of small actions followed, including a cavalry charge by moonlight at Kassassin in which the Household Cavalry, fighting their first action since Waterloo, inflicted heavy loss on the retreating Egyptians.

By 12th September the build-up was complete and Wolseley had concentrated his force six miles east of the Egyptian entrenchments, which ran out due north for four miles from Tel-el-Kebir and were manned by 25,000 troops with 75 guns. He planned a dawn attack, coming out of the sun, on a two-brigade front with two in reserve, after a night approach march from a start-line just under four miles from the enemy positions; the Indian contingent was to advance on a parallel axis south of the freshwater canal and the cavalry was to be prepared to exploit success. Direction was kept by the stars and although the line of advance veered very slightly northwards — fortuitously as it happened since it enabled the left brigade to bypass an advanced redoubt — the timing and silence were well kept. At first light the Highland Brigade on the left and the 2nd Brigade on the right, supported respectively by the 4th and Guards Brigades, went at the trenches with the bayonet. Some sharp fighting ensued, particularly on the Highlanders' front where they met stubborn resistance from some Soudanese regiments, and the Royal Marine Light Infantry, the left battalion of the 2nd Brigade, suffered 80 casualties fighting through its objective. However, with the Cavalry Division and Royal Horse Artillery swinging wide round the position to threaten the rear, the enemy left gave way and by six a.m. the fighting was over, with the Egyptian Army in flight towards Cairo. The heaviest casualties were sustained by the Highland Brigade, the 2nd Highland Light Infantry losing 74 while the 1st Black Watch, 1st Gordons and the Camerons averaged 50 apiece. The two reserve brigades and the Indian contingent were hardly engaged. The British and Indian cavalry kept up an unremitting pursuit, entering Cairo on the afternoon of the 14th, capturing the city and receiving the surrender of Arabi and his army. Wolseley had carried out an excellent campaign,

† Some 16 companies of the 2/21st, 58th and 94th spread between Pretoria, Marabastadt, Lydenburg, Rustenburg, Wakkerstroom, Standerton and Potchefstroom.

masterly in concept and execution, for which he was promoted full general, but instead of the viscountcy he had confidently anticipated, he had to make do with a barony, which did nothing to improve his relations with his royal chief, the Duke of Cambridge. Though the Khedive's authority was restored, it was also clear that if the Canal was to be kept safe, a British garrison would have to remain in Egypt.

British involvement in Egyptian affairs would inevitably lead, sooner or later, to intervention in the Khedive's provinces in the Soudan, where a revolt against Egyptian rule under a Moslem prophet, the Mahdi, had been gathering momentum since 1881. In 1883 an Egyptian army under a British officer, Colonel Hicks, was cut to pieces near El Obeid by the Mahdi's Dervish horde, which thereafter controlled the Soudan except for a few hemmed-in Egyptian garrisons. Sir Evelyn Baring, the British Agent in Egypt, advised the Government that either the Soudan must be annexed or the garrisons withdrawn. Reluctant to involve itself in affairs in the Soudan, which did not directly threaten the Canal, the British Government counselled withdrawal but were unwilling to commit British troops to effect it, other than making available to the Khedive the services of Charles Gordon, last met in China and now a major-general, who had had previous experience in the country. Gordon went out to the Soudan with orders to evacuate the Egyptian garrisons but by May 1884 he was cut off from Egypt and besieged in Khartoum.

If the British Government was unmoved by a rebellion in the heart of the Soudanese desert, trouble on the shores of the Red Sea was a different matter. In 1883 Osman Digna, chief of the Hadendowa tribe between Suakin on the coast and Berber on the Nile, declared for the Mahdi and annihilated an Egyptian column sent to suppress him. A 4,000-strong British force of two infantry brigades and the 10th Hussars under Major-General Graham was despatched to Suakin, whence they marched out westwards to encounter Osman Digna's army at El Teb on 29th January 1884. Though the enemy host came on with fanatical courage against Graham's square, every attack broke in the face of volleys from the Martini-Henry rifles backed by Gatling guns. A fortnight later Graham offered battle again at Tamai, this time with each brigade forming its own square so as to provide mutual support. The leading face of the 2nd Brigade square advanced too fast, thus causing a gap in its tight formation into which the Hadendowa poured, giving the 1st Black Watch and 1st York and Lancasters a hard close-quarter fight, until the supporting fire of the 1st Brigade and the dismounted cavalry enabled them to reform and drive the enemy away into the desert. The way to Berber, still held by an Egyptian garrison, was now open but Graham was ordered to evacuate eastern Soudan, leaving a garrison at Suakin.

By mid-1884 it had become clear that Gordon would be unable to withdraw from Khartoum, even if he had ever intended doing so, and indeed was in grave danger. In the face of mounting public opinion Gladstone, the Prime Minister, reluctantly and belatedly gave his assent to the despatch of a relief expedition under Wolseley. The latter planned to sail his force up the Nile to Korti — no easy task against the swiftly flowing cataracts — and from there send 3,000 men under Major-General Earle up the remaining 500-mile stretch of the river to Khartoum, while a 2,000-strong flying column under Brigadier Herbert Stewart was to strike across the 150 miles of desert, which formed a chord across the arc of the Nile between Korti and Metemmeh, and then make a dash to Gordon's rescue. The greater part of this column, which included a Naval Brigade, a squadron of the 19th Hussars, and the 1st Royal Sussex, was to be made up of a Camel Corps, formed of specially picked men from the Household and Line Cavalry regiments† and the Foot Guards in England, and infantry regiments in Egypt, organized into Heavy, Guards and Mounted Infantry Camel Regiments. The Guards Regiment also included a comapny of Royal Marines. The collection of the necessary supplies, boats, camels and other animals, plus the training of the Camel Corps, consumed months of valuable time and it was not until the end of the year that Wolseley was able to advance from Korti, by which time Gordon's position had grown increasingly perilous.

While Earle's men pulled away up the Nile, Stewart set out across the desert on 30th December. On 17th January 1885, near the wells of Abu Klea, some 15,000 Dervishes suddenly advanced against the column which hastily formed square. Swinging round the front and left of the square, the yelling horde threw themselves at the left rear face held by the Heavy Camel Regiment, whose line had been bulged outwards by the baggage camels in the centre. A naval Gardner gun jammed, as did many of the Martinis from the rapid fire, and within seconds the Heavies were fighting desperately with their bayonets, a weapon to which they were unaccustomed, as the Dervishes swarmed into the square. Had it not been for the steadiness of the Mounted Infantry who poured fire into the enemy flank from the left face and the Guards on the far side who turned their rear rank about, Stewart's 2,000 could have been overwhelmed, but gradually the position was restored and the Dervishes made off. Two days later they attacked again at Abu Kru, but as a Grenadier officer described: *"The square was at once halted, and volley after volley poured into the black mass. As they got within 400 yards, the volley-firing became a continuous roar of musketry, and hundreds fell beneath the well-directed fire of the Mounted Infantry and ourselves. Aiming low, and firing as steadily as on parade, our men mowed the Arabs down like grass; not*

---

† 1st and 2nd Life Guards, Royal Horse Guards; 2nd, 4th and 5th Dragoon Guards; 1st and 2nd Dragoons; 5th and 16th Lancers.

one got within eighty yards of the square".(6) Metemmeh was found to be strongly held by the enemy but just above it, at Gubat, two steamers were waiting with 150 Soudanese troops on board, sent by Gordon with news that he was still holding out but could not last much longer. Unfortunately command of the column now devolved on the indecisive Colonel Wilson, Stewart having been mortally wounded at Abu Kru, and four days elapsed before he sailed with the Soudanese and 20 men of the Royal Sussex, dressed in red tunics as Gordon had particularly requested. Three days later Wilson arrived off Khartoum, only to find that it had fallen two days before and that Gordon was dead. There was nothing for it but to withdraw the Desert Column back to Korti.

Meanwhile the River Column had made slow progress up the Nile and though Earle defeated the Dervishes at Kirbekan, at the cost of his own life, his force had only covered about 200 miles before it too was recalled. By mid-March the whole relief expedition was once again concentrated at Korti. Wolseley, bitterly disappointed at the failure, wrote in his diary, *"What an ending to all our labour, and all our bright hopes, is this"*, laying the blame on Gladstone, *"that it was owing to his influence, active measures for the relief of Gordon were not undertaken in time".(7)*

Although Gordon was dead, the Government still had hopes of crushing the Mahdi by using Berber as a base for future operations, to which it was planned to build a railway from Suakin. To cover its construction, Graham was again sent to Suakin with 13,000 men, consisting of one cavalry and three infantry brigades, one Guards, one Line and one Indian; he was later joined by a 500-strong contingent from New South Wales — the first time Colonial troops had co-operated in a British overseas expedition. Osman Digna, who was still active in the area, attacked Graham at Hasheen on 20th March 1885 but was beaten off with heavy loss. Two days later a British and Indian force under Major-General McNeill was surprised by Dervishes while constructing an intermediate outpost at Tofrek. The cavalry vedettes failed to spot the enemy who, creeping forward through scrub and rocks, suddenly rushed the troops while they were eating their midday meal with their arms piled. All was confusion, the baggage animals and their drivers stampeded, some of the Indian infantry panicked and the Hadendowa warriors plunged with their long swords into the centre of the position. Fortunately the Royal Marines and 1st Berkshires kept their heads and threw themselves into rallying squares, from which their volleys, supported by fire from the 15th Sikhs and 28th Bombay Infantry, gradually drove the enemy off, but not before 100 men had been killed and 140 wounded. For their steadiness on this occasion the Berkshire Regiment was granted the Royal title.

A few more skirmishes followed but support for Osman Digna was beginning to fade. The railway was going ahead, when in May the British Government, alarmed at the possibility of war with Russia,† ordered the cessation of all operations in the Soudan. Graham's force was withdrawn except for a garrison at Suakin and British troops on the Nile were pulled back to the general area of Aswan. A last battle with the Dervishes was fought on the penultimate day of 1885 at Ginniss — an engagement chiefly notable as the last occasion on which the British infantry fought in red.*

The Mahdi died soon after Gordon, being succeeded by the Khalifa Abdullah. Although the Soudan was to be left to its own devices for a while, it was clear that, with continued Dervish raids across the Egyptian frontier, the country would eventually have to be re-occupied. It was decided that, to defend the southern frontier and prepare for the next round, Egypt must contribute to its own defence. To this end a complete reorganization of the Egyptian Army was undertaken by seconded British officers, while the 'fellahin' were drilled and trained by British N.C.Os., the likes of Kipling's *"Sergeant Whatsisname"* who had *"a charm for making riflemen from mud".(8)* The work was begun soon after Tel-el-Kebir by Sir Evelyn Wood, the victor of Kambula, continued under Sir Francis Grenfell and completed by Sir Herbert Kitchener. Kitchener had been commissioned into the Royal Engineers in 1871 and after spending most of his service in survey and intelligence duties in the Middle East, had been one of the officers appointed in 1883 to work under Grenfell. In 1892, at the age of 42, though only a colonel in the British Army, he was made Sirdar, or Commander-in-Chief of the Egyptian Army. By the late nineties the rabble that had been scattered by the Mahdi had been transformed into a well-disciplined and properly-trained fighting force of 16 infantry battalions, ten of Egyptian 'fellahin' and six of Soudanese, ten squadrons of cavalry, one horse and four field batteries, an eight-company camel corps and ancillary services. Most units had between three to five British officers and a British colour-sergeant or sergeant-instructor; other officers were mainly Turks, Circassians or Albanians. For ten years from 1885 the Egyptian Army was broken-in on numerous small expeditions along the southern frontier until its first major test came in 1896. In response to a request for a division on the Nile from Italy, whose troops had just suffered a serious reverse in Abyssinia, Kitchener was instructed to advance to Dongola. With an all-Egyptian force he

† See Chapter 15.

* Grey and Khaki had been worn on the Nile and in the eastern Soudan but red was worn at Ginniss to overawe the Dervishes.

Gen Sir Harry Smith
in general officer's full dress c1860.

5909-128

Lt-Gen Lord Chelmsford, c1879
Lithograph published by the Whitehall Review
8th March 1879.

6910-309

Maj-Gen Sir Garnet Wolseley,
in service dress, c1873.

Field Marshal Lord Kitchener, in
service dress, c1900.
Photogravure after A.S. Cope,
published by the Autotype Company, c1900.

5910-264

Grenadier Guards awaiting the dervish attack at Omdurman, 2nd Sept 1898.

7305-42-106

defeated the Dervishes at Ferket and Hafir,† seized Dongola and then, a year later, after the British Government had made up its mind that the time was ripe for the reconquest of the Soudan, he pushed on to Abu Hamed and Berber, while at the same time beginning the construction of a railway forward from Wadi Halfa towards Berber. The stage was now set for the final defeat of Mahdism.

In April 1898 Kitchener's army of one British and three Egyptian brigades, all of four battalions*, advanced against a 12,000-strong Dervish force under the Khalifa's lieutenant, Mahmud, which was holding a 'zareba' + on the River Atbara, 40 miles south-east of Berber. At dawn on the 8th the attack went in with three brigades in line and one in reserve. First into the zareba were the Camerons, leading the British brigade, which charged through the breach made by the Highlanders, driving the Dervishes towards the river, as the Egyptian and Soudanese battalions came in on the other side. Within 40 minutes it was all over, Mahmud was captured, and only 4,000 of the enemy managed to escape to join the main Dervish army at Omdurman, on the west bank of the Nile at Khartoum.

Kitchener now delayed for four months to escape the worst of the summer heat and to build up and prepare his force for the final attack on Omdurman. Having been reinforced by an additional British brigade†† and the 21st Lancers, he advanced in late August and took up a semi-circular position behind a zareba backing on to the Nile, where his artillery support would be increased by three gunboats which could also bombard Omdurman eight miles away. Among his battalion and company commanders were men who within 20 years would become household names under very different conditions; commanding the XIIIth Soudanese was one of the few survivors of Isandhlwana, Horace Smith-Dorrien; Captain Henry Rawlinson led a company of the Rifle Brigade; the 7th Squadron of Egyptian Cavalry was under a Captain Douglas Haig; while attached to the 21st Lancers was a subaltern of the 4th Hussars, Lieutenant Winston Churchill, whose thrusting manner antagonized everyone, from his brother officers to the Sirdar himself.

Just after six a.m. on 2nd September a vast mass of Dervishes was seen coming on across the desert; 40,000 men on camels, horses and on foot, armed with spears, swords and rifles, advancing in a huge arc against 22,000 Lee-Metford magazine rifles and Martini-Henrys,**ranged in two ranks standing and kneeling behind the zareba , and supported by 44 field guns and 20 Maxim machine guns. The artillery opened fire first, then, as the Dervishes came within extreme rifle range, the Grenadier Guards began section volleys at 2,000 yards, followed by the Royal Warwicks, and soon the whole zareba blazed fire as each battalion took it up. Despite their numbers, the speed of their advance and, above all, the dauntless courage with which they came on again and again, the Dervishes stood no chance against this concentrated fire of modern weapons. As a war correspondent wrote: *"It was not a battle, but an execution".(9)* Nevertheless, Kitchener did not have it all his own way. The Egyptian cavalry and camel corps on the extreme right were in serious danger of being overwhelmed until the fire of a gunboat drove off their attackers. The 21st Lancers, in action for the first time in their history, charged 300 Dervishes on an apparently open plain, only to be engulfed in a hidden ravine filled with thousands of the enemy, stabbing, slashing and hamstringing the horses. They fought their way through, losing five officers, 69 men and 119 horses, before dismounting on the far side and opening fire with their carbines. At the start of the campaign the regiment had endured some ribaldry on account of its lack of active service, but they emerged from their charge to become, in contemporary public opinion, the heroes of the battle and with three Victoria Crosses to their credit.++The most critical moment of the day occurred after Kitchener had ordered a general advance, when Macdonald's Soudanese brigade on the right flank became separated by a mile from its nearest formation and was attacked from its right rear by 20,000 Dervishes returning from their struggle with the Egyptian cavalry. Hector Macdonald was nothing if not a fighter: as a colour-sergeant in the 92nd Highlanders he had been commissioned in the field during the Afghan War and had fought to the end at Majuba. Now his forceful person-ality and powers of leadership held his four battalions, one Egyptian and three Soudanese, to their discipline, firing into the Dervish mass until, with their ammunition running low and bracing themselves to meet the charge with their bayonets, his men were joined on their right flank by the Lincolns, who had come across the field to their aid at the double. The Lincolns' rapid fire drove off the Dervishes and the whole line resumed its victorious march into Khartoum, as the remnants of the Khalifa's brave warriors dispersed into the desert.

† After Ferket he was reinforced by one British battalion, the 1st North Staffords.

* British: 1st Royal Warwicks, 1st Lincolns, 1st Seaforth, 1st Camerons.

+ An entrenched camp surrounded by a thick thorn fence.

†† 1st Grenadier Guards, 1st Northumberland Fusiliers, 2nd Lancashire Fusiliers, 2nd Rifle Brigade.

** The Eygptian and Sudanese battalions had the older rifle.

++ Captain Kenna, Lieutenant Montmorency and Private Byrne.

Mahdism was crushed, Gordon was finally avenged and the Victorian Army had fought the last of its battles against savage enemies. In all such wars it had usually behaved with steadiness and discipline, faced moments of extreme danger with courage, and endured searing heat and harsh terrain with fortitude; yet it had fought in the tactical formations of Waterloo. Closing ranks in line or square may have served best to resist the massed charge of fanatical warriors, particularly when the firepower of such formations was enhanced by quick-firing weapons, but the Army was beginning to ignore the possibility that not all enemies might fight in this way. A year after Omdurman it was to learn what a handful of regiments had learned nearly two decades before, that close order would not suffice against an enemy armed with weapons similar to its own.

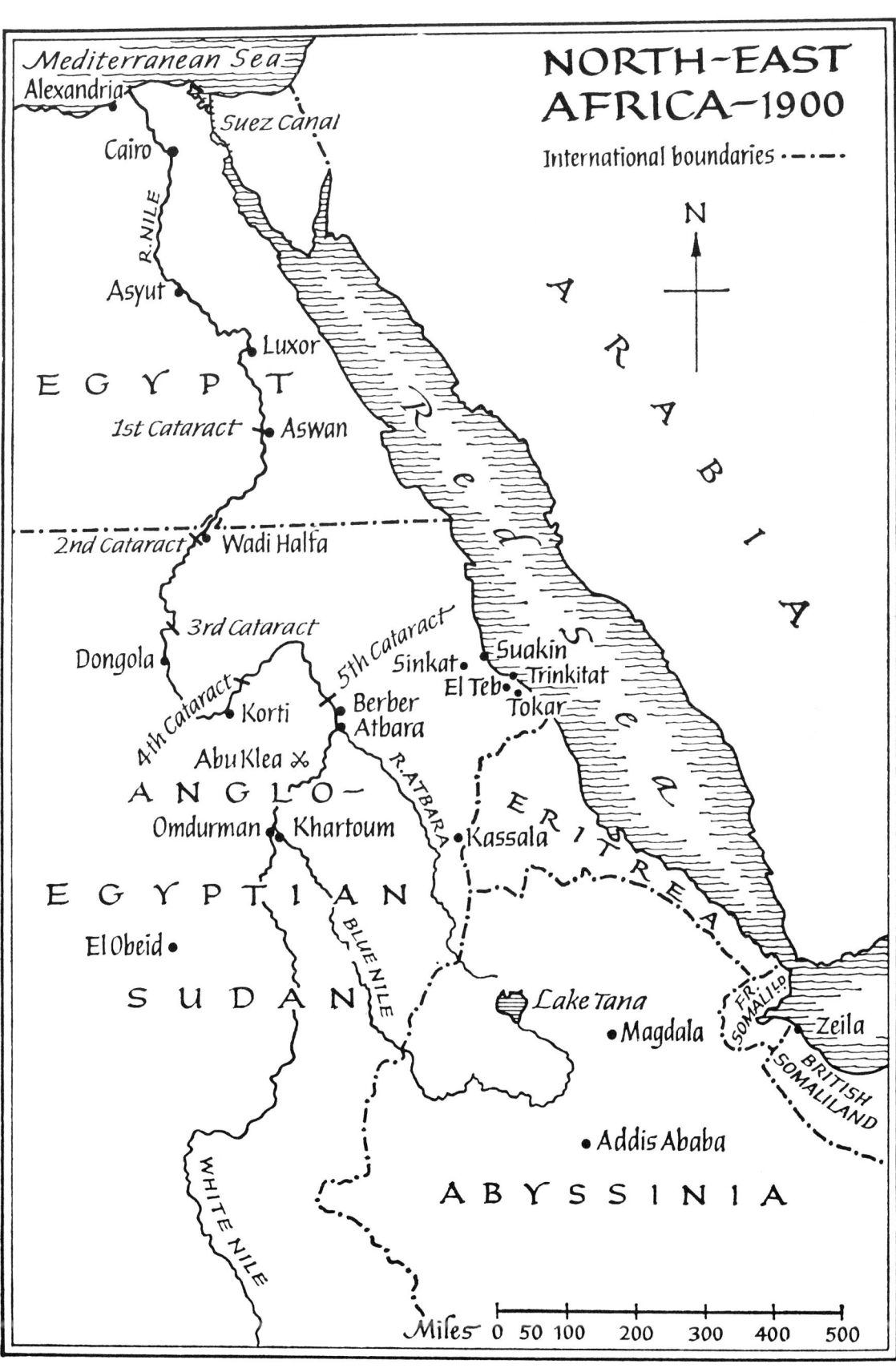

Boer War 1900
6309-38-40
Halt of City Imperial Volunteers – first view of the Veldt – Orange River SA

General Sir Redvers Buller in
South Africa, 1900
Pen and ink sketch by
S. M. Rowlandson   7802-3

Boer commando c1900
6808-40-4

Grenadier Guards in action at Brandwater Basin, South Africa, 1901   6806-355

General Sir George White VC in
service dress, 1900
Chromolithograph by Vanity Fa
14th June 1900   7312-

CHAPTER 18
THE LAST OF THE GENTLEMEN'S WARS
1899 – 1914

To the British public, far removed from the scene of its Army's activities, defeats like Maiwand, Isandhlwana and Majuba assumed the same magnitude as those sustained by the Austrians and French at the hands of the Prussians, though they forgot, for example, that the Austrian casualties at Sadowa were 15 times greater than the total losses of the entire Zulu War. However the nation's confidence in its soldiers was easily restored by victories like Ulundi and Omdurman which so conveniently blotted out the memories of earlier reverses, that when real disaster overtook the Army, as it did in the closing months of 1899, dismay and disbelief struck the country. Although patriotic and imperial fervour re-asserted itself, bringing aid to the hard-pressed soldiers, realisation began to dawn that the Army was hopelessly unfitted for the new century.

Following the discovery of gold in the Transvaal in 1886, the great influx of foreigners, mainly British, had so threatened Boer supremacy that the republic's President, Paul Kruger, always wary of British intentions, had determined to mitigate the influence of these 'Uitlanders' by denying them the vote and other rights. Kruger's suspicions had been further heightened by the ill-fated raid of Dr. Jameson, a henchman of the great imperialist, Cecil Rhodes, in support of the Uitlanders at Johannesburg. Having secured an alliance with the sister Boer Republic in the Orange Free State, Kruger began to build up his military strength while refusing to accede to the British Government's negotiations on behalf of the Uitlanders. On 9th October 1899 Kruger issued an ultimatum, demanding the withdrawal of British troops from his frontiers and the recall of the reinforcements which the Government, alarmed at Boer intransigence, had ordered to be sent from India and elsewhere in September. On the 11th 24,000 Boers from the Transvaal and the Orange Free State invaded Natal, lesser forces laid siege to the small British garrison at Mafeking and the centre of the diamond industry at Kimberley, while others rode into Cape Colony to raise the Cape Dutch.

Despite warnings since 1896 by the Intelligence Department at the War Office of the Boer's ability to put 50,000 mounted riflemen into the field, armed with Mauser rifles and Krupp artillery from Germany; despite an appreciation that 200,000 men would be needed to defeat the Boers by the Commander-in-Chief in South Africa, General Butler, who was recalled for his pessimism and supposed Boer sympathies; and notwithstanding the urgings of Wolseley, by then C-in-C of the Army, that the 9,000-odd British garrison at the Cape and in Natal should be strengthened, no action had been taken by the Government to increase the British military presence in South Africa beyond the belated despatch of the 10,000 reinforcements in September. Not until 20th October did the transports carrying an army corps of 47,000 men begin to leave England under the command of Sir Redvers Buller, a V.C. of the Zulu War, one of the most experienced of Wolseley's favoured officers and now, somewhat to his own misgivings, appointed to the chief command in South Africa.

Before Buller's army could arrive, Sir George White, the subjugator of Burma in 1885 and now commanding in Natal, checked the Boer advance at Elandslaagte, which enabled his advanced brigade at Dundee to withdraw after a laborious march to Ladysmith. Elandslaagte, the first British victory of the war and, as it turned out, the last for some time, was marked by a fine charge in the old style by the 5th Lancers and the Imperial Light Horse, a colonial regiment raised from Uitlanders, and a splendid attack led by Colonel Ian Hamilton, one of the few British officers who had a healthy respect for the Boers, having been at Majuba; armed with this experience, he warned his men, the 1st Devons, 1st Manchesters and 2nd Gordons, to maintain a very open order as they advanced, contrary to the current tactical practice.

After this success, however, White's ambitious attack on the Boers at Lombard's Kop, just outside Ladysmith, ended in complete failure, part of his force† being compelled to surrender while the rest withdrew into the town. By the end of October, four cavalry regiments, nine battalions, six field batteries and various Natal colonial units were entirely surrounded and cut off by the Boers. Fortunately the latter made no attempt to push southwards but contented themselves with tightening their grip round the 14-mile defensive perimeter that White established to protect Ladysmith. Most of the positions and the town itself, which contained 7,000

---

† Elements of the 1st Gloucesters, 1st Royal Irish Fusiliers and the 10th Mountain Battery, Royal Artillery.

civilians, were dominated by the Boer positions from which their heavy guns daily harassed the besieged, soldiers and civilians alike. It was this bombardment, together with an increasing shortage of food as the siege progressed, that caused the greatest trouble to the defenders; both had to be countered by sorties against the gun emplacements and the imposition of a strict rationing system. Conditions within Ladysmith worsened as the weeks dragged by but all were sustained by hopes of relief from the south.

When Buller arrived at the Cape in late October he realised that his first priority of an advance on the Boer republics must be delayed until White had been relieved, a task he intended to undertake himself. However he was faced by imperious demands for relief from Cecil Rhodes, who was locked up in Kimberley, the defence of which was being conducted by Colonel Kekewich and part of the Loyal Regiment with far more success than Rhodes was prepared to admit. Buller therefore began to disperse his force by detaching 10,000 men of the newly-arrived army corps under Major-General Lord Methuen for the relief of Kimberley, while he advanced with 30,000 to force the line of the River Tugela, prior to breaking through towards Ladysmith. He further detached a brigade under Major-General Gatacre to operate against a small Boer force that had invaded Cape Colony.

Methuen's division drove the Boers from some high ground at Belmont, though not without considerable casualties, particularly in the Guards Brigade whose men attacked in close order. The Boers stood again at Enslin until Methuen launched another assault when they fell back to the Modder River. Realising that frontal attacks against high ground held by very mobile marksmen were proving expensive in men without inflicting commensurate losses on the enemy, Methuen tried to turn the Boer defences on the Modder by a flanking attack across the river. The troops advanced with great spirit but Methuen lost control of the battle and was only spared further casualties by the Boers evacuating the position during the night. Now only one obstacle remained before Kimberley was reached, a low ridge at Magersfontein. Appreciating that the Boers would make a determined stand here, Methuen planned to approach the ridge under cover of darkness and attack with Major-General Wauchope's Highland Brigade† at first light.

The Highlanders advanced just after midnight in drizzling rain with each battalion in a tightly packed formation, one behind the other with the Black Watch leading, to avoid men going astray in the dark. At about 4 a.m., with the ridge looming ahead, the brigade halted to open out in attack formation. Just as they began to deploy, the ground in front of them erupted in a blaze of rifle-fire, coming not, as had been anticipated, from the high ground, but from trenches dug at the foot of the slope. With most of the Highlanders still closely packed together, the Boers could not miss despite the poor visibility *"It was hellish"*, a Black Watch corporal wrote, *"how any man escaped, God alone knows. Men were falling all round. There were some men who rallied and re-rallied; others again, the less said about the better".(1)* Wauchope was killed early on, the battalions became hopelessly mixed, panic spread and those who did not run were pinned down in the open where they were to lie all day under a blazing sun. The British artillery came into action, the Guards Brigade moved forward on the right flank and attempts were made to rally the Highlanders, but everywhere the Boers held firm. The next day Methuen retired to the Modder River. His attempt to relieve Kimberley had been bloodily repulsed and, with one of his three brigades broken and demoralised, a renewal of the offensive was out of the question. The fact that the blow had fallen on the Highland regiments, who to the public at large were among the cream of the Army, seemed to magnify the defeat.

Magersfontein was fought on 11th December. On the day before, further east, Gatacre was surprised by a Boer force at Stormberg. His experience in command of a brigade during the Relief of Chitral and of the British division at Omdurman had somehow failed to teach him the need for reconnaissance and security when moving in unknown country, with the result that his two battalions, the 2nd Northumberland Fusiliers and 2nd Royal Irish Rifles, were ambushed and badly cut up. The regimental officers and men did their best to retrieve their general's errors but over 500 were taken prisoner. Like Methuen, Gatacre was compelled to withdraw.

Worse was to follow, for on 15th December Buller launched 15,000 men in a frontal attack across open ground against strong Boer positions holding the line of the Tugela at Colenso. The battle was characterized, on the British side, by the inept, in some cases foolhardy, handling of the attack by Buller and his subordinates, contrasting with the stoical bravery and endurance of the troops; and on the Boer side, by the accuracy of their musketry and artillery, added to the almost complete invisibility of their positions. Two examples suffice to illustrate this unhappy day. Colonel Long, commanding the Royal Artillery, ordered the 14th and 66th Field Batteries to take up firing positions well ahead of the advancing infantry and within 300 yards of some Boer trenches. His gunners fought their guns until the last man was shot down, and although a gallant attempt was made to save the guns, for which six V.Cs were awarded*, ten of them fell into Boer hands. Major-General Hart,

---

† 2nd Black Watch, 1st Highland Light Infantry, 2nd Seaforth and 1st Argylls.

* Major Babtie, R.A.M.C., Captains Schofield, R.H.A., Reed, R.A., and Congreve, Rifle Brigade, Lieutenant Hon. F. Roberts, 60th Rifles, and Corporal Nurse, R.A. 18 Royal Artillery N.C.Os. and drivers were awarded the D.C.M.

commanding the Irish Brigade† which attacked on the left. marched his men into the assault with his battalions in the close, parade-ground order of quarter-column. When the leading companies of the Royal Dublin Fusiliers were within 200 yards of the river, the Boers opened fire with rifles and artillery. The closely-packed Irishmen went down in scores but driven on by their fiery general, who had no patience with taking cover, they plunged into the river which in places was ten feet deep and had barbed wire concealed under the water. After the battle the Boer commander, Louis Botha, wrote of the Irish Brigade's attack: *"They were driven back time and time again. No less than five times they charged and I never want to see finer bravery than I saw there".(2)* By 11.30 a.m., having suffered over a thousand casualties with nothing gained, Buller lost heart and ordered a general retirement. So depressed was he at this failure that he even signalled White in Ladysmith suggesting that the latter should capitulate. The V.C. in command in Ladysmith was to prove of sterner stuff than the V.C. in command on the Tugela.

With three serious reverses in one week –"Black Week" as it was called –, with Kimberley and Mafeking still beseiged, and with more than a division's worth of troops cut off in Ladysmith, Government, War Office and public had little to celebrate at Christmas 1899. Clearly a heroic leader was needed if Britain's honour was to be saved and a handful of Boer farmers taught the lesson they deserved. The only general that nation and Army could trust was the man Wolseley had always disliked, partly for his fame and popularity, partly for his opposition to many of the causes Wolseley had espoused, his rival for the highest post in the Army – Lord Roberts of Kandahar, known and loved by all the lower ranks as "Bobs". Since his triumphs in the Afghan War, Roberts had held the chief commands in Madras and in India. In 1895 he had been promoted field-marshal and, having been passed over as successor to the Duke of Cambridge in favour of Wolseley, he had been appointed Commander-in-Chief, Ireland. Now, aged 67 and on the brink of retirement, he was offered the chief command in South Africa with Kitchener as his chief of staff. He had just heard that his only son had been killed, winning a posthumous V.C. at Colenso, but he nevertheless answered the call of duty. On 23rd December he and Kitchener sailed from Southampton.

The events of "Black Week" woke Britain up to the fact that she was faced with a major war in South Africa, not simply another colonial insurrection. The Militia was embodied to free Regular units at home and overseas for active service; some Militia battalions were sent to the Cape and to Mediterranean stations such as Malta. Thousands of Yeomanry and Volunteers, liable only for home defence, offered their services for overseas. The former were organized into regiments of Imperial Yeomanry, which were to prove invaluable in offsetting the shortage of Regular mounted troops, while the first and most famous of the latter, the City of London Imperial Volunteers – the C.I.Vs. – a force of all arms formed from all the London Volunteer units, sailed for South Africa in early January 1900 amid scenes of huge patriotic enthusiasm. The Empire, too, responded to the mother country's hour of need, Canada, Australia and New Zealand all sending contingents, whose men, together with those of numerous colonial corps already raised in South Africa, being usually of a higher calibre than the British Regular and often accustomed to horses and wide, open spaces, adapted quickly to the mobile warfare of the Boers.

Roberts planned to leave the relief of Ladysmith to Buller while he concentrated his forces near Modder River for a major thrust on Pretoria, via Bloemfontein, the two Boer capitals, relieving Kimberley on the way. To give himself more scope for manoeuvre and reduce his dependence for supplies on the railway system, he set Kitchener to organizing a vast supply train based on animal transport. Taking a leaf out of the Boer book he also built up his mounted arm with particular emphasis on mounted infantry – troops who used horses for rapid movement but fought on foot; some of these were Regular cavalry who turned in their swords and lances, others were infantrymen hurriedly taught to ride, while still more were provided by the Dominion and colonial volunteers and the Imperial Yeomen.

While Roberts was making his preparations during January, Buller launched another attack in Natal, this time at the dominating feature of Spion Kop on the right of the Boer line along the Tugela. The attacking infantry scaled the hill during darkness but, when day broke, found themselves overlooked by Boers on higher ground whose devastating fire caused heavy casualties. Further reinforcements were sent up but, unable to advance, were pinned down in the same confined area. At nightfall the survivors were withdrawn. Buller tried again on 5th February at Vaal Krantz but once more manoeuvred his unfortunate troops into an untenable position. Not until 27th February, the anniversary of Majuba, after four days' costly assaults on the Boer left, was Buller able to break out at Pieter's Hill and send his horsemen riding for Ladysmith. Much of the heaviest fighting had again fallen on the Irish regiments whose gallantry and losses were commemorated, at the Queen's command, by the formation of the Irish Guards.

† 1st Royal Inniskilling Fusiliers, 1st Border Regiment, 1st Connaught Rangers, 1st and 2nd Royal Dublin Fusiliers.

After holding out for more than 100 days, White's garrison at Ladysmith, tired out by their constant vigilance and weak from short rations, greeted the leading squadrons of the Imperial Light Horse and Natal Carbineers with cheers and thankfulness that their ordeal was over. Of the original garrison of 14,000, only 2,000 were pronounced medically fit enough to pursue the retreating Boers. Sir George White, whose indomitable spirit had been the mainstay of the defence, was in failing health and had to be invalided home. Buller followed a few months later. His generalship had proved sadly lacking, largely through self-doubt and indecision, but for all the setbacks and casualties his army had sustained, he never lost the affection and trust of the private soldier, for whose welfare he was ever solicitous.

Meanwhile, on the same day as Pieter's Hill, Roberts over in the west had won a great victory. In the month following his arrival on 10th January, he had re-organized the army into four infantry divisions, each of two four-battalion brigades and three field batteries, a cavalry division of three brigades and seven horse batteries, two brigades of mounted infantry and sundry corps troops, including further units of mounted infantry and batteries of heavy guns and howitzers. In all the force totalled some 26,000 infantry, 7,500 mounted troops and 120 guns; besides British Regulars and the C.I.Vs. — the first Volunteers ever to serve abroad — it included Australians, Canadians and South African units. The offensive began on 11th February. Sending the 1st Division under Methuen up the Kimberley railway line to fix the Boers holding the Magersfontein position and to delude them of his real intentions, Roberts despatched the Cavalry Division under Lieutenant General French on a wide flanking march to the east of Magersfontein with orders to relieve Kimberley at all costs, while the 6th, 7th and 9th Divisions followed in their wake. Brushing aside all Boer opposition, French advanced with great speed and entered Kimberley on the 15th, by which time the 6th Division had reach Klip Drift on the Modder, some 20 miles east of Magersfontein. By now the Boer commander, Piet Cronje, surprised by the rate and direction of the British advance, which he had believed must be dependent on the railway line, belatedly realised that he was being outflanked, and began to withdraw eastwards from Magersfontein along the line of the Modder towards Bloemfontein. Encumbered by a mass of slow-moving ox-waggons, his rate of movement gave time for French's cavalry to ride south-east from Kimberley to head him off at Paardeberg, while the infantry divisions closed in to complete his encirclement. Kitchener, temporarily in command while Roberts was away sick, launched a few costly frontal attacks against the Boer positions dug in along the river bank, but on Roberts' return it was left to shell-fire and the threat of starvation to force the Boers to submit. On Majuba Day Cronje surrendered with 4,000 men. Just over a fortnight later, after driving through two Boer forces guarding the road to Bloemfontein, Roberts' army marched into the Orange Free State capital.

A six weeks' delay now followed, owing to a severe epidemic of enteric fever, the need to secure the railway from Bloemfontein southwards to Cape Colony, and the amassing of supplies and reinforcements for the next stage, the capture of Pretoria. There were by now in South Africa the equivalent of 15 divisions, of which three were mounted, the largest field army Britain had ever assembled. About a quarter of this force was in Natal; two divisions, the 1st and 10th, were around Kimberley; and the 3rd and 6th were garrisoning Bloemfontein and protecting the lines of communication. This dispersal was necessary owing to the many Boer detachments still at large in the country through which the advance had passed. The remainder, five infantry and two mounted divisions, were available for a great sweep up the general axis of the railway line to Pretoria, which began on 3rd May. Encountering only slight opposition as the Boers fell back, Roberts pressed northwards with three divisions and French's cavalry, protecting his right and rear with the other formations, as Methuen advanced on his left from Kimberley. On the 31st Johannesburg surrendered, all the riches of the Transvaal thus passing into British hands, and on 5th June Roberts entered Pretoria as President Kruger, his government and main army made off to the east. Meanwhile Mafeking, never seriously in danger, had been relieved on 17th April and the Boers driven from northern Natal by Buller's men who linked up with Roberts' army in early July. From Pretoria the British troops drove east towards Portuguese East Africa, dispersing the Boer rearguards and forcing Kruger to take refuge in Portuguese territory in late September. Thus in a seven months' campaign, by firm and consistent direction of a simple strategic plan and concentration of superior numbers against the main Boer armies, Roberts had avenged the earlier disasters of the war, broken the enemy into fragments and swept through their two republics which were annexed as British colonies. At the end of 1900 he was recalled to succeed Wolseley as Commander-in-Chief, leaving the final conclusion of hostilities to Kitchener.

This, however, was to prove a great deal more difficult than was thought at the time. Although Roberts' campaign had driven the two Boer presidents and their governments from their capitals, there were many armed Boers still in the field in both republics who had no intention of giving in without a fight. Under such determined and skilful leaders as Botha, De Wet, De La Rey and Smuts, they split themselves up into small commandos and a guerilla warfare, striking at lines of communication, at isolated British detachments and luring forces sent after them into ambushes. From the northern Transvaal right down to the borders of Cape Colony these

highly mobile, elusive and daring bands ranged far and wide, inflicting casualties and damage out of all proportions to their numbers. One of their greatest 'coups' was the defeat by De La Rey of a column under Lord Methuen who, with 600 of his men, was taken prisoner.

Kitchener disposed of some four times the total Boers in the field but large numbers of his men were tied down in garrison and other duties. He set about a systematic clearance of the vast territory by sectioning off areas with barbed-wire fences guarded by blockhouses. Each of these areas was then swept clear of Boer forces, following which they were denuded of shelter and sustenance by burning the farms and crops therein, and concentrating the women and children into camps. It was a slow, laborious and often brutal business but Kitchener kept up a ruthless and relentless pressure, gradually wearing the Boers down until finally, nearly two years after the fall of Pretoria, war weariness took its toll of all but the most recalcitrant and peace was signed on 31st May 1902. A magnanimous policy towards the defeated republics gave them internal self-government within the Empire in 1907 and in the following year the Union of South Africa was formed.

Though the Army had eventually triumphed, the Boer War had imposed great burdens upon it and revealed many defects in the late Victorian military system's capacity for modern war. If the events of the war have been somewhat cursorily described here, it is because the lessons learned from it were of greater importance to the Army than the actual operations, which on the whole were conspicuous more for the immense distances marched than for battles fought. The *"Report of His Majesty's Commissioners on the War in South Africa"*, published in 1903, had harsh words to say on almost every aspect of the Army's organisation, training, administration and its men, from Wolseley, the Commander-in-Chief, down to the private soldier.

Despite the Director of Military Intelligence having repeatedly emphasised, since 1896, the likelihood of war with the Boers, *"no plan of campaign ever existed for operations in South Africa"*,(3) a state of affairs that stemmed from the lack of a proper General Staff at the War Office and inertia on Wolseley's part. The dearth of a uniform system of staff tasks and duties had led to muddle and inefficiency among the various headquarters staffs in the field, and demonstrated that the establishment of the Staff College had not yet overcome the defects in command and control that had been such a feature of the Crimean War. The Army's field guns had proved inferior in performance to the European models possessed by the Boers and serious manufacturing faults had been disclosed in small arms and ammunition. Medical facilities had been severely stretched by the scale of the campaign and poor field hygiene had resulted in more casualties from disease than from enemy action. Although the new Army Service Corps, formed incidently by Buller in 1888, had performed well, its resources were greatly extended, and lack of administrative planning prior to the outbreak of war had necessitated a great deal of improvisation as the campaign progressed, both in the provision of wheeled and animal transport and many items of ordnance stores. The vulnerability to modern weapons of the Army's tactical methods and its generally poor standard of fieldcraft compared to the enemy had been demonstrated over and over again in the early weeks of the war. Nor were these improved by a lack of professionalism in the knowledge and performance of their duties by the general run of officer for whom *"keenness is not the correct form"*.(4) Many N.C.Os, too, had proved reluctant to face up to their responsibilities. The British Regular soldier, particularly from the Army at home rather than in India where the men were more mature and fully trained, had compared poorly in physique, intelligence and resourcefulness with the Boer, the colonial and even the Volunteer and reservist. *"Modern warfare is just a bit beyond him,"* wrote an infantry officer, *"he has neither the intellect of a highly educated man, the instinct of a savage or the self-reliance of the colonial. He is a good fellow but a terribly thick-headed one. To think for himself is not what he is accustomed to".(5)* All in all the investigation into the Boer War revealed that the Army was out of date and ill-prepared, both in size and efficiency, for war in the early twentieth century.

The seriousness of the position was accentuated by the growing military strength of other nations, particularly Germany whose industrial strength since the unification of the country in 1871 had turned it into a major European power, with ambitions to become a world power, rivalling if not outstripping Britain. The growth of the new German Navy which had begun in 1900 demonstrated the Kaiser's expansionist intentions and the possible threat of invasion from Germany began to feature in much British literature of the period. Furthermore Britain, by contracting the "Entente Cordiale" with France in 1904 in an attempt to end her isolation, might find it necessary to put a British army into Europe in the event of German aggression to preserve, as so often had happened in the past, the integrity of the Low Countries and the Channel Ports. Against this background it was clear that no time should be lost in modernizing the country's land forces from top to bottom.

The task was begun by St John Brodrick, the Secretary of State for War, continued with the reforms recommended by a committee under Lord Esher and published in 1904, and completed by Lord Haldane, who became Secretary for War in 1905 and was to prove one of the ablest and far-sighted holders of that office. In 1903 the Committee of Imperial Defence was set up under the Prime Minister, consisting of the political

and professional heads of the Navy and Army with intelligence advisors, to survey the world-wide strategic needs of the Empire. Reform of the higher direction of the Army began in 1904 with the abolition of the post of Commander-in-Chief and the establishment of the Army Council, the formation of a General Staff and the division of responsibilities within the War Office into clearly-defined departments. The Army Council, under the War Secretary, consisted of four military members, each the head of his department in the War Office, and two civilians, known as the financial and civil members, whose collective task was to consider and decide on future policy. At the head of the General Staff was a new appointment, the Chief of the General Staff, the senior serving officer of the Army, whose department was responsible for operations, intelligence, staff duties and training. All matters broadly concerned with men — their recruitment, terms of service and well-being — became the province of the Adjutant-General's Department, while the Army's material needs — transport, supply, quartering, movement, stores and equipment — was the concern of the Quartermaster-General. The fourth military member of the Army Council was the Master-General of the Ordnance whose duties embraced armaments and fortifications. This strict division of staff responsibilities was continued down through every level of command in the Army, so that each intermediate headquarters had its "G", "A" and "Q" branches. To provide trained officers to fill staff appointments the Staff College was enlarged and its syllabus revised, while an Indian Staff College was established at Quetta; to ensure that all staffs worked to uniform procedures, official manuals were published. These new methods became adopted by all dominion and colonial forces, after which the titles of the General Staff and its Chief were dignified by the word "Imperial". Initiative and an increased sense of responsibility were encouraged by de-centralizing many of the War Office's functions to administrative districts, into which the country was divided, whose headquarters would relieve field force commanders of much day-to-day administration, thus leaving them free to train the units and formations under their command for war.

Previously, higher formations had not been formed until after the outbreak of hostilities but henceforth all units were to be allocated in peacetime to the brigades and divisions with which they would go to war. Those stationed at home were earmarked to form an expeditionary force of six self-contained infantry divisions, each of three four-battalion brigades, with their own divisional cavalry squadron, artillery, engineers, supply and transport train (A.S.C.) and three field ambulances (R.A.M.C.); and a cavalry division of four three-regiment brigades, also with its own supporting arms and services. An infantry division totalled 18,000 men with 76 guns† and 24 machine-guns, the cavalry division 9,000 men, 10,000 horses, 24 guns (13-pounders) and the same number of machine-guns. These figures represented the war establishment which would be made up by the recall of reservists, for which a comprehensive mobilization plan was devised.

To provide a second line for the Regular Army, Haldane re-organized the auxiliary forces. The Militia was re-modelled as the Special Reserve, with the role of finding drafts for the Regular units and also the provision of men for certain garrison and lines of communication duties. From 1908 the Yeomanry and Volunteers were re-shaped into the Territorial Force, liable for service anywhere within the United Kingdom but not abroad unless its members so volunteered. It was organized on identical lines to the Regular Army, though lacking its latest weapons and equipment, to form 14 cavalry brigades and 14 infantry divisions including Services. They were to be embodied in the event of mobilization and were to be ready for war after six months' intensive training. In peacetime they would be called out for annual training by the War Office but they were to be raised and administered, though not commanded, by County Associations under the Lords Lieutenant. Their formation commanders were all Regular officers whose staffs were also part-Regular. The mounted regiments retained the word "Yeomanry" in their titles, and the infantry battalions developed closer links with their Regular comrades of the county regiments by dropping the name and appurtenances of the old Volunteers and simply becoming higher numbered battalions of those regiments. To provide a reserve of at least partly-trained officers, the Volunteer Corps that had existed for some time at schools and universities were converted into Officers Training Corps; those schools which did not possess such corps were encouraged to form them.

A considerable body of opinion in the country, to which Lord Roberts lent powerful support, argued that the Territorial Force would not be adequate for home defence and the possibility of a German invasion demanded some form of conscription or national service. However such was the confidence in the Royal Navy's ability to prevent any serious invasion, and so reluctant were politicians of all parties to impose any statutory obligation on the British public to play a part in its own defence, that the national service case went by default.

As befitted a modernized army there were new uniforms, weapons and equipment. All the troops in South Africa had been clothed in khaki of a yellow-ish brown shade but the cotton drill material had proved too thin and been replaced by serge. In 1902 a khaki serge uniform of a darker shade, more suited to European conditions, was introduced for all purposes except ceremonial occasions, on which full dress in the traditional colours was still worn. The slough hat, which had enjoyed great popularity in the Boer War, was at first adopted

---

† 54 18-pounders, 18 4.5-inch howitzers, and 4 60-pounders.

British officers on manoeuvres in India, c1900

7712-41-154

General Lord Kitchener as Commander-in-Chief India with his staff at the Delhi Durbar, 1903

Indian Infantry on manoeuvres c1905

6904-53-37

British and Indian officers of the 21st Pioneers c1905

7712-41-32

as the service headdress but gave way to the flat-topped peaked cap. New accoutrements based on a leather bandolier, a type of ammunition carrier that had proved superior to the old pouches, was introduced in 1903, but was superseded five years later by a scientifically-designed personal equipment made of webbing, which all fitted together in one assembly; mounted troops, however, retained the bandolier. A new rifle was introduced, the Short Lee-Enfield with a clip-filled magazine holding ten rounds; this was issued to cavalry as well as infantry since it was clear that the role of cavalry was changing from shock action to that of mounted infantry. The artillery were re-equipped with quick-firing guns of the type mentioned above and the number of batteries increased, each "brigade" of three having its own ammunition column. Motor transport began to appear in the Army Service Corps and the new field ambulances of the Royal Army Medical Corps; in peacetime these were on a very reduced scale but schemes were drawn up for the requisitioning of motor vehicles on mobilization. The potential of the aeroplane as an instrument of war had not greatly engaged the minds of military thinkers until the results obtained by aerial reconnaissance during the 1912 manoeuvres hastened the growth of a new body, the Royal Flying Corps, which by 1914 was to have 63 aircraft for scouting purposes.

In parallel with the reorganizing and re-equipping of the Army, its training and tactical methods received a complete overhaul. A uniform training cycle was instituted, starting in the winter with the training of the individual soldier in his duties, weapon handling and physical fitness, passing on in the spring to squadron/ company/ battery training, and continuing, as the year progressed with regimental/battalion, brigade, and divisional training, until the culmination was reached with army manoeuvres in the autumn. Great emphasis was placed on developing a high standard of marksmanship, the use of ground, movement in extended order and the covering of such movement by fire. To facilitate the handling of the battalion in such tactics, the old, unwieldy eight or ten companies were abandoned in favour of a four-company organization. The killing power of the machine-gun had been amply demonstrated in the Russo-Japanese War of 1904-05 but its high rate of fire raised problems of ammunition carriage and re-supply, and although each regiment and battalion had two such guns, more trust was placed in fieldcraft and rapid, accurate rifle-fire. The cavalry, though still equipped with sword and lance, also devoted great attention to musketry and learned to march on foot to spare their horses, so that they were fresh for their chief roles of reconnaissance and screening the movements of the infantry. All this intensive training required space, and a new military centre to rival Aldershot was begun at Tidworth to utilise the broad acres of Salisbury Plain. For the annual army manoeuvres large tracts of the country were taken over and small towns and villages, that scarcely ever saw a soldier in the normal course of events, swarmed for a few weeks with khaki columns.

In the face of all this activity a fresh sense of purpose gripped the Army at all levels. A new school of thinking officer, bred in the Boer War, was coming forward in the upper echelons, a school typified by such as Douglas Haig, last encountered as a captain at Omdurman, and now distinguishing himself in Haldane's reformed War Office as Director of Military Training, or Horace Smith-Dorrien, who during his tenure of command at Aldershot around 1907 did much to improve the soldier's welfare and self-reliance by getting the regimental officers to interest themselves in their men as individuals. The example and drive of such officers percolated downwards through the Army in staffs and units alike, breeding a keen though always understated professionalism which had been so lacking prior to the Boer War.

As the British Army was being re-fashioned, so too in India was a new broom at work. Indian troops had not been committed in South Africa but to their chief command there came in 1903 Lord Kitchener, fresh from his successful conclusion of the war. Although the three Presidency armies had been abolished in 1895 in favour of four commands,† each of the latter retained independent control over the troops which were more or less permanently localized within their areas, the chief role being internal security. It was, for example, exceptional for a Madras regiment to serve outside the confines of the Madras Command. Kitchener regarded the internal security role as a matter for the police and quite secondary to what he saw as the prime function of the Army in India, the defence of the North-West Frontier against the possibility of a Russian invasion for a period of up to 12 months without outside assistance. This required the breaking down of the localization, the stationing of the bulk of the army within reach of the threatened zone, in Sind and the Punjab, and the opportunity for all regiments to have experience of frontier conditions. Kitchener renumbered all the Indian regiments in a single sequence, the cavalry from 1st-37th and the infantry from 1st-130th; he further abolished the old Presidency designations so as to unify them all into one single Indian Army. Under the new system, for instance, the 1st Madras Lancers became the 26th Light Cavalry and the 29th Bombay Infantry (2nd Baluch) became the 129th Baluchis; only the ten regiments of Gurkha Rifles, the Corps of Guides and the three Body-guards remained outside this renumbering. British officers were no longer gazetted to the Indian Staff Corps but to regiments of the Indian Army. As in England, all British and Indian units were distributed among newly-formed brigades and divisions with which they would fight in the event of war. By 1914 there were in India

† See Chapter 15.

Royal Irish Fusiliers on manoeuvres, 1908   6807-514-6

Manoeuvres on the Curragh, Ireland, 1913   6810-64-47

the equivalent of ten divisions, 230,000 men in all of which a third were British. No consideration was given to the earmarking of an expeditionary force for employment outside India until 1913 when, in response to a request as to what troops could be spared in the event of war in Europe, the Government of India informed the Army Council that it could count on two — possibly three — infantry divisions and one cavalry brigade. As it turned out when war eventually came, two infantry and two cavalry divisions were to be sent to France, some three divisions to the Middle East, and most of the British Regular units withdrawn, their place being taken by Territorials.

During his time as Commander-in-Chief, Kitchener had wrenched the Army in India out of the nineteenth century and done much to prepare it for modern war. However his work had been limited by financial restrictions. Much of its equipment and weapons were out of date, it was short of many essentials, particularly of artillery and transport, and although it had been brought to a high professional standard of efficiency, it was still basically a Frontier-orientated army, whose modernization was some way behind that of the British Army at home.

In pursuance of the spirit of co-operation engendered by the "Entente Cordiale", the British and French General Staffs had, from 1906, embarked on a series of discussions as to the action to be taken in the event of hostilities with Germany. From 1911 a scheme was worked out in detail for the landing of a British army of 160,000 men in France and for its concentration near the Belgian border around Le Cateau on the left of the French Army. All the mobilization plans to achieve this were perfected and rehearsed, and arrangements made for the recall of garrisons from abroad. As Europe began to form into armed camps following the murder of an Austrian Archduke at Serajevo by a Serbian student on 28th June 1914, it became clear that all the preparations of the previous decade were soon to be put to the test. Austria's determination to punish Serbia brought Russia to the rescue of her fellow Slavs in the Balkans. Russian mobilization was countered by Germany's mobilizing in support of her ally, Austria, and sending an ultimatum to France, who was bound by treaty to Russia. Last-minute efforts to maintain the peace were of no avail as the long-matured plans for war gained an inexorable momentum. France mobilized on 1st August and Germany declared war on her two days later. On the 4th, in accordance with a plan drawn up years before to strike out France before turning on Russia, the Kaiser's armies invaded neutral Belgium to deliver an overwhelming blow against the French left and rear.

The violation of Belgian neutrality brought Britain off the fence. The Territorials had been embodied on 3rd August and on the 4th, the day war was declared, general mobilization was ordered. Between 12th-17th August the British Expeditionary Force was transported to France and by the 20th its concentration was complete. All Haldane's great work, all the carefully laid plans had been brought to fruition, and just over 99 years after its last great battle on European soil, a British army was once again preparing to fight where its forefathers under Wellington and Marlborough had toiled before. Indeed on the night of the 21st the outposts of the 1st Lincolns and 1st Royal Scots Fusiliers of the 3rd Division overlooked the very ground where in earlier times as North's and Mordaunt's they had battled for eight hours on the bloody field of Malplaquet. In some respects the regiments of the B.E.F. were not dissimilar to those of past wars: no conscripts filled their ranks; they were still largely recruited from the poorer classes and officered by the gentry; they were sustained by regimental pride and a sense of national superiority over any foreigner; their weapons, though obviously greatly improved in design and performance, were essentially of the same basic type and on the battlefield events still moved at the speed of the man on foot or horse. The difference lay in the fact that the B.E.F. of 1914 was *"in every respect incomparably the best trained, best organized and best equipped British Army that ever went forth to war".(6)*

CHAPTER 19
ARMAGEDDON
1914 – 1918

Although the British Expeditionary Force sent to France in 1914 was as good, man for man, as any of the enemy or allied armies, it was by comparison very small. Two of its divisions had been held back for home defence by Lord Kitchener, who was appointed Secretary of State for War on the outbreak of hostilities, so that initially it only comprised one cavalry and four infantry divisions, some 100,000 men in all. The infantry was grouped into two corps, the 1st and 2nd Divisions forming the I Corps under Haig, the 3rd and 5th the II Corps under Smith-Dorrien. In overall command was Sir John French who had made a name for himself as a cavalry commander in the Boer War. When the B.E.F. took up its position on the extreme left it had on its right the 13 divisions of the French Fifth Army, whose line was prolonged down to the Swiss frontier by four more armies. Germany deployed a million and a half men in the west of which three armies — 34 infantry divisions and five of cavalry — formed the right wing, wheeling through Belgium and north-west France to pin the French back against their own frontier defences. The Belgian Army, only slightly larger than the B.E.F., put up a gallant resistance but, hopelessly outnumbered, was compelled to withdraw to Antwerp, leaving nothing between the B.E.F. and the 320,000 men of the German First Army under Von Kluck on the outermost flank of their right wing.

After completing its concentration on 20th August, the B.E.F. prepared to advance in conformity with the French plan for an offensive on all fronts, unaware that this plan was already foundering badly. On the 23rd, having been warned of Von Kluck's approach by patrols of Allenby's Cavalry Division, the B.E.F. took up a defensive position at Mons into which the leading German corps blundered unexpectedly. The brunt of the ensuing assault fell upon Smith-Dorrien's II Corps lining the Mons Canal. Throughout the day six German infantry divisions came on supported by a heavy weight of artillery fire but all along the line their dense masses crumbled in the face of the musketry of the 3rd and 5th Divisions, so diligently practised in peacetime. As a German account put it: *"Well entrenched and completely hidden, the enemy opened a murderous fire...The rushes became shorter and shorter and finally the whole advance stopped...With bloody losses, the attack gradually came to an end".(1)*

Despite this cheering success in their first battle, the B.E.F. was compelled to withdraw to conform with the French armies which everywhere were falling back. So began the retreat from Mons, 14 days of hard marching in unusually hot weather for nearly 200 miles with only three or four hours' rest a day, which, coming after the marches up to the concentration area and the battle of the 23rd, was to prove increasingly fatiguing for the troops, many of whom were reservists, particularly for the II Corps on whom the advance pressed hardest. Conscious of his men's weariness, Smith-Dorrien chose to rest them on the night of the 25th at Le Cateau but this much-needed halt earned them a hard fight the next day. Once again the accuracy and rapidity of their rifle-fire checked the German onslaught which towards the end of the day gradually slowed down, permitting the British battalions to break contact one by one and resume the retreat. Smith-Dorrien's line had been reinforced by the fortuitous arrival of the 4th Division from England the day before the battle; on the 30th this Division and an independent brigade were formed into the III Corps under Lieutenant-General Pulteney.

Though short of food and sleep and notwithstanding their casualties and disillusion with the continued retreat, the men of the B.E.F. remained indomitable. Sir John French on the other hand was beginning to form the pessimistic view that only a complete withdrawal from the Allied line could save his force. Dissuaded from this drastic course by Kitchener's personal intervention, he was then prevailed upon to co-operate in the great counter-offensive which Marshal Joffre, the French Commander-in-Chief, was preparing to launch on the Marne against the now-tiring German armies, whose advance had swung southwards east of Paris, thus exposing their right flank to Joffre's re-grouped armies.

The Battle of the Marne saved Paris and shattered German hopes of a quick victory over France. Their armies fell back to the north bank of the Aisne from which the Allies tried to dislodge them on 13th September. Attacking between the French Fifth and Sixth Armies, the B.E.F. secured a lodgement on the enemy bank with

'The Old Contemptibles' British infantry at the Battle of Mons, August 1914. 7404-25-3
Photograph of an oil painting by W.B. Wollen, 1918.

Recruits for the New Armies, 1914.

Haig's I Corps pushing forward strongly on the right into the weakest German sector along the ridge of Chemin des Dames. Their advancing lines were completely overlooked by the German artillery observers but their widely extended attack formations, so different from the close order adopted by the Germans and French, minimised the number of casualties from shell-fire; their steady advance moved a German officer to remark: *"Splendid, we are all filled with admiration".(2)* However Haig's chance of breaking through was baulked by the sudden appearance of the leading corps of a fresh German army and, though his men reached the ridge, when they resumed the attack next day, they were strongly counter-attacked by the newly-arrived troops. Heavy fighting followed all along the B.E.F. front with both armies gradually beginning to entrench themselves the better to hold on to their positions. The fighting on the Aisne continued for a fortnight but by 1st October, with mounting casualties and little gain to either side, a stalemate had set in.

It was now clear to both Allies and Germans that no decision was likely on the Aisne but that to the west, as far as the Channel coast, both sides had an open flank which each began to try and exploit by transferring troops north-westwards — the so-called "Race to the Sea". In the course of this movement the B.E.F. resumed its place on the left of the French so as to be near the Channel ports whence it derived all its reinforcements and supplies. Towards the end of October the B.E.F. was taking up positions in the low-lying country of Flanders around the town of Ypres. Though the I and II Corps had lost heavily in the first two months' fighting, the 6th Division had now joined the 4th in the III Corps, and Rawlinson's IV Corps of the 3rd Cavalry Division and the 7th Division — formed largely of battalions which had returned from overseas garrisons — was moving up from Ostend. At the end of the month the Lahore and Meerut Divisions of the Indian Corps arrived, to be thrown into the fiercest fighting of the war so far. Facing battle and weather conditions that no sepoy had ever dreamed of, short of modern equipment and with some still wearing the thin khaki drill in which they had come from India, these brave men of the "martial races" responded nobly to this fearful challenge.†

The great German effort at Ypres to break through to Calais lasted from 20th October till mid-November. It was a battle of bitter ferocity in which the B.E.F., positioned between the Belgians on the left and the French on the right, were always outnumbered and out-gunned, short of artillery ammunition and fighting from shallow trenches which gave little protection against the quantities of German high explosive shells. With few reinforcements to replace the heavy casualties, battalions shrank to the size of companies, even platoons. Yet the line held, the divisional, brigade and battalion commanders somehow plugging the critical gaps in the defence, the company officers and men meeting attack after attack with their devastating musketry. On 31st October a major crisis came with a German break-through at Gheluvelt on the Ypres-Menin road against the I Corps front. As the line gave way in the face of overwhelming numbers, confusion was made worse by shells knocking out the commanders and staffs of the 1st and 2nd Divisions. Then, in this great struggle of corps and armies, the position was miraculously regained by a single battalion. The 2nd Worcesters, only 350 strong, advanced under heavy shell-fire and re-captured Gheluvelt; the line was restored. Never again would the action of so small a force — *"the last flourish of the old British Regular tradition"(3)* — be able to influence the outcome of a battle.

The Germans made one final thrust on 10th November, by which time the British battalions were down, on average, to about a quarter of their war strength; some had less than 100 men and only nine out of a total of 84 battalions had more than 300. 13 German divisions attacked out of the fog but only one, the Prussian Guard, managed to force a breach and that finally petered out when nothing lay before it but a few scattered strong-points and the gun line where the 18-pounders were firing over open sights. A counter-attack went in led by the 2nd Oxfordshire and Buckinghamshire Light Infantry, who threw back the remains of the Kaiser's Guard as their forbears, the 52nd, had routed Napoleon's Guard at Waterloo.

The battle ended in deadlock. With both sides digging themselves in, the lines of trenches soon ran from the sea to the Swiss frontier and the war of manoeuvre changed to one of sieges, which was to last for four years and would be dominated by heavy artillery, the machine-gun and barbed wire. The expert rifle shooting of the British Regulars, only acquired by years of practice in peacetime and so dominant a feature of the 1914 battles, would no longer be pertinent in a war of masses and high explosive and in any case would be unavailable. The old Regular Army had died at Ypres but not without setting an example of unflinching courage and high resolution to those that would follow them. Of the original B.E.F., 90,000 were casualties and those that remained, supported by the first of their Territorial comrades to reach France,* would have to hold the line until a new army could be formed.

When the war began, Lord Kitchener, with a foresight not shared by many, had predicted a long campaign and set out to create a mass army. He called at first for 100,000 volunteers; he got, by the end of the year,

---

† It was in this fighting that the first V.Cs. ever awarded to Indian soldiers were won, the first recipients being Sepoy Khudadad Khan of the 129th Baluchis and Naik Darwan Sing Negi of the 39th Garhwal Rifles.

* The first of the Territorial Force to go into action were the Oxfordshire Yeomanry on 7th October 1914 and the London Scottish who put up a great fight at Messines on 1st November.

228

1,186,337. By September 1915 the figure would have risen to two and a quarter million. Ignoring Haldane's pre-war plans for the Special Reserve and the Territorial Force, which had already been doubled and had volunteered for overseas service, Kitchener built his New Army round the framework of the old Regular Army, forming "Service" battalions of the county regiments and grouping them into complete divisions. By October 1914 18 New Army divisions had been formed but they were divisions in numbers only. There were few instructors to train them, no weapons, no uniforms, no accommodation, no trained staff to man their headquarters. Old Boer War, even pre-Boer War, Regular officers and N.C.Os. had to be dug out of retirement to command them, though such men had no knowledge of modern conditions. Nevertheless, sustained by little more than their own enthusiasm, the New Army slowly began to assume the semblance of a fighting force. In the meantime the main burden on the Western Front had to be borne by France for the B.E.F., though re-organized in late December 1914 into the First and Second Armies under Haig and Smith-Dorrien respectively, could only muster 11 British and Indian infantry divisions and Allenby's Cavalry Corps. †

The situation on the Western Front in 1915, and indeed later, was one wherein the Germans, ensconced on French soil behind a formidable trench system, often on dominating ground and backed by plentiful artillery, could defend or attack as they so wished; the Allies could only attack and attack frontally at that. Furthermore the artillery they needed to ensure success in no way matched the enemy's, either in calibre of guns or quantities of ammunition available. For the British, this deficiency in heavy armaments was aggravated by the uncontrolled recruiting for the New Army which had drawn many skilled men from factories that in any case were not adapted for mass production of munitions. Not until June 1915, when Lloyd George was made Minister of Munitions, was production put on an efficient footing and even then a year would elapse before its fruits reached the armies in the field. In the meantime the British Army was still in duty bound to assist its French allies.

An offensive at Neuve Chapelle in March failed through shortage of fire support and lack of reserves at a cost of 12,000 casualties. Before it could be renewed, the Germans attacked at Ypres using a new weapon, poison gas, but a stand by the 1st Canadian Division, which cost them a third of their strength, and the German failure to commit reserves prevented a break-through. British counter-attacks to recover lost, though largely worthless ground, resulted in nearly 60,000 more casualties. Further attacks in May at Aubers Ridge and Festubert in support of a French offensive brought British losses for 1915 up to 100,000 and put paid to the last few remnants of the old Regulars. The final British effort for the year in France was made in September when, using gas to compensate for the dearth of artillery, Haig's First Army, now largely composed of Territorial divisions, attacked at Loos. After penetrating the forward positions, Haig called for reserves to exploit success but these, held too far back under the direct control of Sir John French, had to make a long approach march which prevented them from reaching the battle area until after darkness had fallen. They were the first of the New Army divisions. Tired, hungry and ignorant of the situation, these untried and barely trained troops were thrown into a pitiable baptism of fire. Caught by the enemy artillery and machine-guns in the darkness, they fell into confusion and only the arrival of the Guards Division prevented the earlier success turning into disaster. This failure, coming on top of the earlier set-backs, finished Sir John French's tenure of command; he was recalled to England and replaced by Haig. French's former chief of staff, Sir William Robertson, the only man who had ever reached the rank of field-marshal after starting his career as a private soldier, was made Chief of the Imperial General Staff.*

Though these offensives had cost Britain dear with little commensurate gain, her main strategic effort in 1915 had been made elsewhere. As early as January Kitchener, likening the German lines in France to a fortress that could not be assaulted or completely invested, concluded that *"the lines may be held by an investing force, whilst operations proceed elsewhere".(4)* Such a strategy had many a precedent in Britain's earlier continental wars, but with mixed success, whereby sea-power was used to assail the enemy on the periphery, while allies engaged his main land forces. In 1915 it had, besides Kitchener, a number of supporters, including Winston Churchill, the First Lord of the Admiralty, but the commanders in France were not among them, believing the war could only be won by defeating the German Army on the Western Front, to which all Britain's resources must be devoted. Once the Government was seized with the idea, the only question was where? Numerous possibilities were canvassed but gradually attention became focussed on the idea of a swift blow against Germany's ally, Turkey, an idea buttressed by an appeal for a diversion from Russia who was currently hard-

† The Indian troops served on the Western Front throughout 1915 but the majority were later withdrawn to serve in other theatres where the climate was more suited to them.
* One of the most famous stories of Robertson was the way he informed Smith-Dorrien of his sacking by French for a justified but unauthorised withdrawal at Ypres in 1915: " 'Orace, you're for 'ome".

pressed by the Turks in the Caucasus. If Constantinople could be taken, Germany might be deprived of an ally; the Suez Canal — against which one Turkish attack had already been resisted by Indian troops — would be secured; Italy and the Balkans might be induced to join the Allied cause; and Russia could be succoured through warm-water ports. Turkey's defeat would also free other Indian and some British troops by then facing another Turkish army in Mesopotamia, now Iraq. The scheme crystallized into a plan for forcing the Dardenelles with a purely naval force but when this failed on 14th March, due largely to delays which lost all hope of surprise, the need for a supporting land operation against the Gallipoli Peninsula became inescapable.

The command was given to General Ian Hamilton, the veteran of Majuba and Ladysmith, who had less than 40 days to create an army and staff and plan an assault landing, a hazardous venture of which no one had any experience and to which the enemy were now well-alerted. All he could be spared was the 29th Division, composed of the last Regular battalions from overseas garrisons, a hastily improvised Royal Naval Division of sailors and marines, short of artillery and services, a Territorial division, an Indian brigade and the Australian and New Zealand Army Corps (A.N.Z.A.C.) of 39,000 magnificent but not fully trained men. France also contributed a division. The shortage of guns and ammunition then affecting the Western Front was reflected in Hamilton having less than half the number of guns his force was entitled to. Whatever the defects of his army, whatever the perils that lay ahead, all ranks were infected with a wonderful and unique enthusiasm for this imaginative enterprise, and as they sailed from their base in the Aegean Sea *"they went like kings in a pageant to imminent death".(5)*

Within 24 hours of the landing on 25th April hundreds of these men had indeed gone to their deaths. Half-way up the west coast of the Peninsula the Anzacs stormed ashore but their initial success was stopped by a Turkish counter-attack which prevented them reaching the high ground. The 29th Division landed on the southern tip at Cape Helles on five beaches, the main assault going in at what were known as W and V Beaches. The former was the most heavily defended locality and as the leading battalion, the 1st Lancashire Fusiliers, reached the shallows, they were met by a hail of machine-gun and shell fire and coils of barbed wire concealed under the water. The battalion strove desperately to fight its way through, winning six Victoria Crosses in the process,† but had it not been for one company which got ashore on a flank to enfilade the Turkish defences, the Fusiliers must have been massacred. Nevertheless it was done, though at fearful cost, and, as the follow-up battalions landed a beachhead was secured. At V Beach the carnage was even greater. The assault troops, Dublin and Munster Fusiliers and the Hampshires, landed partly from open boats and partly from an old collier, the 'River Clyde', which was run aground so that the men could charge ashore from holes cut in her sides. The men in the boats were shot to pieces by machine-guns and the 'River Clyde' grounded in water too deep for the heavily laden troops to wade through. Only by means of lighters, heroically held in place by sailors, could the soldiers hope to dash for the beach in quick rushes but the enemy fire took a heavy toll. By the end of the day Hamilton's men had seized precarious footholds at Cape Helles and at Anzac Cove but neither force had been able to link up with the other and all the dominating ground was still in Turkish hands. There was nothing for it but to dig in and, in the weeks that followed, the same stalemate caused by trench warfare as already existed in France was imposed at Gallipoli.

By mid-July the beachhead at Helles had been extended inland for three miles and the Anzacs had beaten off a major counter-offensive, but nearly 40,000 men had been lost since the landing, a high rate of disease adding to the effects of enemy action. In August, having received a fresh corps of New Army divisions, Hamilton launched holding attacks from Helles and Anzac Cove while the new troops were put ashore at Suvla, three miles north of the latter. The landing was effected without loss, the bulk of the Turks in that sector being furiously engaged by the Australians, but once ashore the inexperience of the junior commanders and the inertia of their elderly leaders failed totally to exploit the lack of enemy in front of them. With the lost opportunity at Suvla, the Gallipoli campaign was doomed. Hamilton, who had done all he could to offset his serious deficiencies in numbers and equipment, was recalled in October and the new commander, Sir Charles Monro, advised evacuation. By brilliant planning and masterly deception the whole force was got off the Peninsula without the loss of a single man over two nights: from Suvla and Anzac on 19th/20th December and from Helles on 8th/9th January. The expedition begun with such high hopes had been a failure and a costly one at that, with nearly 214,000 casualties of which 145,000 were due to disease and sickness. On the credit side, heavy losses had been inflicted on the Turks of the order of 300,000 which, added to their casualties in the Caucasus, would ultimately seriously impair their military effort.

At the end of 1915, however, the Turks were not only victorious at Gallipoli but in Mesopotamia they had thrown back the Indian Expeditionary Force. Earlier successes had led to General Townshend being sent forward

---

† Major Bromley, Captain Willis, Sergeants Richards and Stubbs, Corporal Grimshaw and Private Kenneally. This number of V.Cs. won by one unit in a single action has only ever been exceeded by the 24th at Rorke's Drift.

World War I - Middle East 'Gallipoli Peninsula - The Landing of 2nd Battalion Hampshire Regiment from H.M.R. River Clyde, April 25th, 1915". Print of painting by Charles Dixon 1920.   7307-40

The 1st Buckinghamshire Battalion at Pozieres during the battle of the Somme, 23rd July 1916.   5911-303
Painting, oil on canvas, by W.B. Wollen.

Indian Cavalry in Palestine, 1918.   Print after F.A. Stewart   5102-47

British Army nurses with an ambulance column in Salonika, 1916.

Nestlé's Milk
- Magic in the Kitchen -

with a force of 17,000 in an over-ambitious attempt to capture Baghdad. Townshend found his path blocked by a greatly superior Turkish army and had no option but to retreat to Kut-el-Amara where, due to the weariness of his men, he decided to make a stand. By the end of December Townshend, who as a junior officer had been besieged in Chitral in 1895, found himself entirely hemmed in and closely invested at Kut. On 29th April, the relieving forces having been less successful than they had been at Chitral, he was forced to surrender with all his near-starving men, most of whom were Indians who had borne up valiantly till the end.

None of these ventures in the east had had any effect on the situation on the Western Front to which the centre of gravity returned in 1916. The British strength in France had now grown to 38 infantry and five cavalry divisions through the entry into the field of the New Army and further Territorial formations, a force of just over a million men. These were grouped into corps, two or three of which formed an army. With battalions, brigades and even divisions swallowed up in these huge organizations, each larger than anything commanded by Marlborough or Wellington, *"a man seemed to lose his identity as an individual"*, an officer wrote, *"one seemed to be engulfed in the colossal panoply of war".(6)* In 1916 there were four such armies, holding a continuous line of 70 miles from Ypres to the Somme valley near Bray. Behind the front a vast administrative organization had been built up, stretching back to the bases of Havre, Rouen and Boulogne, of railways, hospitals, supply dumps, rest areas, workshops, reinforcement depots, field bakeries, bath units, postal and pay offices, all providing the great range of facilities necessary to maintain a mass army in the field. To have achieved such an immense expansion of the logistic services in just over a year of war was a triumph of organizational skill, which owed much to pre-war civilian expertise acquired by many men now in uniform.

There was a great deal else that was new. Heavier guns with an adequate supply of ammunition were now at the front. For the first time since the seventeenth century body armour re-appeared in the shape of a steel helmet. Other throwbacks to the past were the re-introduction of hand grenades and mortars. The increasing dominance of the battlefield by the machine-gun had seen the withdrawal of such guns from battalions and their concentration into divisional companies of the newly formed Machine Gun Corps. Battalions received instead 16 lighter automatic weapons of an American design, the Lewis Gun. The vulnerability of infantry attacking frontally over open ground against barbed wire and machine-guns had led to the development of an armoured and tracked vehicle, called for security reasons a tank. This was primarily the brain-child of Colonel Ernest Swinton who, with the support of Winston Churchill, had persevered with the project against considerable scepticism and opposition until, following the first official trial in February 1916, 150 had been ordered. Unfortunately acute production difficulties had been encountered and it was not until August that the first 60 tanks reached France. Each tank was armed with either two 6-pounder guns or two machine-guns and required a crew of eight, the officers and men concerned being designated the Heavy Section of the Machine Gun Corps.

The infantry tactics based on fieldcraft, marksmanship and fire and movement which had been developed to such perfection by the old Regular Army, were deemed by the British command to be beyond the attainment of a hastily raised and trained mass army. Fire and movement there still was but the fire now took the form of a massive artillery bombardment which, it was thought, would so obliterate the German wire, trenches and machine-gun posts, that the infantry divisions, advancing across No-Man's-Land in an easily taught and controlled formation of successive, carefully aligned waves, would only have to winkle out the few enemy survivors with bomb and bayonet. As Sir Basil Liddell Hart wrote, these infantry tactics saw *"a revival of formations that were akin to the eighteenth century in their formalism and lack of manoeuvring power".(7)* Once the infantry had broken through the enemy lines, the cavalry divisions were to flood through the breach and restore mobility to the operations. Such were the tactical principles on which hopes for 1916 were pinned.

Haig believed that, owing to the standard of training and lack of experience, not only of the troops but also of the staffs at all levels, his army would not be ready to take the offensive until mid-August. However, in response to pleas from the French, who since February had been under constant pressure at Verdun, he agreed to attack in July with the main effort to be made, again at French request, on the Somme, where the British right adjoined the French left. The date was fixed for 1st July and the task given to Rawlinson's Fourth Army of 18 divisions whose attack, on a frontage of some 14 miles held by six German divisions, was to be preceded by a week's bombardment from 1,500 guns, the greatest British artillery concentration ever to be mounted. 11 divisions were to lead the attack with five in close reserve, the remaining two, with three cavalry divisions, forming the Fourth Army reserve. In addition another corps of three divisions and the headquarters of a reserve army under General Gough were kept as a further reserve under Haig's own hand. The Third Army was to mount a subsidiary attack to the north. Although conscription had at last been introduced in Britain in January, the assault divisions were largely from Kitchener's New Army, the enthusiastic volunteers of 1914-15 who were the best of Britain's manhood. As they moved up to their assembly areas they were in high spirits, eager to show their mettle.

Advance 18 pounder field gun, camouflaged, Western Front, c1916.   Contemporary photograph. 5303-31-172
Imperial War Museum

kers Mk I .303 machine gun c1914-1918. 7407-42
AF Enfield Lock

Tank F4 at Wailly, 21st October 1917. During special training at the Tank
Driving School in preparation for the Battle of Cambrai.

Siege Battery Royal Artillery at Bapaume, 1918.

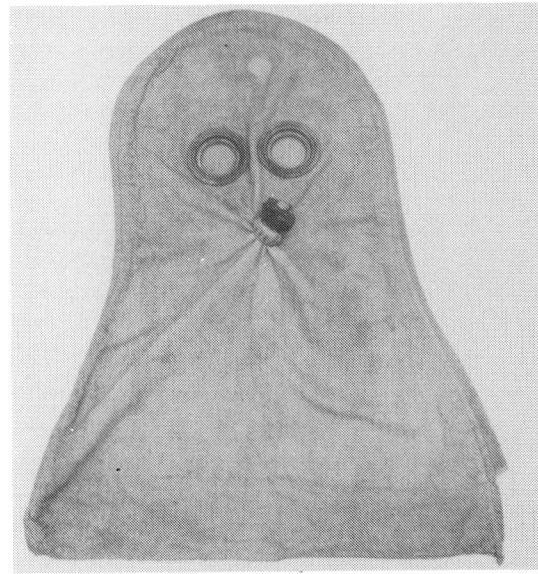

Gas mask c1916. London Irish Rifles Museum.

The Somme, a rolling terrain of chalk downland, had been a relatively peaceful sector of the front which had given the Germans ample opportunity to perfect their defences with deep trenches and dug-outs, villages and dominant features turned into strongpoints, and the whole system covered by thick belts of barbed wire. Moreover, on almost every part of the sector, the Germans held the high ground, with good observation into France, so that any attack would have to be made uphill and in full view. This advantage, coupled with poor British security and the long preliminary bombardment, left the Germans in no doubt that an attack was imminent.

As the sun came up on 1st July, giving promise of a blazing hot day, the bombardment grew to a terrible climax. At 7.30 a.m. the waiting infantry rose from their trenches and advanced at a slow walk with bayonets fixed, wave after wave of Britain's citizen army. Within minutes men began to fall in hundreds, soon in thousands, as the German machine-gunners, emerging deafened but unscathed from their deep dugouts, poured an unremitting stream of lead into the serried ranks of the attackers. Some fell as they emerged from their trenches, many more in No-Man's-Land, while the few who reached the German forward positions found the wire uncut by the bombardment. The scene observed by a battalion commander of the 36th (Ulster) Division attacking Thiépval was typical of the whole:

"I see rows upon rows of British soldiers lying dead, dying or wounded in No-Man's-Land. Here and there I see an officer urging on his followers. Occasionally I can see the hands thrown up and then a body flops on the ground. I perceive heaped up masses of British corpses suspended on the German wire in front of the Thiépval stronghold, while live men rush forward in orderly procession to swell the weight of numbers in the spider's web. I lose sight of the 10th (Royal Irish) Rifles and the human corn-stalks, falling before the Reaper".(8)

Thiépval, only some 400 yards from the Ulstermen's trenches and one of the first day's objectives, was not to fall until 27th September.

By the end of this dreadful day, despite heroic efforts by the raw, inexperienced soldiers, most of the Fourth Army were back in their trenches; only on the right had the 18th and 30th Divisions of the XIII Corps reached their objectives, having penetrated about a mile beyond the German front line, while to their left the 21st Division of the XV Corps had secured a narrow tongue of territory about half a mile deep. All else was failure and at the appalling cost of over 57,000 men, of whom nearly 20,000 had been killed. Never had a British Army suffered such losses in a single day. At Waterloo Wellington had held a frontage of about four miles with 34 British battalions and won a decisive victory at a cost of 7,000 killed and wounded. On 1st July 1916 29 battalions of the VIII Corps attacked on a similar frontage and lost 15,000 without gaining a single foothold in the German line. The failure was due partly to lack of any surprise, partly to the ineffectiveness of the bombardment, too high a proportion of the artillery being only 18-pounder field guns, but most of all to a lack of training and the rigid tactical formations imposed on the troops. The day was only redeemed by the unwavering courage and fortitude of these civilian soldiers who had picked up the torch from the old Regulars and who despite their punishing experience would continue to hold it high in the weeks that followed.

For there was to be no let up. The French were still locked in a death struggle at Verdun and since it was clear that no rapid break-through was possible on the Somme, Haig set himself to wear down the German strength by a process of attrition – keeping up a constant pressure but with only limited assaults. For 140 days fighting raged up and down the Fourth Army front as British, Canadians, Australians and South Africans struggled forward to gain a few yards and then steeled themselves to meet the inevitable German counter-attacks, both sides sustaining bloody losses. From Beaumont Hamel in the north, down through Thiépval, Pozières, High Wood, Deville Wood, to Guillemont in the south, the shattered, wasted ground was fought over time and time again. On 15th September the first tanks were put in to lead an attack by the III, XIV and XV Corps but of the 49 available, only 32 reached the start line and several of these broke down during the attack. Furthermore the surprise effect of these new weapons was greatly diminished by their being split up in twos and threes along the front instead of being used for one concentrated punch as recommended by their advocates. Though many, including the Germans, remained sceptical of the tank's value, Haig perceived their possibilities and urged that production should be increased.

In the meantime the attrition and the slaughter ground on as slowly the weary divisions pushed up on to the high ground until the early winter rains brought the great offensive to a close. In four and a half month's fighting the line had been pushed forward at best no more than seven miles, at worst about a mile, for a cost of 415,000 casualties. It had been *"the glory and graveyard of Kitchener's Army". (9)* Though territorial gains were slight, Haig's strategy of attrition had inflicted enormous casualties on the Germans. largely because of their policy of counter-attacking every British advance, and their fighting spirit was severely damaged. A German soldier wrote: *"Our losses are dreadful . . . . . this is almost unendurable. If only peace would come".(10)*

The disappointment caused by the failure of the Somme offensive to break through was to some degree mitigated by success against the Turks. After Townshend's surrender at Kut, his commander, Sir John Nixon,

Short Magazine Lee Enfield Mk III* c1914-1918

was replaced by General Maude. Having been reinforced from India to a strength of some 400,000, Maude went over to the offensive in December 1916, driving the Turks north-westwards from Kut and advancing on Baghdad. On 11th March 1917 his Territorial and Indian divisions entered the city and the greater part of Mesopotamia was firmly in British hands. Further west, General Murray drove the Turks from the Sinai Desert in 1916, thus securing the Canal, but two costly failures to overcome their strong defences at Gaza led to his replacement in April by Allenby, who was given an additional 100,000 men with orders to take Jerusalem by Christmas.

These troops were sorely needed on the Western Front in 1917 for although the army in France now totalled over 1,200,000 men forming 64 divisions, the brunt of the fighting from now on was to be borne chiefly by the British. Shattered by its losses at Verdun, the French Army's morale crumbled after a disastrous offensive in Champagne during May, after which serious mutinies broke out. Order was restored by General Pétain but a long period of recuperation would be needed before France's fighting ability was restored. Moreover, with Russia collapsing into revolution, everything now depended on Haig's capacity to keep the Germans occupied.

In April he had begun an offensive at Arras as a diversion for the French in Champagne. With greatly improved artillery support and less costly infantry tactics, considerable and worthwhile gains were made - notably the magnificent capture of the dominating Vimy Ridge by the Canadian Corps. But with the cavalry helpless against modern firepower and with insufficient tanks, the advances could not be exploited and the Germans were able to fall back to fresh positions. The collapse of the French offensive brought the battle at Arras to a close.

Haig now planned to make the major British thrust for 1917 in the region around Ypres with the ultimate aim of clearing northern Belgium and denying the German U-Boats the use of Ostend and Zeebrugge. As a preliminary, there occurred one of the most successful feats of arms yet seen on the Western Front: the capture of the Messines Ridge by General Plumer's Second Army to cover the right flank of the main offensive to follow. Messines was a masterpiece of careful planning and preparation and demonstrated what could be achieved by surprise, a principle of war hitherto accorded little recognition by the British command. At 3.10 a.m. on 7th June, 19 huge mines containing nearly a million pounds of explosive were detonated under the German trenches on the Ridge, the culmination of weeks of patient and perilous tunnelling by British sappers. Before the colossal noise of the explosion had died away, 12 British, Australian and New Zealand divisions advanced rapidly behind a rolling barrage fired from over 2,000 guns. By mid-afternoon all objectives had been captured and defences prepared, against which every German counter-attack failed totally.

The optimism inspired by this brilliant operation was sadly not to be fulfilled. The third Battle of Ypres opened on 31st July and was to last for three and a half terrible months, until it finally floundered to a halt in the quagmires that surrounded the remains of a Flemish village which has given its name to one of the most appalling episodes in the Army's long history – Passchendaele. Since Haig still pinned his faith to a prolonged, preliminary bombardment to pave the way for the infantry of Gough's newly-formed Fifth Army, the offensive was foredoomed. Not only was no surprised achieved, but the continual barrage played havoc with the complex drainage system of this low-lying country and, with the particularly heavy and almost unceasing rainfall of that summer, the terrain was soon impassable – *"a lunar landscape of shell-craters, one touching another, filled with water or sludgy clay that could almost wrench the boots off your feet".(11)* Yet week after week Haig, ever-mindful of the need to grip the Germans in battle, urged on the attacks with the endless bombardment from both sides churning the ground into an evermore impenetrable morass. The stoic infantry plodded forward in the teeming rain again and again. Those that were not drowned in the soggy acres of black mud and rain-filled shell-holes were mown down by the interlocking fire-zones of the German machine-guns, spewing out death from massive concrete bunkers sited in depth. Some progress was made when a brightening of the weather coincided with the handing over control of the battle to Plumer, but in October the rain came down again and all the brave endeavour dissolved in mud and blood. So removed were the high command from the troops' suffering that when General Kiggell, Haig's Chief of Staff, visited the front for the first time in November, he is supposed to have wept, crying *"To think that we asked men to fight in that!".(12)* Nothing worthwhile had been gained, the Germans still held the Belgian ports and though their troops had suffered grievously, both in casualties and morale, they could better afford such losses as they could now draw men from the Eastern Front where Russia was out of the war. As for the British soldiers, the horrors of Third Ypres, its nightmare battles and endless privations, had started to sap their spirits. No mutinies split their ranks, as in the French Army, and they continued to do their duty, no matter how awesome, but with conscripts increasly filling the depleted armies, the bright courage and infectious enthusiasm of Kitchener's volunteers were becoming as much things of the past as the stolid endurance and sardonic humour of the Regulars.

One ray of hope pierced the gloom that descended upon the closing months of 1917. On 20th November, at 6.20 a.m., a barrage of 1,000 guns suddenly burst forth upon part of the massively fortified Hindenburg Line, constructed by the Germans after the Somme battles. As soon as the guns opened fire, a mass of 378 tanks

rolled forward closely followed by eight divisions of Byng's Third Army, moving in files behind the protection of the armour. Leading the attack in person was Major-General Elles, commanding what was now known as the Royal Tank Corps. The Germans were taken completely by surprises as everywhere the tanks crushed the wire, shot up the machine-gun posts and rolled great wooden fascines into the trenches so that they could pass over. By the end of the day the Hindenburg Line in front of Cambrai had been overrun and the advance had penetrated to between three and four miles on a six-mile front, taking 6,000 prisoners and 100 guns, a greater penetration in one day than had been made in months on the Somme or at Ypres. After this startling success, however, the attack bogged down. The tank crews were exhausted, there were no reserves of tanks, and with the German reserves hurriedly coming forward, the two cavalry divisions which had been poised to exploit the break-through could achieve nothing. Indeed on the 30th the Germans put in a major counter-attack, recaptured most of the ground lost, and were only denied further gains by being brought to a halt by the Guards Division and the 2nd Tank Brigade. Notwithstanding the disappointing end to the Battle of Cambrai, the combination of surprise with the concentrated use of tanks had revealed a way of breaking the deadlock of trench warfare.

In Palestine, too, Allenby's fulfillment of his directive to capture Jerusalem by Christmas had demonstrated that subtlety was a better weapon than the bludgeon. With the reinforcements he had received giving him numerical superiority over the Turks, part of whose strength had been whittled away by the Arab revolt led by Colonel Lawrence, Allenby planned to break through the Turkish lines between Gaza on the coast and Beersheba, 30 miles to the south-east. By a series of ruses and a feint attack he deceived the Turks into thinking his main effort would be made against Gaza, thus forcing them to commit their reserves. Having then seized Beersheba by an encircling movement with his cavalry, he launched his decisive attack against the enemy's weakened centre and broke through, splitting the retreating Turks into two divergent groups and swinging right to capture Jerusalem, which he entered on 9th December.

After losing a number of his British formations due to a crisis on the Western Front in the spring of 1918, as will be seen later, Allenby was unable to resume the offensive until September, after he had been reinforced from India and Mesopotamia. He now intended not only to breach the Turkish line, which stretched from just north of Jaffa on the coast to the River Jordan, but to effect the total destruction of the Turkish armies by disrupting their supply line of the Hejaz railway from Damascus, knocking out their headquarters, and blocking their lines of retreat. Once again he brought the arts of deception into play to indicate preparations for an assault up the Jordan valley, while he secretly concentrated the mass of his infantry on the coastal flank with three cavalry divisions, Yeomanry, Australians and Indians, close behind. While Lawrence's Arabs blew up the railway in the Turkish rear and aircraft bombed headquarters and telephone exchange, the infantry put in their surprise attack on 19th September, rolling the Turks back north-eastwards from the coast towards the hilly interior, as though opening a door. Through the gap, led by armoured cars, poured the cavalry divisions, riding hard up the coast for 30 miles before swinging east at Megiddo to seize the passes across the Carmel range and block all the Turks' escape routes to the north. Only a few narrow paths eastwards down to the Jordan remained open but as the broken Turkish armies struggled down them they were bombed incessantly by British aircraft. While the enemy troops west of the Jordan were rounded up, the retreat east of the river of the only remaining Turkish army was constantly harassed in flank by the Arabs and finally headed off by Allenby's cavalry near Damascus, which fell on 1st October. On the 23rd the 5th Cavalry Division rode into Aleppo, 200 miles to the north. In a brilliant campaign marked by surprise, mobility and a skilful deployment of all arms, Allenby had routed the Turkish armies in Palestine, advanced 350 miles and taken 75,000 prisoners, all in just over a month for a loss of only 5,000 casualties – an achievement in every way different from the terrible slogging matches of the Western Front. Never again would horsed cavalry play such a decisive role in war and the Battle of Megiddo was a fitting close to a long and gallant epoch which had begun with the Ironsides of the New Model Army.

Turkey was now on her last legs. The final defeat of her army in Mesopotamia had taken place the day Aleppo fell. The surrender of Bulgaria, Germany's ally in the Balkans, to the Allied force which, since 1915, had maintained a precarious and unfruitful lodgement at Salonika in Macedonia and had at last taken the offensive in September 1918, now left that force free to menace Constantinople. On 30th October Turkey capitulated.

Despite these victories in the Near East, events on the Western Front in 1918 had proved beyond all doubt that the war could only be won by wearing down the German Army's will to fight in France and Flanders. German divisions had been pouring west and, although Russia's exit from the war had been balanced by America's entry in 1917, the latter's military build-up had been slow, and by early 1918 only four and a half divisions had arrived in France. They lacked training and equipment but each was larger than the British or French division which had had to be reduced from 12 battalions to nine†. By late January the German strength

† The 1918 type British division was in fact handier than the 1914 type, and with 36 Lewis guns instead of two Vickers machine-guns per battalion, plus brigade machine-gun and mortar companies, had much greater firepower.

had risen to 177 divisions with 30 more on the way, while the Allies' had fallen to an equivalent of 173, due to a shortage of French manpower and the despatch of an Allied force, including one British corps, to bolster the Italians after their collapse at Caporetto in 1917.

After the failures and losses of the previous year the Prime Minister, now Lloyd George, had conceived a growing dislike and distrust of Haig and his ally, Robertson. His ploys to reduce Haig's powers and subordinate him to the French had resulted in the replacement of Robertson as C.I.G.S. by a politically favoured general, Sir Henry Wilson, well known in the Army as a schemer and a man of proven poor judgement. Lloyd George was keen to sack Haig but, afraid to do so and unable to think of a successor, contented himself with removing his chief staff officers. More detrimental to the B.E.F.'s fighting strength was his decision to hold back in England 607,000 trained men, and to send Haig only 100,000 reinforcements instead of the 605,000 asked for. By this means Lloyd George deprived Haig of the ability to mount a spring offensive. To add to Haig's difficulties, he had agreed in December to take over an additional 30 miles of front between the Somme and the Oise from the French; at that time a German attack had seemed most likely east of Rheims against the French but by February 1918 all the indications were that it would fall on the British.

When it came, on 21st March, with a ferocity and power outclassing all previous offensives, 63 divisions hurled themselves against Haig's weakest sector, the 70 miles of front between Arras and the Oise held partly by the right of Byng's Third Army but chiefly by the 11 thinly spread divisions of Gough's Fifth. Preceded by only a short but intense bombardment and greatly aided by fog, the Germans achieved total surprise. Their attack was spearheaded by specially-trained assault troops, whose task was to infiltrate through weak points in the British lines prior to heading for the rear areas, while pockets of resistance were left for the follow-up formations to deal with. Many of Gough's battalions were overwhelmed in the opening minutes, others, though surrounded, fought on till they were overrun or their ammunition ran out. Further north Byng's men from better positions were able to put up a stiffer resistance, but by the 24th the Fifth Army, mostly survivors of Third Ypres, was on the verge of collapse, having fallen back 15 miles. Amiens, a vital railway junction, lay within reach of the leading German divisions and a gap was being driven between the British and French. In a time of crisis General Foch was appointed Supreme Commander to co-ordinate the Allied effort, but in the very speed and depth of the German advance lay the seeds of its own downfall. As Allied reserves were hurried to the threatened sector, the German momentum waned through exhaustion of their troops and supply difficulties, and by the beginning of April the offensive ground to a halt within nine miles of Amiens and 30 of the coast. The British troops had suffered 160,000 casualties and the battered Fifth Army was in some disarray after its struggle against overwhelming odds. Determined to a have a scapegoat, Lloyd George insisted on Gough's dismissal.

As the Allies drew breath, the Germans struck again on 9th April, this time on the Lys south of Ypres against Horne's First Army and the southern sector of Plumer's Second. Unfortunately the first blow fell on a part of the front held by a Portuguese division† which that very day was to be relieved by two British divisions but was meanwhile holding the whole corps front. Completely outmatched, the Portuguese gave way and the Germans swept through the gap heading for Hazebrouck, a rail centre crucial to the defence of Flanders only 13 miles away. The British divisions on either flank tried to contain the thrust with, to the south, some success, but northwards they too were stretched to hold their ground. By the evening of the 10th the enemy had broken through on an 18-mile front, their farthest advance having penetrated some seven miles. There were few reserves and things looked desperate. On the 12th Haig issued his famous Order of the Day: *"Every position must be held to the last man. With our backs to the wall and believing in the justice of our cause, each one of us must fight on to the end".(13)* And fight on they did, gradually slowing the German advance down, as reserves began to come up from the south to strengthen the depleted ranks. The 4th Guards Brigade halted the Germans within five miles of Hazebrouck and held them until supported by the Australians. Although the enemy continued to exert pressure on the northern half of the breach, under the calm and wise direction of Plumer this second great onslaught was brought to a standstill.

The British armies had suffered 240,000 casualties in resisting these attempts to knock them out but the Germans had lost 350,000. Furthermore, if the latter were to win, they had to do it before the Americans arrived in large numbers. Therefore at the end of May they tried again, this time against a quiet French sector on the Aisne where, by an ill-fated chance, the British IX Corps had been sent to rest after the battles on the Lys. In this attack the 2nd Devons of the 8th Division earned a citation in the French Orders of the Day and the Croix-de-Guerre by sacrificing themselves almost to a man in a gallant stand at Bois des Buttes, which gave time for fresh defences to be prepared in rear. The German attack actually reached the Marne, which had seen no fighting since 1914, but there it was stopped by the French and the first of the Americans. Once more the Germans came on, further east from Rheims on 15th July, but as the defence fell back before them, Foch's long-prepared counter-stroke burst against their right flank and drove them back almost to where their line had been in May.

---

† Portugal had entered the war on the Allied side in March 1916. Its troops had trained in Britain and the Portuguese Corps was under command of Horne's First Army.

Field Marshal the Earl Haig of Bemersyde, KT, BM.
Photogravure by Annan & Sons after the painting by Sir James
Guthrie.   5905-82

Field Marshal Lord Plumer. Portrait, oil on canvas, 1925.

Field Marshal Lord Allenby, 1921.   7005-40-1

General Lord Rawlinson of Trent. Portrait, oil on canvas, by
Oswald Birley, 1925.
                                              5201-32

The enemy were now in sore straits. Though they had inflicted heavy losses, they had nowhere achieved a significant break-through, their reserves were used up, their high casualties were affecting their morale and they were growing short of trained and experienced junior leaders. Above all they knew that thousands of fresh, eager Americans were now pouring across the Atlantic. Their fortunes were definitely on the wane and the initiative had passed to the Allies.

During the breathing space afforded to Haig by the battles on the French front, he had reconstituted his armies with reinforcements from the Near East, Italy and England and he had received fresh supplies of tanks, including a new light tank, the "whippet", capable of 8 m.p.h. in contrast to the 3 m.p.h. of the heavier models. On 8th August Rawlinson's Fourth Army once again attacked on the Somme where it had suffered so terribly two years before. This time complete surprise was achieved and headed by 500 tanks the Australian and Canadian Corps broke clean through the German line. 21,000 prisoners were taken and though the advance was slowed, then halted on the 12th, the moral, rather than the material defeat inflicted inspired Ludendorff, the German Chief of Staff, to call 8th August *"the black day of the German Army"*.

While the French and Americans began pounding away in the south, Haig launched a series of blows in the British sector. No sooner had the momentum of the Fourth Army's advance died down, than it was the turn of the Third Army to its north. By the beginning of September the Germans facing these two armies were back behind the Hindenburg Line from which they had mounted their spring offensive, a withdrawal which also forced them to pull back on the Lys, enabling the First and Fifth Armies to regain the ground lost in the April fighting. Although the Germans, particularly their machine-gunners and artillery, were still putting up a stubborn resistance, the quality of the bulk of their infantry was no longer what it was, the attrition battles of 1916-17 and the failure of the spring offensive having taken their toll. Haig's perception of this, and his conviction that, of the Allied forces, the British Army was most capable of a sustained offensive, enabled him to convince Foch that victory could be won in the autumn, rather than postponing the attempt until 1919. All the Allied armies were to combine in a simultaneous attack, from the Belgians and the Second Army in the north down to the Americans on the Argonne, the whole line exerting a concentric pressure on the great German salient bulging westwards between Ypres and Verdun; the main burden would fall on the British First, Third and Fourth Armies facing the heaviest weight of enemy troops holding the Hindenburg Line between Cambrai and St. Quentin, a formidable barrier of steel and concrete defences sited in depth and covered by copious belts of wire.

Between 27th September and 5th October, 35 British and Dominion divisions smashed through this intricate defence system, threw back a superior number of enemy formations, and took nearly as many prisoners as the three concurrent French, American and Belgian offensives achieved together. Coming after four years of terrible fighting on a scale no British army had ever endured before, in which the operations of 1918 alone had already cost 450,000 casualties, the breaking of the Hindenburg Line was an outstanding feat of arms and a superb demonstration of the British and Dominion soldiers' unshaken determination and fighting spirit, which amply justified Haig's confidence in them. If increased reliance for leading attacks was now being placed on the offensive capabilities of the Dominion troops, who man for man were of a higher calibre than the conscripts largely filling the British ranks,† it was nevertheless the 46th Division of North Midland Territorials which secured the most striking success of the break-through. Facing a sector where the German defences were strengthened by the St. Quentin canal flowing through a steep-sided cutting, the North and South Staffordshire battalions of the 137th Brigade swam or rafted their way across the obstacle under heavy fire, thus enabling the division to penetrate the enemy positions to a depth of three and a half miles, taking 4,200 prisoners and 70 guns for a loss of only 800 casualties. This magnificent feat cleared the right flank of the Australian Corps which advanced to widen the breach and shatter the main enemy defences.

After a week's fighting the whole Hindenburg Line, which had taken two years to complete, was in British hands, open country lay beyond, and the Germans opened negotiations for an armistice. Though a month of often heavy fighting still remained, the Germans were falling back all along the Western Front and soon the British armies were advancing in country that had seen no action since 1914. On the day the armistice was signed, 11th November, the Canadian Corps entered Mons where the original B.E.F. had begun the war four long years before.

At the end of the Great War – surely a more appropriate nomenclature than the more prosaic World War I now in common usage – the British Army that had finally won through to victory was a very different force from its predecessor of 1914. On the outbreak of war there had been 750,000 Regular, Special Reserve and Territorial soldiers available for service, exclusive of the Indian and Dominion armies. Between 1914-18 4,971,000 men had enlisted of which three million were volunteers. The B.E.F. in France had grown from the original one cavalry and four infantry divisions to three cavalry and 51 infantry divisions, to which the Dominions added another ten divisions; a further 18 divisions, all British, were in Italy, the Near and Middle East, India and at home. The titanic struggle had drawn men from all walks of life into its ranks so that for the first time in

---

† The Canadian Army was recruited by a system of selective call-up; Australia and New Zealand still relied on volunteers.

its history the Army was representative of British society as a whole. Men who before the war would never have considered applying for a commission — or indeed been thought suitable to hold one — found themselves commanding platoons, companies, battalions, even brigades. The county regiments had risen to an unprecedented number of battalions, the Royal Fusiliers for example having 26, and new regiments had appeared in the Army List: the Welsh Guards, formed in 1915 to complete the national representation in the Brigade of Guards; the Royal Tank Corps and the Machine Gun Corps, the latter disbanded after the war, which had both made the highest contribution to victory and the formation of the Women's Auxiliary Army Corps . . . . . more active duties. The formation of the Royal Corps of Signals in 1920 reflected the plethora of communications modern war required. The dominant role of artillery and the need for heavy guns of larger calibres than any ever used before had seen a great expansion of the Royal Artillery, while the siege nature of most operations had demanded a similar growth in the Royal Engineers. The increases in the Royal Army Medical Corps, the Army Service Corps, the Army Ordnance Corps (both granted the Royal title after the war) and other administrative services to cope with the scale and complexity of the fighting had resulted in there being more men in the rear areas than in the front line. Nevertheless the essential support they had provided for the fighting troops had made a vital contribution to victory and naver had a British field army had such comprehensive and effective logistic backing.

When the war ended over 700,000 of one of the finest generations Britain has ever produced were dead and more than another two million had been wounded, many of them maimed for life.† Their sacrifice and the heroic endurance of the survivors had not only helped save Europe from German militarism but had ensured that the prestige of the British soldier, whether Regular, Volunteer or Conscript, together with that of his Dominion and Indian comrades, stood high, perhaps highest, among all combatant nations. For this, much credit must be given to the British supreme commander on the Western Front, Field-Marshal Sir Douglas Haig. This stubborn and unimaginative man was to be remembered chiefly in the post-war era for the butcher's bill of the Somme and Passchendaele. Yet, unshaken by the responsibilities of four unbroken years in high command and undeterred by intrigues against him, his strong self-discipline, invincible self-confidence and iron resolution had never faltered, even at the darkest hours of the war. A shadowy and remote figure to his men and embarassingly inarticulate in their presence*, his prestige and determination had nevertheless held them together through defeat and the critical days of Spring 1918 so that they could ultimately advance to a great and final victory. In his apparent coldness and lack of feeling for his men he seems to parallel Wellington but, unlike the Great Duke, he was to devote the rest of his life to the welfare of those who had served him. Though never possessed of the spark of genius that makes a great general, Haig's untiring endeavours brought the Army through the most testing ordeal it has ever faced.

---

† The total casualties of the armies of the British Empire was 3,190,235 of which 908,371 were fatal.

* When presenting prizes to the winning team in a cross-country race, he congratulated them with the words *"You have run well. I hope you will run as well in the presence of the enemy".(14)*

Sanctuary Wood, Western Front, 1917.   7606-56-44

CHAPTER 20
PROPER SOLDIERING AGAIN
1919 – 1939

At the end of the Great War Britain for the first time had an army that was similar to those maintained by most major powers since the previous century: a force recruited by conscription and organized for war on a massive scale which involved the whole nation. By September 1920 most of this had changed. Conscription was ended, the wartime soldiers were demobilised, the great formations of corps and armies disappeared and the service battalions formed during the war disbanded. The Army shrank in strength from some four million to a quarter of a million. Officers and men returned to what the pre-war Regulars called "proper soldiering": the old-established round of regimental life with its alternating cycle of home and foreign service, its ranks filled once more by voluntary enlistment and its social content reverting to the pattern of the past – the soldiers drawn largely from the unemployed and poorest classes, the officers from the public schools. It was more than a return to 1914 for then the Army had been preparing itself for a European conflict. From 1919 the Government laid down that all defence planning was to be based on the assumption that there would be no major war for ten years and thus the Army's 'raison d'être' became what it had been in the late Victorian era, the policing of the Empire. Before this time-honoured state of affairs could be fully resumed, there were a number of hang-overs from the war years to be dealt with, one of which required a sizeable deployment of troops within the British Isles.

The centuries-old struggle by Irish nationalists for independence had again erupted at Easter 1916 with an armed uprising in Dublin. The German support on which the republicans, or Irish Volunteers, had counted was not forthcoming, the rising was bungled and within five days British troops had restored order. However, although the rebellion had received little mass support at the time, the subsequent execution of the rebel leaders generated a great wave of sympathy and anger in Catholic Ireland. The General Election of 1918 saw the return of many nationalist, or Sinn Fein, M.Ps. for Irish constituencies, who refused to take their seats at Westminster and set up their own parliament in Dublin, declaring an independent Irish republic. In January 1919 the revived Irish Volunteers, now renamed the Irish Republican Army, began a guerilla war against the Royal Irish Constabulary, attacking police barracks, ambushing their patrols and murdering loyalist sympathisers. British troops were put in to support the police and many a man who had survived the Western Front now met his end from an I.R.A. bullet in the back as they patrolled, raided and searched for arms and rebels. It was a type of war for which the troops, most of whom were very young and only recently enlisted, were quite untrained, but gradually, often by harsh experience, they learned the skills of counter-guerilla operations. It was an unpleasant and bitter campaign which lasted until a truce was arranged in July 1921. Ireland, with exception of the six Protestant counties in the north, was granted self-governing Dominion status within the Empire as the Irish Free State. British troops prepared to evacuate southern Ireland, handing over their barracks to the new Irish Army whom they were to see, in the civil war which immediately followed, chastise the still rebellious I.R.A. with far greater severity and harshness than they had ever been allowed to exert. By the end of 1922 the large garrison that the Army had maintained in Ireland for over 200 years was no more.

After the Armistice in 1918 a British army of occupation was stationed in Germany on the Rhine around Cologne until 1926, after which it was reduced and transferred to Wiesbaden where it remained until 1929. Smaller contingents were sent to supervise plebiscites in disputed areas arising out of the re-drawn frontiers decided at the Treaty of Versailles; the final such plebiscite occurred in 1934 when 1,500 British soldiers policed the voting in the Saar Valley. The last British troops to see action in the immediate aftermath of the Great War were those which had been sent to north and south Russia after the 1917 collapse to try and re-constitute some sort of anti-German front with elements hostile to the revolution. When these elements, or "White" Russians, became embroiled with the Bolsheviks, the British forces were involved in the fighting but all were withdrawn in 1919. The vacuum left in Iraq by the downfall of the Turkish Empire was filled by a British mandate against which the Arabs revolted in 1920, an uprising which took 60,000 British and Indian troops five months to subdue. A renewal of hostilities with Turkey almost occurred in 1922, when forces of Kemal Attaturk's new

Turkey, which had been driving the Greeks from territory the latter had been awarded in Asia Minor, confronted a small British force under General Harington holding the crossing to the Gallipoli Peninsula at Chanak. Fortunately naval and military reinforcements reached Harington before shots were exchanged and a difficult situation was resolved by negotiation.

Apart from dealing with these smouldering embers of the Treaty of Versailles and acting in support of the civil power in the unsettled industrial areas of the United Kingdom, a task the Army at home was compelled to undertake until the country settled down after the General Strike in 1926, the post-war British soldier resumed his old role of imperial policeman, above all in India. Nearly a million and a half Indian soldiers had served with devotion and loyalty in the war, not only in France and the Near and Middle East, but also against German colonies in Africa and China; others had remained in India to keep the peace on the still turbulent North-West Frontier and maintain internal security within the sub-continent. In India they had been supported by British Territorial battalions sent out on the outbreak of war to release Regulars for active service. The rising tide of Indian nationalism, most prevalent in the towns and among the educated middle classes, had remained quiescent during the war in the hope that, when peace came, the Indian Army's contribution to victory would be recognized by the grant of Dominion status for India. Although in 1918 measures were introduced to associate Indians more closely with certain areas of administration, nothing approaching self-government materialized and, in the absence of any likelihood of it so doing in the near future, discontent fermented by the nationalists broke out into serious rioting in the cities in 1919. Troops had to be used to restore order, sometimes with more force than was either desirable or necessary, notably at Amritsar where General Dyer ordered a detachment of Gurkhas to fire on a crowd, of which 379 were killed and 1,200 wounded. Far from teaching the nationalists a lesson as Dyer intended, this incident merely served to increase hostility between government and governed. Rioting diminished but in 1921 Mahatma Gandhi began his campaign of, first, non-co-operation and then civil disobedience.

The Indian Army remained hardly affected by political agitation; this was largely due to the sepoy's faith in his British officers and his strong loyalty to his regiment. This was highly creditable to him and indeed most fortunate because, concurrent with the internal unrest, there was serious work to be done on the Frontier. In May 1919 the newly-crowned Amir Amanullah of Afghanistan sought to consolidate his position and prestige in the eyes of his unruly people by an invasion of India, which he believed was too war-weary to resist effectively. Thus began the Third Afghan War. Most of the British troops available were Territorials eagerly awaiting repatriation for demobilisation and whose morale at the prospect of a frontier campaign was less than high, while the Indian Army was also suffering from the strains of the Great War. Furthermore there was a shortage of artillery and machine-guns, and the irregular levies who garrisoned the advance posts proved unreliable. Nevertheless a division from Peshawar managed to check a superior force of Afghan regulars backed by swarms of tribesmen in the Khyber Pass and forced them to retire on Jellalabad; a success which greatly improved the troops' morale. Plans for a counter-offensive were delayed by tribal raids against the communications back to Peshawar and then further interrupted by news of the main Afghan attack southwards in the Tochi-Kurram area. The Waziristan Militia manning the outposts mutinied and went over to the enemy, forcing the abandonment of all the forward positions and the concentration of the only available Regular troops in the vicinity – two battalions of Sikhs and Gurkhas and a squadron of cavalry – at Thal, covering the entrance to the Kurram Valley, where they were soon closely invested by a large Afghan force. Though under constant attack, they held out from 26th May until 1st June when a relief force from Peshawar under General Dyer, already under a cloud for the Amritsar riots, attacked and routed the besieging forces. Realising that he had underestimated the British powers of resistance, the Amir asked for an armistice which was granted.

The Afghan troops withdrew but hostile tribal activity continued for several months, particularly in Waziristan, where the tenacious resistance of the dissidents was fiercest and continued long after other tribal areas had been pacified. Several reverses were inflicted on the British and Indian troops and not until March 1924 was an uneasy peace imposed on the territory. The country was opened up with metalled roads and a permanent garrison established at Razmak in the heart of Waziristan, consisting of one British and five Indian battalions with supporting arms and services. From here and other frontier garrisons, columns could be rapidly assembled to march out and nip trouble in the bud. There was always trouble in this territory but it rose to a height between 1936-38 when the activities of a notorious malcontent, the Faqir of Ipi, involved the Razmak and Bannu brigades on almost constant operations which, despite the use of modern artillery, armoured cars, machine-guns and aircraft, had not changed greatly since the previous century. As had always been the case, this tribal warfare taught the British and Indian soldiers how to march, shoot and live under active service conditions, skills which were difficult to acquire anywhere else during this period.

The Indian Army had gone through the Great War on the organization instituted by Lord Kitchener in 1903†. Between 1921-22 36 of the Indian cavalry regiments were amalgamated in pairs, a loss of individual regimental identity avoided by only three regiments: the Guides Cavalry and the two oldest, the 27th and 28th Light Cavalry (formerly the 2nd and 3rd Madras Lancers) raised in 1784, but even these two had to change their numbers to 16th and 7th respectively, while the Guides were numbered 10th. Thus from the 39 regiments pre-war, the Indian cavalry had shrunk to 21 regiments, ranging in seniority from Skinner's Horse (1st Duke of York's Own) to the Central India Horse (21st King George V's Own). The pre-war single-battalion infantry regiments had raised second battalions during the war, some even having third and fourth battalions, but maintaining them at war strength had posed many problems, particularly when companies were composed of different classes — Sikhs, Punjabi Mussulmans, Rajputs, Dogras and so on. This led to a complete re-organization of the Indian infantry in 1922, with the aim of building a system of recruitment and reinforcement that could withstand the pressures of war without sacrificing the traditions of the old regiments. Most, but not all of the wartime battalions were disbanded after 1918, so that the majority of regiments had reverted to a single battalion. The new system involved the grouping together, usually in sixes, of regiments with similar traditions and class composition into 20 large regiments in each of which five of the former regiments became active battalions while the sixth formed a depot battalion to train and supply recruits to the other five. Thus, for example, the 14th, 15th, 45th, 36th, 47th and 35th Sikhs of the 1903 designations became the 1st-5th and 10th (Training) Battalions of the 11th Sikh Regiment. Even the Guides Infantry, which hitherto had always remained un-numbered, were drawn into the new system, their first battalion becoming the 5th of the 12th Frontier Force Regiment and their second the 10th of the same.* In the event of any future wartime expansion, each of the 20 regiments could raise additional battalions numbered between 6th and 9th while the expanded 10th Battalions would continue to supply reinforcements. The ten two-battalion regiments of Gurkha Rifles remained outside this system. It is a sad commentary on the decline of the once-proud Madras Army of the old East India Company that there now remained only one Madras regiment, the 3rd, among the 20 new ones and even that was disbanded by 1928; however several battalions of the six Punjab regiments could trace their ancestry to the old Madras Native Infantry of the days of Clive and Stringer Lawrence.

A major innovation in the Indian Army after the Great War was the decision to open the King's Commission to young Indians who would be trained exactly as their British counterparts at Sandhurst. There had of course been Indian officers for years, the subadars and jemadars, but these were all men risen from the ranks, receiving their commissions from the Viceroy. It was intended that the career of a King's Commissioned Indian officer should parallel that of a British second-lieutenant in a British regiment. This decision was followed in 1923 by a further scheme for the very gradual "Indianization" of all Indian units, beginning with eight regiments and, depending on its success, later spreading to others; since it would take about 25 years for the first King's Commissioned Indian officers to reach lieutenant-colonel, the process would be extremely lengthy. Both schemes were hedged about with difficulties and objections from British and Indian sources alike†, and the failure rate of Indian cadets at Sandhurst proved embarassingly high. To remedy this slow and unsatisfactory progress, a committee, largely composed of eminent Indians, was set up, as a result of which, in 1933, the Indian Military Academy was established at Dehra Dun to train potential Indian officers on a three-year course, and the Indianization scheme was expanded to cover more regiments. The I.M.A. proved highly successful and by 1938 was turning out 56 Indian officers a year.

Outside India the Army had other policing tasks in the twenties and thirties. In 1927 the large British and European population of the International Settlement at Shanghai was threatened by the civil war in China and a British division of two brigades from home and one from India was hurriedly despatched to garrison it. Its opportune arrival forestalled any trouble and by the end of the year most of the division had been withdrawn. Nearer home, the growth of nationalism in Egypt had resulted in sporadic violence and rioting from 1919 onwards which Allenby, now the High Commissioner, quelled effectively by the deployment of mobile columns. In 1922 Egypt was recognized as an independent sovereign state but a British garrison remained to ensure the external defence of the country, particularly of the Suez Canal, and the protection of European nationals. Britain retained control of the Soudan and this, together with the continued British presence in Egypt, caused increasing resentment among the Egyptians, leading to a mutiny of their troops in the Soudan. A dangerous situation faced the single British battalion in the country but the arrival of another permitted the disarming of the mutineers to be carried out without further trouble. Thereafter all the Egyptian troops and officials were evacuated from the Soudan, the government being completely taken over by the British and the garrison fixed

---

† See Chapter 18.

* The 1st-4th Battalions being formerly the 51st-54th Sikhs (all Frontier Force). Since each had formerly been junior to the Guides, the latter took precedence on parade.

+ See Philip Mason, "A Matter of Honour"(1974)pp.453-466

The 1st Bn Northamptonshire Regiment, the last British troops to leave Southern Ireland, marching from Phoenix Park through Dublin to embark for England, 15th December, 1922.

Highlanders on guard in Shanghai, 1927.   7112-30-70

Medium tanks on manoeuvres c1930.   6112-362-1

at two British battalions. The Soudanese units of the Egyptian Army, whose forbears had given such good service in Kitchener's 1898 campaign, were re-constituted under British command as the Soudan Defence Force.

In addition to its defensive role in Egypt, the British garrison also formed the strategic reserve for the Near and Middle East. After the war the policing of many areas of British responsibility, notably the protectorates in Palestine and Iraq, had been allotted to the Royal Air Force but occasions arose when ground troops were essential, often in a hurry. Up to the 1930s the conveyance of troops, whether for routine movement or to meet an emergency, had always been by ship, but the growth of the Royal Air Force now permitted a speedier means. In October 1931 an outbreak of pro-Greek rioting in Cyprus had been quelled by the swift arrival of a company of the King's Regiment flown from Egypt. Today the movement of troops by air is commonplace but in the early thirties it was a novelty, and when a complete battalion was put in the air in 1932 it created a considerable impression internationally. In Iraq the R.A.F. airfields were defended by a local force under British officers called the Iraq Levies whose rank and file were Assyrians, from a tribe whose leaders were at odds with the recently formed Iraqi national government. Alarmed by the possibility of mutiny among the Iraq Levies and the consequent danger to his airfields, the R.A.F. commander in Iraq asked for military assistance from Egypt. Between 22nd-28th June the whole of the 1st Northamptons were flown from Ismailia in nine Vickers Victoria aircraft and deployed to the threatened areas in Iraq where they disarmed the Levies and took over guards on the airfields. The sudden appearance of a complete battalion, literally "out of the blue" ensured a rapid calming down of a potentially explosive situation, much as in the previous century the mere sight of a British warship anchoring off a trouble spot had been enough to restore order.

The Northamptons had only recently arrived in Egypt from Palestine where, from 1929, the growing disturbances between Jews and Arabs, following the Balfour Declaration setting up a Jewish national home in the country, had required a sizeable deployment of troops to maintain the peace, since rioting, and the guerilla warfare and terrorism which followed, were beyond the capacity of the Royal Air Force. The Army found itself facing a warlike situation not dissimilar to that which it had encountered in Ireland a decade before — ambushes, bombings, assassinations — against which counter-insurgency techniques had to be quickly developed, but their effect was frequently hampered by political considerations. Some measure of order was restored but the impossibility of reconciling the Jewish and Arab points of view ensured it was only temporary. In 1937 an Arab uprising of even greater ferocity broke out which required the deployment of a complete division in Palestine. While politicians and officials endeavoured to devise a settlement, the troops and police persevered with their thankless task of internal security, until the whole intractable problem became overshadowed by events in Europe.

For the Army at home the twenties and thirties were a difficult and makeshift period of reductions, financial neglect and consequent shortages of men and material imposed by the "ten-year rule" mentioned above and the generally pacifistic climate of the country which was nurtured by the fond belief that the Great War had been "the war to end wars" and by the trust placed in disarmament and the League of Nations. No sooner had the Army reverted to being an all-Regular force after general demobilisation than further reductions were inflicted upon it. In 1922 the three regiments of Household Cavalry were reduced to two by the amalgamation of the 1st and 2nd Life Guards, and the Cavalry of the Line shrank from 28 regiments to 20 by the amalgamation of 16 regiments . Certain infantry regiments, which pre-1914 had had four Regular battalions, were reduced to two in common with the remainder and, following the setting-up of the Irish Free State, five of the Irish regiments were disbanded: the Royal Irish, which had first seen action under William III; that great fighting regiment of the Peninsula War, the Connaught Rangers; the Leinsters, raised in Canada as the 100th Foot as an expression of loyalty during the Indian Mutiny; and those valiant descendants of the old East India Company's Europeans, the Royal Munster and Royal Dublin Fusiliers. The Royal Irish Rifles were re-christened Royal Ulster Rifles which, with the Irish Guards, the Royal Inniskilling and Royal Irish Fusiliers now remained as the only infantry representatives of their country, although Irishmen from north and south continued to enlist in the Army as they had always done. The Irish cavalry regiments suffered amalgamation but not disbandment.

Such money as the Government was prepared to spend on defence going largely to the other two Services, the Army found itself starved of equipment and since the many overseas commitments required the foreign service battalions to be kept up to strength, those at home dwindled to little more than drafting units. On manoeuvres certain weapons had to be represented by flags and other devices, while bodies of troops could only be indicated on occasions by a length of tape held between two men. Furthermore the Army's victory in 1918 had bred a complacency and reluctance to change among the higher ranks which, owing to the bottleneck in promotion caused by the reduction of the Army, continued to be filled by senior veterans of the Great War, each growing older and more set in his ways as the war years receded into the past.

† 3rd and 6th, 4th and 7th Dragoon Guards; 5th Dragoon Guards and 6th Dragoons; 13th and 18th, 14th and 20th, 15th and 19th Hussars; 16th and 5th Lancers (the 16th taking seniority as the 5th had been disbanded from 1799-1861), 17th and 21st Lancers.

British troops fighting off an ambush on their convoy, Palestine, c1935.

Mountain artillery in action during the Mohman Expedition, NW Frontier, 1935.   6006-123-1-60

A machine gun picquet of the 3rd Gurkha Rifles, NW Frontier of India, 1937.

Although there was little the Army's senior officers could do to wean government and the electorate from their indifference to the Army's needs, their conservatism contributed to the delay of its modernization. Above all this manifested itself in the question of mechanization and, in particular, the tank. This battle-winning weapon had been pioneered by the British and after the war a group of forward-thinking officers began to consider a new type of mobile warfare, quite different from the static siege operations of the Western Front, based on the German infiltration tactics of 1918 but using mechanized and armoured formations, of which the tank would be the central feature, supported by aircraft. This group found expression in the powerfully-argued writings of Colonel J. F. C. Fuller and Captain B. H. Liddell Hart, who at first tried to instigate reform from within the Army. But, if tanks and motor vehicles were the weapons of the future, then clearly the horse had had its day, a sentiment repugnant to the senior officers who were cavalrymen as well as to many of their juniors in all branches of the service, for whom the horse was an intrinsic part of their military and social lives. Speaking in 1925, Earl Haig voiced the thoughts of many when he said: *"I am all for using tanks and aeroplanes but they are only accessories to the men and the horse, and I feel sure as time goes on you will find as much use for the horse as you have done in the past".(1)* Nevertheless the War Office did not entirely close its mind to new ideas. The Royal Tank Corps was still in existence, albeit only five battalions strong; plans were afoot to convert the 11th Hussars and 12th Lancers to armoured cars, the first cavalry regiments to lose their horses; and in 1927 an "Experimental Mechanized Force" was formed on Salisbury Plain – only to be disbanded a year later. In the late twenties and early thirties this was to be the pattern – for every step forward, a step back – with everything hampered by governmental limitations on expenditure.

In 1933 Adolf Hitler's Nazi Party came to power in Germany and embarked on a rapid expansion and modernization of the small army that had been allowed to Germany under the Treaty of Versailles. By this time Fuller and Liddell Hart had left the Army but continued to argue their case publicly in books, newspapers and periodicals. Their teachings were eagerly seized on in Germany where by 1935 the first three armoured, or 'panzer', divisions had been formed. The year before Britain had at last acquired its first permanent armoured formation, the 1st Tank Brigade. This was followed by the mechanization of the 2nd Cavalry Brigade whose three regiments† exchanged their horses for tanks but only of the lightest kind and armed only with machine-guns. This formation, together with another cavalry brigade similarly equipped, formed the Experimental Mobile Division with, attached to each brigade, a new type of mounted infantry, the motor battalion, a role appropriately given to the 1st Rifle Brigade and 2nd King's Royal Rifle Corps. In 1938 it was re-designated the 1st Armoured Division; however in armament and in armour its capabilities were greatly inferior to its German counterparts. Still, this was some progress and alongside it there were further improvements in the shape of the gradual substitution of mechanical transport for the horse variety in the Royal Artillery, Royal Engineers, the Infantry and the Services; wireless was replacing older methods of communication; the Lewis gun was being superseded by a new light machine-gun of Czechoslovak design, the Bren; and certain infantry regiments were being converted to machine-gun battalions armed with the old but proven Vickers gun.

The gradual rearmament and modernization since 1934 was given a fresh impetus when Mr. Hore-Belisha was made Secretary for War in 1937; this was accelerated by the Munich crisis over Czechslovakia in 1938, by which time the obviously aggressive intentions of the Axis powers, Germany, Italy and Japan, were making another war a real possibility. Hore-Belisha was instructed to make *"drastic changes"* by the Prime Minister, Neville Chamberlain, who was shocked by *"the obstinacy of some of the Army heads in sticking to obsolete methods".(2)* He instituted a number of improvements to conditions of service in an attempt to stimulate recruiting and appointed younger officers to the Army Council. With more progressive minds at the head of the Army some advance was made in the mechanization programme and the building up of the anti-aircraft defences - increasingly important in view of the growing strength of the German Air Force — but, obstructed by the conservatism and caution with which the stagnation of the previous decade had infected even the more progressive elements in the Army, these belated attempts at modernization fell far short of what the needs of the international situation required.

Furthermore there was still controversy about the tank and its tactical employment. Unlike the German armoured divisions, fast-moving formations of all arms designed for deep penetration on the lines advocated by Fuller and Liddell Hart, British armour was evolving into two distinct types: slow-moving and heavily-armoured tank brigades to co-operate with infantry divisions in the pattern of the Great War and the fast, lightly-armoured but, compared with the German machines, under-gunned cruiser and light tanks with which the armoured divisions were to be equipped for tank warfare. By 1939 there was still only one armoured division, not yet fully operational, which, with four infantry divisions, was earmarked as a new British Expeditionary Force for France; a second was in the planning stage, and a third, also not yet fully equipped, was in the Middle East with another two infantry divisions.

---

† Queen's Bays, 9th Lancers and 10th Hussars.

Vickers Limited

After the Munich crisis the Territorial Army† had been re-organized to provide one armoured, three motorized and nine infantry divisions. It also took on responsibility for the anti-aircraft defence of the country and numbers of Yeomanry regiments and infantry battalions were converted to units of the Royal Artillery and Royal Engineers (searchlights). By March 1939 it was clear that this force would be too small for the war that now seemed inevitable and all existing Territorial units were duplicated so as to provide a total of 26 divisions. Shortly afterwards it was announced that from July all men aged 20 would be conscripted for six months training with the Regular Army, followed by three and a half years with the Territorials. These conscripts, the first ever in peacetime, were dignified by the ancient name of "Militiamen".

Thus, as Europe moved towards its second great conflict 20 years after the last had ended, the Army presented a changed aspect from its predecessors in 1914. The horse had vitually disappeared from its ranks; it had an armoured force, albeit a slender one with tanks whose design and performance left much to be desired; the field artillery had a new gun, the 25-pounder; anti-tank weapons were coming into production for the artillery and infantry; and its supporting services were now motorised. Even the drill had been simplified, men parading in threes instead of fours, new personal equipment was being issued, and a novel uniform had been devised. Known as "battle dress", this was a capacious costume with concealed buttons, many pockets and an unfortunate short blouse top which tended to leave an uncomfortable gap at waist level; though presumably well-intentioned it was without doubt the most unsoldierly garb ever inflicted on the Army.*

Despite all these innovations, the B.E.F. that went to France after the outbreak of hostilities on 3rd September 1939 was, in its readiness for war, a feeble instrument when measured against the magnificent divisions of 1914. Whereas the latter had been ten years in the making, the former was the product of two years' hurried, confused and often inadequate modernization. A bitter price was soon to be exacted for the stagnation and lost opportunities of the inter-war years, for which some blame lay at the Army's door but more attached, as so often in past wars, to politicians and public for their neglect of and lack of interest in the Army's needs in peacetime.

---

† Its title had been changed from Territorial Force in 1920.

* As headdress, the old undress field service cap of the late 1890s was resurrected in a khaki version. This had an unfortunate tendency to fall off, particularly when worn perched over the right ear in the manner affected by wartime soldiers.

Territorial Army 1938, men of the 23rd London Armoured Car Company (Sharpshooters) receiving orders.

CHAPTER 21
THE GREATEST FEATS OF ARMS
1939 – 1945

The opening months of hostilities in 1939 were in marked contrast to those of 1914. Instead of the astonishing scenes of patriotic fervour with long queues of eager volunteers at the recruiting offices, Britain took up the challenge in a mood of grim necessity and, with conscription instituted at the outset, men of military age now waited to be called up. Far from being plunged immediately into heavy fighting, the B.E.F. that sailed to France found itself constructing field defences along the Belgian border in continuation of the Maginot Line which guarded France's frontier with Germany. With the solitary armoured division held back in England, the B.E.F., under the command of General Lord Gort, V.C., consisted initially only of four infantry divisions, each of three-battalion brigades, divisional field and anti-tank artillery, and a cavalry regiment equipped with light tanks and Bren-gun carriers. Two divisions formed a corps which had additional field, medium and anti-aircraft guns, plus a machine-gun battalion. During the seven quiet months of the so-called "phoney war" the B.E.F. was built up to ten infantry divisions organized into three corps and one army tank brigade with its heavy "Matilda" tanks, designed for co-operation with infantry.

The extraordinary peaceful opening to the war was shattered by the German onslaughts against Denmark and Norway in April 1940, followed a month later by their invasion of the Low Countries. The first British troops into action were a hurriedly organized and ill-equipped force of three Territorial brigades landed in southern and central Norway in mid-April but, under-trained and without air support, they were completely outmatched and had to be withdrawn just over a fortnight later. In the north, around Narvik, the 24th Guards Brigade with French and Polish troops held out longer but they too had to be evacuated in early June.

The new German method of waging war with fast-moving armoured divisions supported by aircraft conquered Holland, Belgium and France in the short space of six weeks. While part of their invading forces kept up a continual pressure against the B.E.F. and the northern French armies, which had advanced into Belgium to meet the offensive on the River Dyle, their main thrust surged out of the Ardennes with paralyzing speed and broke through to the coast at Abbeville in ten days, splitting the Allies apart. The B.E.F. retreated behind the Scheldt with their backs to the sea and, as the Germans swung north from Abbeville towards Boulogne and Calais, were soon under increasing pressure from three sides. A successful counter-stroke by the 1st Tank Brigade halted a German armoured division, but by 27th May the outlook was so grim that Lord Gort was ordered to evacuate what he could of the B.E.F. through Dunkirk. That some 225,000 British troops were got away safely from Dunkirk was due largely to the Royal Navy and Royal Air Force, but much credit was also due to a magnificent delaying action at Calais by the 2nd King's Royal Rifle Corps, 1st Rifle Brigade and the Territorials of the Queen Victoria's Rifles. Their sacrifice deprived Britain's only armoured division, which had never left England, of its highly-trained motor battalions. By 4th June the B.E.F., defeated but with its discipline still intact, was safely back in England; all its heavy equipment had been lost but at least its trained men had survived to form a nucleus around which new forces could be built.

In the summer of 1940 Britain and the Empire, under the leadership of Winston Churchill, stood alone against a victorious Germany whose 150 divisions occupying the whole of western Europe posed an invasion threat the like of which had not been faced since the Napoleonic Wars. In the British Isles there were only 15 under-equipped divisions, only one of which was armoured, supplemented by the middle-aged and elderly volunteers of the Home Guard, raised like the Volunteers of the 1790s for local defence. While the Royal Air Force, aided by the men and women of Anti-Aircraft Command, fought their great battle against the German 'Luftwaffe's' attempt to gain air superiority for the projected invasion, the Army prepared to defend the home country, at the same time reorganizing and re-training for future operations. While fresh divisions were formed and equipped, partly from British factories now on full war production and partly from the United States, Churchill ordered the raising of special forces known as "Commandos", after the highly mobile Boer units of the South African War, for offensive raiding attacks against the enemy coastline. In emulation of the German paratroops, which had proved so successful in Holland, a start was made in forming Britain's own Airborne

Anti-Aircraft gun in a London park, 1939.

7605-31-8

General Sir Alan Brooke, later Lord Alanbrooke, 1940.

Field-Marshal Earl Wavell, 1945.

6305-46-1

6710-87

Field-Marshal Sir Claude Auchinleck. Painting, oil on canvas, by Edward Seago, 1964.

Field-Marshal Earl Alexander of Tunis c1943. Imperial War Museum.

7901-13

Field-Marshal Lord Montgomery. Painting, oil on canvas, by Margaret Grose, 1946.

6705-79

Field-Marshal Lord Slim. Portrait, oil on canvas, by Leonard Boden, 1966.

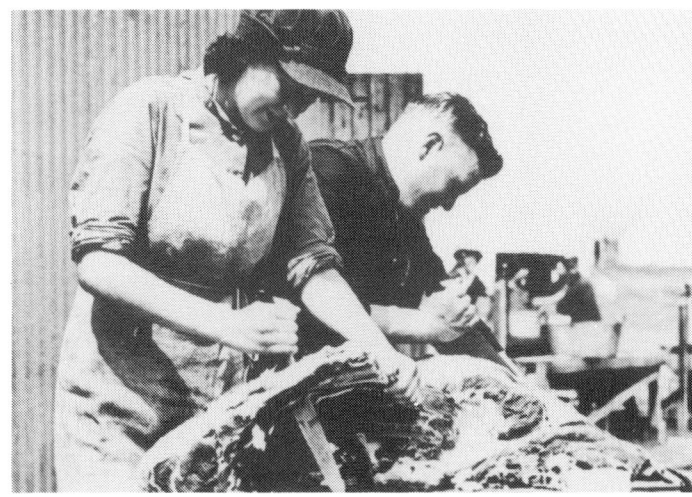

A member of 11th Company, Auxiliary Territorial Service, assisting in the preparation of rations c1940.

Members of the ATS completing the servicing of Cromwell Tanks c1940.

Forces which grew into the Parachute Regiment, the Glider Pilot Regiment and the Special Air Service, the two latter subsequently forming part of the Army Air Corps.†

Though the activities of such special forces would help sustain Britain's offensive spirit, they could not by themselves influence the direction of the war. After the successful outcome of the Battle of Britain the threat of invasion diminished, but any possibility of re-entering Europe was temporarily out of the question. Only on the periphery of the enemy's domains was there opportunity for offensive land operations. As in 1808, when the French invasion of the Iberian Peninsula had afforded Britain the chance to strike at Napoleon's armies, so in 1940 did the invasion of Egypt from Libya by Italy, which had declared war in June, present a similar chance to attack Germany's ally, and by so doing clear the North African coastline, thus winning a springboard from which an invasion of southern Europe could be launched. Such a strategy would also protect Britain's vital oil supplies in the Middle East against any Italian attack from its African possessions.

So began the war in the desert, a campaign destined to swing back and forth across the 600-odd miles between Alexandria in Egypt and Benghazi in Cyrenaica and one to which the main effort of the British Army and its Indian and Dominion comrades would be devoted for over two years. The battleground was a predominantly flat plain of rock and sand, broken only by the occasional low ridge and hillock, and devoid of human life and habitation except for the scattered townships along the Mediterranean shore. The desert provided no food and no water, no shelter from the blazing sun by day or the cold winds at night. On such a featureless terrain

"desert warfare resembled war at sea. Men moved by compass. Each squadron of tanks made great sweeps across the desert as a battle-squadron at sea will vanish over the horizon. One did not occupy the desert any more than one occupied the sea. Always the essential principle was that desert forces must be mobile: they were seeking not the conquest of territory but combat with the enemy. We hunted men, not land, as a warship will hunt another warship and care nothing for the sea on which the action is fought".(1)

To oppose the Italian Tenth Army of seven divisions, the British commander in Egypt, General Sir Archibald Wavell, could only dispose of the Western Desert Force under General O'Connor, consisting of the 7th Armoured and 4th Indian Divisions*, which had already displayed their excellent morale and training during their harassment of the laborious Italian advance into Egypt in September. The Italians had halted at Sidi Barrani where they established a series of fortified camps on a 50-mile front. On the night of 8th-9th December O'Connor pushed the 4th Indian Division through to the rear of the camps, which were then rolled up in succession, while 7th Armoured advanced through the gap to block the Italians' retreat. By 11th December five Italian divisions had been destroyed. O'Connor pushed on in pursuit of the remainder, driving them out of Bardia, Tobruk and Benghazi with the 6th Australian Division which had replaced 4th Indian, withdrawn after Sidi Barrani for a new campaign in East Africa. As the Italians fled along the coast road, 7th Armoured were cutting across the desert to head them off at Beda Fomm, 50 miles south of Benghazi, where, on 8th February, the enemy surrendered. In two months O'Connor's 30,000 men had routed the Italian Tenth Army, taking 130,000 prisoners and 400 tanks for the loss of only 500 men killed. After the grim events of 1940 it was a miraculous and cheering achievement.

O'Connor was all set to drive on to Tripoli but in early 1941 Wavell was faced with many problems. The campaign to eject the Italians from Abyssinia and Eritrea, for which 4th Indian had been withdrawn to join other Indian, British, South African and East African forces, began in February and was to last until the enemy surrendered in May. Troops had to be found to remove pro-German elements threatening the security of the oil pipeline through Iraq in April, and two months later a short campaign had to be mounted against former French allies in Syria where German influence was gaining the upper hand. Worst of all the Germans launched an offensive into the Balkans, overrunning Yugoslavia and invading Greece, which had been successfully withstanding the Italians since the latter's attack in October 1940. Though they could ill be spared, Wavell sent two divisions of Australians and New Zealanders with a British armoured brigade to aid the Greeks in April and a further 14,000 to hold Crete. The Empire troops fought magnificently but, with the Germans deploying their armoured strength in Greece under complete air superiority and a mass airborne landing on Crete, neither could be held and both campaigns ended in evacuation with much vital equipment abandoned.

The withdrawal of forces for the Balkan campaign having halted O'Connor on the border of Tripolitania, the Germans were able to reinforce their Italian allies with two armoured divisions forming the 'Afrika Korps' under a highly skilful mechanised commander, General Rommel. The experienced veterans of O'Connor's Western Desert Force had now been replaced by the partially trained and incomplete 9th Australian Division,

† The Parachute Regiment was formed on 1st August 1942 and the S.A.S. in June 1941 in North Africa. The Glider Pilot Regiment and the A.A.C. were formed in February 1942, the S.A.S. not becoming part of the latter until 1944. The Glider Pilots were disbanded after the war.

* One British and two Indian brigades. Both divisions were mostly Regular soldiers.

the 2nd Armoured Division and an Indian motorized brigade. When Rommel launched a lightning attack at the end of March 1941 these proved no match for his 'panzers' and within a fortnight he had reached the Egyptian frontier. However he had failed to capture Tobruk into which he had driven the Australians who were to hold out there for eight months, posing a constant threat to the Axis lines of communication. Wavell counter-attacked in June with the original components of the Western Desert Force, 7th Armoured and 4th Indian Divisions which, with 22nd Guards Brigade, had been re-constituted as XIII Corps, but his armour was scattered by Rommel's anti-tank defence. The attack failed, Wavell was sent to India as Commander-in-Chief and Sir Claude Auchinleck took over his command in the Middle East. XIII Corps having now been joined by XXX Corps, the forces in the Western Desert were designated the Eighth Army under General Cunningham, who had conducted the conquest of East Africa.

He was not, however, to be so fortunate against Rommel. For the next year the operations in the desert were to be dominated materially and morally by the German general and the 'Afrika Korps', whose tanks and anti-tank guns were in every respect superior to the British and whose tactics were more daring, speedier and altogether better co-ordinated whether in attack, withdrawal or defence. Cunningham's costly offensive in December 1941 foundered in a great tank battle at Sidi Rezegh and its momentum was only regained by Auchinleck taking over personal command of the battle. Though Rommel was pushed right back beyond Benghazi, he swiftly recovered and drove the Eighth Army rearwards 300 miles to Gazala. Here, after a three month pause to build up supplies, he struck again, routing the British armour, capturing Tobruk and advancing at great speed until by 30th June 1942 he was back in Egypt and only 60 miles from Alexandria. He had totally out-generalled Cunningham's successor, Ritchie, who at Gazala had had a preponderance of tanks, and the Eighth Army, despite having fought stubbornly, had been consistently out-manoeuvred. Rommel himself put his finger on it when he said that British soldiers displayed *"an extraordinary bravery and toughness combined with a rigid inability to move quickly".(2)*

Auchinleck again had to take over direct command of the Eighth Army and under his resolute leadership Rommel's headlong pursuit was finally and decisively halted at Alam Halfa on 3rd July. The Germans were now exhausted, their tank strength had shrunk and their greatly extended lines of communication were under increasing attack by the R.A.F. With reinforcements and supplies of a new American tank of vastly improved design, the Sherman, now reaching the Middle East, Auchinleck would soon be well placed to go over to the offensive. However he was to be deprived of the chance for Churchill decided on a complete change of command and sent out Generals Alexander and Montgomery, the former as Commander-in-Chief and the latter to take over the Eighth Army.

Montgomery, one of the Army's most serious and dedicated soldiers, immediately set about eradicating the inferiority complex to which the Eighth Army had become prone regarding the 'Afrika Korps', by forbidding any further plans for withdrawal and by infecting his new command from top to bottom with his own dynamic and aggressive personality. As a young officer in the Great War he had observed how remote senior commanders were from their fighting troops and was determined that every man in the Eighth Army should know him and his intentions. The troops in the desert were soon talking about the new general and a fresh mood of optimism began to spread through all ranks. Montgomery quickly proved he was as good as his words. When Rommel attacked again at Alam Halfa on 31st August, he so accurately predicted the German intentions that he was able to deploy his armoured divisions precisely where they could inflict maximum damage on Rommel's 'panzers'. After a week's fighting the enemy were back where they had started from. Montgomery did not pursue for he was not yet confident that his army was as fully trained and familiar with the new weapons and equipment as he required. As the preparations continued, Montgomery was everywhere, inspecting, lecturing and inspiring his men. By October the Eighth Army's confidence and morale was fully restored to a high degree, it outnumbered the Germans in tanks by nearly five to one and in men by just under four to one, although with the Italians added in, this reduced to nearly two to one. Montgomery disposed of three British armoured and two infantry divisions, four Empire divisions† and smaller formations of Greek, Polish and French troops, organized into the X, XIII and XXX Corps, of which the former was all armoured.

The flanks of Rommel's 60-mile long defences at El Alamein were secured by the sea in the north and the salt-marsh of the Qattara Depression in the south; his minefields and anti-tank defences were five miles deep. To enable the minefields to be cleared by infantry and engineers, Montgomery would have to attack at night. He planned to drive two corridors through the enemy positions facing XXX Corps on the seaward flank and immediately launch X Corps' armour close behind the infantry, thus drawing in Rommel's 'panzer' divisions to attack the British tanks in position. Meanwhile the infantry divisions were to break up the enemy infantry by what he called *"crumbling"* operations against their flanks and rear. An elaborate deception plan was to indicate that the main attack would come in the south on the XIII Corps front.

† 1st, 7th and 10th Armoured, 44th and 51st (Highland); 4th Indian, 9th Australian, 1st New Zealand and 1st South African.

The attack went in at 21.40 hours on 23rd October under cover of a bombardment fired from a thousand guns. The battle was to last for 12 days during which, due to the stubborn German resistance, the fighting assumed an attrition quality reminiscent of the Great War struggles. Despite the slow, dogged progress and several set-backs, Montgomery never lost control and in their essential features the operations conformed to his anticipated pattern, as he later described:

"The break-in had given us the tactical advantage; the dog-fight which followed reduced the enemy's strength and resources to a degree which left him unable to withstand the final knock out blow. The dog-fight demanded rapid regrouping of forces to create reserves available for switching the axis of operations as the situation required; in this way the initiative was retained and the battle swung to its desired end. Tactical surprise was an important factor; the break-in achieved it completely for the enemy had expected our main thrust in the south. In the final thrust again the enemy was deceived; he had prepared for it in the extreme north, and concentrated his German troops to meet it. It was delivered against the Italians, two miles south of the German flank".(3)

By 3rd November Rommel saw that he was beaten and began to fall back. The armoured divisions wheeled north to trap him but he was too quick for them. Nevertheless a great and decisive victory had been won at last. As the Eighth Army pounded in pursuit up the familiar coast road through Sidi Barrani, Tobruk, Gazala and Benghazi they passed the old battlefields they would never see again for this time Rommel was pulling right back to the Tunisian border.

As the Eighth Army raced westwards, a new front was opened in North Africa. On 8th November an Anglo-American force under the American, General Eisenhower, landed in Morocco and Algeria. The British component of this force was to be General Anderson's First Army of which only the 78th Division took part in the initial landings. This division made a dash along the coast from Algiers to try and reach Tunis but after bitter fighting was forestalled on Christmas Day, when within 15 miles of the city, by the Germans who were pouring troops into Tunisia to reinforce Rommel. Heavy winter rains slowed down the Allied build-up and prevented any further advance. By February 1943 when movement again became possible, the Firist Army, now consisting of the V Corps† with the IX Corps then disembarking from England, was holding a line running inland from the coast some 40 miles west of Tunis, which was continued to the south by the U.S. II Corps. Meanwhile the Eighth Army, having taken Tripoli on 23rd January, was approaching the defences of the Mareth Line on the southern Tunisian border.

On 17th February Rommel, now commanding all German forces in Tunisia, broke through against the U.S. II Corps, an attack which seriously threatened the rear of the First Army until halted by a gallant stand of the 26th Armoured and 1st Guards Brigades near the Kasserine Pass. During this offensive General Alexander assumed overall command of both British armies and was given responsibility for the conduct of all land operations in Tunisia. While German forces in the north continued to engage the First Army, Rommel threw his main weight against Montgomery at Medenine but his three armoured divisions suffered so heavily from the Eighth Army's carefully sited anti-tank defence and concentrated artillery fire that the attack failed.

On 20th March Montgomery began his assault on the Mareth Line. The first attack, on the coastal flank, was repulsed but drew in the German reserves. To hold them there Montgomery attacked next in the centre while he sent Lieutenant-General Horrocks with the 1st Armoured and New Zealand Divisions on a wide out-flanking movement round the landward end of the Mareth Line to cut in behind the enemy's fixed defences. Preceded by a carpet of bombs dropped by low-flying aircraft, Horrocks' attack began in the evening and continued throughout the night, a most tricky manoeuvre for armour in broken country, but it was brilliantly successful. The now battered Germans fell back to the Wadi Akarit from which they were again driven by the Eighth Army and pursued to Enfidaville. Meanwhile the First Army had been fighting its way forward through difficult mountain country to the north. In early May it was reinforced by the veteran 7th Armoured and 4th Indian Divisions from the Eighth Army in preparation for Alexander's final offensive. On 7th May 7th Armoured entered Tunis and by the 11th the remaining Axis forces had been trapped in the Cape Bon Peninsula. The following day they surrendered, a quarter of a million prisoners falling into Allied hands. The war in North Africa had been brought to a triumphant conclusion.

The British forces in North Africa were now re-organized. All the armoured divisions except the 7th and some of the infantry returned to England to prepare for the invasion of north-west Europe, while the Eighth Army was re-constituted with the 7th Armoured, 50th, 51st, 78th and 1st Airborne Divisions, which were to be joined by two fresh formations, the 1st Canadian and 5th Divisions, for the invasion of Sicily; this was to be followed by landings in Italy. As time went on this compoition would change, some divisions being transferred elsewhere while others came in, including the 4th, 8th and 10th Indian Divisions who were to take part in some of the most severe fighting of the Italian campaign. In the broken and mountainous terrain of the Italian

† 46th, 78th and 6th Armoured Divisions.

Royal Fusiliers man an advanced post in France, 1940.   Imperial War Museum.

The commander of 7th Indian Brigade during Operation 'Crusader', November 1941.   7409-79-88

Sherman tanks of the 9th Lancers in North Africa, 1942.   7711-143-33

17 pounder anti-tank gun in action, Tunisia c1943.   Contemporary photograph.   Imperial War Museum.

Sten sub-machine gun Mk II, 1939-1945.   6510-204-6

Anti-tank projector, Piat c1942.   7806-28

7409-79-41

Evacuation of the wounded after the relief of the Admin Box, Kohima, February 1944.

Peninsula the operations would assume a very different aspect from the wide-ranging, fast-moving war in the desert but the experienced formations of the Eighth Army would adapt to it as readily as they had to the long hauls across Cyrenaica and Tripolitania. However it was to prove a slow, arduous and often desperate business, frequently under the vilest weather conditions in country that always favoured the defence, and demanding endurance of a high order without any of the compensating exhilaration so many had found in the desert.

From their landing on 10th July, it took the Eighth and U.S. Seventh Armies just over five weeks to conquer Sicily, but the stiff German resistance, particularly against the Eighth Army, which had the hardest terrain to negotiate, enabled Kesselring, the German commander, to evacuate his troops and equipment to the Italian mainland.

On 3rd September the 1st Canadian and 5th Divisions of the XIII Corps landed on the toe of Italy, followed a few days later by the 1st Airborne and 78th Divisions seizing Taranto; within a fortnight the Eighth Army had occupied southern Italy as far north as Bari on the Adriatic. Meanwhile, Mussolini having fallen from power in late July, Italy capitulated on 8th September. The next day the British X Corps and U.S. VI Corps, forming the U.S. Fifth Army, landed at Salerno, 30 miles south-east of Naples but the Germans, unperturbed at the loss of their Italian allies, resisted so strongly that the Salerno beachhead remained a precarious lodgement until the approach of the Eighth Army on the 16th caused the enemy to pull back. While the Fifth Army pushed on to Naples which fell on 1st October, the Eighth moved over to the east of the Appenines to capture the important airfields at Foggia.

Kesselring now planned to exact a heavy price from Alexander's two armies for every yard of Italian soil by utilising the natural features of the country, the mountains and a series of rivers — the Volturno, Sangro, Rapido, Garigliano and the Liri — all of which would have to be crossed before the Allies could assault his main defences on the Gustav Line, centering on the massive monastery of Monte Cassino built on a mountain top and dominating Route 6 which led up the Liri Valley to Rome.

After the Eighth Army had battled forward across the Sangro in November-December and the Fifth had crossed the Garigliano in January 1944, it was decided to assist the assault on the main Gustav Line by a diversion 60 miles in its rear with a landing at Anzio just south of Rome. The British 1st and U.S. 3rd Divisions got ashore on 22nd January but, though later reinforced by six more divisions, were powerless to break out and there they remained under heavy German pressure until 23rd May, unable to influence the great struggle around Monte Cassino.

The Eighth Army now had a new commander, General Leese, Montgomery having gone home to prepare for the invasion; it was upon that Army, or its formations loaned to the Fifth, that the main burden of the ferocious fighting for Cassino fell. It began with the epic attempts of the New Zealanders, the 4th Indian and the 78th Divisions in February and lasted for three of the most bitter and bloody months the British armies were compelled to endure in the war. The precipitous mountains, the appalling weather and the tenacious resistance of the Germans all conspired to defy the heroic efforts of British, Dominion and Indian troops, yet their endeavours and those of their allies tied down 26 German divisions which otherwise could have been sent to northern Europe. Not until May, when Alexander managed to concentrate 13 divisions between Cassino and the west coast, was he able to break through the Gustav Line, Cassino itself finally falling to the Polish Corps of the Eighth Army. On 4th June the Americans entered Rome.

Two days later the long-awaited and long-prepared-for Second Front opened when the British Second Army under General Dempsey with the U.S. First Army on its right landed at dawn on the Normandy coast. In overall command of the land operations was Montgomery, the most experienced Allied battlefield commander. On the British right XXX Corps landed on "Gold" beach near Arromanches, while on its left the 3rd Canadian Division and beyond it the 3rd British Division of I Corps landed on "Juno" and "Sword" beaches respectively to the west of the River Orne. The seaborne assault was preceded by parachute and glider-borne landings of the 6th Airborne Division to protect the left flank of the 3rd Division by destroying an important coastal battery and securing high ground to the east of the Orne, together with the bridges over it; all hazardous tasks which were accomplished with great daring and skill. With the aid of the specialised tanks of the 79th Armoured Division, the assaulting infantry stormed ashore through the intricate beach defences and by the evening of D—Day each of the British beachheads had been linked up, although the efforts of the 3rd Division to take Caen, its prime objective, were thwarted by the presence of a German armoured division around the town.

The Normandy countryside afforded every advantage to a defender, with small fields bounded by thick-set hedges growing above stout banks and intersected by sunken lanes. Attacking through it became a series of small infantry battles with tanks supporting as and when they could see to do so and after the enemy anti-tank guns had been winkled out by the infantry.

Montgomery's overall plan was to hammer away with the Second Army around Caen so as to induce the Germans to concentrate their strength against the east end of the bridgehead, thus ultimately permitting the

Americans to break out in the west against relatively weak opposition. Gradually Dempsey's infantry and tank assaults drew in the German 'panzer' divisions, but such was the density of enemy troops facing him, that the inevitably slow progress caused Montgomery's superiors to question his handling of the battle. However he never deviated from his plan and, following the Second Army's capture of Caen on 8th July and a further massive offensive ten days later, his persistance was fully vindicated. By the end of July the British and Canadians were facing six 'panzer' divisions while the Americans were opposed by only two. On the 25th the Americans burst through the weakened German defences, driving south and then east. Just over three weeks later the bulk of the German formations which had been committed in Normandy were trapped in a pocket between the British, Canadians and Americans at Falaise from which few effective formations escaped.

With the great battle in Normandy won, the Allies began racing across France towards Germany. Eisenhower now assumed overall command, Montgomery taking over 21st Army Group which formed the left flank of the Allied advance with Crerar's First Canadian Army on the Channel coast and Dempsey's Second Army† on its right. On 3rd September the Guards Armoured Division entered Brussels and on the following day 11th Armoured Division captured the vital port of Antwerp, although failure to clear the Germans from its approaches along the Scheldt was to render it unusable until November. With their supply lines greatly extended by the rapidity of their advance and with German resistance stiffening on the borders of Holland and Germany, the Allied advance lost its momentum.

Eisenhower had intended to enter Germany on a broad front with the British and Canadian armies advancing through Belgium and Holland north of the Ardennes, while the three American and one French armies attacked between the latter and Switzerland, all keeping in step with one another. Montgomery urged that all administrative resources should be concentrated for one overwhelming thrust on the less well-fortified northern flank designed to envelop Germany's industrial heartland in the Ruhr, prior to pressing on to Berlin; in this scheme the major part would be played by his own 21st Army Group. The proposal caused heated controversy and considerable ill-feeling between the Americans, by now the dominant partner of the Alliance, and Montgomery. Eisenhower decided to compromise by pushing the U.S. First Army north of the Ardennes on Montgomery's right to strengthen the northern flank's advance but forbidding any immediate attempt against the Ruhr.

On 17th September Montgomery launched Operation "Market Garden", the great airborne assault to seize the bridges over the rivers Maas, Waal and Rhine to prepare a corridor through which Horrocks' XXX Corps would drive north to the Zuider Zee. *"With this one sabre-stroke Montgomery intended to cut Holland in two, outflank the Siegfried Line and establish Second Army beyond the Rhine on the northern threshold of the Ruhr. If all were to go well, the armour would reach the Zuider Zee on the fourth or fifth day, but the hazards were great — especially for the airborne forces".(4)*

This ambitious undertaking could well have succeeded had it not been for hasty planning, poor intelligence and bad weather after the initial landing which hampered further airborne operations. Two U.S. airborne divisions seized the bridges over the Maas and Waal while XXX Corps, headed by the Guards Armoured and 43rd (Wessex) Divisions, began its advance. Meanwhile the British 1st Airborne Division* under Major-General Urquhart had been landed at Arnhem where the farthest bridge crossed the Rhine 60 miles from XXX Corps' start line. The six battalions of the Parachute Regiment and the three of the Airlanding Brigade+ were not only dropped some way from the bridge but also found themselves under almost immediate and heavy-attack by two S.S. 'panzer' divisions. Such was the opposition that only Lieutenant-Colonel Frost's 2nd Parachute battalion managed to fight its way through to the bridge where it resisted successive German assaults to dislodge it with the greatest gallantry and determination. The epic fight by this battalion of a new regiment, with only light weapons against tank and infantry attacks,was in the true tradition of the several such last-ditch stands put up on earlier occasions in the Army's long history. However they and the rest of their airborne comrades, by then fighting desperately from a slowly contracting perimeter on the outskirts of Arnhem, battled in vain for XXX Corps could not reach them. The Guards Armoured Division, led by the Irish Guards group, came up against a well-sited anti-tank defence and, since their movement was restricted by the boggy nature of the ground to the use of a single road, they could only proceed on a one-tank front. In an operation in which speed was of the essence, any delay on such a narrow axis of advance was fatal to the chances of reaching the 1st Airborne in time.

On 22nd September the Guards' route was completely blocked when their leading tanks were within five and a half miles of Arnhem bridge, where the last remnants of Frost's heroic battalion had been finally overrun the day before. An attempt by 43rd (Wessex) Division to strike across country to reach the Rhine was held up and on the 24th Urquhart signalled: *"Unless physical contact is made with us early 25th Sept. consider*

† VIII, XII and XXX Corps.
* 1st and 4th Parachute Brigades, 1st Airlanding Brigade (glider-borne) and 1st Polish Parachute Brigade.
+ 7th King's Own Scottish Borderers, 1st Border Regiment and 2nd South Staffords.

Bren machine gun Mk III, 1944. 6602-86-2

Bedford wagons of 12th Corps, Royal Engineers, at the Saint-Gabriel Waterpoint, Normandy, 1944.
Contemporary photograph.   Imperial War Museum.

5710-8-83
Italy 1944, an AEC armoured car of the 10th Indian Division crossing a Bailey Bridge.

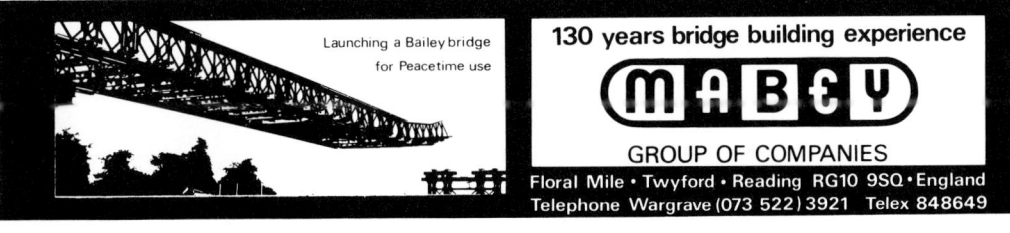

it unlikely we can hold out long enough. All ranks now exhausted. Lack of rations, water, ammunition and weapons with high officer casualty rate . . . . Have attempted our best and will do so as long as possible".(5) An attempt by the 4th Dorsets of the 43rd Division to cross the Rhine and reach the Airborne perimeter failed with the loss of over half the battalion and on the morning of the 25th Urquhart was ordered to withdraw that night. Of his original 10,000 men, only just over 2,000 got back to safety across the Rhine. For all their heroism and endurance, and the unfaltering efforts of the Guards Armoured Division, which had been constantly in action for the previous five months, Operation "Market Garden", Montgomery's bid to end the war in 1944, was a failure. Although all its objectives up to Nijmegen on the Waal had been taken, its prime target was the Rhine crossing and that still remained in German hands.

In the winter of 1944 the Germans launched a sudden and unexpected offensive against a weak American sector of the Ardennes with the aim of recapturing Antwerp. This city was at last available to the Allies as a port after heavy fighting by British and Canadian infantry to clear the enemy from Walcheren and the banks of the Scheldt. The eventual containment of the enemy advance in the so-called "Battle of the Bulge" was an American affair, although during its critical phase Eisenhower placed all the U.S. formations on the northern flank of the salient and control of their operations in Montgomery's hands. The chance of pulling the Americans' chestnuts out of the fire was an opportunity the British Field-Marshal undertook with some relish, and the confrontation between the simply-dressed Montgomery, in black beret and battle-dress, and the be-helmeted and be-pistolled American generals when he told them what they were going to do was not an altogether happy occasion.

Meanwhile in Italy Alexander's operations had been hampered by the withdrawal of formations to France, but he had nevertheless pushed on up the peninsula until brought to a halt by the Gothic Line running between Leghorn and Ancona. The Eighth Army's attack east of the Appenines, followed by the Americans towards Bologna, came near to breaking through to the Po Valley, but terrible weather halted the armour and the two Allied armies were compelled to spend a harsh winter in the mountains north of Florence.

In early January 1945 the 21st Army Group had heavy fighting as the First Canadian Army (of whose 13 divisions nine were British) slogged south-westwards through mud and rain against fierce opposition in the Reichswald Forest to clear the west bank of the Rhine, until it linked up on 3rd March with the Americans to the west of Wesel. On the night of 23rd-24th March the Second Army forced the crossing of the Rhine under cover of an immense bombardment and pushed ahead to join up with the 6th Airborne Division, which had been dropped to the east of the river to facilitate the quick build-up of the bridgehead. By the end of March the Allies had surrounded the Ruhr and Montgomery was all set to head straight for Berlin. To his astonishment, Eisenhower now decided to make the main effort towards Dresden with the U.S. armies, leaving the Russians to take Berlin, while the 21st Army Group was left to protect the American northern flank by an advance on Bremen and Hamburg.

XXX Corps met some still fanatical resistance but the Germans were now on the point of collapse. Hamburg fell on 2nd May to the 7th Armoured Division, ending the last lap of its long journey from the Western Desert which had begun in 1940, and on the same day 11th Armoured, 6th Airborne and the 5th Divisions reached Lübeck and the Baltic coast. Two days later all German forces in Holland and north-west Europe surrendered to Montgomery on Lüneburg Heath, hostilities actually ceasing at 8.0 a.m. on 5th May. Three days earlier, as the Eighth Army rolled into Venice and Trieste to complete its saga of victory since Alamein, the Germans in Italy had surrendered. The long struggle against Hitler's great tyranny was over.

As the weary British, Dominion and Indian soldiers in Europe savoured their triumph, far in the East the struggle with Japan went on. Japan had entered the war in December 1941 when the Eighth Army was making its first and ill-fated offensive against Rommel's 'Afrika Korps'. The Japanese onslaught against British possessions in the Far East had carried all before it with a ferocity and speed for which the weak and ill-equipped British and Indian formations were quite unprepared. Hong Kong fell swiftly and on 7th December the Japanese invaded Malaya, heading fast through the jungle southwards towards Singapore. To defend the entire Malayan Peninsula, General Percival had only the 9th and 11th Indian Divisions† guarding the east coast and northern border respectively, and two Malay brigades in Singapore, all without tanks and aircraft; he later received the 8th Australian Division which took up position in the south in Johore. These widely extended formations were completely outfought by the fast-moving Japanese and, although some battalions put up a stout resistance, by 31st January the last British rearguard, found by the Argyll and Sutherland Highlanders, withdrew across the causeway on to Singapore Island. On 8th February two Japanese divisions came ashore while a third attacked down the causeway. The tired, beaten troops held out for a few days but when the island's water supply was captured, Percival saw no alternative but surrender. On the 15th 70,000 men fell into Japanese hands, including the unfortunate 18th (East Anglian) Division which had been plunged into the last days of the fighting straight off their troopships from England. It was *the greatest British surrender and military disaster since Yorktown in 1781". (6)*

---

† Both were under strength, having only two brigades each.

Next to fall was Burma. There were only two weak divisions in the country and, after Rangoon in the south was captured in early March, they were compelled to fall back along the few roads and tracks that ran north for 900 miles towards India. The Japanese never attacked frontally but, on encountering any defensive position, they would hold its attention with feint attacks, while other forces pushed round a flank through the thick jungle to come in some way to the rear of the defenders, blocking their retreat. Thus the outnumbered British and Indian troops were constantly being outflanked and surrounded, cut off from their supplies, and with the advance guard of any retreating formation as heavily engaged as the rear guard. Any long retreat is demoralizing, as was seen at Corunna and Mons, but when retreating columns are expecting always to be headed off, it is doubly so. As the remnants of the Burma Corps toiled over the last range of hills into India in May, the monsoon broke with torrential intensity. This slowed up the Japanese pursuit but inflicted terrible suffering on the exhausted troops, as their Corps Commander, General Slim, described:

"Ploughing their way up slopes, over a track inches deep in slippery mud, soaked to the skin, rotten with fever, ill-fed and shivering as the air grew cooler, the troops went on, hour after hour, day after day. Their only rest at night was to lie on the sodden ground under the dripping trees, without even a blanket to cover them. . . All of them, British, Indian and Gurkha, were gaunt and ragged as scarecrows. Yet, as they trudged behind their surviving officers in groups pitifully small, they still carried their arms and kept their ranks, they were still recognizable as fighting units. They might look like scarecrows but they looked like soldiers too".(7)

Although the fighting in North Africa and Europe had been hard and fierce, the conditions under which it was conducted were never as grim or obnoxious as those endured in Burma by the British and Indian Armies, and later by men of the King's African Rifles and Royal West African Frontier Force, between 1942-45. They fought in a jungle-covered mountainous terrain with few communications other than narrow tracks, in an ennervating climate of steamy heat and torrential rain, with their health always vulnerable to tropical disease and the unfamiliar and prevalent existence of loathsome insects and reptiles. Even when out of the line their rest areas were frequently little better than the battle area they had just left; not for them the pleasures of Mediterranean beaches or the amenities of French towns. The lack of communications greatly aggravated the provision of supplies forward and the evacuation of casualties rearward, while the devoted work of the medical services had to be carried out under primitive conditions in which the dangers of infection abounded. Above all there was the enemy. The Japanese soldier displayed a fanatical bravery and ferocity which equalled, if not surpassed, anything encountered among the savage enemies of the Victorian era, coupled with modern fighting skills of a high order and total familiarity with the jungle. The concept of surrender was alien to his philosophy, so that few Japanese prisoners were ever taken, while Allied soldiers who fell into his hands could expect extreme privations if not brutal death. After the failure of the first British counter-offensive in the Arakan in January 1943, the morale of the troops in Burma, particularly of those in the rear areas, began to be infected by rumours *"picturing the Japanese as the super bogy-men of the jungle, harping on their savagery. . . . . and the general hopelessness of expecting ever to defeat the enemy".(8)* Thus when the British and Indian divisions in Burma were re-organized as the Fourteenth Army and the command given to General Slim, he had to instil into his men the will to win before he could hope to defeat the Japanese.

The first lift to morale came from the offensive operations far behind the enemy lines conducted by the 77th Independent Indian Infantry Brigade under their unconventional commander, Brigadier Orde Wingate. Wingate had acquired a reputation as a guerilla leader before the war in Palestine and during the Abyssinian campaign. Although viewed with suspicion by more orthodox officers, his theories on deep penetration had impressed Wavell, now Commander-in-Chief India, who sanctioned his plan to attack Japanese rear areas and communications in the heart of Burma in mid-1943. Although his Chindits, as they were popularly known, suffered heavy casualties, they proved it was possible for British soldiers to overcome both the jungle and the Japanese and that, by relying on supplies dropped from the air, conventional lines of communication were unnecessary.

Slim now began to train and educate his army. He taught them to use the jungle as the Japanese used it, as cover for stealthy, cunning manoeuvres round a flank or to the rear. He accustomed them to the idea of supply and casualty evacuation by air so that if outflanked or surrounded they could fight on without concern for their rearward communications. Above all he set out to explode the myth of the Japanese superman and to convince his men that they could and would win. Slim had started his career in the Royal Warwicks† but spent most of his service in the Indian Army, so knew how to inspire and win the confidence of all his men, whether British, Indian or Gurkha. While the retraining went on, he also ensured that his fighting troops would not want for the best of equipment, supplies and medical services, in which he received every assistance from the Commanders-in-Chief India, first Wavell and then Auchinleck.

† A regiment that also gave the Army Field Marshal Montgomery.

At the end of December 1943 Slim launched a limited offensive down the Arakan coast with the 5th and 7th Indian Divisions. Steady progress was being made when on 4th February 1944 the Japanese swung wide round the offensive's eastern flank and cut in across the rear at the Ngakyedauk Pass, surrounding the 7th Division and driving to the coast to block the 5th's retreat. Very fierce fighting followed but Slim put the two divisions on air supply and then attacked the Japanese rear with the 26th Indian and 36th British Divisions. It was now the Japanese who were surrounded and, as the days passed, their supplies ran out. Since they would not surrender, they had to be ruthlessly destroyed and by the 24th it was all over in the Arakan. As Slim wrote: *"For the first time a British force had met, held and decisively defeated a major Japanese attack".(9)*

The Japanese had hoped to draw all Slim's reserves down to the Arakan in preparation for their main offensive further north against Imphal and Kohima which opened in March. At Imphal was a vast supply dump linked by a road passing through Kohima to the railhead 130 miles north at Dimapur. Once these places fell, the enemy would have secured the main communications that linked Burma with India. Preferring to fight close to his supplies rather than forward in the hilly jungle, Slim pulled back the 17th and 20th Indian Divisions from their advanced positions in the south around Tiddim to join the reserve division of the IV Corps, 23rd Indian, on the Imphal plain. Both divisions had to fight their way back against Japanese hooks to head them off but managed to link up with the 23rd at Imphal where the whole IV Corps was soon surrounded and subjected to heavy and persistent attacks. Kohima was held against 15,000 Japanese by a scratch force built round the 4th Royal West Kents and the Assam Regiment whose unyielding resistance distracted the enemy commander from pressing on to Dimapur. The fighting at both places was protracted, bloody and often at close quarters: at Kohima the forward positions of the West Kents were only separated from those of the Japanese by the District Commissioner's tennis court. Showing complete disregard for death, the enemy pressed his attacks with great fury but both at Kohima and Imphal the dogged defence just held.

Meanwhile Slim was bringing aid to the battered garrisons. The successful operations in the Arakan enabled him to fly in two brigades of the 5th Indian Division to Imphal, its third brigade going to Dimapur, and the 7th Indian to Kohima, where it was joined by the 2nd British Division flown up from southern India. Gradually these formations forced their way forwards, pressing against the rear of the Japanese surrounding the besieged areas. On 18th April a brigade of the 7th Division led by the 1st/1st Punjabis broke into the perimeter at Kohima but they could only take over the defence from the worn-out garrison as the Japanese onslaughts continued unabated. Throughout April, May and into June, with the monsoon turning the battlefield into a sea of mud, there was no let-up in the dreadful struggle, but by mid-June there was evidence that the Japanese were out of supplies and many of their troops were starving with nothing to eat but grass. As the Fourteenth Army kept up the pressure, Kohima and Imphal were at last able to link up. On 8th July the Japanese commander ordered what was left of his forces to fall back on Mandalay. Five of his divisions had been destroyed as fighting formations and at least two others had been badly cut up. Though they had lost 50,000 killed, only 600 had been taken prisoner, a clear indication of their fanaticism. The Fourteenth Army, which suffered 16,700 casualties, had saved India, inflicted a crushing defeat on the enemy, and had proved that British, Indian and Gurkha soldiers were more than a match for the Japanese. Yet their great victory was barely noticed in England where all eyes were on the operations in Normandy; small wonder they called themselves "the Forgotten Army".

While the battle raged on the borders of India, Wingate had led a larger, glider-borne expedition into northern Burma to inflict maximum damage in the Japanese rear and to sever the communications of an enemy force facing a Chinese army under the American General Stilwell far in the north. The Chindits set up their strongholds from which they sallied out to harass the Japanese but much of the impetus went out of the operations when Wingate himself was killed in an aircraft crash early on. Nevertheless they endured much hard fighting which assisted Stilwell in his advance south to capture the important communications centre of Myitkina in early August.

Having driven the Japanese from the borders of India, Slim planned a great offensive for the complete re-conquest of Burma in 1945. The enemy still had three armies in the field: the Twenty-Eighth on the Arakan coastal sector; the remains of the Fifteenth, which had been beaten at Imphal, in the centre along the Irrawaddy around Mandalay, guarding the approaches to Meiktila further south where their main administrative area was situated; and the Thirty-Third in the north facing Stilwell's Chinese. The Fourteenth Army now consisted of the IV, XV and XXXIII Corps. While Stilwell and Christison's XV Corps pinned down the Japanese in the north and the Arakan respectively, Slim intended to strike first from the north and west across the Irrawaddy at Mandalay with Stopford's XXXIII Corps to entice the Japanese reserves to that area. Then Messervy's IV Corps,

† Unlike the homogeneous brigades of Indian divisions in North Africa and Italy, the brigades of those in Burma at this time usually consisted of one British, one Indian and one Gurkha battalion, as had been the practice in India for some years.

having moved southwards in secret down the Myitha Valley, was to bear east, cross the Irrawaddy well below Mandalay and drive for Meiktila, seizing the Japanese administrative area and cutting off the enemy armies in the centre and north from Rangoon. The great north-south waterway of the Irrawaddy, between 1,500—2,000 yards wide, presented a formidable barrier to Slim's grand design, and since the projected area of operations was almost completely devoid of motorable roads, nearly all supplies and reinforcements would have to be sent in, and casualties evacuated, by Dakota aircraft flying between India and airstrips constructed by engineers in the wake of the advancing troops. During the course of the offensive 96% of all supplies to the Fourteenth Army were to go in by air.

Despite the hammering they had received at Imphal, the Japanese rear guards of their Fifteenth Army put up a stiff resistance west of the Irrawaddy as the XXXIII Corps converged on the river during January. On the night of the 15th, the 19th Indian Division seized a bridgehead across the river east of Shwebo, which was then savagely counter-attacked by two Japanese divisions for the next three weeks but managed to hold firm. However, with the 2nd British and 20th Indian Divisions closing up to the Irrawaddy further south, one of the enemy divisions was withdrawn into reserve. Meanwhile the IV Corps, its secret march screened by the 28th East African Brigade, was also approaching the river, some 70 miles north-west of Meiktila.

The provision of sufficient craft to pass the Fourteenth Army across the mighty Irrawaddy required a huge effort of logistical improvisation and its successful accomplishment was a tribute to the skills of Slim's British and Indian engineers. Between 12th-15th February the 20th Indian Division was ferried across to establish a bridgehead around Myinmu, against which the Japanese mounted counter-attacks of increasing intensity. At the same time 7th Indian Division of IV Corps began their crossing to the south. As Slim had hoped, the Japanese commander believed this was only a diversion to lure him from the Mandalay area where the main threat, posed by 19th and 20th Indian, seemed to be; to confirm him in this belief, Slim pushed the 2nd Division across the Irrawaddy between 19th and 20th Indian, some ten miles downstream from Mandalay. All XXXIII Corps were now on the east bank, poised to attack the bulk of the Fifteenth Army.

Exactly as planned, the 17th Indian Division and 255th Tank Brigade passed through 7th Indian on the IV Corps front and raced for Meiktila, surrounding it on three sides. As always, the Japanese fought to the last man but, after two days bitter hand-to-hand fighting, this vital centre of the enemy effort in Burma was in Slim's hands. Too late the Japanese commander, Kimura, realised he had been duped but immediately reacted with speed to recapture Meiktila. Withdrawing divisions from the Arakan and from the north, where Stilwell's pressure had been diminished by Chiang Kai-Shek's demand for the return of his Chinese troops, he threw them against the IV Corps in a series of all-out assaults beginning on 12th March. Communications between the 7th and 17th Divisions were severed but Slim brought forward his last reserve, the 5th Indian Division, flying one brigade into Meiktila under heavy enemy artillery fire and sending the other two to 7th Indian. This reinforcement enabled this division to throw back the attacks against it and advance to link up with the 17th at Meiktila. By 29th March IV Corps had restored the situation and the remains of the decimated Japanese divisions withdrew to the east.

Meanwhile the XXXIII Corps had advanced out of their bridgeheads to complete the destruction of the Fifteenth Army. 19th Indian fought its way against fanatical resistance into Mandalay itself, while the 2nd and 20th swung round to the south, cutting off any chance of retreat in that direction and driving the scattered enemy eastwards into the hills. Two Japanese divisions made a last-ditch stand east of Meiktila in April but their cause in Burma was finished. The Fourteenth Army poured south towards Rangoon, supported by a seaborne landing mounted by the XV Corps which had been pressing down the coast. The 26th Division went ashore on 3rd May, only to find that the Japanese had gone. On the day the German armies surrendered in north-west Europe, the re-conquest of Burma was finally completed, but the Fourteenth Army's magnificent achievement was once again overshadowed by events in the West. A major amphibious operation for the re-capture of Malaya was now planned, but before it could be put into effect, the Japanese, harried across the Pacific by the Americans, were bludgeoned into final surrender by the atomic bomb.

The war in Burma was the final and fittingly triumphant conclusion of that great comradeship in arms between the British and Indian Armies which for over 200 years had defied the enemies of Crown and Company. Together the British private, Indian sepoy and Gurkha rifleman had endured many campaigns in the past and now they had fought and conquered in the last and most difficult of all. The all-British formations and units of the Fourteenth Army had demonstrated how will, courage and stamina could overcome a totally alien climate and terrain, infested with a ferocious Asiatic enemy, for which their Western, usually urban backgrounds and previous training had ill prepared them. But the defeat of the Japanese Army in Burma was chiefly a triumph for the Indian Army, both in the forward battle area and in the support echelons stretching back into India itself. It had grown from a strength of 189,000 in 1939 to 2,500,000 in 1945 and, unlike the British Army, every Indian and Gurkha soldier was a volunteer. In the nineteenth century it had always been policy to stiffen each Indian

brigade in the field with a British battalion, an arrangement which had continued up until 1943 (except in North Africa and Italy for administrative reasons). After Imphal Slim concluded that Indian battalions had nothing to learn in the way of fighting spirit from their British counterparts, whose great strength – regimental 'esprit de corps' – he thought had been weakened by the haphazard wartime system of reinforcement; henceforth he brigaded Indian units with Indian, and British with British. He considered they fought better that way and it simplified their maintenance. He conceded that British troops were superior in technical skill and education but in bravery and endurance, both physical and moral, the Indian and Gurkha soldiers were their equal and in some respects superior. Nor were the latter any longer dependent on their British officers, as Lord Roberts, himself a great protagonist of Indian troops, had once maintained they always would be; by 1944 all battalions had their quota of King's Commissioned Indian officers, as well as their subadars and jemadars, and some of them were commanding battalions. Much of the credit for the high standard of the Indian formations was due to Auchinleck's work as C-in-C India in preparing them for the field and to Slim's outstanding leadership and powers of command. For his part Slim repaid their loyalty and trust with high praise: *"My Indian divisions after 1943 were among the best in the world. They would go anywhere, do anything, go on doing it and do it on very little".(10)*

During the six years of the Second World War the British Army lost 144,079 killed, just over a fifth of the total that fell in the Great War. In 1945 its strength stood at three million. Of these about 6% were women, serving chiefly in Queen Alexandra's Imperial Nursing Service and the Auxiliary Territorial Service, the successors to the W.A.A.C. of 1917; others belonged to smaller organizations such as the Mechanized Transport Corps, formed in 1939, and the First Aid Nursing Yeomanry, a much older unit dating from 1909 which lost its nursing function prior to 1939, but one to which many of the women who performed deeds of singular heroism in enemy-occupied Europe belonged. Considerable numbers of women served alongside men in the batteries and searchlight units of Anti-Aircraft Command. Generally, however, the increase in the number of women in uniform was a reflection of the huge growth in the Army's "tail" in proportion to its fighting troops, occasioned by the technological complexities of modern war. The expansion of the Royal Army Service Corps to cope with supply and transport problems in such widely varying conditions as the Western Desert and the Burmese jungle even embraced the creation of its own fleet. At its greatest strength the Royal Army Ordnance Corps mustered 138,000, two and half times greater than Wellington's entire army in the Peninsula in 1813. The advances in medical science and, after 1941, a greatly improved system of casualty clearance and evacuation, together with mobile surgical teams, permitted the Royal Army Medical Corps to give much speedier and more efficacious treatment than in the Great War and which resulted in many more lives saved than was ever possible in former times. The need for prompt repair and regular maintenance of the vast diversity of weapons and equipment brought into service during the war led to the creation of a new and rapidly expanding corps, the Royal Electrical and Mechanical Engineers, whose men and facilities were divided into four echelons, ranging from light aid detachments attached to front-line units to more or less static base workshops. To provide a labour force under military discipline for the multitudinous non-specialist tasks required to maintain an army in the field, the Royal Pioneer Corps and the Non-Combatant Corps were formed in 1939.† Two other new corps whose duties are self-evident from their titles, the Intelligence Corps and the Army Catering Corps, were formed in 1940 and 1941 respectively.

The Royal Artillery, often considered by enemy commanders to be the most professional of the British fighting Arms, grew to a huge size, manning field (including self-propelled), medium, heavy, anti-tank and anti-aircraft guns. The tasks of the Royal Engineers were manifold, from clearing minefields and building bridges under fire, to constructing airfields, roads, pipelines and every sort of undertaking necessary for the Army to live, move and fight, all of which saw the Corps grow to a strength of 280,000 men. Though the front-line troops of both armour and infantry faced many crucial situations during the war, seldom, if ever, were they failed by their supporting gunners and sappers. Equally the fast-moving operations of the Second World War greatly enhanced the importance and growth of the Royal Corps of Signals who, though often hindered by the poor quality and slow production of reliable wireless equipment, earned their right to be included among the Arms, rather than the Services.

The Royal Armoured Corps, formed in 1939, included the old Cavalry of the Line, the Royal Tank Regiment, the Yeomanry and numbers of new regiments as the war progressed, six of which were designated Dragoons (22nd and 25th), Hussars (23rd and 26th) and Lancers (24th and 27th). Its fighting formations increased from two armoured divisions and a tank brigade in 1939 to 28 armoured brigades in 1945. Although various types of tanks were produced during the war - Valentines, Crusaders, Covenanters, Churchills and Cromwells - British tank design never matched the German, and not until the American Sherman reached the

† The former did not receive the Royal title until after the war, when it was also granted to the Military Police, the Pay, Veterinary, Education and Dental Corps. The Non-Combatant Corps was disbanded after the war.

armoured divisions in large numbers were British tank crews able to compete on equal terms with the German 'panzers'. That the old cavalry spirit had not been killed by mechanization was amply demonstrated by the record of such regiments as the 11th Hussars whose armoured cars screened the 7th Armoured Division in advance and retreat from the first Western Desert offensive in 1940 until the capture of Hamburg in 1945. The old "divisional cavalry" of infantry formations were replaced in 1941 by regiments of the specially formed Reconnaissance Corps.†

Despite the greatly increased mechanization of all aspects of war, the infantry remained "The Queen of Battles". Although the newly-raised parachute and commando units earned much popular acclaim, and deservedly so, it was the old regiments of Foot Guards and Infantry of the Line that, as always, bore the brunt of battle, with rifle and bayonet, machine-carbines, grenades, mortars, light and heavy machine-guns, and the fearsome Piat (Projector Infantry Anti-Tank). As mentioned earlier, infantry reinforcements tended more and more to be sent wherever the current need was greatest regardless of their original regiments, so that a Seaforth Highlander might find himself serving in a Royal Sussex battalion one year, only to become a Welch Fusilier the next. Thus the deep-rooted regimental loyalties so characteristic of the Regular Army gave way to more transient attachments, with the focus of men's sense of belonging perhaps centred more on the division than the regiment. Nevertheless this did not preclude individual regiments performing feats of arms comparable with any of bygone days as, for example, the four days stand against superior numbers by the 2nd Hampshires* in Tunisia, which ended with a bayonet charge from which only 120 men came back alive, or the action of the 2nd Rifle Brigade against the German armour at Alamein, when their 6-pounder anti-tank guns, together with those of 239th Battery R.A., destroyed or knocked out 57 tanks and self-propelled guns.

Compared with their forbears of the Great War, the British soldiers of 1939-45 were predominantly conscripts, were better educated, more sceptical of authority, and less able to withstand casualties and hardships over long periods. The wartime Army became more democratic, with officers drawn from all walks of life and passing through the ranks before gaining their commissions. In these circumstances a more personal, more informative style of leadership was required from senior officers than the remote direction of Haig and his army commanders. This the Army received in full measure from such men as Wavell, Auchinleck, Alexander and above all Montgomery and Slim, all of whom had experienced the follies of the Great War and were resolved not to repeat them. Furthermore the Army was fortunate in having at its head as C.I.G.S. a man with the intellectual and executive capacity of Field-Marshal Lord Alanbrooke. Assuming his high office at the darkest stage of the war, he had to deploy all his great qualities of patience, tact, foresight and grasp of conflicting issues to contend, not only with problems posed by the enemy, but also with the vigorous leadership and forceful character of Winston Churchill, whose schemes, if fertile, were sometimes impractical, and later with Britain's reduced status as junior partner in the Anglo-American Alliance. For the greater part of this long and complex war Alanbrooke safeguarded the Army's best interests and supervised its operations with a sure hand.

† Disbanded, with the new cavalry regiments, after the war.
* Accorded the Royal title after the war, together with Lincolnshire and Leicestershire Regiments.

British armour and infantry advancing through a German town, March 1945.   7503-63

The Colour Party of the 1st Bn Somerset Light Infantry, the last British unit to leave India, 28th Feb, 1948.

6009-136-4

Women's Royal Army Corps, c1950.
Girls acting as plotters on the Royal Artillery.

CHAPTER 22
RETREAT TO REFORM
1946 – 1980

Following the Second World War there was to be no return to the traditional round of peacetime soldiering as had occurred after 1918. Occupation forces had to be found for western Germany, Berlin, Austria and the disputed territory around Trieste, claimed by both Italy and Jugoslavia. Garrisons in Austria and Trieste were maintained until 1955 and 1954 respectively, but as the wartime alliance with Soviet Russia changed into the Cold War, so the army of occupation in Germany became a bulwark against the threat from the East as the British Army of the Rhine (B.A.O.R.), subsequently, from 1949, forming part of the military forces of the North Atlantic Treaty Organisation (N.A.T.O.), a role which has continued with growing importance up to the present day. At the end of the war three divisions had been sent to subdue a Communist uprising in Greece where, though later reduced in strength, troops remained until 1950.

Outside Europe the pre-war sabotage and terrorism in Palestine erupted again in the autumn of 1945, this time perpetrated by the Jews with the view to establishing an independent Zionist state. The thankless task of combating an increasingly ruthless and violent insurrection – a foretaste of what was to be the lot of the Army in many parts of the world over the next three decades – fell upon the 1st Infantry Division, recuperating from the Italian campaign, the veterans of the Rhine crossing, 6th Airborne Division, and temporarily the 3rd Division. This bitter campaign tied down 70,000 troops and cost the lives of 223 officers and men before Palestine was finally evacuated in June 1948.

The aftermath of Japan's defeat found British occupation forces in French Indo-China and the Dutch East Indies embroiled with nationalist insurgents until the spring of 1946 when the former colonial powers resumed responsibility for these territories. In India, despite the British Government's readiness to yield to the national political parties' demands for independence, the transfer of power was not accomplished without mass anti-British rioting and looting in the major cities, followed by the first of the communal riots between Hindus and Moslems, to control which British battalions, largely consisting of young soldiers conscripted since the end of the war, had to be called out in support of the police. The partition of the sub-continent into a Hindu India and a Moslem Pakistan, with total independence from 15th August 1947, not only brought to an end the British regiments' efforts to control the growing communal violence and savagery, but also terminated the long and splendid partnership between the British and Indian Armies. Henceforth the regiments of the latter were to be split between India and Pakistan with only four regiments of Gurkha Rifles, the 2nd, 6th, 7th and 10th, each of two battalions, continuing in allegiance to the British Crown. The last task of the old Indian Army fell to one of its finest components, the Punjab Frontier Force, which for six terrible weeks endeavoured to maintain order amid a welter of slaughter while the new boundary was settled in the Punjab. In the end the intolerable strain of preserving its impartiality proved too much and on 2nd September 1947 the Punjab Frontier Force was disbanded after a hundred years incomparable service.† From Independence Day the British regiments were gradually withdrawn from the sub-continent which for so long had been such a central feature of their existence, until on 28th February 1948 the 1st Somerset Light Infantry trooped their Colours through the Gateway of India at Bombay, forming the rear guard of the Army in India as 194 years before the old 39th Foot had been its advance guard.

Although the Labour Government which had come to power in 1945 was keen, both for ideological and economic reasons, to disengage from military commitments overseas, it was clear that, with large numbers of wartime soldiers being demobilised, some conscription would have to be retained if Britain was to fulfill her responsibilities in the unsettled post-war world. In July 1947 the National Service Act was passed to become effective on 1st January 1949. This imposed an obligation on men conscripted of initially one, and from 1950, two years with the Colours, followed by a further obligation of three and a half years' service with the Territorial Army, which was reconstituted in March 1947 to provide a reserve of nine divisions. By this means

† The Corps of Guides, which perhaps best typified the traditions of the Punjab Frontier Force, now forms part of the Pakistan Army.

Montgomery, who was appointed C.I.G.S. in 1946, obtained a Regular Army of over 350,000, rising to nearly 418,000 in 1951, the largest it had ever been in peacetime and for the first time, other than in war, consisting mostly of conscripts.

In 1946 the break-down of Cardwell's regimental system for the Infantry, which had become apparent during the war, was finally recognized by the introduction of the Group (later Brigade) organisation. Regiments were to be grouped together from between eight to two per group under regional designations or those which reflected a common tradition.† Although each regiment was to retain its individual identity, its officers and men were henceforth liable for posting to any regiment within the group. No sooner had this break with past peacetime practice been inflicted on the Infantry, than it was announced that all Line regiments would reduce to a single Regular battalion. Thus, with ten battalions of Foot Guards, three of the Parachute Regiment and eight of the Brigade of Gurkhas, the post-war strength of the Infantry stood at 85 battalions as opposed to 138 pre-war. Although by 1951 the overall strength of the Army would be more than twice what it had been in 1939, the Infantry now represented only about a fifth of the total, instead of half pre-war, the balance being accounted for by an increase in the size and numbers of headquarters, the other Arms and particularly the Services which totalled 42% of the whole.

In the decade following the introduction of National Service, the Army was stretched to the limit. Although Palestine and India no longer claimed large quotas of troops, there was the Rhine Army and the other European garrisons to be maintained, a reserve in the Middle East spread over Egypt, Libya, Cyprus, Somaliland and the Soudan, further garrisons in the Far East and smaller forces in Gibraltar, Malta and the Caribbean. In many of these places and in others more and more troops would have to be committed to the counter-insurgency operations which so often preceded the gradual withdrawal from Imperial responsibilities ordained by successive governments in the face of the growing clamour for independence in Asia and Africa, coinciding with Britain's reduced circumstances after the war. In addition to these tasks, many of which were simultaneous, Britain had to contribute troops for a major war in Korea under United Nations command.

The longest and ultimately most successful of the National Service Army's campaigns was the struggle to save Malaya from a take-over by the country's predominantly Chinese Communist Party under its leader Ching Peng, who had been prominent in resisting the Japanese occupation. The Communists' campaign of murder and intimidation began in June 1948 and made considerable headway, due to the uncoordinated policies of the colonial authorities, a lack of intelligence on which the security forces could base their operations, and the dense tropical jungle which, since it covered four-fifths of Malaya, greatly favoured the guerillas' movements and hampered those of the troops and police. Not until 1950, when General Sir Harold Briggs was appointed director of all counter-terrorist operations under Sir Henry Gurney, the High Commissioner, did matters begin to improve. Briggs established a system of joint committees with civil, military and police representatives at every level, from his own headquarters right down to local districts, where the district officers, police superintendents and battalion or company commanders worked out the detailed operations applicable to their sector. He then set out to deny the terrorists their sources of shelter, supplies and information among the population by concentrating the villagers into safe and protected areas, and instituting checks on the movement and sale of all food supplies. These measures, together with the constant patrols, cordons, curfews and ambushes necessary to hunt down and destroy the guerillas, ate up troops so that from 1950 there were deployed two armoured car regiments and 24 infantry battalions, drawn not only from British regiments but also including eight battalions of Gurkhas, five of the Malay Regiment, two of the King's African Rifles and one from Fiji. Later they would be joined by Australians, New Zealanders and Rhodesians. Among the British troops was a Guards Brigade, serving for the first time in their history east of Suez.

The British battalions, largely consisting of National Servicemen, usually did a three-year tour in Malaya but, owing to the turn-over of the young conscripts, always had a proportion of men who were new to the jungle and had to be taught rapidly how to live and move in it. The Gurkhas on the other hand, being all Regulars, enjoyed a continuity of manpower which bred a wealth of experience, so it was not surprising that the highest number of guerillas killed or captured was obtained by a Gurkha battalion, the 1st/10th, who accounted for 300. Nevertheless the National Servicemen, most of whom came from urban backgrounds, learned quickly the arts of jungle operations and the record number of enemy casualties inflicted by a British battalion was achieved by one with a high National Service content, the 1st Suffolk, who in three years put 195 terrorists out of action at a loss to themselves of 12 killed and 24 wounded. The battalion's success was reflected in the award of two D.S.Os. and nine M.Cs.

---

† Lowland (4 regiments), Home Counties (7), Lancastrian (8), Yorkshire (7), Midland (4), East Anglian (5), Wessex (5), Light Infantry (6), Mercian (4), Welsh (3), North Irish (3), Highland (6), Green Jackets (2). The Brigade of Guards and the Parachute Regiment remained outside this system.

Men of the 3rd Bn, Royal Australian Regiment crossing the Taedong River during the expedition of Pyongyang, Korea c1952.
Soldier Magazine.

British troops patrolling the streets of Port Said, Egypt 1956.   Soldier Magazine.

In 1952 General Sir Gerald Templer took over as combined High Commissioner and Director of Operations. He appreciated that the solution to the Malayan problem lay *"not in pouring more soldiers into the jungle, but.... in the hearts and minds of the Malayan people".(1)* By his determined, forceful and energetic leadership, his tireless travelling, his sympathetic understanding for the ordinary people coupled with a stern but just treatment of the recalcitrant, he set himself to win the co-operation of the local population. At the same time he sought to involve them more in the fight against terrorism by increasing the number of Malay battalions, strengthening the Home Guard which protected the resettled villages and improving the police. All the while the patient combing of the jungle by the troops continued and, as Templer's *"hearts and minds"* policy began to take effect, so the flow of information to the security forces increased, with the guerillas being forced more and more on to the defensive. When Templer left in 1954 the initiative had swung to the security forces and the number of terrorists in the field had been cut by a third. It was to take another six years before these were finally mopped up but in 1957 Malaya was granted its independence under a stable government and on 31st July 1960 the long emergency was finally declared at an end. It had cost the lives of 70 British officers and 280 men and 159 Gurkhas.

On 25th June 1950 the North Korean Army, well equipped with Russian tanks and artillery, invaded South Korea. Four under-strength and ill-prepared United States divisions were hurriedly shipped across from Japan but by mid-August the Americans and South Koreans had been driven back to the south-east corner of the country around the port of Pusan. In response to a plea for help from members of the United Nations by the Supreme Commander in Japan, General MacArthur, the first British contingent consisting of the 1st Middlesex and 1st Argylls, forming the 27th Infantry Brigade under Brigadier Coad, sailed from Hong Kong and landed at Pusan on 29th August. The brigade, joined two months later by the 3rd Royal Australian Regiment, was soon in action, first holding part of the line defending Pusan, and then playing a prominent part in the counter-offensive which drove the North Koreans back up the length of the peninsula to the Chinese border on the River Yalu. This great advance seemed to betoken victory but with November came news that the Chinese were pouring across the Yalu, bringing with them the first bitter onset of the terrible Korean winter.

It was now clear that the U.N. forces were in for a long, tough struggle which indeed was to last until mid-1953 as the fighting swung back and forth across the mountainous terrain in extremes of heat and cold until both sides settled down in the last year of operations to a trench warfare reminiscent of 1914-18. Before the war ended, four armoured regiments and 15 infantry battalions were to fight in Korea. The 27th Brigade were at first dependent on the Americans for their artillery and logistic support but with the arrival of 29th Infantry Brigade Group in November 1950, units of the Royal Artillery, Royal Engineers, Royal Signals and all the Services joined their armoured and infantry comrades. With the coming of further Australian, New Zealand, Canadian and Indian troops, the initial contribution of two battalions grew into the 1st Commonwealth Division, formed on 28th July 1951.†

During the mobile operations of 1951-52 the high quality of the British troops was exemplified by the great stand of the 29th Brigade – C Squadron, 8th Hussars, 1st Royal Northumberland Fusiliers, 1st Gloucesters and 1st Royal Ulster Rifles – on the Imjin River in April 1951. Holding a 10-mile front with open flanks they withstood unrelenting mass attacks by three Chinese divisions trying to break through down the most direct route to Seoul, the South Korean capital. Owing to the wide gaps between the battalions and the overwhelming numbers of the enemy, the latter were able to penetrate right into the heart of the brigade area and the Gloucesters on the left, with C Troop, 170 Mortar Battery, Royal Artillery in support, became cut off from the rest of the brigade. Though they inflicted heavy losses on the Chinese, the Gloucester companies were gradually forced from their positions until the whole battalion was surrounded and concentrated on one hill feature. There, under the inspiring leadership of Lieutenant-Colonel Carne, they fought it out back to back, as their forbears, the 28th, had done at Alexandria, until their food, water and ammunition was almost exhausted. Early in the morning after the third night's fighting, Carne learned there was no hope of relief and was ordered to break out if he could. 46 men of one company managed to fight their way through, but most of the other survivors fell into Chinese hands to endure brutal treatment, indoctrination and privations for two years. During the course of their magnificent stand, the Gloucesters won two V.Cs.,* two D.S.Os., three M.Cs., two D.C.Ms. and eight M.Ms.; furthermore the whole battalion and the Royal Artillery mortar troop were awarded an American Presidential Citation which recorded: *"Without thought of defeat or surrender this heroic force demonstrated a superb battlefield courage and discipline. Every yard of ground they surrendered was covered with enemy dead until the last gallant soldier of the fighting battalion was overpowered by the final surge of the enemy masses".*

† 25th Canadian (three Canadian battalions), 28th Commonwealth (two British and one Australian) and 29th British Brigades (three British).

* Lieutenant-Colonel Carne and Lieutenant Curtis, Duke of Cornwall's Light Infantry attached 1st Gloucesters (posthumous).

Support Company, 3rd Bn Royal Australian Regiment on jungle patrol, Malaya, 1959.   Soldier Magazine.

Troops trial version of 7.62mm self-loading rifle.   Pattern Room, Enfield   7802-51

2nd Bn 2nd Gurkha Rifles in Borneo 1960.

Though the Gloucesters attracted the greatest glory from an admiring public, their stand was only part of the great fight put up by the Fifth Fusiliers, the Ulsters and other elements of the 29th Brigade in holding their ground for as long as possible before breaking through the encircling Chinese in a bloody fighting withdrawal. All three battalions fought in the highest traditions of the British infantry, displaying a stubborn endurance and refusal to be beaten. Two years later the same qualities were demonstrated by the 1st Black Watch and 1st Duke of Wellington's in defence of the position known as the Hook during the trench warfare at the close of the war. Whether Regulars, National Servicemen or Reservists, of whom large numbers had been recalled to fill the ranks of the 29th Brigade, the British troops in Korea proved beyond doubt that the post-war Army was as formidable in battle as any of its predecessors.

While the Korean War and the Malayan emergency were at their height, fresh commitments arose in Africa and the Middle East. In 1952 the 1st Lancashire Fusiliers had to be hurriedly despatched to Kenya where a sinister organisation known as Mau Mau drawn chiefly from the Kikuyu tribe were beginning a murderous campaign against Europeans and other Africans. The lessons learned in Malaya proved invaluable in defeating this insurrection but it took four years and the services of 11 British battalions and the King's African Rifles before the last of the Mau Mau gangs were hunted from their forest hide-outs and their revolting oath-taking practices eliminated.

Two years after the Mau Mau revolt had broken out the Army had another uprising on its hands, this time in Cyprus where the underground organisation EOKA led by the Greek general Grivas, which favoured union of the island with Greece, began the now familiar pattern of riots, assassination and sabotage, followed by guerilla attacks from their lairs in the Troodos mountains and tangled country-side. By October 1955 one Royal Marine Commando and two infantry brigades were deployed to combat this new threat, reinforced by the 16th Parachute Brigade three months later. By April 1956 there were 15 fighting units in Cyprus, maintaining order against rioting mobs in the towns and combing the mountain villages and forests in search of the elusive Grivas and his followers.

Britain now found itself in the unfortunate position of having to quell an armed and increasingly dangerous revolt in the very country to which it had just begun to transfer its Middle East Command from its previous base in Egypt. Ever since the end of the war that country had been trying to rid itself of the British presence by civil disorder, murder of the unwary and hit-and-run shooting attacks; attacks which continued even after the British forces quitted Cairo and Alexandria and moved into the Suez Canal Zone in 1947. In 1952 King Farouk was deposed by a military junta from which Colonel Nasser emerged as the new leader of Egypt. Since it was clear to the C.I.G.S., Field Marshal Sir John Harding, that to maintain troops in the Canal Zone without the co-operation of the Egyptian Government was impractical, negotiations were begun for its evacuation which finally took place in mid-1956. The enthusiasm of the Egyptians at seeing the British leave was only equalled by the relief with which the 70,000 strong garrison shook the sand of the hated Canal Zone off their boots. However in moving to Cyprus the Middle East Command had merely exchanged one hostile environment for another, which by late 1956 showed no signs of abating despite numerous successes against the EOKA gangs.

Furthermore the Army had not seen the last of Egypt. In July 1956 Nasser nationalized the Suez Canal Company which led in November to the ill-fated Anglo-French Suez expedition. The operation was beset by the politicians' indecision and prevarication, plus countless planning and logistic difficulties, which disclosed Britain's unreadiness for such a venture. The initial air and seaborne assaults by the 16th Parachute and Commando Brigades, notably the seizure of Gamil Airport by the 3rd Parachute battalion making the first airborne attack since the war, were successfully accomplished with dash and daring. However the world had changed since Wolseley had brought the Egyptians to heel 74 years before and the recapture of the Canal, which militarily might well have been attainable, proved politically impossible.

Nasser's moral, though hardly military, victory at Suez and his emergence as the personification of Arab nationalism spelled further problems for Britain and yet more tasks for the Army as Cairo Radio spewed out its daily tirade of hate and propaganda all over the Middle East. Tribal uprisings on the borders of the Aden Protectorate found the Army engaged on operations in a terrain very similar to those which generations of soldiers had experienced on the North-West Frontier, although the tribes were scarcely of the calibre of the Pathans and Afridis; nor could the local forces, the Aden Protectorate Levies, whom the British regiments supported, be compared with the old Indian Army. In 1958, at the request of the King of Jordan whose position was threatened by Nasser's intrigues, the 16th Parachute Brigade flew into Amman while the 1st Cameronians were landed at Aqaba. With this timely reinforcement a volatile situation was calmed down without bloodshed. On the other side of Arabia, in the Trucial States of the Persian Gulf, a small British garrison had been assisting the British-officered Trucial Oman Scouts to keep the peace since 1951. In 1957 help was sought by the Sultan of Muscat and Oman in ejecting some very active rebels operating out of the mountainous part of Oman. This commitment lasted for nearly a year and was brought to a successful conclusion by an extremely

daring and brilliantly conducted destruction of the rebel strong-holds by the 22nd Special Air Service Regiment and the Life Guards. The S.A.S. had been reformed as a Regular unit during the Malayan emergency and their invaluable work there and in Oman ensured their survival as an element of the Regular Army. Two regiments of this corps had formed part of the Territorial Army since 1947.

Throughout all this hectic period of the late fifties there had been sporadic and fortunately small emergencies in the Caribbean and British Guiana. The Cyprus troubles, bedevilled by the difficulty of operating among a population largely sympathetic to the insurgents, and by 1958 occupying 26 major units, dragged on until 1959 when the island was granted its independence with two bases retained for British use on the south coast. To be relieved of this onerous and often unpleasant campaign was providential for in 1961, yet another fresh assignment beckoned. Feeling himself threatened by Iraq, the Ruler of Kuwait asked for British assistance. In the height of the Arabian summer infantry and armour were rushed from the United Kingdom, Cyprus, East Africa and Aden but, as in Jordan, the rapid response proved sufficient to deter the Iraqis. The troops found nothing more formidable to fight than the intense heat though this proved bad enough, particularly for the 3rd Carabiniers and the 11th Hussars in their tanks and armoured cars. By October all troops had been withdrawn, either to their former bases or south to the Gulf states.

With Malaya, Kenya, Cyprus and the Middle East emergencies now concluded and as a host of new national flags were run up to replace the Union Jack all over Asia and Africa, the Army had a pause to draw breath and assimilate the major changes to its structure which had begun in 1957. Then, the Conservative Minister of Defence, Mr Duncan Sandys, had announced the gradual termination of National Service and the reversion, from 1st January 1963, to an all-volunteer Regular Army. The news was greeted with enthusiasm both by potential conscripts, who would now avoid the discipline and duties imposed on their elders — something many of their parents would later regret — and by the Regulars who, though conscious of the debt the Army owed to countless National Servicemen, were keen to be free of the time and manpower-consuming problems connected with the training of and functioning with a transient and generally reluctant soldiery pre-occupied with its "demob" date.

In the course of this return to Britain's traditional method of manning her forces, the overall strength of the Army would reduce from the 373,000 with the Colours in 1957 (excluding the Gurkhas) to 165,000, although in the event 180,000 would be required to meet the needs of the Rhine Army, the few remaining responsibilites of the Near, Middle and Far East and the Caribbean, plus a strategic reserve at home. Sizeable reductions would be made in the staffs of headquarters, depots and base installations, but in addition a weighty axe was to fall upon the Royal Artillery, which was to be lopped of 20 regiments over and above the 14 it had lost in 1954 with the disbandment of Anti-Aircraft Command, and upon the Infantry, which was to be cut from 77 battalions to 60 (excluding the Gurkhas). The Royal Armoured Corps was to reduce from 30 regiments to 23. Despite the size of the Gunners' cut, the scheme bore heaviest upon the R.A.C., eight of whose regiments were already the product of amalgamations in 1922, and the Infantry, whose regiments, though all able to trace an unbroken lineage back to the 1881 reorganisation, had lost their second battalions after the war. Now, with only one Regular battalion apiece, it was clear that some would lose their individuality and titles which over the years had become as precious as the numbers had been before the upheaval of 1881. The method chosen, both in the R.A.C. and the Infantry, was the amalgamation in pairs of 14 and 30 regiments respectively, plus the loss to the Grenadier and Coldstream Guards of their 3rd Battalions. A further blow to all Line regiments, amalgamated or not, was the changeover from their treasured individual cap badges to a new badge common to all regiments of a particular administrative brigade (formerly group). These brigades were reorganised so that after the amalgamations, each would contain three or four regiments with a common brigade depot and promotion rolls.†
The principal factor in selecting regiments for amalgamation was the recruiting potential both of the revised brigade areas and of individual regiments. Thus, in a predominantly rural area, such as the East Anglian Brigade's, all five regiments suffered amalgamation despite the Royal Norfolk's, Suffolk's and Bedfords' seniority as 9th, 12th and 16th Foot, with the also senior Royal Lincolns(10th) being transferred from the Midland Brigade as a partner for the Northamptons. In the Royal Armoured Corps selection was based on sparing the regiments amalgamated in 1922 and depriving the largest and most junior Royal Tanks of three of their eight regiments.

Between 1958-61 these amalgamations* took place amid a mixture of emotions in which fortunately a recognition of the inevitable and a determination to make the new unions succeed prevailed in most cases. In an army whose members, particularly the younger element, were less conservative than their forbears, the reorganisation was accepted with less reluctance than the 1881 changes. Only north of the border was there

---

† This involved the formation of a new brigade, the Fusilier (Royal Northumberland, Royal and Lancashire Fusiliers) and the transfer of the Oxfordshire and Buckinghamshire Light Infantry from the Light Infantry to the Green Jackets Brigade. The Midland Brigade was re-titled Forester Brigade (Royal Warwick, Royal Leicesters and Sherwood Foresters).
* See Appendix A.

outright defiance, where the marriage between the Lowland Royal Scots Fusiliers and the Highland Light Infantry to form the Royal Highland Fusiliers (though of the Lowland Brigade) was only accomplished after the replacement of the two Colonels of Regiments by serving officers. At one point the Gordons had been considered as possible partners for the H.L.I., but when Field Marshal Templer, then C.I.G.S., mentioned that regiment's name, the portrait of a former C.I.G.S. and Colonel of the Gordons fell from the office wall with a crash, the glass cracked from corner to corner!

Once the amalgamations were over and the last National Servicemen released, the new and old regiments eagerly looked forward to a period of stability in which to build the reformed Regular Army. However, for the Infantry this was not to materialize for the War Office saw the amalgamations as only the first step in producing a more flexible Infantry Arm, capable of withstanding changing strategic needs and possible further reductions. There were some who favoured the abolition of the regimental system altogether, replacing it with a Corps of Infantry on the lines of the Royal Artillery, a measure abhorrent to most, though not all, infantrymen. Since the brigade system already permitted cross-posting between regiments, it was decided to retain it for the present but, to ensure its viability, as many brigades as possible must have four regiments. Furthermore it would be much tidier administratively if the brigades were to convert themselves into large regiments, each of four battalions or three in the case of the smaller brigades. In 1963 the Forester Brigade was broken up, the Royal Warwicks being elevated to the status of Fusiliers to form the fourth regiment of that brigade, while the Royal Leicesters and Sherwood Foresters performed the same service for the East Anglian and Mercian Brigades respectively. The Army Council bilked at enforcing the large regiment concept, merely encouraging brigades to adopt it; initially only three, East Anglian, Home Counties and Green Jackets were prepared to comply, becoming the Royal Anglian and Queen's Regiments, each of four battalions, and the Royal Green Jackets of three.

Shortly before the East Anglian Brigade obliged the Army Council, that body had also assumed a new style as a result of the current fashion for large organisations. On 1st April 1964 the War Office was relegated to being the Army Department of the enlarged, tri-service Ministry of Defence whose minister was promoted to Secretary of State. The Secretary of State for War was demoted to Minister of Defence for the Army, the Army Council was downgraded to the Army Board and the C.I.G.S. lost the "Imperial" from his title. All this change to the Army from 1958 onwards was perpetrated, somewhat surprisingly, by a Conservative Government. Much of it, nevertheless, was beneficial to efficiency.

The Territorial Army emerged unscathed from the 1958 amalgamations and the old county regimental cap badges were still seen in its ranks. However since 1955 only two of its divisions had an active role as reinforcements for N.A.T.O. while the remaining six were allotted purely to home defence tasks which included support for the Civil Defence Corps. With this mundane role strengths fell and in November 1960 18 battalions were reduced, bringing amalgamation into the T.A. Five years later, with a Labour Government now in power and committed to reducing defence expenditure, the axe fell on the Territorials. Their eight divisions were disbanded and a much smaller force, the Territorial and Army Volunteer Reserve (T.A.V.R.), took its place, consisting solely of individuals, certain specialised units chiefly of the Services, and 24 major units of the fighting Arms, known as the Volunteers, all destined for the reinforcement of B.A.O.R. Due to public pressure the remaining old T.A. units were spared at the last minute to form a lightly-equipped force for home defence under the aegis of the Home Office, but the Labour Government were determined to get rid of them, and after a short period in which these devoted part-time soldiers struggled on under their own resources without any Government backing, they were ultimately consigned into limbo in 1969, together with the Civil Defence Corps, thus depriving the country of any means of coping with the chaos that would ensue after a nuclear attack. The old T.A. had undoubtedly been in need of an overhaul and the T.A.V.R., for its size, was a much improved force. However the almost malignant spurning of public spirited citizens' efforts not only lost a valuable reservoir of disciplined manpower but also struck at the whole concept of part-time voluntary service. Fortunately a later Conservative Goverment went some way to improving the nation's home defence capability by enlarging the T.A.V.R. Recently the present Government has restored its old title of Territorial Army.

Meanwhile the new Regular Army had found fresh fields for its endeavours. From 1962-64 British, Gurkha, Malay and later Australian and New Zealand troops had been protecting the three British dependencies of North Borneo, Brunei and Sarawak on the north coast of Borneo which was shared with Indonesia. Trouble came first from insurgents within the territories, followed by guerilla raids sponsored by Indonesia and finally invasion by Indonesian regular troops. First into action were the 1st/2nd Gurkhas, soon joined by the recently amalgamated Queen's Own Highlanders. Before the "confrontation" as it was called, with Indonesia was over, all eight battalions of Gurkha Rifles, on whom the brunt of the operations fell, were engaged+, plus, on different

---

The most recent Victoria Cross awarded in the British Army went to Lance-Corporal Rambahadur Limbu of the 2nd/10th Gurkha Rifles for great gallantry and superb leadership in Borneo on 21st November 1965.

A patrol of the Parachute Regiment in the Troudos Mountains of Cyprus, May 1961.

An armoured car patrol of the 11th Hussars in the Dhala Mountains, Aden 1961.

276

New uniforms of the British Army 1961

occasions, 15 British battalions of whom the 1st Green Jackets and 1st Argylls completed three separate operational tours in the country. Armoured car support was provided by the Life Guards, Queen's Dragoon Guards, Queen's Royal Irish Hussars and the 4th and 5th Royal Tanks. The maximum strength deployed was in early 1965 with 13 battalions, 22nd S.A.S., two armoured car regiments, two and half artillery regiments and three squadrons of engineers. Together they were responsible for halting incursions across a mountainous and jungle-covered frontier nearly 1,000 miles long, plus an even longer and equally vulnerable coastline to their flanks and rear. There were few roads, so that helicopters and light aircraft were at a premium for movement and logistic support. The confrontation ended with the fall from power of Indonesia's President Soekarno. That this last of the Army's Far East expeditions was completed so successfully, securing the confidence of the inhabitants and domination over the enemy, was due to the skill and professionalism of the troops and the masterly handling of the campaign by successive Directors of Operations, Major-Generals W.C.Walker and George Lea, both veterans of the Malayan emergency with which conditions in Borneo had many similarities.

While this little war was proceeding, other British troops had been summoned to the aid of the newly independent countries of East Africa — Tanzania, Uganda and Kenya — where their armies, drawn from the former King's African Rifles, were in a state of mutiny, a situation that had never occurred in that force before independence. A prompt response by the few units still remaining in Kenya and from Aden ensured a swift return to normality.

By now Aden itself was building up for trouble. It began with a fresh outbreak of tribal uprisings in the hinterland of the Protectorate which had remained tolerably quiescent if not peaceful since the earlier skirmishes of 1955-58. The six weeks' operations in 1964 known as the Radfan War were designed to deter the dissident bands from raiding out of their mountain strongholds against the desert road connecting Aden with the small town of Dhala on the Yemen border where there was a British garrison. 45 Royal Marine Commando and the S.A.S. seized the nearest hill positions used by the dissidents and the little war culminated with a drive by the 3rd Parachute Regiment up the Bakri ridge leading to the main enemy bases, while 1st/1st East Anglian, soon to be the 1st Royal Anglian, scaled and occupied the 5,500ft Jebel Huriyah the highest peak in the Radfan.

Skirmishing in the hinterland continued for another two years but the chief centre of trouble now shifted to Aden Colony where two rival nationalist groups, egged on as usual by Nasser, began the customary campaign of murder and intimidation, despite the British Government's undertaking to grant independence by 1968. This unpleasant episode, the last of Britain's colonial wars, was fought out against the vicious gangs of both groups who relied chiefly on grenades, rocket launchers and the manipulation of hysterical mobs, amid the squalid alleys and bazaars of Aden town and the neighbouring area of Sheik Othman. The security forces' task was greatly aggravated by political restraints, the hostility of the populace, the unreliability of the police and briefly the treachery of both the police and the local forces. The latter resulted in the murder of eight unarmed Royal Corps of Transport men as well as a party of Northumberland Fusiliers who were shot down by the Armed Police in the very police barracks the Fusiliers used as a headquarters. The troops moved in a blaze of publicity made possible by television; a medium which, despite its occasional nusiance value, permitted the publicity-conscious Lieutenant-Colonel Mitchell of the Argylls to demonstrate to the British public how regimental pride could overcome adversity. Unfortunately his robust methods with terrorists, which could have been applauded in a earlier age, did not entirely commend themselves to his superiors. It was perhaps a sign of the times that the fine, but more self-effacing achievements of the 1st Lancashire Regiment and 1st Parachute Regiment, in keeping the cauldron of Sheik Othman under control, won the award of the D.S.O. for their respective commanding officers, Lieutenant-Colonels Downward and Walsh. Perhaps they understood better than Mitchell that times were changing and, with British power now greatly reduced in the world, more circumspect methods of dealing with insurgency were expected than those which had prevailed in the days of Empire. By November 1967 one of the rival factions had virtually succeeded in eliminating the other and the British Government negotiated with the victors for the transfer of power and evacuation of the troops. After the most frustrating and unrewarding operations since the war, this always unpopular station was finally handed over after 128 years occupation and the Army left its barren rocks without regret.

With the emergencies in Borneo and Aden now over, the long retreat from Imperial responsibilities had finally come to an end. After 22 years of almost ceaseless operations since the war in mountains, bush, desert and jungle, for generations the traditional background to the British soldier's activities, the Army came home, leaving only a handful of battalions scattered about the globe. Despite the growing might of Soviet power, the Labour Secretary of Defence, Mr Denis Healey, seized the opportunity to extend the reductions he had already inflicted on the Territorials to the Regular Army. In 1967 he demanded as a sacrifice three Royal Armoured Corps and four Royal Artillery regiments plus eight infantry battalions, and in the following year another R.A.C. regiment and a further nine battalions, three of them Gurkhas; subsequently four of the British battalions earned a reprieve. More amalgamations followed and for the first time, sadly, two disbandments: the

Troops boarding a Comet Aircraft of RAF Transport Command 1962.

Troops manning the peace line in the Falls area of Belfast, 11th September, 1969.

Cameronians, that old regiment of Covenanters formed in 1689, and the York and Lancasters, 65th and 84th Foot. Even the Household Cavalry were not to escape, a partner for the Royal Horse Guards being found by the promotion of the 1st Royal Dragoons above the heads of the more senior regiments of Dragoon Guards to form the Blues and Royals. Three brigades, Fusilier, Light Infantry and North Irish, converted themselves into large regiments, the better to absorb the loss of their junior members†. The next year the earlier loyalty of the Queen's and Royal Anglian in becoming large regiments was rewarded by the abolition of their fourth battalions. Furthermore it soon became apparent that regiments which had resisted this concept in order to retain their identities had lost nothing, for both the large regiment and brigade system were scrapped in favour of still larger groupings: the formation of five administrative divisions – Scottish, Queen's, King's, Prince of Wales's and Light. In keeping with the egalitarianism of the times, the Brigade of Guards was forced to become the Guards Division.

Although administratively convenient, and although individual regiments preserved their identities (the large regiments remaining as such) and even regained their own cap badges, the divisional system virtually ended the close links between counties and regiments; now a Hampshire man opting to join his county regiment could find himself serving in the Staffordshire or Cheshire Regiments. Perhaps in an army which prides itself on looking forwards, even closing its collective mind to the past, and in a society which seems to favour large organisations, such things will not matter in the future. After all, men from all over the British Isles serve happily together in the Royal Artillery and Royal Engineers, and even in bygone days the numbered regiments of foot required no common recruiting ground to consolidate their regimental cohesion. Time and the recruiting figures will tell how destructive or otherwise the breaking down of the county connections with the Infantry has been.

The Labour Government announced its defence policy in 1968 to be that: *"Britain's defence forces, apart from those needed to meet certain residual obligations to dependent territories....should....be concentrated in Europe".(2)* Apart from small garrisons such as Hong Kong, Belize (formerly British Honduras), Gibraltar and in Cyprus, either securing the sovereign bases or in the United Nations force which since 1964 had been striving to keep Greeks and Turks from each others' throats, the new policy confined the Army to B.A.O.R. and a strategic reserve in the United Kingdom. Important though these undoubtedly were, suddenly there seemed no longer any likelihood of the urgent operational tasks which so often had provided a spur to recruiting and a sense of purpose within the ranks. Well-meaning schemes to employ soldiers as a sort of labour corps – or Military Aid to the Civil Community as it was officially called – were being considered, when out of the blue sprang a new, unforeseen role, full of urgency. On 14th August 1969 the Prince of Wales's Own Regiment of Yorkshire were sent on to the rioting streets of Londonderry to relieve the hard-pressed Royal Ulster Constabulary. Within days more troops were deployed in Belfast and by October ten battalions were policing Ulster. Soon, with the emergence of the gunmen and bombers of the I.R.A. on to the troubled scene, the troops' task grew from riot control to quelling urban, and later rural, terrorism, the role familiar to many from Cyprus and Aden. This time it was in their own backyard.

The Army's often thankless work in Northern Ireland has now lasted longer than any other of its post-war commitments, except Malaya, and still continues. The chief burden, as always, has been borne by the Infantry, ably supported by regiments of the Royal Armoured Corps and Royal Artillery, which, as in other emergencies, have converted themselves into temporary infantrymen with results worthy of the best-trained battalions. The Royal Military Police, both men and women, have given invaluable support to the R.U.C. and the bravery and technical skill of the bomb disposal squads of the Royal Army Ordnance Corps have been beyond praise. In addition to their operational tasks, the Royal Engineers and Royal Corps of Transport, indeed all the Services, have stepped into the breach when civilian resources have foundered. Backing up the Regular Army has been the part-time Ulster Defence Regiment, formed in 1970 from men and women in the province, who volunteer their services, often at great risk to themselves and their families.

Subjected to greater political restraints than any imposed elsewhere, the Army has had to operate among a population many of whom are bitterly opposed to its presence, if not actively supporting the I.R.A. Its every activity has been exposed to, and sometimes hindered by the national press and television, some of whose attitudes seem more critical of their own Army than its opponents. It has been acting for most of the time under a Government numbering among its supporters elements traditionally hostile to it, and elected by a nation induced since Suez into uncertainty about its Imperial past and military operations generally. Despite this less than whole-hearted support for its endeavours, the Army has combated an armed insurrection within the United Kingdom with the highest degree of professional competence, discipline and a forbearance under severe provocation unparalleled by any other nation's security forces.

The constant round of crowd control, searches, patrols and checks have nurtured the leadership qualities of junior officers and N.C.Os. to a standard which is the envy of their N.A.T.O. allies. The Army's active operations so close to home for the first time since the eighteenth century, and its efficient performance of more peaceful duties in aid of the civil power, have begun to make thoughtful members of the British public more

† See Appendix A.

105mm light gun manned by 13 (Martinique 1809)
Light Battery, Royal Artillery, on Salisbury Plain, 1975
It can fire a 35lb shell up to 11 miles.
Army PR

A soldier of the 2nd Bn Royal Regiment of Fusiliers on
exercise in Germany with a Sterling sub-machine gun c1977.
Army PR

Chieftain main battle tank, 1978.
Armed with a 120mm rifled gun which is auto stabilised and equipped with a laser range finder, the tank weighs
54 tons and has a crew of four.
ARM   Army PR

Naval and military assistance to the Vietnamese refugees from the freighter Skyluck as they came ashore on the island of Lamma, one of Hong Kong's outlying islands, after the ageing freighter grounded on the rocks. Seamen from the Royal Naval patrol craft HMS Yarnton, which was despatched to the scene, and soldiers from the 1st Battalion, The Royal Green Jackets joined officers from the Royal Hong Kong Police Force in the rescue operations, 1979.

sympathetically aware of their soldiers than ever before in peacetime. On the other hand, the seemingly endless Ulster commitment occupying some 13,000 men, coupled with the need to keep B.A.O.R. at a high state of readiness in the face of massive Warsaw Pact forces, plus further Governmental reductions of the defence budget, have resulted in an Army too small for its job (although but for Ulster it could have been even smaller), with consequent overwork, turbulence to the lives of its members and their families, and a drop in training standards for the N.A.T.O. role†. When these unhappy effects are aggravated by shortages of equipment and politicians' reluctance to pay soldiers properly for their unsettled and often dangerous services, it is not surprising, as has been proved often in the past, that valuable trained men leave. Neglect of the Army by its political masters has been a recurring theme in its history since the seventeenth century. Through those masters, the nation gets the Army, in material terms, it is prepared to pay for. In moral terms it has often got better than it deserves. There have been signs that some of the nation are beginning to wish for less neglect of their Army's needs, to which the new Conservative Government returned to power in 1979 under Britain's first woman Prime Minister, Mrs Thatcher, has responded by making an improvement to the Army's pay one of its first priorities.

Although Britain has once again reverted to an all-volunteer Regular Army, it differs in many ways from its forbears. It is smaller than it has ever been since the mid-nineteenth century, totalling some 140,000 of which 5,000 are women; these are backed by about 58,000 of the T.A.* which, when embodied, are fully integrated into the Regular Army. A few small overseas tasks remain but the long years of Imperial policing are over and the Army has returned to defend its home country. This is achieved under the collective defence afforded by the nation's membership of N.A.T.O., which requires the first permanent deployment in peacetime of British forces in Europe. Thus the Army's chief commitment is the maintenance of the 55,000 troops in Germany, organised to provide the I British Corps of four armoured divisions, each mustering two armoured and three mechanized infantry battle groups, and a more lightly equipped, motorised formation known as the 5th Field Force+. The balance of the Army held back in the United Kingdom, including the T.A., is organised for three tasks: the reinforcement of B.A.O.R. on to a war footing; forces earmarked for assignment to the Supreme Allied Commander, Europe; and troops to secure the home base.

Notwithstanding the repercussions of the burdensome task in Ulster and deficiencies in men and equipment imposed by financial stringency, the soldiers of today display a high morale and professional competence, only ever equalled in peacetime just prior to 1914. Its discipline is steadfast and the relationship between officers and men good, though both rest more on recognition of efficiency and sensible man-management than the more automatic respect for rank and position of the past. The social changes in the country over the last two decades are reflected in the Army by a narrowing gap between the backgrounds of officers and men. No longer is a commission the prerogative of the aristocracy and the gentry, and officers are now drawn predominantly from classes which traditionally viewed the Army with dislike, if not contempt, while promotion from the ranks has ceased to be exceptional. With this new type of officer has come a change in attitude to military life. No more is the Army and the regiment regarded as a pleasant and exclusive club, to join which was a privilege that outweighed the meagre financial rewards. Today the Army is a professional career like any other, in which personal advancement is important, the regiment a stepping-stone to greater things, and for which rewards commensurate with effort and ability are expected. As for the men, while unemployment still brings in recruits, the hand-outs of the Welfare State make this a less fruitful source than in the past and, as with the officers, more emphasis has to be placed on providing a worthwhile career to attract the better type of man an increasingly technical force requires. The days of the "old sweat", contentedly passing his time between the company stores and the wet canteen, are over. In appearance too, the Army is greatly changed. The impractical and hideous battle dress disappeared with National Service, being replaced by a khaki uniform similar to officers' service dress, but for most of the time soldiers go about their duties in businesslike clothing of camouflaged material. Above all today's Army prides itself on being totally up-to-date and progressive, more so than ever before, which leaves little time or inclination for reflection on the past glories and traditions that meant so much to earlier generations.

Yet links with over 300 years service to the Crown linger on. The Household Cavalry are still seen in the mid-Victorian splendour of helmet and cuirass, while the scarlet and bearskins of the Foot Guards swing past on the Queen's Birthday Parade in the same steady ranks that scaled the heights above the Alma. In recent years

---

† The Defence White Paper of 1975 required the Army to reduce by a further 15,000 men. 6,000 of these were restored in 1978, at least on paper, but without any reduction in commitments.

* This now includes 80 major units (battalion or equivalent), of which 56 are of the fighting Arms, and 200 minor units (company or equivalent), predominantly of the Services.

+ A battle group is an all-arms formation in which either tanks or mechanized infantry predominate. The Field Force contains an armoured reconnaissance regiment, three battalions and supporting artillery, engineers and services.

The Prime Minister, the Rt. Hon. Margaret Thatcher, is introduced to two members of the 1st Royal Anglian Regiment by Lt.Gen. Sir Timothy Creasey, KCB, OBE, GOC Northern Ireland; at Girdwood Park on the 29th August 1979, during her flying visit following on the assassination of Earl Mountbatten of Burma and the Warren Point ambushes, two days previously.

the Cardwellian blue spiked helmets, fusilier caps and riflemen's busbies have re-appeared on infantry bandsmen, drummers and buglers to rival the feather bonnets and Highland regalia of the Scottish regiments' pipers and musicians. Even a modern service like the Royal Corps of Transport has reverted to the costume of one of its predecessors, the Military Train, for its band. Despite pre-occupations with urban guerillas and armoured warfare, the modern Army's ceremonial has a precision and panache comparable with any of former days, and as its regiments march or drive past the battle honours and insignia won over the centuries show bravely on their Colours and Standards. Few regiments now remain unamalgamated but all of them, from the only surviving link with Cromwell's New Model Army, the Coldstream Guards, to the products of Healey's newer model, like the Royal Irish Rangers, all still loyally observe and remember on special days the chief deeds and glories of their antecedents.

It is good that they do so for, in an age where the regiment and what it stands for seems of lesser significance than formerly, such memorials help keep alive that great strength of the Armies of Britain, that unique quality that has set them apart from those other nations — regimental pride. Field Marshal Templer once rebuked a plea for a Corps of Infantry with the words: *"Do you not realise that the regimental system of the British Army is and always has been the envy of the world?"(3)* Our soldiers have ever been at their best in tight corners, facing great odds. Be it the Gloucesters on the Imjin, the Parachute Regiment at Arnhem, or the Devons at Bois des Buttes; the 24th at Rorke's Drift or, since they learned in the same school, the Guides at Kabul; the Balaclava charges of the Heavy and Light Brigades; the dwindling line of Hoghton's brigade at Albuera; the 15th Light Dragoons routing four French battalions at Emsdorf; the bloody field of Fontenoy where the 1st Guards stood unyielding under the French fire and the 34th won their laurel wreath for covering the retreat; the Royal Irish under Marlborough and at Namur; or even before the beginnings of a standing army when the Whitecoats fought to the last under the moonlight at Marston Moor; in all these instances, and many more besides, men have been sustained by a corporate sense of belonging, a determination not to let their comrades and their regiments down. If the time should come when British soldiers have to stand against a mass assault across the North German plain, it is to be hoped that the same pride in their regiments may help fortify their courage in what would be the most terrible and overwhelming onslaught the British Army has ever had to endure in its long history.

APPENDIX A

REGIMENTS AND CORPS OF THE BRITISH ARMY IN 1979 AND THEIR CHIEF FORBEARS

For reasons of space regiments' main titles only are given, e.g. The 9th Queen's Royal Lancers are shown as 9th Lancers, The Middlesex Regiment (Duke of Cambridge's Own) as Middlesex Regt. The dates in brackets are those of regiments' formation, amalgamation or major change of title.

HOUSEHOLD CAVALRY
Each one regiment plus one mounted regiment of two squadrons.

Life Guards (1922)
- 1st Life Guards (1788) . . . .
  - 1st Troop, Horse Guards (1660)
  - 1st Troop Horse Grenadier Guards (1678)
- 2nd Life Guards (1788) . . . .
  - 2nd(3rd) Troop, Horse Guards (1660)
  - 2nd (3rd) Troop, Horse Grenadier Guards (1702)

Blues and Royals (1969) . . . .
- Royal Horse Guards (Blue) (1750) . . . . Royal Regiment of Horse (1661)
- 1st Royal Dragoons (1751) . . . . Royal Regt of Dragoons (1683) . . . . Tangier Horse (1661)

ROYAL ARMOURED CORPS
All one regiment unless otherwise stated.

Queen's Dragoon Guards (1959) . . . .
- 1st King's Dragoon Guards (1746) . . . . 2nd Horse (1685)
- Queen's Bays (2nd Dragoon Guards) (1746) . . . . 3rd Horse (1685)

Royal Scots Dragoon Guards (1971) . . . .
- 3rd Carabiniers (DG) (1922) . . . .
  - 3rd Dragoon Guards (1746) . . . . 4th Horse (1685)
  - 6th Dragoon Guards (Carabiniers) (1788) . . . . 9th Horse (1685)
- Royal Scots Greys (2nd Dragoons) (1877) . . . . Royal North British Dragoons (1707) . . . . Royal Scots Dragoons (1678)

4th/7th Dragoon Guards (1922) . . . .
- 4th Dragoon Guards (1788) . . . . 1st Irish Horse (1746) . . . . 6th (5th) Horse (1685)
- 7th Dragoon Guards (1788) . . . . 4th Irish Horse (1747) . . . . 10th (8th) Horse (1688)

5th R. Inniskilling Dragoon Guards (1922) . . .
- 5th Dragoon Guards (1788) . . . . 2nd Irish Horse (1747) . . . . 7th (6th) Horse (1685)
- 6th Inniskilling Dragoons (1751) . . . . Inniskilling Dragoons (1689)

Queen's Own Hussars (1959) . . . .
- 3rd Hussars (1861) (Light Dragoons 1818) . . . . 3rd Dragoons (1685)
- 7th Hussars (1807) (Light Dragoons 1784) . . . . 7th Dragoons (1690)

Queen's Royal Irish Hussars (1958) . . . .
- 4th Hussars (1861) (Light Dragoons 1818) . . . . 4th Dragoons (1685)
- 8th Hussars (1822) (Light Dragoons 1775) . . . . 8th Dragoons (1693)

9th/12th Lancers (1960) . . . .
- 9th Lancers (1816) (Light Dragoons 1783) . . . . 9th Dragoons (1715)
- 12th Lancers (1816) (Light Dragoons 1768) . . . . 12th Dragoons (1715)

Royal Hussars (1969) . . . .
- 10th Hussars (1806) (Light Dragoons 1783) . . . . 10th Dragoons (1715)
- 11th Hussars (1840) (Light Dragoons 1783) . . . . 11th Dragoons (1715)

13th/18th Hussars (1922) . . . .
- 13th Hussars (1861) (Light Dragoons 1783) . . . . 13th Dragoons (1715)
- 18th Hussars (1858)

14th/20th Hussars (1922) . . . .
- 14th Hussars (1861) (Light Dragoons 1776) . . . . 14th Dragoons (1715)
- 20th Hussars (1861) . . . . HEIC 2nd Bengal European Light Cavalry (1858)

15th/19th Hussars (1922) . . . .
- 15th Hussars (1807) . . . . 15th Light Dragoons (1759)
- 19th Hussars (1861) . . . . HEIC 1st Bengal European Light Cavalry (1858)

16th/5th Lancers (1922) . . . .
- 16th Lancers (1816) . . . . 16th Light Dragoons (1759)
- 5th Lancers (1861) . . . . 5th Dragoons (1751-99) . . . . Royal Irish Dragoons (1689)

17th/21st Lancers (1922) . . . .
- 17th Lancers (1822) . . . . 17th Light Dragoons (1763) . . . . 18th Light Dragoons (1759)
- 21st Lancers (1897) . . . . 21st Hussars (1861) . . . . HEIC 3rd Bengal European Light Cavalry (1858)

Royal Tank Regiment (1939) (Four regts.) . . . . Royal Tank Corps (1917) . . . . Heavy Section, Machine-Gun Corps (1916)

Royal Yeomanry (TA) (1965) . . . .
- Royal Wiltshire Yeomanry (1794)
- Sherwood Rangers (1794)
- Kent & County of London Yeomanry (1961) . . . .
  - Royal East Kent Yeomanry (1830)
  - West Kent Yeomanry (1831)
  - 3rd County of London Yeo. (1902)
  - 4th County of London Yeo. (1939)
- North Irish Horse (1902)
- Berkshire & Westminster Dragoons (1961) . . . .
  - Berkshire Yeomanry (1831)
  - Westminster Dragoons (1901)

Queen's Own Yeomanry (TA) (1971) . . . .
- Queen's Own Yorkshire Yeomanry (1956) . . . .
  - Yorkshire Hussars (1794)
  - Yorkshire Dragoons (1803)
  - East Riding Yeo. (1903)
- Ayrshire Yeomanry (1803)
- Cheshire Yeomanry (1794)
- Northumberland Hussars (1819)

Wessex Yeomanry (TA) (1971) . . . .
- Royal Wiltshire Yeomanry (1794)
- Royal Gloucestershire Hussars (1830)
- Royal Devon Yeomanry/1st Rifle Volunteers (T) . . . .
  - Royal 1st Devon Yeo. (1831)
  - Royal North Devon Yeo. (1831)
  - 4th Devons . . . . 1st Devon Rifle
  - (TA) (1881)   Volunteers (1852)

Queen's Own Mercian Yeomanry (TA) (1971) . . . .
- Warwick & Worcester Yeomanry (1956) . . . .
  - Warwickshire Yeomanry (1794)
  - Worcestershire Hussars (1831)
- Staffordshire Yeomanry (1794)
- Shropshire Yeomanry (1795)

Duke of Lancaster's Yeomanry (TA) (1971) . . . .
- Duke of Lancaster's Yeomanry (1819)
- 40th/41st Royal Tank Regiment (1956)

ROYAL REGIMENT OF ARTILLERY
Regiments: 21 Regular, 6 TA. Batteries: 4 Regular, 3 TA.

Royal Horse Artillery (1862) . . . .
- Royal Horse Artillery (1793)
- HEIC Bengal, Madras, Bombay Horse Artillery (1800)

Royal Artillery (1862) . . . .
- Royal Artillery (1801) . . . .
  - Royal Artillery (1716)
  - Royal Irish Artillery (1756)
- HEIC Bengal, Madras and Bombay Foot Artillery (1748)

Honourable Artillery Company (TA) (1668) . . . . Guild of St George (1537)

CORPS OF ROYAL ENGINEERS

Royal Engineers (1862) . . . . { Royal Engineers (1855) . . . . { Royal Engineers (Officers) (1787) . . . . Engineer Officers (1757)
{ HEIC Bengal, Madras and Bombay Engineers (1764) { Royal Sappers & Miners (1813) . . . . Royal Military Artificers (1772)

Royal Monmouthshire Royal Engineers (TA) (1872) . . . . Monmouthshire Trained Bands (1577)

ROYAL CORPS OF SIGNALS

Royal Corps of Signals (1920) . . . . Corps of Royal Engineers (see above)

INFANTRY
All regiments one battalion except where stated.

Guards Division
Grenadier Guards (1815) (2 Regular battalions) . . . . 1st Foot Guards (1685) . . . . King's Royal Regiment of Guards (1660)

Coldstream Guards (1670) (2 Regular battalions) . . . . Lord General's Foot Guards (1660) . . . . Colonel Monck's Regiment (1650)

Scots Guards (1877) (2 Regular battalions) . . . . Scots Fusilier Guards (1831) . . . . 3rd Foot Guards (1713) . . . . Scots Regiment of Guards (1660)

Irish Guards (1900)

Welsh Guards (1915)

Scottish Division
Royal Scots (1881) . . . . 1st Foot (1633)

Royal Highland Fusiliers (1959) . . . . { Royal Scots Fusiliers (1881) . . . . 21st Foot (1678)
{ Highland Light Infantry (1881) . . . . { 71st Foot (1777)
{ 74th Foot (1787)

King's Own Scottish Borderers (1881) . . . . 25th Foot (1689)

Black Watch (1881) . . . . 42nd Foot (1739)
73rd Foot (1786)

Queen's Own Highlanders (1961) . . . . { Seaforth Highlanders (1881) . . . . { 72nd Foot (1778)
{ 78th Foot (1793)
{ Cameron Highlanders (1881) . . . . 79th Foot (1793)

Gordon Highlanders (1881) . . . . { 75th Foot (1787)
{ 92nd Foot (1794)

Argyll & Sutherland Highlanders (1881) . . . . { 91st Foot (1793)
{ 93rd Foot (1800)

51st Highland Volunteers (1967) (3 TA battalions) . . . . Territorial (1908) and Volunteer (1881) battalions of Highland regiments

52nd Lowland Volunteers (1967 & 1971) (2 TA battalions) . . . . Territorial (1908) and Volunteer (1881) battalions of Lowland regiments

Queen's Division

Queen's Regiment (1966) . . . . { Queen's Royal Surrey Regt. (1959) . . . . { Queen's Royal Regt. (1881) . . . . 2nd Foot (1661)
(3 Regular, 2 TA battalions) { East Surrey Regt. (1881) . . . . { 31st Foot (1713)
{ 70th Foot (1758)
{ Queen's Own Buffs (1961) . . . . { Buffs (1881) . . . . 3rd Foot (1572)
{ Royal West Kent Regt. (1881) . . . . { 50th Foot (1755)
{ 97th Foot (1824)
{ Royal Sussex Regt (1881) . . . . { 35th Foot (1702)
{ 107th Foot (1862)....HEIC 3rd Bengal Europeans (1854)
{ Middlesex Regt. (1881) . . . . { 57th Foot (1755)
{ 77th Foot (1787)

Royal Regiment of Fusiliers (1968) . . . . { Royal Northumberland Fusiliers (1881) . . . . 5th Foot (1674)
(3 Regular, 2 TA battalions) { Royal Warwickshire Fusiliers (1963) (Regiment 1881) . . . . 6th Foot (1673)
{ Royal Fusiliers (1881) . . . . 7th Foot (1685)
{ Lancashire Fusiliers (1881) . . . . 20th Foot (1688)

Royal Anglian Regiment (1964) . . . . { 1st East Anglian Regt. (1959) . . . . { Royal Norfolk Regt. (1881) . . . . 9th Foot (1685)
(3 Regular, 3 TA battalions) { Suffolk Regt. (1881) . . . . 12th Foot (1685)
{ 2nd East Anglian Regt. (1960) . . . . { Royal Lincolnshire Regt. (1881) . . . . 10th Foot (1685)
{ Northamptonshire Regt. (1881) . . . . { 48th Foot (1741)
{ 58th Foot (1755)
{ 3rd East Anglian Regt. (1958) . . . . { Bedfordshire & Hertfordshire Regt. (1881) . . . . 16th Foot (1688)
{ Essex Regt. (1881) . . . . { 44th Foot (1741)
{ 56th Foot (1755)
{ Royal Leicestershire Regt. (1881) . . . . 17th Foot (1688)

King's Division
King's Own Royal Border Regt. (1959) . . . . { King's Own Royal Regt. (1881) . . . . 4th Foot (1680)
(1 Regular, 1 TA battalions) { Border Regt. (1881) . . . . { 34th Foot (1702)
{ 55th Foot (1755)

King's Regiment (1958) (1 Regular, 1 TA bn) . . . . { King's Liverpool Regt (1881) . . . . 8th Foot (1685)
{ Manchester Regt (1881) . . . . { 63rd Foot (1756)
{ 96th Foot (1824)

Prince of Wales's Own Regt of Yorkshire (1958) . . . . . . { West Yorkshire Regt (1881) . . . . 14th Foot (1685)
{ East Yorkshire Regt (1881) . . . . 15th Foot (1685)

Green Howards (1881) . . . . 19th Foot (1688)

Royal Irish Rangers (1968) (2 Regular, 2 TA bns) . . . . . . { Royal Inniskilling Fusiliers (1881) . . . . { 27th Foot (1689)
{ 108th Foot (1862)....HEIC 3rd Madras Europeans (1854)
{ Royal Ulster Rifles (1922) . . . . Royal Irish Rifles (1881) . . . . { 83rd Foot (1793)
{ 86th Foot (1793)
{ Royal Irish Fusiliers (1881) . . . . { 87th Foot (1793)
{ 89th Foot (1793)

Queen's Lancashire Regt (1970) . . . . { Lancashire Regt (1958) . . . . { East Lancashire Regt (1881) . . . . { 30th Foot (1714)
{ 59th Foot (1755)
(1 Regular, 1 TA btn) { South Lancashire Regt (1881) . . . . { 40th Foot (1717)
{ 82nd Foot (1793)
{ Loyal North Lancashire Regt (1881) . . . . { 47th Foot (1741)
{ 81st Foot (1793)

King's Division Contd.

Duke of Wellington's Regiment (1881) . . . . 33rd Foot (1702) / 76th Foot (1787)

Yorkshire Volunteers (1967) (3 TA bns) . . . . Territorial (1908) and Volunteer (1881) battalions of West and East Yorkshire Regts, Green Howards, Duke of Wellington's

Prince of Wales's Division

Devon & Dorset Regt (1958) . . . . {Devonshire Regt (1881) . . . . 11th Foot (1685) / 39th Foot (1702) {Dorset Regt (1881) . . . . 54th Foot (1755)

Cheshire Regt (1881) . . . . 22nd Foot (1689)

Royal Welch Fusiliers (1881) (1 Regular, 1 TA bn) . . . . 23rd Foot (1688)

Royal Regiment of Wales (1969) . . . . {South Wales Borderers (1881) . . . . 24th Foot (1689) / 41st Foot (1719) (1 Regular, 2 TA bns) {Welch Regiment (1881) . . . . 69th Foot (1756)

Gloucestershire Regt (1881) . . . . 28th Foot (1694) / 61st Foot (1756)

Worcestershire & Sherwood Foresters Reg (1970) . . . {Worcestershire Regt (1881) . . . . 29th Foot (1694) / 36th Foot (1702) (1 Regular, 1 TAVR, bn) {Sherwood Foresters (1881) . . . . 45th Foot (1741) / 95th Foot (1823)

Royal Hampshire Regiment (1881) . . . . 37th Foot (1702) / 67th Foot (1758)

Staffordshire Regt (1959) . . . . {South Staffordshire Regt (1881) . . . . 38th Foot (1705) / 80th Foot (1793) {North Staffordshire Regt (1881) . . . . 64th Foot (1756) / 98th Foot (1824)

Duke of Edinburgh's Royal Regt (1959) . . . . {Royal Berkshire Regt (1881) . . . . 49th Foot (1743) / 66th Foot (1756) {Wiltshire Regt (1881) . . . . 62nd Foot (1755) / 99th Foot (1824)

Wessex Regiment (1967) (2 TA bns) . . . . Territorial (1908) and Volunteer (1881) battalions of Devons, Dorsets, Gloucesters, Royal Hampshires, Royal Berkshires, Wiltshires

Mercian Volunteers (1967) (2 TA bns) . . . . Territorial (1908) and Volunteer (1881) battalions of Cheshires, South and North Staffords

Light Division

Light Infantry (1968) (3 Regular, 3 TA bns) . . . . {Somerset & Cornwall Light Infantry (1959) . . . . {Somerset Light Infantry (1881) . . . . 13th Foot (1685) / 32nd Foot (1702) {Duke of Cornwall's Light Infantry (1881) . . . . 46th Foot (1741) / 51st Foot (1754) {King's Own Yorkshire Light Infantry (1881) . . . . {105th Foot (1861)....HEIC 2nd Madras Europeans (1839) {King's Shropshire Light Infantry (1881) . . . . 53rd Foot (1755) / 85th Foot (1793) {Durham Light Infantry (1881) . . . . 68th Foot (1756) / 106th Foot (1861)....HEIC 2nd Bombay Europeans (1826)

Royal Green Jackets (1966) (3 Regular, 1 TA bns) . . . . . . {1st Green Jackets (43rd & 52nd) (1958) . . . Oxfordshire & Buckinghamshire Light Infantry (1881) . . 43rd Foot (1741) / 52nd Foot (1755) {2nd Green Jackets (KRRC) (1958) . . . . King's Royal Rifle Corps (1881) . . . . 60th Foot (1756) {3rd Green Jackets (RB) (1958) . . . . Rifle Brigade (1816) . . . . 95th Rifles (1800)

AIRBORNE FORCES
Parachute Regiment (1942) (3 Regular, 3 TA bns)

Special Air Service Regiment (1941) (1 Regular, 2 TA regts)

Army Air Corps (1942) (Reconstituted 1957)

BRIGADE OF GURKHAS
2nd Gurkha Rifles (1906) (2 Regular bns) . . . . 2nd Gurkha Regt (1861) . . . . HEIC Sirmoor Battalion (1815)

6th Gurkha Rifles (1903) . . . . 42nd Bengal Native Infantry (1861) . . . . HEIC Cuttack Legion (1817)

7th Gurkha Rifles (1907) . . . . 2/10th Gurkha Rifles (1903) . . . . 8th Gurkha Rifles (1902)

10th Gurkha Rifles (1901) . . . . 10th Madras Infantry (1st Burma Gurkha Rifles) (1895) . . . . 1st Burma Infantry (1891)

Queen's Gurkha Engineers (1960) . . . . 50th Field Engineer Regt RE (1951) . . . . 67th Field Squadron RE (1948)

Queen's Gurkha Signals (1954) . . . . Gurkha Brigade Signal Squadron (1948)

Gurkha Transport Regiment (1965) . . . . Gurkha Army Service Corps (1958)

Ulster Defence Regiment (1970) (11 battalions)

DISBANDED INFANTRY REGIMENTS
In 1922 (each 2 Regular bns)
Royal Irish Regiment (1881) . . . . 18th Foot (1689)

Connaught Rangers (1881) . . . . 88th Foot (1793) / 94th Foot (1823)

Leinster Regiment (1881) . . . . 100th Foot (1858) / 109th Foot (1862)....HEIC 3rd Bombay Europeans (1853)

Royal Munster Fusiliers (1881) . . . . {101st Foot (1861) . . . . HEIC 1st Bengal Europeans (1756) {104th Foot (1861) . . . . HEIC 2nd Bengal Europeans (1839)

Royal Dublin Fusiliers (1881) . . . . {102nd Foot (1861) . . . . HEIC 1st Madras Europeans (1748) {103rd Foot (1861) . . . . HEIC 1st Bombay Europeans (1661)

In 1968 (each 1 Regular bn)
Cameronians (Scottish Rifles) (1881) . . . . 26th Foot (1689) / 90th Foot (1794)

York & Lancaster Regiment (1881) .... { 65th Foot (1758)
84th Foot (1793)

SERVICES

Royal Army Chaplains Department (1858) .... Army Chaplains (1796) .... Regimental Chaplains (1662)

| Royal Corps of Transport (1965) | Royal Army Service Corps (1888) | Military Train (1857-69) | Land Transport Corps (1855-56) | Royal Waggon Train (1802-33) | Royal Waggon Corps (1799) |
| .... | .... | .... | .... | .... | .... |

Royal Army Medical Corps (1898) .... { Army Medical Staff (Officers) (1873) .... Regimental Surgeons (18th Cent. - 1872)
Medical Staff Corps (1884) .... Army Hospital Corps (1856) .... Medical Staff Corps (1855)

Royal Army Ordnance Corps (1922) .... { Army Ordnance Department (1894) .... Ordnance Store Branch (1877) } .... Board of Ordnance (1418)
Army Ordnance Corps (1896) .... Ordnance Store Corps (1881)

Royal Electrical & Mechanical Engineers (1942) .... { Royal Engineers
Royal Army Service Corps
Royal Army Ordnance Corps

Royal Military Police (1926) .... { Military Mounted Police (1877)
Military Foot Police (1885)

Royal Army Pay Corps (1893) .... Army Pay Department (Officers) (1878) .... Regimental Paymasters .... Army Agents (17th Cent.)

Royal Army Veterinary Corps (1903) .... Army Veterinary Department (Officers) (1881) .... Regimental Veterinary Surgeons (1796)

Royal Military Academy Band Corps

Small Arms School Corps (1929) .... { Small Arms School (1919) .... School of Musketry (1902) .... Royal Corps of Musketry Instructors (1853)
Machine-Gun School

Military Provost Staff Corps (1906) .... Military Prison Staff Corps (1901)

Royal Army Education Corps (1920) .... Corps of Army Schoolmasters (1846) .... Regimental Schools (1812)

Royal Army Dental Corps (1921) .... Royal Army Medical Corps

Royal Pioneer Corps (1940) .... Auxiliary Military Pioneer Corps (1939)

Intelligence Corps (1940)

Army Physical Training Corps (1940)

Army Catering Corps (1941)

Army Legal Corps (1978) .... Army Legal Services Staff List (1948)

General Service Corps (1942) (in abeyance)

Queen Alexandra's Royal Army Nursing Corps (1949) .... Queen Alexandra's Imperial Military Nursing Service (1902) .... Army Nursing Service (1881)

Women's Royal Army Corps (1949) .... Auxiliary Territorial Service (1938) .... Women's Auxiliary Army Corps (1917-18)

COMMAND OF THE ARMY 1485 - 1980

LORD HIGH CONSTABLE

1485 - 1521   3rd Duke of Buckingham

CAPTAIN - GENERAL

1638   Earl of Arundel and Surrey (Earl Marshal)

COMMANDERS - IN - CHIEF

1660 - 70	1st Duke of Albemarle, KG (Captain-General)
1674 - 90	1st Duke of Monmouth, KG
1690-- 1	1st Earl of Marlborough (temporary)
1691	1st Duke of Leinster and 3rd Duke of Schomberg (temporary)
1702	1st Duke of Marlborough (Captain-General)
1702 - 12	Prince George of Denmark, KG (Generalissimo)
1712 - 14	1st Duke of Ormond, KG (Captain-General)
1744 - 46	2nd Earl of Stair, KT
1745	Marshal George Wade
1745 - 57	HRH Duke of Cumberland, KG (Captain-General)
1757 - 63	1st Earl Ligonier, KB
1766 - 70	Marquis of Granby
1778 - 82	1st Lord Amherst, KB (General-on-Staff)
1782 - 3	Hon. Henry Seymour Conway
1793 - 5	1st Lord Amherst, KB (General-on-Staff)
1795 - 1809	HRH Duke of York and Albany, KG,GCB,GCH (Captain-General)
1809 - 11	Sir David Dundas, Bart., KB
1811 - 27	HRH Duke of York and Albany, KG,GCB,GCH
1827 - 28	1st Duke of Wellington, KG,GCB,GCH
1828 - 42	1st Viscount Hill, GCB,GCH,KC
1842 - 52	1st Duke of Wellington, KG,GCB,GCH
1852 - 6	1st Viscount Hardinge, GCB
1856 - 95	HRH Duke of Cambridge, KG,KT,KP,GCB,GCSI,GCMG,GCIE,GCVO
1895 - 1900	Field-Marshal 1st Viscount Wolseley,KP,GCB,OM,GCMG
1900 - 4	Field-Marshal 1st Earl Roberts, VC,KG,KP,GCB,OM,GCSI,GCIE,VD

CHIEFS OF THE GENERAL STAFF

1904 - 8	Lieutenant-General Sir Neville Lyttelton, KCB
1908 - 9	General Sir William Nicholson, GCB

CHIEFS OF THE IMPERIAL GENERAL STAFF

1909 - 12	General Sir William Nicholson, GCB
1912 - 14	Field-Marshal Sir John French, KP,GCB,OM,GCVO,KCMG
1914	General Sir Charles Douglas, GCB
1914 - 15	Lieutenant-General Sir James Wolfe Murray, KCB
1915	Lieutenant-General Sir Archibald Murray, GCB,GCMG,CVO,DSO
1915 - 18	General Sir William Robertson, GCB,GCMG,GCVO,DSO
1918 - 22	Field-Marshal Sir Henry Wilson, GCB,DSO
1922 - 26	General 10th Earl of Cavan, KP,GCB,GCMG,GCVO,GBE
1926 - 33	Field-Marshal Sir George Milne, GCB,GCMG,DSO
1933 - 36	Field-Marshal Sir Archibald Montgomery-Massingberd, GCB,KCMG
1937 - 39	General 6th Viscount Gort, VC,GCB,CBE, DSO,MVO,MC
1939 - 40	General Sir Edmund Ironside, GCB,CMG,DSO
1940 - 41	Field-Marshal Sir John Dill, GCB,CMG,DSO
1941 - 46	Field-Marshal 1st Viscount Alanbrooke, KG,GCB,OM,GCVO,DSO
1946 - 48	Field-Marshal 1st Viscount Montgomery of Alamein, KG,GCB,DSO
1948 - 52	Field Marshal Sir William Slim, GCB,GCMG,GBE,DSO,MC
1952 - 55	Field-Marshal Sir John Harding GCB,CBE,DSO,MC
1955 - 58	Field-Marshal Sir Gerald Templer, GCB,GCMG,KBE,DSO
1958 - 61	Field-Marshal Sir Francis Festing, GCB,KBE,DSO
1961 - 64	General Sir Richard Hull, GCB,DSO

CHIEFS OF THE GENERAL STAFF

1964 - 65	General Sir Richard Hull, GCB,DSO
1965 - 68	General Sir James Cassels, GCB,KBE,DSO
1968 - 71	Field-Marshal Sir Geoffrey Baker, GCB,CMG,CBE,MC
1971 - 73	Field-Marshal Sir Michael Carver, GCB,CBE,DSO,MC
1973 - 76	General Sir Peter Hunt, GCB,DSO,OBE
1976 - 79	General Sir Roland Gibbs, GCB,CBE,MC
1979 -	General Sir Edwin Bramall, KCB,OBE,MC

REFERENCES

CHAPTER 1
1. Hall's Chronicle, quoted Journal of the Society for Army Historical Research (J.S.A.H.R.), Vol.XVI, p.65.
2. Quoted C.C.P.Lawson, "History of the Uniforms of the British Army", Vol.1(1940),p.190.
3. Quoted Cecil Sebag-Montefiore, "A History of the Volunteer Forces" (1908),p.21.
4. 1557, Act 2, Mary, quoted G.Jackson Hay, "The Constitutional Force", (1905),p.88.
5. "A Survey, or Muster of the Armed and Trayned Companies in London, 1588 and 1599",J.S.A.H.R., Vol.IV,p.68.
6. Captain Barnaby Rich, quoted Corelli Barnett, "Britain and Her Army" (1970)(Barnett, "Britain's Army")p.42.
7. Quoted J.S.A.H.R., Vol.XII,p.68.
8. Bishop Burnet, quoted Barnett, "Britain's Army",p.76.

CHAPTER 2
1. Quoted John Buchan, "Oliver Cromwell" (1934), p.135.
2. Quoted M.M.Reese, "Master of the Horse" (1976),p.180.
3. Thomas Carlyle, "Cromwell's Letters and Speeches"(1904), quoted Buchan, op.cit.,p.158.
4. Buchan, op.cit.,p.163. Quoted in ibid.,p.165
5. Quoted in ibid.,p.192.
6. Quoted in ibid.,p.192.
7. Quoted in ibid.,p.197.
8. Carlyle, op.cit., quoted in ibid.,p.204.
9. Quoted in ibid.,p.205.
10. Holles, "Memoirs", quoted in ibid.,p.207,fn.1.
11. Quoted in ibid.p.215.
12. Ibid.,p.295.
13. Quoted in ibid.,p.324.
14. Hon.J.W.Fortescue, "A History of the British Army", 13 Vols., (1899-1930),Vol.I.p.245.
15. Ibid.,p.285.

CHAPTER 3
1. Quoted David Chandler, "Marlborough as Military Commander"(1973), (Chandler "Marlborough")p.31.
2. Ballad, "The Battle of the Boyne", quoted Lewis Winstock, "Songs and Music of the Redcoats, 1642-1902"(1970),p.25.
3. Letters of Samuel Noyes, Chaplain to the Royal Scots, J.S.A.H.R., Vol.XXXVII,p.37.
4. Quoted J.S.A.H.R., Vol.XXVII,p.8.
5. Quoted in ibid.,p.9.
6. Hon.J.W.Fortescue, "The Last Post"(1934), quoted R.E.Scouller, "The Armies of Queen Anne" (1966)p.322.

CHAPTER 4
1. Quoted J.S.A.H.R., Vol.XXIII,p.161.
2. Quoted Elizabeth Longford, "Wellington – The Years of the Sword" (1969)p.322.
3. "The Life and Diary of Colonel John Blackadder"(1824), quoted Peter Young and J.P.Lawford (ed.) "History of the British Army"(1970)p.27.
4. Dr Hare, Marlborough's chaplain, quoted David Green, "Blenheim" (1974),pp.47-48.
5. Quoted in David Chandler, "The Art of War in the Age of Marlborough"(1976)(Chandler, "Art of War")p.53.
6. Quoted R.E.Scouller, "The Armies of Queen Anne"(1966)p.185.
7. Ibid.,p.217.
8. Chandler "Marlborough",p.75.

9. Quoted Corelli Barnett, "Marlborough"(1974) (Barnett "Marlborough")p.87.
10. Captain Robert Parker "Memoirs"(1746), quoted in ibid.,p.87.
11. Noyes, op.cit.,p.149-150.
12. "Letters of the First Lord Orkney during Marlborough's Campaigns", quoted Barnett, "Marlborough",p.166.
13. Peter Drake, Irish captain in the French service, quoted ibid.,p.169.
14. MSS Autobiography of General Hawley, J.S.A.H.R., Vol.XXV,pp.152-3.
15. According to remarks made to the regiment, then 9th (East Norfolk) Regiment of Foot by General Bainbridge in 1848.
16. Quoted Barnett, "Marlborough",p.211.
17. Quoted Chandler, "Marlborough",p.258.
18. Barnett, "Marlborough",p.239.
19. Quoted in ibid.,p.240.
20. "The Flying Post" 29th August 1710, quoted J.S.A.H.R., Vol.XXV,p.15.
21. Quoted Chandler, "Marlborough",p.298.
22. Quoted in ibid.,p.294.
23. Quoted in ibid.,pp.314,328.

CHAPTER 5
1. Public Record Office WO IV, Vol.29,26.10. 1728, quoted J.S.A.H.R., Vol.XXI,p.144.
2. Quoted Fortescue, op.cit.,Vol.II,p.20.
3. Ibid.,p.36.
4. Letter, Major Charles Colville, 21st Foot, quoted J.S.A.H.R., Vol.XXVI,p.118.
5. Letter, Mr Kendal, private gentleman in the 3rd Troop of Horse Guards, quoted J.S.A.H.R., Vol.XI,p.170.
6. Colville, op.cit.
7. Ibid.
8. Kendal, op.cit.,p.169.
9. Letter to Charles James Hamilton, quoted J.S.A.H.R., Vol.VI,p.95.
10. Quoted Fortescue, op.cit.,Vol.II,p.115.
11. Colonel H.C.B.Rogers, "The British Army in the 18th Century"(1977), p.204.
12. Letter, Edward Wortley Montague, quoted J.S.A.H.R., Vol.XXVII,p.169.
13. Letter, quoted J.S.A.H.R., Vol.XXXV,p.184.
14. Quoted John Prebble, "Culloden"(Penguin 1967)p.101.

CHAPTER 6
1. Winston S.Churchill, "A History of the English-Speaking Peoples", Vol.III(1957)p.123.
2. Quoted Fortescue, op.cit.Vol.II,p.279.
3. Captain John Knox, 43rd Foot, "Historical Journal of the Campaigns of 1757, 1758, 1759 and 1760", quoted C.C.P.Lawson, "A History of the Uniforms of the British Army", Vol.II(1941) p.46.
4. Letter, James Wolfe, quoted Francis Parkman, "Montcalm and Wolfe", Vol.II(1901)p.93.
5. Letter, "Boston Newsletter" of 6th July 1758, quoted J.S.A.H.R., Vol.LV,p.187.
6. Letter, officer of the 60th Foot, 14th July 1758, quoted J.S.A.H.R., Vol.I,p.13.
7. Quoted Parkman, op.cit.p.93.
8. Quoted Russell Gurney, "History of the Northamptonshire Regiment"(1935)p.35.
9. Quartermaster Sergeant John Johnson, 58th Foot, "Memoirs of the Siege of Quebec and Total Reduction of Canada",MSS.
10. Knox,op.cit.,quoted Oliver Warner, "With Wolfe to Quebec"(1972)p.167.
11. Johnson,op.cit.
12. Quoted in Lt-General Sir Reginald Savory, "His

Britannic Majesty's Army in Germany during the Seven Years War"(1966)p.viii.
13. Quoted Fortescue,op.cit.Vol.II p.495.
14. Quoted Savory,op.cit.p.184, fn 1.
15. Quoted in ibid.,p.323. fn 1.
16. Journal, 1758-62, quoted in J.S.A.H.R., Vol. LIV,p.83.
17. Ibid.,p.83.
18. Ibid.,p.85.
19. Quoted Savory,op.cit.p.421, fn 1.
20. Colonel Mauvillon, staff officer to Prince Ferdinand, quoted John Mollo, "Uniforms of the Seven Years War"(1977)p.19.
21. Colonel Riedesal, quoted Savory, op.cit.p.354.

CHAPTER 7
1. Diary of James Miller, 1745-50, J.S.A.H.R., Vol.III,p.217.
2. Ibid.,p.225.
3. Forde's report to Madras, quoted Philip Mason, "A Matter of Honour", (1974),p.90.
4. Quoted Mason, op.cit.,p.121.
5. Smith's report, quoted in ibid.,p.69.
6. Ibid.,p.70.
7. Fortescue, op.cit., Vol.III,p.128.
8. Wilks, "History of Mysore", quoted in Sir Patrick Cadell, "History of the Bombay Army" (1938),p.93.
9. Quoted Cadell, op.cit.,p.98.
10. Fortescue, op.cit.,Vol.III,p.492.

CHAPTER 8
1. Quoted Fortescue, op.cit.,Vol.III,p.167.
2. Quoted in ibid.,p.398.
3. Quoted in ibid.,p.242.
4. Quoted in ibid.,p.411.
5. Sergeant Ancell, 58th Regt., "Circumstantial Journal of the Long and Tedious Blockade and Siege of Gibraltar", quoted Thomas Gilby, "Britain at Arms" (1953)p.157.

CHAPTER 9
1. Quoted Gilby, op.cit.,p.49.
2. Letter of his brother, Lord Paget, J.S.A.H.R., Vol.XXXII,p.103, n.74.
3. Quoted Barnett, "Britain's Army",pp.236-7.
4. Ensign T.B.George, 80th Foot, J.S.A.H.R., Vol.XLVII,p.241.
5. Quoted Richard Glover, "Peninsular Preparation 1795-1809" (1963),p.178.
6. Quoted in ibid.,p.179.
7. General Sir Henry Bunbury, "The Great War with France"(1854), quoted Rogers, op.cit.,p.227.
8. Quoted Carola Oman, "Sir John Moore"(1953), p.257.
9. Quoted Glover, op.cit.,p.3.
10. Wellington's Despatches, quoted Longford, op.cit.,p.88.
11. Quoted in ibid.,p.88.
12. Quoted in Gilby, op.cit.,p.193.
13. Quoted in Fortescue, op.cit.,Vol.V,p.66.
14. Quoted T.H.McGuffie, "Recruiting the Ranks of the Regular Army during the Napoleonic Wars", J.S.A.H.R., Vol.XXXIV,p.53.
15. Quoted Glover, op.cit.,p.224.
16. Quoted in ibid.,p.223.
17. Ibid.,p.43.

CHAPTER 10
1. Quoted Barnett, "Britain's Army",p.254.
2. Quoted Douglas Bell, "Wellington's Officers" (1938),p.220.
3. John Kincaid, "Adventures in the Rifle Brigade"(1830),p.58.

4. Wellington, quoted Longford, *op.cit.*,p.286.
5. Wellington, quoted Michael Glover, "Wellington's Army"(1977),p.145.
6. Quoted Michael Glover, "Wellington as Military Commander"(1968),p.211.
7. Quoted Longford, *op.cit.*,pp.328 and 218.
8. Marshal Bugeaud, quoted C.W.C.Oman, "Wellington's Army"(1912),pp.91-92.
9. George Bell, "Rough Notes of an Old Soldier" (1956 edn.),p.46.
10. *Ibid.*,p.83.
11. Quoted Michael Glover, "Wellington's Army", p.171.
12. Kincaid, *op.cit.*,p.182.
13. Quoted Longford, *op.cit.*,p.488.
14. Cavalie Mercer, "Journal of the Waterloo Campaign"(1870), quoted John Naylor, "Waterloo" (1960),pp.145,149.
15. Quoted Naylor, *op.cit.*,pp.169-170.
16. Longford, *op.cit.*,p.477.
17. Quoted in *ibid.*,p.490.
18. Sergeant Cooper, "Rough Notes of Seven Campaigns", quoted Gilby, *op.cit.*,p.194.
19. Kincaid, *op.cit.*,p.245.

CHAPTER 11
1. J.H.Stocqueler, "The Old Field Officer" (1853), quoted Philip Mason, *op.cit.*p.140.
2. Madras subadar, quoted Mason, *op.cit.*,p.23.
3. Holt McKenzie, quoted in *ibid.*,p.196.
4. Florentia Sale, "A Journal of the Disasters in Afghanistan 1841-2"(1843), quoted in *ibid.*,p.223.
5. *Ibid.*,p.224.
6. J.S.A.H.R., Vol.XLV,p.222.
7. Major Waddington, 22nd Foot, J.S.A.H.R., Vol.LV,p.133.
8. Quoted Gilby, *op.cit.*,p.251.
9. Lieut.Taylor, Governor-General's Bodyguard, quoted Marquess of Anglesey, "A History of the British Cavalry 1816-1919", Vol.I.(1973),p.250.
10. Quoted Donald Featherstone, "At them with the Bayonet"(1968),p.140.
11. Quoted Gilby,*op.cit.*,p.251.
12. Hookum Singh, quoted Featherstone, *op.cit.*, p.142.
13. Quoted Featherstone, *op.cit.*,p.147.
14. Lord Hardinge and Captain Unett, 3rd Light Dragoons respectively, quoted in Anglesey, *op.cit.*, p.257 and 278.
15. Brigadier Ashburnham at Ferozeshah, S.A.H.R., Vol.XI,p.70.
16. J.S.A.H.R., Vol.XXX,p.56.

CHAPTER 12
1. Fortescue, *op.cit.*,Vol.XI,p.32.
2. Quoted Elizabeth Longford, "Wellington, Pillar of State"(Panther edition, 1975)p.460.
3. A Regimental Officer (Colonel C.T.Wilson, Coldstream Guards), "Our Veterans of 1854"(1859) p.38.
4. Barnett, "Britain's Army",p.286.
5. A Regimental Officer, *op.cit.*,p.20.
6. Quoted Michael Barthorp, "Crimean Uniforms-British Infantry"(1974)p.116.
7. Quoted W.Baring Pemberton, "Battles of the Crimean War"(1962)p.86.
8. Major Patullo, 30th Foot, quoted in *ibid.*, p.130.
9. Quoted in *ibid.*,p.164.
10. Sergeant T.Gowing, 7th Royal Fusiliers, "A Soldier's Experience"(1895)p.109.
11. General Sir George Higginson, "Seventy One Years of a Guardsman's Life"(1916)p.276.

12. Royal Warrant dated 5th February 1856, quoted D.H.Parry, "Britain's Roll of Glory"(1895) p.285.

CHAPTER 13
1. J.B.Norton, British Resident, quoted in James Hewitt(ed.) "Eye-Witnesses to the Indian Mutiny"(1972)p.4.
2. Philip Mason, *op.cit.*,p.286.
3. Captain William Hodson, quoted Michael Edwardes, "Battles of the Indian Mutiny"(1963) p.49.
4. Lieutenant-General Sir Francis Tuker(ed.), "The Chronicle of Private Henry Metcalfe, 32nd Foot"(1953)p.38.
5. Quoted in James Hewitt, *op.cit.*,p.145-6.
6. "A Lady's Diary of the Siege of Lucknow" (1858), quoted in *ibid.*,p.149.

CHAPTER 14;
1. Calcutta Gazette Extraordinary of 23rd April 1859, quoted in Col.J.P.Robertson, "Personal Adventures and Anecdotes of an Old Officer"(1906) p.268.
2. Fortescue, *op.cit.*,Vol.XIII,p.554.
3. Quoted Barrie Rose, "The Volunteers of 1859", J.S.A.H.R., Vol.XXXVII,p.101.
4. Sidney Herbert, Secretary for War, quoted in *ibid.*,p.102.
5. General Sir Ian Hamilton, "Listening for the Drums"(1944)pp.119-120.

CHAPTER 15
1. Quoted W.H.Hannah, "Bobs — Kipling's General"(1972)pp.127-8.
2. Quoted in Arthur Swinson, "North-West Frontier"(1969 Corgi edition)p.186.
3. Report of the Committee enquiring into the attack on the Kabul Residency, quoted in Col. G.J.Younghusband, "The Story of the Guides"(1908) p.97.
4. Quoted in W.H.Hannah, *op.cit.*,pp.174-5.
5. Quoted in Col.H.D.Hutchinson, "The Campaign in the Tirah"(1898)p.71 fn.
6. *Ibid.*,p125.
7. Eyewitness account, quoted in *ibid.*,p.219.
8. Quoted in *ibid.*,p.219.
9. "The Young British Soldier" from "Barrack Room Ballads".

CHAPTER 16
1. J.S.A.H.R., Vol.XXXIV,p.60.
2. Diary of Corporal John Mitchell, 58th Foot, quoted Michael Barthorp, "To Face the Daring Maoris"(1979)p.103.
3. Quoted John Selby, "The Paper Dragon" (1968)p.87.

CHAPTER 17
1. J.S.A.H.R., Vol.XXXVIII,p.149.
2. James McKay, "Reminiscences of the Last Kafir War"(1970 edition)p.145.(1st Edition 1871).
3. *Ibid.*,p.156.
4. Private Robert Head, 2/24th Foot, letter, quoted Donald R.Morris, "The Washing of the Spears"(1966)p.420.
5. Diary of Corporal William Roe, 58th Foot.
6. Count Gleichen, "With the Camel Corps up the Nile"(1889)p.158.
7. Wolseley's Journal of the Relief Expedition in Adrian Preston(ed.), "In Relief of Gordon",(1967) p.136.
8. Rudyard Kipling, "Pharoah and the Sergeant".

9. G.W.Steevens, "With Kitchener to Khartum" (1898)p.264.

CHAPTER 18
1. Letter of Corporal "A.W.", 2nd Black Watch, J.S.A.H.R. Vol.XX,p.199.
2. Quoted Kenneth Griffith, "Thank God We Kept the Flag Flying"(1974)p.200.
3. "Report of H.M.Commissioners on the War in South Africa"(1903), quoted in Barnett, "Britain's Army",p.341.
4. "Report of the Committee appointed to consider the Education and Training of the Officers of the Army"(1902), quoted in *ibid.*,p.343.
5. MSS Diary of Captain Barton, 2nd Northamptonshire Regiment.
6. Brig-Gen. Sir James Edmonds, "Military Operations, France and Belgium, 1914"(1933)p.10.

CHAPTER 19
1. " 'Die Schlacht bei Mons' ", quoted Edmonds, *op.cit.*,p.94.
2. Quoted in *ibid.*,p.383.
3. John Terraine, "The Great War"(1965)p.90.
4. Quoted in *ibid.*,p.124.
5. John Masefield "Gallipoli"(1916), quoted in E.W.Sheppard,"Redcoat"(1952)p.201.
6. Lt-Col Graham Seton Hutchinson, "Warrior" (1932)p.139.
7. B.H.Liddell Hart, "The Real War",(1930)p.253.
8. F.P.Crozier, 9th Royal Irish Rifles, quoted Gilby, *op.cit.*,p.199.
9. Liddell Hart, *op.cit.*,p.264.
10. Quoted Terraine, *op.cit.*,p.264.
11. Charles Carrington, "Soldier from the Wars Returning"(1965), (Arrow Edition 1970)p.215.
12. Quoted Hutchinson, *op.cit.*, p.229 and in *ibid.*, p.230
13. Quoted Liddell Hart, *op.cit.*,p.431.
14. Quoted in *ibid.*,p.415.

CHAPTER 20
1. Quoted Peter Young & J.P.Lawford(ed.) "History of the British Army"(1970)p.249.
2. Quoted in *ibid.*,p.250.

CHAPTER 21
1. Alan Moorehead, war correspondent, quoted Ronald Lewin(ed.), "Freedom's Battle. Vol.3: The War on Land"(1969),p.57.
2. Quoted Gilby, *op.cit.*,p.165.
3. Field-Marshal Viscount Montgomery of Alamein, "El Alamein to the River Sangro"(1948) p.25.
4. Chester Wilmot, war correspondent, quoted Lewin, *op.cit.*,p.270.
5. Quoted Cornelius Ryan, "A Bridge Too Far" (1974)(Coronet edition 1975)p.508.
6. Barnett, "Britain's Army",p.447.
7. Field-Marshal Viscount Slim, quoted Lewin, *op.cit.*,pp.113-114.
8. *Ibid.*,p.158.
9. *Ibid.*,p.231.
10. Quoted in Philip Mason, *op.cit.*,p.509.

CHAPTER 22
1. Quoted Gregory Blaxland, "The Regiments Depart"(1971)p.101.
2. Supplementary Statement on Defence Policy 1968 (Cmnd.3701).
3. Quoted Blaxland, *op.cit.*,p.472.

INDEX

Figures in bold refer to Illustrations.

Abercromby, Lt-Gen James (1706-81), 68, 70
Abercromby, Sir Ralph (1734-1801), **108**, 109, 111
Aboukir Bay (1801) 110
Abraham, Plains of (1759) 72, (1760) 73
Abu Klea (1885) 209
Abu Kru (1885) 209
Abyssinia 192, 202, 203, 252
Aden 192, 272, 273, **275**, 277
Afghanistan 137, 140, 183, 185, 188, 242
Afghan Wars, 1st (1838-42) **139**, 140, 183; 2nd (1878-80) 185, **187**; 3rd (1919) 242
Agra 113
Ahmedabad (1780) 88
Airey, Maj-Gen Richard (1803-81), 158
Aisne (1914) 225, 227, 237
Aix-la-Chapelle, Treaty of (1748) 64, 65, 67, 81
Alam Halfa (1942) 253
Alamein, El (1942) 253, 254
Alanbrooke, 1st Viscount, Field Marshal, A.F. Brooke (1883-1963), **250,** 265
Albermarle, 1st Duke of see Monck, George
Albuera (1811) 120, 126, 127
Alexander of Tunis, 1st Earl, Field Marshal R.G.L. Alexander R.L.G.
        (1891-1969), **250;** Commander-in-Chief 253;
        North Africa 254; Italy 257, 260; leadership 265
Alexandria (1801) **108**, 110-111
Aliwal (1846) 141, **143**
Allenby, 1st Viscount, Field Marshal E.H.H. Allenby (1861-1936), 225, **228;**
        captures Jerusalem 235, 236; Indian High Commissioner 243
Alma (1854) 156, **159**, 163
Almanza (1707) 50
Almeida 120
Almenara (1710) 53
Amherst, Field Marshal Jeffrey (1717-97), 68, 70, **71**, 72, 73, 78 92, 106,
Amiens, Treaty of (1802) 111, 114, 201, 237
Amoaful, (1874) 201, 202
Amritsar 242
Anderson, Lt-Gen K A N 254
Anglesey, 1st Marquis and 2nd Earl of Uxbridge, H.W. Paget (1768-1854), in Holland
        110; at Corunna 117; at Waterloo 126, 130
Anne, Queen (1665-1714) 35, 40, 43, 53, 55
Anson, Gen. George (1797-1857), 166, 168
Antwerp 64, 225, 258, 260
Anzio (1944) 257
Arabi Pasha 208
Arakan (1943-44) 262
Arcot (1751) 82
Arms, Assize of 10
Army Board 274
Army Council 220, 274
Arnee (1782) 88
Arnhem (1944) 258, 260
Arogee (1868) 203
Arras 54, 235, 237
Array, Commissions of 10, 15, 19
Ashanti Wars, 2nd (1873-74) 201, 202; 3rd (1895-1900) 202
Assam Regiment 262
Assaye (1803) 113
Astley, Sir Jacob (1579-1652) 17
Atbara (1898) 212
Auckinleck, Field Marshal Sir Claude (b. 1884) **250,** 253, 265
Aughrim (1691) 38
Austerlitz (1805) 114, 116
Australia 194, 200, 229, 237, 239, 253, 268-271; 6th, 8th, 9th infantry divisions 252
Austrian Succession, War of (1742-48) 59-64
Badajoz (1812) 120, 123, 125, 126
Balaclava (1854) 155, 158, **159, 160,** 161, 163
Bangalore, siege of (1791) 111, **112**Barrosa (1811) 120
Belize 279
Beresford, Gen William C, (1768-1854) **118,** 120
Blenheim (1704) 44, 46-47, **48,** 49, 50
Belmont (1899) 216
Boer Wars (1880-81) 207-208; (1899-1901) 215-219
Boulogne, siege of (1544) **11, 39**Bosworth (1485) 9
Boyne (1690) 38
Brandwater Basin (1901) **214**
Brandywine (1777) 95
Bronkhorst Spruit (1880) 207
British Army
        discipline (1688) 36, (1748) 65, (1795) 106-107, (1820) 154;
        pay (c.1557) 15, (1688) 36, (1775) 91, (1820) 154, (1885)175;
        purchase of commissions (1688) 36, (1720) 58, (1748) 65, (1795)
        106-107, (c.1820) 164, (1871) 181, recruits (1642) 21, (1702) 44,
        (1720) 58-59, (1748) 67, (1775) 91, (1803) 114, (1835) 154,
        (1920) 241;

establishment   (1661) 33; (1691) 38; (1702-12) 46; (1722) 58; (1748) 67;
               (1793) 106; (1818) 153; (1859) 177; (1914) 225; (1922) 245;
               (1951) 268; (1963) 273; (1979) 282
organisation   (1702) 44, 46
reductions in   (1818) 153; (1922) 245; (1957-63) 273-274; (1967) 277, 279
reform of: under Duke of York 106-109; under Castlereagh 114; as a result of Crimean
             War 175-177; under Cardwell 178, 180-181; under Haldane 222, under Ho
             under Hore Belisha 247.
expeditionary forces (1914) 224-225, 227-228, 237, 239; (1939) 249
Regiments:
    Cavalry: The Life Guards 31, 62, **131**, 209, 245, 273, 277
               Royal Horse Guards 31, 38, 61, 62, 74, 76, 106, 130, 193, 198, 207
               1st Dragoon Guards 35, 49, 74, 76, 106, 130, 193, 198, 207
               2nd Dragoon Guards 35, 38, 49, 60, 74, 76, 106, 202, 245, 273
               3rd Dragoon Guards 35, 38, 49, 60, 74, 76, 106, 202, 245, 273
               4th Dragoon Guards 35, 158, 209, 245
               5th Dragoon Guards 35, 49, 106, 125, 158, 209, 245
               6th Dragoon Guards 35, 49, 76, 166, 169, 245
    Dragoon   7th Draggon Guards 49, 76, 245
               1st Royal Dragoons 33, 61, 106, 130, 158, 209, 279
               2nd Dragoons 46, 49, 55, 74, 76, 130, 158, 163, 209
               3rd Dragoons 35, 50, 61, 125, 137, 142
               4th Dragoons 35, 50, 125, 158, 163
               5th Lancers 209, 245
               6th Dragoons 61, 74, 76, 130, 158, **159**, 245
               7th Dragoons 109, 110, 193
               8th Dragoons 47, 50, 113, 158, 174, 270
               9th Dragoons 55, 136, 142, **167, 168, 169** 168, 169, 173, 186, **255**
               10th Dragoons 55, 74, 76, 109, 209, 245
               11th Dragoons 76, 110, **149,** 158, **160,** 247, 263, 273,
               12th Dragoons 55, 110, 136, 204, 257   247
               13th Dragoons 55, 158
               14th Dragoons 55, 142, 171, 174, 245
               15th Light Dragoons 65, 67, 76, 78, 102, 106, 109, 245
               16th Light Dragoons 67, 93, 106, 136, 141, **143**, 209, 245
               17th Light Dragoons 67, 92, 93, 96, 158, **160,** 174, 207, 245
               18th Hussars 245
               19th Light Dragoons 113
               19th Hussars 183, 209, 245
               20th Hussars 183, 245
               21st Hussars 183, 212, 245
               22nd Light Dragoons 136
               22nd Dragoons 264
               23rd Light Dragoons 136
               23rd Hussars 264
               24th Lancers 264
               25th Dragoons 264
               26th Light Dragoons 110
               26th Hussars 264
               27th Light Dragoons 113
               27th Lancers 264
               29th Light Dragoons 113
Foot Guards 46, 50, 64, 76, 78, 96, 106, 109, 111, 117, 124, 158, 161, 209, 216, 268
Grenadier Guards 31, 40, 49, 50, 62, 106, 110, 130, 133, 158, **159**, 193, **211, 214**
Coldstream Guards 31, 35, 40, 62, **148,** 158, 193, 273, 284
Scots Guards 35, 53, 62, 158
Irish Guards 217, 245, 258
Welsh Guards 240
Infantry:
    1st Foot   31, 36, 37, 40, 46, 49, 61, 64, 110, 136
    2nd Foot   31, 37, 50, **147,** 204
    3rd Foot   33, 49, 53, 62, **90,** 126, 206
    4th Foot   **51,** 64, 202, 203
    5th Foot   35, **60,** 76, 78, **101,** 172, 212, 216, 270, 272, 277
    6th Foot   35, 64, 204, 212, 261, 274
    7th Foot   35, 40, 157, 158, 240, **255,** 280
    8th Foot   35, 49, 61, 62, 64, 76, 169, 173, 185, 186, 245
    9th Foot   35, 50, 137, 141, 273, 277
   10th Foot   35, 49, 142, 212, 224, 273,
   11th Foot   35, 50, 61, 62, 76, **90,** 215, 237, 284
   12th Foot   35, 61, 74, 75, 100, 102, 194, 195, 196, 204, 268, 273
   13th Foot   35, 61, 137, **266,** 267
   14th Foot   35, 106, 195, 196, 202
   15th Foot   35, 49, 70, 72, 279
   16th Foot   49, 50, 53, 273,
   17th Foot   50, 274
   18th Foot   40, 50, 53, 144, 196, 145
   19th Foot   62, 157
   20th Foot   49, 62, 70, 74, 75, 95, 109, 212, 228, 272
   21st Foot   40, 49, 61, 62, 95, 208, 224, 274
   22nd Foot   70, 140
   23rd Foot   44, 49, 61, 62, 74, 75, 96, 110, 111, 157, 163, 200, 201
   24th Foot   49, 76, 142, 206, 284

25th Foot 62, 64, 74, 75, **90**, 110, **147**, 191, 250
26th Foot 37, 44, 49, 272, 279
27th Foot 106, 217, 245
28th Foot 50, 62, 70, 72, 103, 106, 110, 111, 126, **162**, 215, 270, 272, 284
29th Foot 127, 142
30th Foot 188
31st Foot 62, 126, 137, 141, 142
32nd Foot 62, 142, 168, 169, 172
33rd Foot 50, 61, 62, 76, 93, 96, 103, 111, 157, 202, 203, 272
34th Foot 62, 217, 258
35th Foot 50, 70, 72, 209, 210
36th Foot 50, **112**, 227
37th Foot 49, 64, 67, 74, 75, 229, **230**
38th Foot 59
39th Foot 82, 83, 85, 100, 189, 260, 267
40th Foot 59, 70, 95, 109, 110, 111, 194, 195, 196
42nd Foot 55, 62, 68, 95, 110, 158, **162**, 201, 202, 208, 209, 272
43rd Foot 59, 70, 107, 124, 196, 204 277
44th Foot 59, 68, 137, 198
45th Foot 59, 70, 202, 204, 274
46th Foot 59
47th Foot 59, 72, 216
48th Foot 59, 68, 70, 72, 126, 127, 189, 191, **244**, 245
49th Foot 110, 210
50th Foot 56, 141, 142, 196, 262
51st Foot 74, 75, 100, 144
52nd Foot 107, 125, 130, 133, 169, 227
55th Foot 68
56th Foot 100
57th Foot 127, 196, 270
58th Foot 70, 72, 100, 110, 111, 195, 207, 208
59th Foot 198
60th Foot 68, 70, 72, 107, 124, 142, 165, 166 168, 188, 194, 204, 207, 247, 249
61st Foot 100, 142, 169
62nd Foot 95, 141
63rd Foot 81, 215
64th Foot 171, 212
65th Foot 195, 196, 209, 279
66th Foot 126, 186, 188
67th Foot 186, 198, 265
68th Foot 109, 196
69th Foot **131**
70th Foot 196
71st Foot 88, 96, 109, 130, 133, 174, 193, 216, 274
72nd Foot 100, 185, 186, 188, 204, 212
73rd Foot 193, 194, 204, 216
74th Foot 113, 204, 208
75th Foot 168, 169, 173, 189, 204, 208, 274
76th Foot 113
77th Foot 157
78th Foot 113, 171, 173, 216
79th Foot 110, 158, 208, 210
80th Foot 141, 144, 194, 258
83rd Foot 243
84th Foot 85, 169, 171, 172, 279
85th Foot 109
86th Foot 174, 216
87th Foot **121**, 215, 245, **223**
88th Foot 157, 174, 206, 217, 245
89th Foot **162**
90th Foot 110, 111, 172, 206
91st Foot 204, 216, 260, 270, 277
92nd Foot 110, 111, 116, 186, **187**, 188, 207, 208, 215
93rd Foot 158
94th Foot **121**, 207, 208
95th Foot 100, 157
The Rifle Brigade
107, 125, 127, 130, 133, 155, 157, 174, 201, 204, 212, 247, 265, 279
96th Foot 195
97th Foot **101**
99th Foot 195
100th Foot 245
101st Foot 101, 183, 228, 245
102nd Foot 183, 217, 229
103rd Foot 183, 217, 245
104th Foot 183
105th Foot 183, 191
106th Foot 183
107th Foot 183
108th Foot 183
109th Foot 183

Corps:
  Royal Horse Artillery, formation 109; 110, 125, 130, 186, 188, 208
  Royal Armoured Corps 264, 273, 277
  Royal Tanks Corps 236, 240, 247, 264, 277
  Machine Gun Corps 232, 240
  Royal Artillery, formation 55, 58; 67, 74, 82, 124, 126, 175-176, **179**, 183, 194-196, 198, 202, 206, 215-216, 233, 240, 247-248, **265**, 270, 273, 277, 279, **280**
  Corps of Royal Engineers, formation 109; 125, 175, 183, 194-195, 198
  Royal Corps of Signals 264, 270
  Special Air Service Regiment 252, 273, 277
  Royal Army Chaplain's Department 177
  Royal Corps of Transport 110, 176, 240, 264, 277, 284
  Royal Army Medical Corps 176, **197**, 240, 264
  Royal Army Ordnance Corps 176, 240, 264
  Corps of Royal Electrical and Mechanical Engineers 264
  Corps of Royal Military Police 264
  Royal Army Pay Corps 177, 264
  Royal Army Vetinary Corps 264
  Royal Army Education Corps 264
  Royal Army Dental Corps 264
  Royal Pioneer Corps 264
  Intelligence Corps 264
  Army Catering Corps 264
  Women's Royal Army Corps 240
  Reconnaissance Corps 265
  Non-Combatant Corps 264
Armies:
  1st Army (1914-18) 228, 237, 239,; (1939-45) 254
  2nd Army (1914-18) 228, 235, 237, 239; (1939-45) 257-258
  3rd Army (1914-18) 232, 236-237, 239
  4th Army (1914-18) 232, 234, 239
  5th Army (1914-18) 235, 237, 239
  8th Army (1939-45) 253-254, 257, 260
  14th Army (1939-45) 261-262
Army Corps:
  I Corps (1914-18) 225, 227
  II Corps (1914-18) 225, 227
  III Corps (1914-18) 225, 232
  IV Corps (1914-18) 227; (1939-45) 262-263
  V Corps (1939-45) 254
  VIII Corps (1914-18) 232; (1939-45) 258
  IX Corps (1914-18) 237; (1939-45) 254
  X Corps (1939-45– 253, 257
  XII Corps (1939-45) 258
  XIII Corps (1914-18) 234; (1939-45) 253, 257
  XIV Corps (1914-18) 234
  XV Corps (1914-18) 232, 234; (1939-45) 262-263
  XXX Corps (1939-45) 253, 257-258, 260
  XXXIII Corps (1939-45) 262-263
Armoured Divisions:
  Guards 2, 258, 260
  1st 253
  2nd 253
  7th 252-254, 260, 265
  10th 253
  11th 258, 260
  46th 254
  79th 257
Infantry Divisions:
  Guards (1854) 155, 161; (1914-18) 236
  1st (1809) 125; (1900) 218; (1914-18) 225, 227; (1939-45) 257, 267
  2nd (1809) 125; (1854) 155, 157-158, 161; (1900) 218; (1914-18) 225, 227; (1939-45) 263
  3rd (1809) 125; (1812) 126; (1854) 158; (1900) 218; (1914-18) 225, 227 337; (1939-45) 257, 267
  4th (1809) 125; (1811) 126; (1854) 155, 161; (1914-18) 225
  5th (1914-18) 225, 236; (1939-45) 254, 257, 260
  6th (1813) 125; (1900) 218; (1914-18) 227
  7th (1900) 218; (1914-18) 227
  8th (1914-18) 237
  9th (1900) 218
  18th (1914-18) 234. (1939-45) 260
  21st (1914-18) 232
  29th (1914-18) 229
  30th (1914-18) 234
  36th (1939-45) 262
  43rd (1939-45) 258, 260
  44th (1939-45) 253
  50th (1939-45) 254
  51st (1939-45) 253-254
  78th (1939-45) 253-254

Airborne Divisions:
    1st 254, 257-258
    6th 257, 260, 267
Armoured Brigades:
    26th 254
    1st Tank 247
    2nd Tank 236
Infantry Brigades:
    1st Guards 254
    4th Guards 237
    22nd Guards 253
    24th Guards 249
    27th 270
    29th 270, 272
    137th 239
      1st Parachute 258
      4th Parachute 258
      16th Parachute 272
      1st Airlanding 258
Brunei 274
Brunswick, Army of 78, 91, 95, 130
Buckingham, 1st Duke 2nd Creation, George Villiers (1592-1628), 19
Buller, Gen Sir Redvers (1839-1908), 176, **214**, 215, 216, 217, 218
Bunkers Hill (1775) 92
Burgoyne, Gen John (1722-1792), 91, 92, 93, **94**, 95, 96
Busaco (1810) 120, 126
Buxor (1764) 86
Cadogan, 1st Earl, William (1675-1726), 44, 49, 50, 54
Cadiz, expeditions to 16, 19, 120, 123
Caen 257-258
Cairo 109, 110, 11, 208, 272
Calais, Loss of 10, 15; 227, 249
Calcutta, The Black Hole of 83
Cambrai (1917) **233**, 236
Cambridge, Field Marshal, George, Duke of (1819-1904), 155, 158, **159**, 176,
        177, 181, **182**, 209
Camden (1780) 96
Campbell, Sir Colin, Baron Clyde (1792-1863), 158, **164**, 173
Canada, 67-68, 70, 72-73, 91, 193; 1st Army (1939-45) 258, 260; 1st division
        (1914-18) 228, (1939-45) 254, 257; 3rd division 257
Canton (1857) 192, 198
Cape Colony 204, 216, 218, 219
Cape Mounted Rifles 204
Caridgan, 7th Earl, J.T. Brudenell, (1797-1868), 155, 158, **160**, 161
Cardwell, Edward, Viscount Cardwell (1813-1886), 178, 180, 181, **182**, 268
Caribbean 16, 30, 59, 96, 194, 268, 273
Carleton, Gen Guy, 1st Baron Dorchester (1724-1808), 92-93, 95-96
Castlereagh, Viscount, Robert Stewart, (1769-1822), 106, 114, 117, 120
Cawnpore 116, 168-169, **170**, 171-173
Channel Islands 33, 100
Charles I (1600-49), calls out northern militia 19; **20**, forces of (1642) 21; at
        Naseby 27; 31
Charles II (1630-1685), lands in Scotland 29; enters London 30; standing
        army 31, 33, 32, **34**, 36, 79
Chelmsford, Gen Frederick, 2nd Baron (1827-1905), 206-207, **211**
Cherbourg (1758) 78
Chillianwallah (1849) 142, **143**, 144
China, native troops (1900) **199**
Chitral, siege (1895) 188, **190**
Chobham, camp at **143**
Churchill, W.S. (1874-1965), 212, 229, 232, 249, 253, 265
Cintra, Convention of 117, 120
Citudad Rodrigo (1812) 120, 123, 126
Clinton, Gen Sir Henry (1738-1795), 91, 92, 95, 96, 100
Clive, Robert, Baron Clive (1725-1774), 82, 83, **84**, 85, 86
Colenso, (1899) 216, 217
Concord (1775) 91, 92
Conscription, 16, 24-25, 44, 232, 241, 249, 267, 273-275
Coote, Lt-Gen Sir Eyre (1726-1783), 83, **84**, 85, **87**, 88, **90**
Cornwallis, Charles, 1st Marquis (1738-1805), 91, 96, **97**, 100, 111
Corunna (1809) 117
Cotton, Field Marshal Sir Stapleton, Viscount Combermere (1773-1865), 126
Craufurd, Maj-Gen Robert (1764-1812), 117, 125
Crimean War (1854-56) 155-65, **160, 162**
Cromwell, Oliver (1599-1658), **20**, and Eastern Association 23; at Marston Moor 24;
        24; and cavalry tactics 25; in Ireland 29; Lord Protector 30; 46
Culloden (1746) **51, 63**, 64
Cumberland, William Duke of (1721-1765), **56, 57**, at Fontenoy 62; **63**, at Culloden
        64; and Army reforms 65; 70, 74
Cyprus 245, 268, 272-273
Delhi 116, **134**, Ridge 168-169; 171, 173, Durbar (1903) 221
Dettingen (1743) 61, 62, 64

Dover, Treaty of (1670) 33
Dunbar (1650) 29
Dundas, Gen Sir David (1735-1820), 107, 109
Dundas, Henry, 1st Viscount Melville (1742-1811), 106, 109, 110
Dunkirk (1658) 30; 31, 59, (1940) 249
Edgehill (1642) 23
Egypt 109, 110, 111, 192, (1882) 208; 210, 243, 245, 252, 253, 268, 272
Eisenhower, Gen Dwight (1890-1969), 254, 258, 260
Elandslaagte (1899) 215
Eliott, George 1st Baron Heathfield (1717-1790), **97, 98**, 100, 102
Elizabeth I (1533-1603), **14**, 15, 16, 79
Elizabeth II (b1926), **151**
El Obeid (1883) 209
El Teb (1884) 209
England, Civil Wars (1642-50) 21-30
Eugene, Prince of Savoy (1663-1736) 46, at Blenheim 47, 49; at Oudenarde
        50; at Malplaquet 53
Exeter 23
Fairfax, Gen Thomas, 3rd Baron Fairfax of Cameron (1612-1671), 17, 23-25, 27, 29
Falkirk (1746) 64
Ferozeshah (1845) 141, 144
Flodden (1513) 13
Fontenoy (1745) 62, 64, 67
Fort: Duquesne 68; Edward 95; Garry 193-194; Gulistan 189; Moro 74; St. David 81,
        85; St. George 79, **80**, 81-82, 171; Ticonderoga 68, 70, 90, 95;
        William 83; William Henry 68
Fortifications **12**, vulnerability of 13; coastal 33; 38
France 13, 19, 29, 33, 38, 40, 42-43, 47, 49, 50-51, 54, 59, 61, 67-68, 70, 72-75,
        78-79, 81-82, 85, 86, 88, 103, 109, 111, 117, 120, 123, 125, 130-131,
        133, 135, 153, 156, 158, 161;
        Army 13, 40, 47, 49, 50, 51, 61, 62, 67, 68, 70, 72, 73, 76, 96, 116,
        130, 133;
        Revolution 103, War of 111-114
Fraser, Brig-Gen Simon (d. 1777) **94**
Frazer, Augustus 126
French, Field Marshal Sir John D.P. (1852-1925) 218, 225, 228
Fuentes d'Onoro (1811) 120, **122**, 126
Fuller, Maj-Gen J.F.C. (1878-1966) 247
Gallipoli (1915) 229, **230**
Galway, 1st Earl, H de Massue de Ruvigny (1648-1720), 38, 47, 49, 53
Gandamak (1842) 137, 186
Gatacre, Lt-Gen Sir W.F. (1843-1906), 216
Gate Pa (1865) 196
Gazala (1942) 253, 254
Gentlemen-at-Arms 13, 31
Gentlemen pensioners 13, 15
George I (1660-1727), 55, 58
George II, (1683-1760), 59, at Dettingen 61; 65, 67
George III (1738-1820), 92
Germain, George, 1st Viscount Sackville (1716-1785), 74, at Minden 75, 76; and
        America 92-93, 95-96, 100
Germantown (1777) 95
Germany 10, 13, 15, 4 1, 58, 95, 163, (1914-18) 228-240 passim; (1939-45)
        249-65 passim
Gibraltar 49, 55, 58, 59, **98, 99**, 100, **102**, 268, 279
Gill, L Cpl **131**
Gingindhlovu (1879) 206
Ginkel, G de, 1st Earl of Athlone (1630-1703), 38, 44
Ginniss (1885) 210
Glenshiel (1719) 55
Godolphin, Sidney, 1st Earl (1645-1712) 43, 44, 53
Gold Coast Regt 202
Gordon, Gen Charles George (1833-1885), 198, 209, 210
Goring, George, Baron Goring (1608-1657), 17, **20**, 24
Gough, Field Marshal Sir Hugh, 1st Viscount (1779-1869), **138**, 141, 142, 166, 196
Gough, Gen Sir H (1870-1963), 232, 235, 237
Graham, Lt-Gen Sir Gerald (1831-1899), 209, 210
Granby, Marquis of, John Manners, (1721-1770), 76, **77**, 78
Grand Alliance, The 37, 43, 47
Green Brigade, in service of Sweden 17, 31
Guildford Courthouse (1781) 96
Gujerat (1849) 144
Gustavus Adolphus, King of Sweden, tactics used by 17
Hafir, Field Marshal Sir Douglas (1861-1928) 212, 222, 225, 227, **228**, 232, 234-235,
        237, 239, 240
Haldane, Viscount (1856-1928), 219, 220, 224, 228
Hanover, 40, 43, 49, 55, 59, 61-62, 67, 74-76, 116;
        Army 75, 100, 102, 130
Hasheen (1885) 210
Havelock, Sir Henry (1795-1857), **164**, 171, 172
Hawley, Lt-Gen Henry (1679-1759), 64

Henry VII (1457-1509), 9, 10
Henry VIII (1491-1547), **11,** 13, **145**
Hepburn, Sir John (1598-1636), 17, 18
Hesse 49, 74, 75, 76, 78;
       Army 43, 75, 91, 93, 96, 106
Hill, Gen Rowland, 1st Viscount Hill (1772-1842), **118,** 123, 125, 130
Hong Kong 260, 279; Regt 198
Hopton, Ralph, 1st Baron Hopton (1598-1652), 23
Hore-Belisha, L (1893-1957), 247
Hounslow Camp 35
Howe, Gen Sir William, 5th Viscount Howe (1729-1814), 70, at Quebec 72; 91,
       assessment of 92; at Bunkers Hill 92; 93, **94**
Hyderabad 85, 11, 140, Nawab of 81, Nizam of 85, 86, 111
Imjin River (1951) 270
India, Madras Presidency 79, 81-86, 88, 111; Bengal Presidency 83-85. 165-167, 169;
       Bombay Presidency 79, 86, 135, 140; East India Company 79, 81,
       82-83, 85-86, 88, 111, 113, 135, 137, 165, 168, 174, 183
Indian Army, Madras Army 84, 136-137, 171, 174, 183-184; Bengal Army 84, 85,
       135-137, 140-141, 144, 165-167, 169-171, 174, 183-184;
       Bombay Army 79, 84, 136-137, 171, 174, 183-184, 188
Regiments:
   Cavalry: Fane's Horse 198
            Guides Cavalry 247
            Probyn's Horse 188, 198
            Skinner's Horse **139, 148**
            1st Punjab Cavalry 183
            2nd Bengal Light Cavalry 171
            2nd Punjab Cavalry 183
            3rd Bengal Light Cavalry 166
            3rd Bombay Cavalry 188
            3rd Punjab Cavalry 183
            4th European Light Cavalry 183
            4th Madras Cavalry 113
            4th Punjab Cavalry 183
            5th Bengal Light Cavalry 137, 147
    5th Eu5th European Light Cavalry 183
            5th Punjab Cavalry 183
            6th Bengal Cavalry 135
            12th Bengal Cavalry 186
            13th Bengal Lancers **190**
            27th Indian Light Cavalry 243
            28th Indian Light Cavalry 243
   Infantry:
            1st Bengal Europeans 141, 142, 168
            1st Bengal Fusiliers 169
            1st Bengal Native Infantry 83
            1st Bombay Grenadiers188
            1st Bombay Native Infantry 83
            1st European Madras Fusiliers 169
            1st Punjab Infantry 169, 183, 189, 262
            1st Sikh Infantry 183, 189, 200
            2nd Bengal Europeans 142, 168
            2nd Gurkha Rifles **134,** 168, 186, 188, 189, 267 **271,** 274
            2nd Punjab Infantry 169, 173, 183, 186
            2nd Sikh Infantry 183, 188
            3rd Bombay Europeans 174
            3rd Bombay Native Infantry 88
            3rd Gurkha Rifles 169, 191, **246**
            3rd Punjab Infantry 183
            3rd Sikh Infantry 183, 188, 189
            4th Gurkha Rifles 188
            4th Punjab Infantry 173, 183
            4th Sikh Infantry 144, 183
            5th Bengal Native Infantry 137
            5th Gurkha Rifles 183, 186, 188
            5th Punjab Infantry 183
            6th Bombay Native Infantry 135
            6th Gurkha Rifles 267
            6th Punjab Infantry 183
            7th Bombay Native Infantry 135
            7th Gurkha Rifles 267
            7th Rajput Regt 200
            8th Bombay Native Infantry 88
            10th Gurkha Rifles 267, 268, 274
            13th Bengal Native Infantry 172
            14th Sikh Infantry 188
            15th Sikh Infantry 185, 188, 210
            19th Bombay Native Infantry 166
            20th Bombay Native Infantry 166
            21st Pioneers **221**
            23rd Pioneers 188
            23rd Punjab Regt 203

            24th Punjab Regt 188
            25th Bombay Native Infantry **138,** 174
            25th Punjab Regt 188
            28th Bombay Native Infantry 210
            29th Punjab Regt 186
            30th Bombay Native Infantry 186
            32nd Punjab Pioneers 189
            34th Bengal Native Infantry 166
            36th Bengal Native Infantry 144
            36th Sikhs 189, 191
            37th Bengal Native Infantry 137
            38th Bengal Native Infantry 166
            39th Garwal Rifles 227
            40th Madras Native Infantry **134**
            45th Rattrays Sikhs **187,** 189
            46th Bengal Native Infantry 144
            48th Bengal Native Infantry 172
            54th Bengal Native Infantry 137, 166
            71st Bengal Native Infantry 172
            74th Bengal Native Infantry 166, 168
            129th Baluchis 227
Corps of Guides, 147, 168, 183, 186, 267, 284
Punjab Fronier Force 144, 185, 267
Madras Sappers and Miners 202
Mohmand Field Force 189
Divisions:
   Infantry:
      4th 252, 253, 254, 257
      5th 262, 263
      7th 262, 263
      8th 254
      9th 260
      10th 254, **259**
      11th 260
      17th 262, 263
      19th 263
      20th 262, 263
      23rd 262
      26th 262
Brigades:
   Infantry:
      7th **255**
      77th 261
Indian Mutiny (1857-59) 165-174
Indonesia 274, 277
Inglis, Maj-Gen Sir J.E.W. (1814-1862), 172
Inkerman (1854) 161
Ireland, and Elizabeth 1 16; and Cromwell 29; 35, and James II 37-38; 100, 241, 244
       278-279, 283
Ireton, Henry (1611-1651), 23, 29
Isandhlwana (1879) 206
Italy 10, 13, 43, 49, 55, 109, 163; (1939-45) 252, 254, 257, **259,** 260, 267
Jacobite Rebellions (1715) 55, 58, 70, 80, (1745) 70, 80
James I (1566-1625), 19
James II (1633-1701) 33, enlarges army with militia funds 35; 36, 37, and Boyne 38;
       43
Jenkins Ear, War of (1739) 59
Kabul 137, 140, 185, 186, **187,** 188
Kaffir Wars (1846) 203, 204; (1850-53) 155; (1877) 206
Kambula (1879) 206
Kandahar 137, 185, 186, **187,** 188
Kassassin (1882) 208
Khartoum 209-210, 212
Killiecrankie (1689) 37
Kimberley 215-218
King's African Rifles 203, 261, 268, 272, 277
King's German Legion 116, 117, 124, 125, 127
Kirkee (1817) 135; 137
Kitchener, Field-Marshal, Lord H.H. (1850-1916), 210, **211,** 212, in Boer War 217-219;
       221, and Indian Army reorganization 222, 224, 243; and Secretary
       of State for War 225; and New Army 227, 228; 243
Koheroa (1863) 196
Kohima **256,** 262
Korean War 268, **269,** 270, 272
Kruger, Paul 215, 218
Kumasi 201, 202
Kut-el-Amara 232, 234, 235
Ladysmith, siege of (1899) 215-218
Laing's Nek (1881) 207
Lake, Gen Gerard, 1st Viscount, (1744-1808), 113, 135, **138**
Landen (1693) 40
Laswari (1803) 113, **138**

Lauffeld (1747) 64, 67
Lawrence, Sir Henry (1806-1857), 142, 168, 169, 172
Lawrence, John L.M. (1811-1879), 168, 169
Lawrence, Maj-Gen Stringer (1697-1775) 81, 82, **84,** 85, 86
Le Cateau 224; (1914) 225
Leicester, 1st Earl (4th creation) (1532-1588), 16-17
Leipzig (1813) 123
Le Marchant, Maj-Gen J.G. (1766-1812), 125
Lenon, Lt 198
Lexington (1775) 91, 92
Liddell Hart, Basil H 247
Ligny (1815) 130
Ligonier, Field-Marshal John (1680-1770), 62, 64, 67
Lombards Kop (1899) 215
Lords Lieutenant 15, 16, 19
Lostwithiel (1644) 24
Louis XIV of France, plans for domination of Europe 33; and Spanish
             Netherlands 37, 43; 40, 49, 50, 53
Louisburg, Nova Scotia 65, 68, **69,** 70
Low Countries **see** Netherlands
Lucan, 3rd Earl, G.C. Bingham, (1800-1888), 155, **160,** 161
Lucknow 168-169, 171, 172
Lynedoch, Baron, Gen T. Graham (1748-1843), 120, 123, 125
Mafeking, siege of (1899) 215, 217, 218
Magdala (1868) 202, 203, **205**
Magersfontein (1899) 216, 218
Mahratta War (1803-05) 113, 135, 137
Maiwand (1880) 188
Majuba (1881) 207, 270 208
Malaya 192, 260, 268, 270, **271,** 272, 273; Malay Corps of Guides 200;
             Malay Regt 268
Malplaquet (1709) **51,** 53, 44
Maori Wars (1843-48) 194-196
Market Garden Operation (1944) 258, 260
Marlborough, Duke of, John Churchill (1650-1722), at Sedgemoor 33; joins William
             III 35; victory at Walcourt 37; assessment of 44; **45,** tactics
             of 46; his supply system 47; at Blenheim 47, 40; at Ramillies
             49; at Oudenarde 50; **52,** at Malplaquet 53; 54, 59
Marne (1914) 225, 236
Marston Moor (1644) 24
Meanee (1843) 140
Militia 9, 33, 35, 38, 64, 107, 153-153; and Henry VII 10; and Henry VIII 13;
             reformed 15; and Elizabeth 1 15, 16; and James I 19; and
             Charles 1 19; and the Civil War 21; and Charles II 31; and
             James II 35, 36; militia acts 10, 15, 19, 31; militiamen 248
Minden (1759) 75, 76, **77,** 100
Minorca 50, 55, 58, **90,** 100, 109; Regiment 110
Modder River (1809) 216   (1899)
Monck, George, 1st Duke of Albermarle (1608-70) 17; in Scotland 29; joins Charles
             II 30-33, **34;** and Coldstream Guards 35
Mons 40, 50, 53; trereat from 225, **226,** 239   retreat
Montgomery, Field Marshal B.L. (1887-1976), **250,** 253, 254, 257, 258, 260,
             261, 265, 267
Moore, Gen Sir John (1761-1809), 107, **118,** system of training 109-10; and
             light division 107, 109-10, 114, 116; at Alexandria 110-11;
             retreat of to Corunna 117
Mysore War (1767-69) 86
Namur (1694) 40, 54
Napier, Sir Charles (1782-1853), **138,** 140, 142, 144
Napoleon I (1769-1821); 110, 116-17, 130, 133, 135, in Egypt 109; possibility of
             advance on India 111; prepares to invade Britain 114; in Spain
             116-117, 120; defeated at Leipzig 123-124; return from Elba
             127; at Waterloo 133
Naseby (1645) 27
Netherlands 16, 17, 30, **33,** 37, 38, 43, 47, 49, 50, 53, 54, 55, 62, 64, 103, 106,
             107, **108,** 110
Newburn (1640) 19
New Model Army 29, 31, organisation 25; tactics 27; disbandment 27-28
Newbury (1644) 24
New Zealand 194, 239, 252, 268, 270; infantry division 257
Nicholson, Brig-Gen John (1821-1857), 142, **164,** 169
Nieuport (1600) 17
Nightingale, Florence (1820-1910), 161
North Atlantic Treaty Organisation 267, 279, 281
Ohaewai Pa, Siege of (1845) 195
Omdurman (1898) **211,** 212
Orakau (1865) 196
Ordnance, Board of 21, 37, 46, 55, 58; Master General of 13, 36, 43, 46
Oudenarde (1708) 50
Outram, Lt-Gen Sir James (1803-1863), **164,** 172, 173
Paardeberg (1900) 218
Palestine **230,** 236, 245, **246,** 267
Passchendaele (1917) 235
Peiwar Kotal (1878) 185-186
Philiphaugh (1645) 27
Picton, Lt-Gen Sir Thomas (1758-1815), **118,** 125, 130, **131**
Pinkie (1547) 15
Pitt, William, 1st Earl Chatham (1708-1778), Secretary of State 67-68; and
             Wolfe 70; strategy against French Canada 74; 78
Pitt, William (1759-1806), 103, 109
Plassey (1757) 83
Portugal 43, 79, 116-117, 120, **122,** 123-127, 237
Pozieres (1916) **230,** 234
Preston (1648) 29, (1715) 55
Prestonpans (1745) 64
Quatre Bras (1815) 130
Quebec 68, **69,** 70, 72, 73, 92, 93
Radfan War (1964) 277
Ragland, Lord Fitzroy Somerset (1788-1855), 155, 157, 158, **160,** 163
Ramillies (1706) 46, 49, 50
Rawlinson, Henry Seymour, 1st Baron (1864-1925), 212
Red River Expedition (1870) 181, 193, 194
Rhodes, Cecil (1853-1902), 215, 216

Riflemen, Experimental Corps of 107
'River Clyde' 229, **230**
Roberts, Field Marshal F.S., 1st Earl (1832-1914), in 2nd Afghan War 185, 186, 188;
             187, and Boer War 217, 218, 220
Roleia (1808) 117
Romme, Field Marshal Erwin (1891-1944), 252, 253, 254
Rorke's Drift (1879) **205,** 206
Roses, Wars of (1455-1485) 9-10, 12
Rottenburg, Baron de (1757-1832), 107, 109
Royal Hospital, Chelsea 36, 59
Rupert, Prince, Count Palatine of Rhine (1619-1682), **20,** 23, 46 at Breda 17;
             tactics of 21; defeat at Marston Moor 24; defeat at Naseby 27
Russell, William H (1820-1907), 161
St. Malo (1758) 78
Salamanca (1812) 117, **121,** 123, 125, 126
Saratoga (1777) **94,** 95, 96
Sarawak 274
Schomberg, F. H. 1st Duke (1615-1690), 37, 38
Scots Brigade 19
Sedgemoor (1685) 33
Self Denying Ordnance (1644) 25
Seringapatam (1799), 111, **172**
Seven Years War (1756-63) 67-78, 83, 85, 91, 92, 96
Sherpur 186, 187
Sherriffmuir (1715) 55
Sikh War (1845-46) 140-142, **143**
Skippon, Maj-Gen Philip (d 1660), 17, 25, 27
Slim, W. Field Marshal, The Viscount, (1891-1970), **250,** 261, 262, 263, 264, 265
Smith, Sir Henry (1787-1860), 141, 142, 204, 206, **211**
Smith, Joseph (1733-1790), **84,** 86, 88
Smith-Dorrien, Gen Sir H.L. (1858-1930), 212, 222, commands 2nd Corps 225,
             commands 2nd Army
Somme (1916) **230,** 232, 234, 237, 239
Soudan Defence Force 245
Soudan War (1884) 209, 210
Spain, 17, 19, 30, 43, 47, 53, 55, 67, 74, 91, 100, 102, 116, 117, 118, 123,
             superiority of infantry 10; Elizabeth at war with 15, 16;
             Spanish Armada 16; War of Jenkings Ear 59; American war of
             War of Independence 96; and Gibraltar 106
Spanish Succession, War of (1702-13) 40, 47-54, 55, 59, 67
Spion Kop (1900) 217
Steenkirk (1692) 40, 58, 59
Stillwater (1777) 95
Stormberg (1899) 216
Talavera (1809) 120, 126, 127
Tamai (1884) 209
Tarleton, Gen Sir Banastre (1754-1833), 96
Tel-El-Kebir (1882) 208
Templer, Field Marshal Sir Gerald (1898-1979) **frontis,** 270, 274, 284
Territorial Army 220, embodied 224; 229, 248, reconstituted 267; reduction 274; as
             TAVR 274, 282; Territorial Force 220, 229, 248
Tibet (1903-04) 191
Tippoo Sultan 88, 111
Tofrek (1885) 210
Torres Vedras, Lines of 120, 126
Tournai, Capture of (1513) 13, 53, 62
Trained Bands, 13, 15, 16, **18,** 21, 23, 26
Trenton (1776) 93
Ulundi (1879) 207
United States of America 43, 58, 59, 67, 68, 73, 74, 76, 127, 193, 236, 239, 258, 260;
             War of Independence (1776-83) 91, 93, 95, 96, 100, 102
Utrecht, Treaty of (1713) 55, 74
Uxbridge, Earl of **see** Anglesey
Vaal Krantz (1900) 217
Valenciennes (1793) **104**
Vere, Sir Francis (1560-1609), **14,** 17, 33
Vimiero (1808) 117
Vittoria (1813) **121,** 123, 126
Volunteers 177-80, 220
Wade, Field Marshal George (1673-1748), 55, 58, 61, 62, 64
Walcourt (1609) 37
Waterloo (1815) **129,** 130, **131,** 133, 135, **148**
Wavell, Field Marshal Archibald, 1st Baron (1883-1950), **250,** 252, 253, 261, 265,
Wellington, 1st Duke, Sir Arthur Wellesley (1769-1852), 103, **119,** 130, 133, 135
             comments on British troops 44; at Assaye 111; at Assaye
             113; at Copenhagen 116; in Peninsular War 120, 123-124;
             assessment of 124-127, 133; organisation of Army 124-126;
             at Waterloo 130, 133
West Indies 59, 73, 91, 96, 100, 103, 106; West India Regts 194, 201-202
White, Field Marshal Sir George (1835-1912), 191, **214,** 215, 216, 217, 218
White Plains (1776) 93
William III (1650-1702), 36, 42, 43, opposes French domination of Europe 33;
             lands at Torbay 35; in Scotaldn 37; in Ireland 37, 38; takes
             Namue 40
Winchester, Statue of (1285) 10; superceded (1553) 15; 19
Wingate, Maj-Gen O.C. (1903-44), 261-262
Wolfe, Maj-Gen James (1727-59), 65, **71,** at Culloden 64; at Quebec 68, 70, 72;
Wolseley, Field Marshal Garnet, Viscount Wolseley (1833-1913), and Red River
             expedition 194, 201; and Ashanti War 202; and Zulu War
             207; and Egypt 208; and Soudan 209, 210, **211;** and Boer
             War 215, 219; and Roberts 217
Wood, Field Marshal Sir Evelyn (1838-1919), 206, and Zulu War 207; and
             Egyptian Army 201   210
Worcester (1651) 29, 30
World War I (1914-18) 225-240, **226, 230, 231, 233, 238**
World War II (1939-45) 249-265, **255, 256, 259, 265**
Yeomanry (1803) 114; (1854) 153; (1908) 220; (1939) 264
Yeomen of the Guard 9, 10, 13, **14,** 31, **145**
York, Duke of, Frederick Augustus (1763-1827), **104-105** in Netherlands 103;
             Army reforms 106-107, 114; in Holland 109-110
York Chasseurs 106
Yorktown (1781) 100
Zulu War (1879) **205,** 206, 207

Whilst every care has been taken in compiling this publication, and the contents thereof, the Author, the National Army Museum,
Seagull S.A., other contributors and participants and the printers and distributors cannot accept responsibility for any errors,
howsoever caused.
Compiled and edited by the National Army Museum, London, England, and Seagull S.A., Guernsey, C.I.
All origination and typesetting by Hastings Printing Company, Hastings, Sussex, England.
Machining and plates by Anchor Press Ltd., Tiptree, Essex, England.
Colour printing by A. Wheaton Company, Exeter, England.
Binding by Wm. Brendon & Sons Ltd., Tiptree, Essex, England.
This book is printed on Bowater Nimrod Cartridge 100 g/m² supplied by William Guppy & Son Ltd.